The capability approach developed by Nobel Laureate Amartya Sen has become an important new paradigm in thinking about development. However, despite its theoretical and philosophical attractiveness, there has been scepticism about the usefulness of the approach for purposes of measurement and policy analysis. This volume addresses these issues in the context of poverty and justice. Part I offers a set of conceptual essays, some of which debate the strength of the often misunderstood individual focus of the capability approach. Part II investigates the techniques by which we can measure and compare capabilities, and how we can integrate them into poverty comparisons and policy advice. Finally, Part III looks at how we can apply the capability approach to different regions and contexts. Written by a team of international scholars, *The Capability Approach* is a valuable resource for researchers and graduate students concerned with the debate over the value of the capability approach and its potential applications.

FLAVIO COMIM is Director of the Capability and Sustainability Centre at St Edmund's College, University of Cambridge.

MOZAFFAR QIZILBASH is Professor of Politics, Economics and Philosophy at the University of York.

SABINA ALKIRE is Director of the Oxford Poverty and Human Development Initiative (OPHI) at the University of Oxford.

The Capability Approach

Concepts, Measures and Applications

Edited by

FLAVIO COMIM,
MOZAFFAR QIZILBASH
and
SABINA ALKIRE

CAMBRIDGE
UNIVERSITY PRESS

CAMBRIDGE UNIVERSITY PRESS
Cambridge, New York, Melbourne, Madrid, Cape Town, Singapore,
São Paulo, Delhi, Dubai, Tokyo, Mexico City

Cambridge University Press
The Edinburgh Building, Cambridge CB2 8RU, UK

Published in the United States of America by Cambridge University Press, New York

www.cambridge.org
Information on this title: www.cambridge.org/9780521154529

© Cambridge University Press 2008

First published 2008
First paperback printing 2010

A catalogue record for this publication is available from the British Library

ISBN 978-0-521-86287-5 Hardback
ISBN 978-0-521-15452-9 Paperback

Contents

Figures

Tables

Contributors

Sabina Alkire	Director, Oxford Poverty and Human Development Initiative (OPHI), University of Oxford
Antonio Andracchio	Researcher, Centre for International Development, Bologna
Pier Giorgio Ardeni	Full Professor of Political Economy and Development Economics, University of Bologna
Enrica Chiappero-Martinetti	Associate Professor in Economics, University of Pavia and Director of the Human Development, Capability and Poverty International Research Centre (HDCP-IRC) at the Institute for Advanced Study, Pavia
Kanchan Chopra	Director, Institute of Economic Growth, University of Delhi
Flavio Comim	Director of the Capability and Sustainability Centre (CSC) and Fellow of St Edmund's College, University of Cambridge and Fellow of Universidade Federal do Rio Grande do Sul, Porto Alegre (UFRGS), Brazil
Tom De Herdt	Vice-chair and Director of MA programmes, Institute of Development Policy and Management (IOB), University of Antwerp
Séverine Deneulin	Lecturer in International Development, University of Bath
Laurent Derobert	Fellow, University of Avignon
Jean-Luc Dubois	Director of Research, Centre of Economics and Ethics for Environment and Development (C3ED), Institute of Research for Development (IRD), University of Versailles Saint Quentin-en-Yvelines (UVSQ)

Anantha Kumar Duraiappah	Chief, Ecosystem Services and Economics, United Nations Environment Programme
Sara Lelli	Assistant Professor, Università Cattolica del Sacro Cuore, Piacenza
Santosh Mehrotra	Senior Adviser, Planning Commission, Government of India
Fotis Papadopoulos	Researcher, Athens University of Economics and Business
Mozaffar Qizilbash	Professor of Politics, Economics and Philosophy, University of York
Ingrid Robeyns	Senior Researcher in Political Theory, Radboud University Nijmegen, The Netherlands
Sophie Rousseau	Researcher, Centre of Economics and Ethics for Environment and Development (C3ED), Institute of Research for Development (IRD), University of Versailles Saint Quentin-en-Yvelines (UVSQ)
Caterina Ruggeri Laderchi	Economist, The World Bank
Kirsten Sehnbruch	Senior Scholar and Lecturer, Center for Latin American Studies, University of California at Berkeley
Miriam Teschl	Lecturer, Robinson College, University of Cambridge
Panos Tsakloglou	Professor, Athens University of Economics and Business
Elaine Unterhalter	Reader in Education and International Development, Institute of Education, University of London
Shahin Yaqub	Social Policy Specialist, UNICEF Innocenti Research Centre

Acronyms

APF	adaptive preference formation
ANOVA	analysis of variance
BI	Bamako Initiative
CA	capability approach
CVP	Chakriya Vikas Pranali
DPEP	District Primary Education Programme
EGS	Education Guarantee Scheme
ECHP	European Community Household Panel
EU	European Union
FHH	female-headed household
GDI	gender-related development index
GDP	gross domestic product
GNP	gross national product
HCI	Head-Count Index
HP	Himachal Pradesh
HLSS	Household Living Standard Survey
HDI	Human Development Index
HDI	Human Development Indicator
IF	Institution-Freedom
INE	Instituto Nacional de Estatìstica
IFPRI	International Food Policy Research Institute
MP	Madhya Pradesh
MHH	male-headed household
MANOVA	Multivariate Analysis of Variance
MSF	Médecins Sans Frontières
MDGS	Millennium Development Goals
MIMIC	multiple indicators and multiple causes
NFE	non-formal education
OECD	Organisation for Economic Co-Operation and Development
PRI	panchayati raj institutions

PSBH	Panel Study of Belgian Households
PGI	Poverty Gap Index
SEM	Structural Equation Modelling
SPGI	Squared Poverty Gap Index
UNDP	United Nations Development Program
UNESCO	United Nations Educational, Scientific and Cultural Organization
VEC	Village Education Committee

Acknowledgements

In 2001 a conference was organised at the University of Cambridge to study concepts, measures and applications of Amartya Sen's capability approach. The conference – entitled 'Justice and Poverty: Examining Sen's Capability Approach' – was hosted by St Edmund's, New Hall and Lucy Cavendish colleges and sponsored by the British Academy. Particular thanks go to the heads of these three Cambridge colleges, respectively, Sir Brian Heap, Mrs Anne Lonsdale and Baroness Perry of Southwark, for their encouragement and support.

The conference was conceived and convened by Frank Carey and Flavio Comim, and organised by Angels Varea and Kohei Watanabe. It involved thirty-eight paper presentations, as well as working group sessions on different topics. Amartya Sen, Sabina Alkire and Mozaffar Qizilbash gave the three invited talks. Frank Carey made a series of inspirational and humane interventions, inviting participants not merely to exchange intellectual ideas but also to think concretely about how these might serve the poorest of the poor. Carey's comments set a moral tone that ran through the event. The conference culminated in a plenary session at which Professor Sen addressed issues raised by working groups. We are particularly grateful to Professor Sen for his generosity and engagement.

This conference proved to be a turning point in organising scholars interested in the capability approach. Conferences have been held every year subsequently, with the 2002 conference on 'Promoting Women's Capabilities: Examining Nussbaum's Capabilities Approach' also organised under the leadership of Frank Carey and Flavio Comim in Cambridge. Annual conferences now provide the primary opportunity for members of the Human Development and Capability Association (HDCA), which was launched in 2004, to meet and exchange ideas. It is to that Association that all profits from this book will be donated.

Once papers were submitted for consideration, the three editors divided these between them, with Comim and Qizilbash taking primary responsibility for oversight of the refereeing of individual papers, while each editor also took responsibility for comments on his or her own paper. The entire volume was also subjected to anonymous review by Cambridge University Press. From 2006 Alkire saw the manuscript through to production.

The editors would like to express their appreciation to all those who made this book possible. We are especially grateful to the authors for their considerable patience in tolerating numerous delays, as completion of this project took much longer than we hoped. We would also like to express our gratitude to those who refereed papers, including the many papers not included in this volume: Elizabeth Anderson, Tony Atkinson, Pip Bevan, David Bridges, Debbie Budlender, Frank Carey, Meghnad Desai, Jean Drèze, Anantha Giri, Charles Gore, Stephan Klasen, Wiebke Kuklys, Achille Lemmi, Francis McHugh, Gay Meeks, Leonardo Monasterio, Mathias Nebel, Makiko Omura, Onora O''Neill, Vijayendra Rao, Nicolas Sagovsky, Frances Stewart, Diana Strassmann, Simon Szreter and Katarzyna Zawalinska. For research and editorial assistance we are greatly in debt to Afsan Bhadelia for her expert and cheerful assistance.

We should also like to express our gratitude to Sage Publications for permission to reproduce excerpts from their books and to the Lauren Rodgers Museum of Art in Mississippi for permission to use the Millet crayon drawing on the cover.

Finally, we thank Chris Harrison and the staff at Cambridge University Press for their work on production, particularly for managing to secure the cover artwork, as well as all those people, too numerous to mention, who gave patience, encouragement and insights along the way.

Introduction

SABINA ALKIRE, MOZAFFAR QIZILBASH
AND FLAVIO COMIM

Amartya Sen's capability approach has generated remarkable interest in recent years. This volume brings together a selection of papers initially presented at an international conference on the capability approach (CA) held at St Edmund's College, Cambridge in 2001. This conference marked an important turning point in research on the capability approach. It brought together many young scholars who were interested in the approach as well as others who had been working on it for some time. The conference was initially motivated by issues relating to the usefulness of the approach in the particular contexts of poverty and injustice. However, conference papers covered a wide range of topics relating to concepts, measurement and other applications. In this volume, the papers are categorised in terms of these broad and overlapping areas. In 2002 a follow-up conference explored Martha Nussbaum's version of the approach, and annual conferences have been held in subsequent years.[1] Numerous initiatives have since emerged, including the Human Development and Capability Association (www.hd-ca.org). In part as a result of these initiatives, but also quite independently of them, a large literature on the capability approach has emerged.

Amartya Sen's 1980 Tanner lecture, 'Equality of What?', set out a broad agenda for debate and further research. While the approach has been extensively discussed, Sabina Alkire suggests in Chapter 1 that work in this area is still at a relatively early stage. The drawing on the cover of this volume – a version of Jean-François Millet's 'Les Premiers Pas de l'Enfance' ('The First Steps of Childhood') – shows a child taking its first tentative steps, supported by her mother. Only time will tell

---

[1] Nussbaum 1988, Nussbaum 1990, Nussbaum 1992, Nussbaum 1993, Nussbaum and Sen 1993, Nussbaum 1995, Nussbaum 1995, Nussbaum, Glover and World Institute for Development Economics Research 1995, Nussbaum 1998, Nussbaum 1998, Nussbaum 2000, Nussbaum 2000, Nussbaum 2001, Nussbaum 2002, Nussbaum 2003, Nussbaum 2005, Nussbaum 2006.

whether this image provides an appropriate metaphor for this early phase of work on the capability approach. Part of the value of bringing together a set of papers in a volume of this sort is that these papers allow us to assess how far the approach has gone and to define – however tentatively – potential directions for work on the approach. The volume brings together a diverse set of voices, each of which engages with the approach in its distinct manner. However, we emphasise that many of the chapters engage critically with different aspects of the approach, freely questioning and wrestling with it. Indeed, such critical engagement is a common theme of this volume. We hope to bring out the flavour and nature of this engagement in what follows through reference to relevant chapters in this introduction.

At this stage, it is not entirely foreseeable which directions will be pursued in future work on the capability approach and how fruitful they will turn out to be. If we return to the Millet crayon drawing, part of what engages our attention is the unpredictability of the child's first steps and the hope – and anxiety – that unpredictability generates. The steps of a child are powered by its unique curiosity, temperament and circumstances. Similar unpredictability is evident in the emerging literature on the capability approach. It is part of what makes this literature both intriguing and exciting. We hope that this volume will convey some of that excitement.

Concepts

The central concepts involved in the capability approach are capability and functioning. Functionings are what Sen (1999: 75) calls 'the various things a person may value being and doing'. Examples include being adequately nourished, being in good health, avoiding escapable morbidity, being happy, having self-respect, and taking part in the life of the community (Sen 1992: 39). There is no definitive list of basic functionings because different sets will be relevant to different groups and in distinct settings (Sen 2005: 157–160). A person's capability 'represents the various combinations of functionings (beings and doings) that the person can achieve' (Sen 1992: 40). To this degree, the person's capability reflects her freedom or (real) opportunities. Sen has used these concepts to analyse the quality of life, egalitarian justice and poverty *inter alia*. He has demonstrated the insights which arise from a capability or functioning-based analysis in comparison with analyses which exclusively use information on resources, or income, or 'utility' (when this is understood as happiness or desire satisfaction). The capability approach thus broadens the informational basis used in normative evaluations.

To illustrate some of these ideas, consider the quality of life of the painter Vincent Van Gogh, in the winter of 1889. At that time Van Gogh painted an interpretation of Millet's 'The First Steps of Childhood'.[2] It is certainly true that Van Gogh had little income and that he was heavily dependent on his brother for financial support. However, if we considered his position *only* as regards income or resources we would have a very limited understanding of the quality of his life. In the months when he was working on this painting – as well as other paintings based on Millet's work – he was extremely unwell and had recurrent fits. To this degree, he was clearly deprived in terms of Sen's functioning 'being in good health'. In addition, these paintings were created in the asylum of Saint-Rémy de Provence where he did not have people who could sit for portraits. As a consequence, his brother Theo sent him some black and white reproductions of works by Millet and Eugène Delacroix, which he worked from. Van Gogh's choice of 'The First Steps of Childhood' as a subject reflected the limited opportunities or capability he had. His limited opportunities involved a form of disadvantage which may not be adequately captured through an analysis which merely checked his level of 'utility' (in terms of happiness or desire satisfaction), partly because he may have learned to adjust to the circumstances he found himself in.

Capability and functioning remain intimately connected but independently useful concepts in Sen's writings. Because capability is a collection of functionings a person can achieve, capability is evaluated in the 'space' of functionings, thus functionings are integral elements of capabilities. However, the focus on capability directs our attention to freedom and opportunity – which functionings cannot do. Sen does not claim that capability is all that matters; functionings retain ongoing value in themselves. He also leaves open the relative importance of capability as opposed to functionings as well as the relative weights to be given to different capabilities or

[2] Van Gogh's interpretation is to be found in the Metropolitan Museum of Art in New York.

functionings (Sen 1992: 49–53 and 1999: 76–77). These are some of a range of ways in which the approach is intentionally open-ended and incomplete.

In addition to capability and functioning, Sen defines a third core concept, agency. On his account, an agent is 'someone who acts and brings about change' (Sen 1999: 19). The agency aspect is important in assessing 'what a person is free to do and achieve in pursuit of whatever goals or values he or she regards as important' (Sen 1985: 203). In some writings, agency – as well as capability – figures centrally. For example, the approach adopted in Drèze and Sen's book *India: Development and Participation* as well as many of Sen's single-authored writings 'puts human agency (rather than organisations such as markets or governments) at the centre of the stage' (2002: 6). When Roland de Leeuw notes that Van Gogh initially had as a 'social objective' that his Millet paintings would be presented to a local school – presumably to expose young people to Millet's work – it is agency which is relevant (de Leeuw 1996: 466). Of course, Van Gogh's aim if realised would also mark an achievement in terms of functionings, as regards 'taking part in the life of the community'.

Sen uses a range of distinctions in his writings on freedom and development. To clarify his conceptual framework and to avoid potential confusion, we introduce two further terms: 'opportunity freedom' and 'process freedom' (Sen 1999; 2002: chapters 19–21). While 'opportunity freedom' refers to what people have opportunity or ability to achieve, 'process freedom' refers to 'the *process* through which things happen' (Sen 2002: 585). Clearly capability is closely related to opportunity freedom; agency relates to personal process freedoms.

As might be expected given the richness of foundational concepts, several interpretations of the scope of the capability approach are used in the wider literature and indeed in this book. These can be charted between two poles: one narrow and one broad, with the broad subsuming the narrow. The capability approach proposes that the comparison or evaluation of advantage or deprivation (whether or not through measurement) should occur in the space of capabilities *inter alia* (rather than simply utility or commodities), or in some sensible approximation of capabilities such as a vector of achieved functionings. The *narrow* interpretation sees the approach primarily as identifying capability and functionings as the primary informational space for certain exercises. The *broad* interpretation views the capability approach as providing a more extensive and demanding evaluative framework, for example by introducing human rights or plural principles beyond the expansion of capabilities – principles which embody other values or concerns such as equity, sustainability or responsibility.

Both interpretations can be found in Sen's writings. Like the narrow interpretation, the *broad* interpretation argues that the quality of life should be evaluated primarily in the space of capabilities. However, information on capabilities alone is not sufficient. Other considerations (such as rights, process or agency) would enter the overall evaluation of states of affairs in this framework. To illustrate, consider an example which Sen has used recently. The example starts from the well-known claim that in similar conditions women live longer than men. It might be possible, Sen suggests, to equalise people's capability as regards their life chances. However, pursuing such equality, perhaps by discriminating against women in the distribution of health care, would violate process freedom (Sen 2002: 660–661 and 2005: 156; see also Tsuchiya and Williams 2005). On a narrow interpretation, this example can be used to illustrate the limits of the capability approach. By contrast, on a broad interpretation, the very same example might be used to show how the capability approach introduces additional distributional considerations (see also Sen 1985 and 2000). In both the narrow and broad interpretations, the capability approach is viewed as a tool for evaluation – comparing situations with respect to the real opportunities they offer, among other things.

Sen (1984, 1990 and 1999) also frames the objective of development as an 'expansion of capabilities'. This has led to an interest in identifying courses of action or policies that would further this objective. So going beyond the capability approach as an *evaluative space* or *framework*, we can identify a third preoccupation in the literature on the capability approach and, relatedly, human development which focuses on generating *prospective* policies, activities and recommendations. This preoccupation is central to the discussion in the section on measurement and other applications later in this introduction. The chapters in this volume, nonetheless, span all three aspects of the literature.

Much of the philosophical literature is concerned with debates relating to the capability approach as an evaluative space and its relationship to, and perceived merits and weaknesses in comparison with, other approaches. Contributions have included a wide range of papers on justice, happiness, needs and opportunities.[3] Chapters by Alkire, Mozaffar Qizilbash and Ingrid Robeyns engage critically with these issues. Alkire traces the boundaries of the approach and distinguishes evaluative and prospective aspects. Robeyns investigates the ability of the capability approach to address feminist concerns and shows that it can be seen as a 'gender-sensitive evaluative framework'. She expresses a worry raised elsewhere in the literature about the 'under-specified' nature of the approach.[4] Qizilbash considers the extent to which Sen's approach contrasts with the views of happiness, poverty and gender justice in John Stuart Mill's writings. He finds the two approaches remarkably similar in spite of the fact that one is a leading critic, while the other is one of the founders, of utilitarianism.

Another theme in the debate is the relationship between the individual and society in Sen's writings on capability.[5] Chapters by Alkire, Séverine Deneulin, Robeyns and Miriam Teschl and Laurent Derobert engage critically with this debate at the conceptual level. Alkire argues that many criticisms of the so-called 'individualism' of the capability approach arise when the capability approach is drawn upon to generate 'prospective' recommendations (rather than evaluations in the broad or narrow sense). She clarifies that prospective recommendations generated in the capability literature inevitably draw upon institutions and intermediary processes and do not posit Robeyns' methodological individualism, so the criticisms, while accurate in substance, misattribute an individualism that the capability approach lacks.

Deneulin is unconvinced that Sen's capability approach can give sufficient importance to what Charles Taylor has called 'irreducibly plural goods'. She puts forward the notion of 'socio-historical agency' as central

---

[3] Cohen 1989, Cohen 1993, Anderson 1995, Qizilbash 1996, Qizilbash 1996, Alkire and Black 1997, Qizilbash 1997, Qizilbash 1998, Anderson 1999, Anderson 2000, Arneson 2000, Alkire 2002, Qizilbash 2002, Anderson 2003, Sumner 2004, McGillivray 2005, Stewart 1988, Doyal and Gough 1991, Doyal and Gough 1992, Rawls 1993, Sugden 1993, Gasper 1996, Sugden 1998, Dworkin 2000, Pogge 2002, Roemer 2002, Robeyns 2003, Sugden 2003, Griffin 1986, Pattanaik and Xu 1990, Pattanaik and Xu 1998, Pattanaik and Xu 2000, Pattanaik and Xu 2000, Carter and Ricciardi 2001, Pettit 2001, Sen 2001, Carter 2004, Olsaretti 2005, Robeyns 2005, Robeyns 2005, Robeyns 2005, Beitz 1986, Arneson 1989, Rawls and Kelly 2001, Comim 2005, Alkire 2006, Sumner 2006.

[4] See Hill 2003, Qizilbash 2005.

[5] Gore (1997), Evans (2002), Stewart and Deneulin (2002), Sen (2002), Gasper and van Staeveren (2003) and Stewart (2005) *inter alia*.

in the promotion of capabilities, bringing into perspective an empirical illustration of capability expansion in Costa Rica. Her chapter can be read as making the case for a further broadening of the informational basis of the capability approach – when this is used as the basis for prescriptions – to include Paul Ricoeur's notion of 'structures of living together' which belong to a particular historical community but are irreducible to individual relations. Deneulin's argument suggests that in its current form the approach is not just incomplete but potentially misleading.

Robeyns distinguishes between ethical individualism – where the ultimate unit of concern is the individual – and methodological and ontological individualism – which hold that social phenomena can be explained by reference to individuals alone, and that society is merely a sum of its individual parts. She defends ethical individualism, arguing that it is necessary for an adequate account of the wellbeing of women and children. Teschl and Derobert explore how a person's agency and identity influences their choice of functionings from their 'capability set' – the set of vectors of functioning from which they choose. They note the powerful role that a person's diverse social identities can have in influencing their choices. In spite of the apparent contrast between Sen's alleged 'individualism' and the focus on community in the 'communitarian' literature, Teschl and Derobert find that Sen's position is closer to that of one leading figure in that literature – Michael Sandel – than either Sen or Sandel might acknowledge.

Measures and applications

Given that evaluation of capability raises a challenging array of issues of measurement, aggregation, comparison, vagueness, etc., it is with good reason that a growing literature explores these issues. Sen has distinguished three ways in which the capability perspective can inform empirical and quantitative measurement work: the 'direct approach' – which 'takes the form of directly examining and comparing vectors of functionings or capabilities'; the 'supplementary approach' – which involves 'use of traditional procedures of interpersonal comparisons in income spaces but supplements them with capability considerations'; and the 'indirect approach' – which 'remains focussed on the familiar space of incomes, appropriately adjusted' (Sen 1999: 82–3). *Each of these approaches is seen as a way of giving 'practical shape to the foundational concern'* (Sen 1999: 81).

In this introduction, we interpret the notion of 'application' broadly so that it covers the various ways in which a conceptual approach can be given a practical shape or value. Applications matter, not only because intellectual effort can contribute to practical change and inform policy-making but also because they can reshape understanding and contribute towards better conceptualisations of social phenomena and assessment procedures. Some applications involve measurement, but measurability is not a necessary condition for giving practical shape or value to a conceptual approach. The wide range of capability applications described in this book may contribute to shaping and illuminating the insights of the capability approach and can provide further refinements of its conceptual foundations.

The measurement literature includes examples of the direct, indirect and supplementary approaches at work. The direct approach is the most ambitious way of applying the capability approach. Attempts to pursue it typically address the multi-dimensional nature of wellbeing, inequality or poverty when these are understood in terms of capability or functionings. For this reason, some applications of the capability approach are close relatives of other approaches to multi-dimensional measurement. A large literature on such multi-dimensional measurement of wellbeing, poverty and inequality has emerged.[6]

Some of the issues which arise for multi-dimensional measurement are illustrated in Figure 0.1 with respect to poverty. The vertical axis represents achievement in terms of some indicator(s) for some domains. The horizontal axis shows the time across which achievement is measured, which may include future as well as present poverty. A specific level, or range of levels, of achievement constitutes a poverty threshold, or fuzzy poverty band, for each domain which may change

---

[6] Bourguignon and Chakravarty 1999, 2003, Majumdar and Subramanian 2001, Majumdar and Subramanian 2002, Atkinson 2003, Kuklys 2005, Pattanaik and Xu 1990, Schokkaert and Van Ootegem 1990, Klemischahlert 1993, Foster 1994, Gravel 1994, Puppe 1995, Chakraborty 1996, Chiappero-Martinetti 1996, Dutta and Sen 1996, Puppe 1996, Bossert 1997, Diener and Suh 1997, Ok 1997, Brandolini and D'Alessio 1998, Gravel 1998, Ok and Kranich 1998, Pattanaik and Xu 1998, Qizilbash 1998, Sugden 1998, van Hees and Wissenburg 1999, Bossert 2000, Burchardt 2000, Chiappero-Martinetti 2000, Cummins 2000, Klasen 2000, Pattanaik and Xu 2000, Gekker 2001, Fleurbaey 2002, Fleurbaey 2002, Atkinson 2003, Cummins 2003, Robeyns 2003, Sugden 2003, Qizilbash 2004, Robeyns 2004, Drèze and Sen 1989, Drèze and Sen 1991, Drèze and Sen 1991, Drèze and Sen 1997, Tsui 1999, Drèze and Sen 2002, Tsui 2002, Grusky, Kanbur and Sen 2006.

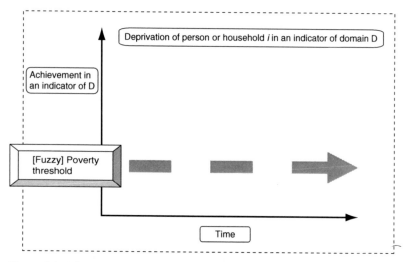

Figure 0.1 Schematic overview of multi-dimensional poverty for individual *i*

over time. This is represented by the broken arrow in the diagram. If a person or group falls within the fuzzy poverty band it is ambiguous whether they are poor. Multidimensional measurement would include information of this sort for each dimension.

Recurrent questions in this literature comprise the following. Which are the *domains* or dimensions that will be included, and on what basis?[7] Which *indicator(s)* best represent each domain or functioning, and on what grounds will these be selected? What is the poverty *threshold* for each indicator, or, if a fuzzy threshold is defined, what are the upper and lower boundaries of the fuzzy poverty band? How does one represent the *interaction* between different indicators and the interactions between dimensions of poverty and identify substitutes and complements? In those cases in which it is necessary to aggregate across domains, how is this achieved and what *relative weights* are set for various domains? And how does one *aggregate* across individuals? Various approaches to multi-dimensional poverty measurement propose clear answers to these questions. A multi-dimensional measure of poverty – the human poverty index – which Sen developed with Sudhir Anand (Anand and Sen 1997) is an example of such a particular measure which is inspired by the capability approach. Decisions about

[7] Alkire 2002, Robeyns 2005, Clark 2003, Clark 2005.

the selection of dimensions, indicators and weights are made in all the multi-dimensional measures of human development – most obviously in the Human Development Index (or HDI), developed by the United Nations Development Programme (UNDP) – and related measures of gender inequality (McGillivray and White 1993; Anand *et al.* 1994; Streeten 1994; Anand *et al.* 1995; Anand and Sen 1997; Anand and Sen 2000; Anand and Sen 2000; Sen 2000; World Bank 2000; Ogwang and Abdou 2003; McGillivray 2005).

While there is a significant overlap between applications of the capability approach and other approaches to multi-dimensional measurement, the capability approach is distinctive inasmuch as it stresses that capabilities and functionings have value in themselves: 'intrinsic value'. Income, by contrast, is seen as having 'instrumental value' – value as a means to the realisation of other ends. While some 'indirect' applications of the capability approach use income as a proxy measure for certain capabilities (see Anand and Sen 2000 and Klasen 2000), income is not usually seen as a dimension of wellbeing itself. Furthermore, the fact that income has an instrumental rather than intrinsic value can influence the form in which income enters into a multi-dimensional measure.[8] This is one among a number of instances where the capability approach as a conceptual framework has implications for measurement. Tracing out such implications is a central theme of Flavio Comim's chapter. Drawing on the writings of both Nussbaum and Sen, he shows the relevance of the approach – understood broadly as an extensive evaluative framework – to measurement issues. Comim also illustrates his claims in various concrete contexts, discussing empirical work carried out in research projects aiming to measure capabilities.

Figure 0.1 also allows us to address a question which has been neglected in the literature on capability: how to handle time? It locates any individual's or group's achievement in a relevant dimension in time. If relevant information is available across time, we would then be able to judge whether a person's failure to achieve a minimally adequate level in some dimension is merely temporary or 'chronic'. This would be one way to link work on capability to work on 'chronic poverty' (Hulme and Shepherd 2003). By locating people or groups in time, Figure 0.1 illustrates how one might study capability dynamics. It also allows one to consider whether or not a person or group situated at

---

[8] Anand and Sen 2000: 99–102 discuss this point in relation to the HDI.

some point in time might become poor in the future. Such 'vulnerability' is a rich research theme (Morduch 1994; Dercon and Krishnan 2000) which has just started to be explored in the literature on the capability approach. While some commentators have discussed how time might be addressed in the capability perspective (Comim 2005), there is scope for further work on these topics. In Chapter 8, Fotis Papadopoulos and Panos Tsakloglou address the time dimension explicitly. They develop an approach to the measurement of social exclusion using the capability approach. They discuss some practical problems involved in using the CA: from an elaboration of a list of functionings and weighting issues to an evaluation of chosen capabilities. In their chapter, if deprivation in certain dimensions occurs for a number of periods in time, it constitutes social exclusion.[9]

Applications of the capability approach have also used techniques to capture the vagueness of notions such as poverty, wellbeing and inequality more explicitly than other work on multi-dimensional measurement. Enrica Chiappero-Martinetti argues that the capability approach's ability to address complex problems without imposing artificial precision is a strength and that fuzzy measures provide one technique by which to capture this strength in empirical analyses – for example of poverty. Sara Lelli compares fuzzy measures with factor analysis using Belgian data. She investigates the empirical consequences of using particular techniques to the operationalisation of the capability approach. She shows how factor analysis could be a helpful device for defining a limited number of easily interpretable dimensions of capabilities and how fuzzy set analysis could be used to qualify the transition from membership to non-membership among different capabilities' characteristics. She finds that the results that emerge from using these two techniques are remarkably similar. Qizilbash suggests that fuzzy poverty measures might be understood as measures of 'vulnerability', though he contrasts such 'vulnerability' from other definitions in much recent work.

While a number of studies look at a comprehensive set of dimensions of wellbeing, inequality and poverty, others focus on a smaller subset of such capabilities or functionings. Work which selects such a subset of capabilities or functionings often shows that approaches that focus on

---

[9] For an alternative approach to the measurement of social exclusion using the CA, see Bossert, D'Ambrosio and Peragine 2004.

income alone are inadequate. Many of Sen's applications of the capability approach have taken this form (Sen 1984; Drèze and Sen 2002). Using Peruvian household survey data, Caterina Ruggeri Laderchi explores the policy relevance of using indicators of, and 'production functions' for, health and education rather than income. Because these capabilities are particularly significant, she takes the position that indicators of morbidity and functional illiteracy are adequate indicators for them. She finds that capability analyses provide more policy-adequate guidance than income analyses. In the context of Mozambique, Giorgio Ardeni and Antonio Andracchio explore one of the central tenets of the CA, that resources are imperfect indicators of wellbeing, arguing that women in female-headed households are not necessarily poorer than men in the space of resources, but that they are much more vulnerable when seen in the space of functionings (such as health and education), providing evidence for a phenomenon known as 'feminisation of poverty'. Kirsten Sehnbruch uses the capability approach to develop a broad index of the 'quality of employment'. She shows that, in the context of the Chilean labour market, this index illuminates a range of policy-relevant issues which would otherwise not be highlighted.

These chapters are among a range of applications of the capability approach that empirically demonstrate the relative strength of analysis and accuracy of policy advice that arise from a reliance on functionings rather than monetary measures, and suggests that these replace or at least supplement standard income, expenditure or consumption measures.[10] At the very least, the findings in these chapters thus make a strong case for using what Sen calls the 'supplementary approach' in certain contexts. In fact, such an approach seems to be implicit in a wide range of policy contexts, as can be seen in the formulation of the 'Millennium Development Goals' (where income poverty headcount indices are supplemented by a wide range of other indicators). Finally, there is now a significant econometrics literature which focuses on the question of how one might adjust income measures to reflect the different rates at which individuals transform income into capability and functioning. This literature pursues what Sen calls the 'indirect

---

[10] For a summary of applications of the approach which distinguish the distinct nature of findings and policy conclusions see Kuklys 2005: 25–28. See also Chiappero-Martinetti's chart in this volume (Table 9.1).

approach'. It has been insightful in the context of disability (Kuklys 2005; Zaidi and Burchardt 2005) and may be useful in other contexts.

In some attempts to apply the capability approach, the question of where information on *freedom* enters – as agency measures for specific dimensions[11] or in other ways – also arises. Often it is also noted that while achieved functionings are easily observed, a person's capability is not. Some of those who are sceptical about the usefulness of the capability approach view this problem as a fatal flaw. Others – including Sen (1999: 81–82 and 131) and some contributors to this volume (including Comim, Ruggeri Laderchi and Chiappero-Martinetti) – follow a more constructive strategy. While there have also been some attempts to focus specifically on capability rather than functionings in applied work, this is an area where there is scope for further work.[12] However, worries about this issue have not held back work on measurement which is guided by the capability perspective. For those researchers who are looking for tools to use in applying that perspective, the literature provides a rich menu of options, or at least a starting point and set of challenges, for further work. If capability-based measurement is in its early stages then the tools which are at hand may be somewhat rudimentary – rather like the spade and barrow in Millet's 'The First Steps of Childhood' – but there are already many such tools as well as clearly defined possibilities for the use and development of techniques which can be explored.

As noted at the beginning of this section, while measurement can help to make a conceptual approach an object of practical value, measurement is not a necessary condition for the application of such an approach. While much of the conceptual and measurement literature has focused on the capability approach as identifying an appropriate space for evaluation, as noted earlier a rich literature has also emerged on generating prospective policies, activities and recommendations, particularly in the context of development conceived as capability expansion. The capability approach has proven to be a powerful tool in this arena quite independent of any work on measurement. At the most general level the approach has changed the language of policy work and public discussion on topics such as poverty, the quality of life and inequality. Part of the reason for this change has been the success of Sen's work on hunger and on the Indian

---

[11] Alkire 2005.
[12] Haverman and Bershadker 2001, Burchardt 2005 and Xu 2002.

economy, much of it co-authored with Jean Drèze (Drèze and Sen 1989 and 2002). However, Sen's collaboration with the United Nations Development Programme on various *Human Development Reports* has also led to the widespread use of the language of capability at the policy level and in public discussion and debate. While the HDI has been the most visible form in which the capability approach has had an impact on the policy world, this change in the language of policy and public discussion also needs to be noted.

There are many different areas such as health,[13] disability[14] and education[15] where the capability perspective has influenced the language of policy and public discussion. To illustrate, in the context of education the use of capabilities language has been introduced alongside the widespread use of the notion of 'human capital'. Because the capability approach focuses on the intrinsic value of various abilities and is not merely concerned with skills which are of instrumental use, it introduces a new dimension to some educational debates. While the use of the capability perspective in discussions about education may be fruitful, existing applications of the approach have also been criticised. In this volume, Elaine Unterhalter extends Sen's views on the role of education to enhance human wellbeing. She argues that education appears under-theorised in the capability approach. One could follow Robeyns' suggestion by supplementing the CA with additional theories. However, Unterhalter argues that the operationalisation of the CA by inclusion of complementary social theories could be 'problematic' as these theories could modify the features of the evaluative space used for normative assessments and how it is understood. She takes issue with Drèze and Sen's apparent equation of *schooling* with substantive freedom because of the many suboptimal or even harmful effects that poor-quality schools may have because of gender bias, violence, incendiary curricula, and so on.

Aside from having a pervasive influence on the language of public policy and discussion, specific policy proposals have also been generated by the capability approach. To this degree, conceptualising deprivation in terms of capability or functionings has an instrumental importance (Sen 1999: 131–132). In *Development as Freedom*, Sen challenges a

---

[13] Sen 2002, Sen 2002, Anand, Peter and Sen 2004, Anand and Dolan 2005.
[14] Burchardt 2004, Terzi 2005, Terzi 2005, Nussbaum 2006.
[15] Unterhalter 2003, Walker 2003, Walker 2006.

policy which focuses on lowness of income as a criterion for a transfer or subsidy. He suggests that while there are well-known incentive problems associated with income-targeted policies – particularly to do with the manipulation of information – focusing on capability or functioning deprivation may avoid these problems. There have been exceptional cases where even a focus on capability deprivation may not get round this problem – such as famine situations where a child has been used as a 'meal ticket' (Sen 1999: 133). However, such cases are likely to be rare. Tom De Herdt evaluates this argument in the context of the relative ineffectiveness of a food relief project run by *Médecins Sans Frontiers* in Kinshasa in the Congo. The data cited in his chapter do suggest that parents might use their children as a 'meal ticket'. However, De Herdt claims that if one includes capabilities such as 'the ability to appear in public without shame' (which Sen often cites), one can explain the data without resorting to the 'meal ticket' argument. De Herdt explores the use of capability-oriented reasoning in understanding incentive incompatibilities in eradicating malnutrition among children, and proposes indicators for programme performance – a common theme of this book.

Several other chapters engage with the policy dimension of Sen's work as it is articulated in *Development as Freedom* in particular. Significantly, at the level of policy prescriptions, *Development as Freedom* identifies five 'instrumental freedoms' which can be seen as 'crucially effective means' to the expansion of other salient capabilities. Instrumental freedoms include political freedoms, economic facilities, social opportunities, transparency guarantees and protective security (Sen 1999: 38–40). In this work, as in related work on hunger and the Indian economy, Sen explores the important role that institutions, including democratic institutions and the market, play in development. He also emphasises the critical importance of agency, which can be expressed in public debate, social movements and democratic practice. The book thus explores applications that put human freedom more at the centre of development and, importantly, are feasible. Nonetheless, Kanchan Chopra and Anantha Kumar Duraiappah, and Santosh Mehrotra suggest that the capability approach is incomplete without studies of the role that institutions play in supporting the evolution of capabilities over time. In the context of two case studies in India, Chopra and Duraiappah illustrate the importance of informal institutions in facilitating capability expansion. Mehrotra engages with democratic arrangements and the nature of participatory interventions in the characterisation of instrumental freedoms in India. Echoing Sen's emphasis on the importance of the practice of democracy, Mehrotra argues that certain forms of local participation are crucial during exercises of democratic decentralisation in order for these to realise the promised expansion of capabilities. His concern with successful social interventions in operationalising the CA is shared by many other contributors in this book.

Finally, Jean-Luc Dubois and Sophie Rousseau, and Shahin Yaqub stress the importance of time. Dubois and Rousseau see capability as a useful concept in the context of poverty policy. They argue that enhancing capabilities can be a poverty-prevention policy primarily because it can reduce a person's vulnerability (understood as the probability of having his/her own situation worsening in the face of a dramatic event). Dubois and Rousseau engage critically with the capability approach by suggesting that its static emphasis to date is insufficient. Shahin Yaqub explores 'the lifecourse approach to capabilities'. He argues that interventions which affect capabilities at an early stage in life can be a crucial factor in influencing the chances that a person will escape poverty at a later stage in life. He shows how time affects individuals' command over commodities, their 'personal utilisation functions' and the implications of their choices. Thus policies which aim at capability expansion must consider the lifecourse in prioritising interventions.

Concluding remarks

This book engages with a wide range of issues from disputed conceptual points to very practical concerns about public policy and discussion. This introduction has attempted to highlight certain gaps in the literature and pathways which might be pursued. At the same time, it has gathered together some of the themes in the diverse chapters. Critical engagement with Sen's writings on capability emerges as a central theme. So while we have stopped well short of summarising the chapters, our introductory remarks aim rather at enticing readers to look more closely at the chapters that follow. Just as 'The First Steps of Childhood' mark the end of a phase in a human life and hint at possibilities, we hope that this book allows readers to appreciate what has been achieved while anticipating and encouraging further research on the capability approach.

Cited references

Alkire, S. (2002) *Valuing Freedoms. Sen's Capability Approach and Poverty Reduction* (New York, Oxford: Oxford University Press).

Alkire, S. (2005) Subjective quantitative studies of human agency, *Social Indicators Research* (74), pp. 217–60.

Alkire, S. (2006) Needs and capabilities, in *The Philosophy of Need*, S. Reader (ed.) (Cambridge: Cambridge University Press).

Alkire, S. and R. Black (1997) A practical reasoning theory of development ethics: furthering the capabilities approach: Policy arena, *Journal of International Development* (9), pp. 263–79.

Anand, P. and P. Dolan (2005) Equity, capabilities and health, *Social Science & Medicine* (60), pp. 219–22.

Anand, P. and A. K. Sen (2004) *Public Health, Ethics, and Equity* (Oxford: Oxford University Press).

Anand, S. and A. Sen (1997) *Concepts of Human Development and Poverty: A Multidimensional Perspective* (New York: UNDP).

Anand, S. and A. Sen (2000) Human development and economic sustainability, *World Development* (28), pp. 2029–49.

Anand, S. and A. Sen (2000) The income component of the human development index, *Journal of Human Development* (1), p. 83.

Anand, S. and A. K. Sen (1994) *Human Development Index: Methodology and Measurement* (New York: Human Development Report Office UNDP).

Anand, S. and Sen, A. K. (1995) *Gender Inequality in Human Development: Theories and Measurement* (New York: Human Development Report Office UNDP).

Anderson, E. (1995) Book review of 'Inequality Reexamined', by Amartya Sen, *Economics and Philosophy* (11), pp. 182–8.

Anderson, E. (1999) What is the point of equality? *Ethics* (109), pp. 287–337.

Anderson, E. (2000) Beyond homo economicus: new developments in theories of social norms, *Philosophy and Public Affairs* (29), pp. 170–200.

Anderson, E. (2003) Sen, ethics and democracy, *Feminist Economics* (9), pp. 239–61.

Arneson, R. (1989) Equality and equal opportunity for welfare, *Philosophical Studies* (56), pp. 77–93.

Arneson, R. (2000) Perfectionism and politics, *Ethics* (111), pp. 37–63.

Atkinson, A. B. (2003) Multidimensional deprivation: contrasting social welfare and counting approaches, *Journal of Economic Inequality* (1), p. 51.

Beitz, C. (1986) Book review of 'Resources, Values and Development', by Amartya Sen, *Economics and Philosophy* (2), pp. 282–90.

Bossert, W. (1997) Opportunity sets and individual well-being, *Social Choice and Welfare* (14), pp. 97–112.

Bossert, W. (2000) Opportunity sets and uncertain consequences, *Journal of Mathematical Economics* (33) pp. 475–96.

Bossert, W., C. D'Ambrosio and V. Peragine (2004) Deprivation and social exclusion, CIREQ, 23. *Cahiers de recherche, 2002–2004.*

Bourguignon, François and Satya Chakravarty (1999) A family in multi-dimensional poverty measures, in *Advances in Econometrics, Income Distribution and Scientific Methodology: Essay in Honor of C. Dagum* (New York: Physica-Verlas).

Bourguignon, François, and Satya Chakravarty (2003) The measurement of multidimensional poverty, *Journal of Economic Inequality* (1), pp. 25–49.

Brandolini, A. and G. D'Alessio (1998) *Measuring Well-being in the Functioning Space* (Banco d'Italia Reseach Department).

Burchardt, T. (2003) Disability, capability and social exclusion, in *Understanding Social Security: Issues for social policy and practice*, J. Millar (ed.) The Policy Press.

Burchardt, T. (2004) Capabilities and disability: the capabilities framework and the social model of disability, *Disability and Society* (19), pp. 736–51.

Burchardt, T. (2005) Are one man's rags another man's riches? Identifying adaptive expectations using panel data, *Social Indicators Research* (74), pp. 57–102.

Carter, I. (2004) *A Measure of Freedom* (Oxford: New York).

Carter, I. and M. Ricciardi (2001) *Freedom, Power and Political Morality* (Basingstoke: Palgrave).

Chakraborty, A. (1996) On the possibility of a weighting system for functionings, *Indian Economic Review* (XXXI), pp. 241–50.

Chiappero-Martinetti, E. (1996) Standard of living evaluation based on Sen's approach: some methodological questions, *Politeia* (12), pp. 47–53.

Chiappero-Martinetti, E. (2000) A multidimensional assessment of well-being based on Sen's functioning approach, *Rivista Internazionale di Scienze Sociali* (108), pp. 207–39.

Clark, D. A. (2003) Concepts and perceptions of human well-being: some evidence from South Africa, *Oxford Development Studies* (31), pp. 173–96.

Clark, D. A. (2005) Sen's capability approach and the many spaces of human well-being, *Journal of Development Studies* (41), pp. 1339–68.

Cohen, G. A. (1989) On the currency of egalitarian justice, *Ethics* (99), pp. 906–44.

Cohen, G. A. (1993) Equality of what? On welfare, goods and capabilities, in *The Quality of Life*, M. Nussbaum and A. Sen (eds.) (Oxford: Clarendon Press), pp. 9–29.

Comim, F. (2005) Capability and happiness: possible synergies, *Review of Social Economy* (63), pp. 161–76.

Cummins, R. A. (2000) Objective and subjective quality of life: an interactive model, *Social Indicators Research* (52), pp. 55–72.

Cummins, R. A. (2003) Normative life satisfaction: measurement issues and a homeostatic model, *Social Indicators Research* (64), pp. 225–56.

Dercon, S. and P. Krishnan (2000) Vulnerability, seasonality and poverty in Ethiopia, *Journal of Development Studies* (36), 25–53.

Diener, E. and E. Suh (1997) Measuring quality of life: economic, social, and subjective indicators, *Social Indicators Research* (40), pp. 189–216.

Doyal, L. and I. Gough (1991) *A Theory of Human Need* (New York: Guilford Press).

Doyal, L. and I. Gough (1992) Need satisfaction as a measure of human welfare, in *Mixed Economies in Europe: An Evolutionary Perspective on their Emergence, Transition and Regulation*, W. Blaas and J. Foster (eds.) (Brookfield, VT: E. Elgar).

Drèze, J. and A. Sen (1991) Public action for social security: foundations and strategy, in *Social Security in Developing Countries*, E. E. Ahmad *et al.* (eds.) (Oxford: Clarendon Press).

Drèze, J. and A. K. Sen (1997) *Indian Development: Selected Regional Perspectives* (Delhi, Oxford and New York: Oxford University Press).

Drèze, J. and A. K. Sen (1989) *Hunger and Public Action* (Oxford, New York: Clarendon Press, Oxford University Press).

Drèze, J. and A. K. Sen (2002) *India, Development and Participation* (New Delhi, New York: Oxford University Press).

Dutta, B. and A. Sen (1996) Ranking opportunity sets and arrow impossibility theorems: correspondence results, *Journal of Economic Theory* (71), pp. 90–101.

Dworkin, R. (2000) *Equality and Capability* (Cambridge: Harvard University Press).

Evans, P. (2002) Collective capabilities, culture, and Amartya Sen's development as freedom, *Studies in Comparative International Development*, 37(2), 54–60.

Fleurbaey, M. (2002) Development, Capabilities, and Freedom, *Studies in Comparative International Development*, (37)(2), 71–77.

Fleurbaey, M. (2002) Equality of Resources Revisited, *Ethics*, (113), pp. 82–105.

Foster, J. (1994) Normative measurement: is theory relevant?, *American Economic Review* (84), pp. 365–70.

Gasper, D. (1996) Needs and basic needs: a clarification of meanings, levels and different streams of work, *Institute of Social Studies Working Paper* No. 210 (The Hague, Institute of Social Studies).

Gasper, D. and I. van Staeveren (2003) Development as Freedom – and as What Else?, *Feminist Economics*, (9:2/3).

Gekker, R. (2001) On the axiomatic approach to freedom as opportunity: a general characterization result, *Mathematical Social Sciences* (42), pp. 169–77.

Gore, C. (1997) Irreducible social goods and the informational basis of Amartya Sen's capability approach. *Journal of International Development*, 9(2), pp. 235–50.

Gravel, N. (1994) Can a ranking of opportunity sets attach an intrinsic importance to freedom of choice, *American Economic Review* (84), pp. 454–8.

Gravel, N. (1998) Ranking opportunity sets on the basis of their freedom of choice and their ability to satisfy preferences: a difficulty, *Social Choice and Welfare* (15), pp. 371–82.

Griffin, J. (1986) *Well-being: Its Meaning, Measurement, and Moral Importance* (Oxford: Clarendon Press).

Grusky, D. and R. Kanbur (2006) *Poverty and Inequality* (Stanford: Stanford University Press).

Haverman, R. and A. Bershadker (2001) The inability to be self-reliant as an indicator of poverty: trends for the U.S., 1975–97, *Review of Income and Wealth* (47), pp. 335–60.

Hill, M. (2003) Development as empowerment, *Feminist Economics* (9), pp. 117–35.

Hulme, D. and A. Shepherd (2003) Special issue: conceptualising chronic poverty, *World Development* (31), pp. 403–24.

Klasen, S. (2000) Measuring poverty and deprivation in South Africa, *Review of Income and Wealth* (46), pp. 33–58.

Klemischahlert, M. (1993) Freedom of choice – a comparison of different rankings of opportunity sets, *Social Choice and Welfare* (10), pp. 189–207.

Kuklys, W. (2005) *Amartya Sen's Capability Approach: Theoretical Insights and Empirical Applications* (Berlin: Springer).

Majumdar, M. and S. Subramanian (2001) Capability failure and group disparities: some evidence from India for the 1980s, *Journal of Development Studies* (37), pp. 104–40.

Majumdar, M. and S. Subramanian (2002) On measuring deprivation adjusted for group disparities, *Social Choice & Welfare* (19), pp. 265–80.

McGillivray, M. and H. White (1993) Measuring development? The UNDP's Human Development Index, *Journal of International Development*, 5(2), pp. 193–9.

McGillivray, M. and A. Shorrocks (2005) Inequality and multidimensional well-being, *Review of Income and Wealth* (51), pp. 193–9.

Morduch, J. (1994) Poverty and vulnerability, *American Economic Review* (84: 2), pp. 221–5.

Nussbaum, M. (1988) Nature, functioning and capability: Aristotle on political distribution, *Oxford Studies in Ancient Philosophy, Supplementary Volume*, pp. 145–84.

Nussbaum, M. (1990) Aristotelian social democracy. *Liberalism and the Good*, R. B. Douglass, G. M. Mara and H. S. Richardson (eds.) (New York: Routledge), pp. 203–52.

Nussbaum, M. (1992) Human functioning and social justice. In defense of Aristotelian essentialism, *Political Theory* (20), pp. 202–46.

Nussbaum, M. (1993) Non-relative virtues: an aristotelian approach, in *The Quality of Life*, M. C. Nussbaum and A. K. Sen (eds.) (Oxford: Clarendon Press), pp. 242–69.

Nussbaum, M. (1995) Aristotle on human nature and the foundations of ethics, in *World, Mind, and Ethics: Essays on the Ethical Philosophy of Bernard Williams*, J. E. J. Altham and R. Harrison (eds.) (Cambridge: Cambridge University Press). pp. 86–131.

Nussbaum, M. (1995) Human capabilities, female human being. *Women, Culture, and Development: A Study of Human Capabilities*, M. C. Nussbaum and J. Glover (eds.) (Oxford, New York: Clarendon Press, Oxford University Press). pp. 61–105.

Nussbaum, M. (1998) The good as discipline, the good as freedom, in *Ethics of Consumption: The Good Life, Justice and Global Stewardship*, D. Crocker and T. Linden (eds.) (Lanham, MD, Oxford: Rowmand and Littlefield Publishers), pp. 312–41.

Nussbaum, M. (2000) Aristotle, politics and human capabilities: a response to Antony, Arneson, Charlesworth and Mulgan, *Ethics* (111), pp. 102–40.

Nussbaum, M. (2000) *Women and Human Development: The Capabilities Approach* (Cambridge: Cambridge University Press).

Nussbaum, M. (2001) Adaptive preferences and women's options, *Economics and Philosophy* (17), pp. 67–88.

Nussbaum, M. (2003) Capabilities as fundamental entitlements: Sen and social justice, *Feminist Economics* (9), pp. 33–59.

Nussbaum, M. C. (1998) Public Philosophy and International Feminism, *Ethics* (108) (4), pp. 762–96.

Nussbaum, M. C. (2005) Women's bodies: violence, security, capabilities, *Journal of Human Development* (6), pp. 167–84.

Nussbaum, M. C. (2006) *Frontiers of Justice: Disability, Nationality, Species Membership* (Cambridge, MA: The Belknap Press of Harvard University Press).

Nussbaum, M.C. and J. Glover (eds.) (1995) *Women, Culture, and Development: A Study of Human Capabilities* (Oxford, New York: Clarendon Press, Oxford University Press).

Nussbaum, M.C. and A.K. Sen (1993) *The Quality of Life* (Oxford: Clarendon Press).

Ogwang, T. and A. Abdou (2003) The choice of principal variables for computing some measures of human well-being, *Social Indicators Research* (64), pp. 139–52.

Ok, E.A. (1997) On opportunity inequality measurement, *Journal of Economic Theory* (77), pp. 300–29.

Ok, E.A. and L. Kranich (1998) The measurement of opportunity inequality: a cardinality-based approach, *Social Choice and Welfare* (15), pp. 263–87.

Olsaretti, S. (2005) Endorsement and freedom in Amartya Sen's capability approach, *Economics and Philosophy* (21), pp. 89–108.

Pattanaik, P. and Y. Xu (1990) On ranking opportunity sets in terms of freedom of choice, *Recherches Economiques de Louvain* (56), pp. 383–90.

Pattanaik, P.K. and Y.S. Xu (1998) On preference and freedom, *Theory and Decision* (44), pp. 173–98.

Pattanaik, P.K., and Y.S. Xu (2000) On diversity and freedom of choice, *Mathematical Social Sciences* (40), pp. 123–30.

Pattanaik, P.K., and Y.S. Xu (2000) On ranking opportunity sets in economic environments, *Journal of Economic Theory* (93), pp. 48–71.

Pettit, P. (2001) Capability and freedom: a defence of Sen, *Economics and Philosophy* (17), pp. 1–20.

Pogge, T. (2002) Can the capability approach be justified?, *Philosophical Topics* (30), pp. 167–228.

Puppe, C. (1995) Freedom of choice and rational decisions, *Social Choice and Welfare* (12), pp. 137–53.

Puppe, C. (1996) An axiomatic approach to 'preference for freedom of choice', *Journal of Economic Theory* (68), pp. 174–99.

Qizilbash, M. (1996) Capabilities, well-being and human development: a survey, *The Journal of Development Studies* (33), pp. 143–62.

Qizilbash, M. (1996) The concept of well-being, *Economics and Philosophy* 14, pp. 51–73.

Qizilbash, M. (1997) Pluralism and well-being indices, *World Development* (25), pp. 2009–26.

Qizilbash, M. (1998) The concept of well-being, *Economics and Philosophy* (14), pp. 51–73.

Qizilbash, M. (1998) Poverty: concept and measurement, Research Report No. 12, Sustainable Development Policy Institute, and paper presented at the annual conference of Development Studies Association, University of East Anglia, September 1997.

Qizilbash, M. (2002) Development, common foes and shared values, *Review of Political Economy* (14), pp. 463–80.

Qizilbash, M. (2004) On the arbitrariness and robustness of multi-dimensional poverty rankings, *Journal of Human Development* (5), pp. 355–76.

Qizilbash, M. (2005) Sen on freedom and gender justice, *Feminist Economics* (11), pp. 151–66.

Rawls, J. (1993) *Political Liberalism* (New York: Columbia University Press).

Rawls, J. and E. Kelly (2001) *Justice as Fairness: A Restatement* (Cambridge: Mass., Harvard University Press).

Robeyns, I. (2003) Sen's capability approach and gender inequality: selecting relevant capabilities, *Feminist Economics* (9), pp. 61–92.

Robeyns, I. (2005) Assessing global poverty and inequality: income, resources, and capabilities, *Metaphilosophy* (36), pp. 30–49.

Robeyns, I. (2005) Bibliography on the capability approach, 2004–2005, *Journal of Human Development* (6), pp. 421–26.

Robeyns, I. (2005) The capability approach: a theoretical survey, *Journal of Human Development* (6), pp. 93–114.

Robeyns, I. (2003) Does the gender division of labor result in unjust inequalities?, paper presented at the annual meeting of the American Political Science Association, Philadelphia Marriott Hotel, Philadelphia, PA, July 9.

Robeyns, I. (2004) Changing times: work and leisure in postindustrial society (book review), *Feminist Economics* 10, pp. 155–9.

Roemer, J. E. (2002) Equality of Opportunity: A Progress Report, *Social Choice and Welfare* (19), pp. 455–71.

Schokkaert, E. and L. Van Ootegem (1990) Sen's concept of the living standard applied to the Belgian unemployed, *Recherches Economiques de Louvain* (56), pp. 429–50.

Sen, A. (1980) Equality of What?, *Tanner Lectures on Human Values*, S. McMurin (ed.) (Cambridge: Cambridge University Press).

Sen, A. (1984) Family and food: sex bias in poverty, in *Resources Values & Development*, A. Sen (ed.) (Cambridge, MA: Harvard University Press). pp. 346–68.

Sen, Amartya K. (1985) Well-being, agency and freedom: The Dewey Lectures 1984, *The Journal of Philosophy*, 82, 169–221.

Sen, A. K. (1990) Development as capability expansion, in *Human Development and the International Development Strategy for the 1990s*, K. Griffin and J. Knight (eds.) (London: Macmillan).

Sen, Amartya K. (1992) *Inequality Re-examined* (Oxford: Clarendon Press).

Sen, Amartya K. (1999) *Development as Freedom*, 1st edn (New York: Knopf Press).

Sen, A. (2000) A decade of human development, *Journal of Human Development* (1), p. 17.

Sen, A. (2001) Reply, *Economics and Philosophy* (17), pp. 51–66.

Sen, A. (2002) Health: perception versus observation, *British Medical Journal* (324), pp. 860–61.

Sen, A. (2002) Why health equity?, *Health Economics* (11), pp. 659–66.

Sen, Amartya K. (2005) Human rights and capabilities, *Journal of Human Development*, 6, 151–66.

Stewart, F. (1989) Basic needs strategies, human rights and the right to development, *Human Rights Quarterly*, (11), pp. 347–74.

Stewart, F. (2005) Groups and capabilities, *Journal of Human Development*, 6(2).

Stewart, Frances and Severine Deneulin (2002) Amartya Sen's contribution to development thinking, *Studies in Comparative International Development*, (37), 61.

Streeten, P. (1994) Human development: means and ends, *American Economic Review* (84), pp. 232–37.

Sugden, R. (1993) Welfare, resources and capabilities: a review of inequality re-examined by Amartya Sen, *Journal of Economic Literature* (XXXVI), pp. 1947–62.

Sugden, R. (1998) The metric of opportunity, *Economics and Philosophy* (14), pp. 307–37.

Sugden, R. (2003) Opportunity as a space for individuality: its value and the impossibility of measuring it, *Ethics* (113), pp. 783–809.

Sumner, A. (2004) Economic well-being and non-economic well-being: a review of the meaning and measurement of poverty, *WIDER Research Paper #2004/30*.

Sumner, L. W. (2006) Utility and capability, *Utilitas* (18), pp. 1–19.

Terzi, L. (2005) Beyond the dilemma of difference: the capability approach to disability and special educational needs, *Journal of Philosophy of Education* (39), pp. 443–59.

Terzi, L. (2005) A capability perspective on impairment, disability, and special needs: towards social justice in education, *Theory and Research in Education* (3), pp. 197–223.

Tsuchiya, A. and A. Williams (2005) A 'Fair Innings' between the sexes: are men being treated inequitably?, *Social Science & Medicine* (60), pp. 277–86.

Tsui, K. (1999) Multidimensional inequality and multidimensional generalised entropy measures: an axiomatic appproach, *Social Choice & Welfare* (16), pp. 145–58.

Tsui, K. (2002) Multidimensional poverty indices, *Social Choice & Welfare* (19), pp. 69–93.

Unterhalter, E. (2003) Crossing disciplinary boundaries: the potential of Sen's capability approach for sociologists of education, *British Journal of Sociology of Education* (24), pp. 665–69.

van Hees, M. and M. Wissenburg (1999) Freedom and opportunity, *Political Studies* (47), pp. 67–82.

Walker, M. (2003) Framing social justice in education: what does the 'capabilities' approach offer?, *British Journal of Educational Studies* (51), pp. 168–87.

Walker, M. (2006) Towards a capability-based theory of social justice for education policy-making, *Journal of Education Policy* (21), pp. 163–85.

World Bank (2000) *World Development Report, 2000/2001: Attacking Poverty* (New York: Oxford University Press).

Xu, Y. (2002) Functioning, capability, and the standard of living – an axiomatic approach, *Economic Theory* (20), 387–99.

Zaidi, A. and T. Burchardt (2005) Comparing incomes when needs differ: equivalization for the extra costs of disability in the UK, *Review of Income and Wealth* (51), pp. 89–114.

1 | *Using the capability approach: prospective and evaluative analyses*[1]

SABINA ALKIRE

'Anxiety is the mark of spiritual insecurity. It is the fruit of unanswered questions. But questions cannot go unanswered unless they first be asked. And there is a far worse anxiety, a far worse insecurity, which comes from being afraid to ask the right questions – because they might turn out to have no answer. One of the moral diseases we communicate to one another in society comes from huddling together in the pale light of an insufficient answer to a question we are afraid to ask.'[2]

The focal question

The focal question of the conference that gave rise to this volume was how Amartya Sen's capability approach, which appears to have captured the interest of many, could be put to use in confronting poverties and injustices systematically and at a significant level. The often-discussed issue beneath that question is whether the research sparked by the capability approach gives rise to more effective practical methodologies to address pressing social problems. Of course ensuing applications are not the only grounds on which to examine a proposition – its theoretical implications, its measurability, or its conceptual coherence might also be fruitfully examined, for example. The extent to which specific applications and techniques embody the approach – their accuracy and limitations – might also be of interest. But in the context of poverty and justice it would appear directly relevant to evaluate

---

[1] Parts of this chapter are taken from the keynote address in Cambridge 2001; the remainder of that address has been published as Alkire 2005. I am grateful for input from the participants in the 2001 Capability Conference in Cambridge, research assistance from Afsan Bhadelia, as well as particular comments from Séverine Deneulin, Ingrid Robeyns, Mozaffar Qizilbash, and Amartya Sen. Errors remain my own.
[2] Merton 1955: xiii.

concrete applications and consequences, whatever else we also examine. Such a sharp focus might generate anxiety. For even if income approaches to poverty reduction shed but a pale light on the subject, it may be that, after scrutiny, we must concede that the capability approach in practice can do no better – or, perhaps, that we do not yet know.

Yet this seems a necessary question. Many have been attracted to the 'promise' that the capability approach and *Development as Freedom* seem to hold. Some writings assert its benefits (at times with rather more enthusiasm than evidence) or suggest that the approach be extended in a particular direction, or respond to certain pressing questions. The studies in this volume often demonstrate a more constructive and proactive tack. They view the capability approach as a work in progress, develop various applications of it, critically examine which insights various techniques embody, and/or debate whether and how these analyses demonstrably differ from alternative approaches. If this matter-of-fact methodology is adopted, it does not matter one whit whether the authors of such research were ostensibly 'critical of' Sen's capability approach or appeared to harbor some affection for it. The value-added of the capability approach in comparison with alternative approaches would be (or fail to be) evident in the empirical analyses and applications and policies to which it gives rise – indeed in the capabilities that were (or were not) expanded. The proof would be in the pudding.

While the demand for exquisite pudding seems inexhaustible, the demand for a more robust approach to poverty reduction is not too feeble either. There seems to be a confluence of political and intellectual forces seeking to advance development activities in ways not unsympathetic to the capability approach. For example, some development agencies, non-government organizations (NGOs), and governments are sustaining their support for the Millennium Declaration and associated Millennium Development Goals (MDGs) – in which poverty is defined as multidimensional and encompasses a range of functionings rather than income alone. Some national poverty reduction strategies are harnessing democratic public debate about priorities and processes, and including the poor in the debate. Some direct poverty reduction activities seek to empower poor persons to be active agents in social and political structures, as well as within the home. However imperfect the initiatives are that advance the MDGs, democratic practices, or empowerment (for example), they signal that there might be a demand for adequate applications of the capability approach. Further, they signal the importance of using the approach well, lest the practical applications settle for something less.

However, the focal question is actually quite difficult to assess: *does the research sparked by the capability approach give rise to more effective practical methodologies to address significant social problems?* More to the point, *the question might be mistakenly construed.* The difficulty in part relates to the different views of what in fact the capability approach *is* – for there are broader and narrower interpretations of it – and what aspects of it various applications or techniques instantiate. It also overlooks some lacunae in the approach, where it needs to borrow from other areas of research or where cross-fertilization with parallel new literature has not yet taken place. But most of all, the question, in the commonly articulated way that I have phrased it, is not actually an appropriate question for *assessing* the capability approach – at least not when this is understood as an evaluative framework. Rather, the question is, itself, a fundamental *application* of the capability approach. A primary evaluative role of the capability approach is precisely to assess which of two states of affairs have expanded human freedoms to a greater extent or what kinds of freedoms have expanded (or contracted) in each. Is the capability approach a baker or a taster; a pudding-maker or the puddings' judge?

This chapter maps, for the purposes of discussion, the possible conceptual boundaries of the capability approach – and notes significant boundary disputes. It refracts the major discussions on individualism and on the use of the capability approach that appear in other chapters and in the surrounding literature, and proposes some salient research questions and areas.

Evaluative framework: limitations

The capability approach gives rise to a normative proposition. The proposition is this: that social arrangements should be primarily evaluated according to the extent of freedom people have to promote or achieve functionings they value. Put simply, progress, or development, or poverty reduction, occurs when people have greater freedoms.

Thus, in addition to providing descriptive information, the capability approach provides an evaluative (often also called normative) framework for assessing alternative policies or programs or options.[3] An evaluative framework in this sense compares two or more states of affairs with respect to a limited set of variables. These might be capability sets or key functionings such as being able to be healthy, well nourished, safe; being able to make your views heard or have a livelihood. Such analyses enable pairwise comparison of alternatives or states of affairs, and inform a subsequent normative choice.

As we discussed in the introduction, this framework can be interpreted in narrow or broad ways:

- The *narrow* interpretation sees the approach primarily as identifying capability and functionings as the primary informational space for certain exercises.
- The *broad* interpretation also views capabilities as the primary informational space but is considerably more demanding. As capabilities are heterogeneous, to compare states of affairs requires *principles* such as equity or sustainability or responsibility in addition to the traditional efficiency. As the identification and prioritization of capabilities entails value judgements, and as comparison using plural principles may generate partial orderings, a third component of the broad approach may be the *process of social choice* (democracy, committee, participation, etc).

In either interpretation, the capability approach might be likened to a sophisticated balance upon which two states of affairs or alternative courses of action can be analysed and compared. Unlike a simple balance that may gauge the weight of only one kind of vegetable at a time, the capability approach – in theory – gauges the weights of plural variables (n-tuples of functionings) simultaneously. In a narrow view, in which information is restricted to capability sets alone, it asks, for each course of action, questions such as which capabilities expanded or contracted? For how many people? By how much and for how long? To deepen assessment, the variables might be compared against several criteria, not 'capability expansion' alone. Thus in a broader view other questions would be assessed, such as were human rights protected? Could people participate? In either view, the balance will often be comparing incommensurable capabilities. A mango may be greater in weight, sweeter in taste and roughly equal in texture in comparison

---

[3] Robeyns 2005, Sen 1992.

with an avocado. Alternatively a state of affairs may be better in terms of educational capabilities but worse in terms of health capabilities, or educational capabilities could be better for some groups and worse for others.

Because of this complexity, in many cases the balance (capability approach) will be unable to identify one course of action as 'best' as a whole – dominating one or several others in every respect. It may be able to discard a set of options that is clearly worse.[4] From the set of possible 'better' options, an informed value judgement will need to be made between the alternatives (the process of this decision will vary, although it should be open to public scrutiny and debate), and such a choice both exercises freedom and creates identity. Even in this case, the capability approach 'balance' has done a great deal of work in clarifying the salient valuational issues that inhere in alternatives, as well as in ruling out courses of action that are dominated entirely by other alternatives.

Understood as an evaluative framework, the capability is actually a limited structure. Its limitations are regularly overlooked. In particular, many who use the capability approach understandably intend that it will (also) *generate* a set of alternative activities, policies, or institutions that would expand capabilities more than the current set, or than a set generated by a traditional or alternative approach.

I would argue that we may need to separate two emphases: **prospective**, and **evaluative**. Both are important but distinct, and the distinctions are noteworthy. The capability approach as an *evaluative framework* undertakes comparative assessments of states of affairs by comparing capabilities or freedoms (*inter alia*). A *prospective application* of the capability approach, in contrast, is a working set of the policies, activities, and recommendations that are considered, at any given time, most likely to generate considerable capability expansion – together with the processes by which these policies/activities/recommendations are generated and the contexts in which they will be more likely to deliver these benefits. The prospective approach thus relates to the project of advancing *Development as Freedom* as well as to many applications advocated in the *Human Development Reports*, in *Hunger and Public Action, India: Development and Participation* and elsewhere. It might draw on the predictive tradition within economics, insofar as accurate

---

[4] Sen 1997.

predictions are used to inform recommendations. To these two we should add a third relevant application of the capability approach, *descriptive analyses*, but it seems sufficient to the purposes of this chapter to confine attention to these two.

The terms 'prospective' and 'evaluative' are only possible words, and one hesitates to pick any terms in a discussion with a long legacy within economics, development economics, and other disciplines. John Neville Keynes, in *The Scope and Method of Political Economy*, cites three roles of political economy: positive, normative, and what he calls 'an art' (which provides rules as to how to attain given ends).[5] In a twice-reprinted article on economic methodology, Sen describes instead description, prediction (concerned also with causality), and evaluation. 'At the very least, the subject of economics includes three diverse, though interrelated, exercises: (1) predicting the future and causally explaining past events, (2) choosing appropriate descriptions of states and events in the past and the present, and (3) providing normative evaluation of states, institutions, and policies' (p. 584).[6] Other exercises might be considered in addition to these three, 'such as using economic arguments for political advocacy (Myrdal, 1953; 1958) or seeing "the rhetoric of economics" as an object of direct importance' (p. 585). Sen also acknowledges various overlaps between the three: for example some but not all descriptive exercises have *implicit predictive content* (pp. 586–7). We will return to this point later.

Prospective and evaluative analyses: complementarities

One inherent limitation of an evaluative framework may be that it focuses on comparing and fully assessing alternatives in terms of their effects on human capabilities and other relevant variables, rather than on making recommendations. Of course evaluations may and often do feed into recommendations, but the *focus* of the exercise is different and importantly so. An evaluation takes time patiently to explore the benefits and disbenefits of different states of affairs/courses of actions as these appear to diverse groups and to people in different situations or with different values. It asks, of these two situations, which is more

---

[5] Colander 1992.
[6] The second of these might be disputed by Lionel Robbins, who wrote, 'Whatever Economics is concerned with, it is *not* concerned with the causes of material welfare as such' (Robbins 1932, p. 9).

desirable, even, more just? It does so knowing that often there will not be a single 'best' answer, but some partial ranking among alternatives may be feasible.

Evaluative analyses are fundamentally concerned with comparisons of states of affairs at one point in time or with streams of capability-related benefits and costs of states of affairs across several time periods. They refer, ultimately, to information on how people's capabilities expanded and contracted. Because of this focus, information on causal chains enters only insofar as it affects endstates. Naturally, as Sen has argued, a sufficiently rich description of outcomes may include some account of their generative processes – such as whether they respected human rights (goal rights) or unfolded through a participatory process. But the primary evaluative focus is *whether* capabilities have expanded, rather than *how and why* such expansion occurred.

Yet, as was noted above, another question that rightly attracts many is precisely which alternatives would *advance* human capabilities more fully, which *prospective* recommendations could or should arise from the capability approach. Prospective analyses have a different emphasis: one on causality, probability, and assumptions. Their main objective is not to compare two states of affairs but to identify which concrete actions are likely to generate a greater stream of expanded capabilities, the better state of affairs.

Prospective analyses cover an equally essential set of questions related to issues of process and causality (how and why): what incremental changes to existing institutional, social, cultural, political and economic structures would expand certain capabilities, and how durable, equitable, and sustainable such expansions would be. Prospective analyses identify the highly productive investments that will leverage a greater yield of capabilities than alternatives.

A central example of prospective analysis is the kind of empirical scrutiny that underlies the identification and advocacy of 'instrumental freedoms' in *Development as Freedom*.[7] Instrumental freedoms are a class of freedoms that, in addition to forming part of the objective or

---

[7] *Development as Freedom* identifies five 'instrumental freedoms' that 'tend to contribute to the general capability of a person to live more freely'. They are:
  1) *Political freedoms*, e.g. democracy, the freedom to scrutinize and criticize authorities, to enjoy a free press and multi-party elections.
  2) *Economic facilities*, e.g. people's opportunity to have and use economic resources or entitlements.

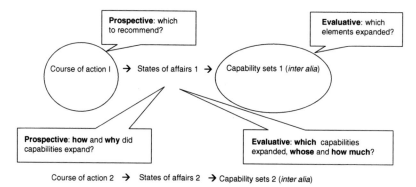

Figure 1.1 'Prospective and Evaluative Analyses: Distinct but integrally related'

'end' of development, are also 'crucially effective means' to the expansion of other salient capabilities.[8] Sen argues that instrumental freedoms can be identified empirically: 'This acknowledgement [of freedom as a crucially effective means] can be based on empirical analysis of the consequences of – and the interconnections between – freedoms of distinct kinds, and on extensive empirical evidence that indicates that freedoms of different types typically help to sustain each other.'[9]

Of course these two analyses are inter-related and indeed overlapping. A good example of this is Ruggeri Laderchi's capabilities production function in this volume. It crosses the boundary while maintaining conceptual clarity, being an empirical estimation of capabilities in which poverty is defined exclusively in capability space (and to that extent, an evaluation) but including a production function in order that the analysis generates useful policy advice. Similarly, Sehnbruch's chapter develops an index that includes a fuller set of indicators for

---

3) *Social opportunities*, e.g. people's ability to have health care, to be educated, and to live in a society where others likewise enjoy these goods.
4) *Transparency guarantees*, e.g. the ability to trust others and to know that the information one receives is clear and honestly disclosed.
5) *Protective security*, e.g. social protections for vulnerable people that prevent abject deprivation.
   Sen 1999: 38–40.
[8] IADB 'Ethics' p. 10.
[9] IADB pp. 10–11; the footnote reads: 'The evidence is discussed in Amartya Sen, *Development as Freedom*.'

work-related capabilities, but it develops this for the purpose of policy recommendation in Chile.

The capability approach evaluates which course of action expanded capabilities more, whereas prospective applications of the capability approach and human development recommend and advocate courses of action that expand capabilities more than alternative courses of action.

Implications: the individualism criticism

One motivation for distinguishing the evaluative and prospective foci is that several major 'boundary disputes' of the capability approach concern this distinction. One such dispute focuses on the alleged individualism of Sen's approach. Critics argue forcefully that an evaluative framework whose constituent elements are the capabilities of *people* (individuals) is misleading (see Deneulin, Dubois and Rousseau, and Teschl and Derobert in this book, and De Herdt and Deneulin 2007). The main force of this criticism is that, although the capability approach's emphasis may be purely evaluative, the larger context of many evaluations is indeed to guide prospective recommendations. And, the critics argue, prospective analyses and recommendations that do not carefully scrutinize the role of collective actions, institutions, and other social structures in creating individual capabilities will be deeply flawed. Below I state the debate in its own terms, then explore how the prospective–evaluative distinction relates to this debate.

Ethical individualism

In Chapter 3 Robeyns explains that Sen's capability approach embraces ethical individualism but does not defend methodological or ontological individualism. This distinction is of cross-cutting importance, precisely because the 'individual' focus of the capability approach is often misunderstood or inaccurately criticized. Robeyns' distinction is this: *ethical individualism* 'postulates that individuals, and only individuals, are the *ultimate* units of moral concern. This, of course, does not imply that we should not evaluate social structures and societal properties, but ethical individualism implies that these structures and institutions will be evaluated *in virtue of* the causal importance that they have for individuals' well-being'. *Ontological individualism* – which Robeyns argues the capability approach does not support and nor should feminists – holds that 'society is built up from only individuals and nothing than individuals, and hence is nothing more than the sum of individuals and their properties'. Explanatory or *methodological individualism* presumes 'that all social phenomena can be explained in terms of individuals and their properties'.

Robeyns argues that feminists should support ethical individualism – because moral theories that take an alternative unit of moral concern such as the family, the social group, or the community will systematically overlook any existing or potential inequalities *within* these units. For example, the deprivations particular to women and children have regularly been overlooked by analyses that focus on the household unit. Further, she observes a key factor which others neglect – hence the tremendous value of this chapter. She observes that 'a commitment to ethical individualism is not incompatible with an account of personhood that recognizes the connections between people, their social relations, and their social embedment'. Criticisms that Sen's capability approach is ontologically or methodologically individualist thus misconstrue the approach.

It may be observed, in light of the previous discussion, that ethical individualism pertains to the capability approach as an evaluative framework (and often, as a critical piece of a theory of justice). It does not speak to the task of *how to promote capabilities* – the task of human development, of creating 'development as freedom'. As mentioned above, most individualist criticisms of the capability approach's individualism focus on this latter task (and at times allege, contra Robeyns and also inaccurately, that the capability approach requires that prospective recommendations to expand capabilities be methodologically individualist). Because a great deal of cross-cutting practical relevance turns on these criticisms it would be useful to consider them carefully.

Critiques

Séverine Deneulin criticizes the capability approach for focusing too much on evaluative rather than prospective analysis (these terms are not, however, employed). While not methodologically individualist, the capability approach exudes too little interest in conditions of capability expansion. She argues in Chapter 4 that without studying structures of living together, the capability approach is unable to generate the kind of recommendations needed to *promote* capabilities; thus it cannot advance its own objective of expanding capabilities. 'In the light of the Costa Rican development path, assessing development on the basis of individual capabilities, or irreducibly social goods that are of intrinsic value to individual lives … would miss out … certain structures of living together that make the whole process of development and expansion of individual capabilities possible' (p. 114). In other words, an evaluative analysis that accurately analysed individuals' capabilities would 'miss out' the institutions or movements or public policies that in part created and sustained those very capabilities, and this information might be deeply relevant to others who are attempting to expand those same capabilities.

This omission would not be particularly important if the capability approach was always used merely to compare and evaluate states of affairs, but this is not the case – it has what Sen referred to as 'implicit predictive content'. In practice, Deneulin observes, the capability approach often 'becomes a guiding theory for development practice'. As Ruggeri Laderchi and Sehnbruch's chapters demonstrate, the empirical evaluation feeds into policy advice. Yet because the capability approach is intended as an evaluative framework, and focuses only on individual capabilities, Deneulin makes the further claim that it 'directs attention *away* from the examination of the structures of living together and historical explications of these structures, which are responsible not only for the conditions of life of individuals today but have also affected past generations and will affect future ones' (p. 115).[10]

Deneulin remains unconvinced that the capability approach can ascribe adequate importance to what Charles Taylor calls 'irreducibly social goods', which might include aesthetic values as well as cultural and political practices. To extend the informational basis of the capability approach, she draws on Paul Ricoeur's notion of 'structures of living together' (Ricoeur 1992) – 'structures which belong to a particular historical community, which provide the conditions for individual lives to flourish, and which are irreducible to individual relations and yet bound up with these' – to recognize the importance of such goods for development. She argues that an evaluation of Costa Rica's success based on individual capability expansion alone would inevitably miss the role that structures of living together played in facilitating the exercise of agency of certain individuals whose actions built that

---

[10] Italics mine.

success.[11] It is crucial to this argument that the value of these structures does not derive entirely from the intrinsic value they have for human flourishing – they also have an instrumental value, affecting the future stream of freedoms that a community will be able to enjoy.

What Deneulin challenges is not ethical individualism – for her approach 'still *ultimately* judges development by individuals' lives'. She challenges the assumption (which she ascribes to those using the capability approach) that evaluation can be delinked from prescription. Should the informational set required for an evaluative assessment be chosen because it has best identified the objectives of ultimate value? Or should it be chosen because it provides sufficient information on which to base further recommendations? Sen's and Robeyn's defense of the capability space has focussed on the former; Deneulin's critique arises from her focus on the latter.

Frances Stewart also advocates that the research and policy agenda related to the capability approach give more attention to 'groups' and to 'group capabilities'. In 'Groups and Capabilities' she defines groups as 'ways of categorising people in ways that represent common affiliations or identities'.[12] She identifies three ways that group membership affects people's capabilities. First, the benefits of belonging to a group may be of intrinsic importance, thus expanding people's well-being – to provide self-esteem, positive human relationships and so on. Also, a person's capabilities may be directly affected by 'how well the group they identify with is doing' (p. 187). Second, 'groups are important instrumentally in determining efficiency and resource shares'. For example, collective action groups of poor persons can enable them to expand many quite different capabilities (p. 189). Third, 'groups influence values and choices. Groups could also exert negative influences on capabilities through these same three mechanisms. Given these three critical roles, analysis of what makes for "good" groups and what makes for "bad" groups becomes a critical part of any research agenda, and of policies towards the promotion of capabilities and human well-being' (p. 190).

Leaving aside Stewart's point on the influence of groups on values – a point which merits inspection and reflection but lies beyond the scope

---

[11] In his analysis de Herdt does consider the relationship between shame and agency. To some degree, this seems to account for the relationship between social and historical conditions and agency which is central to Deneulin's concerns.

[12] Stewart 2005, p. 186. See also Stewart 1996, Stewart and Deneulin 2002.

of this chapter – we can observe that Deneulin's and Stewart's criticisms of the capability approach stem from their intention to *use* the approach in a 'prospective' sense: to create recommendations as to, as Stewart puts it, 'the promotion of capabilities and human well-being'. Their criticisms are not, actually, criticisms of the individualism of the capability approach. Rather, they are criticisms that the capability approach's focus on evaluative analysis leaves unspecified the methods of prospective analysis. In particular, it does not specify the importance of including groups, and structures of living together, in prospective analyses. This is indeed a criticism, but of a different kind. To remedy this they suggest that the vocabulary of capabilities acknowledge group or collective capabilities – a suggestion echoed by others[13] – and that greater attention be paid to the production of capabilities by groups and collective activities. Deneulin makes the stronger claim that the capability approach's emphasis on information on capabilities 'directs attention away' from attention to the very structures that might be most relevant.

These salient issues will be discussed below:

1. Should we talk about collective or group capabilities?
2. How can 'prospective analyses' of the capability approach proceed?
3. Does the focus on individual capabilities divert attention from prospective analyses?

Terms: collective and group capabilities

One proposition that many have put forward is that the language of capabilities should include the capabilities of groups or collectivities. Indeed many would argue that collective capabilities are of intrinsic importance – meaning by 'intrinsic importance' what Stewart identified, namely they indicate capabilities that individuals would not be able to enjoy, directly or indirectly, *except* through their participation in the group. In this case, the term 'collective' or 'group' serves to acknowledge and draw the analysts' attention to the fact that the person's enjoyment of these capabilities (causally) is – at present and probably also in the future – contingent upon their participation in the group, so changes to the group are very likely to affect this person's

[13] Evans 2002, Ibrahim 2006, De Herdt and Deneulin 2007.

capabilities. This title would thus convey something of importance: 'Not only is this freedom a "being or doing" I value and have reason to value; *I could not enjoy it alone*, without the group.' Stewart gives this example: 'In a study of a sex-workers association in Calcutta, Gooptu found that an enhanced sense of self-respect was an important outcome of the formation of this group. As one member put it, "I felt I was released from a closed room and could see the sunlight"' (Gooptu 2002, p. 236). Such information on the provenance of existing capabilities is vital, Stewart and Deneulin argue, to the design of social structures that promote such capabilities.

Moreover the term captures something of the person's experience. For example, consider a good community chamber orchestra in which Ana plays the viola. It has just given a breathtaking performance in which the chamber group, as it were, spoke the music as one voice and even seemed to breathe together. The musicians also get along quite well, and several are friends. Ana deeply values her participation in this group, in which she is inspired, challenged, able to express herself musically, and enjoy friendships. It could be accurate to refer to her capability as her individual 'capability to play viola in a challenging chamber group' plus her 'capability to enjoy friendships with chamber group members'. Yet the words that come to Ana's mind are different – she would say that she values 'our capability to play good chamber music together'. Much of the aversion to the so-called 'individualism' of the capability approach may rest in part on this dissonance between a person's immediate experience of the group as inherent to the capability (collective marketing group, savings and credit group, family, indigenous or cultural community) and the language of individual capabilities. Collective terms better reflect the experience.

Yet the same term, group or collective capabilities, could also be understood as claiming (asserting) that every member of the group/collectivity who enjoyed those capabilities valued them.[14] It is this kind of assertion of which Sen and Robeyns, as feminists, are wary, and for this reason are reluctant to endorse the term or ascribe 'intrinsic' importance to social structures. If instead Ana detested playing the viola (although she could), did not like the members at all, and was forced to play in the chamber group because her grandfather was first

---

[14] This could also be an example of the group influencing a person's own values and preferences, which Stewart raises but which we will not take up now.

violinist, she might still play beautifully in the breathtaking concert. And her grandfather might then declaim that all group members enjoyed 'the capability to play good chamber music together', omitting the fact that Ana did not value that capability at all! In this situation, the locus of the value judgement (that c_1 is a collective capability) might lie with the group leader or with a subset of group members, who make this claim on behalf of others. By appearing to ascribe intrinsic importance to collective capabilities (without consulting all those implicated), this approach forfeits the ability to give a more nuanced and differentiated account of how any given social structure (family, group, tradition), at any given point in time, affects diverse members of it. Robeyns argues that feminists should endorse Sen's ethical individualism, that ultimately the capability approach must focus on individuals. Thus we can accurately assess the capabilities each person actually values and has reason to value, and not stop short at the border of groups – which can, unfortunately, be considerably more destructive towards some members than Ana's grandfather.

So in favor of the term collective capabilities are two arguments:

(i) Given that many descriptions have implicit prescriptive content, and that the purpose of many examinations of capability is to inform efforts to improve these, it is useful to signal to the analyst that not only is the capability valued by individual i but without the wider social group, this capability could not be enjoyed.

(ii) When the group contributes to an individual's capability in one of the two 'intrinsic' ways that Stewart describes, a collective term also 'strikes the ear' as being a more accurate description of the person's experience than describing only their own benefit.

Against it is the position that:

(i) The term collective capabilities could assert, on behalf of each member of the group, that the capability in question was valued by each member or expanded their capabilities uniformly. In fact, participation in the group may often affect different people's capabilities differently, and people may also value the effects of group participation differently. In particular, a group that benefits one subset of members may at the same time harm another, and a claim that a structure or group 'provided a collective capability' may overlook some significant dis-benefits or heterogeneities.

The arguments under discussion are each, it seems, reasonable and could be mutually compatible in a rich enough analysis; the outstanding question is what to *call* capabilities that i) a person herself values but ii) could not enjoy alone. More important than the terms used are the clarity with which the analyses consider each and every one of these insights and concerns, not omitting any, and explain the adopted terms accordingly.

Methods of prospective analyses

When seen as an evaluative framework, the capability approach raises a focused set of questions, some or all of which might enter the analysis: what capabilities should be selected for the evaluation? How are these to be measured or otherwise described? How are relative weights to be set? What is the timeframe of the evaluation? How are distributional issues in capability space to be discussed? And so on. In contrast, *prospective* analyses are inherently heterogeneous, and the capability approach thus far has not explicitly specified a methodology for them. It seems that the methods will be plural and the questions will vary by discipline, level of analysis, policy audience, region and context. Deneulin, Stewart, and others observe that one component of prospective analyses which will be relevant across many contexts and sectors will be the component of groups and social structures. Indeed Deneulin also traces how Sen, and Drèze and Sen's work has actively done so.[15] But we can see immediately that the structure of their suggestion is not confined to the individualism discussion. Many others who are engaging in prospective applications of the capability approach likewise advocate attention to ecosystems, to local institutions, to gender issues, to vulnerability, or to other considerations. So we will broaden the discussion from the incorporation of social structures in prospective analysis to the much broader discussion of how to use, apply, or (awkward though it sounds) 'operationalize' the capability approach in different disciplines and contexts. As is at once evident, the question also merits much more systematic attention than can be given here.

Many of the chapters in this volume engage in prospective analyses, although of course not by that name. At the same time many of them

---

[15] In this volume. See also Deneulin 2006, Deneulin 2002, Deneulin, Nebel and Sagovsky 2006, Stewart and Deneulin 2002.

articulate, in one way or another, a lack of confidence regarding their methods, and a wistfulness that there might be a clear methodology for such analyses, such that they might be undertaken with confidence and rigour.[16]

As others' discussion is particularly focussed on Sen's version of the capability approach, we will start there. In discussing the heterogeneous methodologies appropriate for descriptive, predictive, and evaluative exercises, Sen argues (in that chapter as well as elsewhere) that methodology should be guided by 'what serves the goals of the inquiry' (p. 595) – given that these goals will vary significantly. For example, 'As far as prediction is concerned, the role of value judgements is typically rather limited', although 'the importance of values in motivating predictive inquiries of different kinds has also to be acknowledged' (p. 596). Sen stresses, thus, the need for methodologies to go beyond certain boundaries without specifying what they should be. In a similar vein, Malenbaum's early review of *Resources Values and Developments* observes that in its introduction as well as contents Sen 'warns that the neatness and elegance of social welfare theory in traditional development economics . . . must now give way to the inelegances posed by real development experience. "Uncomfortable aspects" of the application of theory force descriptive and predictive analysis into new institutional requirements in societies seeking economic advance.' And again, 'he envisages complex tasks in disciplines not usually mastered by economic experts in growth and development' (p. 403).

Many have tried to distil characteristic features of Sen's analysis.[17] It may be sufficient for our purposes instead to give an example. Drèze and Sen explore certain structures of service provision – mostly related to nutrition, education, and health care – and try to identify crucial 'instrumental freedoms' for public policy investment and collective action. Their applied work, like that of an increasing volume of others',

---

[16] I have tried to sketch observations about these processes in Alkire 2005, p. 126ff and in Alkire 2006 'Instrumental Freedoms and Human Capabilities' mimeo (on the difficulty and procedures for undertaking empirical assessments of instrumental freedoms in terms of capabilities and plural principles).

[17] These have been done by Alkire 2002, Atkinson 1999, Basu and López Calva 2002, Bohman 1996, Clark 2005, Crocker 2006, Crocker 1992, Crocker 1995, Fukuda-Parr 2003, Gasper 2002, Gasper 1997, Kuklys 2005, Malenbaum 1988, Nussbaum 2003, Omkarnath 1997, Pressman and Summerfield 2002, Qizilbash 1996, Robeyns 2000, Stewart 1996, Stewart and Deneulin 2002, Streeten 2000, Walsh 1995 among others.

demonstrates how prospective analyses draw on, and go well beyond, the capability approach as an evaluative framework and how such analyses do indeed examine institutions, social structures, and groups *inter alia*. The conversations that arise in response to such applications are also crucial to improving the methodologies.

Prospective analyses: education in India

The various analyses by Drèze and Sen demonstrate the thorough, many-faceted kinds of analysis which explore prospective connections between development actions and human capabilities. Consider their 2002 analyses meant to inform public policy as well as advocacy priorities in India. Here are some of the footprints of that exploration, which begins with a description of the potential intrinsic value of education as well as its instrumental value in expanding other capabilities. One possible cause of low education was that education is not actually valued in the eyes of the parents and the communities. However, a parent survey found keen interest among parents in children's education and indeed in girls' education also. Another possibility was that the need for child labor prohibited deprived families from sending children to school – again this was not substantiated empirically. Rather, the barriers appeared to be the affordability of books and uniforms, the distance to schools, and the anticipated returns to education – which are stronger for boys than for girls. Perhaps the strongest barrier was the low quality of education – ramshackle schools, large class sizes, a complex curriculum structure, and unmotivated teachers. Further analysis showed that a significant contribution to the low quality of education was the weak motivation and accountability of government teachers to school inspectors or to the parents and local community.

The analysis then turned to observe that the Indian constitution (Article 45) urges states to provide free and compulsory education for children up to 14 years old (exploring in passing how 'compulsory' education could enhance 'freedom'). Political parties have reiterated this commitment, promising to increase educational expenditure. Instead, government of India figures show that expenditure declined from 4.4 per cent of gross domestic product (GDP) in 1989 to 3.6 per cent in 1997.[18] The analysis implied there might be scope as well as

---

[18] Drèze and Sen 2002, p. 166.

cause for parents and others to demand political responses to the ramshackle schools and missing teachers.

To deepen this consideration of pro-active public action by parents, the positive experience of one state – Himachal Pradesh (HP) – in furthering basic education was analysed. Between 1961 and 1991, girls' literacy improved from 61 per cent to 86 per cent and by 1998–9, school attendance was above 97 per cent for both girls and boys – a rate higher than that of Kerala. This advance also took place against considerable odds: HP has many remote areas that are difficult to access, has been overlooked by private or religious schools, and relied economically on child labor. While it is one of the wealthier Indian states, its educational advances were not mirrored in other states of a similar economic level such as the Punjab or Harayana. Drèze and Sen trace the 'virtuous circle' that developed in HP. By drawing on and mobilizing on a strong tradition of local cooperation and collaboration for shared ends, groups created a politically salient impetus to invest in education; a relatively egalitarian economic structure assured that the expansion of education occurred relatively evenly, and that teachers and students were of similar status. Furthermore, because women in HP do regularly work outside the home, education increased their economic capacity, which provided a balanced incentive for girls and boys to attend school and, similarly, to teach school.

On the basis of this analysis of the educational shortcomings, Drèze and Sen advocate political mobilization in support of basic education that would work locally as well as through formal political and economic channels:

What is perhaps most striking of all is that the failures of government policy over an extended period have provoked so little political challenge. … The fact that the government was able to get away with so much in the field of elementary education relates to the lack of political power of the illiterate masses … It also reflects the fact … that the social value of basic education has been neglected not only by government authorities but also in social and political movements.[19]

This account of education and development gives one example of prospective analyses. It first considers the possible *value* of education – intrinsically as well as instrumentally – then examines the *deprivations*

---

[19] Drèze and Sen 2002, p. 187.

that many experience in education, and their causes. Is it that basic education is not *valued* by the relevant group (parents and students)? Are they blocked from taking advantage of it, thus lack the *real* freedom to be educated although they may have formal access? Or are there institutional reasons for non-attendance – in this case deep flaws in the public education system itself? Having diagnosed, as it were, core issues, the analysis turns to actions that people (parents and students as well as public institutions and NGOs) could undertake as *agents* in order to redress the situation.

In Chapter 16 of this volume, Unterhalter, while appreciating the above analysis, also raises omitted considerations that, she argues on the basis of the South African experience, must also be taken into consideration – analyses that uncover the lack of uniformity in the quality and safety of schooling, and also distinguish between the benefits of schooling processes, skills, and outcomes. This kind of discussion – on the methodology and included/omitted variables as well as on the ensuing policy advice – seems certain to advance the capability approach in a 'prospective' sense. But is it enough?

Possible ways forward

What is evident in the example from Drèze and Sen is that the methodology used for their prospective analysis is indeed wide-ranging and incorporates consideration for institutions and structures of living together to some extent, as well as additional considerations that others might advocate. It is also clear that the methodology was context specific and appropriate to the particular analysis; no attempt was made to articulate a methodology that could be implemented uniformly. Underspecification has its dangers (much like the weakness of having an unspecified list of capabilities).[20] If methods for prospective analyses are too open-ended, and researchers must create them anew in each context, then there is a real, practical possibility that they will (unwittingly or deliberately) omit critical variables, or overemphasize others. It seems that the authors in this volume and related literature are calling for a more systematic, long-term, even painstaking

[20] Nussbaum 2003, Robeyns 2005, Sen 2004; Alkire, S. 2007.

development of plural methodologies, across disciplines and regions and institutions and levels of analysis, that are consistent with the capability approach and draw on the strongest techniques. The specification of appropriate methodologies for prospective analyses may assist resulting analyses to carry critical force.

Evaluation of the 'evaluative framework'

A final question is whether the focus on individual capabilities as the ultimate space in which to evaluate states of affairs diverts attention from prospective analyses and thus endangers the approach's efficacy in its own terms. This is a good question.

Yet given the arguments above and the observations of the increasing number of applications of the capability approach, it seems that we are really quite far from living in a danger zone on that point. In many cases both kinds of information will be complementary and indeed essential for a full analysis. Still, a clear account of the form of analyses that authors are undertaking – whether it is evaluative or prospective, for example (or predictive or descriptive if those terms are more relevant), might give them more liberty to investigate the relevant interconnections with gusto and confidence, and to communicate to the readers the limitations as well as the reach of their conclusion.

A few lines in Alexander Pope's poem *The Dunciad* describe:

Poetic Justice, with her lifted scale,
Where in nice balance truth with gold she weighs,
And solid pudding against empty praise.[21]

If we were to picture the scale of poetic justice 'in the hands of the poorest person each of us know,'[22] then the primary aim of those focused on *using* Sen's capability approach as the basis of prospective recommendations is clear: to make solid pudding. Doing so entails enthusiastic involvement by discerning bakers and tasters alike.

---

[21] Alexander Pope *The Dunciad*. Book i, line 52.
[22] Frank Carey, host of the 2001 conference, asked each participant, at the start and close of the event, to picture the poorest person they knew and ask how that person would benefit from their research and their participation in the conference.

Cited references

Alkire, S. 2002. *Valuing Freedoms. Sen's Capability Approach and Poverty Reduction.* New York, Oxford: Oxford University Press

Alkire, S. 2005. 'Why the Capability Approach?' *Journal of Human Development* 6 (1): 115–33

Alkire, S. 2006. 'Instrumental Freedoms and Human Capabilities,' mimeo

Alkire, S. 2007. 'Choosing Dimensions: the Capability Approach and Multidimensional Poverty', in *The Many Dimensions of Poverty*, J. Silber (ed.), New York: Palgrave Macmillan.

Atkinson, A. B. 1999. 'The Contributions of Amartya Sen to Welfare Economics', *Scandinavian Journal of Economics* 101 (2): 173–90

Basu, K. and L. F. López Calva 2002. *Functionings and Capabilities*. México: Centro de Estudios Económicos El Colegio de México

Bohman, J. 1996. *Public Deliberation: Pluralism, Complexity, and Democracy.* Cambridge, MA: MIT Press

Clark, D. A. 2005. 'Sen's Capability Approach and the Many Spaces of Human Well-Being', *Journal of Development Studies* 41 (8): 1339–68

Colander, D. 1992. 'The Lost Art of Economics', *Journal of Economic Perspectives* 6 (3): 191–98

Crocker, D. 2006. 'Ethics of Global Development: Agency, Capability, and Deliberative Democracy – An Introduction', *Philosophy and Public Policy Quarterly* 26 (1/2): 21–7

Crocker, D. 1992. 'Functioning and Capabilities: the Foundation of Sen's and Nussbaum's Development Ethic', *Political Theory* 20

Crocker, D. 1995. 'Functioning and Capability: The Foundation of Sen's and Nussbaum's Development Ethic, Part II', in M. Nussbaum and J. Glover. Oxford: Clarendon Press

De Herdt, T. and S. Deneulin, Eds. 2007. *Special Issue: Individual Freedoms as Relational Experiences, Journal of Human Development* 8: 2, July

Deneulin, S. 2002. 'Perfectionism, Paternalism and Liberalism in Sen and Nussbaum's Capability Approach', *Review of Political Economy* 14

Deneulin, S. 2006. *The Capability Approach and the Praxis of Development.* Basingstoke: Palgrave Macmillan

Deneulin, S., M. Nebel and N. Sagovsky. 2006. *Transforming Unjust Structures: The Capability Approach.* Dordrecht: Springer

Drèze, J. and A. K. Sen 1989. *Hunger and Public Action.* Oxford: Clarendon Press

Drèze, J. and A. K. Sen 2002. *India, Development and Participation.* New Delhi, New York: Oxford University Press

Evans, P. 2002. 'Collective Capabilities, Culture, and Amartya Sen's Development as Freedom', *Studies in Comparative International Development* 37 (2): 54–60

Fukuda-Parr, S. 2003. 'The Human Development Approach: Operationalizing Sen's Ideas on Capabilities', *Feminist Economics* 9 (2–3): 301–17

Gasper, D. 2002. 'Is Sen's Capability Approach an Adequate Basis for Considering Human Development?', *Review of Political Economy* 14 (4): 435–60

Gasper, D. 1997. 'Sen's Capability Approach and Nussbaum's Capability Ethics', *Journal of International Development* 9 (2): 281–302

Gasper, D. and I. van Staveren 2003. 'Development as Freedom – And as What Else?', *Feminist Economics* 9(2/3): 137–61

Gooptu, N. 2002. 'Sex Workers in Calcutta and the Dynamics of Collective Action: Political Activism, Community Identity and Group Behaviour', in *Group Behaviour and Development: Is the Market Destroying Cooperation?*, J. Heyer, F. Stewart and R. Thorp (eds.), Oxford: Oxford University Press

Gore, C. 1997. 'Irreducible Social Goods and the Informational Basis of Amartya Sen's Capability Approach', *Journal of International Development* 9 (2): 235–50

Ibrahim, S. 2006. 'From Individual to Collective Capabilities: The Capability Approach as a Conceptual Framework for Self-help', *Journal of Human Development* 7 (3): 397–416

Kuklys, W. 2005. *Amartya Sen's Capability Approach: Theoretical Insights and Empirical Applications*. Berlin: Springer

Malenbaum, W. 1988. 'Amartya Sen on Future Development Policy and Program: Review Article', *Economic Development & Cultural Change* 36 (2): 401–09

Merton, T. 1955. *No Man is an Island*. New York: Harcourt Brace

Myrdal, G. 1953. *Political Elements in the Development of Economic Theory*. London: International Library of Sociology

Myrdal, G. 1958. *Value in Social Theory*. London: Allen and Unwin

Nussbaum, M. 2003. 'Capabilities as Fundamental Entitlements: Sen and Social Justice', *Feminist Economics* 9 (2–3): 33–59

Omkarnath, G. 1997. 'Capabilities and the Process of Development'. Centre for Development Studies Working Paper, No. 275. Thiruvananthapuram, Kerala, India

Pressman, S. and G. Summerfield 2002. 'Sen and Capabilities', *Review of Political Economy* 14 (4): 429–34

Qizilbash, M. 1996. 'Capabilities, Well-Being and Human Development: A Survey', *The Journal of Development Studies* 33(2): 143–62

Ricoeur, P. 1992. *One Self as Another*. Kathleen Blamey, trans. Chicago: University of Chicago Press

Robbins, L. C. R. 1932. *An Essay on the Nature & Significance of Economic Science*. London: Macmillan

Robeyns, I. 2005. 'The Capability Approach: A Theoretical Survey', *Journal of Human Development* 6 (1): 93–114

Robeyns, I. 2005. 'Selecting Capabilities for Quality of Life Measurement', *Social Indicators Research* 74 (1): 191–215

Robeyns, I. 2000. *An Unworkable Idea or a Promising Alternative? Sen's Capability Approach Re-examined*, Center for Economic Studies Discussion Paper 0030. University of Leuven, mimeo

Sen, A. 2004. 'Capabilities, Lists, and Public Reason: Continuing the Conversation', *Feminist Economics* 10 (3): 77–80

Sen, A. 2004. 'Economic Methodology: Heterogeneity and Relevance', *Social Research* 71 (3): 583–614

Sen, A. 1992. *Inequality Re-examined*. Oxford: Clarendon Press

Sen, A. 1997. 'Maximization and the Act of Choice', *Econometrica* 65 (4): 745–80

Sen, A. 2002. 'Response to Commentaries', *Studies in Comparative International Development* 37 (2): 78–86

Sen, A. 2002. 'What Difference Can Ethics Make?', International Meeting on 'Ethics and Development' of Inter-American Development Bank on Collaboration with the Norwegian Government

Stewart, F. 1996. 'Basic Needs, Capabilities, and Human Development,' in *In Pursuit of the Quality of Life*, A. Offer (ed.). Oxford: Oxford University Press

Stewart, F. 2005. 'Groups and Capabilities', *Journal of Human Development* 6

Stewart, F. and S. Deneulin 2002. 'Amartya Sen's Contribution to Development Thinking', *Studies in Comparative International Development* 37 (2): 61–70

Streeten, P. 2000. 'Freedom and Welfare: A Review Essay on Amartya Sen, Development as Freedom', *Population & Development Review* 26 (1): 153–62

Walsh, V. 1995. 'Amartya Sen on Inequality, Capabilities and Needs: Review Article', *Science & Society* 59 (4): 556–69

Concepts

2 | *Amartya Sen's capability view:*
insightful sketch or distorted picture?[1]

MOZAFFAR QIZILBASH[2]

Introduction

It is now more than twenty-five years since the publication of Amartya Sen's Tanner lecture (Sen 1980) in which he first began to develop what we now know as the 'capability approach' (CA).[3] The approach has evolved and matured quite considerably over time, and its influence and stature have also grown. It now stands as a, if not the only, major alternative to standard welfare economics. There have also been numerous attempts at applying the CA in different contexts. In some ways the CA has 'grown up' and it is an appropriate time to reassess the CA, and to consider its prospects.

Sen's CA gives us a way of thinking about and, in that sense, a 'view' of various interrelated subjects, such as the quality of life, justice, and development. It is a view which is, as Sen repeatedly tells us, *incomplete*, and which is supposed to be open to different accounts of valuation. Sen

[1] Acknowledgements: This is a revised and updated version of a paper I presented at the conference on 'Justice and poverty: Amartya Sen's Capability Approach' in June 2001. Some of the connections between J. S. Mill and Sen I made in an earlier version of one section of this chapter were further developed and extended in an article for *Utilitas* to which Amartya Sen has since responded. Nonetheless, the *Utilitas* article appeared *before* this chapter. I would like to thank Sabina Alkire, Tania Burchardt, David Clark, Richard Cookson, Flavio Comim, Roger Crisp, Indranil Dutta, Des Gasper, Dudley Horner, Bob Sugden, Pasquale Valentini and, especially, Amartya Sen, for their helpful and encouraging comments on earlier versions which were presented at Cambridge and UEA. Some of the work on this chapter began while I was visiting the Southern Africa Labour and Development Research Unit (SALDRU) and was related to a project on 'Poverty, vulnerability and vagueness' on which I worked with David Clark and Dudley Horner, and which was supported by the Department for International Development (DfID). I would like to thank SALDRU for its hospitality and DfID for its support. Any omissions or errors are mine.
[2] School of Politics, Economics and Philosophy, University of York, Heslington, YO10 5DD; email: mq500@york.ac.uk
[3] The lecture was actually first given at Stanford University in May 1979.

stops short of completing the picture, rather like an artist who prefers a sketch with a few sharply executed marks to a more fully worked and developed painting. The view Sen gives us might be seen as a rather masterful sketch. Yet by leaving out a great deal of detail and producing a striking effect by giving some things a particular prominence, a sketch can distort reality. So I shall look at the view Sen 'draws' and ask: is this view an insightful sketch or a distorted picture? The answer, one might suspect, is 'both'. However, in trying to answer this question, I do not give a full assessment, merely a partial appreciation, of the CA.

There are four aspects of Sen's work on the CA that I will concentrate on in assessing it. The first is Sen's strategy in locating himself in relation to those who came before him, and in particular the utilitarian tradition. Inasmuch as one of his aims is to revolutionise normative economics, Sen has spent considerable energy contrasting his approach to that of his utilitarian predecessors, who, he thinks, laid the foundations for modern welfare economics with the idea of 'utility'. In part two of this chapter, I contrast Sen with one of those predecessors – John Stuart Mill. The relative merits of two ways of applying the CA – the 'choice' and 'options' applications – are discussed in part three. In part four, I focus on ways of 'completing' the CA in applying it. Finally, in part five I focus on the level of precision at which the approach works, and whether it works best with a 'broad brush' or a 'sharp point'. In examining this issue, I make various methodological points by applying the CA in conjunction with fuzzy poverty measures. Part six concludes.

Locating Sen's CA: a comparison with J. S. Mill

One of Sen's most important moves in developing the CA is to differentiate it from utilitarianism in the various versions which have emerged since Jeremy Bentham's account of *classical utilitarianism*. Bentham defined 'utility' as 'the property in any object that tends to produce benefit, advantage, pleasure, good or happiness .... or ... to prevent the happening of mischief and pain, evil, or unhappiness' (Bentham 1970: 12). He went on to state that 'an action then may be said to be conformable to the principle of utility ... when the tendency it has to augment the happiness of the community is greater than any it has to diminish it' (Bentham 1970: 12–13). This principle is now typically understood in terms of the idea that morality involves *maximising* the *sum* of 'utility' in society. Bentham's is, of course, only one way of thinking about 'utility' and 'utilitarianism'. Many alternative versions of utilitarianism have subsequently emerged. In some versions the notion of 'utility' is thought of in hedonistic terms as 'pleasure and the absence of pain',[4] while in others it is understood in terms of informed or rational desires (Harsanyi 1982 and Griffin 1986). Not all forms of utilitarianism focus on the sum of utility: an alternative version focuses on average utility.[5] Nonetheless, all varieties of utilitarianism focus on *consequences* (of actions or rules or motives) when judging right and wrong, even though there are different ways of characterising 'consequences'.[6] Sen keeps the focus on consequences in his work,[7] and rejects the *singular* attention to 'utility' – which he terms 'welfarism' – in the utilitarian approach.[8] This singular focus is, he thinks, a mistake. He thinks that the 'space' of 'utility' – whatever interpretation of 'utility' is used[9] – can be distorted, and thus be misleading in judging a person's advantage. Suppose that 'utility' is thought of as 'pleasure and the absence of pain' and consider the battered and harassed housewife who has learned to find pleasure in the small things in life as a survival strategy. As it happens, she can get as much utility as someone who is successful and free but sees no point in the pursuit of pleasure, and her life thus lacks enjoyment. Even if these two people have the same amount of utility, we may not think they are equally well off. Welfarism may, thus, mislead because of its 'mono-concentration' on utility (Sen 2000b: 19). Sen typically rehearses this argument for the various alternative ways in which we might define 'utility' (Sen 1999: 62).

Sen's critique of utilitarianism has proven both powerful and influential. It has led him to develop his own account of the quality of life. The quality of life is, according to Sen, best thought of in terms of the *capability* to achieve the valuable *functionings* – 'beings and doings' – which are constitutive of valuable lives. He usually defines a person's capability in terms of the range of lives she can choose from (Sen 1993: 30–33). In this sense, a person's capability relates to the *positive freedoms* or *opportunities* he or she enjoys and her 'capability set' is the set of vectors or *n-tuples* of functioning from which she can choose. Sen

---

[4] John Stuart Mill sometimes reads it in this sense – see Mill (1962: 257).
[5] See Harsanyi (1982) *inter alia*.
[6] On this see Samuel Scheffler (1988).
[7] See Sen (2000b).
[8] He also rejects 'sum ranking' – the mere adding up of people's utilities. See Sen (1979).
[9] On Sen's uses of 'utility' see Sen (1991b).

sometimes also uses 'capabilities' to refer to specific valuable abilities, such as the ability to appear in public without shame. Some capabilities are thought of as 'basic', relating to the ability to achieve certain crucial functionings, such as avoiding starvation. Others – such as the ability to be socially integrated – are thought of as more sophisticated. The capability view then sees: (1) development as an expansion of (valuable) capabilities or freedoms (Sen 1984a, 1988, 1990b and 1999); (2) capability as an important currency for judgements involving egalitarian justice (Sen 1990a and 1992); and (3) poverty in terms of 'basic capability failure' (Sen 1983 and 1985c). In most statements of the CA – including the original Tanner lecture (Sen 1980) – Sen contrasts this approach with utilitarianism, though sometimes it looks as if he *makes room for* utilitarianism. Sen (1983: 161f and 1993: 48) treats 'being happy' as a valuable functioning which he associates with hedonistic utilitarianism (Sen 1993: 37). But, in Sen's view, 'being happy' is just one among many functionings one might value, and he holds back from giving a full account of valuable functionings.

How plausible is the strong contrast that Sen sometimes makes between his view and classical utilitarianism? If one is looking for a utilitarian philosopher–economist whose stature is comparable to Sen's, one is led to John Stuart Mill. Mill's work – while critical of, and a departure from, Bentham's in some significant respects[10] – is, in other respects, a canonical expression of classical utilitarianism.[11] Indeed, Mill spent much of his life promoting utilitarianism and was the founder of the Utilitarian Society. Reading Mill, we find, again and again, striking similarities with Sen. I shall concentrate on only three aspects of similarity. First, there is Sen's account of development as an expansion of capabilities. He has characterised this expansion in terms of Marx's notion of 'replacing the domination of circumstances and chance by the domination of individuals over chance and circumstances'.[12] In Mill's *The Subjection of Women* we find an interesting and related account of the contrast between what Mill calls the 'modern world' and the 'old' (Mill 1988: 17). Mill's use of the terms 'modern world' and 'old' belong to a different age, but would translate quite

---

[10] See Mill's essay on Bentham in Mill (1962).
[11] For a sensitive, thoughtful and authoritative reading of Mill's utilitarianism see Roger Crisp (1997).
[12] Sen (1990b: 44).

directly into contemporary uses of 'developed world' and 'underdeveloped'. What distinguishes modern institutions and social ideas from the old is, we are told, that 'human beings are no longer born to their place in society, and chained down by an inexorable bond to the place they are born to, but are free to employ their faculties' (Mill 1988: 17). The 'old' world, Mill tells us, is one where people are, in effect, severely constrained, and so, we can conclude, have limited capabilities or freedoms (in Sen's terms). For a utilitarian, Mill's position is remarkably close to the CA.

Echoes of Sen also fill Mill's eloquent advocacy of the causes of liberty (particularly in his celebrated essay *On Liberty*) and gender equality. It is, to my mind, already clear from the text just quoted that, like Sen, Mill is concerned with equality of opportunities. But in writing about it we find him using a vocabulary which is astonishingly Sen-like. He talks of the disadvantages of women in terms of 'disabilities . . . to which women are subject' and the 'higher social functions' which are closed to women (Mill 1988: 20). He also looks forward to a time when '[w]omen in general would be brought up *equally capable* of understanding business, public affairs, and the higher matters of speculation, with men' (Mill 1988: 90; emphasis added). But even more striking is the fact that Mill is aware of the problem posed by the fact that people adapt to their situations and sees that it not only applies to preferences, as Martha Nussbaum (1999: 13) notes, but that it might also apply to *capabilities*, if these are understood as capacities or skills.[13] He tells us that 'in the case of women, a hothouse and stove cultivation has always been carried on of some of the *capabilities* of their nature, for the benefits and pleasure of their masters' (Mill 1988: 22; emphasis added). The observation that capabilities as much as pleasures, or desires, can be distorted by injustice is noted in various ways in the recent literature on the CA (Nussbaum 1988 and Qizilbash 1997a *inter alia*). While Mill may be using the notion of 'capabilities' in a somewhat narrow way here, his remark prefigures the modern literature.

We also find echoes of Sen in Mill's discussion of poverty. Mill, like Sen (see Sen 1995 and 2000c), is hopeful that rational discussion may

---

[13] I discuss Mill's use of terms relating to 'capability' at greater length in Qizilbash (2006a).

help solve social ills, and he thinks that anyone with sufficient intelligence ought to be engaged in solving these ills. In *Utilitarianism*, he tells us: 'Poverty in any sense implying suffering may be completely extinguished by the wisdom of society' (Mill 1962: 266). His picture of poverty is, inevitably, coloured by his utilitarianism. However, while he does not dwell on capabilities, he does use the concept in his discussion, again on a note of optimism. He thinks that everyone with certain:

> moral and intellectual requisites is *capable* of an existence which is enviable; and unless such a person through bad laws, or subjection to the will of others, is denied the liberty to find the sources of happiness within his reach, he will not fail to find this enviable existence, if he escape the positive evils of life, the great sources of physical and mental suffering, and the unkindness, worthlessness, or premature loss of objects of affection. The main stress of the problem lies, therefore, in the contest with these calamities. (Mill 1962: 265–66; emphasis added)

Mill clearly thought that people have the capability to lead valuable or 'enviable' lives, as long as certain necessary conditions are met. In aiming to ensure that these conditions should be met, his goal was to ensure that a human being's capability for living an 'enviable life' was not undermined. To this degree Mill's account is, again, a capability view. Mill can thus be seen as having a concern with capability *as well as* being a utilitarian. In this passage, he is concerned with ensuring that people have the *capability to be happy*. This position may not be seen as a 'capability view' inasmuch as it can be argued that, in Mill's account, capability is not seen as intrinsically valuable, only valuable to the degree that it is connected (instrumentally) to happiness. Nonetheless, Sen's hope is that the capability view can be adopted by people with different views of valuation or of the good life (Sen 1993: 48) and Mill's view might thus be classified as a particular form of capability view. Inasmuch as this is so, the strong contrast which Sen sometimes makes between classical utilitarianism and his capability view is overdone. The picture of the place of Sen's work in relation to the utilitarian tradition is, to this degree, distorted.

It can be argued that had Mill himself seen that the importance he gives to freedom might seriously conflict with some aspects of his utilitarianism, he would have revised certain central elements in his moral writings. The similarity between Sen and Mill may then arise from the confusion, or conflicting elements, in Mill's thought. Mill is, on this view, an 'imperfect' utilitarian.[14] Even if Mill's position is an uneasy hybrid of liberalism and utilitarianism (as Isaiah Berlin suggested),[15] it is still true, nonetheless, that some passages in Mill can be read as articulating a form of *utilitarian capability approach*.[16] Inasmuch as this is a *coherent* notion, the contrast between the capability view and utilitarianism which Sen sometimes draws can be misleading.[17] It is worth noting, nonetheless, that Sen has repeatedly listed Mill as one of those who saw the importance of freedom and he writes that 'the protection and enhancement of liberty supplemented John Stuart Mill's utilitarian perspective very substantially' (Sen 1999: 89). So Sen is quite aware that there is a close affinity between his views and Mill's. Indeed, he sees his work as firmly rooted in a tradition in which Mill is a major figure and he is pleased to acknowledge his intellectual roots, including Mill's influence (Sen, 2006). Furthermore, in developing his own view of 'utility' Sen goes back to Mill's discussion in developing his 'vector view' of utility (Sen 1980–81). While continuing to contrast his approach with utilitarianism (Sen 1999: 58–59), Sen has also noted the merits of utilitarianism – notably its focus on ends rather than means, as well as its attention to people's well-being (Sen 1999: 60).

The choice and options applications of the CA

There is a contrast between Sen and Mill in the passage where Mill discusses poverty, it is in Mill's extraordinary confidence in the capacity of people who are not subjected to the 'positive evils in life' to

This view of Mill is the one that Amartya Sen adopted in his response to an earlier version of this paper.

[15] See Berlin (1969). Christopher Miles Coope (1998) goes further and claims that Mill was not a utilitarian at all.

[16] I expand on this argument and other connections between Mill and Sen in Qizilbash (2006a). See also Sumner (2006) and Sen's response (Sen, 2006). I've tried to update this chapter in the light of the exchange with Sen, though this has not been easy since that exchange occurred much after the first presentation of this chapter.

[17] While Sen (1993) characterises 'being happy' as a valuable functioning, he sometimes characterises 'being happy' as unconnected with the exercise of valuation (Sen 1987: 46). That exercise of valuation is central to his CA. Nonetheless, the valuation of distinct forms of pleasure is central to some sorts of utilitarianism, such as Mill's in which there is the famous distinction between 'higher' and 'lower' pleasures.

achieve happiness. It is because of this confidence that Mill sees no significant gap between the capability to be happy and happiness itself. In Sen's work the equivalent gap is the gap between the capability to lead a valuable life and the valuable life itself, which is constituted by various functionings. Sen distinguishes between the various 'spaces', or kinds of information, which are relevant to the evaluation of the quality of life. This is, in part, because he is very concerned about the different rates at which different people convert income and resources into capabilities and functionings. These different rates are, after all, relevant to making interpersonal comparisons of the quality of life. Sen is surely right in highlighting this point. There is nonetheless one gap which Sen does not focus on much, and that is the gap which Mill thinks can be easily closed: the gap between capability and a valuable life.[18]

This issue can be related directly to Sen's own discussion of the gap between capability and functionings. While he thinks that both are important, the link between them is relevant to the measurement of capability sets. He considers two approaches to measuring capability sets. The first – the 'choice application' of the CA – involves looking at the functioning vector which is actually chosen. The alternative 'options application' of the CA involves looking at the whole range of functionings which is available for choice (Sen 1997a: 200–01). The choice application is a form of 'elementary evaluation' – it focuses on just one element in the capability set. That element may not, however, be 'maximal' – i.e. one that is no worse than any other in the set. Sen tells us that the choice application will focus only on an element that is no worse than any other in the relevant capability set under the assumptions of 'maximisation', as he defines it, and no uncertainty (Sen 1997a: 203). Both assumptions may fail to hold in the context of poverty analysis – where the approach is much used – and there is, for this reason, a strong case to be made for the 'options' application. I shall focus for the moment on the issue of 'maximisation' and put the issue of uncertainty to one side (see Kanbur 1987).

---

[18] While this gap is central to Sen's work, Sen sometimes underplays its importance. In a recent discussion of problems relating to incentives he tells us, for example, that while there is a 'jump . . . from functionings to capabilities . . . it need not be a big jump' (Sen 1999: 131).

For Sen (1997b), 'maximisation' involves picking an alternative which is *no worse than* any other in the set from which choice is made. This allows for rational choice between options which are 'comparable' and choice between options which are 'non-comparable'.[19] Choosing can, of course, itself be a valuable functioning, and the capabilities involved in choosing may be important. However, such capabilities may not be adequately captured by the *capability set* – if this is understood as the set of functioning vectors (or *n-tuples*) from which choice is to be made – considered by itself. They may need independent attention quite aside from the relevant capability set which is being considered. These capabilities can include, for any given capability set: (1) capabilities involved in articulating and identifying the contents of that set; and (2) capabilities involved in choosing from that set. Among the abilities involved in rational deliberation, (2) would include abilities involved in making 'hard choices' – which might emerge when options are difficult to rank. Sen often illustrates problems relating to such choices by referring to the well-known example of Burridan's ass (e.g. Sen 1997b: 765). For the sake of vividness, particularly in the context of poverty, I use an example involving a starving woman, but little depends on the choice of this example. When a starving woman is faced with the choice of which of her starving children to feed, various capabilities – such as the ability to cope with conflict and stress – are relevant. In such conditions, anxiety might threaten to (even if it does not actually) undermine her capacity to choose, *while leaving the set of options she faces unchanged*. Of course, the CA can treat this anxiety as a form of capability or functioning failure (such as a loss of the capability to think clearly). Furthermore, if the woman actually loses the ability to choose, the set of options is no longer a capability set – the capability set is a set from which the woman *can* choose. Similarly, losing the ability to choose is a form of capability failure. This example suggests nonetheless that there may be problems with the options application, if the options application underplays the importance of the capabilities and functionings

---

[19] Options which are 'comparable' are those which can be ranked according to the relation 'preferred or indifferent to' and 'non-comparable' cases cannot be so ranked. Sen (1997b) uses 'preferred or indifferent to' as equivalent to 'at least as good as'.

involved in choice by putting the emphasis on the set of options.[20] So we ought not to be too sanguine – as Mill perhaps was – about the leap from the capability set to valued lives (or functionings), nor focus *exclusively* on the relevant *set of options* in any specific context. While problems with a singular focus on the set of options for choice do not necessarily push us back to the choice application, they do suggest that certain aspects of freedom which Sen distinguishes from capability or opportunity – such as autonomy of choice – matter in understanding poverty.[21]

Incompleteness and capability consequentialism

Sen famously leaves his CA 'incomplete'. There are different aspects of incompleteness. First, there is the issue of the functionings or capabilities which are valuable. Second, there is the issue of what sort of weight or priority to give to *different functionings or capabilities*, in some particular context, involving interpersonal or international comparisons of the quality of life. Third, there is the issue of what weight or priority to give to *different people* in arriving at moral judgements. Each of these areas of incompleteness is important in the context of application. For those who work in the capability space there are also issues about how to measure opportunity and freedom, which are related to these areas of incompleteness. Applying the CA often involves 'filling in the gaps' left by Sen's incompleteness. These issues need urgent attention if only because some doubt the usefulness of the approach on the grounds that it cannot be made 'operational'. For example, Robert Sugden asks whether, given the large array of functionings that people value, and disagreement about these, as well as problems involved in valuing sets, Sen's framework is 'operational' and a 'realistic alternative to the methods on which economists typically

---

[20] It might be argued that in this case it is the set of options itself which might lead to inability to think clearly and that an improved set of options may restore the relevant ability. So the set of options might still be important in this case. A more serious capability failure – e.g. one caused by serious mental illness – may, however, not be reversible once better options emerge. I'm very grateful to Sabina Alkire for pointing this out to me.

[21] On this see Sen's distinction between the 'opportunity' and 'process' aspects of freedom which are most fully discussed in his Arrow lectures (in Sen, 2002). See also Qizilbash (2005).

rely, and the kind of practical cost–benefit analysis which is grounded in Marshallian consumer theory' (Sugden 1993). Sen has nonetheless 'applied' the capability view – and to that degree made his approach 'operational' – in various ways which have not, perhaps, received sufficient attention.

Variations on Sen's approach – such as that developed by Martha Nussbaum – combine the space of capability with some substantive account of values and develop a more complete view which can be used in evaluation. Nussbaum's approach (Nussbaum 1988, 1990, 1992, 1995, 1998, 1999, 2000, 2003 and 2005) is not the only way of making Sen's approach more complete. Inasmuch as Mill's view can be seen as a capability view, his hedonism (combined with his approach to ranking pleasures and the equal weighting of persons in his view) *could be* used as an alternative route. Some contemporary views of well-being are sometimes also seen as potential ways of completing the CA (Griffin 1986, Finnis 1979, Qizilbash 1998 and Alkire 2002 *inter alia*), though some of these views can also be seen as *alternatives* to that approach. This is, of course, one reason why Sen wants to keep the approach incomplete: it can allow for many different approaches to evaluation. His concern with agreement about the importance of the capability space makes him very open at the level of valuation. Indeed, Sen rarely uses *his own work* on values and preferences to develop his work on capability. In particular, he does not use his work on a 'meta-ranking' of preference rankings which can ground an account of morality and value (Sen 1974) in this context. This is particularly surprising because in his work on the measurement of freedom (Sen 1991a), Sen does adopt a preference-based view of valuing freedom and he has connected his work on meta-ranking with the issue of the measurement of freedom in his Arrow lectures (Sen 2002). This makes his view vulnerable to criticism (Carter 1996: 13), for the same sorts of reasons as preference-based views of 'utility' can be criticised. Sen has forcefully rebutted (Sen 1996: 107–12) this criticism in defending the 'reach' of preference-based views. It is important to distinguish here between the use of preferences in the context of *value* and preferences used in the context of an account of *advantage*. Yet if the use of preferences can distort a view of advantage, such use may also distort an account of freedom or opportunity.

It is a mixture of Sen's liberalism and pragmatism that stops him from filling out a list of functionings and the corresponding capabilities in his *theoretical defences* of the CA (e.g. Sen 1985a and b, 1992 and 1993).[22] As regards liberalism, it is a concern with not telling people what functionings are valuable but respecting their autonomy to choose their lists of valuable functionings which, in part, drives Sen to incompleteness. If people define their own lists, disagreement may emerge, and Sen wants to allow for this. Sen's liberalism again echoes Mill, who thought that it was dangerous for government and the law to be treated as 'better judges' than individuals themselves of their 'capacities and vocations' (Mill 1988: 19).

Sen is also quite explicit about his pragmatism.[23] He writes that it is a 'combination of foundational analysis and pragmatic use that gives the CA its extensive reach' (Sen 1999: 86). Pragmatism leads Sen to be quite open-minded, in his more philosophical discussions, about the things that people value. He also thinks that different capabilities might be relevant in different contexts. In his work for the United Nations Development Programme (UNDP), Sen's pragmatism allows him to focus on some specific capabilities or functionings and an arbitrary set of weights. There are two distinct strategies being employed in Sen's work, which need to be distinguished and which may be hard to reconcile.[24]

In his philosophical discussions, Sen avoids using strong views of value, weights, and aggregation. This is also true in some applications of the CA, when he is writing, primarily, for an academic audience. He argues that we can get quite far by focusing on cases where all the relevant capabilities give the same ranking – the so-called 'dominance' approach to ranking (or 'dominance partial order') – and on cases where all relevant weights which people apply give the same answer – the so-called 'intersection approach' (Sen 1992: 46–47 and 1993: 48–49). In this part of his work, Sen has been insistent on allowing for incompleteness, and for some cases which are non-comparable. This has been an old theme in Sen's work and fits with his discussions of the maximisation view of rationality, which allows for non-comparability. It is compatible with some of his applications of the CA (e.g. Drèze and Sen 1995 and Sen 1984b).

---

[22] Sen has recently further explained his position as regards lists. See Sen (2004b) and (2005b).

[23] I discuss this issue further in Qizilbash (2002a).

[24] I have tried to reconcile these strategies in the light of Sen's recent writings on 'public reasoning' (see Sen 2004, 2005a and 2005b) in Qizilbash (2007).

By contrast, some of Sen's work for the UNDP involves using very specific capabilities, functionings, and weights, and also not being especially concerned with the distinction between functionings and capabilities.[25] This part of Sen's work was no doubt heavily influenced by the necessity of working with the policy agenda of human development, which he, along with the late Mahbub ul Haq and others, pushed at the UNDP. Mahbub ul Haq was convinced of the usefulness of a single index to rival gross domestic product at the policy level, and treated the avoidance of such an index, because of issues relating to weights, as 'academic puritanism taken too far' (Haq 1995: 58–59). The success of his work at the UNDP has vindicated Haq's approach. This part of Sen's work is, thus, best seen as part of a collaborative endeavour which helped provide a set of indices which generates complete orderings. Nonetheless, those who think that the components of composite indices – such as the UNDP's human development index (HDI) – are non-comparable may doubt the *meaningfulness* of these measures. There is, thus, a real need to clarify the contrasting approaches.

In trying to make sense of this aspect of Sen's work for the UNDP, I term any approach to normative evaluation (of actions, motives, or rules) which focuses *exclusively* on capability consequences 'capability consequentialism'. While Sen's position differs from many versions of 'consequentialism', it can be thought of as 'consequentialist' in some broad sense (Sen 2000a). Nonetheless, Sen's position cannot simply be characterised as a form of capability consequentialism since he thinks that there are considerations other than capability (such as the process through which choice is made) that matter. So I am using the term 'capability consequentialism' primarily for clarification purposes, rather than to characterise Sen's view.

Suppose first that we have a list of m valuable capabilities which is to be used in some specific context. Furthermore, suppose that individuals are indexed by i, where $i = 1, \ldots, n$ and c_i is a composite measure of individual i's capability. Assume also that, for each person, we have measures relating to each relevant capability. The measure for each

---

[25] Sen (1999: 131) has recently written that the 'assessment of actual capabilities has to proceed primarily on the basis of observing a person's functionings'. He clearly thinks that it is only in some contexts that the distinction between capability and functioning is crucial, and in others data limitations mean that we must simply focus on functionings (Sen 1992: 49–53).

dimension j can be written d_j, where $j = 1, \ldots, m$. There are different functional relationships which could hold between the various d_j and c_i. We might write the general function as follows:

$$c_i = f(d_1, \ldots, d_m) \tag{1}$$

The functional relationship between the c_i and d_j might or might not be additive. We can define various sorts of capability consequentialism. Writing 'social capability' as C, a 'social capability function' takes the general form:

$$C = g(c_1, \ldots, c_n) \tag{2}$$

This is the capability 'equivalent' of the standard Bergson-Samuelson social welfare function, which relates individual welfare levels to social welfare. We can then define:

$$C = \sum_{i=1}^{n} c_i \quad \text{(sum ranking capability consequentialism)} \tag{3}$$

$$C = (1/n)\sum_{i=1}^{n} c_i \quad \text{(average capability consequentialism)} \tag{4}$$

These are the capability 'equivalents' of classical and average utilitarianism. They are not likely to attract Sen himself, because they do not incorporate any inequality aversion. Finally, we can have a variety of capability consequentialism which is concerned with maximising the situation of the least well-off person or group:

$$C = \min(c_1, \ldots, c_n) \quad \text{('Rawlsian' capability consequentialism)} \tag{5}$$

What we have here is a picture of capability consequentialism which mirrors the standard way of distinguishing moral positions in welfare economics, but simply makes capability rather than 'utility' or 'welfare' the key space of evaluation.

In the relevant parts of his work for the UNDP, much of which is co-authored with Sudhir Anand, Sen is actually working with something a little different. In (2)–(5) there is a relationship between the realisation of capability at the individual and social levels. In his work for the UNDP, Sen does not work with the relationship between the individual and society. The data comes in 'aggregate' form (Dutta, Pattanaik and Xu 2003) in the sense that it typically relates to the realisation of specific functionings or capabilities at the social level. The focus is on the relationship between the realisation of specific capabilities or functionings at the social level and an overall judgement of the realisation of capabilities or functionings. I shall use the term 'social valuation function' to refer to this sort of relationship. In its most general form this is the equivalent of (1) at the aggregate level. Writing the capability or functioning level in society in terms of dimension j as D_j (where, as before, $j = 1, \ldots m$), then we have:

$$C = h(D_1, \ldots, D_m) \tag{6}$$

There are then various variations on this that we might consider:

$$C = \sum_{j=1}^{m} D_j \quad \text{(summing dimensions)} \tag{7}$$

$$C = (1/m)\sum_{j=1}^{m} D_j \quad \text{(averaging dimensions)} \tag{8}$$

$$C = \min(D_1, \ldots, D_m) \quad \text{('Rawlsian' dimensions)} \tag{9}$$

It is clear that (6)–(9) are quite different from (2)–(5), though the same functional forms are being used in (3) and (7), (4) and (8) and so on. The *interpretation* of these equations depends on both the functional form involved *and* the nature of the arguments in the functions. Indeed, it might be argued that in applying the CA we should be aiming to estimate functions like (2)–(5) rather than (6)–(9). The focus on 'aggregate' dimension specific data – in the context of international comparisons which are made in the UNDP publications – is primarily the result of data limitations. The HDI is based on a social valuation function which involves averaging dimensions – it is a variation on (8). The gender-related development index (GDI) and the gender empowerment measure (GEM) in the 1995 *Human Development Report* (based on Anand and Sen 1995) also involve an averaging procedure. Nonetheless, in the construction of the particular indices which enter the GEM and GDI, Anand and Sen adopt a methodology – based on the work of A. B. Atkinson (1970) – which involves inequality-aversion (UNDP 1995: 127) to develop a measure of gender inequality for *each dimension*. It is only after inequality-aversion has been allowed for that the indices are averaged to give the GDI or GEM.

It might seem peculiar that Sen's work involves introducing inequality-aversion in the gender context while using a standard averaging procedure (which does not involve adjusting for inequality-aversion) for the HDI. However, there have been attempts to ensure that the income component of the HDI is equity sensitive (Anand and Sen 2000) and Hicks (1997) and Foster *et al.* (2005) have developed versions of HDI which adjust it for inequality. So the issue is very much alive. The human poverty index (UNDP 1997), which is, again, based on the work of Anand and Sen, uses information on certain capabilities or functionings at the aggregate level and also involves a particular form of average. There has also been an attempt to adjust capability-poverty measures for inequality (Majumdar and Subramanian 2001).

Clearly, the project of developing measures based on the CA is very much alive, and not without potential inconsistencies. There are some important points that emerge from this brief discussion of Sen's work. First, Sen has been quite pragmatic in using the available data in applying the CA. This has meant that he has often not been overly concerned about the distinction between capability and functionings indices. He clearly thinks that that distinction is more important in some contexts than others. Second, there are a number of ways of applying the CA and researchers have to decide how to apply it according to the context. There is certainly no 'magic formula' for applying the CA. Finally, Sen has borrowed techniques from standard welfare economics, such as those used in the Atkinson measure, in developing measures inspired by the CA. Indeed, the Atkinson measure was itself, in part, inspired by the earlier *utilitarian* measure of equality developed by Hugh Dalton (Sen 1997b: 37–39). Sen has, thus, been quite pragmatic using techniques which come out of the various traditions he wants to reject.

Broad brush or precise point?

Well before he began his work on capability, Sen knew that there were important problems involved in precise measurement of inequality and poverty. In *On Economic Inequality* (initially published in 1973 and reprinted in Sen 1997a), he tells us repeatedly that the notion of inequality which is important to politics is one which involves 'sharp contrasts' and 'may not provide a scale sensitive enough to order finely distinguished distributions' (Sen 1997a: 6). He tells us that 'the economist's and the statistician's inclination is to look for an ordering complete in all respects, so that the translation of the notion of inequality from the sphere of political debate, which gives the notion its importance, to the sphere of well-defined economic representation may tend to confuse the mathematical properties of the underlying concept' (Sen 1997a: 6). Sen suggests that we might work with a potentially incomplete 'quasi-ordering'[26] and argues that the desire to move towards a complete ordering may be a serious liability in economics.

It has subsequently been pointed out – by Kaushik Basu (1987) – that we need to distinguish inexactness and incompleteness in our judgements. The implication is that Sen's focus on incompleteness (and techniques such as 'dominance partial ordering' and the 'intersection approach') might not be appropriate when dealing with difficulties generated by imprecision and vagueness. Basu has tried to deal with the problem of vagueness by applying Zadeh's fuzzy set theory to the issue of inequality measurement. Others (Cerioli and Zani 1990 and Cheli and Lemmi 1995) have attempted to apply fuzzy set theory to poverty measurement, and Enrica Chiappero-Martinetti (1994, 1996 and 2000) has tried to combine Sen's approach with Bruno Cheli and Achille Lemmi's approach to fuzzy poverty measurement.

While Sen often refers to the literature on fuzzy sets in his work, he has a direct way of dealing with problems of imprecision. In terms of the artistic analogy, the problem caused by imprecision in evaluation often leads Sen to use a rather 'broad brush' rather than a 'precise point' in using the CA. This strategy is, I think, quite central in some of his writings, and has not been well understood. One example of this strategy at work in Sen's writings is in the context of poverty in affluent countries, where he reports (Sen 1992: 114) a study which shows that men born in Harlem in New York City have less chance of reaching the age of forty than Bangladeshi men. Similarly, in making comparisons between India and China, Sen uses strong contrasts *within* India to make important points (Drèze and Sen 1995: chapters 3 and 4). This general strategy of using striking contrasts is also taken up by the UNDP (e.g. UNDP 1994: 98–101) in its *Human Development Reports* in combination with the HDI – which is, of course, a precise measure. Similarly, it is used by researchers in particular contexts, as, for example, in May, Woolard, and Klasen's (2000: 24–25) discussion of South Africa. Like a painter who uses strong contrasts of colour or tone to achieve a particular effect, Sen makes some striking points

[26] A relation like 'more unequal than' or 'poorer than' is a quasi-ordering if it is reflexive and transitive but not necessarily complete.

in this way. Even though this strategy typically involves using precise numbers (such as figures on survival chances or the HDI), the contrasts are so strong that the *precise* numbers do not matter for the point being made.

The second general approach is one which adopts an explicit methodology – like fuzzy set theory – for dealing with imprecision. There are at least two well-known fuzzy set theoretic approaches to poverty measurement. They both involve some level of income or the quality of life above which people are definitely non-poor, a level below which people are definitely poor, and a zone of cases in between where people belong to the set of the poor to some degree (i.e. where it is true to some degree that people are poor). In their important paper, Cerioli and Zani (1990) suppose that there is some set of poor people, A, with ψ_A giving the degree of membership of A, where ψ_A belongs to the [0,1] interval. If someone definitely belongs to the set of the poor, ψ_A is 1; if she is definitely not poor, then ψ_A is 0. If someone belongs to the set of the poor *to some degree*, then $0 < \psi_A < 1$. Cerioli and Zani develop this approach for the case where income is the unique focal variable as well as for the multi-dimensional case. I focus on the multi-dimensional case, which involves an ordinal method of scoring. The scoring procedure works so that if there are two individuals, or classes of individuals, and one has a higher level of deprivation, that person or class gets assigned a lower number. So the lowest score is assigned to the highest level of deprivation. 'ψ_j' is the score equal to or below which someone is definitely poor in dimension j. ψ_j" is the score in dimension j at or above which people are classified as definitely non-poor in dimension j. ψ_{ij} gives the score for individual i in dimension j. Individual i's degree of membership of the set of the poor in dimension j is written z_{ij} and it is set to 1 if $\psi_{ij} \leq \psi_j$' and to 0 if $\psi_{ij} \geq \psi_j$". If $\psi_j' < \psi_{ij} < \psi_j$", then:

$$z_{ij} = \left(\psi_j'' - \psi_{ij} \right) / \left(\psi_j'' - \psi_j' \right) \qquad (10)$$

To get a measure of the degree to which someone belongs to the set of the poor, Cerioli and Zani then suggest that we take a weighted average of the z_{ij}. That gives us ψ_A for the multi-dimensional case.

Cheli and Lemmi (1995), meanwhile, propose a measure which is both fuzzy and 'relative'. 'Relativism' means that, in the income space, both the cut-offs and the way in which membership of the set of the poor varies with income depend on the sample distribution of income. They also use a multi-dimensional framework. Suppose that we write variable x for dimension j as x_j, and that people are ranked according to their achievement in terms of this variable. k gives the rank order of the level of, or class of, achievement, and is set to one for the highest-ranking class or level of achievement, to two for the second highest class or level, and so on. Then $g(x_j^{(k)})$ denotes the degree of membership of the set of the poor for someone ranked (or someone in the class ranked) k in terms of x_j. Cheli and Lemmi (1995: 127) set $g(x_j^{(k)}) = 0$ for $k = 1$. Writing the sampling distribution of x_j arranged in increasing order according to k as $H(x_j)$, then, for $k > 1$, the degree of membership is given by:

$$g(x_j^{(k)}) = g(x_j^{(k-1)}) + \{H(x_j^{(k)}) - H(x_j^{(k-1)})\}/(1 - H(x_j^{(1)})) \qquad (11)$$

This is a membership function for dimension j only. There may be different ways of aggregating across the dimensions. Chiappero-Martinetti (1994, 1996 and 2000) has used this membership function in conjunction with the CA in the Italian context.

Various issues arise when the fuzzy set theoretic approach is used. Some relate to meaning and motivation. How are we to interpret, and make sense of, degrees of membership? Why do they matter? My hunch is that fuzzy poverty measures can be interpreted as measures of 'vulnerability', and the interpretation which Cheli and Lemmi give of their measure, in terms of 'exposure to risk of falling prey to poverty' (Cheli and Lemmi 1995:129), involves a similar intuition. However, the notion of 'vulnerability' used here is not the same as that used in much of the economics literature – where it relates to the risk or probability of *becoming* poor (say, after a change in prices). In the case of vagueness, vulnerability has to do with the possibility of being *defined* as, rather than becoming, poor. I have made the case for this interpretation elsewhere (see Qizilbash 2002b, 2003 and 2006b) using a supervaluationist approach to vagueness (Fine 1996).

In most of the fuzzy set theoretic literature on poverty, imprecision usually relates to the 'bottom line' at or below which someone is classified as poor. However, there may also be imprecision about the dimensions of poverty. The fuzzy set theoretic approaches just mentioned usually assume that the dimensions of poverty are well (i.e. exactly) defined. This issue has received remarkably little attention (see Qizilbash 2003 and Clark and Qizilbash 2005). There has also been little discussion of the distinction between absolute and relative poverty in the literature on the application of fuzzy set theory to a Sen-type approach to poverty. Chiappero-Martinetti assumes that the relativist fuzzy measure of poverty can be used in conjunction with Sen's account of the quality of life. Yet Sen himself has argued that poverty is 'absolute' in the spaces of functioning and capability, while it may be 'relative' in the spaces of income and resources (Sen 1983 and 1985c).

In order to explore this issue further, I use the two fuzzy set theoretic measures just described together with a methodology used in Stephan Klasen's (1997 and 2000) attempt to apply the CA to the South African context. Like Klasen, I suppose that there are various levels of disadvantage in terms of specific dimensions of the quality of life, which are ranked ordinally. For illustrative purposes, I consider just three indicators relating to educational attainment, water source, and source of energy for cooking. In a comprehensive application of the CA, a much broader range of such indices would be appropriate (Klasen, 2000, Qizilbash 2002b and Clark and Qizilbash 2005). The three selected indices are direct (i.e. non-income) indices which can be thought of as picking up important functionings. Data is taken from the South African census of 1996 (rather than the Southern Africa Labour and Development Research Unit data set for 1993, which Klasen uses, and which uses similar categories for classification) and is presented in Tables 2.1–2.3. The data shows the situation of the major social groups – as they are defined in the South African context – i.e. 'White', 'African', 'Coloured', and 'Asian'. It shows the striking difference between the situations of the White and Asian groups as contrasted, in particular, with Africans. In these tables, where possible, the ranking of levels of disadvantage is exactly as in Klasen (1997 and 2000). In defining cut-offs, I use the following 'relativist' method of classification, which takes its lead from the Cheli and Lemmi approach. In that approach, for someone at the worst-off class or level of achievement in terms of some variable, the fuzzy measure takes a value of 1, so that people or households at this level are definitely poor. For any household or person at the highest level of achievement, the measure takes a value of 0, and that household or person is definitely not poor. Values of the fuzzy measures falling between 0 and 1 capture levels of 'vulnerability' (on the interpretation adopted in Qizilbash 2002b and

2003 and Clark and Qizilbash 2002). So, for example, in the case of the source of water, someone with rank 1 has piped water in their dwelling and is definitely not poor, while someone with rank 5 gets access to water from either a dam or river or stream and is definitely poor in this dimension. Everyone falling in between these two rank orders is 'vulnerable'. The Cheli and Lemmi and Cerioli and Zani measures are also given in Tables 2.1–2.3, with Vcz giving the Cerioli and Zani measure and Vcl giving the Cheli and Lemmi measure.

How do the two measures contrast in this context? In the case of energy used for cooking they give rather different pictures. In this dimension, I have followed Klasen and treated those who use wood as the most deprived category and those who use dung as the second most deprived category. Clearly, the 1.6 per cent of Africans who use dung are considerably more vulnerable according to Vcz ($= 0.75$) than they are according to Vcl ($= 0.54$). This difference arises primarily because Vcl is a relativist measure and because a relatively small proportion of the population falls in the categories between electricity and wood use. That implies a surprisingly low Vcl.

The problem here seems to be a fairly deep one: when we are looking at poverty in the functioning or capability space, it is, as Sen (1983 and 1985c) tells us, absolute rather than relative. The nature of energy use which relates to 'basic capability' has little to do with the proportions which occupy the various categories in the sampling distribution. It

Table 2.1 *Energy source for cooking*

| Source | Electricity | Gas | Coal/Paraffin | Dung | Wood |
Rank	1	2	3	4	5
African (%)	30.60	3.30	33.90	1.60	30.50
Coloured (%)	76.00	5.70	7.20	0.54	10.90
Asian/Indian (%)	98.10	1.10	0.50	0.00	0.50
White (%)	97.70	1.80	0.23	0.00	0.21
Total (%)	47.40	2.30	25.20	1.10	23.04
Vcz	0.00	0.25	0.50	0.75	1.00
Vcl	0.00	0.04	0.52	0.54	1.00

Source: Statistics South Africa (1998)
(Data excludes hostels and all unspecified categories have been excluded in calculations)

Table 2.2 *Access to water*

Type Rank	Dam, river, stream 5	Borehole, well etc. 4	Public tap etc. 3	Piped on premises 2	Piped in dwelling 1
African (%)	17.10	6.00	28.59	21.00	27.00
Asian/Indian (%)	0.20	0.57	0.48	1.90	97.60
Coloured (%)	1.60	1.87	5.40	18.66	72.40
White (%)	0.42	2.58	0.18	0.64	96.30
Total (%)	12.50	4.96	21.10	16.75	44.67
Vcz	1.00	0.75	0.50	0.25	0.00
Vcl	1.00	0.77	0.68	0.30	0.00

Key:
Dam, river, stream = dam, river, stream or spring
Borehole, well etc. = borehole, rainwater tank or well
Public tap etc. = public tap, water carrier or tanker
Source: Statistics South Africa (1998)
(Data excludes institutions and hostels and all unspecified categories have been excluded)

Table 2.3 *Educational achievement*

Achievement Rank	None 6	Some primary 5	Complete primary 4	Some secondary 3	Matric 2	Higher 1
African (%)	19.70	19.98	9.30	33.40	10.96	6.60
Coloured (%)	10.06	18.30	9.86	43.53	11.35	6.88
Asian/Indian (%)	2.00	4.17	3.56	45.08	29.99	15.18
White (%)	0.60	0.28	0.21	26.46	38.27	34.06
Total (%)	14.00	15.00	7.00	33.50	17.40	12.70
Vcz	1.00	0.80	0.60	0.40	0.20	0.00
Vcl	1.00	0.83	0.66	0.58	0.20	0.00

Source: Statistics South Africa (1998)
(All unspecified categories have been excluded)

involves a judgement about what level or kind of capability or func-tioning is basic. That does not have to do with *rankings* of levels of disadvantage as such. If this is so, we have little to fear from the use of a relativist fuzzy measure of poverty in the *income* or *expenditure* space.

Relativist approaches may also be useful when using indices such as educational attainment, inasmuch as knowledge is, in part, a resource. Indeed, the difference between the levels of Vcz and Vcl for those who have some, but have not completed, secondary education might be significant because the amount of education one has *relative to others* might matter for certain capabilities such as the ability to secure employment (see Qizilbash 2002b and Qizilbash and Clark 2005). That is relevant to why those who have some, but have not completed, secondary education are more vulnerable if we look at Vcl as compared with Vcz in Table 2.3. A similar point might be made about the difference between the levels of Vcz and Vcl for those whose access to water is from a public tap, water tank, or carrier in Table 2.2. However, we need to be cautious about the use of Vcl in the context of social indicators relating to functionings.

Conclusions

Amartya Sen's CA has generated a very large literature, and I have focused, for the most part, on Sen's own writings. The question I asked at the outset was: is the picture Sen gives us a distortion or an insightful sketch? My answer is: 'both'. In part one of this chapter, I argued that Sen's discussions of utilitarianism have not engaged as much as they might have with the striking similarities between the classical utilitarianism of John Stuart Mill and Sen's own CA. Sen's CA is certainly closer to this part of the utilitarian tradition than one might guess from reading Sen's work, in spite of his many acknowledgements of the influence of Mill on his work. The remainder of the chapter was concerned with different ways in which the capability view is, or can be, applied. There are potential pitfalls involved in both the options and choice applications of the CA. As regards incompleteness, there are two distinct and *potentially* contradictory strategies which Sen pursues. One involves composite indices and complete rankings, while the other is consistent with non-comparability and incompleteness. Both strategies have been quite fruitful in different contexts, but Sen needs to acknowledge and discuss the possible gulf between the two strategies. Given the potential vagueness involved in notions like 'poverty' and 'inequality', Sen's work uses a broad brush very effectively, especially when there are strong contrasts to be made. It can nonetheless be used in conjunction with accounts of vagueness. However, in using fuzzy poverty measures, we need to learn from Sen: poverty in the functioning and capability spaces is not relative, and the use of relativist fuzzy measures combined with social indicators might be misleading.

Cited references

Anand, Sudhir and Sen, Amartya K. 1995. 'Gender inequality in human development: theories and measurement', Human Development Report Office Occasional Paper 19 New York: United Nations Development Programme.

Anand, Sudhir and Sen, Amartya K. 2000. 'The income component of the human development index', *Journal of Human Development* 1: 83–106.

Alkire, Sabina. 2002. *Valuing freedoms: Sen's capability approach and poverty reduction*. Oxford: Oxford University Press.

Atkinson, A. B. 1970. 'On the measurement of inequality', *Journal of Economic Theory* 2: 244–263.

Basu, Kaushik. 1987. 'Axioms for a fuzzy measure of inequality', *Mathematical Social Science* 14: 275–288.

Bentham, Jeremy. 1970. 'An introduction to the principles of morals and legislation', in J. H. Burns and H. L. A Hart (eds.) *The collected works of Jeremy Bentham*. London: Athlone Press.

Berlin, Isaiah 1969. 'John Stuart Mill and the ends of life', in Isaiah Berlin, *Four essays on liberty*. Oxford: Oxford University Press, pp. 173–206.

Carter, Ian. 1996. 'The concept of freedom in the work of Amartya Sen: an alternative analysis consistent with freedom's independent value', *Notizie di Politeia* 12 (43/44): 7–22.

Cerioli, Andrea and Zani, Sergio. 1990. 'A fuzzy approach to the measurement of poverty', in Camilo Dagum and Michele Zenga (eds.) *Income and wealth distribution, inequality and poverty*. Berlin: Springer-Verlag, pp. 272–284.

Cheli, Bruno and Lemmi, Achille. 1995. 'A "totally" fuzzy and relative approach to the measurement of poverty', *Economic Notes* 94: 115–34.

Chiappero-Martinetti, Enrica. 1994. 'A new approach to the evaluation of well-being and poverty by fuzzy set theory', *Giornale Degli Economisti e Annali di Economia* 53: 367–88.

Chiappero-Martinetti, Enrica. 1996. 'Standard of living evaluation based on Sen's approach: some methodological suggestions', *Notizie di Politeia* 12 (43/44): 37–53.

Chiappero-Martinetti, Enrica. 2000. 'A multi-dimensional assessment of well-being based on Sen's functioning theory', *Rivista Internationale di Scienzie Sociali* CVIII: 207–231.

Clark, David A. and Qizilbash, Mozaffar. 2002. 'Core poverty and extreme vulnerability in South Africa', Discussion Paper 2002–3, Economics Research Centre, University of East Anglia.

Clark, David A. and Qizilbash, Mozaffar. 2005. 'Core poverty, basic capabilities and vagueness: an application to the South Africa context', Discussion paper No. 26, Global Poverty Research Group, Universities of Manchester and Oxford.

Crisp, Roger. 1997. *Mill on utilitarianism*. London: Routledge.

Drèze, Jean and Sen, Amartya K. 1995. *India: economic development and social opportunity*. Oxford: Oxford University Press.

Dutta, Indranil, Pattanaik, Prasanta K. and Xu, Yongsheng. 2003. 'On measuring deprivation and the standard of living in a multidimensional framework on the basis of aggregate data', *Economica* 70: 197–221.

Fine, Kit. 1996. 'Vagueness, truth and logic' in R. Keefe and P. Smith (eds.) *Vagueness: a reader*. London: MIT Press.

Finnis, John. 1979. *Natural law and natural rights*. Oxford: Oxford University Press.

Fleurbaey, Marc. 2002. 'Development, capabilities and freedom', *Studies in International Comparative Development* 37: 71–77.

Fleurbaey, Marc. 2006. 'Capabilities, functionings and refined functionings', *Journal of Human Development* 7: 299–310.

Foster, James, Lopez Calva, Luis F. and Szekely, Miguel. 2005. 'Measuring the distribution of human development: methodology and an application to Mexico', *Journal of Human Development* 6: 5–29.

Harsanyi, John. 1982. 'Morality and the theory of rational behaviour', in Amartya K. Sen and Bernard A. O. Williams (eds.) *Utilitarianism and beyond*. Cambridge, UK: Cambridge University Press, pp. 39–62.

Haq, Mahbub ul. 1995. *Reflections on human development*. Oxford: Oxford University Press.

Hicks, Douglas A. 1997. 'The inequality adjusted human development index: a constructive proposal', *World Development* 25: 1283–1298.

Griffin, James. 1986. *Well-being: its meaning, measurement and moral importance*. Oxford: Clarendon Press.

Kanbur, R. 1987. 'The standard of living: uncertainty, inequality and opportunity', in Geoffrey Hawthorn (ed.) *The standard of living*. Cambridge, UK: Cambridge University Press, pp. 59–69.

Klasen, Stephan. 1997. 'Poverty, inequality and deprivation in South Africa: an analysis of the 1993 SALDRU survey', *Social Indicators Research* 41: 51–94.

Klasen, Stephan. 2000. 'Measuring inequality and deprivation in South Africa', *Review of Income and Wealth* 46: 33–58.

Majumdar, Manabi and Subramanian, Subbu. 2001. 'Capability failure and group disparities: some evidence from India for the 1980s', *Journal of Development Studies* 37: 104–140.

May, Julian, Woolard, Ingrid and Klasen, Stephan. 2000. 'The nature and measurement of poverty and inequality', in Julian May (ed.) *Poverty and inequality in South Africa: meeting the challenge.* London and New York: Zed Books, pp. 19–48.

Miles Coope, Christopher. 1998. 'Was Mill a utilitarian?', *Utilitas* 10: 33–67.

Mill, John Stuart. 1962. *Utilitarianism. On liberty. Essay on Bentham. Together with selected writings of Jeremy Bentham and John Austin.* Edited with an Introduction by Mary Warnock. Glasgow: Fontana Press.

Mill, John Stuart. 1988. *The subjection of women.* Susan Okin (ed.) Indiana: Hackett.

Nussbaum, Martha C. 1988. 'Nature, function and capability: Aristotle on Political Distribution', *Oxford Studies in Ancient Philosophy* 6 (Supplementary Volume): 145–184.

Nussbaum, Martha C. 1990. 'Aristotelian social democracy', in Bruce Douglass, Gerald Mara and Henry Richardson (eds.) *Liberalism and the good.* London: Routledge, pp. 203–243.

Nussbaum, Martha C. 1992. 'Human functioning and social justice. In defence of Aristotelian essentialism', *Political Theory* 20: 202–246.

Nussbaum, Martha C. 1995. 'Human capabilities, female human beings', in Martha C. Nussbaum and J. Glover (eds.) *Women, culture and development.* Oxford: Clarendon Press, pp. 61–104.

Nussbaum, Martha C. 1998. 'The good as discipline, as freedom', in David A. Crocker and Toby Linden (eds.) *Ethics of consumption: the good life, justice and global stewardship.* London: Rowman and Littlefield, pp. 312–411.

Nussbaum, Martha C. 1999. *Sex and social justice.* Oxford: Oxford University Press.

Nussbaum, Martha C. 2000. *Women and human development: the capabilities approach.* Cambridge, UK: Cambridge University Press.

Nussbaum, Martha C. 2003. 'Capabilities as fundamental entitlements: Sen and social justice', *Feminist Economics* 9: 33–59.

Nussbaum, Martha C. 2005. 'Women's bodies: violence, security, capabilities', *Journal of Human Development* 6: 167–183.

Qizilbash, Mozaffar. 1997a. 'A weakness of the capability approach with respect to gender justice', *Journal of International Development* 9: 251–263.

Qizilbash, Mozaffar. 1997b. 'Pluralism and well-being indices', *World Development* 25: 2009–2026.

Qizilbash, Mozaffar. 1998. 'The concept of well-being', *Economics and Philosophy* 14: 51–73.

Qizilbash, Mozaffar. 2002a. 'Development, common foes and shared values', *Review of Political Economy* 14: 463–480.

Qizilbash, Mozaffar. 2002b. 'A note on the measurement of poverty and vulnerability in the South African context', *Journal of International Development* 14: 757–772.

Qizilbash, Mozaffar. 2003. 'Vague language and precise measurement: the case of poverty', *Journal of Economic Methodology* 10: 41–58.

Qizilbash, Mozaffar. 2005b. 'Sen on freedom and gender justice', *Feminist Economics* 11: 151–166.

Qizilbash, Mozaffar. 2006a. 'Capability, happiness and adaptation in Sen and J. S. Mill', *Utilitas* 18: 20–32.

Qizilbash, Mozaffar. 2006b. 'Philosophical accounts of vagueness, fuzzy poverty measures and multidimensionality', in Achille Lemmi and Gianni Betti (eds.) *The fuzzy set approach to multidimensional poverty measurement*, London: Kluwer.

Qizilbash, Mozaffar. 2007. 'Social choice and individual capabilities', *Politics, Philosophy and Economics* 6: 169–192.

Qizilbash, Mozaffar and Clark, David A. 2005. 'The capability approach and fuzzy poverty measures: an application to the South African context', *Social Indicators Research* 74: 103–139.

Scheffler, Samuel. 1988. *Consequentialism and its critics*. Oxford: Oxford University Press.

Sen, Amartya K. 1974. 'Choice, orderings and morality', in Stephan Korner (ed.) *Practical reason*. Oxford: Blackwell, pp. 54–67 and reprinted in Sen, Amartya K. 1982. *Choice, welfare and measurement*. Oxford: Blackwell, pp. 74–83.

Sen, Amartya K. 1979. 'Utilitarianism and welfarism', *The Journal of Philosophy* 76 (9):463–489.

Sen, Amartya K. 1980. 'Equality of what?', in Sterling M. McMurrin (ed.) *Tanner lectures on human values*. Cambridge, UK: Cambridge University Press, pp. 195–220 and reprinted in Sen, Amartya K. 1982. *Choice, welfare and measurement*. Oxford: Blackwell, pp. 353–369.

Sen, Amartya K. 1980–1981. 'Plural utility', *Proceedings of the Aristotelian Society* 81: 193–215.

Sen, Amartya K. 1981. *Poverty and famines: an essay on entitlement and deprivation*. Oxford: Oxford University Press.

Sen, Amartya K. 1983. 'Poor relatively speaking', *Oxford Economics Papers* 35: 153–69.

Sen, Amartya K. 1984a. 'Goods and people', in Sen, Amartya K. *Resources, values and development*. Oxford: Blackwell, pp. 509–532.

Sen, Amartya K. 1984b. 'Family and food: sex bias in poverty', in Sen, Amartya K. *Resources, values and development*. Oxford: Blackwell, pp. 346–368.

Sen, Amartya K. 1985a. *Commodities and capabilities*. Amsterdam: North Holland.

Sen, Amartya K. 1985b. 'Well-being, agency and freedom: the Dewey lectures 1984', *Journal of Philosophy* 82: 169–221.

Sen, Amartya K. 1985c. 'A sociological approach to the measurement of poverty', *Oxford Economics Papers*, 37: 669–676.

Sen, Amartya K. 1987. *On ethics and economics*. Oxford: Blackwell.

Sen, Amartya K. 1988. 'The concept of development', in Hollis Chenery and T. N. Srinivasan (eds.) *Handbook of development economics*, Amsterdam: North Holland, pp. 9–26.

Sen, Amartya K. 1990a. 'Justice: means versus freedom', *Philosophy and Public Affairs* 19: 111–121.

Sen, Amartya K. 1990b. 'Development as capability expansion', in Keith Griffin and John Knight (eds.) *Human development and the international development strategy for the 1990s*. London: Macmillan, pp. 41–58.

Sen, Amartya K. 1991a. 'Welfare, preference and freedom', *Journal of Econometrics* 50: 15–29.

Sen, Amartya K. 1991b. 'Utility. Ideas and terminology', *Economics and Philosophy* 7: 277–283.

Sen, Amartya K. 1992. *Inequality reexamined*. Oxford: Clarendon Press.

Sen, Amartya K. 1993. 'Capability and well-being', in Martha C. Nussbaum and Amartya K. Sen (eds.) *The quality of life*. Oxford: Clarendon Press, pp. 51–73.

Sen, Amartya K. 1995. 'Rationality and social choice', *American Economic Review* 85: 1–24.

Sen, Amartya K. 1996. 'Freedom, capabilities and public action: a response', *Notizie di Politeia* 12(43/44): 107–125.

Sen, Amartya K. 1997a. *On economic inequality*, Expanded edition with a substantial annexe by James A. Foster and Amartya Sen. Oxford: Clarendon Press.

Sen, Amartya K. 1997b. 'Maximization and the act of choice', *Econometrica* 65: 745–779.

Sen, Amartya K. 1999. *Development as freedom*. Oxford: Oxford University Press.

Sen, Amartya K. 2000a. 'Consequential evaluation and practical reason', *Journal of Philosophy* XCVII: 477–502.

Sen, Amartya K. 2000b. 'A decade of human development', *Journal of Human Development* 1: 17–23.

Sen, Amartya K. 2000c. 'East and west: the reach of reason', *New York Review of Books* XLVII (12): 33–38.

Sen, Amartya K. 2002. *Rationality and freedom*. Cambridge, Mass.: Harvard University Press.

Sen, Amartya K. 2004a. 'Elements of a theory of human rights', *Philosophy and Public Affairs* 32: 315–356.

Sen, Amartya K. 2004b. 'Dialogue: capabilities, lists and public reason: continuing the conversation,' *Feminist Economics* (10): 77–80.

Sen, Amartya K. 2005a. *The argumentative Indian. Writings on Indian history, culture and identity*. London: Penguin.

Sen, Amartya K. 2005b. 'Human rights and capabilities', *Journal of Human Development* 6: 151–166.

Sen, Amartya K. 2006. 'Reason, freedom and well-being', *Utilitas* 18: 80–96. Statistics South Africa 1998. *Census in brief*. Pretoria: Statistics South Africa.

Sugden, Robert 1993. 'Welfare, resources and capabilities: A review of Inequality Reexamined by Amartya Sen', *Journal of Economic Literature* 31: 1947–1962.

Sumner, L. W. 2006. 'Utility and capability', *Utilitas* 18: 1–19.

United Nations Development Programme (UNDP) (1994, 1995, 1997). *Human Development Report*. New York: Oxford University Press.

3 | Sen's capability approach and feminist concerns

INGRID ROBEYNS

Introduction[1]

There is by now a vast feminist literature arguing that mainstream normative theories (whether they focus on inequality, poverty, well-being, social justice or policy reform) are often false gender-neutral and androcentric. Theories are false gender-neutral and androcentric when they pretend to be theories which apply equally to men and women, but upon closer scrutiny they are focusing mainly on male experiences and interests, thereby ignoring aspects of social institutions, or dimensions of well-being, that are of special importance to women and children. Often these theories have a poor underlying notion of gender, or implicitly rely upon sexist or androcentric assumptions, or incorporate empirical claims about gender issues that are highly contested. Susan Okin's (1989) seminal work in this area criticised several social justice theories, ranging from communitarian to libertarian, for failing to properly incorporate the interests of women and families. Elizabeth Anderson (1999) critiques the 'luck egalitarian' theories within liberal political philosophy for not being able to adequately deal with women's caring responsibilities and the dependency of children, the disabled and frail elderly. Iris Young (1990) and Nancy Fraser (1998) have argued that theories of distributive justice are structurally limited in dealing with key feminist concerns such as the gendered division of labour. Eva Kittay (1999) showed that Rawls's (1971) theory of justice cannot adequately deal with the interests and needs of dependants and caregivers, and

[1] This paper was first presented at the conference on Sen's capability approach at St Edmunds College, Cambridge, summer 2001. I would like to thank Bina Agarwal, Hilde Bojer, Roland Pierik, Amartya Sen, Irene van Staveren and the anonymous referees for comments on an earlier draft, and the Cambridge Political Economy Society Trust and the Netherlands Organization for Scientific Research (NWO) for research funding.

therefore cannot adequately account for inequalities between women and men. In earlier work I have analysed the basic income proposal, proposed by Philippe Van Parijs (1995) and others. While it is often claimed that a basic income would be beneficial to women, the core social structures that create or sustain gender inequality would not be weakened, and might perhaps even be reinforced when a basic income would be introduced (Robeyns 2001). And this is just a short selection – there are many more feminist critiques of normative theories of poverty, inequality, well-being, social justice and policy reform that point at gender biases in those theories.

This chapter is situated in this tradition. My aim is to analyse Amartya Sen's capability approach through a feminist lens. How far does Sen's capability approach address, or have the potential to address, feminist concerns regarding well-being and social justice? Or are there androcentric biases in the capability approach? I will frame my analysis in the context of affluent and technologically advanced societies. In such societies the biological differences between men and women have been reduced mainly to their different roles in the reproductive process (at least, if a person is able and chooses to engage in reproduction). The biological roots of the sexual division of labour have been weakened substantially in these societies, and can be eliminated almost completely in individual cases.[2] Moreover, in these countries average living standards are well beyond those of physical survival. Empirically these countries often coincide with (imperfect) liberal democracies, where every person's idea of the good life would, at least in principle, be respected by the government, and where state and religion are constitutionally separated. In short, I will limit my analysis to countries where cultural, religious and gender norms are relatively liberal compared with other countries. This caveat does not imply that the analysis is irrelevant for societies or communities that are not affluent and technologically advanced and that do not have a liberal constitution and laws. But it seems reasonable that for these countries additional concerns will have to be taken into consideration. For example, a feminist analysis of the capability approach in poor and explicitly non-liberal societies would require extra attention for the impact of cultural, religious and gender norms on human

---

[2] For an account of how this could be done, see Sandra Lipsitz-Bem (1998).

well-being, and for how extreme poverty influences those norms and social institutions.

Sen's capability approach revisited

To start off, I will highlight some aspects of Sen's capability approach that are especially relevant for gender concerns.[3] While I will assume a basic familiarity with Sen's capability approach, it is important to keep in mind that there are several different interpretations of the capability approach, as some scholars interpret Sen within their own paradigm, while other scholars interpret Sen through (implicit or explicit) disciplinary, religious or ideological lenses. In my view, the interpretation that is most faithful to Sen's roots and views understands the capability approach against the background of the crossroads of normative welfare economics and theories of distributive justice in liberal political philosophy.[4]

Sen's core argument is that in making interpersonal evaluations that can feed into analyses of poverty, inequality, justice or development, we should focus on what people are effectively able to do and to be, that is, on their capabilities. Capabilities are real opportunities to functionings, which are beings and doings such as being literate, being well fed, being healthy, being educated, being part of a social network, having a decent job and so forth. Thus, goods or income are not important in themselves, but in what their characteristics enable people to do and to be, that is, in the *capabilities* that a person can generate from these goods and services. The extent to which a person can generate capabilities from goods and services depends on the factors that determine how smoothly this conversion can be made. Three different types of *conversion factors* can be distinguished: social, environmental and personal. The social conversion factors are determined by a number of societal aspects, such as social institutions (e.g. the educational system, the political system, the family, etc), social norms (including gender norms, religious norms, cultural norms, moral norms), traditions,

---

[3] This chapter does not address Nussbaum version of the capability approach (Nussbaum 2000). I have discussed some of the differences between Sen's and Nussbaum's versions in Robeyns (2003b, 2005a, and 2005c).

[4] For a full elaboration of this interpretation, see Robeyns (2005a). For some of Sen's main works on the capability approach, see Sen (1980, 1984a, 1984b, 1985a, 1985b, 1987, 1990, 1992, 1993, 1995, 1999).

and behaviour of others in society (e.g. stereotyping, prejudiced behaviour, racism, sexism, homophobic behaviour and so forth). The environmental conversion factors are determined by the environment in which a person lives, e.g. whether deforestation has caused erosion and flooding which threatens the security of one's shelter. The personal conversion factors are determined by one's mental and physical aspects. These personal characteristics, such as disabilities or bodily vulnerabilities, affect the types and degrees of capabilities one can generate with resources. A healthy person who has a pair of running shoes can use these to train for a marathon, but this is not an option for people with bad knees and certainly not for paralysed people.

Not all capabilities require some good or service as an input. For example, being respected by your peers requires only respectful behaviour from other people, and not necessarily any goods or services. Still, the same category of social and individual factors and parameters which influence the conversion factors also impinge on those capabilities that do not necessarily require the input of commodities. For example, being subjected to a pattern of insults is a violation of a person's capability, and many cases of insult in contemporary society do not rely on any material basis, but often occur via discourses and attitudes. Another example is an incurable and aggressive cancer. If such cancer drastically restricts the capabilities that a person can enjoy, this restriction is to a large extent a direct effect of the cancer and not only via its hampering effect on what this ill person can do with certain commodities. Thus, several of the factors that determine the individual's conversion factor also impinge on the capability set directly.

A person's capability set, which comprises all the capabilities of a person, represents her freedom to achieve well-being and agency – and this is the dimension which Sen proposes as the informational basis for interpersonal comparisons. The choice of achieved functionings from a person's capability set need not be seen as an idealised choice of a purely rational agent who is detached from society; instead, the capability approach explicitly acknowledges the impact of preference formation mechanisms on the preferences that people activate when they make choices, and also the potentially wide range of other social influences on decision making, such as peer pressure, social conformity, expectations from – or commitments to – family and friends and so forth. In addition, certain mental aspects of the person impinge on her ability to choose, for example low self-confidence, or post-traumatic anxieties.

It is important to stress that Sen's capability approach is deliberately an open-ended framework or a broad evaluative paradigm, and not a fully fleshed-out theory. Strictly speaking, the capability approach advocates only that for normative evaluations we should focus on capability sets. Many scholars who have either criticised the capability approach or furthered it have done so against the background of their own discipline or field. In most cases, the capability approach is not sufficiently specified by Sen to provide complete answers to questions central to a specific sub-discipline, and such an analysis requires the integration of additional theories. It will be argued below that this has important consequences for the usefulness of the capability approach to address feminist concerns.

Having laid out the main tenets of the capability approach, we can now turn to develop a feminist analysis. The first question that we need to ask is which aspects of the capability approach make it a framework sensitive to feminist concerns. There are at least three aspects of the capability approach that make it a gender-sensitive evaluative framework: its focus on functionings and capabilities; the key role given to human diversity; and its relation to individualism. We will analyse the first and second aspect in the following section and discuss the particular individualist nature of the capability approach in the next section.

Human diversity and the evaluation of functionings and capabilities

The main characteristic of the capability approach is its focus on doings and beings and the freedom to achieve them, instead of the goods and resources that people can access or possess. In philosophical discussions on social or distributive justice, resources as a focal variable are advocated by many major normative theorists. In normative welfare economics, empirical analyses mostly focus on income, or sometimes consumption or wealth. Sen's aim is to criticise both subfields simultaneously, by proposing to focus on functionings and capabilities, instead of commodities.

Why does Sen advocate capabilities as the relevant evaluative space instead of resources? Capabilities are intrinsically important to people's well-being, whereas resources or commodities are only means to reach a valuable life. In other words, the capability approach focuses on the ends instead of the means of well-being. Why is this important?

People differ in their ability to convert resources or commodities into valuable functionings, hence a similar bundle of commodities will generate different capability sets for different people. While many theories of social justice and well-being acknowledge the importance of human heterogeneity, they either recognise only a limited number of dimensions in which people differ, such as handicaps, or they are unable to sufficiently translate this concern for diversity into their theoretical framework.[5] Sen, however, gives human diversity a central place in his framework. For feminists this is very important, because all too often the agents in mainstream theories are very androcentric, in the sense that, either explicitly or implicitly, this person's characteristics are 'masculine' characteristics, i.e. characteristics which are positively valued by the masculinity norms in dominant gender ideologies.[6] For affluent western societies, these 'masculine' characteristics include that the person would be employed or at least be willing and able to be employed, and has no attachments to other people which might prevent him or her from holding a job. For many women (and very slowly an increasing number of 'new fathers'), this is a model that has never applied to their lives, as they often had to struggle to combine caring responsibilities for children, the infirm and the elderly with their wish and need to have a paid job. Care responsibilities have often been invisible and neglected in mainstream theories of well-being and justice, in particular the constraints which the world of care and the world of paid employment impose on one another, and how these constraints are different for men and women (Okin 1989; Bubeck 1995; Kittay 1999).

The capability approach accounts for human diversity in at least two ways. First, as pointed out above, it focuses on functionings and capabilities as the evaluative space, hence taking into account several dimensions of well-being instead of only one, such as income. Income

---

[5] However, not all theorists of justice are vulnerable to the same degree, and a deeper analysis should distinguish for the different kinds of resources that are being used in this debate. For an analysis of resources as defined in welfare economics, see Kuklys and Robeyns (2005); for an analysis of Rawlsian social primary goods, see Pogge (2002); for a comparison of resources and social primary goods applied to global poverty and inequality, see Robeyns (2005b).

[6] For accounts on how masculinity norms operate, and their importance in understanding the gendered nature of liberal-democratic societies, see Bourdieu (2001) and Kimmel (2000).

might reveal much of the well-being of an idealised independent individual who is working full time, who is in good health and good physical and psychological condition, and who has no major caring responsibilities. But for an unemployed person, or a care taker, or a dependent person, other dimensions of well-being might be much more important for their overall well-being. This is not to deny that income *is* an important determinant of well-being and can serve as a proxy in case other information is lacking or too costly to collect. The point is rather that the more a person deviates from the idealised model of an unattached healthy worker who has substantial control over his life, the more other factors influence the mapping from income into well-being. Feminist theorists have argued that accounting for this kind of diversity is crucial if one wants to develop theories which take into account both men's *and* women's lives, hence if one wants to avoid theories to be androcentric or gender biased. For example, for a young mother the availability of good quality subsidised child care might, next to her income level, be an important determinant of her functionings well-being, whereas this hardly affects the well-being of a single childless person or a parent whose caring responsibilities are taken care of by another person, such as his partner. Public goods, and the social networks on which we can rely, are just two of the aspects that can have a profound effect on our well-being levels. The well-being of diverse people should therefore be based on a *multidimensional metric* that can account for non-financial and non-material constituents – and the capability approach offers this.

The second way in which the capability approach accounts for human diversity is by acknowledging that the conversion of the characteristics of the commodities into functionings can also differ between people. Some of these differences will be individual, whereas others will be structural differences in society, related to gender, class, race, caste and so on. In the case of gender, discrimination is one of those factors influencing conversion, not only for income but for other commodities as well. Suppose a man and a woman have equal access to higher education and receive the same scholarship. Both eventually obtain the same educational degree and both want to use this degree to enable some functionings (like the functioning to lead an interesting life by means of one's profession, the functioning to develop self-esteem, to secure financial autonomy, to be able to provide support for dependent others, to develop interesting social contacts, to reach one's professional ambitions and so on). But since women are discriminated against in the labour market, it will be more difficult for a woman to use her degree to achieve all those functionings, compared with a man with the same degree.[7] More generally, group-dependent constraints, like prejudices, social norms, habits and traditions, can affect the conversion of the characteristics of the commodities into capabilities. The capability approach thus acknowledges the importance of societal structures that impact differently on different groups.

It is important to recognise that the capability approach is not limited to the market but looks at people's beings and doings in market and nonmarket settings. Feminist economists have argued at length that economics needs to pay attention to processes and outcomes in the nonmarket economy too (e.g. Folbre 1994; 2001; Folbre and Nelson 2000; Himmelweit 1995; 2000). This argument applies equally to inequality or poverty analysis: we need to take into account aspects of people's well-being and advantage related to both the market and nonmarket aspects of life. This is crucial for the assessment of gender inequality, as women are spending much more time outside the market economy than men (UNDP 1995; Gershuny 2000). By making inequality or poverty assessments based on aspects of the market economy only, like income, earnings, or job-holding, we exclude from our analysis some aspects of well-being and advantage that affect women's lives more than men's, such as care labour, household work or how much one can rely on non-professional social networks.

Gendered social structures and constraints are important for *all* theories of well-being and justice, but not all theories are equally capable to include those constraints, nor are all theorists equally willing to take these gendered constraints into account. Most justice theorists do not make their account of gender relations explicit and do not respond to feminist critiques, but are implicitly relying on androcentric and gender-biased assumptions. This is strongly at odds with recent social theorising on gender, which generally tends to state that virtually all societal institutions have a gendered character and that for most areas of life this works to the disadvantage of girls and women and to

---

[7] For recent evidence of gender labour market discrimination in Western post-industrial societies, see Goldin and Rouse (2000), MIT Committees on the Status of Women Faculty (2002), Neumark, Bank and van Nort (1996), Valian (1998) and Wennerås and Wold (1997).

the advantage of boys and men (Bourdieu 2001; Kimmel 2000; Lipsitz-Bem 1993; Valian 1998). It is striking that so little of this empirical and theoretical work on gender differences and gender inequalities has been taken on board by social justice theorists. The important question which the capability approach faces is whether its further specification and operationalisation will be equally vulnerable to these androcentric biases.

Individualism and feminism

Sen's capability approach is an ethically or normatively individualist approach, but it is neither ontologically nor methodologically individualistic (Robeyns 2000: 16–18; 2005a: 107–110). To properly understand in which respects the capability approach is individualistic, we should distinguish between ethical individualism on the one hand and methodological and ontological individualism on the other hand. Ethical individualism makes a claim about who or what should *ultimately* count in our evaluative exercises and decisions. It postulates that individuals, and only individuals, are the ultimate units of moral concern. In other words, when evaluating different states of social affairs, we are interested only in the effect of those states on individuals. This, of course, does not imply that we should not evaluate social structures and societal properties, but ethical individualism implies that these structures and institutions will be evaluated *in virtue of* the causal importance that they have for individuals' well-being. In other words, social structures and societal properties should be evaluated, but only if they are important factors impinging upon the well-being of individuals.

At the core of methodological and ontological individualism is the claim that 'all social phenomena are to be explained wholly and exclusively in terms of individuals and their properties' (Bhargava 1992: 19). Ontological individualism states that only individuals and their properties exist and that all social entities and properties can be identified by reducing them to individuals and their properties. Ontological individualism hence puts a claim on the nature of human beings, on the way they live their lives and their relation to society. In this view society is built up from only individuals and nothing other than individuals and hence is nothing more than the sum of individuals and their properties. Similarly, explanatory individualism is the doctrine that all social phenomena can be explained in terms of individuals and their properties.

The crucial point in this discussion, which is also very relevant for feminist concerns, is that a commitment to ethical individualism is not incompatible with an account of personhood that recognises the connections between people, their social relations and their social embedment. Sen's capability approach embraces ethical individualism, but does *not* rely on ontological or explanatory individualism. On the theoretical level, the capability approach accounts for social relations and the constraints and opportunities of societal structures and institutions on individuals in at least two ways. First, by recognising the social and environmental factors which influence the conversions of commodities into functionings, and thus by recognising the wide range of structures, institutions, group memberships and other elements that determine these conversion factors. For example, the capability approach will take into account that in societies where mothers are expected to bear the primary responsibility for child care, the provisioning of child-care facilities will expand the capability for paid work for mothers much more than for childless people or fathers who are not responsible for the daytime care of their children. Similarly, a mother who is embedded in gender-egalitarian and supportive social networks may find it much easier to combine her child-caring responsibilities with her other roles such as a worker, a citizen and a friend.

The second way in which the capability approach can account for the societal structures and constraints is by theoretically distinguishing functionings from capabilities and postulating capabilities as normatively more important than achieved functionings. This implies that there is scope for responsibility in the capability approach, as people could be held responsible for the choices that they make from their capability sets, which will determine their achieved functionings. While Sen has not elaborated which normative theory of responsibility for choice he would want to integrate in the capability approach, there are suggestions in his work that he would take into account the societal structures and constraints on these choices and thus on the normative notion of responsibility. However, Sen's capability approach *allows* those structures and constraints on choices to be taken into account but does not offer such a full account. Strictly speaking, one could also use the capability approach with theories of choice and personal responsibility that do not acknowledge societal structures and constraints, and

these complementary theories have ultimately far-reaching consequences for our evaluative exercises. I will return to this issue in the
following section.

Hence, the capability approach does not rely on ontological or
methodological individualism, while it does embrace ethical individualism. Is this a position that feminists should embrace? Yes, I think so.
Feminists should embrace ethical individualism because this is necessary for women and children to be given their due right and not to be
subsumed under the cover of the well-being of the household, family,
clan or community. Ethically non-individualistic well-being notions,
such as notions of the well-being of the household, family or community, do not recognise that there are often trade-offs between the well-
being of different members of those communities. Non-individualistic
ethical notions of well-being often implicitly justify existing power
relations and hierarchies within these communities, because people in
power are much stronger to determine what counts as 'the well-being
of the household or community'. All too often, girls and women are
low on the societal hierarchy and have less power than other family and
community members. It is deceiving to think that households or communities are altruistic, harmonious units where the well-being of the
weakest members will be given priority. Feminist scholars have pointed
out that thinking of households (and families and communities) as
harmonious units so that the preferences or interests of all members
can be represented by one aggregate preference is not only justifying the
intra-household inequalities that generally work at women's disadvantage but is also empirically shown to be untrue (Agarwal 1997; Folbre
1994, 1997; Komter 1989; Humphries 1982; Nussbaum 2000; Okin
1989; Robeyns 2003a; Woolley and Marshall 1994).

An example could illustrate my claim that the ethical individualist
nature of the capability approach is important for feminists. Take a
household with a certain level of well-being in terms of commodities
and services (income, self-produced goods, caring activities and so on).
Suppose now that there are two adults in this household, a woman and
a man, and that independent of how they divide up the market and non-
market work (or paid and unpaid work), the overall household well-
being will be the same. This ethically non-individualistic well-being
evaluation obviously hides the different effects that different household
arrangements have on the various members of this household: it can
matter a great deal for the individual well-being levels whether there is

a traditional gender division of labour or an equal sharing of paid work, unpaid work and care. It is an old feminist claim, which I cannot defend here, that paid work, unpaid work and care should ideally be equally shared between men and women, or at the very least that societal institutions and power relations between groups should be such that they allow couples to share all kinds of work equally without being significantly disadvantaged by that choice.[8] Women who shoulder the full burden of unpaid work and care lose several capabilities, will have lower achievements on several functionings and are jeopardising their future financial well-being in case the household breaks down. This example would also illustrate that there is much more to well-being than money: even in households where there is an equal sharing or pooling of the earned income, different people can quite likely have different levels of functionings well-being.

At the same time, a feminist analysis would be limited and much less relevant if it were ontologically and methodologically individualistic. The act of caring for other people, which determines to such a large extent the current position of many women in society, highlights that people's capabilities are interconnected and often only co-realisable, that people are in various ways connected to one another, that people's decisions are made with regard to others and that other people's actions, needs and desires influence our actions, freedom and well-being. An ontological individualistic framework would not be able to understand the real processes behind a daughter who gives up her paid job to care for her demented parent, for example. In many cases, the idea of an individual voluntary choice is not appropriate here, as there is no acceptable alternative anyway, as needs of other people might take a higher urgency or priority to our own individual career wishes and life planning. This is important for a feminist analysis, as women are much more called upon for such emergency situations and to help relatives in need. Similarly, a feminist analysis will also be much more powerful if it can transcend methodological individualism. Many of the key concepts which social scientists use to explain gender inequalities, such as gender norms, socio-cultural notions of masculinity and femininity, prejudices and stereotypes, gender identity and gender power

---

[8] See e.g. Folbre (1994), Himmelweit (2000), Okin (1989), Phillips (1999: 91–95), Robeyns (2003a), among many others.

differences, are more powerful and illuminating if their explanation goes beyond individual facts only.

In short, I conclude that any theory of well-being or social justice which wants to be relevant for *all* people and not just for 'detached adults' without day-to-day responsibilities for others, and which wants to be able to understand gender relations and evaluate gender inequalities in well-being, should be ethically individualistic, and methodologically and ontologically non-individualistic. Sen's capability approach fulfils this requirement.

The vulnerability of an underspecified framework

By arguing that a person's capability and not her functionings levels should be the focal variable of our evaluative exercises, and by insisting that individuals are the ultimate units of our moral concern, Sen has given feminists a powerful framework to analyse and criticise some aspects of gender relations. But, as I have already mentioned briefly, there is one major feminist concern with the capability approach and that is its underspecified nature. The underspecified character of the capability approach requires that, before the capability approach can be applied for specific normative analyses, it has to be supplemented with additional theories. These theories include ontological theories about certain aspects of social and individual lives, and explanatory theories giving accounts of why states and processes are the way they are and how we should understand them. These supplementary theories also include normative accounts of the three conversion factors in the capability approach, and a normative theory of choice and personal responsibility. In sum, a wide range of ontological, explanatory and normative accounts that are added to the capability framework before it can be fully operationalised has an impact on our normative analysis in terms of functionings and capabilities.

In this section I want to elaborate on this point by illustrating how a normative assessment can lead to radically different conclusions depending on the theories that we add to the capability approach. I will first present the stylised case of the lives of Harry and Wendy, then show that two different descriptive accounts of Harry's and Wendy's lives and the society in which they live lead to totally different answers to the question as to whether Harry and Wendy are equally well off. Harry and Wendy are an English couple with two children. Harry trained as a computer salesman, whereas Wendy has a nursing degree. Both Harry and Wendy are healthy. When their first child was born, Wendy left her nursing job and became a full-time homemaker. As Wendy doesn't have a paid job, Harry is the only wage earner and he shoulders the responsibility to provide financially for his family. Wendy, meanwhile, not only provides full-time care for her two toddlers but is also responsible for the cleaning, cooking, washing up, shopping, ironing and virtually every other aspect of the management of the household. Harry takes care of the car and does the maintenance jobs around the house.

A *conservative capability analysis* of Harry's and Wendy's well-being would look at a range of capabilities and ask how well both achieve on them. The conservative analysis explains Harry's and Wendy's division of labour by saying that because women tend to have stronger preferences for children, both Wendy and Harry would be better off if Wendy could stay at home while Harry would hold a job. Fair enough, one could reply, but this does not tell us anything about their initial capability sets. There are two possible replies that the conservative account could give. The first variant would say that both had the same capability sets, hence both had equal access to either a job or to specialise in homework. People who subscribe to this kind of theorising assume that men and women have equal opportunities, but that their different preferences explain their differentiated outcomes, including the gender division of labour. In my reading of the literature on equality and justice in political philosophy and normative welfare economics, this is the unarticulated account which many theorists hold. The second variant would say that Harry's and Wendy's capability sets overlap, whereby Harry has easier access to a job but more difficult access to stay at home, for example because of societal expectations. But this second conservative strand would not think that the fact that their capability sets overlap is normatively problematic, as these gender-specific spheres are creating a different but equally well-off life for both men and women. Hence men and women will live lives in male and female spheres, but this should not trouble us because their preferences are different and within each sphere they are leading the kind of life they would want to lead. Hence, men and women are 'different but equal', and while for some specific capabilities the corresponding achieved functionings level will not be the same, their aggregated capability and functionings well-being will be the same. And if there are some men and women who would prefer to spend more time in the other sphere, they are free to do so. This second strand seems to be prevailing among theorists who are culturally conservative, even if their views on economic justice may be quite radical.

The *feminist capability account* has a different evaluation of Wendy's and Harry's well-being levels. Underlying a feminist account would be a theory of gender, which is a theory about what it means to be a woman or a man and how these meanings materialise in different outcomes for men and women. Typically, feminists would not claim that women and men are essentially different species, which would explain their different roles in life, but would argue that gender is a social construction, a societal and cultural feature. The biological differences between women and men are not *explaining* their different positions in society but rather are used to *justify* women's less advantaged position (e.g. Bourdieu 2001; Kimmel 2000; Lipsitz-Bem 1993; Valian 1998). All aspects of social life, such as child socialisation, the design of institutions and so forth, reproduce gender norms. The result is a 'gendered society' (Kimmel 2000), where ultimately not only the institutions are gendered but our identities become gendered as well. Moreover, as Virginia Valian (1998) shows, our cognitive faculties also interact with notions of gender. Both men and women rely on stereotypes when making sense of the staggering amount of information that our brains have to process. One of the elements of these stereotypes is that we value some 'masculine' characteristics positively in men and negatively in women, whereas we value 'feminine' characteristics positively in women but negatively in men. The 'masculine' characteristics are typically those which are valued highly for professions, such as assertiveness, leadership, being able to take initiative and so forth. As a result, women experience a clash between what is expected from them in order to be a good professional and what is expected from them as a woman. Both men and women rely on these stereotypes and therefore both men and women tend to undervalue and unintentionally discriminate against women in professional settings, and undervalue and discriminate against men who are in a non-leadership role in the spheres of nurturing and care.

A feminist capability account would use such a rich theory of gender to argue that at least three elements of the capability approach have to be addressed: gender inequalities in the conversion of resources into capabilities, the gender inequalities in the capability sets, and how gender interacts with choice and personal responsibility.

First, the feminist capability account would point out that women tend to have lower conversion rates when converting the resources into capabilities. The reasons for this can be various, but many are instances of injustice. For example, given gender labour market discrimination, a woman might have the same opportunity to study, but this might not translate into getting the same job. Or women might not have the same opportunity to go out at night because of male violence on the streets. Or women might have a physical voice and the intellectual capacity to think, but both the fact that men tend to interrupt women much more than they interrupt men, and tendencies to consider women as less capable leaders, might lead to the fact that women have fewer opportunities to have their voices heard in public.[9]

Second, the feminist capability account would argue that women's and men's capability sets were not equal in the first place.[10] It might well be that in some areas women's capability sets would be larger than men's, e.g. for capabilities to relate intimately to others or the capability to talk about worries that one has, as dominant masculinity norms tend to suppress these capabilities in boys and men. But in many areas of life, men's capability sets are larger than women's. If it is more difficult for a woman to find a decent job in the labour market, due to gender segregation or gender discrimination, this already restrains her options and makes her capability sets unequal at the outset. Also, gendered norms and expectations work together to restrain the capability sets of men and women differently. For example, it is much easier for a man to be able to combine a job with a family than for a woman to do so. Cross-national empirical evidence shows that mothers adjust their working patterns to accommodate families, while very few fathers do so (Gornick and Meyers 2003). This is partly due to the lack of high-quality subsidised child care in many countries and the fact that many jobs assume that one is child-care free. One could argue that this constraint is making the capability set of parents smaller than non-parents' capability sets, which is true. However, one has to add that gender norms expect women to take on this responsibility in order to conform to dominant expectations. Hence the capability sets of women

---

[9] Empirical evidence for these claims is widespread in gender studies; see e.g. Kimmel (2000).

[10] I have argued this based on an exploratory review of the empirical literature in Robeyns (2003b).

and men are not equal in the first place. Moreover, most feminists would argue that the capability set of the average man is a more advantageous package than the average woman's capability set.[11] This does not imply, however, that feminists should be striving to make women's capability sets equal to men's. On the one hand they would want social policies and societal changes to give men more access to the valuable capabilities which are more frequently in women's capability sets than in men's, such as capabilities to develop an intimate relationship with one's children and other family members. On the other hand, they would also argue that equality on 'male terms', where everyone would have the male capability sets, is simply impossible from a societal point of view (e.g. Himmelweit 2000). If women had the same capability sets which many men have now, including the choice to have a job while your partner bears the primary responsibility for child care, and if all women chose this capability out of the capability set, then society would probably collapse because our society can reproduce itself and take care of its most vulnerable members thanks only to all the non-market work which is mainly performed by women. This also illustrates that the choices of the achieved functionings out of the capability sets are interpersonally interdependent, because it is impossible that both parents would choose to hold a job and leave the child care to the other partner. Good quality subsidised child care might enlarge the capability set of women somewhat in the direction of the capability sets that most men have now without threatening society's existence, but it seems unlikely that we could reproduce ourselves and take care of the most vulnerable members of society if all women had access to men's capability sets and started to choose the same functionings bundles that men are choosing.

A third element of the capability approach which feminists would want to debate are the notions of choice and personal responsibility. Can women and men be held fully responsible for the functionings which they choose from their capability sets? A classical response is that if their real freedom to choose the kind of life they valued most was equal, then their well-being freedom would be equal and we should

---

[11] Obviously, women from higher-class or more privileged ethnic backgrounds or other more advantaged categories will be better off than disadvantaged men from lower social classes or disadvantaged ethnicities and 'races'. I am only making the claim that within each category, women will be worse off than men in capability terms, all things considered (Robeyns 2003b).

respect it if someone chooses a life which leads to lower achieved well-being levels. Otherwise we would be imposing our notions of the good life upon those women and men, which is an act of paternalism.

The classical response of feminists has been that the choices that women are making are often not simple 'voluntary choices' or 'genuine choices'. Feminists would argue that choice reflects both preferences, constraints and a wide range of social and personal influences on our preferences and actual choices, and that we have to analyse these concepts from a gender perspective. The influences on choice are different for men and women, and feminists would argue that for many valuable capabilities the constraints for women are harder. For example, Wendy may have made the actual choice to become a home-maker, but it is highly likely that gender discrimination and segregation in the labour market have made her earnings lower than Harry's, which makes it rational from the point of view which considers the aggregate financial interests of the household that Wendy stays at home. Moreover, Wendy is a nurse, a profession in which women are dramatically overrepresented and which is worse paid than many other professions which require similar skills, training and responsibilities. There is ample evidence that when jobs become more feminised, relative wages go down. Hence wage levels themselves should not be seen as value-free signals stemming from demand and supply, but among other things also as justifying a gender ideology that it is OK to pay less for 'female' work because this work is assumed to be less important, or because women's wages are considered secondary. There are many more gendered constraints that could be discussed here. The bottom line is that feminists would argue that the constraints on choice are different for men and women, and that they are normatively problematic because they reduce women's options to valuable capabilities more than they reduce men's. This is a point that is widely acknowledged in gender studies and feminist theory, even when often phrased in a different vocabulary.

Moreover, the problem with choice and personal responsibility in the capability approach is not only that the constraints on choice are gendered but also that the actual preferences underlying the choice are shaped by gender socialisation and other gendered social and psychological processes. For example, Valian (1998) shows that stereotypes not only lead to unintentional discrimination against women in the professions but also that this ultimately affects their preferences and behaviour. If male assertiveness is rewarded whereas female assertiveness is socially punished, then men will tend to become more assertive, whereas women will tend to become less assertive. Similarly, if showing emotions is socially discouraged for men but not for women, then women will be able to develop and use their emotions whereas men would tend not to do so. Feminists would therefore want to integrate a theory of preference formation into the capability approach. In Wendy's case, feminists would wonder whether Wendy is intrinsically better skilled and more interested in rearing children, or whether Harry would be equally interested in that had he been given the chance to develop this preference and if he lived in a society where it would be considered 'normal' that men share the child rearing with their partners. In such a feminist account, it remains to be seen whether a responsibility concept that strictly distinguishes between a choice (for which one is responsible) and elements beyond one's control (for which one is not responsible) is a useful analytical device. This sharp distinction between choice and circumstances has become a paradigmatic element in many contemporary liberal theories of distributive justice and equality, but it is obvious from the above sketch that the integration of a rich theory of gender will put this notion under severe pressure (Anderson 1999; Young 1990; 2001). We do need a satisfactory normative theory of preference formation, which can then help us to construct a theory of responsibility that does not simply assume away gender as a structuring force in social and individual life.

In conclusion, the stylised example of Harry and Wendy will be analysed quite differently by a conservative capability perspective, or a feminist capability perspective. The former will conclude that Harry and Wendy are likely to be equally well off, whereas the latter will conclude that for most aspects of well-being men's achieved well-being tends to be higher than women's, and that it is crucial to critically examine the constraints on the capability set and the notion of choice in the capability approach.

Conclusion

A feminist analysis of Sen's capability approach differs from feminist analyses of other theories of well-being and social justice, precisely because the capability approach is not a theory but a framework. Sen's capability approach is deliberately underspecified. This means that the capability approach in itself is not sufficiently specified as an evaluative tool, but instead it needs further specification each time we want to operationalise it, that is, to use the capability approach to make an evaluation or a normative analysis. This additional specification includes the integration of explanatory, ontological and normative accounts and theories. It is especially important to integrate additional theories on individual and collective decision-making, preference formation, the nature of gender relations, the gendered nature of societal constraints and social institutions, the nature of caring activities and unpaid work, and so on. They have to be a full part of the explanatory theories that underpin the analysis, but also be integrated in the normative evaluation. While this goes beyond the argument in this chapter, the analysis presented here can be extended to other dimensions of human diversity, such as race, class, ethnicity, age and sexual orientation.

Sen's capability approach has much more potential to address gender issues and feminist concerns than most other well-being and social justice theories. Feminists can use Sen's framework to strengthen their own feminist analyses and make empirical and theoretical applications showing that an integrated gender perspective improves the quality of our research and advances our knowledge. However, feminists should be concerned that the capability approach might be interpreted and applied in an androcentric way. They will have to remain vigilant that the literature on the capability approach does not suffer from the same gender-biased interpretations that have plagued other theories on well-being and social and distributive justice.

Cited references

Agarwal, Bina 1997. ' "Bargaining" and gender relations: within and beyond the household', *Feminist Economics* 3(1): 1–51.

Anderson, Elizabeth 1999. 'What is the point of equality?', *Ethics* 109: 287–337.

Bhargava, Rajeev 1992. *Individualism in the social sciences*. Oxford: Clarendon Press.

Bourdieu, Pierre 2001. *Masculine domination*. Cambridge, UK: Polity Press.

Bubeck, Diemut 1995. *Care, gender and justice*. Oxford: Clarendon Press.

Folbre, Nancy 1994. *Who pays for the kids? Gender and the structures of constraint*. New York: Routledge.

Folbre, Nancy 1997. 'Gender coalitions: extrafamilial influences on intrafamily inequality', in L. Haddad, H. John and H. Alderman (eds.) *Intrahousehold resource allocation in developing countries: models, methods, and policy.* Baltimore: Johns Hopkins University Press, pp. 263–274.

Folbre, Nancy 2001. *The invisible heart. Economics and family values.* New York: The Free Press.

Folbre, Nancy, and Nelson, Julie 2000. 'For love or money – or both?', *Journal of Economic Perspectives* 14(4): 123–140.

Fraser, Nancy 1998. 'Social justice in the age of identity politics: redistribution, recognition, and participation', in G. Peterson (ed.) *The Tanner Lectures on Human Values.* Salt Lake City: University of Utah Press, pp. 1–67.

Gershuny, Jonathan 2000. *Changing times. Work and leisure in post-industrial societies.* Oxford: Oxford University Press.

Goldin, Claudia, and Rouse, Cecilia 2000. 'Orchestrating impartiality: the impact of "blind" auditions on female musicians', *American Economic Review* 90 (4): 715–741.

Gornick, Janet, and Meyers, Marcia 2003. *Families that work. Policies for reconciling parenthood and employment.* New York: Russell Sage Foundation.

Himmelweit, Susan 1995. 'The discovery of "unpaid work": the social consequences of the expansion of "work"', *Feminist Economics* 1(2): 1–19.

Himmelweit, Susan 2000. 'Introduction', in S. Himmelweit (ed.) *Inside the household: from labour to care.* London: Macmillan, pp. xv–xxxiii.

Humphries, Jane 1982. 'Book review of a treatise of the family, by Gary Becker', *The Economic Journal* 92: 739–740.

Kimmel, Michael 2000. *The gendered society.* New York: Oxford University Press.

Kittay Feder, Eva 1999. *Love's labor. Essays on women, equality and dependency.* New York: Routledge.

Komter, Aafke 1989. 'Hidden power in marriage', *Gender & Society* 3(2): 187–216.

Kuklys, Wiebke, and Robeyns, Ingrid 2005. 'Sen's capability approach to welfare economics', in Wiebke Kuklys *Sen's capability approach: theoretical insights and empirical applications.* Berlin: Springer-Verlag.

Lipsitz-Bem, Sandra 1993. *The lenses of gender: transforming the debate on sexual inequality.* New Haven: Yale University Press.

Lipsitz-Bem, Sandra 1998. *An unconventional family.* New Haven: Yale University Press.

MIT Committees on the Status of Women Faculty 2002. *Reports.* Cambridge, Mass.: MIT.

Neumark, David, Bank, Roy J., and Van Nort, Kyle D. 1996. 'Sex discrimination in restaurant hiring: an audit study', *Quarterly Journal of Economics* 111: 915–941.

Nussbaum, Martha 2000. *Women and human development: the capabilities approach*. Cambridge, UK: Cambridge University Press.

Okin, Susan 1989. *Justice, gender and the family*. New York: Basic Books.

Phillips, Anne 1999. *Which inequalities matter?* Cambridge, UK: Polity Press.

Pogge, Thomas 2002. 'Can the capability approach be justified?', *Philosophical Topics* 30(2): 167–228.

Rawls, John 1971. *A theory of justice*. Oxford: Oxford University Press.

Robeyns, Ingrid 2000. 'An unworkable idea or a promising alternative? Sen's capability approach re-examined', *Center for Economic Studies Discussion paper 00.30*. Leuven, Belgium: University of Leuven.

Robeyns, Ingrid 2001. 'Will a basic income do justice to women?', *Analyse und Kritik* 23(1): 88–105.

Robeyns, Ingrid 2003a. 'Does the gender division of labor result in unjust inequalities?', paper presented at the Annual Meetings of the American Political Science Association, Philadelphia.

Robeyns, Ingrid 2003b. 'Sen's capability approach and gender inequality: selecting relevant capabilities', *Feminist Economics* 9(2/3): 61–92.

Robeyns, Ingrid 2005a. 'The capability approach: a theoretical survey', *Journal of Human Development* 6(1): 93–114.

Robeyns, Ingrid 2005b. 'Assessing global poverty and inequality: income, resources and capabilities', *Metaphilosophy* 36(1–2): 30–49.

Robeyns, Ingrid 2005c. 'Selecting capabilities for quality of life measurement', *Social Indicators Research* 74(1): 191–215.

Sen, Amartya 1980. 'Equality of what?', in S. McMurrin (ed.) *The Tanner Lectures on Human Values*. Salt Lake City: University of Utah Press, pp. 196–220.

Sen, Amartya 1984a. 'The living standard', *Oxford Economic Papers* 36: 74–90.

Sen, Amartya 1984b. 'Rights and capabilities', in his *Resources, values and development*. Cambridge, Mass.: Harvard University Press, pp. 307–324.

Sen, Amartya 1985a. *Commodities and capabilities*. Amsterdam: North Holland.

Sen, Amartya 1985b. 'Well-being, agency and freedom', *The Journal of Philosophy* LXXXII (4): 169–221.

Sen, Amartya 1987. 'The standard of living', in G. Hawthorn (ed.) *The standard of living*. Cambridge, UK: Cambridge University Press.

Sen, Amartya 1990. 'Justice: means versus freedoms', *Philosophy and Public Affairs* 19: 111–121.

Sen, Amartya 1992. *Inequality re-examined*. Oxford: Clarendon Press.

Sen, Amartya 1993. 'Capability and well-being', in M. Nussbaum and A. Sen (eds.) *The Quality of Life*. Oxford: Clarendon Press, pp. 30–53.

Sen, Amartya 1995. 'Gender inequality and theories of justice', in M. Nussbaum and J. Glover (eds.) *Women, culture and development: a study of human capabilities*. Oxford: Clarendon Press, pp. 259–273.

Sen, Amartya 1999. *Development as freedom*. New York: Knopf.

UNDP 1995. *Human development report*. New York: Oxford University Press.

Valian, Virginia 1998. *Why so slow? The advancement of women*. Cambridge, Mass.: MIT press.

Van Parijs, Philippe 1995. *Real freedom for all. What (if anything) can justify capitalism?* Oxford: Clarendon Press.

Wennerås, Christine, and Wold, Agnes 1997. 'Nepotism and sexism in peer-review', *Nature* 387: 341–343.

Woolley, Frances, and Marshall, Judith 1994. 'Measuring inequality within the household', *Review of Income and Wealth* 40(4): 415–431.

Young, Iris Marion 1990. *Justice and the politics of difference*. Princeton: Princeton University Press.

Young, Iris Marion 2001. 'Equality of whom? Social groups and judgments of injustice', *The Journal of Political Philosophy* 9(1): 1–18.

4 | *Beyond individual freedom and agency: structures of living together in the capability approach*

SÉVERINE DENEULIN[1]

Introduction

It was a typical summer evening in Talamanca, a small village in the Bri-Bri indigenous reserve in the south of Costa Rica, near the Panamanian border. I had the privilege of accompanying a group of lawyers from the Costa Rican Court of Justice who were working on a popular education project about the Costa Rican constitution. On that evening, some indigenous people met with us in the well-lighted education centre of the village in order to tell us some stories of their lives. With the musical background of animal life in the surrounding equatorial forest, an elderly farmer told us how a primary school had been created in the village in the 1950s. He also shared his experience of how, after falling seriously ill in the 1970s, he was taken by helicopter to the nearby city where he received free medical treatment and how, after remaining for many weeks in hospital without any result, he was cured by going to see the traditional healer of his indigenous community. A young indigenous lady reported how she received support from the Costa Rican state university in her efforts to translate the Bri-Bri language into written form, as well as to write the legends and traditions of her people. The young lady's ten-year-old boy proudly taught us how to breed iguanas (after school, the young boy was helping his family in their iguana breeding farm supported by a government programme designed to protect endangered species). As the evening

[1] Department of Economics and International Development, University of Bath, Bath BA2 7AY. I thank Flavio Comim, Henry S. Richardson, Frances Stewart, Nick Townsend, the participants of the conference and two anonymous referees for helpful comments on a preliminary draft. I also thank Jacqueline García and the family Mora-Ulate for invaluable help during my fieldwork in Costa Rica.

unfolded, so did my understanding of Costa Rica's achievements in promoting the capabilities that people have reason to choose and value.

Costa Rica is a well-known case in development circles of how a country with limited economic resources has been able to provide high levels of quality of life for its people, or in other words has been able to expand the capabilities they have reason to choose and value (Garnier *et al.* 1997; Mesa-Lago 2000a, 2000b). Costa Ricans widely enjoy the capability to live long and healthy lives (life expectancy has increased by thirty years in half a century and reached seventy-six years in 2000), the capability to read and write (the proportion of illiterate people has been reduced from 27 per cent in 1940 to 4 per cent in 2000), the capability to be healthy (infant mortality rates have decreased from 137 per thousand in 1940 to 13 per thousand in 1995, health insurance coverage has expanded from 0 per cent in 1940 to 84 per cent in 1990, the coverage of basic services is almost complete in both rural and urban areas), and the capability to live in a clean and rich natural environment (a large surface of the country's superficies have been declared protected natural areas in order to preserve the rich bio-diversity of its forests).[2]

The thrust of Sen's capability approach is that development be judged 'in terms of the expansion of substantive human freedoms' (Drèze and Sen 2002: 3). These substantive human freedoms are 'seen in the form of individual capabilities to do things that a person has reason to value' (Sen 1999a: 56). Hence, the development of Costa Rica is to be assessed in terms of what Costa Ricans are able to do or be, such as being able to read and write, to live in a clean environment, to live long and healthy lives, or to participate in the life of the community. But is it sufficient to assess development achievements in the space of individual freedoms or individual capabilities, as is implied by Sen's capability approach?

Although his approach has shifted the informational basis of quality of life assessment from income to the capability space, this chapter argues that, by placing individual subjects at the centre stage of his capability approach, Sen maintains a conceptual tension between the individual and his or her society. That tension can survive at the theoretical level but cannot be maintained when the capability approach becomes a guiding theory for development practice.

[2] Data in this paragraph are taken from CEPAL 2001, Estado de la Nación 2001 and Garnier *et al.* 1997.

This tension becomes especially unsustainable in three areas. First, there is a strong rationale for extending the evaluative space of development to non-individual or collective capabilities, and not only insofar as they contribute to guaranteeing the capabilities of individual subjects. Second, because individual value judgements critically depend on a collective framework that gives rise to them and sustains them, assessing development in terms of the capabilities that individuals have reason to choose and value requires setting the subject of development beyond individual subjects. Third, if individual agency is to be central in promoting individual capabilities, as it is in Sen's capability approach, then development theory cannot ignore the socio-historical conditions that make individual agency possible. In that respect, the chapter introduces the notion of socio-historical agency as central in the promotion of capabilities.

Individual freedom in Sen's capability approach

By situating the evaluative space of quality of life in the capability space, that is in what individuals are able to be or do, Sen's capability approach implies that individuals are to be considered as the very subjects of development, both as ends and means of development. Development is to be assessed 'in terms of whether the freedoms that individuals have are enhanced' and development is to be achieved through the 'free agency of individuals' (Sen 1999a: 4). Speaking of the deep afflictions that affect mankind in terms of hunger, malnutrition, preventable diseases, poverty and oppression, Sen underlines the point that 'we have to recognise the role of *individual freedoms* of different kinds in countering these afflictions. Indeed, *individual agency* is, ultimately, central to addressing these deprivations' (Sen 1999a: xii).[3]

Even if individual subjects are at the core of development, both as the ends and means of development, Sen's capability approach does not consider them as detached from the social setting in which individuals breathe and live. It does not separate the 'thoughts, choices and actions' of individual human beings from the society in which they live, since individuals are 'quintessentially social creatures' (Sen 2002: 81). This leads Sen to introduce the notion of 'socially dependent individual capabilities' (Sen 2002: 85), and to assert that

---

[3] Italics added.

the freedom and agency that each individual enjoys are 'inescapably qualified and constrained by the social, political and economic opportunities that are available to us' (Sen 1999a: xii). Individual freedoms are inescapably linked to the existence of social arrangements, and 'our opportunities and prospects depend crucially on what institutions exist and how they function' (Sen 1999a: 142).

Institutions or societal arrangements are of central importance for promoting the freedoms of individuals. For example, the capability of Costa Ricans to be healthy is crucially dependent on the existence of key welfare institutions. The capability of Costa Ricans to live in a clean environment is deeply connected to the collective belief that biodiversity cannot be forsaken for economic interests, and to the existence of a legal and enforcement framework reflecting that collective belief. Equally, the capability of indigenous people to maintain their language and traditions cannot be made possible without an adequate legal framework that fully protects and implements the rights of cultural minorities. This is why, in Sen's capability approach to development, individual freedom is 'quintessentially a social product', because 'there is a two-way relation between (1) social arrangements [such as economic, social and political opportunities] to expand individual freedoms and (2) the use of individual freedoms ... to make the social arrangements more appropriate and effective' (Sen 1999a: 31). Development and the expansion of freedoms cannot occur without the presence of key institutions such as the market, public services, the judiciary, political parties, the media, etc. As Sen puts it, such 'a freedom-centred view [of development] calls for an institutionally integrated approach' (Drèze and Sen 2002: 20).

Despite the crucial role of social arrangements in the construction of individual freedoms themselves, Sen is very reluctant to approach development with a supra-individual subject. Even if social arrangements or institutions are seen as very important elements in enhancing or impeding individual freedoms, they are still to be 'investigated in terms of their contribution to enhancing and guaranteeing the substantive freedoms of individuals' (Sen 1999a: xiii). Institutions do crucially contribute to our freedoms, but 'their roles can be sensibly evaluated in the light of their contributions to our freedom' (Sen 1999a: 142). Sen (2002) underlines that all actions finally bear upon the lives that human beings live, lives which are lived only by individuals and not by some supra-individual subject.

Gore (1997) has developed a forceful critique of Sen's focus on individual capabilities as the informational basis for well-being evaluation and development assessment. He has argued that, like the informational basis of utility and opulence, 'functionings and capabilities [in Sen's capability approach] are seen as objects of value which individuals have [and] which are disembedded from the institutional contexts of human activity' (Gore 1997: 235), and that, hence, Sen's capability approach does not take into account the intrinsic value that these institutional contexts have for individual human well-being. Although it includes social elements by, for example, including social capabilities (such as the capability to participate in the life of the community or to appear in public without shame), or by insisting on the importance of social arrangements in providing the conditions through which individual capabilities will be exercised, Gore argues that the capability approach remains individualist because the 'goodness or badness of social arrangements or states of affairs is evaluated on the basis of what is good or bad *for* individual well-being and freedom and [because it] is also reduced to the good *of* those individuals' (Gore 1997: 242). In agreement with Sen, Gore affirms that the evaluation of states of affairs is to be assessed on the basis of what is good or bad for individuals, but he objects that the valuable constituents of individual human well-being are to be seen in terms of individual properties only. Individual lives contain collective goods as well, and therefore individual human well-being is also to be assessed on the basis of these collective goods.

Gore bases his argument on Charles Taylor's concept of 'irreducibly social goods' (Taylor 1995). Irreducibly social goods are objects of value which cannot be decomposed into individual occurrences, or expressed in terms of individual characteristics. They cannot be reduced to individual acts or choices, since these individual acts or choices are understandable only against a background of practices, understanding, and meaning. For example, the word 'beautiful' can be understood, and has a meaning, only against a further background of meaning. Women with large hips were once upon a time considered as the standard of beauty, while in other contexts only slim women could qualify as being beautiful. Without the irreducibly social good of a language code and cultural practices, an individual uttering the word 'beautiful' would be incomprehensible. Among these irreducibly social goods, one finds, for example, language codes, institutional norms, aesthetic values, ethnic belonging, and cultural or political practices inherent in a given society.[4] According to Gore, the capability approach critically fails to recognise the intrinsic value of these irreducibly social goods, and incorporates them only to the extent to which they affect individual properties. Although irreducibly social goods remain components of individual lives, because these goods have an intrinsic value to human well-being, the informational basis of development, Gore argues, needs to go beyond individual capabilities and incorporate these.

Sen has strongly rejected the critique advanced by Gore, and asserts that his capability approach does indeed include the intrinsic importance and value of irreducibly social goods in the evaluation of individual well-being. For example, it considers democratic freedom, or the ability to take part in and to influence the decisions that affect the life of the community, as a good that cannot be reduced to individual characteristics and that has its locus in the society itself. Sen stresses that democratic freedom is 'a significant *ingredient* – a critically important *component* – of individual capabilities' (Sen 2002: 79). Thus, the level of democracy that characterises a society is an irreducibly social good that fully enters as an ingredient in individual human well-being. However, the importance and value of democratic freedom are relevant only to the extent that it enters as a component of individual human well-being, to the extent that it makes the lives of individuals better. There remains a strong rationale for including irreducibly social goods in the informational basis of development for reasons that go beyond their intrinsic value to the lives of individuals.

---

[4] Taylor (1995) strongly distinguishes the notion of irreducibly social goods from the economic conception of public goods. Like public goods (such as national defence or a dam), irreducibly social goods cannot be secured for one person without being secured for a whole group, but the goods that public goods are producing are the goods of individuals. Taylor gives the examples of a dam and a culture. The dam itself is not good, only its effects are, and its effects are good to individuals. In contrast, an irreducibly social good like a culture cannot be instrumentally valuable to individual goods like a dam would be. Irreducibly social goods cannot be judged through their effects, and are not instrumental to a purpose they serve. A valuable culture, unlike the dam, is an irreducible feature of society as a whole, while the dam is only an instrument and not a feature of society at all.

Structures of living together

It may appear to be a contradiction that a good can at the same time be an irreducibly social good, that is, a good irreducible to any individual component or characteristic, and remain a component of individual lives. Yet this contradiction constitutes the definitional core of irreducibly social goods: they exist beyond individuals but owe their existence to them. Irreducibly social goods could not exist without being endorsed by individuals, since anything that happens does so because individuals make it happen. For example, a language would not exist if individuals had never spoken it, a social norm would not exist if individuals did not endorse that norm in regulating their actions, a particular form of ethnicity would not exist if individuals did not bear the characteristic feature of that ethnicity, etc. But the fact that irreducibly social goods exist only when supported by individuals does not imply that they do not have an existence well beyond individual actions and decisions. For example, although a football team cannot exist without its constitutive elements and cannot win a match without the participation of its players, the football match cannot be reduced to the actions of its players, and the value of the actions of a football team is greater than the value of the actions of its individual members taken separately.

In order to maintain the interconnection between individual actions and irreducibly social goods, the notion of 'structures of living together', introduced by the French philosopher Paul Ricoeur, appears, in my opinion, more appropriate in the context of development to refer to the reality of irreducibly social goods. Structures of living together can be defined as structures which belong to a particular historical community, which provide the conditions for individual lives to flourish, and which are irreducible to interpersonal relations and yet bound up with these.[5] Unlike the notion of irreducibly social goods, the notion of structures of living together directly suggests that irreducibly social goods emerge from the fact that individuals are living together, and that this fact constitutes the very condition under which individual

---

[5] Paul Ricoeur's original definition refers to the notion of institution: 'By institution, we understand the structure of *living together* as this belongs to a historical community, a structure irreducible to interpersonal relations and yet bound up with these' (Ricoeur 1992: 194).

human lives may flourish. But the basic idea is the same. Although sustained by individual components, these structures of living together have an autonomous existence and cannot be reduced to the features of the individuals living in these structures. Referring again to the example of the term 'beautiful', the word has a meaning only against a structure of living together, namely a language. Although a language and its meaning depend on individuals speaking that language and endorsing its meaning, the language has an existence beyond individuals. No individual word would be understood if that structure of living together did not exist. Even apparently individual properties such as personal autonomy cannot exist without certain structures of living together that support personal autonomy (see Raz 1986: 204–6). As Charles Taylor (1995: 135–6) summarises it: 'In one sense, perhaps, all acts and choices are individual. They are, however, only the acts and choices they are against the background of practices and understandings. But this *langue* cannot be reduced to a set of acts, choices, or indeed other predicates of individuals. Its locus is a society.'

It must be noted that, as structures emerge from human beings living together in a particular community, these structures need not always be oriented towards the good living of society. Structures of living together can have a negative effect upon the good living of its members, such as structures of inequalities and oppression caused by an unequal distribution of power. All these are features of a society upon which an individual has little control but which, nonetheless, constrain or promote his or her actions.

I began this chapter with a brief assessment of Costa Rica's success in the light of Sen's capability approach to development. Examining the reasons for Costa Rica's development success illustrates how ignoring structures of living together in the assessment of development misses out a crucial aspect of development.

The reasons that the human development literature has often advanced to explain a country's success in achieving high levels of capabilities are mainly the scope and nature of the public spending in key areas, such as health and education (see for example Ghai 2000; Stewart *et al.* 2000). Costa Rica has obviously fared very well in having adequate public action oriented towards the expansion of individual capabilities. It has the highest social spending ratio in Latin America, it has social services accessible to the whole population in both rural and urban areas alike, and it has a strong emphasis on primary health services and primary education (Mesa-Lago 2000b). Yet, this public action has not emerged from a vacuum.

While Sen has often emphasised that the degree of democratic freedom is central in understanding the social development path of countries (see Alkire 2002: 129–143; Sen 1999b), he does not explore the reasons why some democratic countries are more able than others to take the necessary public action to promote individual capabilities.[6] This chapter argues that, beyond democratic freedom, it is the existence of certain structures of living together which explains the successes and failures of countries to promote the capabilities that people have reason to choose and value.

For example, the various individual capabilities of the inhabitants of the Costa Rican village described in the introduction exist only through a multiplicity of certain structures of living together that have been built up throughout Costa Rica's history.[7] The capability of the inhabitants of the village to read and write has its roots in the certain productive and social structure that was characteristic of Costa Rica at the end of the nineteenth century. This led the government, guided by a liberal elite, to take the decision to impose universal primary education for boys and girls, in rural and urban areas alike (Mesa-Lago 2000a). The poor economic conditions of the country, and the egalitarian character of its productive structure, together with a certain motivational structure of the political elite of the time, allowed this irrevocable decision to be taken without much opposition from the economic elite (IADB 1994).[8] Similarly, the capability of the inhabitants of the village to enjoy efficient health services is due to the social

---

[6] For example, after Costa Rica and Uruguay, Colombia is the third Latin American country that has the most long-standing democracy. Yet, the exercise of democratic freedom in Columbia has not led to the same level of social achievements one could find in other Latin American countries, even those that have known long periods of dictatorships such as Argentina (see Whitehead 2002).

[7] A more detailed description of the reasons behind Costa Rica's development can be found in Deneulin 2005.

[8] It is precisely because of this particular structure of the elite, which did not have to assert its power on the military, that Costa Rica was able to take the decision to suppress its army in 1948. The abolition of the army, far from being a deliberate decision to generate more resources towards social areas, has to be seen within the background of the particular structures of living together that characterised Costa Rica. A similar decision in other countries would have been impossible (see, for example, Torres 2001).

and power structure of Costa Rica and the motivational structures that have inhabited certain leaders at key moments.

The Costa Rican social security system and the provision for universal health services that emerged at the beginning of the 1940s were the results of the actions of a particular leader (Calderón) who had the vision to introduce a social security scheme. Calderón was able to carry out his vision through a key alliance with the communists which enabled him to overcome the opposition of a small economic elite (Wilson 1998). These two decisions, for universal primary education and social security, emerged from the particular motivational and power structures of the Costa Rican society, and opened the path for an even more powerful structure of living together in promoting capabilities, that of a society whose identity is built on its welfare institutions. This social democratic identity has led to the progressive development of complex welfare institutions guaranteeing the conditions for Costa Ricans to exercise key valuable capabilities. (For a description of the evolution of welfare institutions in Costa Rica, see Mesa-Largo 2000a, 2000b; Seligson *et al.* 1997.) Such identity acts as a strong collective capability that belongs to the Costa Rican society as a whole beyond individual reach and control, and explains the high levels of human well-being that Costa Ricans enjoy.

In the light of the Costa Rican development path, assessing development on the basis of individual capabilities, or irreducibly social goods that are of intrinsic value to individual lives such as the capability to maintain one's language and culture or the capability to participate in the political life, would miss out an important component of the development process itself. It would miss out certain structures of living together that make the whole process of development and expansion of individual capabilities possible.

Although Gore's critique was directed at underlining the need to include structures of living together as components of individual human well-being, he did not address Sen's view that states of affairs should be evaluated only according to their goodness or badness *for* individuals. This position, known as ethical individualism (Robeyns 2000), holds that, when evaluating states of affairs, the effects of states of affairs on individuals are what matters, and therefore individual subjects are to be the unit of moral concern. It hence suffices to evaluate structures of living together by looking at their effects, positive or negative, upon individual features such as individual freedoms.

Examining the reasons why individual Costa Ricans enjoy high levels of human freedoms inclines us to conclude that the reality of development is not well captured by ethical individualism, insofar as ethical individualism leads to an excessive focus on existing individual lives, and directs attention away from the examination of the structures of living together and the historical explications of these structures, which are not only responsible for the conditions of life of individuals today but have also affected past generations and will affect future ones. Structures of living together are thus not only to be assessed because they are good for individuals, but also according to whether they promote the collective structures which help individuals to flourish. Beyond the individual capabilities of Costa Ricans to read and write, to live long and healthy lives, to live in a non-polluted environment, to enjoy high levels of democratic freedom, there are collective capabilities which belong to the Costa Rican society (and not to individual Costa Ricans), and in part constitute the conditions of existence of individual capabilities. Because structures of living together belong to a social group of which individuals are members, development cannot be assessed only in terms of whether the freedoms of the individual members of that social group have been enhanced, but has also to be assessed in terms of whether the (collective) freedoms of that social group or collectivity to promote individual freedoms have been enhanced.

One could object that assessing collective structures according to whether they generate collective structures which themselves lead to individual flourishing is still instrumental to individual human well-being. It still ultimately judges development by individuals' lives, and hence such a position is still ethically individualistic, since ultimately the evaluation of states of affairs depends on their effects upon the lives of individuals. However, although this position still appears instrumental and judges states of affairs according to their effects upon individuals, because this position acknowledges that structures of living together constitute the condition of existence of individual lives, this position goes beyond ethical individualism. Individuals are not the *only* unit of moral concern. Structures of living together are units of moral concern *too*. Failing to include them explicitly in the evaluation of states of affairs leads to the loss of important information for development.

Sen's thinking seems to have recently evolved in that direction, moving away from an ethically individualistic approach. In response to critiques accusing his capability approach of focusing 'on individuals and their relation to an overall social context, and not on collectivities' (Evans 2002: 56), Sen seems to have incorporated these critiques into his thinking and moved away from the language of individual capabilities. He now asserts that there do indeed exist capabilities that belong to collectivities and that can only with difficulty be reduced to individual capabilities: 'There are genuine collective capabilities such as the capability of a world nuclear power to kill the entire population of the world through nuclear bombing. Similarly, the capability of Hutu activists to decimate the Tutsis is a *collective capability since the ability to do this is not a part of any individual* Hutu's *life (interdependent as it is)*. There could be also more positive collective capabilities such as the capability of humanity as a whole to cut child mortality drastically' (Sen 2002: 85).[9]

Does Sen's capability approach now contain an insoluble contradiction? Can it affirm the importance and value of *collective* capabilities, while also affirming the importance and value of 'socially dependent individual capabilities' (Sen 2002: 81) which, Sen insists, 'have to be distinguished from what are genuinely "collective capabilities"' (Sen 2002: 85)? It seems difficult to understand why Sen's capability approach should rest on the evaluation of states of affairs in terms of whether the freedoms of (socially interdependent) individuals have been enhanced, and not in terms of whether the freedoms of the collective wholes in which individuals live (such as the freedom of the Hutus not to kill Tutsis) have been enhanced.

If the capability approach is to say something about the success of development policies in bringing about certain outcomes, the informational basis for assessing development cannot only remain at the level of its individual outcomes but has also to include the (collective) processes that are responsible for these outcomes, such as, for example, the power structure of a particular country, its existing social norms, its particular national identity, or its particular political and democratic history. Structures of living together, by the very fact of transcending individual human actions, need to be identified, because they are properties of a collectivity rather than a property of individuals, and these collective capabilities provide the conditions for individual lives to flourish. In addition to the distinction between valuable capabilities

[9] Italics are mine.

(such as the capability to be healthy) and non-valuable capabilities (such as the capability to commit homicide), one would need to distinguish valuable from non-valuable structures of living together, or what Sen has now called collective capabilities that made these individual capabilities possible (such as the valuable collective capability of eradicating child mortality, or the negative collective capability of an ethnic group to kill another ethnic group). Moreover, because individual lives and choices are so affected by structures of living together, one cannot assume that their choices, including what they value, are independent of these structures. I now turn to this issue that will further point towards the need to pay explicit attention to collective capabilities.

Meaning and values

Sen's capability approach does of course recognise this deep entanglement between choices and structures. For example, the capability to move around in a particular society strongly depends upon the presence of public transport, the availability of road infrastructures and the degree of peace in that society. If someone possesses a bike, he will be less able to exercise his capability to move around in a society where civil war rages and where roads have not been maintained than a person who would similarly choose to move around in a peaceful Western European country (Robeyns 2000: 17). But if the latter person has witnessed a terrible traffic accident involving a cyclist, and subsequently is psychologically unable to ride a bicycle again, could one conclude that that person freely chose not to ride a bike? Nussbaum (2000: 88) notes in the context of the capability for play and leisure that people should be free to lead a workaholic life should they choose to do so. But one might wonder to what extent a young professional who apparently *freely* chooses a workaholic life has really made a free decision and not a constrained decision given the work culture of her society. The capability approach seems to pay little attention to how the capability to make free choices should be treated, beyond the provision of adequate information.

As these examples show, the capability approach needs to be able to distinguish to what extent one is free to exercise a certain capability and to what extent this choice is constrained by social norms. But the capability approach does not seem to offer a framework to evaluate whether people have the capability to make free choices. Nussbaum (2000: 82) has emphasised that the capability for practical reason is a pre-condition for the exercise of freedom, but the problem is that one needs to be free in order to be able to access practical reason, and if practical reason is what is thought to enhance freedom, the approach ends up in a circle. If women, when offered literacy classes, refuse to make use of the opportunities after having been offered all the adequate information regarding the value of them attending the classes, can one conclude that they have the capability for knowledge?

Sen has written extensively about the deformation of *preferences* and how these could be socially deformed, but *capabilities* could be socially conditioned and equally severely deformed, even after providing adequate information concerning the wrongness of the choices. Is it a matter of accepting, then, that there is no such thing as free choice and acknowledging that all choices are, ultimately, socially conditioned? Perhaps it would suffice to answer that question by simply acknowledging that what is considered as meaningful and worthy of choice can be understood only against a background of community and history, and that free choice and value judgement are themselves to be understood as being made on the basis of certain internalised beliefs inherent in the specific structures of living together in which individuals live. So it is not a question of identifying those whose capabilities have been deformed as against 'free' individuals, but of accepting that all are subject to restraints and conditioning which affect how they exercise choices.

Somewhat independently of his capability approach, Sen (1985: 183) has discussed how meanings are dependent on social contexts, and that moral valuation depends on one's position. States of affairs (and hence capabilities) are thus always evaluated where the person situates himself. Yet he argues that this does not entail that moral evaluation is necessarily relative. There are choices that can be considered as non-meaningful and even wrong. Sen writes: 'The positionality of moral valuation is perfectly consistent with objectivity of moral values. Moral valuation can be position-relative in the same way as such statements as "The sun is setting". The truth of that statement varies with the position of the person, but it cannot vary from person to person among those standing in the same position' (Sen 1985: 183–4). But if all of us, standing in the same position, value the same objectives, can we say with confidence, in an unchangeable way, that our choices are morally (and objectively) valuable? If, for example, all poor and marginalised people who live beside an elite driven by status symbols, or who are daily invaded by consumerist ways of life through the media, value the capability for self-expression (by buying a cellular phone) rather than the capability to be adequately nourished, can that value judgement be accepted because it is shared among all people in the same position?

As Peter Evans (2002: 58) underlines, the capability approach does not seem to 'explore the ways in which influences on "mental conditioning" might systematically reflect the interests of those with greater economic clout and political power'. And he pursues: 'Sen acknowledges that the "sun does not set on the empire of Coca-Cola or MTV", but he does not explore the implications of these kingdoms for the ability of people to choose the kind of lives they "have reason to value".' The capabilities that people value respond to many forces, including global ones, over which individuals have no control. Rarely, if ever, do people have freedom to decide whether these global forces or new structures (norms) through which they frame their value judgements (such as, for example, consumerism) are valuable or not. How, then, can one judge, for example, the underlying social concerns of a society, as exemplified in consumerism, through which people will choose certain valuable capabilities?

In Sen's capability approach, the privileged structure through which people make their value judgements is through democratic deliberation. Citing Sen's example of an indigenous community which has to choose between 'a traditional way of life' and the 'escape of grinding poverty' (Sen 1999a: 31), UNESCO's *World Culture Report* quickly adds that, in today's structures of inequality, one may wonder what margins people have for 'free' decisions (UNESCO 2000: 34). There are indeed structures of inequalities and power that leave indigenous communities with little choice other than that of 'choosing' a modern way of life, or structures of inequalities and power that leave countries with little option other than that of 'choosing', or rather accepting, through democratic deliberation, to pursue development through the privatisation of public services. The capability approach would require an evaluation of the different structures that lead individuals or collectivities to endorse certain values rather than others. The next section examines a final rationale for explicitly including structures of living together in the informational basis of quality life.

Individual agency and its socio-historical conditions

Political philosophers gathered under the label 'communitarian philo-sophers' (Mulhall and Swift 1992) have long discussed how human agency and freedom cannot be thought of independently of structures of living together. They argue that the latter actually form an integral part of the constitution of the self. They insist that freedom and the capacity for choice are not given, but have to be developed. Before being an agent endowed with the capability to make autonomous choices, a self has to be developed, and this cannot be done without a community, without the relationships one makes with other persons. Community is pre-existent to individuals. It is what gives meaning to the life of its members and gives them identity, in the sense that it is only from their attachment to communities that human beings draw their moral development, their identity, and the meaning of their life.

Agency is not a *tabula rasa*, but is itself the product of certain structures of living together. Insofar as human beings have the power to understand themselves, to interpret what they are and what they do, 'the languages needed for such self-interpretation are essentially social, and community is a structural precondition of human agency' (Mulhall and Swift 1992: 162). For example, a woman who is forced into an arranged marriage often does not have the agency to protest and rebel because the structures of living together that surround her do not provide the preconditions for her to do so. She will find her agency and ability to choose not to enter an arranged marriage only provided that, for example, the education she received at school, or government campaigns for gender equity and dignity, have given her the necessary critical skills to question the established order. In other words, she will have the individual agency to avoid arranged marriage only provided that she receives enough collective support to pursue her choice. Exercising one's freedom of choice, like the freedom to marry the partner one wishes, will require collective action to change the struc-tures and transform them into structures enabling individual human beings to acquire agency and exercise choice.

Referring to the example in the introduction, although writing an oral indigenous language to prevent its loss crucially depends on the individual action and agency of one young lady (in that sense, Sen is right in affirming that individual agency and action are crucial in addressing deprivations), her action is made possible only through the quality of education that she herself received at school and through the support that she encounters with academic institutions that are willing to support her efforts. Only certain structures of living together can give rise to and can sustain her individual agency and actions to preserve the indigenous language. As Evans (2002: 56) points out: 'In practice, my ability to choose the life I have reason to value often hangs on the possibility of my acting together with others who have reason to value similar things. The capability of choosing [and acting] itself may be, in essence, a collective rather than an individual capability.'

The necessary presence of certain structures of living together which make individual agency and action possible is even more obvious when those who are choosing and acting are country leaders. For example, the decision to introduce a social security scheme in Costa Rica at the beginning of the 1940s was made by a single individual, President Calderón (see Rosenberg 1983). However, even though Calderón had the necessary individual agency to pass bold social security reforms and other unprecedented progressive social reforms (such as a Labour Code), he could not have exercised his agency if he had not encountered the necessary collective support and necessary structures of living together to do so. It was through an alliance between his own elite party and the Communist party that the social reforms that would shape the future of Costa Rica's social development were able to be implemented (Wilson 1998). Such a collective action would not have been made possible two decades later in the Cold War, when a very strong anti-communist culture was reigning across the world.

The choice that individuals are making appears thus to be crucially dependent upon the particular socio-historical structures in which they find themselves rather than upon a choice that inheres in their inner self. As a consequence, it seems that if the aim of the capability approach is to address deprivations, it will have to place not individual agency as central to addressing deprivations but rather *socio-historical agency* (what individuals can do in the socio-historical reality in which they are living) as central, and this unavoidably entails a careful consideration of the particular structures of living together that constitute this socio-historical agency.[10]

---

[10] The importance of socio-historical agency in promoting development is further explored in Deneulin 2006.

Conclusion

This chapter has argued that because structures of living together were constitutive of individual capabilities and of people's value judgements, there was a strong rationale to include them explicitly in the informational basis of quality of life and development. As the Costa Rican case study has illustrated, ignoring these implicit structures of living together risks hiding an important, if not the most important, factor of development and the removal of human deprivations. Had the particular structures of living together of Costa Rica been different, the country's social development would probably be very similar nowadays to that of its Central American neighbours.

The chapter has also argued that structures of living together were constitutive of individual agency and that central to addressing deprivations was not as much individual agency as the particular structures that build such agency, what I have called the socio-historical agency. Again, as the Costa Rican case study has illustrated, although its social development is due to key individual actions, these actions would not have been possible without certain implicit structures of living together.

Development is not only a matter of promoting the freedoms that individuals have and that they have reason to choose and value, but, because the subject of development is at the same time both individual and collective, is also a matter of promoting the freedoms that collectivities have and that are worthwhile for the collectivity as such. Therefore, drawing up a 'list' of valuable structures of living together that build up a country's necessary socio-historical agency to promote development, in parallel with Nussbaum's list of valuable capabilities (Nussbaum 2000: 75–77), would be a legitimate route that could be taken.

If development is about enhancing the quality of life of *human* beings, then it cannot ignore that such a human life is a life whose sustenance and meaning can come only *through others* (Aristotle 1995: 16–22). And it cannot ignore that the good of such a human life is brought about neither by the mere collections of private or individual actions, nor by the proper action of a collective subject which sacrifices the parts to itself. It has to acknowledge that the good of humans is brought about by an action that is common to both the collective and individuals into which it flows back, and which, in turn, must rely on it (Meritein 1946: 50).

Cited references

Alkire, Sabina 2002. *Valuing Freedoms.* Oxford: Oxford University Press

Aristotle 1995. *Nicomachean Ethics*, Revised Oxford Translation, Jonathan Barnes (ed.). Princeton: Princeton University Press

CEPAL 2001. *Panorama Social de America Latina y del Caribe.* Santiago, Chile: Comisión Económica para America Latina

Deneulin, Séverine 2005. 'Development as Freedom and Costa Rica's Human Development', *Oxford Development Studies* 33 (3/4): 493–510

Deneulin, Séverine 2006. *Sen's Capability Approach and the Praxis of Development.* Basingstoke: Palgrave/Macmillan

Drèze, Jean and A. Sen 2002. *India: Development and Participation.* Delhi: Oxford University Press

Estado de la Nación 2001. *Estado de la Nación en Desarrollo Humano Sostenible.* San José, Costa Rica: Programa de las Naciones Unidas para el Desarollo

Evans, Peter 2002. 'Collective Capabilities, Culture and Amartya Sen's Development as Freedom', *Studies in Comparative International Development* 37 (2): 54–60

Garnier, Leonardo, R. Grynspan, R. Hidalgo, G. Monge and J. D. Trejos 1997. 'Costa Rica: Social Development and Heterodox Adjustment', in S. Mehrotra and R. Jolly (eds.) *Development with a Human Face.* Oxford: Clarendon Press, pp. 355–383

Ghai, Dharam (ed.) 2000. *Social Development and Public Policy: A Study of Some Successful Experiences.* UNRISD/London: Macmillan

Gore, Charles 1997. 'Irreducibly Social Goods and the Informational Basis of Sen's Capability Approach', *Journal of International Development* 9 (2): 235–250

Inter-American Development Bank 1994. *A la busqueda del siglo XXI: Nuevos Caminos de Desarrollo en Costa Rica.* San José: IADB

Meritein, Jacques 1946. *The Person and the Common Good.* Notre Dame: University of Notre Dame Press

Mesa-Lago, Carmelo 2000a. 'Achieving and Sustaining Social Development with Limited Resources: The Experience of Costa Rica', in D. Ghai (ed.) pp. 277–322

Mesa-Lago, Carmelo 2000b. *Market, Socialist and Mixed Economies: Comparative Policy and Performance, Chile, Cuba and Costa Rica.* Baltimore: Johns Hopkins University Press

Mulhall, S. and A. Swift 1992. *Liberals and Communitarians.* Oxford: Basil Blackwell

Nussbaum, Martha 2000. *Women and Human Development.* Cambridge, UK: Cambridge University Press

Raz, Joseph 1986. *The Morality of Freedom*. Oxford: Oxford University Press

Ricoeur, Paul 1992. *One Self as Another*. Chicago: University of Chicago Press

Robeyns, Ingrid 2000. 'An Unworkable Idea or a Promising Alternative? Sen's Capability Approach Re-examined', *Discussion Paper* 30. Leuven: Centre for Economic Studies

Rosenberg, M. 1983. *Las Luchas por el Seguro Social*. San José, Costa Rica: Editorial Costa Rica

Seligson, M. A., J. Martinez and J. D. Diego Trejos 1997. 'Reducción de la Pobreza en Costa Rica: El Impacto de las Políticas Públicas', in J. V. Cevallos (ed.) *Estrategias para Reducir la Pobreza en América Latina y el Caribe*. Quito, Ecuador: PNUD, pp. 105–192

Sen, Amartya 1985. 'Well-Being Agency and Freedom: The Dewey Lectures 1984', *Journal of Philosophy* 82 (4): 169–221

Sen, Amartya 1999a. *Development as Freedom*. Oxford: Oxford University Press

Sen, Amartya 1999b. 'Democracy as Universal Value', *Journal of Democracy* 10 (3): 3–17

Sen, Amartya 2002. 'Symposium on Development as Freedom: Response to Commentaries', *Studies in Comparative International Development* 37 (2): 78–86

Stewart, Frances, G. Ranis and A. Ramirez 2000. 'Economic Growth and Human Development', *World Development* 28 (2): 197–219

Taylor, Charles 1995. 'Irreducibly Social Goods', in Charles Taylor, *Philosophical Arguments*. Harvard: Harvard University Press, pp. 127–145

Torres, Edelberto 2001. 'Contrapunto entre Reforma y Revolución: La Democracia en Costa Rica y Guatemala', in J. Rovira Más (ed.) *La Democracia de Costa Rica ante el Siglo XXI*. San José, Costa Rica: Editorial de la Universidad de Costa Rica, pp. 21–40

Whitehead, Laurence 2002. *Democratization: Theory and Experience*. Oxford: Oxford University Press

Wilson, Bruce 1998. *Costa Rica: Politics, Economics and Democracy*. London: Lynne Rienner Publishers

UNESCO 2000. *World Development Report on Culture*. Paris: UNESCO

Does identity matter? On the relevance of identity and interaction for capabilities

MIRIAM TESCHL[1] AND LAURENT DEROBERT[2,3]

Introduction

Sen went a long way within economic analysis of well-being. By developing his capability approach to understand people's quality of life, he tried to respond to weaknesses he detected in other theories that dealt with human well-being. In particular, he addressed strong criticism towards the utilitarian approach, no matter how utility might be interpreted. Modern economics employs 'utility' to illustrate everything that an individual maximises and that led to the fact that '(m)athematical exactness of formulation ... proceeded hand in hand with remarkable inexactness of content' (Sen 1999a (1985): 2). Opposing, therefore, this kind of simplification, 'which has the effect of taking a very narrow view of human beings (and their feelings, ideas and actions), thereby significantly impoverishing the scope and reach of economic theory' (Sen 1999a: 3), he proposes a view that sees a person's well-being in terms of his or her 'functionings', i.e. what the person succeeds in doing or being. Functionings are people's achievements and reflect their state of existence. The well-being of a person is the evaluation of this existence. Well-being, therefore, is not concerned only with the possession of commodities or the happiness or desire fulfilment those may produce, it also evaluates the conversion of the characteristics of those goods into functionings according to the person who possesses them. Furthermore, Sen is interested in the freedom a person has in terms of the choice of functionings, which he calls a

[1] Robinson College, University of Cambridge, UK. Corresponding author: Miriam Teschl, mt367@cam.ac.uk.
[2] GREQAM, France.
[3] We are grateful to Philippe Grill, Alan Kirman, Pierre Livet, Stéphane Luchini, Mozaffar Qizilbash and an anonymous referee for helpful discussions and comments on this chapter.

person's 'capability'. Capabilities refer to the functionings a person can achieve (Sen 1999a: 3–15). The evaluation of potential achievements is the assessment of a person's 'advantage' (Sen 1999a: 33). Sen's enticing contribution to the assessment of the quality of life therefore is the idea not only to look at what a person achieves but also to consider the options a person has the opportunity to choose from. This, however, requires an understanding of what a person has reason to value to be and to do and thus a 'thick' theory of the individual. Indeed, Sen presents in relation to his capability approach a very rich conception of the individual that gives not only a view of *what* a person is and does or could be and do but also of *who* the person is.

Other articles besides his contributions to the capability approach equally reflect his rich view of individuals, some of which discuss in particular aspects of a person's *identity*. He claims that people have 'multiple identities', one of which is, for example, being a woman or a man (Sen 1985b, 1990c). This aspect is important if women (or men) suffer from their female (or male) identity because their needs and interests are either neglected or not accurately *perceived* by other people. Other articles consider more specifically the question of a person's 'social identity' and the influences others may have on people's 'self-knowledge' (Sen 2000c). In these contributions he defends the importance of 'reason before identity' (Sen 1999c) and refutes social identity as a determining force of people's behaviour. Sen reiterates his view that people have many identities according to their adherence, membership, activities, etc. Yet, he argues, these identities should be the result of some deliberative choice.

Generally, two different dimensions of identity can be considered. One concerns the rather sociologically inspired idea of people's identification with others or with certain ideas, thus their 'social identity'. Social identity is a categorisation of people in different groups, thus a form of description of individuals, effectuated by attributing particular characteristics to them that result from the participation in and identification with specific groups. The other concerns the more philosophical inquiry into what is and constitutes the identity of a person. This dimension of identity includes among others the question of what it means when a person refers to herself as 'I', thus implying that she has a particular experience of herself and some sort of conscious self-understanding of *who* she is and wants to be. This self-understanding allows her to reflect on her beings and doings and to differentiate between herself and others. In that sense, personal identity goes beyond social identity and does not consider identity as some descriptive characteristic of human beings, but as a process of evaluation and change of a distinctive and selfsame person's beings and doings over time.

In the first part of this chapter we thus argue that Sen presents a very rich view of the individual within the capability approach, without, however, ever linking it specifically to any concerns about identity. Moreover, even when he reflects on the influence of people's social identity on their self-knowledge, he actually does not discuss social identity as such, but presents an account of personal identity. This means that he presents a view of a person who is capable of choosing and changing his group memberships and thus of differentiating himself from the group. And yet, because Sen advances his ideas about identity through the perspective of individuals *as multiple identities*, he gives an unrealistic account of the actual process in which the person engages in order to create her personal identity. People may have multiple identities, but they do not see themselves as multiple identities. But they see and recognise themselves as an 'I' and thus (can) engage in a reflective process, not only about *what* they are and do and have reason to value but also about *who* they are and would like to become. Thus, personal identity might be thought to lie within the capability space because it reflects the evaluative process of a person, who is endowed with certain functionings and who wants to achieve specific capabilities in order to change her functionings. Consequently, to develop an explicit account of personal identity might be a useful contribution to the debate about a person's well-being, especially when evaluated within a capability space. Any form of capability deprivation can then be seen not only as reducing a person's well-being but also as impeding a continuous development of an individual's personal identity.

A second part of this chapter engages in more detail with the question of identity and well-being. Indeed, the question of *identity* has received quite some attention in recent years, even from economists and in particular from Akerlof and Kranton (2000, 2002), who consider identity in relation to economic behaviour and consequently in relation to well-being. They define identity as the social categories to which a person belongs. The membership of these groups causes people to maximise their utility by reducing the distance between their own characteristics and those of the social group. The closer they are to the *ideal* characteristics of their group, the more they enhance their *sense of the self*. Thus in comparison with Sen who discusses social identity but really presents (the baseline of) an account of personal identity, Akerlof and Kranton are talking generally about identity but really develop considerations of a person's social identity only. Indeed, because they base their analysis within a utility-maximising framework, people have an incentive to follow social norms and rules and to stick to their categories simply because it might be too costly to change them. To choose differently than one's social group might arouse resistance from other people who feel threatened in their identity by non-category-consistent choices of a person. This certainly does not give an account of a person who is able to reflect and to decide on the influences of her social group and on *who* she wants to be. Indeed, it seems to be more appropriate to consider a person who desires to engage in non-category-consistent choices within a capability space. Even if this person faces social resistance to her choices, she might still value being a particular person and doing specific actions – and the capability approach allows us to evaluate the extent to which this person thus has the freedom to become and to be *who* she wants to be. The capability approach can conceptually take into account that following specific rules because of a particular group membership does not necessarily express the highest utility the person could achieve *if* the person had no effective choice to do otherwise because of social pressure.

However, what Akerlof and Kranton make clear is that other people's action might influence a person's well-being in terms of identity. In a third part of the chapter we will therefore explore in more detail the dimension of social interaction and the influence not only on people's well-being but also on their self-understanding and personal identity development. Indeed, our claim is that between the purely *social identity* level and the *personal identity* level is a level of social interaction. It is this interaction with other people and not simply one's group membership and identification with others that will have an important impact on a person's self-understanding and thus on personal identity. Indeed, Charles Taylor (1989), for example, thinks that personal identity has to be seen in relation to other people. He suggests that a self-understanding is possible only via the expression and narration of one's life, shaped by common symbols and goods that are prevalent within a given community. In relating to others, a person will learn about him or herself by learning about others. This relation to other people, however, does not exclude that a person recognises herself as being distinct from others. Being in relation with others does not reduce or impede one's personal identity. And yet this claim is true only if relations and interactions with other people indeed contribute to a deepened self-understanding and not to distorted perceptions about oneself. In order to assess this claim, we have again to come back on the evaluation of a person's life in terms of functionings and capabilities. While certain types of relations and interactions with people will indeed enhance the functionings and capabilities of a person, others will not. This then reduces a person's quality of life not only in terms of well-being but also in terms of personal identity.

In the following section we will discuss in more detail Sen's approach in the light of identity. In the next section we will present Akerlof and Kranton's identity approach. Not being fully satisfied by their model, we will try to establish the links with Sen's capability approach. The section after that is concerned with social networks, with people's interactions and the consequences they may have on their capabilities. The conclusion will summarise our approach.

Sen's view of individuals and identity

Sen's capability approach is the result of a fundamental criticism of existing theories of well-being, especially utilitarian ones, and this for several reasons. First, a person's life cannot be judged exclusively in terms of his or her well-being – of which utilities is a reflection (Sen 1987: 40). People may have different goals, commitments or values, which may not coincide or be satisfied with the achievement of well-being. The former is a view of a person in terms of his or her agency, distinct from the latter, i.e. seeing him or her in terms of well-being. Agency and well-being are not unrelated though – to achieve a goal may make people happier, and people's enhanced happiness may make agency goals more achievable. Sen, therefore, is rejecting the idea that well-being is the only subject matter of morality. Second, Sen denies that utility is the best representation of humans' well-being (Sen 1987: 45). If utility is seen in terms of happiness, for example, it may possibly happen that people adjust to their circumstances. A 'subjugated house-wife' (Sen 1999a) may feel gladdened by someone's act of compassion, but her gladness stands in no relation to her suffering. Even in terms of desiring, the utility approach does not go very far, as the oppressed and poor may have ceased to desire much as a result of their experiences. 'Well-being is ultimately a matter of valuation, and while happiness and the fulfilment of desire may well be valuable for the person's well-being, they cannot – on their own or even together – adequately reflect the value of well-being' (Sen 1987: 46). Third, economists are always interested in people's advantage they can achieve by exchanging with others (Sen 1987: 38). Yet advantage may not always be best seen in terms of achievement. A person's advantage rather may be perceived in terms of *freedom* to achieve both, her well-being and her agency goals (Sen 1987: 47).

Sen also criticises to see an index of primary goods, income or other resources as the basis on which to judge people's advantage (Sen 1984: 319–323). Possessing resources does amount to having the means to achieve well-being and freedom. Instead, one should focus on meeting certain requirements to lead a fulfilling life, rather than on income or goods needed to meet those requirements. 'Since the conversion of primary goods and resources into freedom to select a particular life and to achieve may vary from person to person, equality in holdings of primary goods or resources can go hand in hand with serious inequalities in actual freedoms enjoyed by different persons' (Sen 1990b: 115). In fact, if somebody has a physical handicap, the possession of goods may do less for him or her than for any other person.

Given this criticism, Sen proposes his capability approach as an alternative framework for the evaluation of people's well-being. This assessment of the quality of life takes into account a person's functionings, i.e. what he or she is and does, and capabilities, the alternative combinations of functionings that a person can achieve. In this way not only people's well-being and agency *achievements* can be assessed but also their well-being and agency *freedom* (Sen 1993: 35). Sen, therefore, broadens the view of people and allows for the introduction of different sorts of motivations that make people not only look for well-being but also engage in a continuous evaluation of goals and aims other than well-being. Indeed he writes that '(t)here is a particular sphere in which such an agency role may be especially important, and that is *the person's own life*. Various concepts of 'autonomy' and 'personal liberty' relate to this special role of agency in personal life, going well beyond considerations of well-being. The moral foundation of well-being is informationally extremely restrictive, and the agency aspect is much too crucial to leading a life for it to be intrinsically of no moral importance' (Sen 1985a: 186. Italics added). Also, when Sen considers well-being, his interest is oriented much more towards knowing whether a person is well than towards knowing whether she is well off in terms of controlling things *outside* her, such as income, commodities or primary goods. He wants to know about the well-being, which is not something a person commands, 'but *something in her* that she achieves. What kind of life is she leading? What does she succeed in doing and in being?' (Sen 1985a: 195. Italics added). We must not, according to Sen, lose sight of the important personal parameters in developing an approach to well-being, as well as to agency. Indeed, '(a) person's agency aspect cannot be understood without taking note of his or her aims, objectives, allegiances, obligations, and – in a broad sense – the *person's conception of the good*' (Sen 1985a: 203. Italics added). Agency, though, requires responsible agents. A person needs to evaluate her aims and desires and cannot simply refer to her agency freedom just because something intrigues her to be or to do. 'The need for careful assessment of aims, objectives, allegiances, etc., and of the conception of the good, may be important and exacting. But despite this need for discipline, the use of one's agency is, in an important sense, a matter for oneself to judge' (Sen 1985a: 204).

Sen thus elaborates a rich account of the human being whilst enlarging the space of evaluative assessment of people's quality of life to functionings and capabilities. Indeed, his concerns transmit a picture of an individual engaged in a reflective process about the capabilities he wants to achieve and whose achievements will turn into functionings that will motivate a renewed reflection on the capabilities he desires to attain. This process affects a person's self-understanding and is an expression of what we would call the individual's *personal identity*. The consciousness of this process of personal identity formation is articulated in the answer to the question of 'who one is'. Charles Taylor (1989) specifies that this question 'can't necessarily be answered by giving name and genealogy. What does answer this question for us is an understanding of what is of crucial importance to us ... My identity is defined by the commitments and identifications which provide the frame or horizon within which I can try to determine from case to case what is good, or valuable, or what ought to be done, or what I endorse or oppose' (Taylor 1989: 27). The question *who?*, however, is asked within a web of interlocution (Taylor 1989: 36). When asked about *who* one is, then 'to be able to answer for oneself is to know where one stands, what one wants to answer. And this is why we naturally tend to talk of our fundamental orientation in terms of who we are. To lose this orientation, or not to have found it, is not to know who one is. And this orientation, once attained, defines where you answer from, hence your identity' (Taylor 1989: 29).

Seen in this light, Sen's conception of the individual can tell us not only *what* he or she is, does and has reason to value to be and to do but also *who* he or she is, the *who*, that goes above the *what* in the sense that it includes an expressed self-perception and self-knowledge by a person trying to understand and to create his or her personal identity.

The idea of (self) perception has actually intrigued Sen in other writings that were not directly intended as contributions to the capability approach. Especially in his gender-related articles, Sen develops a sensitive analysis in relation to self-perception. Moreover, the very first words of Sen's article on 'Women, technology and sexual divisions' are explicit in relation to *identity*. 'Everyone has many identities,' he writes as the opening phrase (Sen 1985b: 195; see also Sen 1990c: 125). To be a woman or a man is one of them. To belong to a social class, to a certain nation or even to have a certain age contributes to our identity. Depending on the issue under consideration though, the sexual identity may play a more or less important role. Sexual identity is important in assessing well-being. This is so because in many societies, women tend to have an economically inferior position within and outside households. This position influences the *perception* people – men in this case – have about women and their interests. Yet women also adapt to these perceptions and tend to approve of certain asymmetries of power (Sen 1985b: 196). One possible reason for these ambiguities of perception may lie in the fact of who is contributing what to the family's wealth. In many societies, men still are the breadwinners. 'The role of outside earnings seems a strong one in creating a difference within the family' (Sen 1985b: 207). The weight of market-valued income does contribute greatly to an asymmetry of consumption and sustenance when balanced against those 'other activities' done by women. The latter's contribution to the family's wealth and well-being often goes unperceived as a result of being unvalued in economic terms. The disregard of their activities affects the influence women have on bargaining positions related to making decisions and solving conflicts of interests in family affairs. But if women would enter the labour market and start working outside their homes or would attain a better education to be able to find more 'productive' employment in terms of benefits, their status would increase and women would have a greater say in personal and family decisions (Sen 1985b: 205).

Hence, Sen's idea is that a person has multiple identities to which certain interests and needs are related. However, these interests can be wrongly perceived and thus reduce a person's actual well-being. Therefore, in order to increase this person's well-being, he or she has to engage in actions that change the perception of his or her identity. In the particular case of having the identity 'being a woman', this person should accept a job in the labour market in order to increase her woman status through market-valued income. This seems to be a more than plausible argument.

However, if the aim is to change (self) perceptions, the question is whether this reasoning is the appropriate one, that is, whether a person is indeed engaging in this form of reflection in order to decide about suitable actions to change distorted perceptions. Does a person engage in actions in order to change the perception of one of her multiple identities, or does the person choose to do certain things because they are an expression of *who* she is and would like to be? If the latter were the case, then the choice of actions is unrelated to her particular *identities* as such, but refers instead to her *as a person*. These acts would be an expression of this person's personal *identity* and might after all affect the overall status of her different *identities*, but this is not necessarily the first criterion of choice. Arguably, a person rarely perceives herself as a being with multiple identities but rather sees herself as a person with a particular identity. Her aim is to live the life she wishes to live and not to achieve a particular status of her multiple identities. Consequently, an increase in well-being is reflected to the extent that she can become *who* she wants to be without being confronted with distorted perceptions of what she should be and do that impede her personal identity development. To the extent she is confronted with wrong perceptions and cannot be *who* she wants to be, the person might be more interested in trying to find means that make people accept who she is and to make them understand her interests rather than to engage in actions that change the status of her particular identities as such. Hence, while Sen points to the very important issue of perception and its relation to well-being, the entrance to this discussion via multiple identities seems to be the wrong access. If identity matters to a person, it is not her multiple identities as such but her personal identity and the freedom to choose to be *who* she wants to be. By focusing on actions that change the perception of particular 'identities', Sen takes the view of an external observer that recommends a strategy of changing a particular status. While this is a legitimate suggestion for an outside observer, from the point of view of a particular person, this strategy might or might not reflect *who* she wants to be. Indeed, a woman whose contribution to the family's wealth goes unnoticed because it is not valued in money terms might not necessarily want to take on a job in the labour market to contribute to an increase in her social status, but would prefer that her work is appreciated in appropriate terms even if it is not valued in terms of money. The question, of course, is how this can come about.

In more recent articles, Sen started to explore in more detail issues related to identity, in particular to a person's social identity (Sen 1999c, 2000b, 2000c). Geared by the refusal to see individuals as solely acting out of self-interest, he stresses the fact that people's behaviour is influenced by identification with others. 'The idea that a sense of community and fellowship is important for us all is also difficult to ignore, and it relates closely to our conceptions of social identity' (Sen 1999c: 5). Social identity can be important in two different ways: by its delineating role and by its perceptual function. The delineating aspect refers to the adherence to different groups and thus 'can be part of an adequate formulation of any idea of the social good' (Sen 1999c: 13). This means that the participation in a particular group influences people's notion of the social good. However, a person can have multiple identities, as she may be a 'member' of different groups. There is no need, according to Sen, for one overarching identity to rule out any other. There is thus no need to believe in the existence of only one overarching social good. 'A person can be a Nigerian, an Ibo, a British citizen, a resident in the United States, a woman, a philosopher, a vegetarian, a Christian, a painter, and a great believer in aliens who ride on UFOs – each of these groups giving the person a particular identity that may be invoked in particular contexts' (Sen 2000c). Thus the delineating aspect of identities, Sen argues, leaves room for choice and reasoning (Sen 1999c: 14). A person can reflect upon the importance she attributes to the adherence to a specific group seen in the wider context of her multiple identities. And she can choose to belong to certain groups, after proper reasoning, some time in the future. Thus

Sen rejects the idea of 'passively recognising' identities, an idea that, according to his interpretation, prevails in communitarian writings (Sen 1999c: 6). The communitarian perspective sees, according to Sen, the individual as 'discovering' her attachments to different groups rather than choosing them after proper reflection. His main criticism about this idea is that uncritical discovery of one's identity may have dreadful consequences. 'A lack of self-knowledge and the absence of self-criticism often derives from our attachment to one group of people, while spelling brutal disaster for another group of people' (Sen 2000c). In fact, the only 'real' discovery of identity one may make, says Sen, is 'to find out that we have a connection or a descent of which we were previously unaware' (Sen 2000c). In any case, '(c)hoices have to be made even when discoveries occur' (Sen 2000c). Thus, Sen wants to distinguish himself from a communitarian thought that sees the individual embedded within social groups and who cannot reason and perceive him or herself without any relations to others. In contrast, Sen develops the view of an embedded individual who is still capable of reasoning independently of given culture and values.

However, Sen admits that '(i)t is perfectly obvious that one cannot reason from nowhere' (Sen 1999c: 23). This refers to the second important aspect of social identity, its perceptual function. 'There can be little doubt that the communities or cultures to which a person belongs can have a major influence on the way he or she sees a situation or views a decision' (Sen 1999c: 22). However, we still can, according to Sen, reason within a particular cultural belief, with a particular identity. This is so because certain cultural dispositions may influence but not completely determine us. Choices do exist even though we are under the influence of cultural characteristics. Furthermore, within groups or cultures, there is not one unique way to behave or to be. Every human being has the ability to question and to doubt. 'It is hardly ever presumed that, just because a person is born English, or comes from an Anglican background or from a Conservative family or has been educated in a religious school, she must inescapably think and reason *within* the general attitudes and beliefs of the respective groups' (Sen 1999c: 25. Italics in the text).

Sen's analysis demonstrates that a person's *social identity* is undoubtedly an important factor in her life. However, he seems to be less concerned about social identity as such and more about the evaluative processes and choices a person can make in relation to her social identity. And yet, instead of focusing on what this process of choice is and means for the person herself and how it may evolve over time, Sen always discusses this choice through the lenses of a person's participation and identification with specific groups. The question again is whether this is the best entrance point to assess the relation of the individual with her social environment. Here again a person does not think of herself as being *social identities*, but as a person with her own *personal identity*. This means that a person refers to herself as an 'I' and makes decisions that influence her respective beings and doings not only in terms of *what* but also of *who* she is and wants to be. The aim of a person is not to choose different social identities but to create or to choose her own personal identity. The important question to solve, of course, is to what extent a person can and does satisfy her choices concerning her personal identity and not those of her social identities and corresponding obligations.

To some extent, Sen's discussion of social identity as group memberships and identification is also confusing. People can be vegetarians, philosophers, English, etc. he writes. But certainly, a person is not a vegetarian because she belongs to a group of vegetarians, but she is vegetarian because she does not eat meat. This means that a person is vegetarian without ever participating in a social group. Equally, a person does not have an identity as a philosopher because she adheres to a group of philosophers with whom she identifies herself, but because she engages in a certain activity called philosophy and therefore may even oppose her views to those of others. The fact is that a person's simple group memberships do not tell us much about *who* that specific person is. Seen from outside, it might be only a way of knowing *what* she is and thus of describing her in terms of some features or characteristics that she has in common with other people – people the person herself might not even know. Thus, not all social identities imply any active group membership. Certain *social* identities are simply the observed outcome of individuals' decisions based on reflections about how they want to live their life and not on which group they want to participate in. In those cases, there is not any identification with others involved. Equally, a person is not English or French because he necessarily identifies himself with all the English or French, but because he was born in the respective country. A supporter of a football club does not identify himself with his fellow supporters but shares with them the passion for the same football club.

So what actually is identification with others? What does Sen mean when he writes '(o)ur identification with others in one group or another can have a strong influence on our thoughts and feelings, and through them, on our deeds as well' (Sen 2000c)? In what sense does this influence come about? How do people recognise this influence? The answer to these questions requires a specific form of reasoning. Sen, however, does not explore this form of reasoning, but goes straight to people's capacity of choice. And this choice means deciding about the extent of participation in different social identities. As important as this choice is, from the claim that others influence people's feelings and actions to the argument that choice of participation is necessary, something has gone missing on the way. Indeed, how does Sen think that people are choosing their social identities? Is it actually social identity that they are choosing or some other aspect that is related to how people would like to live their life? Our claim is that people have to know to some extent what they are going to choose. One cannot compare the choice of social identities with the choice between an apple and an orange. The difference is that in many cases the chooser is already involved with the object of choice. In that sense, it becomes obvious that the chooser is choosing himself, and the choice is almost by definition much more personal than the simple choice about the extent of participation in a given group.

Given this entanglement between subject, the person and object of choice, his social identity, one must differentiate at least between two situations: one in which the object of choice 'decides' on the subject and one in which the subject decides on the object. While the latter situation means that a person can most evidently choose his social identity by deciding to which school he wants to go, which education to pursue, what job to accept, etc., the former implies more than simply choosing. Indeed, in that case, a person already has a specific social identity by the fact that he was born in a certain country, into a family, network of friends of this family, etc. Hence, the object of choice is not the social identity as such but rather the meanings and consequences this social identity has for the chooser. Here, the choice of identity really requires a person to evaluate his upbringing, education, lifestyle, but also his family's history and finally also the historical, social and political background of the country in which he lives. Most evidently, the result of this 'choice' will equally influence the choices the person will make in the future. Thus, 'reason before identity' is a necessary condition in order to *be* a person, that is, a human being separate and distinct from the social group and able to evaluate its influences on him. But here reason is more than simple choice. While Sen is right to reject strong communitarian views that cannot conceive the person independently of the actual cultural and social background into which he was born, he seems to reject too much when he so vehemently rebukes the idea of someone 'discovering' his identity. His claim that the only thing that can be discovered is some connection or descent of which one was not aware sounds slightly odd in comparison with what some communitarians really understand by 'discovery'. Indeed, Michael Sandel, an author whom Sen criticises several times, writes (1998: 153):

For the subject whose identity is constituted in the light of ends already before it, agency consists less in summoning the will than in seeking self-understanding. Unlike the capacity for choice, which enables the self to reach beyond itself, the capacity for reflection enables the self to turn its lights inward upon itself, to inquire into its constituent nature, to survey its various attachments and acknowledge their respective claims, to sort out the bounds ... between the self and the other, to arrive at a self-understanding less opaque if never perfectly transparent, a subjectivity less fluid if never finally fixed, and so gradually, throughout a lifetime, to participate in the constitution of its identity.

This means that a process of self-understanding is not simply a *choice* about the extent of participation in social groups. It requires that a person understands what he is going to choose. It is evident that 'discovery' alone cannot be all there is in terms of identity. But 'choice' cannot be either. This would disregard the particular nature of the choice itself. Indeed, the choice is not about the participation in particular groups; the choice is about oneself within a given social environment. It is the choice about meanings, values, aims, objectives that a person has and accepts in relation to his life. Meanings, values and aims, of course, that come about in interaction with other people without whom those meanings had no sense. And yet, those interactions do not preclude the choice a person can make in respect of *who* he wants to be as a distinct being from his involvement in a social environment.

Hence, Sen enters this debate by arguing that a person has multiple social identities. A person then would have to choose the extent of participation in these groups or decide to change his participation over time. However, approaching this process of choice through the perspective of social identities does not do justice to the real process of choice a person is engaging in. Arguably, a person does not see himself as *social identities*, but as a person who refers to himself as 'I' and who wishes to make choices that contribute to the development of his *personal identity*. The process of reflection underlying his choices is less concerned with 'what are my social identities?' and 'which social identities do I want to have?' but more with 'who am I?' and 'who do I want to be?'. We can see this choice about one's personal identity ultimately as a choice within a space of capabilities. It is a process of choice and reflection on *who* one wants to be (capabilities) and *who* one is (functionings) and their respective influences on each other. Identity choice is not a choice between two objects, but the choice about one's own subject. The chooser is changed by his particular choice. To understand this process of change, the chooser applies a process of reasoning that is not only limited to this particular choice but requires an understanding of the meaning and value the person attaches to the choice and the change.

To discuss the issue of identity as a matter of choice from a *multiple identities* perspective and not from a *personal identity* perspective finally has its price when we consider more specifically the question of how to evaluate a person's well-being. The price is an inconsistency in Sen's proposed solution to the problems related with people's identity. This becomes clear if we consider again the issue of distorted perceptions of women's interests. Despite all the possible choices a person can make, one cannot choose to be or not to be a woman.[4] It therefore appears that to be a woman whose interests are wrongly perceived is a sort of 'socially determined handicap'. However, Sen introduced his capability approach rightly enough in order to surpass the problem of *physically* handicapped people and their disadvantage in relation to the conversion of goods or resources into capabilities. Moreover, he writes that '(t)he issue of gender cannot be properly addressed if advantage and disadvantage are seen merely in terms of holdings of primary goods, rather than the actual freedoms to lead different types of lives that women and men respectively enjoy' (Sen 1990b: 116). But the solution

---

[4] Of course people can nowadays change their sex and thus choose to be or not to be a woman. However, these choices happen under particular circumstances and we thus assume that nobody changes their sex in order to increase the status of this particular aspect of one's identity.

that Sen proposes in relation to women's 'social' handicap suggests otherwise. Sen argues that if women had access to the labour market, they would be able to 'bring home' market-evaluated money income as men do. It is thus the money they bring home that will eventually affect their bargaining position within the household (Sen 1990c). Hence, it seems that Sen suggests changing distorted perceptions (or 'social handicaps' more generally as we would say) by offering equal access to resources and even more specifically to money income. Thus the problem of social handicaps is not solved within a capability space, but via considerations of equal resources and income. This is inconsistent with Sen's previously cited consideration of gender difference and more generally with his discussion of 'physical' handicaps where he rightly suggests that advantage should not be measured in terms of equal holdings of goods (or resources and income), but in terms of equal capabilities. Money income and access to the labour market is certainly a means for well-being improvement. The question however is whether it is sufficient to change distorted perceptions about women's interests. Money income and labour market access does not yet guarantee that a person actually can or succeeds in living the life she has reason to value, or to be *who* she wants to be. Too many distorted perceptions can come about through the kind of job a person is finally doing. Moreover, simply contributing market-evaluated money income to the household does not necessarily change the traditional role many women still have within the household. Money income is a means to well-being, but not an end.

The access to the labour market and thus to a new social identity can improve women's position in a traditional society. Over time, it certainly will also contribute to a change in perceptions others might have of a particular person (or of a group of people). But this may well be a long way off. Therefore, the underlying idea of our critique is the claim that as much as a person does not think of herself as *being* a sum of certain *social identities*, as much will she not be perceived as such by other people. What ultimately matters are not the different social identities people have but the perceptions associated with particular *people*. If we consider distorted perceptions of interests as a form of capability deprivation for those who suffer from them, then their situation can be improved not only through a change in their social identity but also through a removal of those distorted perceptions. Thus, a change in these perceptions is as much a matter of those who hold those perceptions as of those whom the perceptions are about. This reflects the particular nature of identity: a person's identity is not only changing through her own choices and actions but to some extent also through the choices and actions of others. This leads to the question as to whether choosing a new social identity will alone be sufficient to improve effectively a person's well-being if distorted perceptions are in play. We will try to respond to this question in the following two sections. At the moment we suggest that the development of a *personal identity* approach within the capability space can contribute more to the evaluation of distorted perceptions than a *multiple identity* perspective. A personal identity approach within the capability space does not consider only the access to different social identities and thus *what* the person is and does and could be and do, it also evaluates the freedom to be *who* one wants to be and thus the capability of being free of distorted perceptions.

Introducing 'identity' into the evaluation of the quality of life

There has recently been one attempt to introduce the concept of identity into the assessment of economic outcomes. Akerlof and Kranton (2000, 2002) use psychological and sociological ideas of identity with which they try to explain different economic phenomena. The word 'identity' appears many times in their text and lots of examples are given of how 'identity' influences people's behaviour (especially in 2000). Indeed, there is not one definition of the concept only, rather several ones. Akerlof and Kranton first argue that identity is a person's sense of the self. Later they state that identity is based on social categories, but this would exclude any kind of self-understanding that seems fundamental to identity as an answer to the question of *who* one is. Subsequently, they explain identity as describing a person's self-image as well as her assigned categories, yet they do not account for the use of the word 'self-image'. However, Akerlof and Kranton formulate an interesting model, in which identity is included in the utility function and motivates behaviour.[5] Additionally, in their

---

[5] Identity is represented as a function that depends on one's and others' actions, on the assigned social categories (being a man or a woman for example), on one's own characteristics and on the assigned prescription that are related to one's adherence to certain social categories.

model, one's utility also depends on one's actions as well as on those of others. This basic idea is then incorporated into different models that try to explain gender discrimination in the labour market, poverty and social exclusion and the household division of labour (2000) as well as decisions concerning education (2002). Individuals, for whom the social categories, their own characteristics and the socially assigned prescriptions as well as the reaction of others are assumed to be given, choose the actions that will maximise their utilities. To a certain extent, people can also choose their category assignment – for example through education – and influence in this way their identity and, thus, their behaviour. In their basic model, there are two possible activities and individuals have certain preferences over these activities (2000). Furthermore, there are two social categories. Members belonging to a certain category should in general choose a specific activity. Anyone, therefore, who chooses an activity that does not correspond to her prescribed one will lose some identity that stems from the respective social category she adheres to. A loss in identity will lead to a reduction of a person's utility. Yet these choices will not only influence the agent's identity, they will also spill over to other people's identities and utilities. If an individual chooses an activity that does not coincide with the prescribed one, the other individuals in the same category may lose some identity as a consequence of this individual's action. Therefore, those individuals may 'respond' and act in such a way as to restore their identities. This may cause further losses in identity and utility for the individual who did not choose to conform to the socially expected activity in the first place. Depending therefore on the overall outcome, taking into account all actions and reactions, an individual will do or refrain from doing a certain activity. This is how Akerlof and Kranton can explain gender segregation at the working place for example. Two social categories, men and women, have certain prescriptions for appropriate activities, i.e. the jobs do have some 'auras of gender' (Akerlof and Kranton 2000: 732). If a woman takes on a man's job, she loses identity by doing such work. In the same way, a man would lose identity through the woman's action as he may feel his own self-image to be threatened. Their models also explain, so they argue, that if women's identity is enhanced by homework, they will have a lesser incentive to participate in the labour market. Yet the impact of women's movements, for example, leads to a change of behavioural and attributed prescriptions to the social categories. By reshaping the notions of femininity and masculinity, gender segregation at the labour market will also change. As these models show, identity does influence market outcomes.[6]

Akerlof and Kranton introduced identity into economic modelling because it is, as they say, 'fundamental to behavior' (Akerlof and Kranton 2000: 717). And indeed, 'choice of identity may be the most important "economic" decision people make. Individuals may – more or less consciously – choose who they want to be. Limits on this choice may also be the most important determinant of an individual's economic well-being (ibid.)'. This is certainly a very important point, and yet, one wonders, why restricting the choice of being who one wants to be is related only to consequences on economic well-being. It certainly would affect well-being in general. And Sen would add that the agency aspect of people does not have to be forgotten either. Indeed, as Akerlof and Kranton incorporate their concept of identity into a utility function, even more of the above-mentioned criticism Sen developed towards the utilitarian approach could be put forward. Of special interest in relation to identity is the fact that people may choose according to certain principles that are different from just maximising their utility. People may choose in accordance to *who* they would like to be. This means that one has to understand people's actions, and not, as in the utility approach, just observe them. The drive, of course, to accomplish *who* one wants to be may render the person happy. But it is the whole idea of one's 'life project' that produces happiness and not just single actions. In that sense, utilities or happiness constitute one aspect among others of a person's identity and life project and not, as Akerlof and Kranton propose, identity an aspect of somebody's utilities. However, they state that 'increases or decreases in utility that

---

[6] The more recent paper (2002) applies the *identity*-model to the economics of education. In this model, people, i.e. students, have to choose their social categories and an effort in school. By selecting the social category (leading crowd, nerds or burnouts), they take into account their own characteristics and the ideal characteristics of the respective social category to which they would like to belong. The more their private characteristics differ from the social ones, the higher are the costs of membership. By choosing an effort level, students consider their own actions and the ideal behaviour of the chosen category. The more students deviate from the prescribed behaviour, the higher are their costs in terms of utility loss. Thus, once again, these students have an interest to minimise the distance between themselves, their proper characteristics and actions, and the *self-image* associated to the specific category.

derive from I_j (the identity of individual j) (are called) gains or losses in identity' (Akerlof and Kranton 2000: 719).

Yet what would that mean if we took this sentence literally? It would mean that we are happier the more identity we have. But what is to have more identity? More identity in an Akerlof and Kranton literal sense means that my characteristics fit more closely to those of the social group. Yet clearly, everybody has an identity and it is hard to argue that one has more or less identity just because characteristics fit better to a social group. One of Akerlof and Kranton's examples relates to the fact that husbands lose identity when they do housework and when their wives earn more than half the household income (Akerlof and Kranton 2000: 747). Yet certainly men do not lose their identity by contributing to some household work. Under the depicted circumstances they rather have a conflict between what is expected of them and their own conception and perception of what a man 'naturally' does. This reflects Sen's discussion about misconceived perceptions about women's interests. However, as discussed previously, perceptions can be modified by active reflection and evaluation, as well as changes in the social structures, such as enforcing women's participation in the labour market. However, Akerlof and Kranton's model does not take into account any dynamic perspective that could include changes in perceptions. Moreover, even though Akerlof and Kranton consider the possibility of changing social categories or violating prescriptions, there is no full account given as to what are finally the motivations for people to do that. They just cite examples where people have actually done it, such as woman marines, female trial lawyers or other situations where women take up a 'man's job' (Akerlof and Kranton 2000: 722–723). However, either these women had to renounce some traits of their femininity or, in some cases, they would have been harassed by their male colleagues, who undertook certain humiliating actions against their female co-workers to, as was argued, restore their masculinity. So why did these women choose to occupy these positions in the labour market? To maximise their utility? Utility in terms of happiness? Yet harassed women certainly are not at the maximum of their happiness. Utility in terms of personal satisfaction about their status as 'modern women' then? Seems plausible, yet the harassment is still there, and to argue that their status outweighs the disutility of harassment renders the whole explicative structure once again quite farfetched. If one starts to think about identity, the utility-based approach that tries to deal with it seems to come quite soon to its conceptual limits.

And yet to consider identity in relation to the evaluation of well-being and agency seems to be an important issue. Furthermore, what Akerlof and Kranton do clearly and interestingly illustrate is the influence of people's interaction on their respective identities and their related well-being. However, the consequences of people's being and doing as it was described in Akerlof and Kranton's models seem to be better illustrated in the space of functionings and capabilities. In fact, Akerlof and Kranton's model maximises over actions, thus 'doings' only. The capability space allows consideration of beings as well. And it is somebody's being seen as an ongoing process of self-understanding and self-creation that underlines the idea of personal identity. In a capability space, the fact, for example, that women choose to take on a man's job may be better explained in terms of values, desires and freedoms to act and to be than in terms of pure utilities. A woman may have taken on a man's job because she likes the job, she does not consider it to be purely male work, she wants to become more independent, the job corresponds to what she would like to do and to be, etc., all aspects that do not necessarily have to do with the maximisation of her utility. Especially in regard of identity related capabilities, i.e. being able to be *who* one would like to be, it seems more plausible to understand women's choices of taking men's jobs when situated in a capability space as she may undertake some professional activity even though she may know about the problems she could encounter in the workplace. Just to observe that a woman chose a man's job and to conclude that therefore this act must have given her the greatest utility does not evaluate properly this woman's well-being, especially not if she chose the job in order to be *who* and what she would like to be, but now suffers harassment from her colleagues. The overall assessment of her situation is better analysed in a capability space. If her male colleagues really harass her, then her level of functioning suffers and her capability may of course be improved if the co-workers' behaviour changes. However, one may also argue that men's functionings and capabilities in terms of identity declined by the presence of women working with them. How can this situation be solved? Well, this hints at the important fact that in certain circumstances, people's capabilities may be improved only by considering them in a larger context of people's interaction. Identity is a dynamic concept. Many problems and difficulties arise because one sticks to a certain view of *who* oneself and the other is. This view is often related to some apparently indisputable views of the 'social organisation' and division of labour, which in turn is related to some equally uncontested meanings of what is – in this case – femininity and masculinity. In the end, only by influencing and changing those meanings will we be able to solve the above depicted situation and improve the capabilities of both men, who do not feel threatened by women colleagues any more, and women, who will not be harassed. These changes may indeed occur by interacting with each other in such a way as to be able to get to know who the other is, by eventually realising that one has more points in common than issues that would strictly divide two people, man and woman, at the same working place. What has to be changed are the perceptions, to use Sen's terminology, one has about the other in case it distorts the view about the other's being and doing.

Sen suggested that to improve women's position in society and within their families, they should take on a job in the labour market and earn money-valued income as men do (Sen 1985b: 205). This will indeed help to appreciate women's labour and contribution to the family's wealth and may lead to more respect and acknowledgement of women's being and doing. And yet, as has often been observed, equal division of labour in the labour market does not necessarily lead to the same equality in the private sphere. Women often enough do have to cope with a double shift of official work and household activities. This dichotomy still hints at inherited and uncontested views of what women and men do, about what femininity and masculinity are and mean. In order to change this, it is necessary not only to reflect on the meaning of such characterisations and social organisations but also to consider how men and women interact and evaluate all this in terms of capabilities.

The influence of social interaction on people's capabilities

The standard economic theory depicts individuals as utility maximisers who are not very affected by social relations. This may be a good basis for simple markets, yet for the assessment of the quality of life, this view might be too narrow. Indeed, there is now a growing literature, even within economics, that tries to capture the fact of people's 'embeddedness' in a social context.[7] In addition to financial and human capital, the notion of social capital, i.e. the way people relate to each other, gains momentum. To judge a person's well-being and advantage therefore, we cannot just look at his or her position in an isolated manner but have to see the context in which this relationship takes place. The existence and the nature of social capital has a pivotal function in determining people's functionings and capabilities. Social capital may be a form of constraint, as well as of possibility, and according to that, well-being and advantage have to be evaluated.

Indeed, well-being, agency, identity and social capital may be connected to each other in at least two different ways. First, the social context of people's interaction and the way they relate to each other will have consequences for their identity as well as their well-being and agency. It is within a given social network that a person acquires a more or less reflected self-understanding about *who* she is. Second, somebody's well-being and agency may be improved if the quality of relationship and interaction with others are changed or enhanced. This may indeed be the case if people get to 'learn' about each other's identity, about what is of importance to them and if they consequently change potential ambiguous perceptions about *who* the other is. In this section we cite some possible relations of the way people interact with each other with their identities as defined in the previous sections and, consequently, with their capabilities.

The first point is best demonstrated by some illustrative examples taken from the ever-growing social network literature. As Mark Granovetter argues for 'the strength of weak ties' (Granovetter 1973), so see Beate Völker and Henk Flap, 'weak ties as a liability' (Völker and Flap, 2001). Granovetter studies the social structure of American society, Völker and Flap the case of East Germany. In the American society of the 1970s, weak ties seemed to be indispensable instruments for individuals to seize advantageous opportunities for them (like finding a job) or to become integrated into the community (Granovetter 1973). In East Germany though, at the time of communism, weak relations were suspicious because of the considerable control apparatus the system had established. People 'assumed that every house committee, cadre, working group or brigade had at least one person who was an unofficial informant of the security police' (Völker

---

[7] See for 'embeddedness' Granovetter (1985).

and Flap 2001: 399). Often, weak ties were used only for the provision of material commodities, as goods were short in supply. Political and private issues were discussed within small 'niches', little subgroups of people who were all strongly linked to each other. Indeed, 'niches helped people to develop a sense of identity and individuality, an image of self on the one hand and an image of the world in which one lived on the other' (Völker and Flap 2001: 404). Moreover, in the case of East Germany strong ties were the most important channel for finding a job. Within their niches, people 'tried to escape the "collectivism and communism by design" and searched for more individuality, freedom, or areas of life that were not contaminated by the encompassing ideology of communist lifestyle and norms' (2001: 400). However, the experience of a communist political regime does not mean that all (ex)-communist countries developed similar networks. This becomes clear when we look, as Richard Rose does, at Russia's 'transition' to a modern market economy in comparison with, among others, the Czech Republic (Rose 2000). Indeed, whereas Czechs, even though they lived with communism for several decades, live quite successfully in a modern market society, Russians, equally used to communism, do not as they continue to be hunted by their 'antimodern Soviet legacy' (Rose 2000: 148).

If the characteristic of a modern society is 'the predominance, in both the market and the state sectors, of social capital in the form of large, impersonal bureaucratic organisations operating according to the rule of law (...)' (2001: 147), then antimodern means that these formal, official organisations fail and people tend to turn to semi-transparent, personal relationships with a small number of related and acquainted individuals. Moreover, people try to 'debureaucratise' their relations with formal organisations by personalising them, or by bribing and cajoling individuals in official positions in order to get things done. This system of informal networks with corrupt implications has been more prevalent in Soviet states than in communist states in general. As it thus turns out, a certain legacy of network structures influences the way a society changes or does not change (and thus how people behave) when it is confronted with some new influence, in this case the modern organisation of market economies. In many situations, informal networks may be positive for individuals. However, whereas in modern states informal networks either enhance or at least do not work against formal organisations, in the context of an antimodern society, the existence of informal networks, even though beneficial to individuals, harms the society and its transition towards a modern system. Indeed, as Rose suggests, '(t)he introduction of the market has increased opportunities for overt corruption, that is, the payment of cash to get officials to break rules to the benefit of the recipient'[8] (Rose 2000: 158). That is, informal networks in an antimodern society such as Russia tend to work against modern features.

In terms of personal well-being however, the only reliance on formal organisations in antimodern states would signify greatest vulnerability and social exclusion for individuals as this would imply that they miss important informal connections to procure the necessities of life.[9] Thus, similar types of relations amount to varying degrees of well-being according to social, historical and cultural circumstances. So does access to informal networks without connections to formal organisations amount to a *loss* in welfare, for example, in slum communities in Bangkok, Thailand (Daniere *et al.* 2002: 176ff). This is especially true in relation to environmental and sanitary aspects of people's lives in these slums. Even though certain slums have a rich social capital in terms of interaction and integration among the inhabitants, the missing linkages to government officials do not help solve the problem of water and sanitation, which has negative consequences on their health. Yet socially integrated communities could solve issues of collective waste collection more easily than socially disintegrated and isolated ones. Indeed, it appears that economically and geographically isolated communities are associated with low levels of integration and linkages (Daniere *et al.* 2002: 190).[10] These few examples already show that 'seemingly private decisions (such as with whom to interact) are influenced by institutional contexts' (Völker and Flap: 398). These influences will certainly affect people's identity and self-understanding and arguably go over pure choice aspects of identity. However, these influences can be offset by trying to understand the way people relate

---

[8] Rose maybe exaggerates a little with this judgement. It might be true to some extent that the market does not solve the problem of informal networks and its subsequent corruption, but it does not follow from his arguments that '[...] the market increased opportunities for overt corruption [...]' (Rose 2000: 158).

[9] This, however, is not the case. As Rose states, very few Russians do consistently lack access to informal networks and thus would be, in that sense, socially excluded (Rose 2000: 167).

[10] And/or vice versa?

and interact with each other and what it does to their respective identities as persons living in a given social context. Exploring these aspects of oneself in relation to others will help to achieve a better understanding of those social characteristics and structures that influence people's sense of identity. And it also becomes clearer in what way relations will be of an advantage or a disadvantage in terms of capabilities for people. In certain situations people will benefit from a large set of different kinds of relations, in others they are better off with a small group of well-known people. In some situations, people are better off with little contact to formal organisations, in others with more. '(E)very institutional context leads to specific personal experiences and problems for which no standardised solutions are available' (Daniere *et al.* 2002: 398). Indeed, interactions have to be considered for each specific case and evaluated in terms of capabilities.

The second point may also be visualised by referring to another study conducted by Henk Flap. His research concentrated on the conflicts of allegiance and their influences on the outbreak of violence within a society. His hypothesis is that the more different circles of loyalties would overlap, the less violent a conflict would result than when those loyalties are separated (Flap 1988). Indeed, Robert H. Bates and Irene Yackovlev confirm this hypothesis empirically by analysing ethnicity and conflicts in Africa. Ethnic leaders are more driven into violence if they have to fear political exclusion. '(I)t is diversity, not homogeneity, that lowers the probability of conflict. Separatist solutions may therefore exacerbate, rather than ameliorate, the problem' (Bates and Yackovlev 2002: 330). In a more general, explicative sense, Flap takes what he calls 'circles' to be a collection of people with identical interests or features, either seen in the form of some official association, group or party or as some unofficial classification of people with the same characteristics, status or position within a network of social relations. The overlap of different circles would amount to either the creation of new links between the respective members of those groups, or changing and enhancing the quality of existing links of those groups of people. Especially if these circles have opposing interests, the overlap may induce people to try to understand each other's point and argument, indeed to get to know each other because the overlap leads to the recognition and identification of at least some common interests. The advantage of an overlap is in fact that the newly interconnected people do have to approach themselves from 'both sides'. There is not one set of people that is going to be accepted or included into another group. Those groups do have to try to get to know and to respect the others in terms of their identity for the sake of a better outcome for everybody. We might now say that the reciprocal acknowledgement of each other and of common interests may indeed lead to an improvement in terms of capabilities for those involved in the encounter. Moreover, an overlap also amounts to an expansion of one's identity. The reciprocal inclusion and acknowledgement of interests can be seen as a form of appropriation of identity, a reflection on and an understanding of *who* one is in relation to and with the other.

We may relate this kind of overlap to the example of men and women. Sen argued that women should get paid work in the labour market to change their position within the family. But this situation would amount to a one-sided overlap or inclusion of women into a male-dominated, public labour market. As we argued above, this does not yet mean that men participate to the same extent in household activities, which is an essentially female-dominated, private sphere. Only men's inclusion in the sphere of household and child-rearing activities would complete the overlap. Market recognition is not sufficient to change women's welfare. Even though in many cases women improve their position within the household by getting access to the labour credit market or to land property, they still do not attain the same position as men have and their interests continue to be misperceived.[11] Also, market recognition will not be universally applicable as a solution to changing perceptions as in certain societies and circumstances, women prefer not to enter the labour market and to engage in informal activities as they withdraw in such a way the money they earn from the control of their husbands. Earning some money without the husbands' real knowledge about the amount gained by informal productive activities does indeed lead to more autonomy for these women.[12] This shows that it might be reasonable to accept a vision of what Michael Walzer called 'complex equality', i.e. different spheres, where different goods are distributed to different groups of men and women for different reasons and according to

[11] See for example: Agarwal 1994; Tam 1996; Mayoux 2001. See also Altman and Lamontagne (2004) for an interesting account of culturally influenced intrahousehold allocation of goods.
[12] Commaille 1993: 21–22.

different procedures (Walzer 1983: 26). Equality between men and women may not be fully established, as long as one distributive good, namely market-valued income and its associated importance and authority, also dominates the distribution of influence and power within private spheres. The inclusion of women in the labour market will in most cases improve a woman's position because she gains at least some independence but also experiences and knowledge that may be important for a better perception of herself and her interests. And yet, in terms of complex equality, it would also be important that men are included in household and related activities that are dominantly associated with the private and often female sphere of people's life. Only if men participate in the 'typical' female sphere of activity will they gain knowledge about the interests and needs of women because of their own experience of them. As much as Sen, in reference to Adam Smith, underlines the importance of 'being able to appear in public without shame' (Sen 2000a: 4), as much should it be possible 'to be able to live and to participate in private without shame'. The perception of women will change if what they are and do is understood as well as appreciated for what it is – and this not only through market-valued income. The reciprocal inclusion would amount to some sort of overlap, an overlap of activities that helps not only to get to learn about the other and his or her respective being and doing but also to discover common interests and the advantage to foster them cooperatively.

In a general sense, to have access to different circles is significant for the identification of one's own interests as it allows for a diversified view of oneself that results from the different influences and confrontations within the circles and networks. The recognition of one's interests will also expand the view of agency possibilities in different spheres of activity. However, equally important for a person's capability will be that the other recognises one's interests. This recognition will have an important influence on the perception the other has of oneself. The change of perception can best be achieved when people acknowledge that their interests overlap. Overlapping means that a person shares some interests with some other, without being or becoming exactly the other. It implies that one finds out about *who* one is thanks to the equality as well as difference in relation to the other. However, this difference has the tendency to be understood and valued, and not to be used as a means to dominate the other.

Conclusion

The main idea of this chapter consisted in showing a certain form of paradox in Sen's writing. Even though he has a rich conception of people's identity in his writings in relation to the capability approach, he does not link it with the issue of identity. When he discusses identity, his starting point is the influences people's social identity in terms of group memberships have on their perceptions and actions, but what he really is concerned with is to demonstrate that individuals always have a capacity to reason about their identity and thus to choose which group they want to belong to and to what extent. This process of choice and, as we call it, the creation of a person's personal identity over time can, however, best be considered within a capability space. The evaluative space of capabilities offers a promising context to talk about identity, indeed a much better one than the standard utilitarian framework.

There are several interconnected reasons why the questions of identity and social interaction are important in considerations of people's well-being and agency. First of all, we have to know about the well-being and agency of a person as a *who*, which includes knowing where the person is coming from and where she wants to go. We have to know what is of importance to her. Critics could say that there is not very much improvement for people like Sen's 'subjugated housewife' and her adapted perceptions of how happy she is when we consider her personal identity. What is of importance to her could still be very much adjusted to what is socially expected. But we are concerned with *who* she is, who and what she likes to be and why it matters to her. To know about *who one is* may highlight the gap between what somebody wants to be and the social or relational constraints preventing her from becoming it. If a young woman wants the same working opportunities as men, yet the labour market discriminates against women (who, say, have the 'handicap' to become pregnant), this points to the fact that the value of 'self-realisation', as well as the intrinsic value of being considered equal to men, is not achievable and this woman suffers from inequality in capabilities. Furthermore, to know *who* the person is helps us learn about the social context in which she lives. We cannot say a lot about somebody's well-being if we do not consider her geographical location as well as her framework and set of interactions, in relation to which her life becomes a sense. Sen rightly points out that not to have modern equipment in a society where this is required in order to participate in community life is worse than in a society where this need does not exist (Sen 1999b: 89). Also, to know about somebody's framework and social situation would help to distinguish between a person who 'starves' for some religious reason, for example, and a person who does not have enough to eat (Sen 1993: 40). Finally, people's identity will be formed and influenced by their interactions with others. The way people relate to each other may not affect only their well-being and agency possibilities but also their being and doing in terms of identity as the encounter with the other may always be a source of personal growth as well as evolution – and, sometimes, unfortunately, also of personal disadvantage.

Cited references

Agarwal, Bina 1994. 'Gender and command over property: a critical gap in economic analysis and policy in South Asia', *World Development* 22: 1455–78.

Akerlof, George and Kranton, Rachel 2000. 'Economics and identity', *Quarterly Journal of Economics* 65: 715–53.

Akerlof, George and Kranton, Rachel 2002. 'Identity and schooling: some lessons for the economics of education', *Journal of Economic Literature* 40: 1167–1201.

Altman, Morris and Lamontagne, Louise 2004. 'Gender, human capabilities and culture within the household economy: different path to socio-economic well-being?', *International Journal of Social Economics* 31: 325–64.

Bates, Robert and Yackovlev, Irene 2002. 'Ethnicity, capital formation, and conflict: evidence from Africa', in Gootaert, Christian and van Bastelaer, Thierry (eds.). *The Role of Social Capital in Development: An Empirical Assessment*. Cambridge: Cambridge University Press.

Commaille, Jacques 1993. *Les stratégies des femmes. Travail, famille et politique*. Paris: la Découverte.

Daniere, Amrita, Takahashi, Lois and Naranong, Anchana 2002. 'Social capital and environmental management: culture, perceptions and action among slum dwellers in Bangkok', in Isham, Jonathan, Kelly, Thomas and Ramaswamy, Sunder (eds.). *Social Capital and Economic Development: Well-being in Developing Countries*. Cheltenham: Edward Elgar.

Flap, Hendrik 1988. *Conflict, Loyalty and Violence*. Frankfurt: Verlag Peter Lang.

Granovetter, Mark 1973. 'The strength of weak ties', *American Sociological Review* 78: 1360–80.

Granovetter, Mark 1985. 'Economic action and social structure: the problem of embeddedness', *American Journal of Sociology* 91: 481–510.

Mayoux, Linda 2001. 'Tackling the down side: social capital, women's empowerment and micro-finance in Cameroon', *Development and Change* 32: 435–64.

Rose, Richard 2000. 'Getting things done in an antimodern society: social capital networks in Russia', in Dasgupta, Partha and Serageldin, Ismail (eds.). *Social Capital: A Multifaceted Perspective.* Washington D.C.: The World Bank.

Sandel, Michael 1998 (1982). *Liberalism and the Limits of Justice,* 2nd edn. Cambridge: Cambridge University Press.

Sen, Amartya 1984. 'Rights and capabilities', in Sen, Amartya (ed.). *Resources, Values and Development.* Oxford: Basil Blackwell, pp. 307–24.

Sen, Amartya 1985a. 'Well-Being, agency and freedom. The Dewey Lectures 1984', *Journal of Philosophy* 82: 169–221.

Sen, Amartya 1985b. 'Women, technology and sexual division', *Trade and Development* 6: 195–223.

Sen, Amartya 1987. *On Ethics and Economics.* Oxford: Basil Blackwell.

Sen, Amartya 1990a. 'Millions of missing women', *New York Review of Books,* December 20.

Sen, Amartya 1990b. 'Justice: means versus freedoms', *Philosophy and Public Affairs* 19: 111–21.

Sen, Amartya 1990c. 'Gender and cooperative conflicts', in Tinker, Irene (ed.). *Persistent Inequalities.* New York: Oxford University Press, pp. 123–49.

Sen, Amartya 1993. 'Capability and well-being'. In Nussbaum, Martha and Sen, Amartya (eds.). *The Quality of Life.* Oxford: Clarendon Press.

Sen, Amartya 1999a (1985). *Commodities and Capabilities.* Oxford: Oxford University Press.

Sen, Amartya 1999b. *Development as Freedom.* Oxford: Oxford University Press.

Sen, Amartya 1999c. *Reason Before Identity. The Romanes Lecture for 1998.* Oxford: Oxford University Press.

Sen, Amartya 2000a. 'Social exclusion: concept, application, and scrutiny', *Social Development Papers* 1, Asian Development Bank.

Sen, Amartya 2000b. 'East and West: the reach of reason', *New York Review of Books,* July 20.

Sen, Amartya 2000c. 'Other people', *New Republic,* December 18.

Tam, Tony 1996. 'Reducing the gender gap in an Asian economy: how important is women's increasing work experience?', *World Development* 24: 831–44.

Taylor, Charles 1989. *Sources of the Self. The Making of the Modern Identity*. Cambridge: Cambridge University Press.

Völker, Beate and Flap, Henk 2001. 'Weak ties as a liability. The case of East Germany', *Rationality and Society* 13: 397–428.

Walzer, Michael 1983. *Spheres of Justice. A Defense of Pluralism and Equality*. New York: Basic Books.

6 | Measuring capabilities

FLAVIO COMIM[1,2]

Introduction

The measurement of capabilities is the most pressing challenge ahead for the operationalisation of the capability approach (CA). Yet the idea of measurement would seem *prima facie* inimical to the CA. Measurement in social sciences is usually identified with a narrowness of understanding about the application of concepts and theories. Quite often it involves dismissal of important qualitative information, such as what is important, good, or morally obligatory, focusing sometimes exclusively on quantitative information. In fact, in the jargon of the CA, we could say that measurement might entail a limitation of informational spaces used in evaluative assessments. Thus, in principle, it would seem that it is an error to insist on the measurement of capabilities. Whereas the CA puts forward a proposal for expansion of informational spaces for normative evaluations, assessment by measurement appears to narrow down those spaces, ignoring types of information that cannot be translated into concrete metrics. Sen (1999: 81) notes that the foundational merits of the CA do not

> however, entail that the most fruitful focus of *practical* attention would invariably be measures of capabilities. Some capabilities are harder to measure than others, and attempts at putting them on a 'metric' may sometimes hide more than they reveal. [original emphasis]

Indeed, there are many different ways in which theories can be applied and, contrary to the conventional wisdom found, for instance, in

[1] I would like to express my deepest gratitude to David Crocker, Mozaffar Qizilbash, Angels Varea, Gay Meeks, Sabina Alkire and Des Gasper for their valuable comments and suggestions. The remaining errors are my full responsibility.
[2] Capability and Sustainability Centre, St Edmund's College, Cambridge; UFRGS, Brazil; fvc1001@cam.ac.uk

mainstream economics, the operationalisation of a theory does not need to be limited to quantitative measurement. Yet measurement does not always need to be tantamount to quantification or narrowing of informational spaces. Only in an unduly narrow sense, measurement is equivalent to assigning numbers to units of analysis. Measurement in a broad sense would entail i) clarification of concepts; ii) specification of dimensions that will be chosen as the focal point of analysis; iii) choice of categories to represent the scales in which the evolution of dimensions would be assessed; and iv) organisation of results. The first step in the measurement process consists in clarifying terms and hypotheses to get the concrete meaning of some abstract terms. For instance, one can talk about 'democracy' in very abstract terms without being able to grasp its concrete meaning in specific historical contexts. Measurement processes will push for this translation of abstract terms into entities with operational meaning. Second, measurement entails the specification of the dimensions to be measured. This choice involves the election of some classes of value at the expense of others. For instance, measuring children's development comprises a choice of focal points of analysis (e.g. nutrition, cognitive development, psychological maturity, etc.) that is considered more representative for expressing their overall development. Third, measurement requires choice of scales. These scales do not always need to be translated into numbers. Qualitative scales are commonly used to assess complex problems such as disability (Booth and Booth, 1998). Finally, measurement involves a coherent or systematic way of displaying the results. This is important because results tend to be sample-sensitive and the characterisation of particular realities needs to reflect a story behind the measures. Theories will then guide the final organisation of results.

A measurement framework is useful to solve concrete problems. Generally speaking, theories can be transformed into an object of practical value by i) theoretical applications (use of theoretical arguments to illuminate situations, providing a focus that highlights certain salient feature or facts of theoretical or normative interest); ii) methodological applications (use of theoretical arguments to discuss methodological issues); iii) case-study applications (use of descriptive information to contextualise and examine particular empirical or theoretical issues); and iv) empirical statistical studies (use of statistical analysis involving quantification of parameters and estimation of equations, especially regression analysis to identify causal factors in contrast to mere correlations). Measurement in a broad sense pervades all those uses.

The main objective of this chapter is to analyse a range of conceptual and practical issues involved in the task of measuring functionings and capabilities. It is based on a systematisation of Amartya Sen's and Martha Nussbaum's selected writings, combined with fieldwork experience developed across different projects. With this purpose, the chapter is divided into three parts. The first part examines the conceptual level related to the measurement of capabilities. It investigates conceptual features of the approach that influence the sort of measurement work that can be carried out. The second part focuses on the empirical level related to the measurement of capabilities. It analyses issues such as those of aggregation, weighting and data incompleteness. Finally, the third part discusses empirical work carried out in research projects aiming to measure capabilities.

Part 1: conceptual level

Quantitative information might reveal important features of normative evaluations. On the possibility of measuring well-being, Griffin (1986: 75) argues: 'There are many different scales of measurement, and it would be astonishing if well-being were not measurable on at least one of the less demanding ones.' He maintains that we use a quantitative language whenever we speak of well-being. Carter (1999) seems to take this argument further, stressing the importance of addressing the quantitative attribute of freedom. According to him, the degree of freedom is 'an ineradicable part of liberal discourse and theorizing' (1999: 4). Indeed, measurement is part of daily life when individuals assess different aspects of their actions and states. Expressions such as 'more', 'less', 'better' or 'worse' are used daily to describe our own well-being or the state of the economy or of democracy.

Measurement is necessary for the full fruition of the CA as a framework for practical ethics, potentially applicable to human development and well-being analysis. This claim can be justified on several grounds. It seems evident that much of the CA's added value as a theory for normative evaluations lies in its potential for practical application. So far the approach has undoubtedly secured great admiration as a philosophical incursion into development ethics, but has not yet systematically proved its added value as a distinctive methodology for going about solving practical problems (as utilitarianism has done). It might well be argued that the approach was not intended as an empirical methodology, although its 'architects' have often stressed the importance of using philosophical approaches to solve development problems (see, for instance, Sen, 1999 and Nussbaum, 2000a). One of the most serious practical difficulties faced by the approach – and also one of its greatest merits – is its theoretical under-specification. The CA provides a justification for using broader informational spaces in normative evaluations but offers no guidance about how different informational spaces are to be filled in, combined, or sequenced. This is not due to any flaw in the approach, but to its *bottom-up* nature that requires participation and involvement of those people who are the agents of development change. Instead of being passive beneficiaries of cunning development plans conceived from above and outside, development agents decide together and often democratically their joint ends and means. This helps to prevent 'technological fixes' to development problems but brings an alternative conception for going about measurement that needs to be further explored.

One does not need to despair of the CA, as some of its critics did and still do, in face of this 'measurement challenge'. It seems useful to remember here the original critiques of the CA by Sugden (1993), Ysander (1993), Srinivasan (1994) and Roemer (1996), among many others. In few words, they have suggested that the 'multidimensional-context-dependent-counterfactual-normative' nature of the CA might prevent it from having practical and operational significance. For instance, Sugden (1993: 1953) argues: 'Given the rich array of functionings that Sen takes to be relevant, given the extent of disagreement among reasonable people about the nature of the good life, and given the unresolved problem of how to value sets, it is natural to ask how far Sen's framework is operational.' Similarly, Ysander (1993: 84) comments that 'in an overwhelming number of cases, the investigators failed to observe and measure anything which could, with the best will in the world, be called a capability'. Srinivasan (1994) appears to see in the human development index (HDI) the 'operational face' of Sen's capability approach which, according to him, is vulnerable to the charge of not providing an 'empirically sound' metric. He argues that 'the HDI is conceptually weak and empirically unsound, involving serious problems of noncomparability over time and space, measurement errors and biases' (1994: 241). Roemer's critiques are related to his emphasis on complete orderings and the evidence – as he sees it – that the CA does not provide a complete index of functionings. One might conclude from these critiques that *prima facie*, the approach cannot answer these criticisms and that the approach is not *usable* in practice or has been applied in a flawed way or that Sen did not attach great importance to its practical implications. But this would be a mistake.

Both Nussbaum and Sen have attached great practical importance to the CA. For instance, when discussing the conditions for an 'appropriate' approach to the evaluation of the standard of living, Sen (1987: 20) remarked that 'the approach must nevertheless be practical in the sense of being usable for actual assessments of the living standard'. Similarly, when examining the relation between his substantive claims on inequality and the CA, Sen (1992: 11) stressed that their implications 'are not only of theoretical interest, they also have some practical importance'. This feature of applied knowledge has been analysed by Nussbaum (1990, 1999), who has explained the relevance of the Aristotelian foundations of practical reason. Both have carried out empirical work from a capability perspective, analysing issues such as sex bias, gender gaps, mortality and hunger, among many others. This argument could be opposed on the grounds that Nussbaum and Sen's *claims* about the practical significance of the CA might not prove that the approach does not in fact face additional operational hurdles in comparison to the conventional use of statistics from, say, a utilitarian, libertarian, or resourcist perspective. Moreover, it is not a ready-made recipe-like answer to the problem of providing clear, practical guidelines to development practitioners (researchers, policy-makers, etc.), interested in useful, applied information. To some extent, Sen acknowledges a concern with empirical difficulties in measuring capabilities (e.g. 1985: 46 and 1992: 52). With regard to the range of relevant freedoms, he notes (1999: 24): 'The extensive coverage of freedoms is sometimes seen as a problem in getting an "operational" approach to development that is freedom-centered. I think this pessimism is ill-founded.'

But the challenge remains. Even those sympathetic with the CA have acknowledged that the operationalisation of the approach is still one of the main challenges lying ahead. For instance, Robeyns (2000: 26) has noted that 'despite the fact that Sen published *Commodities and Capabilities* in 1985, the number of *empirical applications* [emphasis added] is still quite limited' and that none of the applications she reviewed was 'using surveys which were specifically constructed to *measure* [emphasis added] functionings'. Supporters of the CA have also remarked on the difficulty in translating the approach into practice: due either to its emphasis on value judgements with high informational requirements or to its multidimensional nature. Alkire (1998: 3) observes that 'Sen has not specified how the various value judgements that inhere in his approach and that are required in order for its practical use (whether at the micro or macro level), are to be made' and that 'without some specification – and simplification – the capability approach cannot be used efficiently'. Chiappero-Martinetti (2000: 3) has argued:

Undoubtedly, the richness of such theoretical argumentation is not easy to translate into practical terms. The capability approach is certainly more demanding at an informational and methodological level if compared with more standard approaches (i.e. income or opulence-centred analysis) to well-being: it is also hard to constrain and to manage in the traditional framework of welfare and poverty analysis, if we want to fully preserve its informative and interpretative contents. These difficulties could partially explain why, up to now, there are relatively few empirical applications that have been able to capture the richness of such a perspective even if many well-being analyses conceptually refer to it.

Now, if the measurement of functionings and capabilities is to be tackled, then we must address many secondary questions that are crucial for the application of the CA. It is important to note that a measurement framework is made of: i) a set of articulated principles that allow the development of procedures and techniques for building capability indicators; and ii) measurement criteria that should be used to assess the quality of capability measurements. The translation of philosophical concepts into empirical variables needs to be faced in order to measure capabilities. This might involve re-stating the main tenets of the CA in a terminology that allows its systematic operationalisation.

Valuational foundation

Measurement of capabilities should be compatible with and informed by the principles of the CA. The CA is a framework for evaluating and assessing social arrangements, standards of living, inequality, poverty, justice, quality of life and well-being. It is not meant to be a substantive theory of these issues in the sense of offering 'the unique blueprint for "the just society"' (DF 286–287; see 254). The main purpose of the approach is to enlarge the *informational space* in normative assessments and to pass the ball to public discussion and democratic deliberation to decide questions of quality of life and justice (and their relation to other values). Thus, in comparison with other ethical approaches, the CA would include in its informational space not only opulence, utilities, primary goods and rights but also functionings and capabilities that individuals and groups have reason to value. Simply put, the valuational exercise required by the CA consists in the identification and possible weighting of valuable things that people are able to be or to do. This valuational exercise at the core of the approach brings different layers of complexity to its measurement:

a) First, it leads to a multiplicity of variables and to a plurality of relevant spaces that are, more often than not, heterogeneous.
b) Second, it requires a solution to the complex issue of the varying importance of different functionings and how people evaluate them. While many functionings can be essential and important for a 'good life', others can be trivial and valueless and even perverse.
c) Third, it requires a solution to the problem of characterising the 'agency aspect' of human life and its relation to individuals' functionings and capabilities to function.

Indeed, the elaboration of a broader informational space is not the only important element in the CA. This space should be shaped by *autonomous actions*, and it is this feature that gives the approach its name. Capabilities are more than simply a compilation of functionings. They should reflect in different degrees a person's *freedom* to live in a way that she would value. As Sen (1999: 53) puts it: 'The people have to be seen, in this perspective, as being actively involved – given the opportunity – in *shaping their own destiny*, and not just as passive recipients of the fruits of cunning development programs' [emphasis added]. Thus, capabilities should also have intrinsic value and be constitutive of a person's being. This means that not only achieved functionings are valuable but also the individual's capability to choose and discriminate among possible livings. While it is simple to argue that this emphasis on freedom or capability reflects the agency aspect of a person, trying to measure it is more difficult. Not just any increase in autonomy counts, only those that reflect an expansion of *valuable opportunities*.

The valuational exercise put forward by the CA has strong Aristotelian roots. Nussbaum and Sen (1988: 315) summarise this influence, observing that the Aristotelian process is characterised by the following features:

i) noncommensurability: treating each of the values as qualitatively distinct, irreducible to each other;
ii) essentiality of the particular: emphasising the particular contexts of choice, the individual history and cultural idiosyncrasies;
iii) role of emotions and imagination: noting the cognitive role of emotions.

Noncommensurability cannot be solved simply by multidimensional approaches to measurement. It involves an assessment of the different dimensions and the choice of appropriate techniques for this end. Multidimensional approaches are a necessary but not a sufficient condition to handle noncommensurability: procedures for solving the trade-offs, conflicts and inconsistencies between different options are needed. Most importantly, perhaps, is the essentiality of freedom for reconciling different noncommensurable aspects of well-being. As Berlin ([1958] 2002: 213–214) observes:

The world that we encounter in ordinary experience is one in which we are faced with choices between ends equally ultimate, and claims equally absolute, the realisation of some of which must inevitably involve the sacrifice of others. Indeed, it is because this is their situation that men place such immense value upon the freedom to choose; for if they had assurance that in some perfect state, realisable by men on earth, no ends pursued by them would ever be in conflict, the necessity and agony of choice would disappear, and with it the central importance of the freedom to choose.

This is indeed dramatically important when addressing the measurement of 'basic capabilities', all of which are considered essential for individuals to live humanly.

Noncommensurability adds complexity, but it should not be seen as a negative feature of the CA. As argued by Nussbaum and Sen (1988: 315): 'This commitment to the qualitative integrity of each value is one of the greatest advantages of this procedure [the CA] over other approaches that might be used (e.g. in some of the literature on development economics) in assessing traditional cultures.' Similar difficulties arise from the fact that measurement, based on the essentiality of the particular, is committed to *principles of low-levels of aggregation of data and discrimination* among different circumstances. Finally, the role of emotions seems to impose insurmountable hurdles for measuring capabilities. However, measurement based on inquiries that are 'reflectively descriptive' might be able to take into account a wide range of emotions and feelings. That is why Sen insists on a selection, weighting and sequencing exercise based on democratic processes and Nussbaum rejects trade-offs among equally valuable capabilities.

In operational terms, individual functionings might be represented by real numbers and a person's actual achievement can be expressed by a functioning vector. For instance, a vector consisting of basic and complex functionings would include being well nourished, sleeping well, psychological and bodily integrity, enjoying friendship, etc. A capability set might then be represented by alternative combinations of functioning vectors that can be achieved. Here, it would be important to represent the *agency freedom* of people. A question remains about how the identification and ranking of valuable capabilities could be measured in this framework. Sen (1992: 44) notes: 'The need for selection and discrimination is neither an embarrassment, nor a unique difficulty for the conceptualisation of functionings and capabilities.' A proper solution requires public discussion and democratic deliberation. Operationally, there are five alternatives for the evaluation of capability sets:

 i) by the value of its highest-valued element;
 ii) by their number of elements;
 iii) by combining a maximal element x with the number n of members of the set (x, n);
 iv) by the option ultimately chosen;
 v) by an *a priori* definition of a set of basic capabilities.

Sen has demonstrated how the assessment of capability sets is negatively related to their number of elements: the value of a set can be reduced when the number of elements is reduced (it is also determined by having opportunities that are not chosen) but it could not be enhanced by an increase in trivial choices (see Sen, 1992: 63). Alternatives i) and iv) and v) seem to be more suitable for the measurement of functionings. In any case, neither i) nor ii) could provide straightforward empirical counterparts for measuring capabilities. The fourth option, based on Samuelson's revealed preference approach, faces the limitation of being used only when data are observable and available. Finally, it should be emphasised that because value selection and discrimination are an intrinsic part of the CA, *a priori* specifications of capabilities should be avoided. Yet there are circumstances, such as those related to poverty assessment, where a compromise with an *a priori* assessment is possible. As argued by Sen (1992: 44–45):

> In dealing with extreme poverty in developing economies, we may be able to go a fairly long distance in terms of a relatively small number of centrally important functionings (and the corresponding basic capabilities, e.g., the ability to be well-nourished and well-sheltered, the capability of escaping avoidable morbidity and premature mortality, and so forth).

A short list of functionings can be offered as a basis for public discussion. Further discussion of procedures for measuring capabilities is required, so that the agency freedom aspect is properly reflected. There is no clear-cut method, but as presented in the empirical part of this chapter, some tested procedures might help to find a way to proceed.

Human diversity

Another important feature of the CA, with consequences for the measurement of capabilities, is its acknowledgement of a 'pervasive human diversity' in the characterisation of individuals. Sen (1992: xi, 117) qualifies this feature as an 'empirical fact' and uses it to emphasise the biased nature of a resource-based approach in the assessment of the capability that a person enjoys. There are many sources of diversity between human beings, from which Sen (1999: 70–71) identifies as the most important those concerning:

  i) personal heterogeneities (e.g., levels of education, age, health status, etc);
 ii) environmental diversities (e.g., political, related to the physical environment, etc.)
iii) variations in the social climate (e.g., local culture, norms, social capital, etc.)
 iv) differences in relational perspectives (e.g., hierarchies, job-relations, etc.)
  v) distribution within the family (e.g., concerning the equality of distribution of resources, fairness, prioritisation, etc.).

These differences will shape the degree of variations in the conversion of resources into capabilities. Consequently, because individuals are diverse, their capabilities cannot be measured alone in terms of the resources that they have available or over which they have command but need to be assessed also in terms of what they are capable of doing and being with these resources. It is important to note that in practice these sources of diversity should not be taken for granted but should be verified empirically. More concretely, they might work as *control variables* (that is, as parametric variables) in the measurement of capabilities.

It is interesting to note that Nussbaum's list of central human capabilities (see e.g. 2000, 2003) is widely used in the measurement of capabilities (see e.g. Biggeri, 2004) without consideration of the *multiple realisability* of its elements. Indeed, she calls attention to the fact that the constituents of her list based on universal principles can be manifested in a wide variety of ways. As she argues (2000: 77): 'Indeed, part of the idea of the list is its *multiple realizability*: its members can be more concretely specified in accordance with local beliefs and circumstances' [original italics]. This suggests that the measurement of central human capabilities should follow a two-stage procedure: first, with the definition of a list of universal human capabilities a group of central capabilities could be set. Second, with the principle of multiple realisability these central capabilities could be further specified according to the particular historical contexts of the societies or individuals investigated. Human diversity can therefore be respected even if one starts from a list of universal principles.

This principle has not been fully appreciated by authors such as Robeyns (2000a), who dichotomise Sen's and Nussbaum's strategies for the elaboration of capabilities lists. Robeyns (2000a: 69) argues that 'if we want to respect Sen's capability approach as a general framework for normative assessments, then we cannot endorse one definite list of capabilities without narrowing the capability approach'. But Nussbaum does not endorse 'one definite list of capabilities'. In fact, the process behind multiple realisability does not seem to be very different from what has been proposed by Sen. This is not to say that there are no other differences between Nussbaum's and Sen's versions of the CA, but simply that the 'list debate' has not entirely appreciated the principle of multiple realisability (please note that Qizilbash (2002) touches on this issue). It is, however, fair to acknowledge that Sen gives much more weight to public discussion and democratic deliberation in selecting, prioritising and specifying capabilities.

It is important to note that the use of lists could also be criticised on the grounds of being built upon an insufficient consensual basis about the nature of the 'good' for human interests. The quest for a universal account of the good, as carried out by Aristotle, might prove elusive. O'Neill (2002: 77) develops this point, arguing that:

Just as a shopping list will not *in itself* contain information that requires some purchases to be given priority over others, so a pluralistic account of human goods does not *by itself* require some goods to be respected at the expense of others.

She argues that the search for a complete account of human good with the ensuing problems in specifying priority orderings among its components is less promising than an alternative based on an account of human obligations. That is why the valuational foundation of the CA and its view on obligations or commitments is so important: it is an answer to the problem raised by O'Neill. The main issue is that sometimes all capabilities cannot be realised at once and then individuals and communities must choose. Be that as it may, different beliefs in the possibility of a universal account of human good can be translated into different strategies for measuring capabilities.

The extent of human diversity in determinate contexts will affect the selection of relevant focal variables. That is, the degree of human diversity will influence the choice of variables on which the analysis focuses and the characterisation of their plurality. As Sen puts it (1992: 3): 'The pervasive diversity of human beings intensifies the need to address the diversity of focus in the assessment of equality.' In operational terms, we could say that the degree of human diversity will influence:

i) the range of conversion rates of resources into functionings and capabilities and;
ii) the nature of the parameters (group or individual) of the conversion rates.

Thus, as far as the issue of income inequality is concerned, the consequence of human diversity can be seen not only in the variation of income-*earning* ability of individuals but also in their income-*using* ability (Sen, 1999: 119). Whereas resourcists have seen the convertibility issue simply in terms of command or access to material means, Sen has stressed the degree of ability that individuals have in transforming resources in valuable functionings.

Human diversity in the CA appears as an 'empirical fact', but in practice it is used as an assumption – of crucial importance – in the critique of the utilitarian and Rawlsian approaches. When engaging in a measurement exercise, the assumption of human diversity should be translated into an empirical hypothesis to be tested. It remains to be seen empirically how diverse human beings are within different communities and societies. Sen (1992: 117) argues: 'There are diversities of many different kinds. It is not unreasonable to think that if we try to take note of all the diversities, we might end up in a total mess of empirical confusion. The demands of practice, as well as reasonable normative commitments, indicate discretion and suggest that we disregard some diversities while concentrating on the more important ones.' Thus, the relevance of this element for measuring capabilities requires that the assumption should have the status of an empirical hypothesis or an 'empirical precondition' to be verified before the application of the approach.

The link between heterogeneity and plurality of values should not be taken for granted. Much more is needed beyond the acknowledgement of the importance of these characteristics. As emphasised by Griffin (1986: 91):

What needs defending is not the mere plurality of values but a certain important picture of how they are related – that they clash, that they all matter, that they all have their day, that there are no permanent orderings or rankings among them, that life depressingly often ties gain in one value to terrible loss in another, that persons may go in very different directions and still lead equally valuable lives – call this picture 'liberalism'.

Measurement of capabilities, in a broader sense, could provide an empirical way of finding out about these relations between different values and their heterogeneity. Simple tools such as correlation matrices might provide insights concerning the links between different values. For example, central basic capabilities (e.g. health, education, security, etc.) could be correlated with each other in order to identify possible synergies or noncommensurabilities among them.

Objectivity

Objectivity is another important characteristic, claimed by the CA, that should be considered when measuring capabilities. Sen (1987: 16) argues that 'the movement in the objectivist direction away from utility may be right' and that the assessment of living standards based on subjective criteria does not provide a reliable picture. Capabilities are best seen as objective properties of the characterisation of individuals' general and specific freedom(s) and not as subjective as individual preferences. Within this context, objectivity must be distinguished from invariance. The same capability may vary in its specification or valuation between societies but be perceived, from the analyst's perspective, as an objective reality. Thus, the use of some subjective measures (such as either some measures of well-being or happiness) to assess 'the good life' can be misleading.[3]

The problem is that the objective conditions lived by individuals can influence their perceptions of their objective realities. Sen (1992: 9–10) has argued that 'the capability perspective is more sensitive than utility-based approaches to problems of entrenched deprivation, which can lead to defensive adjustment of desires and expectations (thereby distorting the metric of utilities)'. This issue, known in the capability literature as the *adaptive preference problem*, has been extensively discussed by Elster (1982) and Nussbaum (2000, Chapter 2). It concerns the use of subjective information in capability assessments. Given the popularity of empirical investigations based on subjective assessments, it is difficult to see how the CA can avoid the adaptive preference problem when many researchers have been using surveys (based on subjective questions) to measure capabilities. In practice, as

---

[3] See Sen's (1993a) argument on 'positional objectivity'. There is no necessary contradiction between subjectivism and objective specification of HWB, as long as positional parameters that influence individuals' observation and understanding are accounted for. In this exercise, particular types of mental tendencies can be excluded, and as Sen points out (1993: 137), 'In the context of scrutinizing the subjective arbitrariness of some views, it remains necessary to examine whether those views could be made to fit positional objectivity only through parametric specifications that invoke special mental tendencies, particular types of inexperience, or constrained features of reasoning. If so, the diagnosis of subjective arbitrariness would remain relevant, no matter whether we also describe those views as positionally objective from that very special position'.

it is argued below, the adaptive preference problem demands triangulation techniques and validation questions to check the accuracy of subjective information. Elster (1982: 238) suggests that adaptive preference formation (APF) can be characterised both 'externally' and 'internally'. The external characterisation of APF has five main features: i) reversibility, distinguishing between changes that occur through preference and learning from those that result from habituation and resignation; ii) endogeneity, in the sense that some preferences are an effect rather than a cause of a restricted feasible set; iii) causality, stressing character planning and differing from deliberate manipulation of wants by other people; iv) evaluation, looking at the processes in which individuals form their preferences; and v) consequential features of preference formation processes instead of simply describing individuals' perceptions of situations. Thus, when change is induced by learning and experience, they do not qualify as 'adaptive' in Elster's interpretation. Yet when they are due to habituation and resignation, expectations are typically adaptive. It is interesting to note that the feature that distinguishes between the two mechanisms (learning vs habituation) of induced preference change is *irreversibility*. Changes such as habituation and resignation involve reversible processes, in Elster's view. In practice, an examination of the historical or dynamic aspects of the processes of capability formation might inform us of the mechanisms of adjustment and correction used by people.[4] So, measurement of capabilities needs 'history'. Other methods of handling adaptive preferences could also be considered, such as Sen's appeal to 'the nature of public participation and dialogue' in the formation of people's values and their identity (Sen, 1999: 152) or Nussbaum's characterisation of awareness processes that would provide a structure within which we can understand the universality of the constitution of human personality (Nussbaum, 2000: 155).

It must be noted that objectivity is a position-dependent characteristic. Sen, in his 1993 *Storrs Lectures on Objectivity*, develops arguments in favour of the notion of 'positional objectivity'. He argues (1993b: 142–143): 'Positional objectivity can be important for ethics as well.

---

[4] Of course, Elster's notion of adaptive preferences is different from Nussbaum's and Sen's notions. For more on that, see Teschl and Comim (2005) and Comim (2005).

The nature of moral decisions makes some positional characteristics inescapably relevant for evaluation and choice.' He criticises the idea of seeing objectivity as a form of invariance. The measurement of capabilities becomes here an issue of parametric specifications of positional characteristics, according to

  i) special mental tendencies;
 ii) particular types of inexperience;
iii) constrained features of reasoning.

These characteristics of measurement related to positional objectivity are clearly linked to the CA's feature of providing a wider informational space for normative evaluations. As Sen (1993b: 144) puts it: 'It is only because of this arbitrary insistence (that judgments of consequences be position-neutral) that consequentialism appears to fail to guide agent-relative choice of actions and accommodate agent-relative values.' This demand for objectivity is clearly influenced by Aristotle (see *Nichomachean Ethics*, Book I, Chapter 7), who believed that an internalist [meaning not merely introspection but sifting through and criticising public beliefs] inquiry was able to yield truth and objectivity in moral assessments. The idea was that an internalist inquiry [in contrast to ascending beyond human experience and history to God, natural law or Platonic forms] could result in a societal consensus able to go beyond superficial individual desires.

The objective characteristic of the CA is also intrinsically associated with its incompleteness as a practical guide to context-dependent evaluations. Commenting on Nussbaum and Sen's (1988) suggestions that the CA should introduce an objective normative account of human functioning, with a procedure for objective evaluation of functionings, Sen writes (1993: 47):

I certainly have no great objection to anyone going on that route. My difficulty with accepting that as the *only* route on which to travel arises partly from the concern that this view of human nature (with a unique list of functionings for a good human life) may be tremendously over-specified, and also from my inclination to argue about the nature and importance of the type of objectivity involved in this approach. But mostly my intransigence arises, in fact, from the consideration that the use of the capability approach as such does not require taking that route, and the deliberate incompleteness of the capability approach permits other routes to be taken which also have some plausibility [emphasis in original].

Here Sen does not seem to be concerned with objective empirical work but with rejecting the idea of universal lists as the goal or result of evaluation. Thus, the sort of objective empirical work that can be conducted from a capability perspective is bound to face the problem of defining coherence among different contexts and informational spaces. Contexts might differ according to variations in space or in time or to particularities resulting from different circumstances. The operational challenge here is how the practical nature of context definition will influence the objective nature of capabilities. This remains one of the most obscure areas in the measurement of capabilities because researchers continue addressing theoretically the problem of adaptive preferences at the same time that they continue using subjective information empirically in the measurement of capabilities (see for instance, Schischka, 2002, for a competent use of subjective information).

Counterfactual nature

Perhaps the most important (and intriguing) characteristic influencing the difficulty in measuring capabilities (through the use of empirical measures) is their counterfactual (or transfactual) nature. Sen (1982 [1980]: 359) describes the notion of counterfactual, explaining that 'it contrasts what is observed with what allegedly would be observable if something else were different'. Ultimately, capabilities are an expression of the degree of opportunities and choices open to individuals in shaping their own actions and destiny. It is not simply about the realisation of these choices. This notion appears in Sen's critique of 'desire-supported morality' in his paper 'Plural Utility', when he argues (1981: 209):

It may be noticed that a basic capability index not only shifts attention from utility to some human functions (e.g., to move freely, not to be hungry), it also shifts attention from actual performance to *capabilities* (what a person *can* do rather than what he *does* do). The entire perspective of *opportunities* as opposed to chosen positions will be missed by any desire-supported morality.

If one is serious about the distinction between functionings and capabilities then one should consider the counterfactual nature of potentialities that will define the capabilities of individuals. The distinction between functionings and capabilities is often blurred or not consistently clear in some of the work that is being carried out using the CA (see the excellent paper by Krishnakumar, 2004 as an illustration).

The point is, as Sen (1987: 1) puts it, that a person 'could have a good deal of *freedom*, without achieving much'. For instance, old people can be pretty healthy without having many choices about their health or other functionings. Capabilities could be high, but for any number of reasons individuals might choose not to realise them; or they might choose to have more of one sort of freedom than of another. Because the informational basis of evaluation in the CA incorporates counterfactual or possible choices and scenarios, it does not correspond to the informational basis that would be derived from a straightforward observation of facts. Yet we know there is a big difference between being healthy and lacking freedom to be healthy or not (e.g. if we were force fed to keep us alive).

Williams (1987: 96) has observed that Sen 'directs our attention to the idea that capability stands to functionings as the possible stands to the actual'. But how can we measure counterfactuals or unobservable variables? And how can capabilities be measured if a capability is a possibility (which can be exercised or not) and not an actuality? The solution, as proposed by Sen, seems to be linked to a close examination of the nature of the counterfactual in question and the possibility of identifying links between counterfactuals and their realisation. In his words (1992: 66):

While this may look like adding to the already heavy informational demand for analysing freedoms, it need not, in fact, make the *practical problems* of such analyses more intractable. Sometimes the nature of counterfactual choices are very easy to guess, e.g., that people would choose to avoid epidemics, pestilence, famines, chronic hunger. The elimination of these unloved things, through public policy aimed at giving people what they would want, can be seen as an enhancement of people's real freedom. In this sense, even *simple observations of realized states* may have direct relevance to the analysis of freedoms enjoyed [emphasis added].

To some extent, this strategy seems to frustrate theoretical arguments about the importance of capabilities vis-à-vis functionings (Sen, 1981: 209). If at the end of the day we are pushed into using functionings when applying the CA, then the idea of capability seems to have less practical relevance. Moreover, the idea of a counterfactual – related to the property of something that is contrary to what is observable – might be better expressed by the concept of transfactual – referring to something that may or may not be observable. Here, capabilities operate on different ontological levels: the empirical level of observed functionings vis-à-vis the level of the structures that support potentialities. It might be very difficult in practice to identify those contexts and circumstances where both counterfactuals and realised states can be approximated, because what we are free to do or be may be very different and sometimes contrary to what we in fact are doing and being. The complexity added by the counterfactual nature of capabilities is furthered by the fact that CA assessments aim to reveal aspects related to autonomous individual choices. Thus, it is not enough to report the simple counting of the number of alternatives available to individuals. Those counterfactual alternatives reflect agency and capacity of deliberation. It should also be noted, as argued by O'Neill (2002: 28), that 'whatever else people think about individual or personal autonomy they do not equate it with mere choice'. So, measurement of capabilities should address the problem of characterising autonomous choices and not just any choices (even if they are about valuable options). When people are forced to face 'tragic choices', e.g. between different central human capabilities (for instance, between drinking clean water or eating), they are far from exercising autonomous choices. Individuals are put in an unfair situation where choices involve a decrease in one of their basic capabilities.

This counterfactual feature of the measurement of the CA has important consequences for the use of available data and choice of techniques. The data needed for measuring capabilities is related to the sort of evaluation intended and to the circumstances. People in a totalitarian society may not realise their democratic capabilities but they still may have them in the sense that they could realise them in democratic contexts, due to their personal endowments. This already results in a very high level of complexity in data collection. And yet the informational basis necessary for the introduction of counterfactual choices seems to impose an even higher demand on the sort of data to be collected for the measurement of capabilities. As discussed below, new techniques will have to be deployed to match this challenge. Econometricians appear to have no difficulty in understanding the counterfactual nature of capabilities. Indeed, they equate it to the *latent* unobservable nature of some variables. For this reason, some like

Krishnakumar (2004: 7), have argued that 'capabilities by definition cannot be directly measured' and that only their respective functionings can. This would imply that 'possibilities' cannot be measured.

Thus, the four conceptual issues briefly presented above, namely valuation, diversity, objectivity and counterfactuality, shape the possibilities and the choice of alternative techniques used for measuring capabilities. More often than not they are totally ignored in capability empirical work. When this happens, the question that remains to be answered is about the real added value of the CA for fieldwork and data analysis. Thus, these conceptual issues represent difficulties that if ignored comport the risk of researchers ending up merely paying lip service to the CA – a practice that has become increasingly common in the literature.

Summing up, it should be stressed that the 'measurement challenge' is real and that the operational difficulties with the CA cannot be easily dismissed or ignored. The CA has proved itself as a successful way of philosophically articulating important dimensions related to social choice, political justice and human development. Both Sen and Nussbaum have provided comprehensive empirical examples on how one goes about using the approach, but so far no practical methodology has been put forward that could be systematically applied. 'Systematic' does not mean 'closed', impervious to individual and democratic deliberation. Rather, it consists in a systematic starting point for well-being assessments. The challenge is to link the main characteristics of the approach to a systematic but open-ended methodology to identify and assess those situations where capabilities were enhanced. Should we avoid pursuing this aim because of the open nature of the approach? Should we limit ourselves to scrutinising Nussbaum's and Sen's empirical work, searching for clues about how empirical work should be carried out? The latter seems unlikely to be a successful avenue because of the contextual feature of the approach. Techniques and methods used by both Nussbaum and Sen (in particular about India) cannot be automatically replicated in other countries. So, a more general approach for generating and handling capability data is needed. To what extent might the CA influence further empirical development work (beyond what it already has)? How do the above conceptual issues interact with the practical elements of development research? In what follows, some answers to these questions are attempted.

Part 2: practical level

The main distinction between this second set of issues and the ones in the previous section is that issues relating to data, multidimensionality, aggregation, weighting and incompleteness are common to many other approaches and are general to empirical work. Whereas some aspects of these issues have already been touched upon in the previous discussion, here they are analysed in a more concrete way in relation to the measurement of capabilities. In the practical work, both sets of issues need to be combined. A measurement framework coherent with the CA cannot ignore its main tenets and shall be able to provide solutions for practical issues, as will be discussed below.

Data

Procedures for measuring capabilities will depend on the sort of data available. It is common to find empirical applications of the CA based on secondary data that cannot go further than exploring multidimensional elements of a wide array of functionings, for example how healthy or nourished or politically active people are (see, for instance, Klasen, 2000). Undoubtedly, the collection of primary data will become more frequent as the approach develops. The absence of primary data related to capabilities should not prevent researchers from exploring capability dimensions in data that have been assembled with other purposes in mind. The difficulties in empirically defining capabilities, based on the characteristics discussed in the previous section, will pervade empirical exercises whether they are based on primary or secondary data.

According to Sen (1985: 26), the most important sources of data for the application of the CA are i) market purchase data, ii) responses to questionnaires and iii) non-market observations of personal status. For instance, in the case of health functionings, data would comprise i) medical costs, including insurance costs, ii) questionnaires involving individuals' perception of their health status or difficulties in accessing medical care and iii) nutrition or illness status. While the approaches based on utility and opulence tend to concentrate on the first and second sources, the CA makes more extensive (but not exclusive) use of the third source. When discussing international comparisons, Sen pointed out the problem of 'limitations of reliable data' (1985: 46) which he defines as the problem of 'lack of demand' for this sort of database, for non-market observations of personal status. Sen (1994) identifies two positions when handling data: the purist position and the most pressing policy problems position. Considering the scarcity of reliable primary information and its arbitrariness, Sen (1994: 318) suggests:

There is a dilemma here. There is merit in being cautious, but at the same time it is not absurd to use – with adequate warning – figures that are considered by statistical organizations which specialize in gathering and reconstructing international data to be the best estimates.

Within the position of most pressing policy problems, emphasis should be given to the *parametric variations* (factors that define the variation in parameters) in the criteria used for measurement, such as:

  i) focal variable (variable(s) chosen for the analysis);
 ii) time stretch (duration or number of time periods);
iii) relativity (other choice of parameters related to the specification of the model);
 iv) unit of aggregation (individual, household or groups).

It is important to note that formally the reference unit of the CA is the individual, but that in practice Sen quite often illustrates his approach by using group or country-level data. For instance, when discussing the existence of sex bias in India, he (1985: 52–58) presents his analysis in terms of the relative performance of different groups. Similarly, when illustrating the differences between judging poverty by income and judging poverty by capabilities (1992: 126–7), he works with data at the national level. Indeed, as Douglas and Ney (1998: 72) have observed, Sen is only formally or nominally concerned with the individual because in practice 'the measures are designed to assess the institutional support for the individual'. Therefore, there seems to be no restriction concerning the reference unit used for measuring capabilities, namely that both individual and social measures can be employed. To a certain extent, the same assessment applies to Nussbaum's work. She formally defines capabilities at an individual level and searches for measures of institutional support for them, like constitutional principles. Nussbaum (1999, 2000) delves into some life stories of Indian women and provides some hints about the sort of empirical data that one should look for in measuring capabilities, but she does not explore those avenues herself.

Sen (1992) argues that it is important to know what data would be useful in principle even though we may not be able to get it. The empirical strategy suggested consists in acknowledging the practical problems of informational availability whenever necessary and searching for practical compromises. He remarks (1992: 53):

The capability approach can, thus, be used at various levels of sophistication. How far we can go would depend on the practical considerations regarding what data we can get and what we cannot. Ideally, the capability approach should take note of the full extent of freedom to choose between different functioning bundles, but limits of practicality may often force the analysis to be confined to examining the *achieved* functioning bundle only [original emphasis].

One might wonder, however, why go to the trouble of engaging in such philosophical and conceptual effort to characterise the counterfactual elements of the CA, in particular, its capability dimension and 'agency aspect', if at the end similar results (to those of the basic needs approach, for instance) will be achieved. This *jump* in going from the CA as a philosophical framework (where capabilities are stressed) to the CA as a strategy for empirical appropriation of reality (where functionings are emphasised) unfortunately seems to be, for many at least, of secondary practical importance. Indeed, Sen (1999: 131) himself argues:

The assessment of capabilities has to proceed primarily on the basis of observing a person's actual functionings, to be supplemented by other information. There is a *jump* here (from functionings to capabilities), but it need not be a big jump, if only because the valuation of actual functionings is one way of assessing how a person values the options she has.

To emphasise, the CA has been quite convincing (if assessed by the number of academics who have already expressed their support for this approach) in arguing for the importance of broadening the informational space given by opulence or utilities, etc. to include functionings and capabilities. And yet, all the rigour applied to scrutinising alternative approaches, including, for example, Rawls's defence of the space of primary goods, seems to be lost when putting into practice the options for attaching an empirical meaning to capabilities.

It appears that the level of difficulty in measuring capabilities will depend on the level of analysis adopted. At a macro level, interpersonal differences are ignored and aggregates on mortality levels or female illiteracy will provide the same information either from a capability or from a Rawlsian perspective. The significant difference between approaches seems to rest on micro-economic studies, where the valuational foundation of the CA allows people to express their 'powers of discrimination' with regard to their well-being or to the good life. This option for microfoundations in normative assessments would not solve completely the problem of measuring freedoms or capabilities as the fundamental theoretical concept of the approach. Having to settle for an 'empirical equivalent' based on achieved functionings seems undesirable as a general strategy coherent with the main value-added by the approach.

Important issues remain to be developed about the structuring of empirical surveys. How should data be collected? What principles can be helpful here? How to choose indicators or variables? What statistical techniques are available to handle the main properties of capabilities? These and other questions, the answers to which are far from being evident, are part of any attempt to carry out primary surveys based on the CA. Some of them will be addressed in the last part of this chapter.

Multidimensionality and aggregation

Multidimensionality is one of the features of the CA most frequently explored empirically. Though not exclusive to this approach, this feature is central to Sen's critique of resources and even access to resources as sufficient indicators of well-being. The argument that 'resources are imperfect indicators of well-being' became one of the main tenets of the CA (see Sen, 1999: 80). If resources were reliable indicators of well-being, we would not need to bother about assessing directly the multidimensional aspects of and important differences among people's lives. Rather, we would simply calculate parametric variations in resources according to personal features. But multidimensionality arises also from a CA critique of the utilitarian approach that promotes an aggregative view of well-being (manifested, for instance, in cost–benefit analysis). The traditional utilitarian view dispenses with multidimensionality and plurality of spaces by focusing on preference satisfaction as the main evaluative space. Nussbaum (1990) has delved into the Aristotelian roots of noncommensurability among different values, showing how it is important to explore many aspects of human well-being. The need to take into account multidimensionality can be justified on the grounds that Rawlsian and utilitarian informational spaces[5] provide distorted metrics of well-being. Possible ways of handling multidimensionality are related to alternative options for aggregation of information.

The link between noncommensurability and multidimensionality appears in Sen's proposal for *the vector view*, back in 1981, based on a multicomponent view of utility. At that time, his aim was to reject the utilitarian calculus as a basis for judgement. The vector view would comprise:

i) nonhomogeneity among values;
ii) noncommensurability;
iii) need for value weights;
iv) moral status of weighting (moral rejection of intensity aggregates).

This view would be related to an objective understanding of aggregation. Before examining that, it is important to remark that there are two possible basic levels of aggregation required by the CA. In the absence of better names, we could call them the *horizontal* and the *vertical* levels of aggregation. We could think of a matrix where different functionings (or capabilities) are in the columns and different individuals are in the rows. In this simple scheme, horizontal aggregation would refer to aggregation of different functionings for one individual. This would imply the reduction or collapse of the multidimensional nature of functionings into one or a couple of aggregates. Alternatively, vertical aggregation would represent the total level of a particular functioning for all individuals in question. It would imply the reduction of interpersonal diversity among individuals. Both horizontal and vertical aggregation could be merged into a unique aggregate representing the general level of functionings across all dimensions for all individuals. This could be averaged to represent a more concrete picture. This figure would be equivalent to the very popular figures of GNP or GDP per capita. It is precisely in the critique against this high level of aggregation (or *conglomerative perspective* as described in the 1997 HDR) that the capability

---

[5] The response to Rawls's plurality of social primary goods and utilitarian reduction of the good to preference satisfaction must of course proceed on very different lines.

approach finds its high intersection with a human development perspective. Chiappero-Martinetti (2000: 7) notes:

In a multidimensional framework the aggregative question also becomes much
more complex because it can be conducted on different and/or subsequent
levels. First, we could be interested in moving from the space of elementary
indicators to the overall evaluation of a given functioning for each unit of
analysis; secondly, the aggregation could involve the whole set of functionings
for obtaining an overall picture of the individual or household standard of
living; finally, we could be interested in merging the individual well-being
assessments into a synthetic index of socio multidimensional well-being.

In developing countries, in particular, where inequality levels are
very high, averaging statistics does not produce very reliable indicators. In these circumstances, both levels of aggregation are achieved at
the expense of de-characterising the data. The CA's emphasis on
multidimensionality can be translated empirically into a principle of
discrimination towards low levels of aggregation with regard to heterogeneous dimensions and individuals. It is conducive to micro-studies
because it tries to isolate the individuals as the main unit of analysis. It
is also dependent on the purpose at hand, as Chiappero-Martinetti
remarked. Thus, as Sen has noted (1987: 33): 'The passion for aggregation makes good sense in many contexts, but it can be futile or
pointless in others.' Disaggregated features are important depending
on the issue to be analysed. Consequently, the degree of human
diversity and the nature of the problem at hand will define the criteria
for selection of the level of aggregation to be used.

  Horizontally, this will imply the definition of the relevant *focal
variables* to be used, that is, the definition of the variables to be focused
on by the analysis and the dimensions to be included. Vertically, this
will lead to the definition of the *unit of analysis* (individuals, households, groups, regions, countries, etc.) to be employed. Measurement
should be pursued as part of an empirical work with analytical purpose. Therefore, the choice of space, selection of particular measures
and unit of analysis would have to be made in the light of that purpose.
Sen (1999: 86) comments:

A general approach can be used in many different ways, depending on the
context and on the information that is available. It is this combination of
foundational analysis and pragmatic use that gives the capability approach
its extensive reach.

It must be noted that for Sen, vertical aggregation is not much of an issue, since he formally defines functionings and capabilities as properties of individuals. His use of other units of analysis would appear to be *derivative* rather than *intrinsic* (Sen, 1992: 117, n.1). That is, intrinsically the unit of analysis is the individual, but other unities can be defined provided that they are derived from or linked to individuals. Thus, in the case of an investigation of inequality between different groups, the interest in groups could be qualified as derivative to the extent that it informs about inequality among individuals placed in different groups – and not because the functionings and capabilities of the different groups are *intrinsically* relevant.

Sen (1992: 133) argues that, whenever desirable, plurality of spaces can be reduced by:

a) 'scrutinised' exclusion of particular elements;
b) combining or uniting elements by some evaluative procedure;
c) using *intersection partial ordering* (techniques of dominance and intersection) to select the common information given by different spaces.

Yet the argument remains that more often than not the CA privileges the study of diversity and heterogeneity instead of subsuming them into aggregates. Aggregation procedures are thus closely related to the identification of capabilities or capability deprivations. For instance, in comparing the nature of deprivation in India and in sub-Saharan Africa, Sen remarks that (1999: 103) he has 'also not attempted to produce an "aggregate" measure of deprivation, based on "weighting" the different aspects of capability deprivation. A constructed aggregate may often be far less interesting for policy analysis than the substantive pattern of diverse performances'. It follows that the CA has an inbuilt principle of discrimination towards lower levels of aggregation.[6]

Weighting and incompleteness

The valuational exercise intrinsic to the CA, whether performed by individuals or groups, consists in identifying and ranking different

---

[6] In this case, what has been called 'principle of discrimination' can be understood as a tendency for using micro, disaggregated data in characterising capability deprivation. It does not imply that one should not consider using higher levels of aggregation (for instance, in the Human Poverty Index) whenever the purpose at hand is international comparability.

valuable functionings and capabilities. This is, indeed, a demanding task. The process of deliberation and judgement involved in evaluating capability sets does not need to be comprehensive or complete for practical purposes. Weights do not need to be precisely specified to have practical significance; they can rather be confined to certain ranges or can cover merely the scope of the decision or of the judgement to be taken in a particular case.

Incompleteness is a deliberate and pragmatic element of the CA. As Sen observes (1992: 46): 'The capability approach can often yield definite answers even when there is no complete agreement on the relative weights to be attached to different functionings.' Techniques such as the *dominance partial order* and the *intersection approach* (for further information on these, see Sen, 1997) can be used without specification of weights. The purpose here is to avoid demanding a precise formulation of a problem that is complex and ambiguous. Given the multidimensional character of values and human diversity, the existence of a plurality of orderings is unavoidable. Part of the justification for adopting partial orderings in interpersonal comparisons is based on what Sen called the 'pragmatic reason for incompleteness'. This is an argument for using whatever parts of rankings are available, rather than doing nothing until a complete ranking is achieved. This argument is tantamount, in practice, to a strategy of identifying contexts in which the CA can be used, trying to draw lessons from particular experiences. In Sen's words (1999: 33):

The motivation underlying the approach of 'development as freedom' is not so much to order all states – or all alternative scenarios – into one 'complete ordering', but *to draw attention to important aspects of the process of development*, each of which deserves attention. Even after such attention is paid, there will no doubt remain differences in possible overall rankings, but their presence is not embarrassing to the purpose at hand [emphasis added].

The selection of weights is not a simple empirical issue in the CA. It is at the heart of an important methodological tenet of the approach: its participatory and democratic nature. The CA is based on a participatory principle that is associated with the process of reflective and reasoned evaluation on the part of individuals about their lives and autonomous actions and with the exercise of participation and consensus building for societies. In fact, Sen criticises the pre-selection or fixed priority principles for weights needed for evaluative judgements.

As he argues (1999: 80): 'If informed scrutiny by the public is central to any such social evaluation (as I believe is the case), the implicit values have to be made more explicit, rather than being shielded from scrutiny on the spurious ground that they are part of an "already available" metric that the society can immediately use without further ado.' However, it is not clear whether this critique would also apply to situations where epidemics, hunger, high levels of deprivation, etc. require immediate action.

To sum up, it can be argued that the measurement of capabilities can be guided by a set of principles derived from the main characteristics of the CA. There are many decisions to be made in the process of choosing data, working with multidimensional indicators, aggregating information, weighting variables and handling incomplete series of observations. The sequence of principles discussed above, related to 'pressing problems', 'discrimination towards lower levels of aggregation' and 'participation', can assist, in association with the main theoretical features of the CA, decisions on i) parametric variations of control variables, ii) handling noncommensurability, iii) choosing focal variables, iv) deciding on the unit of analysis and level of aggregation, v) applying intersection approaches or dominance partial ordering to systematise the information provided by participating individuals that contributed their normative assessments. The use of a sequence of principles is far from being a mechanical exercise. On the contrary, it largely depends on the establishment of a bottom-up framework for systematising the collection of information provided by individuals deliberating together about their capabilities. These principles are the foundation of *a* methodology (among many possible methodologies), a way of systematically proceeding in order to measure capabilities. In what follows, the last section briefly describes empirical work based on these principles and the sorts of issues faced in each particular case.

Part 3: the proof of the pudding

A brief examination of the methodology used in some empirical projects might provide a concrete illustration of the discussion on the measurement of capabilities that occupies us here, although a full description of the empirical results is beyond the scope of this chapter. Three projects were carried out using a simple methodology taking on board the issues raised in the previous discussion on the measurement of capabilities. All three projects shared a concern with applying the CA for assessing human well-being. Two projects ('Você Apita' and 'Globo Repórter') included surveys that were carried out in Brazil during 2003–2004. The other project ('UNEP – Indicators for Sustainable Consumption') involved a survey carried out in three countries, Latvia, Lithuania and Estonia, during 2004.

'Você Apita' is a project sponsored by Fiat in Brazil, as part of its corporate responsibility agenda. It is a unique project operating in more than eighteen cities and involving 26,000 school children from the poorest backgrounds, who attend deprived schools on the outskirts of large cities. These children have little access to general information through books, computers or TVs in their daily lives. The main aim of the programme is to promote children's autonomy or agency in the sense of running or being author of one's own life. So, one could not hope for a programme closer to the main purpose of CA. Interestingly enough, the programme was structured around the contributions of the Brazilian educator Paulo Freire and his concept of *Protagonismo Juvenil* (youth's autonomy or agency) that has many similarities with the CA. As part of the project, each city was allocated one or two 'field agents' to work with participating schools. The first element of the project is awareness raising about safety, environment, traffic, drugs, urban violence, etc. through talks given by NGOs, the police, the Samaritans, and so forth. After this round of awareness raising, students are invited to 'take action', to identify their most pressing problems themselves and to collectively choose a sequence of actions designed to solve these most pressing problems. The complexity of actions that children formulate and carry out is considerable. Within the framework of this project, a survey was carried out with the participation of more than 12,000 children (half of whom were the control sample in the survey). More than 900 teachers were interviewed and the views of the teams of field agents were also incorporated in the research.

The second project was planned in partnership with the Brazilian National TV programme 'Globo Repórter'. The aim of the project was to investigate how people convert resources into functionings and capabilities, one of the basic tenets of the CA. It examined the phenomenon of 'indebtedness' that afflicts the poorest individuals in developing countries. It is not difficult to find trajectories of poverty that start with an illness or an accident and that, through the mechanism of indebtedness, takes people into absolute poverty. Four hundred and fifty interviews were conducted in the city of Porto Alegre during August 2004. Individuals from all different socio-economic backgrounds were interviewed and the results of the analysis were presented in a national TV programme, with in-depth interviews showing that 'resources are an imperfect indicator of well-being': a familiar conclusion for CA researchers, but one that should not be taken for granted as if it were an assumption and not a hypothesis to be tested empirically.

The third project on 'Indicators for Sustainable Consumption', funded by the United Nations Development Programme Regional Office for Europe, involved research work about quality of life and environmental awareness in three Eastern European countries, Latvia, Lithuania and Estonia, comprising a survey with 900 interviews. Different aspects related to the use of capability indicators vis-à-vis subjective indicators and indicators of resources were explored. The project examined the links between capability and sustainability variables and the relation between choices made by individuals and their well-being. The problem of adaptive preferences was at the core of the discussions of sustainable consumption, where choices made by individuals (leading to over-consumption) are often not conducive to higher levels of well-being (in a sustainable way).

All projects were formulated following some principles and guidelines – the foundations of a methodology – that help structuring the measurement of functionings and capabilities according to the characteristics of the CA, as presented above. It is worth stressing that the steps that will be summarised below are meant to be a description of *a* methodology, with the acknowledgement that there are many other methodologies that are coherent with the main tenets of the CA. This fieldwork experience might provide useful information about the main empirical challenges to be faced in measuring capabilities. Some material from these projects is reproduced below for illustrative purposes only.

First step: anthropological exercise

In all three projects, the first step was to collect information (usually qualitative) about the views and ideas of the individuals who would be part of the survey, on the lines of the participatory principle. In the case of 'Você Apita', field agents and teachers were interviewed and teams of researchers observed some children 'in action' in classroom meetings – discussing what they considered pressing problems – and activities. Diaries (including photos, letters, exercises, etc.) produced by all groups of children during three years of the project were also studied. In the case of 'Globo Repórter', the categories of analysis were defined based on a preliminary set of pilot interviews and initial work done by the journalists. Finally, the anthropological exercise (AE) of the UNEP project was based on in-depth conversations with the local partners in the three countries. So, the degree of involvement and participation of individuals in the different AEs was not homogeneous and was subject to what was feasible in each case. The principle of pressing problems, as described by Sen (1994), guided the choice of scope in each situation.

The important point to note is that an AE is needed before structuring the empirical survey. The general aim of this exercise is to understand the categories that individuals in various contexts use in their daily normative assessments. These particular categories would then be structured in a survey to reflect different central human capabilities. This exercise of apprehending context is inherently complex and it may involve the first stages of any assessment project. This is part of a two-stage procedure where categories of analysis are first identified in each context and can later be homogenised to produce comparable results across different contexts. The categories to be used should reflect the CA's concern with reflected evaluation and participation.

Mapping out attitudes of people as expressed in their daily lives allows us to understand, as Elster (1982) has suggested, how individuals historically form their values and views. These results can be checked by using triangulation techniques (for more on that see Singleton and Straits, 1999, Chapter 13) and by collecting and comparing different views about the same reality. For instance, the people who best seem to understand poverty in developing countries are social workers or volunteers who systematically work with the poor. It is common to find them working for charities or for religious institutions. Their views can come close to those held by the Smithian 'impartial spectator', knowledgeable of the complex circumstances shaped by a sequence of historical events and not much distorted by the multiple deprivations to which the poor are subjected themselves. The AE gives a concrete meaning to the principle of discrimination, as discussed above. Figure 6.1 provides a short

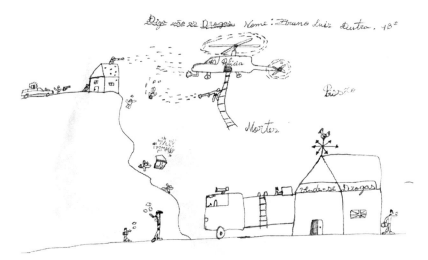

Figure 6.1 Drawing by a Brazilian child carried out as part of the anthropological exercise for 'Você Apita'

illustration of the sort of material used for the AE of the project 'Você Apita' in Brazil.

Second step: structuring the survey

In a CA survey it seems essential to translate the main tenets of the approach into empirical hypotheses. Since there is no theoretical way of finding out how to operate within a diversity of informational spaces, a survey can be structured to settle this conceptual difficulty. Questions can be organised into four categories: i) socio-economic variables (resource based); ii) subjective variables; iii) individual functionings and capabilities; and iv) social functionings and capabilities. The contents of the survey can be defined only after the AEs, setting the questions that were relevant to particular contexts and purposes of the assessment. In the case of the project 'Você Apita', the interviews with the teachers allowed further scrutiny of the problem of adaptive preferences, as if we had a fifth category of analysis consisting of 'external checks and balances' (in order to capture objective dimensions of their assessment that might be ignored by their subjective evaluations). The application of the surveys involved the elaboration of several pilot studies that resulted in the main survey after 1–3 runs of the pilots.

This could also be seen as a way of adjusting the survey to people's normative exercise: categories of analysis were changed to reflect people's evaluation procedures – but within a CA structure. The principle of participation acquires the status of a concrete strategy by combining the AE with the development of adjustment techniques. They help in defining the weighting system and the level of aggregation to be used in the formulation of indicators. In the case of 'Você Apita', surveys with children were designed following pedagogical principles and using drawings and schemes of representation. The principle of discrimination was followed in all surveys and individual positions were used to make assessments.

Third step: facing the CA tenets

A CA survey should be able to reflect people's reflective judgement. To a certain extent, this judgement is captured in the AE, when the main variables to be used are suggested from an examination of people's views. One might wonder whether these views could not be obtained directly from open questions in the survey. The problem here is that, more often than not, answers to open questions are difficult to compare. Comparability is one essential property of any indicator. However, the degree of homogeneity imposed by closed questions, without any AE, would be at odds with the bottom-up participatory nature of the CA. It is here that Nussbaum's principle of multiple realisability seems to be very helpful in linking the AE to the structuring of surveys: the AE is instrumental in defining the main categories to be used in a survey together with their particular realisations. Therefore, the particular questions that are historically and context-specific can be understood as special manifestations of a certain category. For instance, education as a general category has different levels and meanings depending on its historical and spatial context, and on the purpose of the study. The meaning of education, in poor marginalised schools in Brazil, as surveyed in the 'Você Apita' project, was related to the concrete challenges of literacy and bodily integrity in a hostile environment. In contrast, the main issue of education in Eastern Europe was related to the use of knowledge in developing choices conducive to higher quality-of-life standards. In the 'Globo Repórter' project, the particular feature of education that seemed more relevant to the problem at hand was concerned with financial awareness and information assimilation (from the media). Multiple

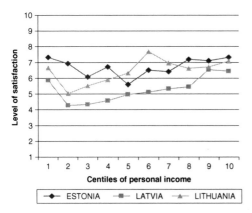

Figure 6.2 Satisfaction and personal income.
*The UNEP project compared subjective well-being with resources and capabilities. A cross-section exercise was carried out to check the correlation between different levels of income with levels of self-satisfaction

realisability is indeed an important feature of the CA (in particular in Nussbaum's version) in linking the objective nature of capabilities with its specific context-dependent meaning.

One important point to be made is that all questions in the survey were designed to be simple and straightforward. These *simple questions* were used to check empirically the relevance of different information spaces for the assessment of capabilities. Questions about subjective well-being were derived from the literature on happiness (Frey and Stutzer, 2002). An illustration of our results for the 'UNEP' survey is given in Figure 6.2.

Questions about resources were based on current living standards and measurement surveys. Questions about capabilities were designed to be i) objective and ii) normative. A ranking exercise was part of the surveys to avoid the common problem of *aggregation of irrelevant (or less important) alternatives*. In many surveys where individuals simply report their views about problems, statisticians compile the information, giving more importance to themes that are quoted more often. In this way, an irrelevant alternative (of lower importance) can be interpreted as the core issue if the evaluative exercise is based only on the frequency with which that issue is mentioned and the ranking order is ignored. For instance, three individuals providing the following assessment rankings (in decreasing order of importance) could reveal [a, b, c], [a, d, c] and [e, f, c] and the statistician could conclude that c is the most important problem due to its higher frequency. This is a common problem in current project assessment in developing countries. However, for the CA, evaluative exercises must be at the centre of the survey design. CA surveys need ranking exercises as a central part of their formulation (they can be done by individuals or communities). Aggregation should then take into account a weighting system elaborated on the basis of ranking exercises.

The counterfactual nature of the CA was dealt with in the formulation of the surveys by creating a category for 'autonomous choice' variables. In doing so, the autonomy of the individuals was assessed by categories that directly represent autonomous actions. This was certainly a short-cut, but not necessarily a bad one. Other options provided by econometrics suggest a different form of short-cut, with positive results (see Lelli, Chapter 10 this volume, Addabo *et al.*, 2004 and Krishnakumar, 2004). The questions posed in the three surveys were based on queries related to people's *attitudes* that were meant to reflect their values and degree of autonomy about particular issues. Another way of working

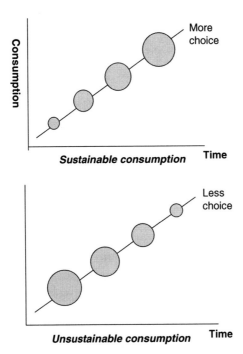

Figure 6.3 Schematic representations of counterfactuals

with the counterfactual nature of capabilities, and the (autonomous) choices that they may involve, was to try a representation of the counterfactual nature of choice affected by a latent dimension.

The above representation plots similar time trends of levels of consumption (factual) that are associated with a sequence of circles (representing a counterfactual range of a choice variable, for instance environmental problems as a proxy for an indicator affecting the intertemporal transmission of capabilities) that might be used to illustrate counterfactual dimensions not usually observed when considering only functionings. The particular underlying mechanisms affecting autonomous choices will depend on the scrutiny of particular situations. The diagrams presented here are just illustrations. In the case of the UNEP project on sustainable consumption, a simple comparison, using the Brundtland (1987) definition of sustainability, allowed the use of the environmental dimension as the counterfactual for choice. A scale was built to represent the potentiality of 'choice' based on the status of the environment. The main point here was to link the counterfactual nature of capabilities with *mechanisms of transmission*[7] of choice. In the particular case of sustainable consumption, the state of the environment represents a counterfactual mechanism of transmission between choices today and (lack of) choices in the future.

Measuring the counterfactual dimension of capabilities can be done by i) a direct identification of dimensions that reflect individuals' autonomous, reflected and critical choices or by ii) an identification of temporal dimensions involved in the process of formation of capabilities. In the latter, the measurement of capabilities might involve clarifications about the mechanisms that prevent autonomous choices. In the first perspective, a cross-section study based on simple questions about individuals' autonomous actions would be necessary. In the second perspective, a time-series or life-cycle analysis would be more appropriate to take into account age-related control variables. The autonomous choices that shape one's life can be better seen as a result of a process of evolution, including mechanisms and informational spaces that intertemporally shape individuals' opportunities.

---

[7] Mechanisms of transmission refer to the elements that intertemporally influence or determine choice behaviour. Thus, consumer choices today might affect consumer choices tomorrow, because by negatively affecting the environment today, they allow less freedom for choice in the future (or for future generations).

Fourth step: choosing indicators

The first questions that need to be answered in a CA measurement exercise are about the nature of the informational spaces used for normative assessments. Here, it is not enough to argue that capabilities are about sets of valuables 'beings and doings', because the precise mechanism for finding out these functionings could be shaped by subjective biases. A two-stage procedure as suggested by Nussbaum and Sen is required for combining *bottom-up participation* with objective information. Another question of concern is about the importance of resources in determining people's capabilities. It is reasonable to acknowledge that very poor people might be in a situation where the best informational basis for assessing their well-being is heavily influenced (e.g. due to their resignation) by their lack of resources (or entitlements), as argued by Sen (1981). The measurement of the three categories of information (resources, subjective and capabilities) allows further clarification about the importance of different informational spaces in a particular situation.

Much of the measurement work might consist in creating capability indicators based on people's valuational exercises. The benefit of using indicators lies in their (desirable) properties of being:

- measurable
- valid (measures that reflect the concept they are intended to reflect)
- reliable (stability in the use of measures that capture the same dimension)
- analytically sound
- user-friendly
- sensitive or responsive to changes in circumstances
- cost-effective
- policy-relevant
- context-dependent
- comparable (based on international consensus about their validity)
- able to articulate a world-view.

There is no single mechanism for creating capability indicators. Here, the best combination to create indicators seems to result from a compromise between conceptual clarity (indicators should reflect the concepts that they are meant to reflect – if one uses the expression 'capabilities', then one should certainly comply with the CA

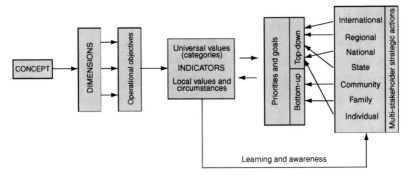

Figure 6.4 Building capability indicators: bringing together concepts and priorities and goals

measurement characteristics) and multi-stakeholder priorities and goals (in the case of capabilities, variables should reflect autonomous normative views). Indicators should also reflect different spatial and temporal scales. Figure 6.4 shows a simplified version of this 'compromise' between investigators and people's deliberations.

When deciding on measurement scales, a whole range of possibilities is open for building indicators involving i) nominal vs interval vs ordinal vs cardinal scales, ii) complete vs partial orderings, iii) the number of response categories, iv) options of codification, v) options for transforming scales (by using e.g. logs) among other possibilities. Reliability and validity tests, as put forward by Singleton *et al.* (1993: 113–129), can also be considered. The process of choosing indicators is influenced by the principles discussed above. The participatory principle is translated into guidelines emerging from multi-stakeholder strategies. The principle of discrimination is used when adapting general capability categories to local values and circumstances. Finally, the principle of pressing problems can help shape the operational objectives of the indicators. Indicators can then be formulated following the main CA features.

Fifth step: statistical analysis

The multidimensional nature of the CA invites the use of a wide array of multivariate techniques, such as ANOVA (analysis of variance), MANOVA (multivariate analysis of variance), factor analysis, cluster analysis, principal component analysis, SEM (structural equation modelling often known as LISREL), fuzzy sets and MIMIC (multiple indicators and multiple causes). These distinct methods differ in the type of measurement scales and on the assumptions they make about the nature of the associations between the different measures and their causal links. Most of the methods currently used for measuring capabilities (e.g. considered by Lelli, Chapter 10 this volume, Ruggeri Laderchi, Chapter 7 this volume, Chiappero-Martinetti, 2000, Krishnakumar, 2004 and Addabo *et al.*, 2004) are based on the assumption of interdependence among the variables. For a recent discussion of the use of these methods in estimating capability functions, see Krishnakumar (2004).

It is important to note that not all surveys need to go through econometrics or multivariate statistical analysis. Qualitative and quantitative indicators can provide valuable direct descriptive evidence about functionings and capabilities (for a good illustration see Biggeri, 2004). In the surveys described above, the 'Você Apita' project (carried out in 2005) was analysed through an econometric study that compared its results by using factor analysis, SEM and MIMIC; for the other two surveys the results of the measures have been reported descriptively. Further econometric analysis of the UNEP project data is under way.

Sixth step: reconciling two levels of analysis

Sen (1999: 81) makes a distinction between two different levels of analysis, namely the foundational level and the practical level. He often keeps these two levels apart, arguing that the imperfections involved in the practical compromises needed to operationalise the CA do not interfere with the truth of the arguments put forward in its support. He suggests that the theoretical merit of the CA does not automatically imply a follow-up with the use of empirical measures based on capabilities. Because the CA follows a context-dependent logic, it can be used in a variety of ways and no sacrosanct empirical formulation should predominate over others. (Indeed, empirical applications might not be even necessary in some contexts.) Sen (1999: 81–83) discusses three alternative practical approaches to the CA, namely i) the direct approach (direct comparison among vectors of functionings and capabilities involving a) total comparison, b) partial ranking or c) distinguished capability comparison),

ii) the supplementary approach (complementing traditional income comparisons with capability considerations) and iii) the indirect approach (adjustment of income based on capabilities). The choice of approach will depend on how the foundational and the practical level are combined. This choice will be *ex-ante* part of the survey design and *ex-post* will lead to some practical adjustment about the best way of linking the survey results with the conceptual arguments behind the project. It will depend on the context and purpose of the application of the CA. The notion of *practical compromise* seems to be part of Sen's argument for the choice of strategy and articulation of the foundation and practical levels. As he puts it (1999: 84–85):

Each of these approaches has contingent merit that may vary depending on the nature of the exercise, the availability of information, and the urgency of the decisions that have to be taken. Since the capability perspective is sometimes interpreted in terribly exacting terms (total comparisons under the direct approach), it is important to emphasize the catholicity that the approach has. The foundational affirmation of the importance of capabilities can go with *various strategies* of actual evaluation involving *practical compromises* [emphasis added].

Each evaluation strategy will have its own context purpose-dependent methodology, shaped by spatial and temporal considerations and unpredictable patterns of normative views defined through participatory mechanisms. Guidelines based on these broad remarks might provide an accurate picture of the real processes of measurement, but they seem to be too general to be useful in an instrumental way. Be that as it may, the last stage of the three empirical surveys presented above consisted in the reconciliation of empirical results with theoretical tenets and deciding on practical compromises about the best portfolio of evaluation strategies.

Concluding remarks

The objective of this chapter has been to examine some issues regarding the measurement of capabilities. It was argued that the solution for apparently unsolvable measurement problems entails the use of the main foundational characteristics of the CA. The analysis was divided into three parts. The first part examined the conceptual level of measurement, where the main features of the CA were briefly described. These features are important: they are the ones that allow the insights of the approach to be translated into capability results. Measurement without them might result in merely paying lip service to the CA, without actually using it. The second part of the chapter explored the empirical level of measurement, bringing into the discussion some general issues of data availability, aggregation, weighting and incompleteness. The last part of the chapter illustrated how some features of the capability space were translated into strategies and methodological decisions.

The chapter argued that the main features of the CA can help shape a measurement framework conducive to capability analyses. Measurement criteria cannot (and should not) be applied mechanically to capability assessments. Rather, they should follow practical considerations related to a series of principles and the relevant purpose of a particular evaluative exercise – including a strong role for participation of those being investigated.

Cited references

Addabo, T., Di Tommaso, M. L. and Facchinetti, G. (2004) 'To what extent fuzzy set theory and structural equation modelling can measure functionings? An application to child well-being,' *Proceedings of the 4th Capability Conference, Pavia*, 5–7 September.

Aristotle. 'Nichomachean Ethics'. In: Ackrill, J. L. (1987) *A New Aristotle Reader*. Oxford: Clarendon Press.

Berlin, Isaiah ([1958] 2002) 'Two Concepts of Liberty.' In: Berlin, Isaiah (2002) *Liberty*. Oxford: Oxford University Press, pp. 166–217.

Biggeri, M., Libanora, R., Mariani, S. and Menchini, L. (2006) 'Children Conceptualizing their Capabilities: Results of a Survey Conducted during the First Children's World Congress on Child Labour.' *Journal of Human Development* 7(1): 59–83.

Brundtland, H. (1987) *Our Common Future – The Brundtland Report*. Oxford University Press (for the World Commission on Environment and Development).

Carter, I. (1999) *A Measure of Freedom*. Oxford: Oxford University Press.

Chiappero-Martinetti, Enrica (2000) 'A Multidimensional Assessment of Well-Being Based on Sen's Functioning Approach.' *Rivista Internazionale di Scienze Sociali* 108: 207–39.

Comim, Flavio (2005) 'Capabilities and Happiness: Introductory Remarks'. *Review of Social Economies*, June.

Comim, Flavio (2001) 'Richard Stone and Measurement Criteria for National Accounts.' In: Klein, Juday and Morgan, Mary (eds.) (2001)

The Age of Economic Measurement. London: Duke University Press, pp. 213–234.

Douglas, Mary and Ney, Steven (1998) *Missing Persons: A Critique of Personhood in the Social Sciences*. London: University of California Press.

Elster, Jon (1982) 'Sour Grapes –Utilitarianism and the Genesis of Wants'. In: Sen, Amartya and Williams, Bernard (1982) *Utilitarianism and Beyond*. Cambridge: Cambridge University Press.

Frey, Bruno and Stutzer, Alois (2002) *Happiness and Economics*. Princeton: Princeton University Press.

Griffin, James (1986) *Well-Being*. Oxford: Clarendon Press.

Klasen, Stephen (2000) 'Measuring Poverty and Deprivation in South Africa'. *Review of Income and Wealth*, 46, 1, March.

Krishnakumar, Jaya (2004) 'Going Beyond Functionings to Capabilities: An Econometric Model to Explain and Estimate Capabilities'. Proceedings of the IV International Capability Conference, Pavia, Italy.

Nussbaum, M and Sen, A (1988) 'Internal Criticism and Indian Rationalist Traditions'. In: Krausz, M. (ed.) *Relativism: Interpretation and Confrontation*. University of Notre Dame Press.

Nussbaum, Martha (1990) *Love's Knowledge: Essays on Philosophy and Literature*. Oxford: Oxford University Press.

Nussbaum, Martha (1999) *Sex and Social Justice*. Oxford: Oxford University Press.

Nussbaum, Martha (2000) *Women and Human Development: The Capabilities Approach*. Cambridge: Cambridge University Press.

Nussbaum, Martha (2003) 'Capabilities as Fundamental Entitlements: Sen and Social Justice.' *Feminist Economics*, 9(2/3): 33–59.

O'Neill, Onora (2002) *Autonomy and Trust in Bioethics*. Cambridge: Cambridge University Press.

Qizilbash, Mozaffar (2002) 'Development, Common Foes and Shared Values'. *Review of Political Economy*, 14(4): 463–480.

Robeyns, Ingrid (2000a) 'An Unworkable Idea or a Promising Alternative? Sen's Capability Approach Re-examined.' In: *Center for Economic Studies Discussion on Paper 00.30*. Unversity of Leuven, mimeo.

Roemer, John (1996) *Theories of Distributive Justice*. Cambridge: Harvard University Press.

Schischka, J. (2002) 'The Capabilities Approach as a Metric for Economic Development: An Application in Nepal'. Conference Proceedings: 'Promoting Women's Capabilities: examining Nussbaum's Capabilities Approach' 9–10 September. Von Hugel Institute, St Edmund's College Cambridge. http://www.ctedmunds.cam.ac.uk/vhi/sen/program1.shtml.

Sen, Amartya (1999) *Development as Freedom*. Oxford: Oxford University Press.

Sen, Amartya (1998) 'Mortality as an Indicator of Economic Success and Failure'. *Economic Journal*, 108: 447, pp. 1–25.

Sen, Amartya K. (1997) *On Economic Inequality*. Oxford: Clarendon Press.

Sen, Amartya (1994) 'Economic Regress: Concepts and Features'. *Proceedings of the World Bank Annual Conference on Development Economics*. Washington: The World Bank.

Sen, Amartya (1993a) 'Capability and Well-Being'. In: Nussbaum, Martha and Sen, Amartya (1993) *The Quality of Life*. Oxford: Oxford University Press.

Sen, Amartya (1993b) 'Positional Objectivity.' *Philosophy and Public Affairs*, 22(2): 126–145.

Sen, Amartya (1992) *Inequality Reexamined*. Oxford: Oxford University Press.

Sen, Amartya (1987) 'The Standard of Living'. In: Sen, A. K., Muellbauer, J., Kanbur, R., Hart, K. and Williams, B., *The Standard of Living: The Tanner Lectures on Human Values*. Cambridge: Cambridge University Press.

Sen, Amartya (1985) *Commodities and Capabilities*. Oxford: Oxford University Press.

Sen, Amartya (1981) 'Plural Utility'. *Proceedings of the Aristotelian Society*, 80, 1980–1.

Sen, Amartya (1980) 'Equality of What?' In: Sen, Amartya (1982) *Choice, Welfare and Measurement*. Cambridge: Harvard University Press.

Singleton, Royce A., Straits, Bruce C. and Miller Straits, Margaret (1993) *Approaches to Social Research*. New York: Oxford University Press.

Singleton, Royce and Straits, Bruce (1999) *Approaches to Social Research*. Oxford: Oxford University Press, third edition.

Srinivasan, T. N. (1994) 'Human Development: A New Paradigm or Reinvention of the Wheel?' *AEA Papers and Proceedings*. Vol. 84, n. 2, pp. 238–243.

Sugden, Robert (1993) 'Welfare, Resources, and Capabilities: A Review of *Inequality Reexamined* by Amartya Sen'. *Journal of Economic Literature*, Vol. 31, n. 4, pp. 1947–1962.

Teschl, Miriam and Comim, Flavio (2005) 'Adaptive Preferences and Capabilities: Preliminary Considerations'. *Review of Social Economies* June.

Williams, Bernard (1987) 'The Standard of Living: Interests and Capabilities'. In: Sen, A. K., Muellbauer, J., Kanbur, R., Hart, K. and Williams, B., *The Standard of Living: The Tanner Lectures on Human Values*. Cambridge: Cambridge University Press.

Ysander, Bengt-Christer (1993) 'Robert Erikson: Descriptions of Inequality'. In: Nussbaum, Martha and Sen, Amartya (1993) *The Quality of Life*. Oxford: Clarendon Press.

PART II

Measures

7 Do concepts matter? An empirical investigation of the differences between a capability and a monetary assessment of poverty

CATERINA RUGGERI LADERCHI[1]

This chapter aims to evaluate the empirical consequences of the theoretical debate on the nature of poverty, focusing in particular on the differences between Sen's capability approach and the mainstream monetary approach. Such an analysis provides a constructive link between theoretical debates and the practice of poverty assessments. In fact, if at the empirical level the association between alternative indicators of deprivations is so strong that different approaches appear as approximately equivalent, the policy relevance of the theoretical debates on the concepts of poverty is greatly diminished. We will explore whether this is really the case with reference to Peru. Beginning with a brief review of Sen's capability approach and its critique of standard monetary-based assessments of poverty, a framework for comparing capability-based and consumption-based approaches is suggested. Our results are then presented, aiming at identifying the relationship between monetary resources and individual achievements by testing for the significance and size of the 'parametric variations' at the core of Sen's argument against identifying poverty with monetary indicators. The findings are, however, also helpful to

[1] The World Bank. The findings, interpretations and conclusions expressed herein are those of the author and do not necessarily reflect the views of the executive directors of the Internationl Bank for Reconstruction and Development/The World Bank or the governments they represent. This work was undertaken as part of my doctoral research while at St Antony's College, Oxford University. The attentive supervision and continuous support of my then supervisor Professor Frances Stewart is gratefully acknowledged, as are the useful comments received at various stages of the work by Pedro Francke, Jesko Hentschel, Taimur Hyat, John Knight, Jaime Saavedra, and Rosemary Thorp and Moises Ventocilla. The usual disclaimers apply.

think of policy priorities in a capability perspective as opposed to a monetary one, as well as for identifying issues on which more work is needed in order to enhance the ability of the capability approach to inform policies.

Introduction

Poverty as a category is hard to define. The word brings to mind a situation of living in 'obvious want and squalor', as already recognised in the definition adopted by Rowntree (Rowntree 1902; Veit-Wilson 1986) in what is acknowledged to be the first scientific analysis of the phenomenon. Nevertheless, the questions of 'with respect to which standard', 'measured in which space' and 'with whose criteria' want and squalor should appear 'obvious' do not lend themselves to straightforward answers, especially if aiming at a definition which might hold across different contexts and time. Monetary measures are generally adopted as they offer apparently straightforward answers to these questions and are widely accessible now due to the large availability of household surveys. But are monetary measures capturing the essence of poverty? And more fundamentally, do they offer the only perspective which might inform policies?

Thorough critiques have exposed the strong assumptions underlying standard monetary-based assessments of poverty (e.g. Townsend 1970, Sen 1983, Chambers 1995), but despite widespread awareness of the main themes of the debate, it is still true that '(e)conomists usually prefer income (or consumption) based measures of poverty' (Baker and Grosh 1994, p. 3). As the choice of any particular concept of poverty is not value-free, and as such cannot be portrayed as a unique and objective representation, it is important to explore alternative concepts and to evaluate whether their adoption translates into different assessments of poverty. This chapter tries therefore to provide a constructive link between the theoretical debate and the practice of poverty assessments by evaluating empirically the differences between an assessment conducted according to standard monetary metric practices and one based on deprivation in basic capabilities.

Is it really the case that at the empirical level the association between alternative indicators of deprivations is so strong that different approaches are approximately equivalent? We will explore the question with reference to Peru. This analysis entails both checking how far different pictures of poverty overlap and trying to understand why. To do so, in part one we will briefly review Sen's concept of capability deprivation, in part two we will discuss how this approach can be compared with standard monetary assessments and present the methodology we are going to adopt. In part three we will then present our empirical analysis, based on Peruvian household data (ENNIV 1994). In part four the relevance of this analysis for policy making will be discussed, and a final section will conclude.

Poverty as capability deprivation

Sen's critiques of the standard practice of measuring poverty build on a critical assessment of the utilitarian assumptions on which the use of the monetary based approach is based[2] and of the claim that poverty consists of a lack of economic welfare (e.g. Lipton and Ravallion 1995). These critiques show how imperfect a proxy for welfare utility is and point to the need for an alternative definition of wellbeing and poverty based on what individuals can do and be in their lives.[3] On this

---

[2] The use of monetary indicators, of income in particular, is at times justified on the basis of right-based arguments. In this sense there is a similarity with Sen's perspective, even though Sen's concern for positive freedom still leaves monetary indicators (if used in a 'sufficiency' rather than in an 'adequateness' perspective) open to the same kind of criticism about 'parametric variations' which will be illustrated below.

[3] More specifically, Sen claims that: (a) the significance of utility maximisation can be questioned as only a 'rational fool' would apply the same criterion to two issues as different as determining market choices and defining one's own wellbeing; (b) market choices might be determined by other factors than pure utility maximisation (as shown, for example, by Prisoner's Dilemma kinds of interactions); (c) even if the utility outcome was the only thing that mattered for the individual, that outcome could be determined by different blends of individual characteristics and objective situations. If utility stands for desire fulfilment or happiness, then both the 'physical-condition neglect' (i.e. the focus only on the mental disposition of a person and not on what that person can do) and the 'valuation-neglect' (i.e. the fact that valuation might be conditional on what appears as reasonable or possible) may affect individual valuation in ways which someone attempting an objective valuation of wellbeing would not subscribe to. Note that the alternative definition of utility as mere description of choices without reference to the underlying psychological conditions, i.e. the revealed preference definition of utility, is even weaker in providing a basis for ethical judgement. In fact, if choice between two options is not linked to an individual attaching any particular value to one choice compared with the other, that choice does not provide any ground for attributing to the chosen option any greater

basis, Sen suggests an alternative conceptualisation in which 'well-being of a person is best seen as an index of the person's functionings' (Sen 1985, p. 25) where the functionings represent the 'doing and beings' of an individual, and where the set of alternative functionings available to the person constitutes his capability set.

This particular conceptualisation of wellbeing lends itself to the analysis of poverty seen as 'capability deprivation' (Sen 1997, p. 210). Poverty, therefore, is not about having insufficient income or consumption, it is about not being able to live a valuable life. In particular, poverty is defined with respect to those capabilities which can be labelled 'basic' in that they entail satisfying certain 'elementary and crucially important functionings up to a certain level' (Sen 1992, p. 45) and in that their fundamental role in determining wellbeing can be largely agreed upon. A list of some basic capabilities for poverty measurement is suggested to include being adequately nourished, leading a long and healthy life, being literate (as a source of access to knowledge and communication or perhaps as the result of a structured and social process of learning) and avoiding homelessness. These are likely to be recognised as part of the absolutist core of needs and agreement can be reached without specifying particular commodity bundles and particular ways of achieving functionings (Sen 1992). Furthermore, this list is encompassed in other lists of fundamental capabilities, such as the one put forward by Nussbaum (1999).[4]

As far as the choice of indicators that can be used for poverty analysis is concerned, it is important to stress that this approach emphasises that: (1) ' the connection [of poverty] with lowness of income is only instrumental;[5] (2) there are influences on capability deprivation *other*

---

social value (Sugden 1993); (d) wellbeing and welfare are different as the former pertains only to purely self-seeking behaviour and the latter includes also the consideration of agency (which includes other goals, values and ideals that are important in individual life despite not increasing an individual's wellbeing); in a welfare assessment one should include also what an individual can do ('advantage') and not only what the individual does.

[4] Note, however, that as discussed below, Nussbaum's language is not identical to Sen's, in particular on the connotation to be given to the 'basicness' of basic capabilities.

[5] In this approach monetary resources play only an instrumental role as they are an input in the capability production function, rather than an intrinsically valuable quantity (or, by extension, a quantity whose relation with the quantity of value is uniform for all individuals, as for example in a utilitaristic approach in which all individuals have the same utility function).

than lowness of income; and (3) the instrumental relation between low income and low capability is *parametrically variable* between different communities and even between different families and different individuals' (Nussbaum 1999, p. 211). The emphasis is, therefore, on indicators which might directly capture the level at which a given functioning is (or could be) achieved rather than on monetary measures.

Despite the success of these ideas in shifting the terms of the debate on poverty, there seems to be a hard-to-defeat implicit assumption by practitioners that the role played by monetary resources in determining shortfalls in capabilities is so central that they can act as proxies for them. In other words, it is assumed that monetary indicators can capture the essence of poverty by driving all the other dimensions of deprivation. This type of consideration seems, however, not to be limited to the ability of monetary resources to capture deprivation in terms of capability, as it extends to the relatively little attention which has been paid generally to operationalise broad and multidimensional concepts of poverty (such as the one adopted by the Social Summit in 1995, WSSD 1995). The following quote well illustrates the point: 'Being poor is related to a wide range of factors including income, health, education, access to goods, geographical location, gender, ethnic origin, and family circumstances. It is difficult to measure poverty in such a way as to capture its multidimensional nature, but a commonly used measure of poverty is the income or consumption of individual or households' (World Bank 1996, p. 2).

It seems to us, however, that unless it is proven that income or consumption can really do a good job in capturing all the other relevant dimensions of deprivation, the need to develop new indicators of poverty cannot be ruled out. Further, the idea that one indicator captures effectively the core of deprivation seems to be closely associated with a disregard for the circumstance that different dimensions of deprivation might call for different types of intervention, and that it is not guaranteed that a policy will have a synergetic effect on all aspects of deprivation.

Comparing alternative approaches to poverty measurement

Different concepts of poverty are based on assumptions and values which, as such, are not amenable to empirical testing. One might, however, test whether adopting indicators such as those suggested by Sen's analysis provides us with a different assessment and understanding of poverty than a money-metric one.

Not many studies in the literature have explored this type of issue. Among them, a paper by Gertler and Van der Gaag (1990) tested the extent to which those who are poor under one definition are classified as poor also by other definitions using data from Côte d'Ivoire. Their approach was based only on tests of association between different indicators and did not tackle the question of why the realities captured by different definitions differ and which are the consequences of those differences for policy. Further, Chaudhuri and Ravallion (1994) point out how purely statistical measures of associations conceal important value judgements. Considering the percentages correctly identified and exposing the kind of targeting errors made seems to us, therefore, a more useful approach than calculating measures of association as one can explicitly consider the value judgements required to evaluate the trade-offs entailed by the choice among indicators. In the case of Gertler and Van der Gaag (1990), these value judgements are reinforced by the fact that, despite the results of their tests of association, the authors seem to judge the indicators on the basis of the total percentage of cases ranked consistently with one preferred indicator (i.e. equivalent per capita consumption).[6]

An interesting example of comparison between indicators of poverty explicitly rooted in a capability framework is Klasen's (2000) analysis of monetary and non-monetary deprivation in South Africa. The latter was measured with a deprivation measure obtained by aggregating indicators of 'basic capabilities as well as stated priorities in the population' as identified by the questionnaire. Apart from presenting a methodology for the construction of aggregate indicators of non-monetary deprivation, the paper is particularly interested in exploring the correlates of different types of deprivation to discuss the relation between such an aggregate measure and a standard monetary poverty

---

[6] In urban areas only anthropometric indicators seem to be picking up significantly different (in statistical terms) people, while in rural areas the food ratio (the percentage of household expenditure devoted to food) and per capita floor area also appear to be uncorrelated with the preferred measure. As the other measures are not picking up different people according to their test, then any other (as for example adult school attainment) could be used instead of the preferred one (i.e. consumption per equivalent adult).

measure. From the comparisons of how the two types of indicators identify poverty, in fact, important differences in identifying the poorest of the poor emerge, with clear relevance for targeting purposes. Note, however, that in this paper the adoption of a composite indicator prevents him from trying to model the causes of non-monetary deprivation, so that his multivariate analysis remains descriptive in nature and allows him only to describe the characteristics of those who are deprived rather than attempting to explain why they are deprived.

In contrast with those other studies in this paper, as already mentioned, we are not interested only in assessing whether there is a significant discrepancy in the way the approaches suggested by different indicators identify the poor but also in understanding why this is the case and which consequences for policy these differences entail. The investigation of the 'why' question is central to our analysis as Sen has put forward a clear explanation of what drives the difference between assessing poverty by focusing on means (such as monetary resources) and ends (basic capabilities) as indicators of poverty, and it is this causal link which we are explicitly going to test.

Referring to how the capabilities approach has been formalised (Sen 1985) allows us to illustrate the role played by the parametric variations between individuals in the claim that a focus on monetary resources is inappropriate to capture capability deprivation. A simple representation of the way resources are mapped into functionings is provided by the following production function for the achievement b and the individual i living in household h (composed by him and other o members):

$$b_i = f_i(c(x_i(y_h, t_i, t_o, d_h, z_h, l)) + \varepsilon_i$$

with $f_i \in F_i$ and $F_i = [f_i | f_i = (t_i, t_o, d_h, z_h, l)]$ and where y_h is a measure of household resources, t_i is a set of individual characteristics, t_o represents a set of characteristics of other members of the household, d_h is a set of demographic characteristics of the household, z_h is a set of public goods available to the household, l is a location variable capturing other area-specific influences. These factors influence the basket of goods and services (x)[7] whose characteristics (extracted by c) are then combined according to one of the utilisation functions (f) available to

---

[7] Note that this statement aims explicitly at leaving indeterminate the choice mechanism leading to the goods and services consumed, as in line with the whole

the individual. ε_i is an individual specific error term which we assume to be normally and identically distributed.

As b_i is just one of the possible achievements which individual i can achieve in terms of a given capability, the empirical analysis of capabilities production functions seems daunting. The estimation can, however, be simplified when analysing poverty, as we consider basic capabilities which entail satisfying 'elementary and crucially important functionings up to a certain level' (Sen 1992, p. 45). At the basis of the concept of basic capabilities, in fact, is the idea that some minimal level is deemed to be of intrinsic importance. This implies that an individual able to reach levels of functioning above that minimal level would do so because of the inherent importance of that level of achievement. In other words, when focusing on basic capabilities we can reduce a measure of *freedom to achieve* to a measure of *achievement*.[8]

In terms of our implicit capability production function this implies that for a given basic capability b^*_i, we can define a b_{line} as the intrinsically valuable minimal level in the given dimension and set

$$b^*_i = 1 \text{ if } b_i \supset b_{line}$$

$$b^*_i = 0 \text{ if } b_i \subseteq b_{line}$$

where b_{line} is an appropriately specified 'crucial level'.

This formulation implies that the relation between resources and basic capabilities can be easily estimated with limited dependent variable techniques. In this way we can test for the existence, size and significance of differences between individuals with different characteristics, belonging to different kinds of households and living in locations with different access to public goods. As these differences drive the parametric variations which Sen claims distort a picture of

---

capability approach we are not assuming that such choice is necessarily utility maximising.

[8] An alternative way of looking at this issue, though one grounded on a somewhat different perspective, is the classification by Nussbaum (e.g. Nussbaum 2000) of different types of capabilities. She contrasts basic capabilities (i.e. 'the innate equipment of individuals that is the necessary basis for developing the more advanced capabilities, and a ground of moral concern', p. 84) with internal capabilities (i.e. 'developed states of the person herself that are, so far as the person herself is concerned, sufficient conditions for the exercise of the requisite functions') and combined capabilities (i.e. internal capabilities *combined with* suitable external conditions for the exercise of the function').

deprivation based on monetary resources, this procedure allows us to test whether this distortion exists. Further it allows us to highlight which factors particularly limit individual achievement of basic capabilities – this last one of key importance for the identification of poverty reduction interventions. Finally, the limited dependent variable models we adopt to estimate the production function for the functioning b_i illustrated above can be seen as equivalent to estimating a conditional demand functions (Behrman 1990). This similarity will provide us with useful guidance in the analysis, as well as with terms of comparisons for the results, even if we do not share in the utility-maximising assumptions from which these models are generally derived.

Choosing indicators of basic capabilities

Before presenting our empirical results, there are two important questions that need to be addressed: the choice of basic capabilities and of indicators. As far as the first choice is concerned, a very minimalist view is taken here of which 'elementary and crucially important functionings' are to be chosen, focusing only on health and education.[9] Our pragmatic choice of capabilities glides over the ethical question of what makes a life valuable, but this does not make our empirical analysis irrelevant, given that our concerns lie in the fungibility of indicators and provided that health and education are at least part of any concern with deprivation in basic capabilities.

The choice of the indicators of deprivation to use in this type of analysis deserves careful scrutiny. Our concern has been to reconcile data availability with consistency with Sen's model. A first criterion for the selection has therefore been to choose available indicators that truly represent functionings, i.e. that represent individual achievements.[10] It has already been mentioned that we take health and education to be valuable in themselves. One needs, however, to decide which among the possible indicators of these dimensions can be taken to identify an

---

[9] These two capabilities seem to command widespread consensus in the literature (e.g. Doyal and Gough 1991) and are seen as central in the consensus interpretation of Sen's ideas, emerging both from his writings and in the way his ideas have been popularised indirectly in the human development paradigm (e.g. UNDP 1990).

[10] Access variables, such as distances to given amenities, for example, have been excluded.

elementary and crucial functioning, and where to set the line between adequacy and deprivation. The two issues are actually intertwined, as by choosing an indicator one is also often implicitly setting the extent of deprivation: depending on the indicator (e.g. primary school attendance vs. secondary school attendance) chosen, one is implicitly deciding for how many people deprivation in that respect will be binding.[11]

One simple solution to both the problem of identifying the lower end and of identifying one or more indicators for a given basic capability is to select for each capability an indicator which identifies a non-negligible proportion of the population as deprived in a given dimension.[12] This procedure, however simple, anchors our definition of deprivation to the more constraining aspects of each basic capability within the context analysed. It seems reasonable to assume that, of the many possible aspects of each capability, not all might prove equally constraining for individuals living in different contexts.[13] This way of

---

[11] Note that the issue of the definition of the lower end applies also to monetary indicators. We will not debate this issue explicitly, but we will rely on the poverty line which is mostly used in the recent literature on Peru. We are in fact aiming at comparing the capacity of poverty measurement as generally performed to capture deprivations in other dimensions.

[12] Other solutions could, in contrast, centre on synthesising the information conveyed by several indicators of one capability into a composite indicator (for example, by factor analysis or by using fuzzy aggregation), or on using correlational analysis (used quite often in the literature, see for example McGranahan 1972 discussing indicators of development and using correlations as a validation criterion). These statistical techniques aim, in fact, at identifying the single indicator within a given dimension which captures more of the information carried by the others. The importance of that indicator then lies in it being tightly interdependent with other aspects of the same phenomenon which has to be measured. We have no problem, however, in acknowledging that different indicators capture different aspects of the same capability as we try to identify the one whose deprivation is more binding in a given context. Further, these alternative ways of operationalising the measurement of each capability are more data intensive, which can complicate matters even more considering that, as also discussed below, different indicators recorded in our data might be group specific, so that aggregation of different aspects might blur the type of deprivation being recorded and the identification of the determinants (as opposed to simple correlates) of the deprivation itself.

[13] One could, of course, question whether this way of proceeding implies that the 'objective core' defining human wellbeing is in this view exceedingly relativised. This does not seem to involve, however, a greater extent of contextualisation of the analysis (though admittedly one 'external' to the objects of the analysis, rather than arising from their opinion) than the need to reach an informed

proceeding at the same time keeps our sample size for empirical estimation of reasonable size for reliable inference.

Following these criteria and the literature discussing strengths and weaknesses of various indicators,[14] we considered as indicators of capability deprivation[15] morbidity and – for the subsample of children aged 12–15[16] – failure to reach functional literacy (four years of schooling). This analysis deals therefore with both a group-specific and a more universal indicator of deprivation. At the same time it is insensitive to other differentiations among groups of individuals (the most obvious being gender). Some of the characteristics on the basis of which individuals are differentiated will be considered in our analysis as factors which can potentially affect the way resources are translated into capabilities. At the same time, it is worth acknowledging that some of these individual characteristics could affect not only the way resources are translated into capability (in the case of gender, for example, consider a gender-based allocation of resources which disfavours women) but also the way in which deprivation is defined for those different groups (such as, for example, a gender-based definition of deprivation in health). To advance in this direction, further research, possibly supported by participatory methods to identify group-specific indicators, could be pursued, though it falls beyond the scope of this chapter.

An aside on subjective morbidity data

Given the absence of objective morbidity data, we decided to adopt self-reported morbidity, which affects around 31 per cent of the

consensus on the dimensions along which an evaluative exercise is conducted, often stressed in Sen's writings.

[14] Various contributions in Feachem *et al.* 1992 offer a good discussion of morbidity indicators. A variety of indicators of educational achievement is present in the literature. For a discussion with respect to the Latin American case, see Wolff *et al.* (1994).

[15] It should be noted that the analysis performed here considers indicators one by one. We are not dealing here, therefore, with the issue of how to value a vector of different indicators (all the relevant functionings at once).

[16] Of the various indicators one could have adopted we selected one which could capture a contemporary deprivation in education, that is why we focused on an indicator which could be constructed for the 12–15 age group. We did not consider adult deprivations in education as it would have been very hard to disentangle the causal relation, especially because of the difficulty of finding good instruments to overcome simultaneity bias.

population.[17] As the use of this type of indicator is contested, a more extensive discussion of this type of information is in order.

The ENNIV survey we use provides a self-perceived indicator based on a 'tracer list' including a list of symptoms as well as diagnosed malaria or other illness in the last four weeks.[18] This introduces an element of objectivity into the assessment, as symptoms 'have the characteristic of observability, even if they are not actually observed' (Idler 1992, p. 42).[19] Nevertheless, cross-national comparisons show that seemingly objective self-perceived data of the kind available to us are influenced by cultural factors (or by the different socio-economic circumstances which might prevail in different contexts), therefore making interpretation difficult (e.g. Murray *et al.* 1992). Further, within a given context, the discrepancies between morbidity profiles obtained through self-perceived rather than observed indicators is unclear,[20] though they are seen as reflecting 'valuation neglect', i.e. all the factors which affect the subjective ideal of health with respect to which the individual defines his own condition.[21]

Against this discouraging view of subjective indicators of morbidity, it is important to consider that information on many experiences of illness cannot but be subjective (some conditions could not possibly be

---

[17] The other indicators we considered adopting were being sick for more than a week and being sick and in bed for more than a week, but adopting them seemed to imply restricting ourselves to the analysis of a very small group of the population (about 11 per cent and 2 per cent of the population appeared to fall into these two groups, respectively).

[18] A note of warning is needed concerning the long recall periods involved, as well as the empirical evidence which points to self-perceived rates being increased by respondents being prompted by tracer lists (see Murray *et al.* 1992). Other sources of bias might emerge from the wording, timing of the inquiry and reporting by proxy respondents (in this case limited to younger members of the household).

[19] In this sense, therefore, the information available to us on morbidity is more objective than synthetic global assessments in which individuals are required to rank their health status from 'excellent' to 'poor'.

[20] Extensive research done on US data in the 1950s found that the extent of the variance between the two kind of assessments differed a lot depending on the causes of disease (see Murray *et al.* 1992).

[21] Empirical evidence points to the significance of an income effect in identifying oneself as sick (Murray *et al.* 1992), as well as hinting that the lower the opportunity cost is (because of paid sick leave and similar factors), the greater the recognition of morbidity. Also education has an important bearing on self-perceived morbidity, as it affects not only awareness of health issues but also the perception of what it is possible to achieve.

identified without self-reporting of suffering), though greater concern is caused by discrepancies in the profiles of conditions which should be measured by both objective and self-reported indicators.[22] Further, these critiques are based on the idea that the value of self-reported assessments lies in proxying (however imperfectly) objective indicators. In contrast, it has been suggested that 'if I think I am ill, then, by definition, I *am* ill', while measures of observed morbidity are more oriented at capturing disease than illness (Murray *et al.* 1992). This could mean, therefore, that self-reported measures of morbidity are capturing a different aspect of health than objective measures. While the former might be characterised by 'false positives' and 'false negatives' (Murray *et al.* 1992), they reflect an aspect of health whose importance for policy purposes cannot be overlooked.

The point is reinforced by considering that research on global self-assessments of health status[23] (e.g. Idler *et al.* 1991, Idler 1992) has found that they provide much better predictions of mortality than more objective indicators, once the subjective responses have been made conditional on a variety of socio-economic and 'objective' health-related indicators. Such evidence suggests that self-assessed health measures capture something which is relevant not only to a subjective definition of health but also to as objective a measure of health as mortality. Further evidence (see Cummins 2000) suggests that the association between objective and subjective measures is stronger when 'objective life quality decreases to low levels' (p. 7). This seems in line with recent emphasis on self-reported measures of health in the context of developing countries (see Feachem *et al.* 1992) because of their economic and non-economic effects.[24] We will, therefore, rely on this self-reported

---

[22] A third category of conditions that cannot be identified except through external observation also exists, together with the above-mentioned conditions which need to be subjectively revealed and those which should emerge both through objective and self-reported diagnoses.

[23] Global self-assessments of health status are given by the subjective classification of one's health into a limited number of categories going from 'excellent' to 'poor'.

[24] The list of the effects of adult illness beyond those in terms of personal sufferings spans from consequences on 'health of other adult members, on medical treatment costs, and on non-medical consumption, investment, production, earnings and income distribution' to the 'costs of the coping mechanisms that households and communities use to mitigate or to insure against the consequences of adult ill-health' (Feachem *et al.* 1992, p. 161).

indicator as we trust that it captures an aspect of health that cannot be dismissed in an evaluation of wellbeing, though we acknowledge that it does not represent the only possible representation of morbidity and that it would be valuable to complement it with more objective data.

Before proceeding to our empirical analysis, it is worth underlining two important dimensions of heterogeneity which characterise our selection of indicators. The first is that they reflect the circumstance that different functionings indicators are appropriate for different groups (e.g. morbidity data can be collected for the whole sample, while low achievements in school can be identified only for those of school age). This implies that when adopting the capability approach to target policies, one might have to map an individual indicator to the household level. A second and more important difference among these indicators is that they are bound to have different degrees of association with household monetary resources. It is nevertheless true that if we take them as indicators of intrinsically important deprivations, even if they appear to be 'perversely' related to resources as one can expect the self-reported morbidity indicator to be, this should not represent an appropriate criticism.

The methodology

On the basis of what we have discussed in the previous subsections, we can now briefly lay out our methodology. We will consider first health, then education, taking up one indicator at a time. Initially we will consider the way they identify deprivation as opposed to monetary indicators. As this part of our analysis has some analogies with the debate on targeting, it is worth noting that the tables of our descriptive analysis are of the kind shown below.

In terms of targeting accuracy, if we take the objective to be identifying a non-monetary deprivation, then a monetary one identifies correctly the observations in Groups A and D, while Group B represents a targeting

Table 7.A

	Non-deprived in non-monetary dimension	Deprived in non-monetary dimension
Non-poor	Group A	Group B
Poor	Group C	Group D

error I (i.e. an error of omission or '*F*-mistake') (Cornia and Stewart 1995, p. 351), while Group C represents a targeting error II, i.e. an error of inclusion of the non deprived or '*E*-mistake' (ibid.). We will then proceed to an in-depth analysis of the factors which influence the way resources are transformed into capabilities by estimating the capabilities production functions presented earlier. Our estimates should help us understand why some people who are deprived in monetary resources are not deprived in other dimensions, or why monetary resources might not be enough to avoid other important forms of deprivations. Finally, we will draw conclusions on what has been learned from these analyses, as well as presenting some simple simulations which will highlight the policy relevance of the findings.

The empirical results

In this section we will present our comparative analysis of indicators of basic capabilities and of monetary poverty indicators. It has been performed on the ENNIV 1994 survey for Peru,[25] a survey moulded on the LSMS type. Before proceeding, a snapshot of monetary poverty in 1994 is presented, as it will make a useful background to what follows.

More than half of the population of Peru was deemed to be in monetary poverty according to an expenditure-based indicator which captures the inability to buy a minimal basic consumption basket, while one in five people could not buy a minimal food basket (extreme poverty). Disaggregating the FGT indices for poverty and extreme poverty shows wide variations in the regional pattern of the indices, with rural areas faring worse than average under all profiles, especially relative to Metropolitan Lima. To the information shown it can be added that indigenous people, who represent the majority of rural people, together with larger households are more likely to be poor even when other socio-economic characteristics are taken into account. Other important characteristics of the poor are that they have lower access to sanitation and electricity, a circumstance reflecting both their inability to afford it and the characteristics of the places where they live (Ruggeri Laderchi 1999).

---

[25] For more information on the survey and the monetary poverty lines adopted, see Moncada *et al.* 1996.

Table 7.1 *Monetary poverty in Peru 1994*

	Incidence (headcount)	Depth (poverty gap)	Severity (FGT($\alpha = 2$) index)
TOTAL	53.16	19.08	9.31
Lima	41.30	11.55	4.59
Urban coast	51.84	17.76	8.36
Rural coast	61.47	24.29	12.14
Urban Sierra	51.54	18.37	9.19
Rural Sierra	64.71	26.58	14.12
Urban Selva	42.96	14.49	6.43
Rural Selva	70.21	28.47	14.83

Table 7.2 *Extreme monetary poverty in Peru 1994*

	Incidence (headcount)	Depth (poverty gap)	Severity (FGT($\alpha = 2$) index)
TOTAL	18.68	5.29	2.24
Lima	5.18	1.10	0.34
Urban coast	12.24	2.83	1.00
Rural coast	23.87	6.42	2.33
Urban Sierra	12.73	3.28	1.28
Rural Sierra	37.71	12.19	5.67
Urban Selva	11.94	2.18	0.58
Rural Selva	38.61	10.93	4.70

The relation between morbidity and monetary poverty

In this subsection we test how consistent the identification of poverty by morbidity and monetary indicators is. As Table 7.3 shows, the patterns of self-perceived morbidity and consumption poverty are such that not even the hypothesis of complete randomness can be rejected. Many cases are as consistently as inconsistently classified by both indicators, making one a very bad predictor of the other.

We have also considered an alternative cut-off point for the identification of poverty by focusing on extreme consumption poverty (Table 7.4).

Table 7.3 *Self-reported morbidity vs. consumption poverty (18550 observations)*

	Non-sick *	Sick *	Total
Non-poor	68.65	31.35	100.00
	53.32	55.10	53.87
	36.98	16.89	53.87
Poor	70.17	29.83	100.00
	46.68	44.90	46.13
	32.37	13.76	46.13
Total	69.35	30.65	100.00
	100.00	100.00	100.00
	69.35	30.65	100.00

For every category the row, column and overall percentage are presented
*in the last four weeks, Pearson test of association: $F(1,357) = 2.0739$
$P = 0.1507$

Table 7.4 *Self-reported morbidity vs. extreme consumption poverty (18550 observations)*

	Non-sick *	Sick *	Total
Non-poor	69.73	30.27	100.00
	81.78	80.36	81.35
	56.72	24.63	81.35
Poor	67.73	32.27	100.00
	18.22	19.64	18.65
	12.63	6.02	18.65
Total	69.35	30.65	100.00
	100.00	100.00	100.00
	69.35	30.65	100.00

For every category the row, column and overall percentage are presented
*in the last four weeks, Pearson test of association: $F(1,357) = 1.7580$
$P = 0.1857$

The number of cases consistently identified by extreme consumption poverty and morbidity rises to 63 per cent of the total observations. At the same time, only one in five of the morbidity cases would be identified by focusing on those in extreme poverty. The association between the variables appears again statistically insignificant, showing that by focusing on those reporting morbidity implies picking up a completely different group of people than a monetary approach would suggest.[26]

Capabilities production functions: morbidity

In analysing our data on morbidity we are well aware that 'causes of socio-economic patterns in self-perceived data are difficult to determine' (Murray *et al.* 1992). This also explains why comparatively few studies have analysed data of this kind. Some analysis is, however, available from a study of early LSMS surveys (Murray *et al.* 1992) on Côte d' Ivoire, Ghana and Peru. It is of particular interest as it provides us with a picture from the first round of the ENNIV data collected in 1985/86. In Peru, correlations were found among morbidity and age (older people reporting greater morbidity), size of the household (smaller households reporting more morbidity, for both adults and children), gender (with women reporting greater morbidity and in particular pregnant women reporting greater and longer illnesses than non-pregnant women), area of residence (urban areas being characterised by greater reporting, though illnesses were 'perceived to be less disabling than in rural areas') and total household expenditure (reported morbidity increased from 34 per cent for the lowest quartile to 41 per cent for the highest). In the Peruvian study no regression analysis was performed, but nevertheless its descriptive analysis provides a benchmark against which to compare our findings.

Trying to make sense of those other factors lying behind the pattern shown above, we have estimated the determinants of reported morbidity, controlling for the individual and household variables mentioned above, as well as for education (which is actually the single factor to which most attention has been devoted when estimating adult morbidity functions, e.g. Behrman and Wolfe 1989, Strauss *et al.* 1993), the

---

[26] This result could be seen as a reflection of the self-reported nature of the data, with richer people being able to afford the time and resources of considering themselves ill. We have argued above for the value of this type of health indicators, so we will limit ourselves here to the consideration that, once these indicators are recognised to capture deprivation, their not being related to monetary poverty is not a validation criterion when starting from a different approach to the definition of poverty such as the one under consideration here.

demographic and ethnic structure of the household as well as social service provision and location. We also present a tobit model of the number of days respondents reported they had been sick. The use of the tobit is justified by reference to an unobservable health variable, which upon reaching some threshold level appears as number of days of sickness. The tobit has also been run taking into account a series of dummies to purge the estimates of the fixed effects associated with different departments.[27] The potential endogeneity of household resources has been tested adopting the Rivers and Vuong (1988) two-stage procedure. Household per capita expenditure was instrumented by ownership of real assets and of consumer durables.[28] The hypothesis of weak exogeneity could not be rejected, however, so in the models included in Table 7.5 expenditure appears non-instrumented.

The weak exogeneity of household expenditure from morbidity is of interest as one would expect that household resources are affected by participation in the labour market or by productivity-related wage differentials linked to household members' health. Several considerations are in order. First of all inasmuch as savings or assets which can be easily liquidated are available, consumption and health might not be jointly determined in the same period, especially if the illness is of a temporary kind. Further, the link with the labour market is less strong at the upper end of the income distribution, where people are more likely to enjoy some work-related welfare provision against illness. One can argue therefore that while for the rich the link between morbidity and income does not exist, for the poorest a link exists but that is through 'objective' (and severe)[29] disease, which may be weakly correlated to the subjective dependent variable we examine here.[30]

---

[27] Due to problems of convergence we could not use district-level fixed effects.

[28] The joint significance of the regressors of this first stage was $F(37,308) = 160.93$ Prob $> F = 0.0000$.

[29] As not working because of illness is likely to depend on the perceptions of health held, it seems most likely that the illnesses which affect work behaviour are at least those whose impairing effect is truly disruptive for work and can therefore be considered as severe.

[30] When running the same models on younger cohorts for which parental education variables could be obtained (i.e. for individuals who still have cohabiting parents), weak exogeneity is rejected. The amount of time spent by parents with sick children rather than at work is one possible mechanism responsible for this endogeneity.

Table 7.5 *An analysis of morbidity*

	Probit		Tobit	Fixed effects ♣
	Coef.	dF/dx	Coef.	Coef.
	t		t	t
Household per capita	0.038**	0.012	0.556**	0.458**
expenditure	4.270		4.566	5.135
Age	0.003	0.001	0.104*	0.098*
	1.015		2.166	2.360
Age squared	0.00007	0.00003	0.001	0.001
	1.717		1.097	1.582
Gender	0.119**	0.040	1.642**	1.728**
	4.646		4.581	4.959
Years of schooling	−0.061**	−0.021	−0.811**	−0.876**
	4.920		4.833	6.152
Years squared	0.002*	0.001	0.021*	0.026**
	2.393		2.000	3.072
Indigenous	0.060	0.018	0.452	0.359
	1.163		0.677	0.585
Female-headed	0.091	0.032	1.226	1.367**
household				
	1.775		1.782	2.735
Age of the head	−0.002	−0.001	−0.019	−0.021
	1.462		0.819	1.298
Size of the household	−0.007	−0.003	−0.120	−0.173*
	0.671		0.852	2.156
Ratio of children in the	0.277	0.089	3.749	2.651
household	1.760		1.797	1.786
Availability of public	−0.183*	−0.058	−2.264	−2.337**
water in the	2.194		1.920	2.758
household				
Availability of public	0.098	0.032	1.566	1.528
sewage in the	1.019		1.181	1.740
household				
Time to reach a health	−0.001	0.000	−0.009	−0.002
facility*	1.173		0.798	0.272
Time to be attended in	0.001	0.000	0.014	0.007
a health facility*	1.283		1.437	1.205
Community literacy	0.791**	0.226	12.266**	3.642
rate*	3.074		3.528	1.682

Table 7.5 (*cont.*)

	Probit		Tobit	Fixed effects ♣
Urban areas	0.011	0.004	−0.284	0.741
	0.134		0.257	1.071
Constant	−0.735**		−13.310**	−11.607**
	4.801		6.433	3.929

*significant at the 5% level
**significant at the 1% level
♣fixed effects run at the department level

Weak exogeneity in this case could therefore reinforce the scepticism about using self-reported morbidity data. Without repeating the arguments already discussed about why this analysis is of interest, it is worth noting that the Hausman test in the Rivers and Vuong (1988) procedure is a general specification test. The finding might therefore also reflect the difficulty in finding appropriate instruments for the first stage among the available variables.

Monetary resources appear as strongly and positively correlated with both a higher probability of reporting illness and longer duration morbidity in the three models presented. Other aspects of our findings, however, challenge the exclusive reliance on simple correlations (as done in Murray *et al.* 1992) of other studies, which, as already mentioned, have found that ageing is generally associated with reporting greater illness. Age, for example, does not significantly affect the probability of reporting morbidity, though it affects its duration. Note, in contrast, that the significance of gender is quite in line with the reporting pattern identified in other developing countries,[31] where a gender differential seems to hold strongly over the life cycle, and also when focusing on activity of daily living (ADL) measures (Strauss *et al.* 1993).

Years of schooling play a significant role in all our models, as has been reported elsewhere. This finding has been found to persist when one controls for individuals and parental background (e.g. Behrman Wolfe

---

[31] In Thailand and Pakistan, however, when respondents answered about other members of the household they tended to report greater morbidity for boys than for girls, possibly because of cultural biases (Murray *et al.* 1992). In our data, however, this is not the case: morbidity was reported for 1265 out of 3556 girls under 15 and 1290 out of 3562 boys under 15.

1989, Strauss *et al.* 1993). The claim is that this variable is doing more than picking up individual specificities (which would favour both scholastic achievements and better health), suggesting that education improves the technology with which resources are transformed into health. Note also that the diminishing returns of education would not reverse the effects of education over the relevant range (e.g. only after thirty-nine years of education in the case of the tobit). To test this hypothesis we tried to impose some form of control for parental characteristics by considering their education. Given the nature of our data, however, we could do so only on a smaller and younger part of our sample (3980 obs., average age 13.5). For all the parental education variables which were tried, the effect was to make own years of schooling insignificant. Given, however, the young age of these individuals, it does not seem surprising that their own schooling is not significant in determining their health status.

Ethnicity and female headship of the household do not play independent roles in determining whether people are sick or not. Individuals in female-headed households are, however, sick for longer when considering department-level fixed effects.[32] The age of the head of the household has also been controlled for. As we were already controlling for individuals' ages, these controls have been inserted to capture for some of the background characteristics of the individual. In this sense people living in households with older heads have experienced an 'older technology' in transforming health inputs into health (most likely low parental education is the main characteristic of such an older technology). Again, this type of effect did not prove significant. The size of the household diminishes the probability of being sick, though significantly so only when looking at the days of illness and controlling for departmental idiosyncratic features. The percentage of household members below five, the other household demographic variable we considered, does not appear to affect reported morbidity.[33]

We included a set of variables to control for provision of social services both at the household and at the community level. Of these, access to public water reduces both the probability and the severity of illness when considering the fixed effect model. This is interesting as

---

[32] This might well depend on who is effectively answering the questionnaire, as the head is answering for all the members of the household.

[33] Different reasons, ranging from expected maternal depletion to care-related factors or to the higher vulnerability of children to illness suggested that this variable was to be considered.

public water can play an important role in determining gastrointestinal infections, especially in children. The two findings can possibly be reconciled by considering that the latter affect mostly children and that later in life individuals have a greater resistance to this kind of disease. The variables that should capture access and quality of health (which one would expect to play a role)[34] surprisingly do not seem to be doing so. The last variable of this group is the percentage of adults in the community who have not attended school sufficiently to gain functional literacy. Similar variables have been used by others (e.g. Behrman and Wolfe 1989) to proxy prices on the ground that 'relative prices broadly defined (i.e. to include infrastructure as well as nominal prices) usually are systematically related to the size of the urban area and the extent of education of the population in which one resides' (Behrman and Wolfe 1989 p. 650). In that study using Nicaraguan data, the literacy variable did not prove significant, while in contrast we find it significant when considering day of illness and controlling for fixed effects. One could argue that its significance is either because the community literacy rate proxies prices or because of some more general effect through the impact of schooling on the environment one lives in.[35]

Finally, we wanted to control for the claim discussed above that in urban areas more morbidity is reported but it is perceived to be less disabling. Though the signs of the urban area dummy are compatible with this hypothesis in our first two models, this variable is insignificant throughout. It seems likely, therefore, that in other studies the association between urban areas and morbidity was picking up the effect of some of the other variables for which we are controlling.

Morbidity: summing up

This analysis, as already remarked, points to a complex relationship between resources and reported morbidity. From our descriptive analysis it appeared that they are not associated in a statistically significant way, though by modelling morbidity we have been able to go beyond the correlations which were found by others in an earlier round of the same survey. Of the factors which were significantly associated with

---

[34] For example, Gertler and Van der Gaag (1990), estimating a model of medical choices in Peru using data from a previous round of ENNIV, found a significant effect of the time needed to travel on each of the choices.

[35] Also this one, as with the other community variables, might be problematic as it averages over the small number of observations included in every PSU.

Table 7.6 *The impact of education and access to public water on the probability of reporting morbidity, by decile*

	1st decile	5th decile	Top decile
Probability of being ill if			
Average years of schooling	32.6	31.2	34.1
One year of schooling more than average	31.2	30.5	33.6
Impact of years of schooling on probability	−1.4	−0.7	−0.5
Probability of being ill if			
No access to public water	33.5	34.3	37.7
Access to public water	29.6	30.5	34.9
Impact of access to water on probability	−3.9	−3.8	−2.8
Marginal effect of expenditure	1.22	1.19	1.32
Mean expenditure	665	1750	7448
Incidence of morbidity (%)	28.01	31.3	35.8
Average years of schooling	5.25	7.39	9.89
Percentage of households without access to public water	62.77	73.56	79.59

morbidity in the 1985/1986 study (Murray *et al.* 1992), age does not appear as significant, nor does the size of the household (it appears significantly only when explaining the number of days of illness and controlling for unobservable district-specific characteristics). Further, we do not find that the urban–rural divide matters in terms of reporting morbidity as described by Murray *et al.* (1992).

In Table 7.6 above we have elaborated our results further, exploring the effects of both education and access to public water on morbidity. We find that both education and public water provision have the greatest effect for the poorest. At the same time the 'perverse' effect of affluence on illness is the strongest for the richest. These two effects combined are such that investing in the education of the poorest would provide 'returns' in terms of self-reported morbidity almost three times as high as those for the richest.

Children's educational achievements and monetary poverty

The association between low educational achievement for the 12–15 year age group and monetary poverty is strong and significant. Even

Table 7.7 *Children's educational achievements vs.*
consumption poverty (1779)

	Having had five years of schooling	Not having had five years of schooling	Total
Non-poor	87.6	12.4	100.0
	45.7	22.4	40.5
	35.5	5.02	40.5
Poor	70.9	29.1	100.0
	54.3	77.6	59.6
	42.2	17.4	59.6
Total	77.6	22.4	100.0
	100.0	100.0	100.0
	77.6	22.4	100.0

For every category the row, column and overall percentage are presented
Pearson test of association: $F(1, 341) = 50.8184$, $P > F = 0.000$

so, one in five of the children of this age group who have not yet achieved functional literacy are to be found in non-poor households (Table 7.7). At the same time, however, 70 per cent of the poor children in this age bracket have had at least five years of primary education, which shows that poverty in itself is not sufficient to hinder the chances of a child to reach this minimal level of education within a reasonable amount of time.

Table 7.8 focuses on those in extreme poverty. Adopting this lower poverty line implies that the majority of children without the fifth grade are now non-poor. As adopting this lower poverty line implies that the percentage of poor declines between Table 7.7 and Table 7.8 by roughly two-thirds, and a similar decline occurs in the group of those who despite being poor are not deprived in education, these tables illustrate that those among the poor children who have achieved our minimal educational target are equally spread among the monetary poor (i.e. they are not concentrated among the bottom poor or the richest of the poor).

Household resources are associated with this deprivation, with the exception of the second bottom decile which shows lower deprivation than the third one. Such a strong association suggests that a pure investment model of education – in which individuals' efficient choice

Table 7.8 *Children's educational achievements vs.*
extreme consumption poverty (1779)

	Having had five years of schooling	Not having had five years of schooling	Total
Non-poor	82.2	17.8	100.0
	83.0	62.2	78.4
	64.5	13.9	78.4
Poor	60.9	39.1	100.0
	17.0	37.8	21.6
	13.6	8.5	21.6
Total	77.6	23.4	100.0
	100.0	100.0	100.0
	77.6	23.4	100.0

For every category the row, column and overall percentage are presented
Pearson test of association: $F(1, 341) = 55.7746$, $P > F = 0.000$

Incidence of self-reported morbidity and average number of days ill, by hh pc expenditure decile

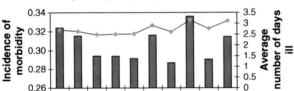

Figure 7.1 The distribution of reported morbidity by decile
*We have also graphed the average number of days of sickness of those who reported morbidity trying to capture the seriousness of their illness. As the figure shows, there is much more than household per capita expenditure driving the morbidity pattern, in line with the 1985 findings reported above.

of the level of schooling is determined only by the (expected) benefits of schooling and by its cost – does not capture important features of the Peruvian reality.[36] Liquidity constraints and availability of schooling

---

[36] Our indicator could be reflecting also individual specific characteristics determining repetition or drop-outs, but those should be averaged out when considering the aggregate picture as in the figure above.

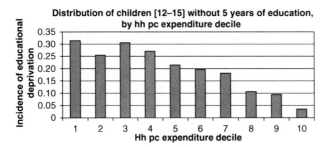

Figure 7.2 Graph showing how children without the fifth grade of primary schooling are distributed by deciles

facilities are plausible candidates for such an outcome. Further, education might have some consumption characteristics such that individuals pursue it for its intrinsic value.

Empirical studies controlling for the family background of the individual have found that income might be partially proxying other things. For example, Behrman and Wolfe (1987) estimates of children's schooling using fixed effects for the mothers' sibling see the effect of household income (which was found already small and not significant in the standard case) reduced by two-thirds. However, Behrman (1990) reports results from a Thailand study showing that income had a positive though decreasing effect on post-primary continuation rates and that this effect does not change when controlling for parental schooling or for some community characteristics.

Harbison and Hanuschek (1992), reviewing an extensive body of literature in the USA and the developing world, present a grouping of the variables which have been adopted in the literature to explain educational production. Apart from income and socio-demographic variables to capture family inputs which we have already mentioned, they list aggregate summaries of socio-demographic characteristics of other students in the school to capture peer inputs, and teachers' characteristics, schools' organisation and community factors which should capture school inputs. Such a wealth of information is not generally available in household surveys and the ENNIV is no exception. In our estimates we have tried to find variables which could capture as many as possible of these effects. We are well aware, however, that 'the estimated models of educational performance undoubtedly fail to capture many of the truly important inputs to the educational process' (Harbison and Hanuschek 1992, p. 25).

Capabilities production functions: children's achievements

Table 7.9 shows our estimates of the determinants of children aged 12–15 without five years of schooling. Household resources appears as strong and significant determinants of children's schooling achievements. The model presented shows the effect of the variable non-instrumented. We also tested for weak exogeneity of household resources with the Rivers and Vuong (2SCML) two-stage estimator[37] – as we could not, *a priori*, exclude the possibility that child labour might help the household to afford sending the children themselves to school, or that, more generally, child schooling decisions might be jointly determined with the household labour supply. Such a specification did not allow us, however, to accept the hypothesis of endogeneity.

The other determinants we considered included age and gender among the child's individual characteristics. We tried alternative specifications of the age variable, but as we are dealing with a restricted age range, the best specification was the one presented with one dummy for children aged fourteen and fifteen. This specification suggests that for those children the probability of not having yet achieved the five years of schooling is lower than for those one or two years younger. Gender, in contrast, plays no statistically significant role, though it is interesting to see that the effect would be one of decreasing the chances of low achievement in school for females.

The parental variables we have considered control for parental background and ability as well as for direct educational achievements. Of these, father years of schooling has a strong and significant effect, while mother education has a lesser impact and is significant exactly at the 5 per cent level. The effect of ethnicity in lowering the chances of low achievement is not significant. Similarly, the size of the household does not have a significant coefficient. Household composition (as measured by the proportions of children under seven and children aged 7–11), in contrast, significantly affects children's performance in school. These

---

[37] Also in this case we tried instrumenting with household assets and durables.

Table 7.9 *Children aged 12–15 without five years of schooling*

	Probit	
	Coef. t	dF/dx
Household pc. expend. (000)	−0.204** 3.21	−0.038
Age 14–15	−0.363* 2.54	−0.068
Gender	−0.068 0.60	−0.013
Father years of schooling	−0.064** 3.36	−0.012
Mother years of schooling	−0.043* 1.97	−0.008
Indigenous	−0.067 0.33	−0.012
Size	−0.020 0.54	−0.004
Proportion of children less than 7 yrs old in the household	1.029* 2.04	0.192
Proportion of children 7–11 yrs old in the household	0.506** 3.42	0.108
Time to school (minutes)	−0.005 0.93	−0.001
School with no water and sewage	0.066 0.39	0.012
Urban areas	−0.273 1.75	−0.051
Constant	0.408 0.92	
N of observations	959	
Joint significance of the regressors	$F(12,290) = \text{Prob} > F = 0.0000$	

*significant at the 5% level
**significant at the 1% level

demographic variables suggest that while having more younger children implies a greater number of household chores to be performed (especially for elder daughters, though we did not find any significant effect by gender of the child), when siblings are older this effect diminishes. We also considered two variables to capture access and quality of schooling. They proved insignificantly correlated with low achievements, which perhaps should not come as a surprise given how little they reflect the quality aspects which are likely to affect schooling performance.[38] Finally, there seems to be little difference between rural and urban areas.

Children's achievements: summing up

This subsection explored the relationship between monetary resources and children's educational achievement. Household per capita resources were found to be an important determinant of children's educational achievements. At the same time we found that being poor was not an obstacle to having attained five years of schooling for many of the 12–15 year olds. Our two-way tables showed a rather homogeneous distribution of the children with five years of schooling within the poor, and similarly our figure showed that for the four lowest deciles of the distribution there seemed to be little variation in the incidence of this deprivation. When we investigated the determinants of deprivation in children's achievements we could identify parental characteristics and household composition as important conditioning factors.

In Table 7.10 we have investigated the effectiveness of household resources and parental education for different expenditure deciles. One year of paternal education reduces the chances of children having a low achievement in school by 1.5 per cent for both the lowest decile and the fifth one, while reducing them only by 0.2 per cent for those in the top decile. Household resources would need to increase by half to achieve the same result for those in the lowest decile – by 5 per cent of those in the top decile. Similar effects, though smaller, hold for

---

[38] We also tested for interactions between parents' education and school quality variables following Birdsall (1985), where a partial substitutability between public inputs (less available where distance is greater) and private ones was hypothesised, but could not find any significant effect.

Table 7.10 *The impact of parental education on the probability of low educational achievement for children aged 12–15, by decile*

	1st decile	5th decile	Top decile
Prob. of low educational achievement if			
Father with avg. years of education	29.3	20.5	1.6
Father with 1 year of edu. more than avg.	27.8	19	1.4
Impact of 1 year of paternal education on probability	1.5	1.5	0.2
Equivalent expenditure	970	2075	7800
Change in expenditure			
In absolute terms	305	325	352
As a proportion of average exp.	1.459	1.186	1.047
Prob. of low educational achievement if			
Mother with avg. years of education	27.4	19.8	1.8
Mother with 1 year of edu. more than avg.	26.3	18.8	1.6
Impact of 1 year of maternal education on probability	−1.1	−1	−0.2
Equivalent expenditure	870	1950	7655
Change in expenditure			
In absolute terms	205	200	207
As a proportion of average exp.	1.308	1.114	1.028
Meme			
Mean expenditure	665	1750	7448
Incidence of low achievement (%)	31.42	21.44	3.57
Avg. years of paternal education	5.63	7.96	11.15
Avg. years of maternal education	4.76	6.93	10.24

one more year of maternal education. The last section of the table, showing the proportion of children with low educational achievements, reveals that they are ten times more likely to occur in the lowest decile than in the top one, while parental years of schooling are about twice as many in the latter than the former.

Due to the impact of parental education variables, the table seems to carry important policy implications. It shows in fact that even in households at the bottom of the distribution of monetary resources, one extra year of parental education has an effect equivalent to the one of a substantial increase in household resources. This indirectly sheds light on the understanding of an important mechanism of intergenerational transmission of non-monetary poverty.[39] At the same time, throughout this subsection we have identified a strong responsiveness of children's education to household income. The consideration that children who proceed with their studies at a better pace have an opportunity of becoming more productive and getting better jobs sooner (if they ever attain enough education to access those better jobs), together with the consideration of the high responsiveness of children's education to household resources, seems to point to the possibility of spurring a virtuous circle. Improving education for the poorest would have, among other effects, that of increasing children's education in the future and hence possibly also their productivity, their future incomes and their ability to provide a life less scarred by monetary and non-monetary poverty for their children.

Conclusion

In this chapter we have tried to assess whether a profile of deprivation rooted in Sen's capability approach provides us with different insights than one based on economic welfare, using Peruvian household survey data. As we have argued that checking only for statistical association between indicators hides important value judgements, we estimated capabilities production functions for achievements in education and health. This allowed us to draw empirical conclusions on the quantitative importance of the parametric variations which affect individuals' ability to convert household resources into capabilities. At the same time we could identify the constraints to individual achievements

---

[39] It seems unlikely that any of the parents of the children considered has opportunities for adult schooling. So it is likely that what we observe here is the effect of parental education acquired before the children were born. In principle one could question whether parental education would have the same effect and whether, on the basis of the costs of provision, it would prove an efficient poverty-reduction tool.

which were more binding, so that acting upon them would offer greater leverage for policy action.

We started by checking the congruence of the way observations are classified by monetary and non-monetary indicators. It was found that despite their statistical association (only our morbidity indicator was not significantly associated with monetary poverty),[40] some other important factors were driving individual achievements. For example, one in five children with low educational achievement (falling behind at school) is in a non-poor family.

We then considered explicitly the factors which could be driving these results by estimating capability production functions modelling the various dimensions of deprivation. Our estimates indicated that individual, household and community characteristics, in different ways and to varying degrees depending on the context, do affect the way resources are translated into individual achievements. This suggests that if one is interested in capturing deprivation in basic capabilities, a monetary indicator would not be sufficient or appropriate. Further, important policy priorities for the eradication of capability poverty emerge from this analysis, as illustrated by our simulations of the relative magnitude of the effects of some non-monetary factors as compared with household resources on the probability of being deprived.

This analysis not only shows the important contributions that the capability perspective offers for policy making, it also points to important implications for its operationalisation, which are shared by other multidimensional concepts of poverty. Reading across our results, in fact, suggests a considerable heterogeneity. The measures we chose as indicators of basic capabilities were different in their association with monetary poverty, in their responsiveness to additional household resources, and in the extent to which we could identify other factors which were constraining the effectiveness of household resources in bringing about capability improvements. Also the types of variables which drive those parametric variations are rather heterogeneous in the different cases we considered. Not all

---

[40] As shown by the Chi-squared test provided underneath Tables 7.3 and 7.4 and referring to a simple correlation. In Table 7.5 we found household resources as significant determinants of morbidity – this was, however, conditional on all the other regressors being taken into account.

Table 7.A.1

Definition of variables	Average	Note
Monetary poverty	0.53	Household per capita consumption levels deemed insufficient to cover the cost of covering basic food and non-food needs
Extreme monetary poverty	0.19	Household per capita consumption levels deemed insufficient to cover the cost of a basic food basket
Self-reported morbidity (all sample)	0.31	Having been ill in the last four weeks
Failure to reach functional literacy	0.22	Children aged 12–15 with less than four years of schooling
Age	26.05	Years of age
Age square	1079.26	Years of age squared
Gender	1.51	(1 man, 2 woman)
Years of schooling	7.33	Years of completed education
Years of schooling squared	74.67	Years of completed education squared
Indigenous person	20.97	Declaring to speak indigenous language
Female-headed household	0.14	
Age of the head	48.12	
Size of the household	6.16	
Proportion of children (0–5) in the household	0.12	
Proportion of children (0–7) in the household	0.17	
Proportion of children (7–11) in the household	0.14	
Availability of public water	0.70	Water provided by the public utility (either in the house/building where the household lives, or through a public fountain)

Variable	Value	Description
Availability of public sewage	0.58	Connection to the public sewage network in or outside the house
Time to reach a health facility	31.17	Community average of the time travelled by individuals to reach a medical facility for a health check or treatment
Time to be attended in a health facility	50.50	Community average of the time individuals waited to be visited or treated by medical personnel
Community literacy rate	0.15	Community average of the answers to the literacy questions on reading and writing ability
Urban areas	0.64	
Household per capita expenditure (000)	2.16	
Father years of schooling	7.68	
Mother years of schooling	6.66	
Time to school	17.27	Time travelled to reach school
School with no water and sewage	0.22	The school attended has functioning connections to the public water and to the public sewerage networks
Children 14 or 15	0.10	Dummy identifying children aged 14 and 15 years

of them are directly relevant as policy variables, though they might provide useful clues for targeting specific interventions. Further, they do not have the same type of effect on different deprivations and some variables even ended up having an opposite effect, as in the case of household resources which significantly contribute to increased morbidity while reducing deprivation in education. At the same time a useful (and comforting) result of our analysis, much in line with available evidence from other countries (e.g. Strauss and Thomas 1993, Behrman 1990), is that there seem to be things which are unequivocally good in terms of improving capability or more generally wellbeing as measured in non-monetary terms, such as, for example, education.[41] The reasons behind these results in relation to specific deprivations have been discussed already, but it is worth underlining how the adoption of a multidimensional framework brings about the need to make sense of this diversity.

Cited references

Baker, Judy and Grosh, Margaret 1994. 'Measuring the effects of geographic targeting on poverty reduction', Living Standards Measurement Survey Working Paper n. 99, Washington D.C.: the World Bank

Behrman, Jere R. 1990. 'The actions of human resources and poverty on one another. What we have yet to learn', Living Standards Measurement Survey Working Paper n. 74, Washington D.C.: the World Bank

Behrman, Jere and Wolfe, Barbara 1987. 'Investments in schooling in two generations in pre-revolutionary Nicaragua: the roles of family background and school supply', *Journal of Development Economics*, 27: 395–419

Behrman, Jere and Wolfe, Barbara 1989. 'Does more schooling make women better nourished and healthier?', *Journal of Human Resources*, 24: 644–663

Birdsall, Nancy 1985. 'Public inputs and child schooling in Brazil', *Journal of Development Economics*, vol. 18: 67–86

---

[41] Education appears therefore to perform a double role, both as basic capability and as a possible determinant of other capabilities of the individual or of other members of the household. In this sense, together with being a 'basic' capability in a Sen sense, it also falls into the category of 'internal' capabilities in the Nussbaum sense – though neither author focuses on the possible implications for others.

Chambers, Robert 1995. '*Poverty and livelihoods: whose reality counts?*', Discussion Paper 347, Brighton Institute of Development Studies

Chaudhuri, S. and Ravallion, M. 1994. 'How well do static indicators identify the chronically poor?', *Journal of Public Economics*, 53: 367–394

Cornia, Giovanni Andrea and Frances, Stewart 1995. 'Two errors of targeting', in Van de Walle, Dominique and Kimberly Nead (eds.) *Public spending and the poor. Theory and evidence* Baltimore: Johns Hopkins University Press for the World Bank, pp. 350–386

Cummins, Robert A. 2000. 'Objective and Subjective Quality of Life: An Interactive Model,' *Social Indicators Research*, 52: 55–72

Doyal, D. and Gough, I. 1991. 'Who Needs Human Needs?' In: Doyal, L. and Gough, I. *A Theory of Human Need* Basingstoke: Macmillan

Feachem, Richard G.A., Kiellstrom, Tord, Murray, Christopher J.L., Over, Mead and Phillips, Margaret A. 1992. *The Health of adults in the developing world* New York: Oxford University Press for the World Bank

Gertler, Paul and Van der Gaag, Jacques 1990. *The willingness to pay for medical care: Evidence from two developing countries* Baltimore: Johns Hopkins University Press for the World Bank

Harbison, Ralph W. and Hanuschek, Eric A. 1992. *Educational performance of the poor. Lessons from rural North East Brazil* New York: Oxford University Press for the World Bank

Haddad, Lawrence and Kanbur, Ravi 1989. 'How serious is the neglect of intra-household inequality?', *The Economic Journal*, 100: pp. 866–881

Instituto Cuánto (1994) Encuesta Nacional de Hogares sobre Medición de Niveles de Vida (ENNIV) 1994, Lima, Instituto Cuánto

Kennedy, Eileen and Haddad, Lawrence 1994. 'Are pre-schoolers from female-headed households less malnourished? A comparative analysis of results from Ghana and Kenya', *Journal of Development Economics*, 30: 680–696

Klasen, S. 2000. 'Measuring poverty and deprivation in South Africa', *Review of Income and Wealth*, 46(1): 33–58

Lipton, Michael and Ravallion, Martin 1995. 'Poverty and Policy' in Behrman Jere and Srinivasan T.N. *Handbook of Development Economics* 3, Amsterdam: Elsevier

McGranahan, Donald 1972. 'Development indicators and development models', *Journal of Development Studies*, 8: 170–196

Moncada, Gilberto and Webb, Richard 1996. *Como estamos. Analisis de la enquesta de Niveles de Vida*, Lima: Cuanto and UNICEF

Murray, Christopher J. L., Feachem, Richard G. A., Phillips, Margaret A. and Willis Carla 1992. 'Adult morbidity: limited data and methodological uncertainty', Chapter 3 in Feachem *et al.* 1992

Nussbaum, Martha C. 1999. *Sex and social justice* Oxford: Oxford University Press

Nussbaum, Martha C. 2000. *Women and human development. The capabilities approach* Cambridge: Cambridge University Press

Rivers, Douglas and Vuong, Quang H. 1988. 'Limited information estimators and exogeneity tests for simultaneous probit models', *Journal of Econometrics*, 39: 347–366

Rowntree, B. Seebohm 1902. *Poverty. A study of town life* London: Macmillan and Co. 2nd edition

Ruggeri Laderchi, C. 1999. *The Many Dimensions of Deprivation in Peru: Theoretical Debates and Empirical Evidence.* Queen Elizabeth House Working Paper No. 29. University of Oxford

Sen, Amartya 1983. 'Poor, relatively speaking', *Oxford Economic Papers*, 35: 153–169

Sen, Amartya 1985. *Commodities and capabilities* Amsterdam: North Holland

Sen, Amartya 1992. *Inequality re-examined* Oxford: Oxford University Press

Sen, Amartya 1997. *On economic inequality* Oxford: Clarendon Press 2nd edition

Smith, Richard and Blundell, Richard W. 1986. 'An exogeneity test for a simultaneous equation tobit model with an application to labour supply', *Econometrica*, 54: 679–685

Strauss, John and Duncan, Thomas 1995. 'Human resources: empirical modelling of household and family decisions' in Behrman, Jere and Srinivasan, T. N. *Handbook of development economics* 3, Amsterdam: Elsevier

Strauss, John, Gertler, Paul, Rahman, Omar and Fox, Kristin 1993. 'Gender and life-cycle differentials in the patterns and determinants of adult health', *Journal of Human Resources*, 28: 791–837

Sugden, Robert 1993. 'Welfare, resources and capabilities: a review of "inequality re-examined" by Amartya Sen', *Journal of Economic Literature*, 31: 1947–1963

Townsend, Peter (ed.) 1970. *The concept of poverty* London: Heinemann Educational Books Ltd

UNDP 1990. *Human development report* New York: Oxford University Press

Veit-Wilson, John 1986. 'Paradigms of poverty: a rehabilitation of B.S. Rowntree', *Journal of Social Policy*, 15: 69–99

Wolff, Lawrence, Schiefelben, Ernesto and Valuenzela, Jorge 1994. *Improving the quality of primary education in Latin America and the*

Caribbean, World Bank Discussion Paper n. 257. Washington D.C.: the World Bank

World Bank 1996. *Poverty reduction and the World Bank. Progress and challenges in the 1990s* Washington D.C.: the World Bank

WSSD (World Social Summit Declaration) 1995. *Report of the World Summit for Social Development*, Copenhagen 6–12 March

8 Social exclusion in the EU: a capability-based approach

FOTIS PAPADOPOULOS[1] AND PANOS TSAKLOGLOU[2,3]

Introduction

Since the late 1980s, in the political discourses of several European countries the term 'poverty' has been gradually substituted primarily by the term 'social exclusion' and, to a lesser extent, by the terms 'social disintegration' and 'social marginalisation'. Comprehensive definitions of 'social exclusion' used in the academic literature interpret it as the denial of social, political and civil rights of citizens in society or the inability of groups of individuals to participate in the basic political, economic and social functionings of the society [Silver (1994), de Haan (1998)]. In practice, though, policy makers as well as a number of social scientists in EU member-states seem to interpret 'social exclusion' as 'exclusion from the labour market', 'acute poverty and material deprivation' (or both) or, less frequently, 'inability to exercise basic social rights' [Mayes *et al.* (2001), Atkinson *et al.* (2002)]. Few empirical studies investigating aspects of social exclusion can be found in the literature and, among them, there exists little agreement regarding its proper operationalisation.

This chapter builds on earlier work of the authors [Tsakloglou and Papadopoulos (2002a, 2002b)] and attempts to outline a methodology for the identification of population members at high risk of social exclusion based on Sen's concept of capability failure, using the information of the European Community Household Panel (ECHP).

[1] Athens University of Economics and Business.
[2] Athens University of Economics and Business, IZA and IMOP.
[3] Acknowledgements: we are grateful to two anonymous referees for very useful comments and suggestions. The final version of the chapter was written when Panos Tsakloglou was Visiting Senior Research Fellow at the Hellenic Observatory of the European Institute of the LSE. He wishes to thank the members of the Observatory for their hospitality. The usual disclaimers apply.

Social exclusion and capabilities

Earlier studies of social exclusion claimed that 'poverty' and 'social exclusion' differ in two fundamental respects: 'poverty' is unidimensional since it is concerned only with lack of income, whereas 'social exclusion' is multidimensional since it is related to a broad range of aspects of deprivation and, further, 'poverty' is a static concept whereas 'social exclusion' is a dynamic concept [Berghman (1995)]. Both claims are controversial. Although a considerable number of empirical poverty studies equate poverty with lack of income, at least since the pioneering work of Townsend (1979), many social scientists have argued that poverty is a multidimensional phenomenon and several of them have incorporated aspects of multiple deprivation in their analysis. Further, in recent years with the advent of panel data and the extensive use of administrative records, a large number of empirical studies have been devoted to the investigation of dynamic aspects of poverty. In fact, as Sen (2000) points out, social exclusion might not be such a 'new' concept after all. Notions of poverty conceptualised in broader than monetary terms can be found even in Aristotle's *Nicomachean Ethics*, whereas the notions of exclusion and inclusion are at the centre of the concept of poverty used by Adam Smith in the *Wealth of Nations*.

Sen (1985a, 1999, 2000) argues that in order to assess one's well-being it is essential to define the latter in terms of capabilities rather than opulence or utility. Capabilities, as a freedom notion, is much wider than owning commodities or being happy or even fulfilling desires, as with the classic utilitarian approach. People own commodities, which in turn have certain characteristics that are used in order to satisfy various needs. The way people use these characteristics defines their 'functionings'; in other words their achievements. The notion of capabilities represents the freedom that a person has in terms of choice among a wider set of functionings and commodities. Limited choice among 'functionings' can lead to capability deprivation and, in extremis, social exclusion.

A number of practical problems arise when one tries to assess well-being using the capability approach. The problem first concerns the list of 'functionings' that are considered to be important (they may depend on the reference society). The second is a weighting problem on the importance of different functionings, whereas a third problem has to do with the valuation not only of the set of functionings that is chosen but also of the other sets that are not; in other words, the valuation of capabilities. Sen (1983) argues that deprivation in the space of capabilities has an absolute core; it is only in the space of commodities that escaping from a form of deprivation may depend on the reference society. For example, being free or well fed is a universal goal, but the importance of the particular commodities and/or functionings that will guarantee the satisfaction of these needs may depend on the conditions of the society in which the individual lives. In this sense, it is not necessary to observe a conceptual conflict between the capability approach, which has an 'absolutist' core, and an outright relativist approach in Townsend's research tradition [Sen (1983, 1985b), Townsend (1985)]. In order to assess deprivation in the space of capabilities, one might need to take a relative approach in the space of commodities.

Sen (2000) puts social exclusion in this perspective. Social exclusion is a particular form of relational capability deprivation, closely related to the notion of poverty. It is important to note, though, that not all kinds of deprivational situations should be analysed under the concept of social exclusion. The key point that should be kept in mind is the relational aspects of deprivation that can be brought to attention using this notion. The context given to the idea of social exclusion by Sen traces the following broad lines. Social exclusion is connected with poverty in the sense that poverty means poor living and not just having fewer commodities or lower monetary income. Thus, social exclusion, like poverty under the capability approach, is multidimensional. Further, as noted earlier, social exclusion is relational. Sen argues that exclusion from social relations is itself as important as other forms of 'mainstream' deprivation but it can also lead to these other forms, such as employment deprivation, economic poverty, etc. Finally, there is an issue of relativity in addressing this problem in practice, based on society rules and customs. After all, even under the notion of social exclusion as a particular form of relational capability deprivation one needs to establish a connection with the particular society that people run the risk of being excluded from; hence the need for a relative analysis in the space of commodities.

Sen makes two further remarks regarding the way social exclusion can lead to deprivation. First, social exclusion has 'constitutive relevance', in the sense that it has a distinctive importance of its own, no matter what other consequences it has. Moreover, it also has 'instrumental importance', in the sense that there are categories of relational deprivation or even unfavourable inclusion that might not be so bad by nature, but their consequences could lead to far more fierce forms of deprivation. As a result, on the one hand social exclusion can be viewed both as a state and as a process leading to deprivation and, on the other hand, other forms of deprivation may reinforce situations of exclusion. Second, a distinction should be made between 'active' and 'passive' exclusion. The criterion used in this case is whether a policy maker makes a deliberate attempt to exclude from the society particular groups of individuals. This distinction is more important at the level of policy analysis. Sen notes that, even in the case of 'passive' exclusion where there is no direct attempt to exclude, it is the policy maker's responsibility to remedy the possible reasons that lead to exclusion.

Empirical implementation

Data and methodology

The quantification of social exclusion is not an easy task. There is no consensus on a specific method on either 'functioning' and 'capability' valuation. Sen (1985a) suggests that a good approach of researching well-being based on capabilities would be to use 'responses to questionnaires' and 'non-market observations of personal states'. Regarding which functionings are important, Sen (1985a: 30–31) argues that

in the richer countries, the functionings involving longevity, nourishment, basic health, avoiding epidemics, being literate, etc., may have less variation from person to person, but there are other functionings that do vary a great deal. The ability to entertain friends, be close to people one would like to see, take part in the life of the community, etc. may vary a good deal even within a rich country, such as USA or the UK.

On a slightly different note, Sen (2000) suggests that the quantification of social exclusion calls for discrete treatment in areas such as lack of access to health care, lack of educational opportunities, absence of social safety nets, credit market exclusion, lack of facilities for disabled persons, marketing limitations, political and cultural exclusion, employment exclusion, etc. Especially for the latter, Sen (1997) points out that labour market exclusion and social exclusion are not one and the same thing and should not be treated as such, although he admits that long-term unemployment can be both a constitutive and instrumental factor in an exclusionary process.

The data requirements for the operationalisation of Sen's approach are extremely heavy and the information required for its full implementation does not exist in any data set currently available in any country. In this section, we attempt to provide an operational approximation using the information of the first five waves of the ECHP, which cover the period 1994–1998. The ECHP is an ambitious effort at collecting information on the living standards of the households of the EU member-states using common definitions, information-collection methods and editing procedures. It contains detailed information on incomes, socio-economic characteristics, housing amenities, consumer durables, social relations, employment conditions, health status, subjective evaluation of well-being, etc. [Eurostat (1996)]. One of the main objectives of the ECHP is the collection of data that could be used for the analysis of various aspects of deprivation and social exclusion. However, in many cases, the information collected refers to 'functionings' rather than 'capabilities'.[4]

Our general approach is the following. In the first step, we construct static indicators of deprivation in particular fields (proxies for capability deprivation). In the second stage, we 'aggregate' this information in order to derive a static indicator of cumulative disadvantage. In the final stage, we focus on chronic cumulative disadvantage, which can be considered as a reasonable approximation to the concept of 'social exclusion' as outlined above.[5] Throughout the chapter, the unit of

---

[4] For nine EU member-states – Belgium, Denmark, France, Greece, Ireland, Italy, the Netherlands, Portugal and Spain – the ECHP data sets that were provided to the research community contain full information for all (five) waves currently available. In the cases of Germany, Luxembourg and the UK, after the fourth wave the original ECHP data sets were replaced by national panels harmonised, to the extent possible, with the methods and variable definitions of the 'original' ECHP. Information on a number of variables of interest for our analysis is not available in the latter ('harmonised national') panels. Austria and Finland joined the ECHP at later stages of the project, whereas in the case of Sweden a national panel containing relatively limited information was harmonised ex post to fit the ECHP.

[5] Relatively similar approaches have been adopted by Schokkaert and Van Ootegem (1990), Brandolini and D' Alessio (1998), Burchardt *et al.* (1999, 2002) and Klasen (2000) in their analyses of living standards, poverty and/or social

analysis is the individual (population member), although most of the information used has been collected at the household level. All estimates are weighted, using the population weights contained in the ECHP. Four blocks of information are used in order to construct deprivation indicators: income (poverty), living conditions, necessities of life and social relations. The ECHP contains information on several other fields that, under different circumstances, could be exploited for the purposes of the identification of population members at high risk of exclusion (such as current health status, highest education level attained, indebtedness, social security coverage, etc.). This information is not used here for various reasons (quality of information, cross-country comparability, information related to outcomes rather than ability to participate (capability), etc.).

Deprivation, cumulative disadvantage and social exclusion

The first deprivation indicator examined is lack of sufficient income (poverty). The use of such an indicator in the framework of the present analysis is not uncontroversial. However, as Sen (1999: 90) points out, 'while it is important to distinguish conceptually the notion of poverty as capability inadequacy from that of poverty as lowness of income, the two perspectives cannot but be related, since income is such an important means to capabilities'.

Two concepts of 'disposable income' are available in the ECHP. The first is 'net income from all sources during the previous year'. The second is 'current net monthly income'. The former is more comprehensive and, ceteris paribus, more appropriate for empirical poverty research, but, unlike the latter, it is not contemporaneous with the household's characteristics and refers to the year prior to the survey.[6] In the cases of Austria, Belgium, Denmark, France, Greece, Ireland, Italy, Netherlands, Portugal and Spain we were able to match the information on the household's 'net income from all sources during year *t*' with the information on the household's characteristics in year

exclusion in Belgium (among the unemployed), Italy, the UK and South Africa, respectively. See also the axiomatic approaches to the measurement of social exclusion developed by Chakravarty and D'Ambrosio (2003) and Bossert *et al.* (2005).

[6] Note that since both concepts do not contain either private or publicly provided incomes in-kind, they cannot be considered as very good approximations of the concept of 'command over resources'.

$t - 1$. For this group of countries we were able to create a data set with full information for all the variables used in our analysis for waves 2–4 (1995–1997). In the cases of Germany, Luxembourg and the UK we had to use the original ECHP data set for the period 1994–1996, since the 'harmonised national' panels did not contain variables crucial for our analysis. As a consequence, the concept of income used in these countries is 'current net monthly income'.[7]

As Sen (1999: 89) indicates, 'relative deprivation in terms of *incomes* can yield *absolute* deprivation in terms of *capabilities*' (italics in the original). Hence, in line with the current practice of Eurostat, we adopted a relativist approach and the poverty line used in our analysis is set at 60 per cent of the median equivalent income per capita, using the 'modified OECD equivalence scales'. The latter assign a weight of 1.00 to the household head, a weight of 0.50 to each of the remaining adults in the household and a weight of 0.30 to each child. The estimates of the poverty rate derived using this method on the data of the third wave of the ECHP are reported in the first column of Table 8.1. They show that relative poverty tends to be higher in countries with higher levels of aggregate inequality such as the Southern European countries associated with the 'rudimentary' welfare state regime and countries associated with the 'liberal' welfare regime (UK and Ireland) and lower in the low inequality countries of Northern and Central Europe with 'corporatist' or 'social-democratic' regimes.[8] The results of sensitivity analysis are provided in the first three columns of Table 8A1 in Appendix I, as the poverty line rises from 50 per cent to 60 per cent and then to 70 per cent of the median equivalent income per capita. Even though in all countries the poverty rates rise sharply as the level of the poverty line increases, in broad terms the relative ranking of countries hardly changes.

The second deprivation indicator used in this chapter covers the field of living conditions. In this field, the ECHP contains information on

---

[7] In the case of Finland for which we did not have information for a sufficient number of waves, we present only cross-sectional results, whereas due to the limited information available, we were obliged to leave Sweden out of our analysis.

[8] Despite its popularity, an important drawback of the poverty rate as a deprivation indicator is that it is not sensitive to the distance of the deprived individual from the deprivation threshold, that is, the poverty line. This drawback is also common in the rest of the deprivation indicators used in our analysis.

Table 8.1 *Deprivation indicators*

| Country | Proportion of the population in the third wave of the ECHP (1996) classified as deprived according to: | | | |
	Income (poverty)	Living conditions	Necessities of life	Social relations
Austria	13.6	6.8	11.8	5.9
Belgium	15.1	6.8	10.6	8.8
Denmark	10.0	4.6	6.5	4.0
Finland	12.0	3.9	11.5	2.9
France	15.4	6.6	15.2	4.3
Germany	10.3	6.3	11.9	4.7
Greece	22.3	10.6	32.2	2.0
Ireland	19.6	9.7	15.4	0.6
Italy	18.1	9.2	16.0	6.8
Luxembourg	9.2	4.5	7.7	6.5
Netherlands	11.2	4.2	9.9	5.2
Portugal	22.0	19.6	15.9	4.5
Spain	19.7	8.7	15.6	2.3
United Kingdom	23.8	5.5	17.6	1.6

twenty-two items related to the availability of certain household amenities, the existence of particular problems in the accommodation and the enforced lack of a number of durable goods.[9] Naturally, these items are not equally important in all countries. Hence, in order to aggregate the available information into a single 'welfare indicator' in the field of living conditions, for every item under consideration we assigned to each population member living in a particular country and having

[9] The information of the ECHP on household amenities refers to the existence of the following amenities in the dwelling: a separate kitchen, a bath or shower, an indoor flushing toilet, hot running water, heating or electric storage heaters, and a place to sit outside (e.g. terrace or garden). The self-reported information on problems with a household's accommodation refer to the following problems: shortage of space, noise from neighbours or outside, too dark, not enough light, lack of adequate heating facilities, leaky roof, damp walls, floors, foundation etc., rot in window frames or floors, pollution, grime or other environmental problems caused by traffic or industry, vandalism or crime in the area. Finally, the information on enforced lack of durable goods due to financial reasons concerns the following items: car or van (available for private use), colour TV, video recorder, microwave, dishwasher, telephone, second home (e.g. for vacation).

access to a particular item (housing amenity or lack of problem or durable good) a weight equal to the proportion of the country's population living in dwellings not lacking the corresponding amenity or not reporting the relevant problem or not reporting enforced lack of the particular durable good. As a consequence, if a particular item is very rare (common) in a particular country, an individual living in a household with such an item is assigned a low (high) welfare weight. Then, the weights of each person are added and the resulting sum is divided by the sum of the average 'welfare scores' for each item for the entire population.[10] Finally, a cut-off point in the distribution of this welfare indicator is selected and the population members falling below this threshold are defined as persons at high risk of deprivation in the field of living conditions. For the purposes of our analysis, we selected a cut-off point equal to 80 per cent of the median of the distribution of the above welfare indicator. The resulting estimates using the data of the third wave of the ECHP are reported in the second column of Table 8.1. The cross-country differences are substantially larger than the differences reported in the first column of the table. In general, higher aggregate deprivation rates are reported in the poorest EU member-states. Nonetheless, it should be kept in mind that these scores are purely relative, in the sense that they have been derived using national cut-off points. Naturally, the particular threshold selected, like the poverty line selected before, is quite arbitrary. Nevertheless, as the evidence of Table 8A1 shows, the results are fairly robust in terms of the ranking of the various countries when the threshold changes but, of course, not so the share of the population classified as deprived.

---

[10] In algebraic terms, the formula used for the calculation of each person's 'welfare indicator', uj, is:

$$u_j = \frac{\sum_{i=1}^{I} w_i X_{ij}}{\sum_{i=1}^{I} w_i}$$

where I is the total number of items for which information is available (22 items), w_i is the proportion of the country's population living in accommodation with item i and X_{ij} is a variable that takes the value of 1 (0) if individual j lives in a household that is (is not) equipped with item i. For each population member the 'welfare indicator', u_j, takes values between 0 (complete deprivation) and 1 (no deprivation).

The third static deprivation indicator concerns the field of necessities of life. The households that participated in the ECHP were asked a number of questions about their ability to afford (if they wanted to) a number of activities considered as quite basic.[11] The method used for the construction of a deprivation indicator in the field of necessities of life is similar to that outlined above for the construction of a deprivation indicator in the field of living conditions. We first constructed country-specific welfare indicators for each population member based on the proportion of the country's population residing in households where the reference person replied positively to each of the questions asked. After experimenting with several thresholds, we selected a cut-off point equal to 60 per cent of the national median and derived the estimates reported in the third column of Table 8.1. Again, as a general tendency, higher deprivation rates are reported in the poorest EU member-states. As the results of sensitivity analysis reported in the last three columns of Table 8A1 show, in the case of necessities of life the country rankings are not as robust with respect to the threshold used as in the cases of income (poverty) and living conditions. The latter should be attributed primarily to the limited number of items used for the construction of the welfare indicator in the field of necessities of life, which results in a rather discontinuous distribution of welfare scores.

The fourth static deprivation indicator covers the field of social relations. In this case, we classified as deprived those population members aged sixteen or above who reported that they talk to their neighbours 'once or twice a month' or less frequently and, in addition, they meet friends 'once or twice a month' or less frequently and, further, they are not members of a club or organisation (such as a sport or entertainment club, a local or neighbourhood group, a political party, etc.). Children aged below sixteen were assigned the same status – deprived or non-deprived – as the reference persons of their households. The corresponding estimates are reported in the last column of Table 8.1. Unlike the other non-monetary deprivation indicators used

[11] The ECHP contains information on the ability of the households to afford (if they want to) the following: keep their homes adequately warm, pay for a week's annual holiday away from home, replace worn-out furniture, buy new, rather than second-hand, clothes, eat meat, chicken or fish every second day and have friends or family for a drink or meal at least once a month.

in this chapter that are likely, at least to some extent, to be correlated with the financial conditions of the individual and his/her household, this indicator aims to capture non-material aspects of exclusion. Undoubtedly, an individual classified as deprived according to the above definition must live a very isolated life, even if she has the capability to sustain a relatively high material standard of living. Nevertheless, using the information of the ECHP we cannot be sure whether the individual chose to be in this state (unlikely but not impossible) or not.

In the next stage, we proceed to the examination of the 'cumulative disadvantage' experienced by the members of each country's population; that is, the number of indicators according to which each population member is classified as deprived. It should be noted that this approach is not uncontroversial, since it gives equal weight to all deprivation indicators. The corresponding estimates, using the data of the third wave of the ECHP, are reported in Table 8.2. In all countries, the majority of the population is not classified as deprived according to any of the four deprivation indicators. The proportion of the population classified as deprived according to at least one indicator varies between 20.5 per cent in Denmark and 43.5 per cent in Greece. In all countries, substantially fewer population members are classified as deprived according to at least two indicators than according to at least one indicator. The proportion of the population classified as deprived according to three or four indicators varies between 5.5 per cent in Portugal and less than 1 per cent in Luxembourg. Undoubtedly, being classified as deprived according to one criterion only may be due to a chance factor. On the contrary, limiting the group of people at high risk of cumulative disadvantage to those classified as deprived according to three or four criteria would, in most cases, restrict the group to an extremely small number of seriously disadvantaged persons and would not allow any further analysis of the group's characteristics. Therefore, we decided to consider as persons at high risk of (static) cumulative disadvantage those that are classified as deprived according to at least two of the above deprivation indicators. Using this criterion, the population share of the group varies between 3.4 per cent in Denmark and 18.8 per cent in Greece. High shares are also recorded in Portugal, the UK, Italy, Ireland, Spain and France, whereas the corresponding shares in the Netherlands, Luxembourg, Finland and, to a lesser extent, Germany, Austria and Belgium are relatively low.

Table 8.2 *Indicators of cumulative disadvantage (third wave of the ECHP, 1996)*

Country	Proportion of the population classified as deprived* according to:				
	No criterion	At least one criterion	At least two criteria	At least three criteria	All four criteria
Austria	71.5	28.5	7.6	1.6	**
Belgium	70.7	29.3	8.2	2.8	**
Denmark	79.5	20.5	3.4	1.3	**
Finland	76.6	23.4	5.8	1.0	**
France	70.7	29.3	9.4	2.6	[0.2]
Germany	76.7	23.3	7.3	1.9	**
Greece	56.5	43.5	18.8	4.5	**
Ireland	71.0	29.0	10.6	4.2	**
Italy	65.4	34.6	11.3	3.3	[0.2]
Luxembourg	78.5	21.5	5.5	[0.8]	**
Netherlands	77.7	22.3	5.4	1.0	[0.2]
Portugal	60.0	40.0	15.6	5.5	[0.3]
Spain	65.7	34.3	9.9	2.2	**
United Kingdom	67.7	32.3	14.4	3.5	**

* Using the criteria of Table 8.1: income (poverty), living conditions, necessities of life and social relations.
Note: Figures in brackets denote that the estimate is derived from a small number of observations (between 20 and 50), while a double asterisk denotes that there are fewer than 20 observations in the sample.

As noted earlier, one of the characteristics of social exclusion that has been emphasised in the literature is its dynamic nature. Being excluded today may lead an individual into a trap with little prospect of escaping exclusion in the future. Table 8.3 provides estimates about the number of times each country's population members are classified as being at high risk of cumulative disadvantage during a period of three years using the longitudinal sample of the first three waves of the ECHP. Taking into account the evidence of Tables 8.1 and, particularly, 8.2, it is not surprising to find that in all countries the great majority of the population is not classified as being at high risk of cumulative disadvantage in any of the three years. The share of those classified as being at high risk of cumulative disadvantage in at least

Table 8.3 *Indicators of high risk of social exclusion*

Country	Proportion of the population classified as suffering from cumulative disadvantage* during a period of three years (1994–96)			
	Never	At least once	At least twice	Three times
Austria	87.0	13.0	6.1	2.6
Belgium	85.3	14.7	7.5	4.4
Denmark	92.4	7.6	1.5	[0.4]
France	85.2	14.8	6.9	2.9
Germany	87.0	13.0	5.4	1.8
Greece	73.5	26.5	15.6	7.8
Ireland	84.3	15.7	9.8	5.3
Italy	81.0	19.0	9.7	4.6
Luxembourg	88.7	11.3	5.5	[2.1]
Netherlands	91.2	8.8	4.2	1.5
Portugal	75.9	24.1	15.0	10.8
Spain	82.5	17.5	7.1	2.2
United Kingdom	79.8	20.2	13.0	8.0

* Classified in a particular year as deprived according to at least two of the following criteria: income (poverty), living conditions, necessities of life and social relations.

one year varies significantly across countries, from 7.6 per cent in Denmark to 26.5 per cent in Greece. Substantial variation is also observed with respect to the population share of those classified as being at high risk of cumulative disadvantage during all three years, from less than 1 per cent in Denmark to over 10 per cent in Portugal.

Being at high risk of cumulative disadvantage only once may be attributed to a chance factor and does not necessarily provide a strong indication of high risk of social exclusion. Similarly, escaping high risk of cumulative disadvantage only once in a period of three years may also be attributed to a chance factor and should not be considered as a strong indication of low risk of social exclusion. Therefore, we decided to focus on those classified as being at high risk of cumulative disadvantage at least twice during a period of three years and classify them as being at high risk of social exclusion. The corresponding estimates are shown in the third column of Table 8.3. They demonstrate that the cross-country variation is considerable. Only 1.5 per cent of the Danish population are classified as being at high risk of social exclusion, whereas the corresponding proportion for Greece is 15.6 per cent. High proportions are also recorded in Portugal (15.0 per cent) and the UK (13.0 per cent) and relatively low ones in the Netherlands (4.2 per cent), Germany (5.4 per cent) and Luxembourg (5.5 per cent). For the rest of the countries under consideration the relevant share varies between 6.1 per cent and 9.8 per cent.

Population groups at high risk of social exclusion

This approach can also be used for the identification of population groups at exceptionally high (or low) risk of social exclusion within each country, as well as for the quantification of their contribution to the aggregate risk of social exclusion in the country under examination. Such an analysis is performed in this subsection. For the purposes of our analysis, each country's population (balanced sample only) is subdivided into mutually exhaustive and exclusive groups according to seven criteria: employment status of the individual and his/her reference person (household head), educational level of the individual and his/her reference person and the individual's household type, health status and citizenship. The corresponding results are reported in Table 8.4.[12] Two types of estimates are reported. The first is the relative risk of social exclusion of the population group in comparison with the national average (column A). Figures substantially higher (lower) than 1 indicate a high (low) risk of social exclusion in comparison with the rest of the population within a particular country. However, since the population shares of these groups may differ substantially across countries, two identical relative risk factors may represent very different contributions to the aggregate risk of social

---

[12] Due to the very small number of individuals classified as being at high risk of social exclusion in the Danish sample, no such analysis is performed for Denmark. The notation used in Table 8.4 is the following: Austria: A, Belgium: B, Germany: D, Spain: E, Greece: EL, France: F, Ireland: IRL, Italy: I, Luxembourg: L, the Netherlands: NL, Portugal: P and the United Kingdom: UK. Since during a period of three years several changes in status may be observed, for the purposes of our grouping we used the most frequently observed classification. In cases of ties, the allocation between the observed categories was random, with one exception: in the case of employment status, if one of the three observed classifications was 'unemployed', the individual was classified as unemployed.

exclusion. For this reason, we also report the contribution of each group to the aggregate risk of social exclusion; that is, the share of the group's members among those classified as being at high risk of social exclusion (column B).

In the first two panels of Table 8.4 the population members are grouped according to the employment status of the household's reference person and the individual himself/herself, respectively. Since a considerable proportion of the information required for the construction of the indicator of social exclusion was collected at the household level, it is likely that the characteristics of the reference person may be more important than those of the individual for the determination of the individual's risk of social exclusion. Five groups are formed in the first panel of the table: 'Employed full-time', 'Employed part-time',[13] 'Unemployed', 'Retired' and 'Other inactive'. The latter consists mostly of persons engaged in housework and, to a lesser extent, students.

The estimates reported in the first line of Table 8.4 show that in all countries, the relative risk of social exclusion of population members living in households where the reference person is employed full-time is lower than the national average. However, in some countries the relevant risk factor is below 0.2 (Ireland, Belgium, UK), whereas in others it is higher than 0.6 (Luxembourg, Italy, Portugal, Austria). As a consequence, in some countries over 40 per cent of those classified as being at high risk of social exclusion live in households where the reference person is employed full-time (Luxembourg, Portugal, Italy) whereas in others the relevant share is around 10 per cent (Ireland, Belgium, UK). The estimates reported in the second line of the table show that in most countries, the small group of persons living in households where the reference person is employed part-time face a risk of social exclusion higher but, with few exceptions (Ireland, Luxembourg, France), not considerably higher than the national average. Due to its small population share, in no country apart from Ireland is the group's contribution to the aggregate risk of social exclusion higher than 10 per cent. On the contrary, in all countries living in a household whose reference person is

---

[13] Following Eurostat's definitions, the criterion for distinguishing between full-time and part-time employment is whether the individual works more than thirty hours per week.

Table 8.4 *Relative risk factors and contributions to the aggregate risk of social exclusion of particular population groups*

	A		B		D		E		EL		F		IRL		I		L		NL		P		UK	
	A	B	A	B	A	B	A	B	A	B	A	B	A	B	A	B	A	B	A	B	A	B	A	B
Employment status (ref. person)																								
Employed full-time	0.64	35.1	0.17	10.2	0.56	36.5	0.58	33.9	0.58	39.8	0.45	30.6	0.14	8.1	0.76	45.1	0.77	53.4	0.29	17.4	0.69	47.0	0.19	11.9
Employed part-time	0.70	2.9	0.77	1.1	0.69	1.7	2.28	2.0	1.69	1.7	2.78	4.0	4.51	16.3	1.32	1.3	[2.80]	[3.0]	1.15	5.4	0.90	2.0	0.62	1.7
Unemployed	3.18	7.3	4.72	10.0	5.18	19.6	2.63	27.4	1.92	5.2	5.45	18.7	3.42	29.3	4.46	11.1	**	**	5.49	14.0	3.32	10.1	4.11	20.3
Retired	1.26	28.7	1.50	41.7	0.90	22.6	0.87	16.9	1.70	34.6	1.21	29.2	0.31	3.4	0.78	24.6	0.98	23.3	0.68	12.5	1.31	25.3	0.89	17.3
Other inactive	1.71	26.0	3.66	37.0	4.50	19.6	1.70	19.7	2.33	18.6	4.36	17.5	2.57	42.9	2.82	17.9	4.78	19.5	3.63	50.7	1.83	15.6	4.09	48.8
Employment status (individual)																								
Employed full-time	0.53	21.3	0.13	4.1	0.43	16.5	0.38	9.9	0.58	19.1	0.32	12.2	0.11	3.4	0.46	13.9	0.56	20.1	0.15	4.5	0.64	26.9	0.14	5.0
Employed part-time	0.71	2.9	0.11	0.4	0.73	5.1	1.00	1.7	1.27	1.7	0.97	3.1	0.53	2.3	0.80	1.4	1.06	5.2	0.83	10.6	0.88	2.4	0.37	3.0
Unemployed	2.06	4.2	3.07	9.4	3.67	16.5	2.05	21.2	1.44	7.1	3.51	18.9	2.35	11.6	2.69	15.1	[2.27]	[3.0]	3.55	9.9	2.9		2.70	12.9
Discouraged	[1.87]	[0.9]	3.78	3.6	3.45	1.5	2.24	2.8	1.95	0.7	2.66	1.1	3.22	4.4	2.50	5.0	–		–		1.05	0.6	2.39	1.4
Constrained	1.46	11.8	1.82	17.6	1.06	7.7	1.08	21.7	1.09	18.3	2.19	8.4	1.21	21.9	1.38	17.8	1.17	17.9	2.13	10.8	1.51	11.4	2.22	21.3
Precariously employed	[0.86]	[0.2]	0.85	0.9	2.22	1.7	1.53	3.6	1.33	1.9	1.49	0.8	1.81	3.4	2.61	3.4	–		0.0	0.0	1.59	1.8	0.76	0.9
Retired	1.79	12.4	1.31	14.3	0.76	3.0	0.57	4.5	0.97	5.4	1.47	17.0	0.44	2.1	0.80	8.2	1.15	6.0	2.02	24.1	0.49	3.9	1.42	3.6
Other inactive	1.32	22.7	0.89	18.2	0.92	19.5	0.81	8.6	1.81	30.7	1.06	18.4	0.49	2.9	0.76	15.2	0.81	12.7	0.51	7.8	1.50	22.6	0.85	13.8
Aged less than 17	1.17	23.6	1.60	31.5	1.69	28.4	1.31	26.2	0.77	15.1	1.06	20.0	1.67	48.0	1.23	20.2	1.69	35.1	1.46	32.3	1.33	27.4	1.82	38.1
Household type																								
Older household, no children	1.88	20.8	0.86	12.8	0.90	14.2	1.08	9.8	2.05	29.0	1.08	14.2	0.69	4.5	0.96	12.8	0.50	5.8	0.54	7.4	1.80	17.5	0.94	15.1
Younger household, no children	0.86	15.3	0.86	15.8	0.77	20.0	0.90	5.2	0.81	9.7	0.97	19.3	0.78	7.2	0.53	5.0	0.96	18.2	0.80	21.9	0.83	5.2	0.56	12.2
Lone parent household	1.40	6.2	1.74	8.3	3.47	10.0	1.80	4.3	0.86	2.0	2.16	7.8	2.62	11.9	1.09	3.7	1.82	5.0	7.17	26.9	1.51	5.2	3.51	10.1
Couple with children	0.95	36.6	1.09	55.8	1.10	42.8	0.98	47.4	0.48	21.4	0.89	43.4	1.11	67.9	0.93	45.9	1.15	56.2	0.83	39.0	0.59	28.8	1.14	54.4
Other household types	0.77	21.1	0.70	7.3	0.86	13.0	0.97	33.3	1.38	37.9	1.08	15.3	0.47	8.5	1.32	32.6	0.72	14.9	0.57	4.8	1.36	43.3	0.53	8.1

Table 8.4 (*cont.*)

	A		B		D		E		EL		F		IRL		I		L		NL		P		UK	
	A	B	A	B	A	B	A	B	A	B	A	B	A	B	A	B	A	B	A	B	A	B	A	B
Education level (ref. person)																								
Tertiary	0.59	3.5	0.52	20.5	0.36	9.4	0.13	2.1	0.09	1.6	0.21	4.1	0.05	0.6	0.06	0.5	0.13	2.3	0.14	2.7	0.0	0.0	0.23	5.0
2nd stage secondary	0.58	35.0	0.40	15.5	0.93	43.5	0.33	3.6	0.30	7.3	0.59	22.1	0.59	16.5	0.36	11.8	0.39	12.3	0.69	39.5	0.15	1.0	0.61	18.0
Less than 2nd stage secondary	1.94	57.2	1.45	63.9	1.85	45.8	1.30	94.0	1.58	89.3	1.78	73.1	1.48	82.9	1.21	87.5	1.64	85.4	2.23	43.9	1.15	99.0	1.60	75.3
Still in education	1.46	4.2	0.0	0.0	0.64	1.3	0.40	0.3	1.79	1.8	0.89	0.7	0.0	0.0	0.26	0.1	–	–	3.25	13.9	0.0	0.0	0.76	1.8
Education level (individual)																								
Tertiary	0.43	1.8	0.40	8.3	0.43	6.3	0.16	1.6	0.13	1.7	0.23	3.4	0.06	0.4	0.11	0.5	0.07	0.8	0.20	2.4	0.12	0.4	0.23	3.4
2nd stage secondary	0.58	25.9	0.50	11.4	0.77	29.6	0.38	3.7	0.43	8.1	0.66	17.3	0.37	7.8	0.38	9.2	0.28	6.3	0.50	20.0	0.34	2.1	0.55	13.4
Less than 2nd stage secondary	1.79	42.0	1.23	37.1	1.23	32.8	1.25	66.4	1.60	71.9	1.57	51.6	1.23	41.3	1.18	61.7	1.27	54.8	1.44	30.7	1.11	68.2	1.19	43.3
Still in education	1.03	7.1	1.04	9.0	0.79	2.7	0.33	2.4	0.74	2.8	1.13	6.9	0.37	2.6	0.52	4.7	0.41	1.6	2.68	14.7	0.22	1.6	0.38	1.4
Aged less than 17	1.17	23.2	1.60	34.2	1.69	28.7	1.31	25.9	0.77	15.5	1.06	20.9	1.67	47.8	1.23	23.9	1.69	36.5	1.46	32.1	1.33	27.7	1.82	38.4
Health																								
Sick/Disabled	2.71	6.0	2.89	3.6	3.25	6.8	2.18	4.2	2.64	6.4	2.37	6.0	[1.94]	[0.6]	2.26	5.3	[2.73]	[2.9]	3.15	4.5	1.72	9.9	1.79	3.0
Healthy	0.79	94.0	0.84	96.4	0.88	93.2	0.87	95.8	0.85	93.6	0.82	94.0	0.99	99.4	0.89	94.7	0.84	97.1	0.89	95.5	0.83	90.1	0.88	97.0
Citizenship																								
Non-EU	4.31	20.0	1.92	13.5	3.16	5.1	[1.32]	[0.3]	1.31	1.5	3.55	20.3	[0.0]	[0.0]	3.31	1.0	[5.07]	[9.0]	6.39	5.3	2.31	1.3	2.05	2.6
EU	0.85	80.0	0.69	86.5	0.97	94.9	1.00	99.7	0.99	98.5	0.85	79.7	1.00	100	0.98	99.0	0.93	91.0	0.95	94.7	0.98	98.7	0.98	97.4

Notes: – no cases in the group,
** group with 1–20 cases,
[] group with 21–50 cases

Column A: Relative risk factor (proportion of the group at high risk of social exclusion divided by the proportion of all persons at high risk of social exclusion)
Column B: Contribution to aggregate risk of social exclusion (proportion of all persons aged 16+ at high risk of social exclusion who are members of the group)

unemployed is associated with a very high relative risk factor.[14] In the Netherlands, France and Germany the members of this group are over five times more likely to face social exclusion than the average population member, whereas in Belgium, Italy and the UK the relevant relative risk factor is between 4 and 5. At the other extreme, the group's relative risk factors in Luxembourg and Greece are lower than 2. These disparities, combined with the fact that the group's population share varies quite substantially across countries, result in significant cross-country differences with respect to the group's contribution to the aggregate risk of social exclusion. The corresponding contributions are between 20 per cent and 30 per cent in Ireland and Spain but lower than 10 per cent in Luxembourg, Greece and Austria. Cross-country differences are also observed in the next line of the table. In most countries, the relative risk factor of persons living in households whose reference person is retired is close to the national average, the only strong outliers being Greece (risk factor: 1.70) and Ireland (risk factor: 0.31). In most countries between a fifth and a third of those classified as being at high risk of social exclusion are members of the group. The exceptions are on the one side Ireland (3.4 per cent), the Netherlands (12.5 per cent), Spain (16.9 per cent) and the UK (17.3 per cent) and on the other Belgium (41.7 per cent) and Greece (34.6 per cent). Finally, the heterogeneous group of persons living in households whose reference person belongs to the 'other inactive' group appears to face a risk of social exclusion substantially higher than the national average in almost all countries under examination and, in some countries, over a third of those classified as being at high risk of social exclusion are members of this group (the Netherlands, the UK, Ireland, Belgium).

In the second panel of Table 8.4 the grouping factor is the employment status of the population member. The groups used are the same as those used in the first panel of the table, with three exceptions: 'discouraged workers', 'constrained workers' and 'precariously employed'. Such groups appear with increasing frequency as vulnerable population groups in policy debates. The group of 'precariously employed' persons is formed by extracting them from the group of

---

[14] It should be noted that, as Sen (1999, pp. 94–95) points out, it is important to distinguish unemployment as constitutive of capability failure and as a cause of capability failure.

those employed full-time or part-time. They are persons who were in employment in a particular wave of the ECHP but had experienced at least two unemployment spells during the previous five years or one unemployment spell lasting for over one year during the same period and, in addition, they reported that they felt 'extremely' or 'very' insecure in their current employment. The groups of 'discouraged workers' and 'constrained workers' were extracted from the group of 'other inactive' and consist of two types of people who are inactive but not retired. 'Discouraged workers' are those who left the labour market because, as they reported, they believed that there was no proper job for them. 'Constrained workers' are those, mostly females, who reported that they would have liked to have a job but were not searching for one because of housework or caring for children or other people.

Like the results of the first panel of the table, the results of this panel suggest that in all countries those in full-time employment face a substantially lower risk of social exclusion than the rest of the population. Again, a considerable dispersion in the corresponding relative risk factors is observed (from 0.11 in Ireland to 0.64 in Portugal). On the contrary, unlike the first panel of the table, the evidence of the second panel suggests that in most countries persons employed part-time face a lower risk of social exclusion than the average population member, even though the group's contribution to the aggregate social exclusion is higher than the contribution of the group of persons living in households headed by a part-time employee. Presumably, this difference should be attributed to the fact that most of the part-time employees are spouses or children of other household members (reference persons) who are employed full-time. In most cases, the opposite picture emerges with respect to the group of unemployed persons. Their relative risk of social exclusion is always higher than the national average but, in most cases, lower than the corresponding risk of persons living in households whose reference person is unemployed, implying that many unemployed persons live in households headed by persons with a different employment status (presumably employed). In almost all countries, the groups of 'discouraged workers', 'constrained workers' and, to a slightly lesser extent, 'precariously employed' persons face a risk of social exclusion higher than the rest of the population. Only the second of these groups, 'constrained workers', has a relatively high population share in all countries and, as a result, in some countries over a fifth of those classified as being at high risk of social exclusion are members of the group (Ireland, Spain, UK). In line with the results reported in the top panel of the table, both the relative risk and the contribution of the 'retired' to the aggregate risk of social exclusion vary considerably across countries. On the contrary, once the 'constrained workers' and the 'discouraged workers' are excluded from the group, in most countries the remaining members of the 'other inactive' group face a risk of social exclusion lower than the national average. Finally, it is important to note that in all but one of the countries under examination (Greece), children aged below seventeen face a higher risk of social exclusion than adults. In fact, in four countries the contribution of children to aggregate social exclusion is between 30 per cent and 40 per cent (UK, Luxembourg, the Netherlands, Belgium), whereas in Ireland almost one in two population members at high risk of social exclusion is a child.

In the third panel of Table 8.4 the population members are grouped according to their household type. Five groups are defined: 'older household, no children' (persons aged over sixty-four living alone and childless couples where at least one partner is aged over sixty-four), 'younger household, no children' (persons living alone or childless couples aged below sixty-four), 'lone parent household', 'couple with children' and 'other household types'. In this panel, cross-country differences are more striking than in the first two panels of the table.

In the majority of the countries under examination, the risk of social exclusion of the group of older households without children is close to the national average. There are significant exceptions though. The corresponding risk factor is around twice as high as the national average in Greece, Austria and Portugal, whereas the group's relative risk factors in Luxembourg, the Netherlands and, to a lesser extent, Ireland are substantially lower than the national average. These differences, combined with the fact that the group's population share varies substantially across countries, leads to spectacular cross-country differences with respect to the group's contribution to the aggregate risk of social exclusion. Less than 5 per cent of those at high risk of social exclusion in Ireland are members of the group, whereas the corresponding figure in Greece is close to 30 per cent. Unlike the estimates reported in the first line of this panel, the estimates in the second line suggest that in all countries the group of younger households without children faces a risk of social exclusion lower than the national average. Likewise, in most countries the risk of social exclusion of the members of couples with children is close to the national average. However, due to the fact that in all countries this is a large group, in most countries between 30 per cent and 50 per cent of those at high risk of social exclusion are members of the group. There are exceptions though. In Luxembourg, Belgium and the UK over half of those classified as being at high risk of social exclusion belong to the group, whereas in Ireland, despite the fact that the group's risk factor is not very high, over two thirds of those facing a high risk of social exclusion are members of this group. On the contrary, the corresponding shares in Greece and Portugal are lower than 30 per cent. In all countries except Greece, the members of lone-parent households face a higher risk of social exclusion than the rest of the population. In some countries, the corresponding risk factors are extremely high – the Netherlands (7.17) and, to a lesser extent, the UK (3.51) and Germany (3.47). As a consequence, in countries such as Greece, Spain and Italy fewer than 5 per cent of those classified as being at high risk of social exclusion are members of lone-parent households, whereas in Ireland, the UK and Germany the corresponding figure is around 10 per cent and in the Netherlands a staggering 26.9 per cent. Nothing of particular interest emerges from the results for the heterogeneous group of members of 'other household types'.

In the next two panels of Table 8.4, the national samples are grouped according to the educational status of the reference person (fourth panel) and the individual (fifth panel). Using the information of the ECHP, we are able to form only four groups: 'tertiary', '2nd stage secondary', 'less than 2nd stage secondary' and 'still in education'.[15] In several instances in the public discourse, low educational qualifications are cited as one of the main routes to social exclusion. Unfortunately, the information of the ECHP does not allow proper testing of this hypothesis, since the information contained therein on the educational qualifications of population members is not particularly disaggregated. In some countries, the group 'less than 2nd stage secondary' includes almost two thirds of the population members.

The evidence of these panels suggests that, indeed, high educational qualifications are an effective barrier against social exclusion. In all

---

[15] As well as 'aged less than 17' in the fifth panel – a group that was discussed earlier.

countries, the risk of social exclusion of tertiary education graduates or members of households where the reference person has completed tertiary education is significantly lower than the national average and, in most cases, the group's contribution to the aggregate risk of social exclusion is quite small, if not negligible. Moreover, in almost all cases the relative risk factors of upper secondary education graduates or members of households where the reference person has completed the 2nd stage of secondary education that are reported in the second line of these panels are higher than the corresponding estimates reported in the first line of the panels but lower than the national average. However, the cross-country differences in the relative risk factors are quite considerable, ranging from 0.15 in Portugal to over 0.9 in Germany. In all countries, the majority of those classified as facing a high risk of social exclusion have not completed the 2nd stage of secondary education. Nonetheless, primarily due to differences in population shares, the group's contribution to the aggregate risk of social exclusion varies considerably across countries, from around 30 per cent in the Netherlands and Germany to around 90 per cent in Greece and Portugal. Cross-country differences are also reported in the next line of these panels, regarding the small group of students or households headed by students. In most cases, these are low-risk groups, although the evidence of the Netherlands points in the opposite direction.

In the next panel of Table 8.4 the population members are grouped according to their self-reported health status into 'sick/disabled' and 'healthy'. More specifically, the first group consists of those who reported that they had 'bad or very bad health in general' and, in addition, that they were 'severely hampered in daily activities by mental health problem illness or disability', whereas the rest of each country's population members are classified as 'healthy' (including children aged under sixteen, for whom no such information was provided). Although far from uncontroversial, using this classification we can examine the extent to which health factors are associated with the risk of social exclusion in the countries under examination. The results of Table 8.4 suggest that in all countries those classified as 'sick/disabled' face a risk of social exclusion substantially higher than the national average – in most cases between two and three times higher.

In the last panel, the members of the ECHP are grouped according to their citizenship. In almost all countries, poor immigrants from Third

World countries are considered to be among the most vulnerable groups in the society. The information of the ECHP does not allow the classification of the population members according to their citizenship in a way that would be suitable for the purposes of the present work. Here, we use two groups: 'EU citizens' and 'non-EU citizens'. For a number of reasons, the corresponding estimates should be interpreted with great caution. Immigrants, and especially illegal immigrants, are likely to be seriously underrepresented in the sample of the ECHP. Moreover, not all non-EU immigrants originate from poor developing countries and their composition varies considerably across EU member-states. The estimates of Table 8.4 suggest that in almost all countries in which a sufficiently large number of non-EU citizens are included in the ECHP sample, this group faces a high relative risk of social exclusion, especially in countries such as the Netherlands, Luxembourg, Austria and, to a lesser extent, France and Germany. In fact, one in five persons at high risk of social exclusion in France and Austria is a member of this group, while the contribution of 'non-EU' citizens to the aggregate social exclusion is around 10 per cent in Belgium and Luxembourg.

Conclusions

This chapter has outlined a methodology for identifying individuals at high risk of social exclusion in the countries of the EU based on Sen's capability approach, using the data of the ECHP. In the first step, population members deprived in four fields (income, living conditions, necessities of life and social relations) were identified. In the second step, the extent of cumulative disadvantage of these individuals was examined and, in the final step, we identified as persons at high risk of social exclusion those who were found suffering from chronic cumulative disadvantage. Application of this method to the data of thirteen EU countries revealed substantial cross-country differences in the population shares of those classified as being at high risk of social exclusion. The highest levels of aggregate risk of social exclusion were recorded in a couple of southern countries (Greece and Portugal) as well as the UK and the lowest in a number of northern and central European countries (Denmark, the Netherlands, Germany and Luxembourg). Medium levels were observed in the remaining countries (Austria, Belgium, France, Ireland, Italy and Spain).

The final part of the chapter was devoted to the identification of population groups at high risk of social exclusion within the thirteen countries. The results of the analysis revealed a number of qualitative similarities and quantitative differences across the EU. In all countries under examination, lack of full-time employment by either the individual or, especially, the household's reference person was found to be positively and significantly associated with increased risk of social exclusion. The strongest effects were associated with unemployment, precarious employment and other types of inactivity apart from retirement. In addition, the risk of social exclusion was found to be strongly negatively associated with education and, in most countries, positively associated with non-EU citizenship, bad health and lone parenthood.

Appendix I

Table 8A1 *Aggregate deprivation indicators – sensitivity analysis*

	Proportion of the population in the third wave of the ECHP classified as deprived according to:								
	Income (poverty)			Living conditions			Necessities of life		
Country	50%	60%	70%	70%	80%	90%	50%	60%	70%
Austria	7.8	13.6	21.6	2.8	6.8	19.3	6.7	11.8	12.9
Belgium	9.4	15.1	24.2	3.0	6.8	18.5	6.0	10.6	14.0
Denmark	3.7	10.0	19.1	2.3	4.6	14.1	3.3	6.5	8.2
Finland	6.3	12.0	19.5	0.7	3.9	14.2	10.7	11.5	23.1
France	8.5	15.4	23.0	2.5	6.6	20.4	7.7	15.2	18.1
Germany	4.9	10.3	18.6	2.2	6.3	17.4	5.5	11.9	19.1
Greece	16.1	22.3	29.2	4.4	10.6	23.5	22.6	32.2	32.2
Ireland	8.9	19.6	28.7	5.1	9.7	20.8	7.7	15.4	18.1
Italy	12.4	18.1	26.3	3.4	9.2	21.4	14.9	16.0	27.5
Luxembourg	4.0	9.2	19.9	2.0	4.5	13.0	4.8	7.7	15.5
Netherlands	6.7	11.2	20.1	1.3	4.2	15.0	5.3	9.9	15.1
Portugal	14.3	22.0	29.4	13.0	19.6	30.5	15.1	15.9	18.0
Spain	13.7	19.7	27.6	4.4	8.7	22.0	5.8	15.6	15.7
United Kingdom	17.3	23.8	30.9	1.0	5.5	18.4	7.7	17.6	21.2

Cited references

Atkinson A. B., Cantillon B., Marlier E., and Nolan B., 2002, *Social indicators: The EU and social inclusion*, Oxford University Press, Oxford.

Berghman J., 1995, 'Social exclusion in Europe: policy context and analytical framework', in Room G. (ed.) *Beyond the threshold: The measurement and analysis of social exclusion*, Policy Press, Bristol.

Brandolini A. and D'Alessio G., 1998, '*Measuring well-being in the functioning space*', Bank of Italy (mimeo).

Bossert W., D'Ambrosio C. and Peragine V., 2005, 'Deprivation and social exclusion', Centre for Household, Income, Labour and Demographic Economics (CHILD) Discussion Paper No 03/2005.

Burchardt T., Le Grand J. and Piachaud D., 1999, 'Social exclusion in Britain 1991–1995', *Social Policy and Administration* 33: 227–244.

Burchardt T., Le Grand J. and Piachaud D., 2002, 'Degrees of social exclusion: Developing a dynamic multidimensional measure', in Hills J., Le Grand J. and Piachaud D. (eds.) *Understanding social exclusion*, Oxford University Press, Oxford and New York.

Chakravarty S. R. and D'Ambrosio C., 2003, 'The measurement of social exclusion', DIW Discussion Paper 364.

Eurostat (1996) *The European Community Household Panel (ECHP): Survey methodology and implementation*, Theme 3, Series E, Eurostat, Luxembourg.

Haan A. de, 1998, 'Social exclusion: an alternative concept for the study of deprivation?', *IDS Bulletin* 29: 10–19.

Klasen S., 2000, 'Measuring poverty and deprivation in South Africa', *Review of Income and Wealth* 46: 33–58.

Mayes D., Berghman J. and Salais R., 2001, *Social exclusion and European policy*, Edward Elgar, Cheltenham.

Schokkaert E. and Van Ootegem L., 1990, 'Sen's concept of the living standard applied to the Belgian unemployed', *Recherches Economiques de Louvain* 56, 429–450.

Sen A. K., 1983, 'Poor, relatively speaking', *Oxford Economic Papers* 35: 153–169.

Sen A. K., 1985a, *Commodities and capabilities*, North Holland, Amsterdam.

Sen A. K., 1985b, 'A sociological approach to the measurement of poverty: a reply to Professor Peter Townsend', *Oxford Economic Papers* 37: 669–676.

Sen A. K., 1997, 'Inequality, unemployment and contemporary Europe', *International Labour Review* 136: 155–172.

Sen A. K., 1999, *Development as freedom,* Oxford University Press, Oxford.

Sen A. K., 2000, 'Social exclusion: concept, application and scrutiny', Social Development Papers No 1, Asian Development Bank, Manila.

Silver H., 1994, 'Social exclusion and social solidarity: Three paradigms', International Institute for Labour Studies Discussion Paper No 69, ILO, Geneva.

Townsend P., 1979, *Poverty in the United Kingdom: a survey of household resources and standards of living*, Penguin, Harmondsworth.

Townsend P., 1985, 'A sociological approach to the measurement of poverty – a rejoinder to Professor Amartya Sen', *Oxford Economic Papers* 37: 659–668.

Tsakloglou P. and Papadopoulos F., 2002a, 'Aggregate level and determining factors of social exclusion in twelve European countries', *Journal of European Social Policy* 12: 209–223.

Tsakloglou P. and Papadopoulos F., 2002b, 'Identifying population groups at high risk of social exclusion', in Muffels R., Tsakloglou P. and Mayes D. (eds.) *Social exclusion in European welfare states*, Edward Elgar, Cheltenham.

9 Complexity and vagueness in the capability approach: strengths or weaknesses?

ENRICA CHIAPPERO-MARTINETTI[1,2]

So far as laws of mathematics refer to reality, they are not certain. And so far as they are certain, they do not refer to reality.

(Albert Einstein 1922)

All traditional logic habitually assumes that precise symbols are being employed. It is therefore not applicable to this terrestrial life but only to an imagined celestial existence [. . . .] logic takes us nearer to heaven than most other studies.

(Russell 1923, pp. 88–9)

All economists know the economy is complex – very complex. That is one of the reasons why society needs economists – to try to make that complexity somewhat simpler and more understandable.

(Colander 2000, p. 1)

Introduction

Concepts of poverty and well-being, like many – probably most – issues and phenomena relating to the human sciences are intrinsically complex and vague, though no more so than crucial economic concepts such as utility, rationality, or recession. This is largely due to the fact that they involve a plurality of interrelated variables, dimensions, and

[1] University of Pavia; enrica.chiappero@unipv.it
[2] Acknowledgments: An early draft of this chapter was prepared while I was senior research associate at Von Hugel Institute, St Edmund's College, University of Cambridge in 2003. I sincerely thank this institution and, in particular, Flavio Comim for making my stay very comfortable and fruitful. I am very grateful to Sabina Alkire, Ingrid Robeyns, Renata Targetti-Lenti, Italo Magnani for their comments and suggestions to a previous version of this chapter. I owe a special debt of gratitude to Mozaffar Qizilbash for his insightful and incisive comments.

spaces with no clear-cut boundaries between them. While both common sense and some of the social sciences (sociology and psychology in particular) plainly acknowledge the intrinsically complex and vague nature of poverty and well-being, the same cannot be said for economics. Only infrequently mentioned, rarely acknowledged at the foundational level, almost always feared and avoided from an empirical point of view, complexity and vagueness are often perceived in economic analysis as elements of weakness within a theoretical framework, and potential obstacles to its operationalization.

Generally speaking, it is widely believed that overly complex concepts are or can be vague, and that when a concept is not delineated by clear boundaries, it is not accurate. Moreover, theoretical frameworks characterized by an excessive degree of complexity can be difficult to apply at the empirical level, which makes them less appealing. Authors such as Sugden (1993), Srinivasan (1994) and Roemer (1996) have critiqued Sen's capability approach based upon such arguments. The multidimensional and context-dependent nature of this approach, its lack of specificity as to how these dimensions should be selected and assessed, the absence of a rigorous formalization, definite metric, algorithm, or index that provide a full ranking and make it possible to carry out interpersonal comparisons, are all seen as elements of weakness that can seriously preclude the practical application of the approach.[3]

It is interesting to note that the great interest in, and significant support for, the capability approach by scholars from numerous disciplines are often based on a reverse interpretation of the same arguments. Indeed, it is precisely the rich and unrestricted nature of the capability approach that makes it so appealing to many researchers, its usefulness in addressing a plurality of issues within a multiplicity of contexts, its interpretative richness regarding what a good life is, and the attention it focuses on human diversity. Multidimensionality and the lack of narrow, predefined boundaries are here seen as major strengths rather than potential constraints or weaknesses. The aim of this chapter is to discuss to what extent concepts of well-being and poverty are intrinsically complex and vague, what degree of complexity and vagueness is admitted and acknowledged at a foundational level

---

[3] For an excellent and detailed discussion on whether the capability approach should be considered 'an unworkable idea or a promising alternative', see Robeyns (2000).

in this field of research, and how this complexity is preserved, captured, simplified, or simply ignored in the move from the theoretical foundation to its practical application. Special attention will be focused on the capability approach, currently among the richest and most multifaceted frameworks of thought for analysing poverty and well-being. What I will attempt to argue here is that the intrinsic complexity and vagueness of these concepts, which are captured and described in such a clear and holistic manner by the capability approach, should be viewed not as elements of weakness or obstacles but as strengths – the real challenge is to develop methods of evaluation and assessment and to find technical measurement tools able to capture and preserve this richness adequately.

Since its formulation in the mid-1980s, a fair – though not vast – number of empirical applications based on the capability approach have been produced; various statistical tools have been tested, including the fuzzy sets methodology, which has been applied with interesting results.[4] In earlier papers I have tried to describe the advantages and potential of this technique; in this chapter my aim is to clarify in what sense this tool may be considered adequate for capturing the intrinsic complexity and vagueness that characterize the capability approach and the ideas of poverty and well-being that the approach generates.

The chapter is structured as follows: Sections 2 and 3 are devoted to clarifying and qualifying the meanings of complexity and vagueness; Section 4 discusses in what sense the capability approach is a complex and vague theoretical framework; Section 5 focuses on measurement issues related to vagueness and complexity, and compares traditional tools based on classical bivalent logic with tools founded on many-valued logic, with special attention to fuzzy set analysis. The last section draws some conclusions.

Complexity

The meaning of complexity adopted in this chapter is quite restricted, as it refers merely to the nature of concepts such as well-being or poverty, standard of living, or quality of life. More precisely, I will reserve the term *complexity* to describe multifaceted, multidimensional

---

[4] See, in particular, Chiappero-Martinetti (1994, 1996, 2000), Lelli (2001), Clark and Qizilbash (2002) and Baliamoune-Lutz (2004).

concepts consisting of many interrelated elements and patterns for which, generally speaking, the whole cannot be fully understood by separately analyzing its components. From this point of view, what determines complexity is not only the existence of many parts and how they are related or connected to one another but also the necessity of considering them jointly.[5] This means that the whole can be greater than the sum of its parts, so that by looking at the overall picture we are able to capture linkages and details that cannot be fully perceived through a partial and fragmented vision.

For our purposes, it may be useful to distinguish between two different levels of analysis:[6]

a) *intrinsic (or conceptual) complexity*, which pertains to the nature of a given phenomenon, and can be partially or fully reflected in the way in which the phenomenon has been conceived and conceptualized;

b) *complexity in measurement*, which arises as one moves from the elaboration phase of theoretical concepts to their operationalization, and mainly refers to the choice of technical tools adopted for empirical investigations.

With reference to the notion of intrinsic complexity, further distinctions can be made by looking at the degrees of complexity or heterogeneity entailed, which can *be related to*:

i) *the object of analysis*, which refers to the number and the nature of evaluative spaces involved. From this point of view, the degree of complexity increases as the number of dimensions, and the level of specificities of each dimension, grow. This usually happens when, for instance, many dimensions are taken into consideration or a plurality of variables is required for describing a given dimension, or if the spaces involved are characterized by a high level of specificity;

---

[5] This definition is similar to that expressed by Alkire (2002, p. 182): 'By dimension I mean . . . any of the component aspects of a particular situation. The key features of dimensions are that they are *component aspects* of something – in this case human development – that *coexist* with other components.'

[6] This distinction can be partially referred to Sen's distinction between the 'foundational level' and the 'practical level' (Sen 1999), which is discussed in detail by Comim (2001a).

ii) *the unit of analysis*, which relates to the way in which human diversity is accounted for. The degree of complexity goes from the simplest assumption based on the idea of a representative agent to subsequent levels of complexity where group-based analysis and personal and household heterogeneities are taken into account;

iii) *the context of analysis*, which refers to the degree to which structural elements, spatial factors, and environmental diversities are taken into account. Also in this case, the atomistic view of a representative agent living in an undefined and indeterminate place is the simplest and common assumption. Complexity can progressively increase when a plurality of socioeconomic, institutional and environmental contexts, but also heterogeneous social constraints and cultural norms affecting individual well-being, are taken into account;

iv) *the relationships and linkages among each level and element involved*. Complex concepts should be characterized not only by the existence of a multidimensional nature but also by the attention reserved to the connections and linkages existing among the three previous levels of analysis.[7] Intrinsic complexity requires that these linkages be highlighted, the causes and effects of each investigated, their joint effect in affecting, determining, and explaining inequality and deprivation in living conditions understood.

Reviewing the broad range of well-being and poverty approaches currently available in the literature, one quickly verifies that each of them copes with these degrees of complexity in different ways, ranging from highly simplified frameworks to substantial and multifaceted, yet

---

[7] The idea of intrinsic complexity is something that can easily be explained referring to different fields of analysis that carry out their investigations in multidimensional spaces. In medicine, for example, a diagnosis is normally based on a broad number of elements: subjective symptoms expressed by the patient, objective health conditions checked through medical examinations and clinical tests, quantitative data and qualitative information on the health and lifestyle of the patient according to his or her personal features, such as sex, age, and living conditions, as well as the relationships among these different aspects and how they can reciprocally affect each other. A good practitioner knows that he or she cannot make an accurate diagnosis based on a single element or symptom. What this example makes quite plain is, however, not widely accepted in well-being analysis, where the diagnosis of deprivation (mainly in developed countries) is often, if not always, based on a single symptom – namely, the lack of income.

highly differentiated, views of what well-being is. On the one hand, we can find the most basic and common conceptualization of human well-being, which avoids any kind of complexity, restricting the evaluative space to a single dimension as regards both the object and the unit of the analysis. The underlying hypothesis of this purely individualistic and univariate characterization of welfare is that nothing other than income distinguishes individuals, and the amount of income of an individual is all that is required to identify deprivation, evaluate inequalities,[8] or depict quality of life and human well-being in line with the neoclassical perspective. On the other hand, there are more complex and rich schemes that consider multidimensionality from different perspectives and among these, the capability approach is certainly one of the most complete.

The degree of complexity associated with the capability approach will be discussed in detail in Section 4. What I want to emphasize here is that whatever degree of complexity is involved in the theoretical formulation of a concept (*intrinsic complexity*), this should be distinguished from the *technical* issues involved when that concept is translated into a quantitative or qualitative measure of well-being (*complexity in measurement*). Keeping this distinction in mind can be useful for several reasons. First, the two levels of complexity can (though not necessarily must) be closely linked. On the one hand, relatively simple concepts can be hard to measure when imperfect information, lack of knowledge, or imprecise tools are all that is available; on the other hand, concepts and theories with a high degree of complexity can be operationalized with a relatively high degree of accuracy.[9] Second, welfare analysis based on accurate algorithms and advanced analytical tools usually refers to a single evaluative space (namely, income or consumption) and thus on a relatively restricted and rough idea of human well-being, so that it can be difficult to

---

[8] Traditionally this assumption is also included in the axiomatic structure of poverty and inequality index by the symmetry axiom, which assumes homogeneity as regards each characteristic different from income.

[9] Some rightly point out that 'complexity' is not the same thing as 'complicated'. 'A system is complicated if it can be given a complete and accurate description in terms of its individual constituents, no matter how many' (Cilliers 1998). 'Complication is a quantitative escalation of that which is theoretically reducible' (Chapman 1985, p. 370). A complex system, on the contrary, cannot be reduced without losing its true nature (Reitsma 2003).

distinguish between concepts that are genuinely complex and concepts that are instrumentally simple.[10] Third, strong simplifications, which are usually introduced with the empirical implementation of complex concepts, are typically justified by resorting to various arguments: the scarcity of statistical data, the impossibility of carrying out expensive *ad hoc* surveys, the fact that some dimensions are unobservable or only partially and indirectly measurable, or the lack of adequate measurement tools. Without denying the existence of these constraints, I think that the intrinsic complexity of a concept should be preserved, even if not necessarily in its entirety. Furthermore, sometimes complex approaches can be simplified intentionally in order to focus the attention on specific aspects that are relevant to the aims of the empirical investigation, ignoring others that are derivative. But in this case, too, if the richness of the theoretical framework and its spirit is preserved, the empirical assessment will still reflect this complexity to a certain extent.[11]

A final remark: it is evident that the meaning of complexity discussed here is very simple and restricted if compared with the idea of complexity found in the economic thought of authors such as Smith, Marshall, Kaldor, and Hayek, among others, or in more recent complex, non-linear, adaptive systems developed, for instance, by the Santa Fe approach.[12] However, it is worth noting that even if aims, context,

---

[10] On this point, see also Robeyns (2000).

[11] As argued by Sen: 'Even when precisely capturing an ambiguity proves to be a difficult exercise, that is not an argument for forgetting the complex nature of the concept and seeking a spuriously narrow exactness. In social investigation and measurement, it is undoubtedly more important to be vaguely right than to be precisely wrong' (1989). I am in full agreement with this opinion and it is exactly on this premise that the present work is based. However, as I will argue in Section 5, vagueness and ambiguities are similar but not exactly identical concepts. In the case of the capability approach it seems to be more appropriate to refer to vagueness rather than to ambiguity.

[12] See Arthur, Durlauf, and Lane (1997). Complexity has been a recurrent topic in economic theory, from Smith's emphasis on increasing returns and his interest in the economic growth process that involves an increasingly complex pattern of specialization, to Marshall's appeal for substituting biological analogies with mechanical analogies, to more recent and in-depth analyses expressed by von Hayek in 'The theory of complex phenomena' (1967), his critique of a reductionist approach in economics and his idea of 'spontaneous and organised complexity'. But as David Colander points out (2000, p. 34): 'Many earlier economists understood the implications of complexity, of which increasing returns and multiple equilibria are important elements, but they also recognised that they did not have the tools to deal with it formally, and therefore did not

and motivations are entirely different, conclusions are quite similar, namely that the intrinsic complexity that characterizes many (most?) economic phenomena is not always or not adequately taken into consideration in mainstream economics.

Vagueness

Vagueness is another distinctive and persistent feature of many concepts and phenomena. Many propositions in ordinary language are inherently vague, and their meanings almost invariably context-dependent.[13] For instance, 'young' or 'big' or 'beautiful' are vague linguistic concepts in the sense that they do not have exact and universal definitions (various meanings are possible, and clear cut-off points between a given concept and its opposite – such as 'old', 'small' or 'ugly' – do not exist). Moreover, their connotations can change according to the situations to which they are applied (i.e. 'young' or 'beautiful' take on different meanings when they are used to describe a human being or an animal or vegetable species).

Again, it can be useful to keep the foundational level separate from the measurement level, and to distinguish between:

work on them.' Complexity theory today has and makes use of these analytical and computational tools that allows it to introduce hypotheses of non-linearity, to scrutinize an individual's actions and interactions for understanding aggregate behaviour, to stress the adaptive, evolutionary, inductive processes by which agents in the real economy actually learn, to emphasize path dependence and the role of institutional structures. For an interesting attempt to bridge notions of complexity in economic thought and today's complexity theory, see Colander (2000) and, in particular, Comim's and Montgomery's contributions therein.

[13] Russell argued that all natural language expressions are vague, including symbols and logical connectives (Russell 1923, pp. 88–9). However, as outlined by Wright: 'Ordinary language is always more or less vague, but a logically perfect language would not be vague at all: so the degree of vagueness of a natural language is a direct measure of its distance from being everything which it 'logically' ought to be' (Wright 1976, reprinted in Keefe and Smith 2002, p. 151). The intrinsic vagueness of many economic concepts was often noted and remarked upon by Keynes: 'Net-income, being based on an equivocal criterion which different authorities might interpret differently, is not perfectly clear-cut' (Keynes, *Collected Writings*, 1960a, p. 60). Finally, in distinguishing between consumption and investment goods, and finished and unfinished goods, he remarked: 'All these arbitrary distinctions, however, are only arbitrary in a highly a priori sense ... If we had reason to expect that a different set of lines of division would be more appropriate to our psychology of behaviour and decision, we should have to draw them differently' (Keynes, *Collected Writings*, 1960b, p. 433).

v) intrinsic vagueness, *which refers to the nature of a given concept or phenomenon*; and

vi) vagueness in measurement, *which relates to the way in which vagueness can be accounted for.*

In this section attention is focused on the conceptual level of the discourse, whereas discussion on the measurement issue will be postponed to the second part of this chapter.

The historical roots of vagueness go back to the ancient Greeks, who introduced vagueness into philosophy with the sorites paradox,[14] which has fascinated and troubled philosophers for centuries.[15] However, it was only around the 1970s that attention to this topic began to grow significantly, and formal treatment of vagueness became common.

---

[14] Greek paradoxes were usually formulated in terms of a sequence of questions. 'Does one grain of wheat make a heap? Do two grains of wheat make a heap? Do three grains of wheat make a heap? ... Do ten thousand grains of wheat make a heap? It is to be understood that the grains are properly piled up, and that a heap must contain reasonably many grains, If you admit that one grain does not make a heap, and are unwilling to make a fuss about the addition of any single grain, you are eventually forced to admit that ten thousand grains do not make a heap' (Williamson 1994, p. 8).

[15] Galen, in the late second century A.D., wrote: 'According to what is demanded by the analogy, there must not be such a thing in the world as a heap of grain, a mass or satiety, neither a mountain nor strong love, nor a row, nor strong wind, nor city, nor anything else which is known from its name and idea to have a measure of extent or multitude, such as the wave, the open sea, a flock of sheep and herd of cattle, the nation and the crowd. And the doubt and confusion introduced by the analogy leads to contradiction of fact in the transition of man from one stage of his life to another, and in the changes of time, and the changes of seasons. For in the case of the boy one is uncertain and doubtful as to when the actual moment arrives for his transition from boyhood to adolescence, and in the case of the man in his prime when he begins to be an old man. And so it is with the seasons of the year when winter begins to change and merges into spring, and spring into summer, and summer into autumn. By the same reasoning, doubt and confusion enter into many other things which relate to the doings of men in spite of the fact that knowledge of these things is obvious and plain' (Galen, on medical experience). Similarly, Cicero noted: 'Nature has permitted us no knowledge of limits such as would enable us to determine, in any case, how far to go. Nor is it so just with a heap of corn, from which the name (sorites) is derived: there is no matter whatever concerning which, if questioned by gradual progression, we can tell how much must be added or subtracted before we can give a definite answer – rich or poor, famous or unknown, many or few, large or small, long or short, broad or narrow' (Cicero, Academica). Both are quoted in Keefe and Smith (2002, p. 58–60).

The starting point is quite straightforward. Classical logic is bivalent and does not admit vague predicates: a predicate can be only true or false. As Sainsbury writes (1990, pp. 251–2):

According to this classical picture, the job of classificatory concepts is to sort or segregate things into classes by providing a system of pigeon-holes, by placing a grid over reality, by demarcating areas of logical space. Boundaries are what count, for a concept must use a boundary to segregate the things which fall under it from the things which do not.

There is no doubt that the principle of bivalence is applicable and necessary in many cases and contexts: for example, laws must certainly demarcate a boundary between legitimate and illegitimate acts. However, at times it may seem irrational or unfair to draw substantial distinctions in terms of rights and duties based on differences that are often marginal: in this field, too, predicates can be coined intentionally in order to leave their application indefinite in some cases.[16] In all fields of science as well as in ordinary language, there are plenty of concepts and predicates that seem to escape the law of the excluded middle.[17] Keefe and Smith in their excellent book on vagueness (2002) offer numerous examples discussed in philosophy and logic: bald, tall, or heap, but also red or child are usually mentioned as examples of vague propositions. These propositions are vague because, generally speaking,

---

[16] For instance, Tappenden (1995; quoted in Keefe and Smith 2002, p. 21) describes a case where the US Supreme Court coins the phrase 'brownrate' to mean 'with all deliberate speed' in order to avoid specifying a precise speed.

[17] In classical logic, the law of the excluded middle (LEM) is formulated in terms of 'either A or not A' or, equivalently, saying that the union of a set with its complement yields the universal set ($A \cup \bar{A} = U$). Symmetrical to the law of the excluded middle is the law of non contradiction (LNC) that affirms that the intersection of a set with its complement corresponds to the empty set, $A \cap \bar{A} = \emptyset$ or, equivalently, that 'not both A and not A'. Finally, strictly related (and often confused with) to the law of the excluded middle is the principle of bivalence (PoB) stated as 'every statement or proposition is either true or false'. At first glance LEM and PoB do seem equivalent: however, as Mehlberg (1958) and Williamson (1994) clarify, while the former refers to the schema 'A or not A' in the object or language under study, the latter is a meta-linguistic principle that any statement A is either true or false. This means that if the PoB holds it is possible to derive the LEM but the opposite does not necessarily follow. In classical logic this correspondence between PoB and LEM keeps but this is no more true for other approaches to vagueness such as 'supervalutionism' – that violates PoB but keeps the LEM – or 'fuzzy logic' – that rejects the PoB and, generally, does not adhere to the LEM. On this point see also Klir and Yuan (1995).

it can be difficult and sometimes impossible to identify exactly when a rapidly receding hairline turns into baldness, or how tall a person must be to be defined as 'tall', or how many grains of sand make a heap: we cannot do so because sharp boundaries between bald and not bald, tall and not tall, a heap and not a heap, do not exist and because there is a fringe or penumbra of borderline cases regarding which decisive judgements are impossible.[18]

As Qizilbash has pointed out (2002, 2003) in his papers on vagueness and poverty, the predicate 'poor' can also be considered *per se* a vague predicate since i) there can be cases where it is not clear whether or not the predicate applies (when, for example, a person is not clearly poor and not clearly not poor); ii) along a hypothetical scale of wellbeing, an exact point at which a poor person ceases to be a poor person does not really exist; iii) if X is a rich person, with an income of, say, $1 billion, and Y, with an income that is only one dollar less, is also a rich person, then if we carry on, dollar by dollar, along a continuum line of people ranked by amounts of income that are always one dollar less then the previous one, this yields the conclusion that a person with no income is also a rich person, and this is clearly false.[19]

What is wrong is to ignore the intrinsic vagueness inherent in the idea of poverty and to assume that a clear cut-off point exists, and can be drawn, between 'poor' and 'not poor' as the standard approach for measuring poverty has traditionally done, by defining a poverty threshold in terms of income or consumption expenditure.

The problem is more substantial than formal: in drawing a line, sharp boundaries are immediately established and borderline cases are by definition excluded. However, this is not a way to solve vagueness but simply an attempt to ignore it. Moreover, an infinite number of lines might be drawn differently by different researchers; yet this means that the word 'poor' can assume a potentially infinite number

---

[18] It should be noted that not only predicates but also adverbs such as 'very' or 'many' are intrinsically vague: from this point of view, the use of categorization such as 'very poor' or 'extreme poverty' actually increases the degree of vagueness.

[19] Wright (1976) has defined predicates that lack sharp boundaries as 'tolerant' because their application is insensitive to small changes. Tolerance is due neither to laziness on the part of the speaker nor to the lack of information about the objects ('a notion of degree of chance too small to make any difference to their applicability', p. 156); no new evidence would clear up the matter.

of representations (as, in fact, does occur). In any case, the sorites paradox emerges in all its strength: a person with an income y is poor, but a person with an income a hundredth greater is definitively not.

It should be clear from the above definition that the meaning of vagueness used here is not dependent on the nature of the evaluative space that we have chosen for analyzing poverty; the idea of poverty is intrinsically vague, no matter whether it is measured in terms of income or nutrition, physical health or any other relevant – single or multiple – dimension of human well-being. The above three features that identify a vague predicate are fully applicable in all these cases. The crucial point here concerns the meaning and the existence of a cut-off point – that is, the possibility of drawing a line between poor and not poor without coming up against the sorites paradox. Moreover, vagueness is not context-dependent: by and large, phenomena that are intrinsically vague will maintain their nature under any circumstances. Poverty can and should be defined in a different way according to different contexts, but in any space and in any time it will always maintain its intrinsic vagueness. Finally, the 'amount' of vagueness does not depend on the number of dimensions or variables taken into consideration. Vagueness exists even when poverty is identified in a unique space – typically, that of income – or in the case of a plurality of focal variables are taken into account, being related to the indeterminacy about how and whether it is possible to identify in each space thresholds below which a person will be characterized as poor.

Susan Haack (1996) distinguishes respectively between unidimensional and multidimensional vagueness, and points out that in the second case, each single variable may suffer, in addition, from the first kind of vagueness.

This distinction between unidimensional and multidimensional vagueness partially corresponds to the distinction between vertical and horizontal vagueness introduced by Qizilbash (2003). In this paper, Qizilbash traditionally refers the former to the dilemma of the existence of a clear cut-off point below which one must fall to classify as poor, while he identifies the latter in terms of the range of dimensions of poverty.[20]

---

[20] While the meaning of vertical vagueness is clear and refers to the difficulty of drawing a poverty line, some doubt can arise regarding the meaning of horizontal vagueness. With reference to the notion of 'basic needs' and 'basic capabilities', Qizilbash writes (Qizilbash 2003, p. 50): 'In making these notions applicable in any context researchers have to settle on the set of

What is important to stress here is that, as already discussed in the previous section, multidimensionality affects complexity and requires analysis into components and weighting; yet it is not, *per se*, a source of vagueness (which, as a matter of fact, also arises when unidimensional, apparently simple, concepts are involved). In contrast, if the adoption of a multidimensional perspective allows us to draw clearer boundaries around an intrinsically complex concept, then vagueness could be reduced instead of increased.[21] In any case, a clear distinction between complexity and vagueness is important not only at a semantic level but also in terms of the choice of the most appropriate tools to be used for representing and capturing these two distinct though interrelated issues.

The meaning of vagueness discussed here is basically related to the nature of a given concept and seems to adapt quite well to ideas of poverty and well-being, which can substantially be conceived as intrinsically vague concepts.[22] As will be discussed in the following sections, this view would suggest a move away from the classic, bivalent logic, in order to substitute the dichotomy of truth *versus* falsity with a many-valued logic based on *degrees* of truth. This perspective determines what is usually called degree theories of vagueness.[23]

needs or capabilities which count as 'basic'. Vagueness about this set of needs or capabilities is horizontal vagueness.' However, if the problem is to choose among any possible dimensions a set of explicative variables or spaces potentially useful for representing a given concept (poverty in terms of basic needs or basic capabilities), this seems to be more a problem of complexity or selection rather than of vagueness.

[21] John Coates, outlining that the vagueness literature offers a sort of philosophical defence of common sense practice, identifies a different relationship between vagueness and complexity: 'A complex term is defined as a conjunction of simple terms and vagueness arises when we are in doubt as to whether the complete conjunction of elements is required for the application of the term or something less than this complete conjunction' (Coates 1996, p. 157). Again, I think that it seems more useful to conceive complexity and vagueness as distinct features, taking into account the fact that the latter can be present even in the absence of the former.

[22] Even if the measurement of well-being does not formally require the identification of a clear cut-off point such as the poverty line, nonetheless it seems to reasonable to assume that well-being achievements, such as healthy living or education and knowledge, or participation in the social life can be better described in terms of partial fulfillment more than an 'in or out' condition.

[23] Lukasiewicz (1920) was a pioneer of modern three-valued logic, which represents the first step towards the multi-valued logics that were subsequently developed by, among others, Goguen (1969), Zadeh (1975), Machina (1976)

However, this is not the only way to formulate the idea of vagueness. There are theories of vagueness that preserve both classical logic and semantics, such as Williamson's epistemic approach, which conceives vagueness basically as a matter of ignorance of the clear-cut boundaries of a given concept. According to this epistemic view, a clear-cut boundary, for instance, between tall people and all the others, or between poor and not poor people, exists, but we are simply ignorant of where such boundaries lie. From this point of view, vagueness is nothing more than a consequence of our inexact knowledge.[24] Williamson gives an explanation of this source of ignorance in terms of margin for error: when our knowledge is inexact, a belief is reliable only if we leave a margin of error. Reliability increases with the width of the margin and the more accurate our cognitive capacities are, the narrower is the margin needed to achieve a given level of reliability (Williamson 1994, p. 226).

Another theory of vagueness that preserves the simplicity of classical logic is supervaluationism:[25] the central idea here is that vague predicates can be made more precise by taking into account any admissible valuations or precisification criteria. A statement is true (or, better, super-true) if and only if it remains true under every admissible valuation; a statement is false (or super-false) if and only if it remains false under every admissible valuation; otherwise, it is neither true nor false. In this case there is no truth value at all.[26]

and, more recently, Zadeh and Kacprzyk (1992), Klir and Yuan (1995), Hajek (1998), Nguyen and Walker (1999) Edgington (2002). Degree theories, epistemic views, and supervaluationist approaches are all discussed in Keefe and Smith (2002).

[24] Williamson (1994, pp. 216–17) clarifies the meaning of inexact knowledge with several examples: 'Vision gives knowledge about the height of a tree, hearing about the loudness of a noise, touch about the temperature of a surface, ... in each case, the knowledge is inexact. One sees roughly but not exactly how many books a room contains, for example: it is certainly more than two hundred and less than twenty thousand, but one does not know the exact number. Yet there need be no relevant vagueness in the number. The inexactness was in the knowledge, not in the object about which it was acquired.' On the epistemic view see also Cargile (1969) and Jackman (2004).

[25] See Fine (1975), Tye (1989) and for a synthetic description Sorensen (2002). Clark and Qizilbash (2002) apply the supervaluationist approach for measuring poverty in South Africa.

[26] A typical, non-scientific example is the following: 'Toronto is in Canada' is true on each admissible interpretation, so this sentence is true (or super-true); 'Toronto is in Europe' is false on each admissible interpretation, so it is false or super-false. The sentence 'the number of trees in Toronto is even' could be true

Each of these different ideas of vagueness presents advantages and elements of strength as well as weaknesses and theoretical limits[27] and each of these theories requires different measurement tools in order to be adequately represented. The choice among them largely depends on the purpose of the analysis and the contexts in which the vagueness is being considered.

Vagueness and other related concepts

Having described in brief how vagueness is conceived and conceptualized from different theoretical perspectives, it might be useful to offer a few words now on clarifying the similarities and the differences between vagueness and other related concepts such as inaccuracy, generality, ambiguity, and unspecificity. This distinction is not only semantically important but also instrumentally significant in terms of the choice of which measurement tools are most appropriate for capturing and representing different meanings of vagueness.

  i) *Vagueness should be distinguished from inaccuracy.* Russell (1923) defines accurate representation as isomorphism: maps, charts, or photographs all draw closer to this definition in so far as they are accurate. In contrast, a representation is vague when the relation of the representing system to the represented system is not one-to-one but one-to-many. Vagueness is a matter of degree while accuracy represents a sort of ideal limit (Williamson 1994).

 ii) *Vagueness should be distinguished from imprecision (or inexactness)*: here the distinction between measurement imprecision and intrinsic imprecision is important. The former is associated with the degree of exactness with which we can measure a given quantity, and depends on the quantity of available information and the quality of measurement tools as well as the statistical correctness of our measurements. The latter is related to the properties of a phenomenon and not to the measurement of these properties

on some admissible interpretations and false on others, so it is neither true nor false. Of course, the sentence 'the number of trees in Toronto is either odd or even' is true on each admissible interpretation and therefore super-true. See, among others, Williamson (1994).

[27] It has not been clarified, for example, why we are ignorant about where the boundaries of vague predicates lie and whether such knowledge is possible or not. On this, see Keefe and Smith (2002).

(Cox 1994). While the first type of imprecision is negatively related to the degree of exactness of a given measurement tool, the second type does not diminish with an increase in the precision of a given metric.

iii) *Vagueness should be distinguished from unspecificity or under-specificity*: the sentence 'someone is poor' is obviously vague, but only in the sense that is less than adequately informative for understanding in what sense one is poor and how poverty can be identified. This has nothing to do with borderline cases or with the lack of sharp boundaries and thus with vagueness, which will remain even if the amount of available information increases, reducing the lack of specificity.[28]

iv) *Vagueness should be distinguished from semantic ambiguity*, which stems from the existence of multiple meanings attached to one word. A typical example might be the word 'bank', which can be understood as a financial institution but also as a rising ground bordering a lake or a river; or the sentence 'the food is hot', which is ambiguous because hot could refer to the food's temperature but also to the presence of hot spices. It could be, as in these examples, that terms and predicates are both ambiguous and vague; however, while semantic ambiguity may be eliminated by distinguishing between these meanings or by paraphrase or by a plausible interpretation, the same does not hold for vagueness. What is the temperature or the amount of spices that qualify a food as hot or not hot? Is there a precise point at which the food is not hot? These remain vague and intrinsically ambiguous issues.

In contrast, the idea of vagueness as a lack of clear-cut borderlines fits very well with the concepts of indeterminacy (Haack 1996) and fuzziness (Zadeh 1972). From a linguistic point of view, fuzziness has also been defined as referential vagueness (Kempson 1977 and Zhang 1998): the meaning of a lexical item is in principle clear, but it may be hard to decide whether or not the item can be applied to certain objects. In the case of referential vagueness or fuzziness we do not have clear-cut criteria for distinguishing the referential boundaries of sets of poor, tall, or bald people. In line with this distinction, vagueness, fuzziness, and indeterminacy will be used interchangeably in this chapter and

---

[28] Russell also defines unspecificity as generality.

kept conceptually and semantically distinct from other apparently similar but different concepts such as inaccuracy or imprecision. As I will discuss in the next section, intrinsic vagueness and indeterminacy are fundamental properties of the fuzzy set theory, which is a precise, well-specified, accurate tool that appears to be particularly promising for dealing with intrinsically vague and fuzzy predicates.

Intrinsic complexity and intrinsic vagueness in the capability approach

Is the capability approach a complex scheme? According to the taxonomy suggested in this chapter and to common opinion in this field of research, yes, there is no doubt that the capability approach is intentionally and intrinsically complex.[29] However, the prescription to refer to a multiplicity of evaluative spaces for assessing well-being represents only one – probably not the most crucial one – of the qualifying elements of this approach. Many other approaches offer a broad-ranging view of human well-being.[30] What is worth noting is that with the capability perspective, the plurality goes well beyond the prescription of multivariate spaces for assessing well-being, involving other fundamental aspects and levels of analysis. First of all, in this multivariate evaluative perspective two distinct levels or spaces of analysis – the capability space and the functioning space – are brought into focus, distinguishing what individuals *can* do from what they *do*. Second, in most cases – as the empirical applications show – both evaluative spaces are generally interpreted as multidimensional spaces: recurrent functionings such as education, health, participation, and housing are assessed by using a plurality of qualitative and quantitative variables. Third, the way in which the capability approach conceives human diversity is intrinsically pluralistic: it acknowledges how the high degree of heterogeneity in personal features such as sex, age, and physical and psychological conditions makes each person substantially

---

[29] Bourguignon and Chakravarty (2003 p. 26): '. . . . well-being is *intrinsically* multidimensional from the view point of "capabilities" and "functionings" . . .'

[30] See, among others, the contribution of the so-called Scandinavian School with the Swedish approach suggested by Erikson and Aberg (1987) and Erikson (1993) and the Swedish Scandinavian Welfare Study formulated by Allardt. For the Basic Needs school, see Stewart (1985) and Doyal and Gough (1991). For a comparison among different multidimensional approaches to human well-being, see Alkire (2002).

different from the others, generating deep interpersonal variations in the conversion of resources into functionings and capabilities. Fourth, two hypothetically identical people in terms of personal features but living in different households and facing different socioeconomic contexts and different cultural and natural environments will generally have different sets of opportunities and different living conditions.[31] Finally, what makes the capability approach an intrinsically complex (and not only a multidimensional) approach is the attention it focuses on investigating the linkages among the aforementioned layers of analysis: what are the differences and linkages between capability and functioning sets, what kind of practical advantages and technical difficulties are associated with the decision to focus attention on one space or another,[32] how can pervasive human diversities and the environment (*latu sensu*) positively or negatively influence our achievements, and our possibility to achieve our overall freedom, via the conversion factors. Thus, the capability approach is much more than a mere multidimensional framework for assessing poverty and well-being; it offers a broader, richer, and intrinsically complex theoretical scheme for describing the multifaceted nature of poverty, understanding its causes and effects, and investigating interrelated layers of analysis that have traditionally been neglected or not adequately debated. However, while this intrinsic complexity is often (though not always) considered a strength at the conceptual level, it is also generally perceived as a potential drawback due to the indisputable challenges it entails at the methodological level.[33]

---

[31] A different interpretation of layers of analysis and interconnections between individual and social context is offered by Comim (2001b), who distinguishes between poverty as a property of an individual and system-level poverty that 'is due to causes that transcend individual characteristics or circumstances' (p. 2). In another paper, Comim and Kuklys (2002) explore how these two conceptually different levels of poverty, their determinants, and interactions can be empirically measured.

[32] Elsewhere I have argued why it is important to include both spaces in a well-being assessment rather than to choose between them. See Chiappero-Martinetti (1996).

[33] Srinivasan (1994) and Sugden (1993), for example, do not hide their scepticism towards the possibility of making this approach truly operative, while Ysander (1993) points out the fact that 'capabilities are often rather elusive things to catch' and concludes that 'economists may be confused here because they are used to dealing with one of the few aspects of life where the opportunity set can

Is the capability approach a vague scheme? Are concepts of poverty and well-being formulated within this framework vague concepts? With reference to the meaning of vagueness developed in the literature and discussed in Section 3, where a vague predicate is defined as a predicate i) with borderline cases, ii) no sharp boundaries and iii) susceptible to sorites paradoxes, the answer appears quite obvious. Yes, they are undeniably vague, *yet no more and no less so than the most traditional definitions of well-being or poverty usually are.* The existence of vagueness refers to these predicates *per se* and the scarce lack of realism in the assumption that a clear-cut demarcation exists between poor and not poor in unidimensional spaces is simply reproduced and reinforced when many dimensions of well-being are involved.

As Sen himself writes (2003, pp. 5–6), 'There are many ambiguities in the conceptual framework of the capability approach. Indeed the nature of human life and the content of human freedom are themselves far from unproblematic concepts . . . . In so far as there are genuine ambiguities in the underlying objects of value, these will be reflected in corresponding ambiguities in the characterization of capabilities . . . . if an underlying idea has an essential ambiguity a precise formulation of that idea must try to capture that ambiguity rather than attempt to lose it. Even when precisely capturing an ambiguity proves to be a difficult exercise, that is not an argument for forgetting the complex nature of the concept and seeking a spuriously narrow exactness. In social investigation and measurement, it is undoubtedly more important to be vaguely right than to be precisely wrong.' The next section will be devoted to a discussion of these methodological issues.

---

be reasonably well defined and measured' (p. 84). Responses to these criticisms can be found in Sen (1999) and Robeyns (2000, 2003).

As a matter of fact, despite the growing empirical poverty and well-being literature based on or inspired by the capability approach, it is very difficult to find applied exercises that fully and perfectly reflect the richness and complexity of this approach. In most cases functionings instead of capabilities are estimated and few words are spent for justifying this kind of choice (but for an interesting exception see Burchardt 2002); there is not a clear distinction between means and ends and often income is included as a dimension of well-being; linkages among functionings are not always investigated; human diversity and environmental heterogeneity are generally described *ex-post* more than included *ex-ante* in the empirical exercise; conversion factors are rarely mentioned or taken into account. From this point of view, much work must still be done.

From theory to practice: how complex and vague concepts can be measured

In Sections 2 and 3, I investigated intrinsic complexity as multidimensionality, and vagueness as difficulty or appropriateness, at a conceptual level, in 'drawing a line'. In this section, I will discuss complexity and vagueness from a measurement point of view. The main aim is to review how these aspects have been dealt with in multidimensional poverty analyses, with special attention to empirical applications based on the capability approach.

As far as the first aspect is concerned, multidimensionality requires managing a variety of variables (qualitative and quantitative, dichotomous and polytomous, cardinal and ordinal) as well as an analysis into components and weighting. In particular, the methodological issues that must be dealt with are related to layers of complexity associated with:

i) the number and the nature of a plurality of symptoms of deprivation and dimensions of well-being;
ii) the forms of heterogeneity among individuals and circumstances which can affect or generate poverty;
iii) the correlation among variables, dimensions and levels of analysis;
iv) the aggregation across attributes, across units of analysis (i.e. individuals, households, groups) and between attributes and units for establishing an overall deprivation index.[34]

Two different strategies seem to be available for dealing with the first two of the above issues: either to bring multidimensionality back to a univariate approach, or to make use of multivariate techniques. Some examples of the first strategy are the conversion of needs into a money metric by needs-adjusted disposable income, the equivalence scales methodology or the aggregation across various attributes into a single index, followed by the identification of a unique poverty line.[35]

---

[34] On the substantive difference of these different forms and level of aggregation see, among others, Atkinson 2002.

[35] Bourguignon and Chakravarty (2003, p. 27) outline that in this way the concept of poverty essentially remains a one-dimensional concept. They also argue that 'the issue of the multidimensionality of poverty arises because individuals, social observers or policy makers want to define a poverty limit on each individual attribute: income, health, education, etc.' (pp. 27–8). In this paper they also

Factor analysis, structural equation modelling, cluster analysis, log-linear models, principal component analysis, and fuzzy sets theory are examples of the multivariate techniques most commonly used in poverty analysis to reduce, measure, and aggregate deprivation dimensions, as well as to analyze causal relationships among them. Again, if poverty were identified as a shortfall from a threshold on *each* dimension of an individual's or household well-being, a plurality of poverty lines would need to be established. In this case, an additional problem could arise regarding whether or not a given threshold can be defined independently from the others. Moreover, even if both absolute and relative poverty lines could potentially be applied when evaluative spaces other than income are being considered, some authors point out that absolute poverty lines seem more viable compared with relative thresholds, which could be unclear or debatable in some evaluative spaces.[36]

Regarding the issues of aggregation and comparison, the most recent literature on multidimensional poverty measurement is moving essentially in two different research directions, focused respectively on the formulation of multidimensional decomposable poverty indexes and on the extension of dominance stochastic conditions in a multidimensional framework.[37]

There is no doubt that both multidimensional poverty measurement and poverty orderings, compared with the single dimensional approach case, generate some challenging issues. To mention some of the most important: the aggregation order (should we aggregate first across individuals, and then across attributes, or vice versa?)[38] and the procedure for combining deprivation dimensions (how should we choose among union, intersection or other aggregative procedures, and what are the technical and normative implications of this choice?);[39] the

formulate a methodology for combining these different poverty lines into a multidimensional index.

[36] In the case of health, for instance, it seems more reasonable to identify a minimally acceptable level rather than a relative one. See Bourguignon and Chakravarty (2003) and Garcia Diaz (2003).

[37] For the former, see Chakravarty *et al.* (1998), Bourguignon and Chakravarty (2002, 2003), Tsui (2002); for the latter see Atkinson (2002) and Atkinson *et al.* (2002). On multidimensional poverty measurement, see also Maasoumi (1999), Dagum and Costa (2002), Duclos *et al.* (2002), Bibi (2003) and Garcia Diaz (2003).

[38] As Atkinson (2002) points out, there are substantive differences between these two forms of aggregation. On this issue see also Dutta, Pattanaik and Xu (2003).

[39] See Atkinson *et al.* 2002; Duclos *et al.* 2002.

existence and extension of overlapping among these dimensions;[40] the necessity of reformulating the axiomatic structure of multidimensional poverty indexes;[41] and the complexity of extending the stochastic dominance conditions beyond the bidimensional case.[42]

Even so, broad agreement as to the multidimensional nature of poverty bears out the need to solve the measurement problems that it poses, by readapting the methodological tools used in the unidimensional case as well as by experimenting with innovative tools able to preserve the intrinsic complexity of a given phenomenon. There can undoubtedly be a trade-off between the complexity and richness of a theoretical framework on the one hand, and, on the other hand, the degree to which a complex theoretical scheme can be fully formalized, measured, and employed for the purpose of comparison. However, the attempt to simplify complexity by operating (in the most extreme instance) within a single unidimensional space does not really seem to be the right solution.[43]

As far as the second issue is concerned – i.e. how vagueness is measured or dealt with – just as often occurs in the univariate case, in a multivariate setting, too, vagueness is in most cases simply ignored: the assumption that a threshold or a cut-off point can be established for every dimension, without any justification offered as to how realistic or reasonable this assumption is, is still a recurrent approach. If it seems meaningless to affirm, as often occurs, that an individual should be identified as poor if his or her disposable income is equal or lower to a given threshold – say \$1 a day – but *not* poor if this income is one cent higher, then it seems even more controversial to assume that an abrupt, sharp cut-off point exists between sick and healthy men, happy or unhappy women, fully integrated or totally excluded people. It might be more reasonable to assume human well-being, in its various dimensions, as being distributed along a continuum that ranges from a condition of complete deprivation to one of full well-being, whatever the reference space – income, health, knowledge, participation, social life,

---

[40] This refers to the case in which attributes can be substitutes, complements, or have no relation at all.

[41] See Tsui (2002), Bourguignon and Chakravarty (2002, 2003).

[42] See Atkinson (2002); Atkinson *et al.* (2002).

[43] For instance, Kuklys (2003), in measuring well-being in accordance with Sen's approach, makes interesting use of the hierarchical structure of goals for reducing the dimensionality of well-being.

and so forth – being considered. Of course, there are understandable descriptive reasons that justify the choice of a single, conventional poverty threshold – for example, the need to identify, count, rank, and compare those who are poor. However, there is also a substantive issue related to the normative and prescriptive implications of this choice, and this issue is often neglected or not sufficiently taken into consideration. What, for instance, is the standard of living associated with a poverty line conventionally set at half of the mean or median income, or corresponding to $1 a day? Do such thresholds reflect an average standard of living or a 'decent' level of life? Do they represent a minimum or optimal goal for a given society? Or are they related to the amount of economic resources that could be, or should be, allocated for reducing poverty?[44]

Furthermore, the assumption that a single, identical poverty line should be used to identify a sort of homogeneous category – i.e. 'poor people' – seems to be equally questionable. As I pointed out earlier, the capability perspective envisions the relationship between income or resources and capability as something that is mediated and affected by conversion factors, which seriously calls into question the concept of a *single* threshold for *all* individuals, independent of their personal characteristics and circumstances. As Sen himself points out (1992, 1997), in this case what should be considered is not the absolute lowness of income but the inadequacy of a given amount of income for achieving a minimum threshold of capabilities, according to the personal characteristics and circumstances that affect the conversion factors.[45]

As we move from the theoretical to the empirical level, the question that arises is whether the standard tools used in poverty analysis are

[44] The linkage between technical criteria and normative issues is more clearly defined for the so-called *statutory*, official, or political threshold, which corresponds to the minimum amount of income adopted in social or fiscal legislation – for instance, the subsistence income in Belgium (see Atkinson *et al.* 2002). An advantage of this method is precisely that it reflects the political view of poverty; a potential disadvantage is that a statutory threshold also reflects budget constraints and other political factors, meaning that the amount of money in question does not necessarily guarantee that individuals or households will be able to satisfy their basic needs or achieve a decent standard of living.

[45] Bottiroli-Civardi and Chiappero-Martinetti (2006) have suggested an approach based on a plurality of (absolute or relative) poverty lines differentiated by a subgroup of populations, and proposed a reformulation of the FGT class of poverty measures for capturing the between and within poverty components.

adequate for representing the complexity and vagueness that characterize the capability approach. What kind of multivariate techniques
have most frequently been used for operationalizing the capability
approach? Are they coherent with the main features of this approach?

Table 9.1 lists some of the empirical applications of the capability
approach.[46] A review of this table evidences some interesting features:

i) Both micro and macro datasets are used, and a large amount of
   variables and a variety of dimensions are taken into account: from
   a minimum of three to a maximum of over fifty quantitative and
   qualitative variables, and from three to twenty dimensions. None
   of these empirical applications is based on *ad hoc* surveys and all of
   them adapt secondary data according to their respective purposes.
ii) Human diversity is more frequently taken into account when
   empirical applications are based on micro-data. However, few
   studies consider human diversity *ex-ante*, for instance by focusing
   attention on homogenous population sub-groups. In most cases,
   empirical applications refer to the overall population and construct
   only *ex-post* a poverty profile for describing personal or social
   characteristics common to poor people.[47]

---

[46] This list is of course neither complete nor exhaustive. The empirical applications
included have been selected because they are among the best known and most
frequently cited, and because of the variety of methodological tools used. We
have excluded the empirical application of the capability approach, which
takes us back to the univariate case: see, for instance, Lelli (2003) and Kuklys
(2004). We have also excluded some brilliant empirical analyses that use the
capability approach for purposes other than the assessment of well-being. See,
among others, Burchardt (2002) – this paper, for the first time, measures
capabilities rather than functionings, with particular reference to women's
employment in Britain. For a broad, updated survey on the empirical
applications of the capability approach, see the 'Empirical Analysis' section on
www.hd-ca.org

[47] With the *ex-ante* approach, homogeneity among individuals or households is
postulated implicitly, a comparison with a common reference point (the poverty
line) is carried out, and finally a poverty profile is constructed with the aim of
discovering, *ex-post*, which individual or household explicative factors (sex,
race, age, geography, or other characteristics) can generate poverty conditions.
However, this procedure does not seem to be fully coherent with the theoretical
underpinning of the capability approach, since it neglects the fact that *ex-ante*
these differences affect human needs and generate differentiated conversion
rates. It would seem more reasonable to analyze poverty by focusing attention on
homogeneous population sub-groups, or making use of a plurality of poverty
lines (or adjusted equivalence scales when a money metric is used) that attempt to

Table 9.1 *Different methodological solutions tested/applied for operationalizing Sen's capability approach in well-being and poverty analysis*

Reference	Data	No. of variables	Complexity No. of dimensions	Human diversity	Context	Linkages between dimensions or levels	Vagueness Poverty line?	Aggregation across dimensions	across units	overall index	Technique
Sen (1985)	macro	3	3	no	Set of countries	no	no	no	no	no	Descriptive statistics Partial ranking
UNDP (1990) HDI	macro	4	3	no	almost all countries	no	no	yes	-	yes	Normalization through scaling (linear functions) Log transformation for GDP Aggregation by arithmetic mean Complete ranking (human development index)[1]
UNDP (1995) GDI	macro	4	3	yes (ex-ante) gender	almost all countries	no	no	yes	-	yes	Normalization through scaling (linear functions) Log transformation for GDP Equally distributed index Arithmetic mean Complete ranking (gender development index)[1]
UNDP (1997) HPI-1 HPI-2	macro	4	3 (4 in HPI-2)	no	a set of developing vs. industrialized countries	no	in some dimensions (i.e long and healthy life, decent standard of living in HPI-2)	yes	no	yes	Generalized weighted mean with $\alpha = 3$ Complete ranking (human poverty index)[1]

Balestrino, Sciclone (2000)	macro 26	no	Italian regions	yes	no	yes	–	yes	Factor analysis Complete ranking (functioning-based well-being index)[1]
Baliamoune-Lutz (2004)	macro 11	no	almost all countries	no	no	yes	–	yes	Fuzzy sets theory Complete ranking (human well-being index)[1]
Schokkaert, van Ootogem (1990)	micro 46	yes (ex-ante) unemployed	Belgium	yes	yes	no	no	no	Factor analysis Regression analysis
Brandolini, D'Alessio (1998)	micro 20	yes (ex-post)	Italy	yes	yes	yes	yes	yes	Descriptive statistics Sequential stochastic dominance + multidimensional poverty index Partial and complete ranking (functioning deprivation index)[1]
Chiappero-Martinetti (2000)	micro 34	yes (ex post): subgroups of population	Italy	yes	no	yes	yes	yes	Fuzzy sets theory Complete ranking (overall well-being index)
Lelli (2001)	micro 54	yes (ex-post)	Belgium	yes	no	no	yes	no	Factor analysis vs. fuzzy analysis

Table 9.1 (*cont.*)

Reference	Data	No. of variables	No. of dimensions	Human diversity	Context	Complexity — Linkages between dimensions or levels	Vagueness — Poverty line?	Aggregation — across dimensions	across units	overall index	Technique
Klasen (2000)	micro	-	14	yes (ex-post)	South Africa	yes	yes	yes	yes	yes	Principal component analysis / Complete ranking (multi-component deprivation index)[1]
Clark, Qizilbash (2002)	micro	30	20 / 12 (core dim.)	yes (ex-post)	South Africa	no	no	no	yes	no	Fuzzy set theory; supervaluationist approach
Robeyns (2002)	micro	-	14	yes (ex-post) age and gender	UK	between income and functioning	no	only between var. in each dimension	no	no	Descriptive statistics
Kuklys (2003)	micro	15	4	yes (ex-ante)	UK	yes	no	no	yes	no	MIMIC model
Anand et al. (2004)	micro			yes (ex-ante) gender	UK	yes	no	yes	yes	yes	Regression analysis

Note:
(1) denomination of the index as indicated by the author(s)

iii) Linkages between dimensions of well-being and levels of analysis are more likely to be investigated when empirical applications are based on a micro-data set.

iv) Accurate descriptions are generally made of how well-being is distributed in its multiplicity of dimensions and across individuals; however, the 'temptation' to aggregate in a single index in order to make comparisons seems to prevail, even though some authors (e.g. Schokkaert and Van Ootegem 1990) expressly reject this temptation. On the whole, a large number of interesting multidimensional well-being and deprivation indexes have been formulated.

v) A wide range of multivariate and innovative techniques has been tested for selecting dimensions, describing variables, and deriving weighting and aggregate dimensions, including, in particular, factor analysis (Balestrino and Sciclone 2000; Schokkaert and Van Ootegem 1990; Lelli 2001), principal-component analysis (Klasen 2000); structural equation models (Kuklys 2003), and fuzzy set theory (Baliamoune-Lutz 2004; Chiappero-Martinetti 2000; Lelli 2001). Brandolini and D'Alessio (1998) also attempt to apply the sequential dominance for well-being comparisons between population subgroups.

vi) In most of the empirical applications of Sen's approach, vagueness is acknowledged either implicitly or explicitly: rarely are poverty thresholds drawn, but when they are, it is usually for aggregative purposes. When methodological tools such as fuzzy set theory or supervaluationism approach (Clark and Qizilbash 2002) are applied, these choices are motivated precisely by the need to handle the aspect of vagueness.

The above-mentioned empirical applications show that what are often considered 'weaknesses' of the capability approach (too demanding in terms of statistical information, too complex to be operationalized) can be overcome without great difficulty. Most importantly, these applications attempt to preserve and indeed emphasize, as much as possible, the 'strengths' of the approach – its consideration of the heterogeneity of individuals and their contexts and of the intrinsic vagueness of

capture the heterogeneity of personal features and circumstances. On this, see again Bottiroli-Civardi and Chiappero-Martinetti (2006).

well-being and poverty concepts – by adopting a wide range of methodological solutions.

An 'optimal technique' cannot probably be identified among those that have been tested until now, or that operationalization of the capability approach demands a single measurement tool or 'formula'. The broad nature of the approach, its being 'a framework of thought' (Robeyns 2000, 2003), is absolutely compatible with a plurality of techniques and methodological solutions, which must be selected from according to the specific purposes of the empirical investigation in question, and the availability of statistical data. Much more work has yet to be done: new and innovative tools need to be developed and tested, and contributions from other disciplines and fields of research could be very useful in this respect.

Even so, I would like to conclude this chapter by explaining why I consider fuzzy measurement techniques to be particularly promising and powerful for the operationalization of Sen's approach. There are two main reasons for this, one more specific and pragmatic, the other broader and founded on methodological grounds.

From a practical point of view, fuzzy sets theory is more than just a simple generalization of the crisp or classical sets theory.[48] It is a flexible and rigorous mathematical tool that makes it possible to represent quantitative (continuous or discrete) and qualitative variables, to quantify linguistic attributes as well as the so-called hedges or qualifiers[49] making use of a plurality of functional forms. Compared with

---

[48]   A crisp set divides the elements of a given universe into two groups: those that certainly belong to the set (membership value equal to 1) and those that certainly do not (membership value equal to 0). A sharp, unambiguous distinction between these two opposite cases certainly exists. A fuzzy set allows for gradual, continuous values of membership between the whole interval [0, 1], assigning to each element of a given universe a value representing its grade of membership to the fuzzy set. Because full membership and full non-membership to the fuzzy set can still be indicated, respectively, by values 1 and 0, a crisp set can be considered as a restricted case of the more general fuzzy set.

[49]   Linguistic variables are words or sentences expressed in natural language. Age, for instance, is a quantitative variable when expressed in terms of years. It becomes a linguistic variable if we refer to it with a (fuzzy) predicate such as, for instance, old or young. A linguistic hedge or fuzzy quantifier modifies the meaning of a predicate or, more generally, of a fuzzy set: *very*, *close to*, *quite*, *fairly*, are all examples of hedge. In the same fashion as adverbs and adjectives in language, these qualifiers change the shape of fuzzy sets. For instance, applying the hedge *very* to the linguistic variable or fuzzy set of young people, we obtain a

crisp sets theory, it offers a broader class of aggregation functions for combining elementary sets – complement, union, intersection, and averaging operators – where each class of functions is characterized by a properly justified set of axioms and the appropriate aggregation operator can be chosen according to different contexts and purposes.[50] Finally, fuzzy methodology is intuitively appealing, theoretically accessible, and also computationally simple. All these features are important for the operationalization of Sen's approach. First of all, almost all of the empirical analyses cited in Table 9.1 make use of both qualitative and quantitative variables, and the latter are often categorical. Secondly, multidimensionality makes the aggregation process more challenging, adding to the intensity of deprivation in one space and the extension of deprivation in more than one space. The availability of a plurality of aggregation operators makes it possible to capture both the depth and the breadth of dimensions of deprivation, and to make explicit the normative judgements underlying each process of synthesis.

From a methodological point of view, the fuzzy sets theory captures a dimension of uncertainty that traditional statistical tools, based on classical logic and crisp sets, are unable to grasp. From a semantic point of view, there are two categories of uncertainty. The first type is associated with events or statements that are well defined, yet the lack of information, elements of indecision associated with time, the degree of precision of the measurement tools used, or our ability to use these tools in a proper way, make the choice between two or more alternatives unspecified. This type of stochastic uncertainty corresponds to the notion of ambiguity (and broadly to the related concepts of inaccuracy, imprecision, unspecificity, or underspecificity, as described in Section 3) and has been largely and appropriately dealt with by probability theory and statistics.[51]

different fuzzy set, and thus a different representation of the corresponding membership function.

[50] See Zimmerman (1991). For a discussion on the meaning of fuzzy aggregations and their application to multidimensional well-being based on the capability approach, see Chiappero-Martinetti (1994, 2000).

[51] However, in literature fuzzy measures have been formulated with the aim of dealing with ambiguity and generalizing probability as well as other classical measures such as plausibility measures or belief measures. A fuzzy measure assigns a value to each crisp set of the universal set X according to the degree of evidence or belief that a particular element belongs in the set. Klir and Yuan (1995) provide an intuitive example regarding the difference between fuzzy measures and the degree of membership to a given fuzzy set. The example refers

The second type of uncertainty is related to the notion of vagueness as the difficulty in defining sharp boundaries and precise distinctions: fuzzy methodology provides a mathematical tool for dealing with this kind of uncertainty. Thus we have uncertainty as ambiguity and probability theory on the one hand, and uncertainty as vagueness and fuzzy sets theory on the other. Probability and fuzziness are not competing, alternative tools for measuring uncertainty: they are appropriate tools for measuring two different types of uncertainty, and they can complement each other.[52] This distinction is crucial and should be emphasized: even if membership grades and probabilities can take on similar values, they are not the same thing; and substantial differences at the conceptual level exist.[53] As already pointed out, probability is *negatively* related to the amount of information available. Generally,

to jury members who are uncertain about the guilt or innocence of the defendant. The set of guilty people and the set of innocent people are crisp sets with distinct boundaries and very different results: sentence and prison for one and acquittal and freedom for the other. Perfect evidence could assign full membership (the defendant is totally guilty) to one and only one of these two sets (the set of guilty people). However, if we exclude the cases of people who have confessed to their crime or been caught in a criminal act, generally speaking evidence is not perfect and some uncertainty prevails. A fuzzy measure indicates the degree to which the evidence provides proof of the defendant's guilt or innocence, that is, the extent to which it represents the uncertainty associated with two well-defined alternatives. This type of uncertainty, which derives from lack of information (i.e. ambiguity), is totally different from fuzziness, which results from the lack of sharp boundaries (i.e. vagueness). In the former case, a fuzzy measure assigns a value to each crisp set of the universal set (in our example, the two sets of guilty and innocent people); in the latter, a value (a membership degree) is assigned to each element of the universal set (in our example, to each defendant to be judged by jury members). After having expressed their guilty sentence, the jury members must also define the degree to which the defendant can be considered guilty, and this can be included in the interval between 0 and 1, according to different degrees of responsibility for a given crime.

[52] Both the fuzzy sets and probabilities theories belong to a wider and generalized theory of uncertainty that includes the possibility theory and the Demster-Shaferd theory of evidence, among others. Within this large set of theory, possibility theory is closer to the fuzzy sets theory than is probability theory. Zadeh (1978) views fuzziness as a possibilistic, rather than probabilistic, type of vagueness. Klir and Yuan (1995, p. 205) write: 'Probability theory is an ideal tool for formalizing uncertainty in situations where class frequencies are known or where evidence is based on outcomes of a sufficiently long series of independent random experiments. Possibility theory, on the other hand, is ideal for formalizing incomplete information expressed in terms of fuzzy propositions.'

[53] A possible reason for confusion is due to the fact that membership functions ψ_A are usually defined with reference to the interval of real numbers from 0 to 1

as information increases, probability disappears: more information reduces uncertainty, and thus probability values will be smaller as well. In a context of perfect and total information there is no uncertainty, and probability values will be equal to zero. Furthermore, probability is 'time-dependent': if a given event (for example, winning a lottery) has a probability of 0.02 per cent, then it is sufficient to wait and see if the event will occur or not.

In contrast, fuzziness can be *positively* related to the amount of information (the more information available, the greater the vagueness may be, thus weakening the possibility of defining sharp boundaries for a given event or phenomenon) and it does not dissipate with time, since it is an intrinsic property of an event or a given object. A typical example used to clarify the distinction between probability and fuzziness refers to statements such as 'there is a 30 per cent chance of light rain tomorrow'. A greater amount of statistical data and more sophisticated measurement tools could make this statement more precise; in any case, it is sufficient to wait until tomorrow and the probabilistic uncertainty will be solved. However, the fuzziness or vagueness regarding whether or not the rain will be light remains.

The way in which we should interpret membership degrees and probabilities is also different: if a given individual i belongs to the fuzzy subset of poor people with a membership degree equal to 0.7, this does not mean that he or she has a 70 per cent probability of being poor, but that his or her condition of being poor is vague or fuzzy in a measure of 70 per cent. In other words, if probability affirms that through time individual i is poor 70 counts out of 100, fuzzy analysis assigns this membership degree on the basis of the conditions of individual i, and the value does not change if the individual's condition does not change – no matter what the number of observations. Is the fuzzy sets theory the only tool for measuring vagueness, or are other options also available? More generally, how can vagueness be dealt with? Formal treatments of vagueness, which have become common in the last few decades, can be classified according to two main

inclusive. This choice is convenient for normalization and makes the comparison with crisp sets theory immediately evident. However, it is a choice, not a constraint, and any other specification is equally possible. A further distinction between membership degrees and probabilities that is immediately apparent is that the sum of the latter must be equal to one, while there is no such requirement for membership degrees.

approaches: those that seek to preserve almost all of classical logic and those that replace the dichotomy of truth and falsity with a manifold classification. As already discussed in Section 3, the supervaluationist approach and Williamson's epistemic approach, which conceive vagueness basically as a matter of ignorance, are examples of the first group, while multivalued logic and fuzzy logic refer to the second group.

The juxtaposition here is evident: in the former case, the basic assumption is that vague arguments must be 'regimented' (Haack 1996) so that classical logic can be applied; in the latter, vagueness must be accepted and dealt with through the use of many-valued or fuzzy logics. The suggestion of a fuzzy logician is to 'fuzzify' classical logic to obtain a new logic, which is directly applicable to 'unregimented' arguments.[54]

Qizilbash (2003) has discussed and compared these three different philosophical accounts of vague predicates – i.e. epistemic approaches, supervaluationist theory, and degree theories, which include fuzzy sets theory – and applied a supervaluationist approach for measuring poverty and vulnerability in South Africa (Clark and Qizilbash 2002).[55] He underlines the arguments in favor of supervaluationism, contrasting it to the fuzzy approach, which he criticizes for a series of reasons. Among them, he points out that it is not fully clear how membership

---

[54] Susan Haack (1996), in her critique of fuzzy logic, affirms that by assigning membership degrees, for example, to the predicate *tall* rather than settling on an arbitrary cut-off point avoids the need to regiment unidimensional vagueness (or vertical vagueness, to use Qizilbash's definition); yet it does not avoid the need to regiment multidimensional (or horizontal) vagueness and, at this level, introduces further complexities. From her point of view, fuzzy logic simply postpones, rather than eliminates, the need to introduce arbitrary boundaries. The conceptual distinction between complexity and vagueness suggested here, however, should clarify that as they are different issues, they require different methodological solutions.

[55] The application of this approach for measuring poverty necessitates a series of assumptions. As Qizilbash (2003) points out: 'There are certain "admissible" ways of making the predicate "poor" more precise ... If all admissible sharpening of "poor" include some particular dimension of poverty, ... it is a "core dimension"' (pp. 50–1). Then, he assumes that 'there is a range of minimal critical levels, which are involved in admissible sharpenings of "poor" ... and a set of "admissible dimensions" each of which has a range of admissible critical levels associated with it. Finally, "someone is poor (or core poor) ... if she falls at or below the lowest admissible minimal critical level on at least one core dimension"' (Qizilbash 2003, p. 51).

degrees should be interpreted when they are applied for measuring 'vertical vagueness' – that is, vagueness about the critical level below which one should be identified as poor; fuzzy sets theory does not focus on what he calls 'horizontal vagueness' – i.e. vagueness about the dimensions of poverty – nor does it offer criteria for identifying a 'core' dimension of poverty. A clearer distinction regarding the nature and purpose of the fuzzy sets theory *vis-à-vis* the supervaluationist theories and its appropriateness for measuring vertical and horizontal vagueness might be sufficient for addressing these critiques.

On the one hand, as I have tried to show, the aim of the fuzzy methodology is not to 'make more precise' concepts that are intrinsically vague, but to evidence, preserve, and account for this vagueness. The supervaluationist theories recognize the vague nature of many predicates, but their principal aim is to solve vagueness, to get back to the Aristotelian law of true or false, A or not-A, poor or not poor.[56] They are two different alternatives – and significantly different tools – for dealing with 'vertical vagueness' and the choice between them depends on how predicates and concepts are formulated, and thus how the idea of vagueness is conceived.[57] Vagueness plays a significant role in poverty and well-being analysis, taking on a precise meaning that must be preserved, particularly when these phenomena are viewed through the lens of the capability approach. The fuzzy sets theory seems to represent a proper tool for filling the gap between the theoretical formulation of intrinsically vague concepts and their measurement, even while much more work can and should be done in order to adapt this tool to the specific context of multidimensional poverty analysis.

On the other hand, the usefulness of a supervaluationist approach emerges more clearly in what Qizilbash defines as 'horizontal vagueness' (which, however, I think would be better defined as 'intrinsic complexity': see note 18). In a multidimensional setting, it certainly represents an alternative to other multivariate techniques (for example,

[56] Qizilbash writes (2003, p. 50): '. . . supervaluationism can be easily interpreted in the context of poverty measurement. The central concept is that of a specification space, and it is in this space that the notion of *making things more precise, or "sharpening"* them is developed' [italics added].

[57] As also Keefe and Smith recognize: 'Perhaps different ways to model vagueness are useful for different purposes and none is ideal for all' (Keefe and Smith 2002, p. 49).

the factor analysis) for reducing complexity, selecting dimensions, and identifying core poverty.[58]

However, issues such as the choice of what are the relevant dimensions of well-being or what it means to belong to the 'core poor' involve inescapable normative judgements, and the responsibility for such choices should be left to public debate, or discussed within a prescriptive theoretical framework, rather than being left up to mathematical and statistical tools.[59]

Conclusion

Complexity and vagueness are intrinsic and inescapable features of many concepts and phenomena. The aim of science is to remove or to reduce descriptive inaccuracy, imprecision, and inexactness as far as the availability of data, experimental error, and measurement tools permit. However, there is a vagueness and indeterminacy that affects many concepts and phenomena in human as well as in hard sciences and that cannot be removed, since they are aspects that are intrinsic to these concepts and phenomena.

The picture that derives from a multidimensional approach to well-being and poverty analysis is not a simple sum of the parts and neither is it – nor can it be – a clear picture. Some details, in particular, call for our attention; others superimpose, while still others remain in the shadows. Some aspects present sharply defined boundaries, while others are vague and indeterminate. Our minds and our eyes, by their very nature, are able to grasp details and shades of meaning – more generally speaking, to recognize the complexity and richness of what is in front of us – far better than can the conceptual schemes and methodological restrictions that exist in most fields of research, economics *in primis*.

The thesis that I have tried to support in this chapter is that the blurred nature of this picture should be seen neither as constraint nor deficiency;[60] it is rather the *inescapable consequence* that arises when *intrinsically* complex concepts such as those of well-being and poverty

---

[58] As shown by Clark and Qizilbash (2002) who, using survey responses for a sample of South African people, select admissible critical levels and core dimensions of deprivation recurring to the supervaluationist approach.

[59] See Sen (1999).

[60] 'Sometimes a blurred picture may communicate more meaning than a sharp one' (Coates 1996, p. 8).

are being considered. The value of a theoretical framework should be judged by its ability to acknowledge such complexity, represent multi-faceted phenomena, and investigate in-depth relationships, causes, and effects among the plurality of dimensions involved. This is precisely what the capability approach has been able to do.

In this chapter I have suggested that intrinsic complexity (i.e. multidimensionality) and intrinsic vagueness (i.e. difficulty in 'drawing a line') on the one hand, and complexity and vagueness in measurement on the other, should be separated, at least conceptually. In differentiating the two layers of discourse, it becomes possible to clarify why the intrinsic complexity and intrinsic vagueness of this theoretical framework should not be considered a constraint or hindrance that compromises its value. It is the inadequacy of traditional statistical tools in capturing these distinct features that should instead be called into question.

In terms of the measurement issue, the range of multivalued techniques for dealing with multidimensionality is quite wide, as the empirical applications of the capability approach also show, while the choice of tools to account for vagueness is more limited. In this chapter I have emphasized arguments in favor of a fuzzy methodology (i.e. fuzzy logic and fuzzy sets) for operationalizing the capability approach, in an attempt to demonstrate how it seems to be able to account for vagueness as well as complexity better than other techniques which are based on classical, bivalent logic and probability theory.

Cited references

Alkire, S. 2002. *Valuing freedoms. Sen's capability approach and poverty reduction*, Oxford: Oxford University Press.

Anand, P., Hunter, G. and Smith, R. 2005. 'Capabilities and wellbeing: Evidence based on the Sen–Nussbaum approach to welfare', *Social Indicators Research*, 79, pp. 9–55.

Arthur, W. B., Durlauf, S. and Lane, D. (eds.) 1997. '*The economy as an evolving complex system II*', *Santa Fe Institute Studies in the Sciences of Complexity*, vol. 27, Reading, USA: Addison-Wesley.

Atkinson, A. B. 2002. 'Multidimensional deprivation: contrasting social welfare and counting approaches', mimeo, Oxford: Nuffield College.

Atkinson, A. B., Cantillon, B., Marlier, E. and Nolan B. 2002. *Social indicators. The EU and social inclusion*, Oxford: Oxford University Press.

Balestrino, A. and Sciclone, N. 2000. 'Should we use functionings instead of income to measure well-being? Theory and some evidence from Italy', *Rivista Internazionale di Scienze Sociali*, 109: 1–20.

Balestrino, A. and Carter, I. (eds.), 1996. *Functioning and capabilities: normative and policy issues*, Notizie di Politeia, 12, 43/44, Milan.

Baliamoune-Lutz, M. 2004. 'On the measurement of human well-being: fuzzy set theory and Sen's capability approach', Research paper 2004/16, Helsinki: Wider UN.

Bibi, S. 2003. 'Measuring poverty in a multidimensional perspective: a review of literature', mimeo, Québec: Université Laval.

Bottiroli-Civardi, M. and Chiappero-Martinetti, E. 2006. 'Measuring poverty within and between population subgroups', IRISS Working Paper Series 2006–06, IRISS at CEPS/INSTEAD.

Bourguignon, F. and Chakravarty, S. R. 2002. 'Multidimensional poverty orderings', working paper 2002–22, Paris: DELTA.

Bourguignon, F. and Chakravarty, S. R. 2003. 'The measurement of multidimensional poverty', in *Journal of Economic Inequality*, 1: pp. 25–49.

Brandolini, A. and D'Alessio, G. 1998. 'Measuring well-being in the functioning space', mimeo, Rome, Italy: Banca d'Italia.

Burchardt, T. 2002. 'Constraint and opportunity: women's employment in Britain', mimeo, ESRC Research Centre for Analysis of Social Exclusion, London: London School of Economics.

Cargile, J. 1969. 'Thesorites paradox', in *British Journal for the Philosophy of Science*, 20: pp. 193–202. Reprinted in Keefe, R. and Smith, P. 2002: pp. 89–98.

Chakravarty, S., Mukherjee, D. and Ramade, R. 1998. 'On the subgroup and factor decomposable measures of multidimensional poverty', in *Research on Economics Inequality*, 8: pp. 175–194.

Chapman, G. P. 1985. 'The epistemology of complexity and some reflections on the symposium "The science and praxis of complexity" ', mimeo, Montpellier, The United Nation University.

Chiappero-Martinetti, E. 1994. 'A new approach to evaluation of well-being and poverty by fuzzy set theory', in *Giornale degli economisti e annali di economia'*, 7–9: pp. 367–388.

Chiappero-Martinetti, E. 1996. 'Standard of living evaluation based on Sen's approach: some methodological suggestion', in Balestrino A. and Carter I. (eds.), pp. 37–54.

Chiappero-Martinetti, E. 2000. 'A multidimensional assessment of well-being based on Sen's functioning approach', in *Rivista Internazionale di Scienze Sociali*, 58: pp. 207–239.

Cilliers, P. 1998. *Complexity and post-modernism: understanding complex systems*, London: Routledge.

Clark, D. and Qizilbash, M. 2002. 'Core poverty and extreme vulnerability in South Africa', discussion paper 2002–3, The Economics Research Centre, School of Economic and Social Studies, University of East Anglia.

Coates, J. 1996. *The claims of common sense: Moore, Wittgenstein, Keynes and the social sciences*, Cambridge, UK: Cambridge University Press.

Colander, D. (ed.) 2000. *Introduction to complexity and the history of economic thought*, London: Routledge.

Comim, F. 2000. 'Marshall and the role of common sense in complex systems', in Colander, D. (ed.), pp. 155–192.

Comim, F. 2001a. 'Operationalizing Sen's capability approach', mimeo, Cambridge, UK: University of Cambridge.

Comim, F. 2001b. 'System-level poverty and socially sustainable development', mimeo, Cambridge, UK: University of Cambridge.

Comim, F. and Kuklys, W. 2002. 'Is poverty simply about poor individuals?', mimeo, Cambridge, UK: University of Cambridge.

Cox, E. 1994. *The fuzzy systems handbook*, Chestnut Hill, M.A., USA: Academic Press.

Dagum, C. and Costa, M. 2002. 'Analysis and measurement of poverty. Univariate and multivariate approaches and their policy implications. A case study: Italy', in Dagum, C. and Ferrari, G. (eds.).

Dagum, C. and Ferrari, G. (eds.) 2002. *Household behaviour, equivalence scales and well-being*, Berlin: Springer-Verlag.

Doyal, L. and Gough, I. 1991. *A theory of human need*, Basinkstoke: Macmillan.

Duclos, J., Sahn, D. and Younger, S. 2002. 'Robust multidimensional poverty comparisons', *The Economic Journal*, 116, 514, pp. 943–968.

Dutta, I., Pattanaik, P. and Xu, Y. 2003. 'On measuring deprivation and the standard of living in a multidimensional framework on the basis of aggregate data', in *Economica*, 70, 2, pp. 197–221.

Edgington, D. 2002. 'Vagueness by degree', in Keefe. R. and Smith, P. (eds.), pp. 294–316.

Einstein, A. 1922 'Geometry and experience' in his *Sidelights of relativity*, London: Methuen, pp. 25–56.

Erikson, R. 1993. 'Descriptions of inequality: the Swedish approach to welfare research', in Nussbaum, M. and Sen, A. K. (eds.), pp. 67–83.

Erikson, R. and Aberg, R. 1987. *Welfare in transition. A survey of living conditions in Sweden 1968–1981*, Oxford: Clarendon Press.

Evans, G. and McDowell, J. (eds.) 1976. *Truth and meaning*, Oxford: Clarendon Press.

Fine, K. 1975. 'Vagueness, truth and logic', in *Synthese*, 30, pp. 265–300. Reprinted in Keefe and Smith (eds.), pp. 119–150.

Fukuda-Parr, S. and Shiva Kumar, A. K. (eds.) 2003. *Readings in human development*, New Delhi: Oxford University Press.

Garcia Diaz, R. 2003. Multidimensional Poverty, mimeo, York, UK: University of York.

Goguen, J. A. 1969. 'The logic of inexact concepts' in *Synthese*, 19, pp. 325–373.

Haack, S. 1996. *Deviant logic, fuzzy logic: beyond the formalism*, Chicago: Chicago University Press.

Hajek, P. 1998. *Metamathematics of fuzzy logic*, Dordrecht, The Netherlands: Kluwer Academic Publisher.

von Hayek, F. A. 1964. 'The theory of complex phenomena', in *The critical approach to science and philosophy: essays in honor of Karl R. Popper*, Mario Bunge (ed.), New York: Free Press.

Hayek, F. A. 1967. 'The theory of complex phenomena', in *Studies in Philosophy, Politics, and Economics*, Chicago, University of Chicago Press.

Jackman, H. 2004. 'Temporal externalism and epistemic theories of vagueness', in *Philosophical studies*, 117, 1–2, pp. 79–94.

Keefe, R. and Smith, P. (eds.) 2002. *Vagueness: a reader*, Cambridge, USA: MIT Press.

Kempson, R. 1977. *Semantic theory*, Cambridge, UK: Cambridge University Press.

Keynes, J. M. 1960a. *Collected writings of John Maynard Keynes: vol. 7, the 'General Theory' of employment, interest and money*, New York: Palgrave Macmillan.

Keynes, J. M. 1960b. *Collected writings of John Maynard Keynes: vol. 13, The 'General Theory' and after*, New York: Palgrave Macmillan.

Klasen, S. 2000. 'Measuring poverty and deprivation in South Africa', in *Review of Income and Wealth*, 46, 1, pp. 33–58.

Klir, G. J. and Yuan, B. 1995. *Fuzzy sets and fuzzy logic. Theory and application*, New Jersey: Prentice Hall International Editions.

Kuklys, W. 2003. 'Measurement and determinants of welfare achievement– evidence from the UK', mimeo, Cambridge, UK: University of Cambridge.

Kuklys, W. 2004. 'A monetary approach to capability measurement of the disabled – evidence from the UK', Papers on strategic interaction, 8–2004, Jena, Germany: Max Planck Institute for Research into Economic Systems.

Lelli, S. 2001. 'Factor analysis vs. fuzzy sets theory: assessing the influence of different techniques on Sen's functioning approach', Public Economics working paper series 121, Leuven, Belgium: Center for Economic Studies.

Lelli, S. 2003, 'What money can't buy: the relevance of income redistribution for functioning levels', mimeo, Leuven, Belgium: Center for Economic Studies.

Lukasiewicz, J. 1920. 'Philosophical remarks on many-valued systems of propositional logic', in *Polish Logic: 1920–1939*, Storrs McCall (ed.) 1967. Oxford: Oxford Clarendon Press.

Maasoumi, E. 1999. 'Multidimensioned approaches to welfare analysis', in Silber, J. (ed.).

Machina, K. F. 1976. 'Truth, belief and vagueness', in *Journal of Philosophical Logic*, 5, p. 47–78. Reprinted in Keefe R. and Smith P. (eds.), pp. 174–203.

Mehlberg, H. 1958. *The reach of science*. Toronto: Toronto University Press, pp. 256–259. Reprinted in Keefe R. and Smith P. (eds.), pp. 85–89.

Montgomery, M. 2000. 'Complex theory: an Austrian perspective', in Colander D. (ed.), pp. 227–240.

Nguyen, H. T. and Walker, A. 1999. *First course in fuzzy logic*. Boca Rato, Florida, USA: CRC Press.

Nussbaum, M. and Sen, A. K. (eds.) 1993. *The quality of life, wider studies in development economics*, Oxford: Clarendon Press.

Qizilbash, M. 2002. 'A note on the measurement of poverty and vulnerability in the South African context', in *Journal of International Development*, 14, pp. 757–772.

Qizilbash, M. 2003. 'Vague language and precise measurement: the case of poverty', in *Journal of Economic Methodology*, 10, 1, pp. 41–58.

Reitsma, F. 2003. 'A response to simplifying complexity', in *Geoforum*, 34, pp. 13–16.

Robeyns, I. 2000. 'An unworkable idea or a promising alternative? Sen's capability approach re-examined', Discussion Paper 2000.30, Leuven, Belgium, Center for Economic Studies.

Robeyns, I. 2002. 'Gender inequality: a capability perspective'. Doctoral thesis, Cambridge: Cambridge University.

Robeyns, I. 2003. 'The capability approach: an interdisciplinary introduction' mimeo, Amsterdam: University of Amsterdam.

Roemer, J. 1996. *Theories of distributive justice*, Cambridge, USA: Harvard University Press.

Russell, B. 1923. 'Vagueness', in *Australasian Journal of Philosophy and Psychology*, 1, pp. 84–92. Reprinted in Keefe and Smith (eds.), pp. 61–68.

Sainsbury, R. M. 1990. 'Concepts without boundaries', Inaugural Lecture given at King's College, London, 6 November 1990. Reprinted in Keefe and Smith (eds.), pp. 251–264.

Schokkaert, E. and Van Ootegem, L. 1990. 'Sen's concept of the living standard applied to the Belgian unemployed', in *Recherches Economiques de Louvain*, 56, 3–4, pp. 429–450

Sen, A. K. 1985. *Commodities and capabilities*, Amsterdam: North Holland.

Sen, A. K. 1989. 'Economic methodology: heterogeneity and relevance', in *Social Research*, 56, 2, pp. 299–329.

Sen, A. K. 1992. *Inequality re-examined*, Oxford: Clarendon Press.

Sen, A. K. 1997. *On economic inequality. Expanded edition with a substantial annexe* by James Foster and Amartya Sen, Oxford: Clarendon Press.

Sen, A. K. 1999. *Development as freedom*, New York: Alfred A. Knopf Press.

Sen, A. K. 2003. 'Development as capability expansion', in Fukuda-Parr, S. and Shiva Kumar, A. K. (eds.). Originally published in *Journal of Development Planning*, 1989, 19, pp. 41–58.

Silber, J. (ed.) 1999. *Handbook of income inequality measurement*, Boston: Kluwer Academic Publisher.

Sorensen, R. 2002. 'Vagueness', in Zalte E. (ed.), *Stanford Encyclopedia of Philosophy*, available on line: http://plata.stanford.edu/archives/fall2002.

Srinivasan, T. N. 1994. 'Human development: a new paradigm or reinvention of the wheel?', in *American Economic Review*, papers and proceedings, 84, pp. 238–243.

Stewart, F. 1985. *Basic needs in developing countries*, Baltimore, USA: Johns Hopkins University Press.

Sugden, R. 1993. 'Welfare, resources and capabilities: a review of *Inequality Re-examined* by Amartya Sen', in *Journal of Economic Literature*, 36, pp. 1947–1962.

Tappenden, J. 1995. 'Some remarks on vagueness and a dynamic conception of language', in *Southern Journal of Philosophy*, 33, pp. 193–201.

Tsui, K. Y. 2002. 'Multidimensional poverty indices', in *Social Choice and Welfare*, 19, pp. 69–93.

Tye, M. 1989. 'Supervaluationism and the law of excluded middle', in *Analysis*, 49, pp. 141–143.

UNDP, 1990, 1995, 1997. Human Development Reports, Oxford: Oxford University Press.

Williamson, T. 1994. *Vagueness*, London: Routledge.

Wright, C. 1976. 'Language-mastery and the sorites paradox', in Evans G. and McDowell J. (eds.), pp. 223–247. Reprinted in Keefe and Smith (eds.), pp. 151–173.

Ysander, B. C. 1993. 'Comment to Erikson's work "Descriptions of inequality" ', in Nussbaum M. and Sen, A. K. (eds).

Zadeh, L. A. 1975. 'Fuzzy logic and approximate reasoning', in *Synthese*, 30, pp. 407–428.

Zadeh, L. A. 1975. 'A fuzzy set interpretation of linguistic hedges', in *Journal of Cybernetics*, 2, pp. 4–34.

Zadeh, L. 1976. 'A fuzzy algorithmic approach to the definition of complex and imprecise concepts' in *International Journal of Man-machine studies*, 8, pp. 249–291.

Zadeh, L. A. 1978. 'Fuzzy sets as a basis for a theory of possibility', in *Fuzzy sets and systems*, 1, pp. 3–28.

Zadeh, L. and Kacprzyk, J. (eds.) 1992. *Fuzzy logic for the management of uncertainty*, New York, USA: J.Wiley & Sons.

Zhang, Q. 1998. 'Fuzziness – vagueness – generality – ambiguity' in *Journal of pragmatics*, 29, pp. 13–31.

Zimmerman, H. J. 1991. *Fuzzy sets theory and its applications*, Boston: Kluwer Academic Publisher.

10 | Operationalising Sen's capability approach: the influence of the selected technique

SARA LELLI[1,2]

Introduction

A major feature of Sen's theory, characterising well-being as a rich and multifaceted concept, unquestionably lies in its conforming to intuitive notions of what it means to be better off or worse off. Essentially, this account confronts anybody who is willing to assign some kind of concrete shape to functionings and capabilities with a frame of analysis involving, however, analogous issues if compared with the concepts of the living standard traditionally used in practical work. In spite of this, when it comes to working definitions and measurements, its informational richness is often regarded as a worrisome feature.

The existing applications have nevertheless proven to be rather fruitful in terms of the array of suggested techniques. As Atkinson (1999: 185) has stressed, 'there is more than one way in which an idea of this kind [Sen's framework] can be operationally effective'. Focusing on micro applications, the literature has been basically ranging in between the use of simple descriptive statistics, multivariate methods and the 'fuzziness' approach. The adoption of the two latter methodologies has been repeatedly endorsed by Sen himself (1990, 1994 and 1996), emphasising their suitability for his framework. Accordingly, most applications nowadays rely on either of the two techniques.

Meanwhile, increasing attention has been devoted to Sen's approach – at least in some countries – and also by public institutions. At a more

[1] Università Cattolica del Sacro Cuore, Piacenza; Center for Economic Studies, K. U. Leuven.
[2] This chapter greatly benefited from the valuable and attentive comments of Erik Schokkaert. Special thanks go also to Ingrid Robeyns, Enrica Chiappero-Martinetti, Mozaffar Qizilbash, Luc Lauwers, Bruno Cheli and Stephan Klasen for their comments and suggestions. I am grateful to 'Fondazione di Piacenza e Vigevano' for the generous financial support. The usual disclaimers apply.

general level, the advent of the Human Development Index further substantiates the previous claim while stressing the importance of performing supplementary investigations aimed at assessing the reliability of the results emerging from the different methodological approaches. This represents, indeed, both the rationale and the purpose of this chapter, i.e. ascertaining, by means of an illustrative empirical exercise, to what extent the results originated by the implementation of Sen's concepts are influenced by the choice of the specific technique, where the latter takes the form of either factor analysis or fuzzy sets theory. Ideally, procedural decisions should in no way affect the overall results, as any major discrepancy could bring about considerable normative implications, not to mention the potentially significant consequences it could entail in terms of political choices whenever the public institutions' interest towards this approach turned into actual endorsement.

The remainder of the chapter, therefore, is organised as follows. After having sketched the basic notions underlying the capability approach in Section 2, the theoretical foundations of factor analysis and fuzzy sets theory will be briefly reviewed in Section 3. Section 4 will be devoted to the comparative analyses concerning their use in association with well-being measurement. Section 5 will conclude by summarising the findings.

The core concepts of the capability approach

The interpretation of the notion of well-being as not exclusively associated with affluence but with everyone's abilities indeed represents a major feature characterising Amartya Sen's theory.[3] In Sen's view, the capacity of profiting from the available resources is greatly influenced by its utilisation, which in turn depends upon the specific circumstances experienced by the given individual. Hence, goods are not valued as a

---

[3] The terms 'well-being' and 'standard of living' will be used interchangeably, in spite of the distinction made by Sen. For the sake of accuracy, the focus in this work will be on what he defines as 'standard of living', namely the achieved activities and states of being (e.g. having good nutrition) of an individual. 'Well-being', in Sen's view, refers to the range of opportunities the individual has to pursue activities and states of being valuable to him. It has to be measured in the capability space and, consequently, exhibits higher data requirements than available for this study.

consequence of their being possessed; rather, they are evaluated on the basis of the effects that they may engender on the individual, effects that are likely to differ rather seriously according to the various circumstances under which those goods are exploited.

A couple of issues commonly disregarded by traditional welfare economics make up, in fact, the foundation of Sen's thoughts. First, the deep human diversity affects individual well-being through both the heterogeneity of personal characteristics (e.g. intelligence, age, gender, physical conditions) and the specific socio-environmental conditions (e.g. economic infrastructures, social norms, public services). Next, it affects the intrinsic value of one's freedom to choose and achieve. As a consequence of the alleged inadequacy of the availability of goods as a measure of well-being, Sen maintains that although the provided goods could exactly coincide with the ones that would have been selected had the individual had the opportunity to choose, the quality of the life that receives the goods but has not chosen them will be reduced by the mere absence of such a right. 'Acting freely and being able to choose are, in this view, directly conducive to well-being' (Sen, 1992: 51).

Adopting Sen's particular terminology, the two above-mentioned issues may be translated by the notions of *functioning* and *capability*. Functionings are the various doings and beings of a person, the achievements of an individual determined by the particular way in which he is able to 'let the available goods function'. Formally, following Sen (1985), letting x_i be a vector of commodities possessed by person i and selected from the consumption set X_i, c being the function converting the commodity vector into a vector of characteristics of those commodities[4] (thus, the vector of characteristics consumed by person i will be given by $c(x_i)$) and u_i a utilisation function chosen by person i in the set U_i reflecting the specific use of the commodities that the person can make in generating a functioning vector out of the characteristics of the given commodities and in association with his actual abilities, person's i functioning b_i will be expressed as

$$b_i = u_i(c(x_i)) \tag{1}$$

---

[4] Sen adopts, in fact, Gorman-Lancaster's perspective, which enables him to see every commodity in terms of the vector of its characteristics.

Capabilities, instead, are intended to portray one's freedom to choose what kind of life to live and should, therefore, depict the actual autonomy in pursuing and achieving those doings and beings one deems valuable. Depending on two main factors – namely, the consumption set of the person (*i.e.* the set X_i) and the ability to convert commodities into achievements (*i.e.* the set U_i) – capabilities can be described as

$$Q_i = \{b_i|b_i = u_i(c(x_i)), \text{ for some } u_i(\cdot) \in U_i \text{ and some } x_i \in X_i\} \quad (2)$$

In spite of its intuitive appeal, defining the value of the set Q_i has fairly significant and disturbing implications in that the notion of capability implies that hypothetical situations have to be taken into account when evaluating one's living standards. This makes, of course, the measurement of one's capabilities far more difficult than the measurement of one's actual functionings. As a consequence, in what follows, Basu's (1987) suggestion will be taken on and the analysis will exclusively focus on functionings as indicators of one's living standards.

Some theoretical remarks on the adopted methodologies

Identifying functionings by factor analysis

Factor analysis represents a data reduction technique very often used in empirical research in the social sciences with the purpose of summarising the available data (usually test scores or questionnaire responses) in such a way that the researcher can easily grasp the empirical relationships among the variables under consideration. In doing so, factor analysis relies on the assumption that the observed variables are linear combinations of some common underlying dimensions, known as 'factors'.

The factor analytic technique exploits the presumed correspondence between the system of latent factors and the set of observed variables in order to identify the separate dimensions for the given data and determine the extent to which each variable is explained by each dimension. In assessing individual living standards, such methodology is thus considered as a helpful device for solving the problem of defining a limited number of well-interpretable dimensions of well-being. The specific application of this technique to Sen's capability approach basically implies assessing the empirical validity of the following model and subsequently interpreting the different factors in terms of functionings

$$a_{ij} = \lambda_{1j}f_{i1} + \lambda_{2j}f_{i2} + \ldots + \lambda_{pj}f_{ip} + u_{ij} \quad i = 1, \ldots, N; \ j = 1, \ldots, n. \quad (3)$$

which, in matrix notation, reduces to

$$A = \Lambda F + U \tag{4}$$

where A captures the matrix providing the answers of the i respondents on the j items, F represents the matrix of 'factor scores' giving the position of each respondent on the p functionings, Λ captures the matrix of 'factor loadings' showing the association between the answers on the items and the position of the respondents on the functionings and U is the matrix of the residual terms. Each questionnaire response can, thus, be interpreted as a linear combination of a number of common factors contributing to the variance of different observed variables, and of one specific unique hypothetical factor including influences which affect only a specific variable and any other sources of bias.

The determination – carried out on the basis of the matrix A – of the factor loadings constitutes the first and major step of the whole procedure. The information provided by the matrix Λ is what makes the identification of the single functionings possible: since factors serve as predictors in deriving the observed variables and they are assumed – as it will be argued in the subsequent paragraph – to be uncorrelated with each other; the loadings may be interpreted as both regression weights and as correlation coefficients.[5] Hence, they can be seen as indicating the degree of correspondence between each item and the functioning, with higher loadings making the item representative of the functioning. This points to the fact that the derivation of such loadings – as well as of the subsequent factor scores – is performed in accordance with a number of preliminary assumptions whose fundamental implication is that the latent factor scores wholly explain the correlations among the

---

[5] Such coefficients basically play the same role in factor analysis as regression coefficients in regression analysis. Although in both cases the key variable is described as a linear weighted combination of another set of variables plus a residual, the traditional regression techniques postulate the observability of the set of independent variables, while factors just represent hypothetical constructs that can only be estimated from the data.

observed variables and, thus, their estimation has to take place in such a way that they account for the maximum possible amount of the variance of the variables being considered.[6] Therefore, defining R_{AA} as the correlation matrix of the respondents' answers and trusting an estimate for the matrix Ψ,

$$R_{AA} = \Lambda R_{FF} \Lambda' + \hat{\Psi} \tag{5}$$

which, assuming that the common factors are orthogonal ($R_{FF} = I$), can be re-expressed as

$$R_{AA} - \hat{\Psi} = \Lambda\Lambda' \tag{6}$$

where Λ can be defined as

$$\Lambda = Q\Omega^{1/2} \tag{7}$$

Q being the matrix of the eigenvectors of $(R_{AA} - \hat{\Psi})$ and Ω the matrix of the corresponding eigenvalues. However, once computed, the factors have to be interpreted and identified.[7] A rotation of the factors (i.e. a redistribution of the variance in between factors by applying an orthogonal transformation matrix T to the estimated loadings, so as to shift the original $\hat{\Lambda}$ into the new $\hat{\Lambda}^* = \hat{\Lambda}T$) providing a matrix in which each factor displays only a few high loadings is needed. The Varimax procedure – which was selected for the application – complies with such a viewpoint by maximising the variance of the squared loadings in each column of the matrix $\hat{\Lambda}^*$. This implies making the loadings on each factor either high (i.e. close to one) or near zero, so as to sharply indicate the association (or the lack of association) between the variables and the specific factor, thus facilitating the interpretation. Moreover, the choice of an orthogonal rotation method implies the

---

[6] Apart from the necessary hypothesis of some existing underlying structure in the system of observed variables, out of convenience all common factors F are supposed to be standardised and orthogonal; besides, the procedure requires that the residual terms U are uncorrelated with each other while at the same time not correlating with the common factors, have mean zero as well as a specific variance determined by the diagonal elements of a matrix Ψ.

[7] Initial solutions are not useful for such a purpose, both because factors with many large loadings are difficult to identify and because an almost infinite number of mathematically equivalent sets of factors exist, as the same correlation matrix may originate from many different latent configurations of loadings. This particular identification issue is known as the 'rotation problem'.

theoretical assumption of absence of any correlation in between the rotated underlying dimensions, which meets the well-known objections raised by Basu (1987) or Williams in Sen (1987) in what concerns the potential danger of functionings overlapping.[8]

Once the derivation and interpretation of loadings is complete, a last step usually relates to the data reduction goal. From Sen's perspective, the estimation of individual scores conveys an essential meaning, as they can be understood as describing the living standard of the respondents. The procedure (cf. Thomson, 1951) is quite straightforward: according to the basic equation (4) and, given both the observability of the matrix A and the availability of Λ, a least squares technique allows F to be estimated for each respondent. This way, each factor score will result in a linear composite of the optimally weighted variables under analysis.[9]

Identifying functionings by fuzzy sets theory

The idea of a fuzzy set is quite simple in itself. Fuzzy sets are classes within which the transition from membership to non-membership takes place gradually rather than suddenly. In fuzzy sets theory an element is allowed to partially belong to a set. As a result, each set is characterised by a function μ assigning to each of its elements a real number in the interval [0,1] taken to represent its membership value.[10] More formally, let X be a set whose elements are denoted by x, then a fuzzy set A will be defined as a mapping $\mu: X \to [0,1]$. Following such a definition, $\mu(x) = 0$ implies non-membership, $\mu(x) = 1$ stands for full membership, and intermediate values between 0 and 1 denote partial

---

[8] Stephan Klasen kindly drew my attention to the fact that Sen's approach actually does not require the different functionings to be uncorrelated. This is correct; yet I personally subscribe to Basu's warning and believe that, from a theoretical point of view, sorting out the various components of well-being constitutes a wise precautionary measure. Moreover, out of carefulness an oblique rotation on the specific data used in this empirical application was performed as well and it did not produce any modification in the results.

[9] For a thorough description of the technical details concerning factor analysis see, for example, Harman (1976).

[10] Note that the degrees of membership are just conventionally fixed and the choice of the unit interval is, in itself, arbitrary. Furthermore, the set of possible membership values need not necessarily consist of numerical values; it may well be just an ordered set of verbal hedges.

membership. Within the context of well-being evaluation $\mu(x)$ could well represent the grade of membership of an individual to the set A of the population with a high standard of living with respect to a specific indicator (e.g. the frequency of social contacts).

Several methods for assigning degrees of membership have been used and others proposed in the literature. I will confine myself to introducing those measures used in the application.

Selection and estimation of membership functions

It seems to be widely accepted nowadays that the only condition a membership function must really satisfy is that it has to range between 0 and 1. The researcher can legitimately select any curve whose shape is defined according to what suits him best from the point of view of simplicity, convenience or efficiency.

Two main measures – distance and frequency – have proved to be helpful. Advocating an essentially subjective interpretation, the distance concept allows membership to be estimated by similarity judgements: assuming the existence of an ideal perfect element in the set, the degree of membership of any other element is taken to be a function of its relative distance with respect to it. Of course, the distance function has to be specified. A widespread monotonic version is the quadratic *sigmoid* curve (or, alternatively, its reflected image, namely the *logistic* function), defined by three parameters: the zero and full membership values (α and γ, respectively) and the crossover point ($\beta = \alpha + \gamma/2$) whose membership value equals 0.5 and, hence, represents the most doubtful point with respect to the specific attribute under analysis.[11] The key parameters are determined by identifying sharp extreme conditions (i.e. stipulating conditions of absolute deprivation and absolute fulfilment with respect to a given variable), while the derivation of the intermediate degrees of membership for the points falling in the intervals $[\alpha,\beta]$ and $[\beta,\gamma]$ is carried out thanks to a quadratic interpolation leading to the following specification (Sanchez, 1986: 337)

---

[11] This formulation, of course, strongly restricts the nature of the set X, implying that the latter be both ordered and equipped with a multiplication and an addition operator. The graphical representations of the μ functions are given in Figure 10.A.1.

$$\mu(x) = \begin{cases} 0 & \text{if} & x \leq \alpha \\ 2[(x-\alpha)/(\gamma-\alpha)]^2 & \text{if} & \alpha < x \leq \beta \\ 1 - 2[(x-\gamma)/(\gamma-\alpha)]^2 & \text{if} & \beta < x \leq \gamma \\ 1 & \text{if} & x > \gamma \end{cases} \tag{8}$$

An increasing curve such as the sigmoid relies on the claim that when the belief that an element x belonging to the set A strengthens, the value of $\mu(x)$ will increase. Hence, it is best fit for representing notions like 'how often do you go to the cinema?', whereas its logistic counterpart looks more appropriate for depicting negative concepts such as 'financial difficulties'.

Linear membership functions are very popular in common empirical analysis as well, as they are easy to specify, interpret and visualise. These representations presuppose the variables' categories to be equidistant from one another and assume a direct proportionality between the elements of the domain and the membership grade – a very restrictive and not always appropriate assumption. Two main classes of linear representations are prevalent: first, the basic *linear* function depending exclusively on the extreme values of the variable x, and whose increasing version takes the simple following form

$$\mu(x) = \begin{cases} 0 & \text{if} & x = x_{min} \\ \frac{(x-x_{min})}{(x_{max}-x_{min})} & \text{if} & x_{min} < x < x_{max} \\ 1 & \text{if} & x = x_{max} \end{cases} \tag{9}$$

Alternatively, the *trapezoidal* specification postulates the choice of two threshold values, a_1 and a_2 (larger than the minimum and smaller than the maximum), corresponding to the categories of the variable x beneath which a condition of low living standard is evident and above which a situation of high living standard can undoubtedly be assumed, respectively

$$\mu(x) = \begin{cases} 0 & \text{if} & x \leq a_1 \\ \frac{(x-a_1)}{(a_2-a_1)} & \text{if} & a_1 < x < a_2 \\ 1 & \text{if} & x \geq a_2 \end{cases} \tag{10}$$

Two plateaux thus characterise trapezoidal specifications: all the elements of the domain falling within a given plateau share equal membership in the fuzzy set. As argued, however, such a representation requires the preliminary definition of two critical values to separate the definitely deprived and the definitely non-deprived, hence laying open to an obvious critique in what concerns the grounds on which the choice of the thresholds takes place. Usually, the subjective beliefs of the researcher performing the analysis represent the rationale for discriminating among the given categories, thus introducing precise normative assumptions in the whole procedure.[12]

The notion of frequency, meanwhile, has been considered helpful in offering a way out from the issue of a prioristic choices. Some authors have proposed to define the membership grades with reference to the distribution of the considered element in the specific society. Assuming a non-linear and monotonic relation between the indicator variable x and the degrees of membership, Cheli and Lemmi (1995) propose to order the categories of x with respect to the risk of deprivation $k = 1, \ldots, K$ associated with them (the higher k, the lower deprivation, thus the higher one's standard of living) and subsequently make use of the following specification:

$$
\mu(x) = \begin{cases} 0 & if \quad x = x^1; k = 1 \\ \mu(x^{k-1}) + \frac{F(x^k)-F(x^{k-1})}{1-F(x^1)} & if \quad x = x^k; k > 1 \\ 1 & if \quad x = x^K; k = K \end{cases} \tag{11}
$$

where $F(x^k)$ denotes the cumulative distribution of x ranked according to k. From the perspective of the authors, such an approach is intended to allow the membership function to be based exclusively on the empirical evidence; yet, I believe, such a procedure entails specific normative implications as well. The rationale lying behind the choice of any specification by a researcher necessarily implies, in my reading, the implicit adoption of a particular standpoint, entailing precise opinions and/or judgements about the way a line has to be drawn between deprived and non-deprived individuals. Thus, the idea of taking the distribution of an attribute in society to be the key determinant of one's degree of deprivation represents, in this view, some kind of stance.

---

[12] Moreover, the choice of a given specification itself could be interpreted in the light of the precise normative implications it entails: for instance, the trapezoidal specification could be understood as reflecting the idea of equal marginal contributions to the probability to be deprived with respect to a given element.

It emerges quite clearly, therefore, that the process of definition of the building blocks of fuzzy sets theory makes allowance for a significant discretionary power on behalf of the researcher. However, this is just an aspect of the problem, the subsequent step being the combination of the μ functions relating to the single variables by means of appropriate operators, so as to form fuzzy sets, i.e. so as to get a measure of functionings' achievement.

From membership degrees to fuzzy sets: how to aggregate fuzzy subsets

A frequently used class of aggregation criteria is represented by the so-called *averaging operators*. The unweighted means belong to such class. Formally, unweighted averaging operators amount to

$$UA[\mu_A(x), \ldots, \mu_z(x)] = \left[\left(\sum_{i=A}^{Z} \mu_i(x))^{\alpha}\right) \cdot \frac{1}{Z}\right]^{\frac{1}{\alpha}} \tag{12}$$

with $\alpha = 1$ denoting the arithmetic mean, $\alpha = -1$ denoting the harmonic mean and $\alpha = 0$ denoting the geometric mean. Yet the unweighted averaging operators introduce an idea of compensation among the various items under consideration, but confine themselves to a fixed compensation: a rather strict assumption in describing a variety of phenomena.

An often chosen alternative is the frequency-based weighting, relying on the implicit assumption that the smaller the proportion of people exhibiting a low achievement on a specific item, the larger the weight that should be attributed to such an item in the aggregate set, so as to express the idea of some kind of a relief induced by the sharing of a negative experience with other persons. Two formulations have been proposed during the last decade which have become rather widespread in applied fuzzy theory: Cerioli and Zani (1990) suggest taking weights to be equal to the inverse of the proportion of individuals who are deprived with respect to a given item; Cheli and Lemmi (1995) opt for a generalisation of the latter specification, i.e.

$$w_i = -\ln\left[\frac{1}{n}\sum_i \mu_i(x)\right] \tag{13}$$

In spite of the different normative assumptions, these specifications do not seem to provide contrasting evidence with respect to either the traditional equal weighting or subjective judgements.[13] Indeed, Cerioli and Zani's (1990) formula has been empirically tested against the above-mentioned ones, without necessarily yielding considerably dissimilar results (cf. Brandolini and D'Alessio, 1998: 40–41).

A comparative empirical application

The data

The data used in this study are taken from the Panel Study of Belgian Households (PSBH), i.e. the survey whose questions make up the Belgian section of the European Community Household Panel (ECHP). The specific questionnaire was submitted in 1998 to a sample of about 3800 households (corresponding to 7021 individuals). It represents the richest currently available body of data for the purpose of assessing multidimensional well-being in Belgium.

From the overall set of variables (more than 800), a small number of indicators (namely, 54) were selected. Such indicators were classified into seven categories: social interactions, cultural activities, economic conditions, health, psychological distress, working conditions and shelter.[14] This procedure has clear implications for the analysis: first, it means that when operationalising fuzzy sets theory each category has been implicitly taken as denoting a functioning; next, that the factor analytic exercise can be thought of as an attempt to validate the postulated seven-factors structure. It can be remarked that most of the variables are qualitative, either categorical or just dichotomous; moreover, they are rather heterogeneous in that they include both subjective and

---

[13] Cheli and Lemmi propose what they name as a 'totally fuzzy and totally relative' procedure to the measurement of deprivation, defining the membership to the fuzzy set of the deprived people on the basis of the distribution functions of the considered variables (see equation 11) and coupling it with a weighted averaging operator where the weighting system corresponds to the one illustrated in expression (13), which in case of simple dichotomous variables coincides with Cerioli and Zani's one. The reference to sampling distributions makes it possible, according to the authors, to take into account both the social context (by looking at the individual's position in the distribution of a given item within the society) and the relevance of each item (by observing its frequency) when assessing deprivation.

[14] A complete list of the variables used can be found in Figure 10.A.1.

objective indicators, both direct and indirect measures of the given functioning.[15]

Social interactions have been appraised by means of both a direct indicator – i.e. the frequency of contact and meeting with friends – and a group of variables relating to the incidence of a number of leisure activities likely to imply some kind of social relations. Though being perfectly aware of the conceptual weakness inherent to the way this dimension has been depicted (unfortunately, any other specific question on the issue was absent in the survey), it was included to stress the relevance of a functioning accounting for one's social contacts. Similarly, *cultural activities* have been evaluated on the basis of the answers to some questions pertaining both to one's membership in any socio-cultural association and to the regularity in visiting museums or attending conferences, concerts, plays, movies or in participating in creative activities. The *economic status* has been taken to constitute a specific functioning in spite of the debatable nature the latter could be charged with. In the spirit of what is argued by Brandolini and D'Alessio (1998: 33), the available economic resources within the household are interpreted both as a measure of the social status of its members and as reflecting the ease of one's life in terms of available goods and/or services as well as in terms of subjective perception of safety relative to the occurrence of unexpected events. Several items have been considered, among which are the regularity in saving money, individual perceptions concerning both the household's present economic conditions and its successfulness in making ends meet, the existence of difficulties in facing payments or reimbursement of loans or the lack of a number of commodities due to unaffordability.[16]

---

[15] It is well known that the use of subjective information is likely to raise several objections. Hence, being aware that much caution is required when adopting such opinions as indicators of well-being, the potentially distortive effect of each of them was (hopefully) offset by supplementing it with a number of objective variables.

[16] Each of the last two variables pulls together a number of indicators whose summated rating scale has been considered in the analysis: four dichotomous variables for financial difficulties and nine dichotomous variables for non-affordability. Scale reliability was assessed by computing coefficients alpha. The estimates were 0.77 and 0.84 for the financial difficulties and the non-affordability scales, respectively.

The information concerning *health* has been partly directly captured by a self-assessed ordinal variable and partly indirectly extrapolated through dichotomous indicators referring to the presence of illnesses or to recent admission to a hospital. Besides, three continuous variables quantifying the frequency by which a physician is consulted provide additional evidence on the subject. A very interesting negative type of functioning somehow strongly related to one's health, namely *psychological distress*, has been investigated thanks to a group of twelve categorical indicators denoting the occurrence of symptoms such as feeling depressed, sleeping badly, losing appetite or feeling irritable, which play an extremely significant role in determining the mental well-being of a person.

The indicators grouped under the label *working conditions* aim at disentangling some non-economic aspects related to one's activity, in the light of the idea that work satisfaction does not exclusively stem from salary but rather from several psychic advantages as well. Accordingly, a number of non-monetary features such as the person's judgement (on an ordinal scale articulated in six categories) of either his work schedule or his working environment, the position he holds, the number of hours devoted to the job, etc. have been explored, along with two variables sizing up one's possible feeling of overqualification as well as one's potential intention to look for an alternative job. Finally, the *sheltering* conditions are to be interpreted as the result of three main types of indicators: a crowding index, taking note of the household size as well as of possible economies of scale, and a heating availability variable;[17] a subjective ranking depicting the level of satisfaction about one's housing situation; and two summated rating scales corresponding to the occurrence of problems related to the dwelling and/or to its specific location.[18]

---

[17] The crowding index has been computed as the ratio between the total number of rooms and an equivalence coefficient determined on the basis of the OECD scale. Accordingly, the following weights have been used: 1.0 for the first adult; 0.7 for any other adult (18 and over); 0.5 for children (under 18). Only heating has been considered as a result of the extremely poor variation exhibited by other indicators of basic utilities, which made them not appropriate for factor analysis.

[18] Both the dwelling's and the area's scale bring together seven dichotomous variables. The reliability coefficients for these scales are 0.60 and 0.67, respectively. The values are slightly low when compared with the widely used rule of thumb of 0.70; however, I consider them still acceptable.

Assessment of functionings according to factor analysis

The first and basic step in designing a factor analysis focuses on ascertaining that the fundamental statistical requirements associated with the use of such methodology are fulfilled. More precisely, one should make sure that the data matrix displays sufficient correlations to justify the application of this technique.[19] Once this has been done, the factor analytic procedure moves on to the initial computation of the correlation matrix, which is then transformed through estimation of a factor model to obtain a factor matrix. The initial extraction provided fifty-four factors, in line with what was expected but definitely too large a number for any meaningful analysis. Yet the visual inspection of both the scree plot and the eigenvalues made obvious that seven of them already could have been considered sufficient for best representing the data.[20] As a result, only the latter restricted number of factors were retained for subsequent rotation.[21] Conceptual and practical considerations led to the selection of an orthogonal rotation method, namely varimax: from a conceptual point of view, it was best suited for making sure that functionings do not overlap; from a practical point of view, it made the interpretative task easier *vis-à-vis* an oblique solution.

The results stemming from the varimax rotation are presented in Table 10.1. All values have been multiplied by 100 and rounded to the

---

[19] For this reason, the partial correlations between each pair of variables controlling for the effects of all other variables were first inspected. Only in a very few cases did they appear to be larger than 0.30, thus providing some preliminary evidence in favour of the aptness of the selected indicators. Out of caution, Kaiser's measure of sampling adequacy was computed as well. This index, ranging from zero to one, summarises how small the partial correlations are relative to their ordinary counterpart. The overall measure for the sample amounted to 0.89, which according to the commonly used guidelines undoubtedly falls within the range of meritorious values. The inspection of the indices for the individual variables as well revealed a substantial correctness of the data selection, the lowest value being 0.66.

[20] The scree plot graphs the value of the characteristic roots against the roots' factor number in their order of extraction. The shape of the resulting curve is used to evaluate the number of factors to extract. Specifically, the point at which the curve first begins to turn into an approximately horizontal line is considered to indicate the maximum number of factors to extract.

[21] Out of carefulness, factor analysis was performed also for the hypothesis that the economic variables were excluded from the sample. This choice turned out not to affect the results at all.

Table 10.1 *Rotated factor pattern*

	Factor 1	Factor 2	Factor 3	Factor 4	Factor 5	Factor 6	Factor 7
Friends	−5	15	−18	5	−1	4	−12
Sports match	−2	45*	7	0	1	−5	−5
Café	1	57*	2	13	0	−5	4
Restaurant	0	34*	24	37*	1	−9	−6
Disco	5	54*	−10	3	−1	−8	3
Games	3	52*	0	0	1	−7	4
Going out	3	54*	8	21	2	−11	7
Sports practice	−3	38*	13	13	1	−8	−5
Meet ends	−13	5	73*	11	4	−5	−13
Savings	−3	12	61*	9	2	−10	1
Perceived situation	−6	10	46*	11	8	−8	0
Fin. difficulties	9	0	−30*	−7	−1	0	13
Non affordability	8	1	−46*	−10	−1	2	24
Economic satisfaction	−19	−1	61*	10	20	−2	−23
Health status	−24	26	15	9	8	−61*	−1
Chronic illness	10	−12	−7	−2	−1	54*	−1
Recent illness	10	−4	−3	−2	−3	47*	2
Hospital	7	0	0	−5	2	45*	−1
Generalist	8	−12	−9	−9	1	57*	−7
Specialist	15	−2	−1	2	0	47*	5
Other physician	7	−2	2	11	0	10	1
Psychol. problems	24	−5	−4	0	0	29	3
Depressed	71*	−8	−18	−2	−9	19	4
No appetite	44*	6	−6	−5	−5	22	8
Insomnia	49*	−10	−8	1	−6	22	4
Unrested	63*	−3	−7	1	−10	20	9
Nervous	42*	4	−2	−5	−1	3	5
Feel guilty	70*	9	−2	7	−5	−1	9
No concentration	67*	2	2	4	−9	6	8
Weeping	57*	−4	−9	1	2	12	−2
Pessimistic	71*	−4	−9	1	−9	8	3
Irritable	63*	6	0	3	−5	−1	9

Table 10.1 (*cont.*)

	Factor 1	Factor 2	Factor 3	Factor 4	Factor 5	Factor 6	Factor 7
Need reassurance	70*	−7	−3	7	−2	0	3
Out of sorts	75*	−2	−6	0	−7	18	5
Housing satisfaction	−17	−7	19	2	16	5	−53*
Area	13	−2	−15	4	−4	4	46*
Dwelling	11	3	−13	0	−3	2	55*
Heating	4	5	20	17	1	−11	−21
Crowding	−7	−13	−4	16	−3	12	−16
Theatre	2	13	6	63*	3	−6	−2
Cinema	12	45*	−2	34*	−3	−17	6
Concert	1	26	8	60*	3	−5	1
Museum	1	5	10	69*	0	−5	1
Conference	−2	1	8	57*	−1	−6	−2
Creative activity	3	6	4	28	3	0	0
Association	−6	22	12	27	1	1	−6
Work certitude	−6	1	9	1	43*	2	−1
Work type	−10	0	2	3	65*	−2	−3
Number of hours	−7	4	1	−2	61*	3	1
Work schedule	−5	4	3	6	65*	3	3
Working environm.	−9	4	1	2	65*	−2	−3
Work distance	−2	−1	0	1	36*	−2	−5
Job search	−4	16	−1	2	−14	2	2
Overqualified	3	14	−7	0	−23	4	6

nearest integer, so as to improve readability. In addition, the values equal to or exceeding 0.30 have been flagged with an asterisk.[22]

As is immediately obvious, except for a limited number of cases the loadings fall substantially above or below the selected threshold

---

[22] The choice of 0.30 as the threshold value for identifying significant factor loadings is in line with the use of a 5 per cent significance level and the assumption of standard errors being twice those of conventional correlation coefficients.

and their interpretation does not seem to be too problematic. *Factor 1* exhibits extremely high loadings on the twelve items related to the mental attitudes of the respondents, hence confirming the existence of a latent negative type of functioning likely to be named 'psychological distress'. *Factor 2*, instead, visibly collects a number of items suggesting a clear orientation towards a number of leisure activities implying some contact with other individuals: from regularly going to cafés or discothèques to generally hanging out in the evening. In spite of its poor and debatable nature, I interpret this functioning as referring to some kinds of 'social interactions'.[23] *Factor 3* obviously reflects the good 'economic conditions' of the respondents, with large positive weights for saving behaviour, being able to make ends meet, being content with one's financial resources, and almost as large but negative weights for cash shortage and enforced lack of commodities. Moving to *Factor 4*, high-scoring respondents often go to the theatre, visit exhibitions, attend concerts and/or conferences, thus evoking the idea of a rich 'cultural life'; the latent construct is labelled accordingly.

The collection of items on which *Factor 5* exhibits significant loadings visibly echoes people's judgements in relation to their job and may accordingly be thought of as a 'working conditions' functioning. *Factor 6* undoubtedly relates to one's 'health' dimension. However, the signs are such that a high score on this health functioning should be seen as revealing a bad condition. In the subsequent part of the analysis, this construct will thus be reversed in order to facilitate the comparison with its counterpart stemming from the application of fuzziness. Finally, the pattern of loadings characterising *Factor 7* stands out for its focus on the problematic aspects – both in terms of location and of a dwelling's features – related to the housing situation of the respondents, as well as for the relevance attributed to personal dissatisfaction in relation to it. Exactly the same issue as for the fourth factor will have to be faced also for this 'shelter' functioning.[24]

---

[23] Of course, an obvious drawback of the way this dimension has been measured lies in the fact that, for instance, an alcoholic individual would presumably score pretty well on the social interactions functioning though not being necessarily fully integrated in society. Hence, any subsequent interpretation based on this sphere will have to be carefully weighted up.

[24] I feel it is necessary to stress that all functionings will be positively measured in the remainder of this chapter.

The rotated factors substantially confirm, then, the picture that was postulated. The latter can be extrapolated only by computing factor scores. This final step accomplished, seven variables will be available that provide a description of the living standards of the respondents and that are likely to be used, therefore, for subsequent analyses.

Functionings' assessment according to the fuzzy methodology

As previously argued, within the context of the fuzzy procedure each category of selected indicators is implicitly assumed to denote a functioning, thus the first step to be taken concerns the selection and the computation of the most appropriate membership functions to represent each of the fifty-four observed variables.[25] A preliminary action is represented by the identification – for each variable – of two values below and above which the extreme conditions of full membership and non-membership can be ascertained. Besides achieved functionings being the underlying concepts to be represented, full membership will always be associated with the threshold stipulating conditions of absolute fulfilment with respect to a given indicator.[26] This being accomplished, membership grades will have to be specified for all the intermediate categories.

In the light of the fact that membership functions are likely to bring a substantial element of subjectivity into the analysis, I feel it is important to conduct a range of sensitivity tests to determine the robustness of the results to the choice of a particular specification for $\mu(x)$. Accordingly, three different, widely common models have been applied to the intermediate values of the indicators' list. At the outset, the frequency-based approach taken by Chiappero-Martinetti (2000) has been followed, representing most of the membership functions by the above specification (11) or – whenever categories appeared to be equidistant – by the simple linear one depicted in expression (9).[27] Alternatively, both

---

[25] To be more precise, one should talk about only forty-three variables owing to the binary nature of a number of them for whom, obviously, no transformation is needed.

[26] This implies, for instance, that when dealing with the 'frequency of contact with friends' indicator, a membership grade of one will be attributed to the category 'every day' and a zero value will be reasonably ascribed to 'never'.

[27] As far as the use of fuzziness in explicit association with Sen's approach is concerned, Chiappero-Martinetti (2000) unquestionably constitutes the

sigmoid/logistic functions (8) and trapezoidal ones (10) have been defined for exactly the same indicators.[28]

The membership functions so defined will provide a description of each individual's position in relation to each elementary indicator. What is needed for a complete assessment, however, is each one's degree of achievement relative to the aggregated groups of indicators, i.e. the given functionings. The next step resides, therefore, in combining the variables pertaining to the same category by means of adequate operators. In the first model (the 'Cheli and Lemmi'), the indicators have been aggregated by means of compensatory operators whose weighting structure was illustrated in expression (13). The reason for such choice lies specifically in the possibility of comparing these results with the ones by Chiappero-Martinetti (2000). In addition, an aggregation of the same membership functions (the 'Cheli and Lemmi') as well as of the ones arising from the trapezoidal and the S-shaped specifications was performed using the unweighted averaging operators, so as to get three cumulative representations treating all attributes equally. The latter will then be compared with each other for the purpose of emphasising the effect of the selected specifications. Although being perfectly aware of the obvious drawbacks of the symmetric assumption, I'd like to avoid any possible influence stemming from the particular weighting system when confronting the various operationalisations of $\mu(x)$. Ultimately, four different series comprising seven fuzzy sets each will have been derived from the outlined fuzzy procedure, thus bringing about the possibility of drawing significant comparisons both among fuzzy aggregates and between the latter and the previously obtained factor scores, which is precisely the major aim of this chapter.

reference work. For my purposes, this contribution represents the main source of inspiration; moreover, having been the first application of fuzziness to Sen's theory, it constitutes an exclusive yardstick for drawing comparisons with my results.

[28] Being conscious of the highly debatable appropriateness of the linearity assumption for most of the variables in the dataset, I wish to stress that the comparative goal constitutes the only rationale driving this speculative procedure and no further use will be made in the remainder of this study of the so-derived trapezoidal membership functions. It is also worth reiterating that, in determining the threshold values for the latter and the S-shaped functions, a remarkable subjective component has unavoidably been introduced. Figure 10.A.1 presents a detailed list of the adopted membership functions.

Table 10.2 *Pairwise correlations among fuzzy specifications*

	Cheli and Lemmi equal weighting						
	Psychol. distress	Social interac.	Econ. cond.	Cultur. activ.	Working cond.	Health	Shelter
S-shaped	0.93	0.98	0.96	0.95	0.82	0.97	0.85
Trapezoidal	0.88	0.95	0.97	0.91	0.93	0.97	0.88

To what extent do the results differ?

A first glance at correlations and some summary characteristics of the derived functionings

There are no formal connections, in my reading of the methods, between fuzzy sets theory and traditional parametric techniques such as factor analysis. Hence, one cannot easily draw comparisons in quantitative terms between them, relying on either the explained variance or the accuracy of the estimates.[29] As a matter of fact, the obvious measure providing an assessment of the nature and the strength of the relationship between the two methodologies as well as among the various specifications of the membership functions is the Pearson correlation coefficient. Table 10.2 summarises the computed pairwise correlations for the latter curves, all significant at the 1 per cent level.

Immediately, a remarkably strong association emerges, the lowest coefficient amounting to 0.82. Furthermore, though not being reported in the table, an almost perfect relationship between the doings and beings measured on the basis of either the trapezoidal or the S-shaped definitions appears: no matter the considered functioning, the absolute value of the correlation coefficient relating these two specifications permanently equals 0.99.

A first glance at these results seems to suggest the existence of extensive evidence in favour of those fuzzy researchers thinking of

---

[29] Actually, fuzzy sets theory provides also a data reduction technique which, in a sense, evokes the rationale underlying factor analysis. It aims, in fact, at reducing a collection of fuzzy sets to a smaller collection of derived fuzzy sets exhibiting certain properties (namely, the latter should highly overlap with their respective original sets and they should be as few as possible). Thus, while factor analysis essentially depends on correlations, the fuzzy reduction technique mainly relies on overlap coefficients. It could perhaps represent a fruitful direction for future research.

membership grades as exclusively offering an indication, a tendency index on an object assigned by an individual.[30] Accordingly, on account of the resemblance of the various outcomes, one should not be too much concerned about the specifically selected functions denoting an element's belonging to a set. Yet this conclusion leaves one puzzled. If one is not keen on considering membership functions as mere 'rescaling devices' but rather believes that they entail some normative implications as a result of their reflecting specific ethical viewpoints, the outcome of this analysis has to be interpreted as stating that different normative assumptions are likely not to affect the results: a somewhat curious conclusion! More thoughtful considerations, however, reveal that these outcomes come, in a way, as no surprise: the trapezoidal and the S-shaped specifications, for instance, can well be thought of as proxies, while the frequency-based formulation shares several common traits with the sigmoid/logistic curves. Hence, some additional and more radical specifications (i.e. more oriented towards a clear dichotomic partition of the state values) should have probably been investigated in order to further the usefulness of the comparisons, though even from those analyses I would not expect to uncover any major discrepancies, owing to both the presence of several dichotomous variables and the limited number of categories exhibited by the remaining elementary indicators which are being used. What is more, a recent and very interesting work by Filippone *et al.* (2001) somehow confirms the above-mentioned findings: within the context of a thorough analysis of some drawbacks inherent in the 'totally fuzzy and relative' poverty measures, the authors compare the results obtained by applying both of the two different membership specifications and three weighting systems to the same set of elementary indicators, uncovering the irrelevance of both choices and, thus, reaching essentially analogous conclusions with respect to the ones presented here.[31]

---

[30] This interpretation of membership uncovers a clear link with scaling theory. In many cases, actually, membership functions have even been elicited thanks to a suitable method for scaling the subject's perception of an attribute (cf. Norwich and Turksen, 1984). More generally, however, remarkable similarities can be found in between unidimensional scaling and the fuzzy procedure.

[31] The membership function specifications are the original 'Cheli and Lemmi' of expression (11) and a transformed one, always in line with the 'totally fuzzy and relative' approach. The three weighting systems are the one of expression (13), a linear and an exponential one.

Table 10.3 *Pairwise correlations: factor scores vs. fuzzy sets*

| | Factor scores | | | | | | |
	Psychol. distress	Social interac.	Econ. cond.	Cultur. activ.	Working cond.	Health	Shelter
S-shaped	0.95	0.91	0.93	0.85	0.84	0.91	0.74
Cheli & Lemmi EW	0.96	0.93	0.93	0.91	0.89	0.91	0.83
Trapezoidal	0.92	0.89	0.94	0.83	0.88	0.91	0.76

Table 10.4 *Summary characteristics of the selected aggregates*

| | Factor scores | | Fuzzy Cheli and Lemmi | |
	Mean	Std. Dev.	Mean	Std. Dev.
Psychological distress	0.338	0.169	0.321	0.195
Social interactions	0.313	0.164	0.311	0.217
Economic conditions	0.597	0.166	0.582	0.266
Cultural activities	0.286	0.163	0.276	0.233
Working conditions	0.677	0.127	0.589	0.161
Health	0.832	0.090	0.689	0.226
Shelter	0.734	0.123	0.683	0.186

Similar results, however, also emerge from the comparison between the outcomes produced by the two key methodologies: the estimated factor scores (rescaled so as to range, them too, in between zero and one) exhibit an impressively high degree of association with any possible kind of fuzzy aggregate, as depicted by Table 10.3 (also in this case they are all significant at 1 per cent).

In line with these findings, therefore, the picture of the Belgians' living standards emerging from the two techniques bears impressive similitudes, as a look at the summary statistics given in Table 10.4 confirms.

Here, only factor scores and the specific model of fuzzy sets' representation that, in the remainder of the analysis, will be considered as the exclusive term of comparison – namely the 'Cheli and Lemmi' – are depicted. The other models display, in my view, a number of clear limitations owing, on the one side, to the postulated – and rather unrealistic – equal importance assigned to the various elementary indicators and, on the other side, to the excessive rigidity of the linearity assumption underlying the trapezoidal specification. In the light of this, Cheli and Lemmi's approach appears more convincing after all. As the table illustrates, both methodologies seem to suggest the same general picture in what concerns the degree of achievement exhibited by the Belgian sample in a number of doings and beings.

Bearing in mind that any distribution takes on values in the interval [0,1] where zero denotes the minimum level of functioning's fulfilment and one the complete attainment, a relatively high degree of accomplishment can be said to emerge in the material dimensions (shelter, economic and working conditions) as well as in health and in psychological status, while relatively poor realisations concern social interactions and cultural activities.[32] Although already informative, this simple comparison looks rather unsatisfactory as both the matrix of factor scores extrapolated via factor analysis and the fuzzy evaluations of functionings do not lend themselves – as such – to straightforward interpretations. To structure the information contained in both of them so as to make it possible to get an insight into each individual functioning, while at the same time facilitating comparisons based on each technique's capacity to recover data structures that plausibly and intelligibly capture individual well-being, standard multivariate analysis is used.

Multivariate analysis of functionings

Let individual's i achievements on the p dimensions be expressed as a function of his income y_i and of some personal factors π_i

$$f_{ip} = f(y_i, \pi_i) \tag{14}$$

Postulating a non-linear relationship between individual achievements and income, and representing personal factors by a number of socio-economic characteristics, the following regression model can be estimated for both types of functionings (i.e. factor scores and fuzzy aggregates):

---

[32] As already stressed, a note of caution is needed in the interpretation of these results: social interactions and cultural activities are, by far, the conceptually weakest functionings among the derived ones.

$$f_{ip} = a_{0p} + a_{1p}y_i + a_{2p}(y_i)^2 + \sum_{j=3}^{m} a_{jp}x_j + u_p \quad p = 1,\ldots,7. \qquad (15)$$

where x_j denotes a vector containing the observations of all individuals about the socio-economic characteristics j, u_p is the vector of disturbance terms and the as are coefficients to be estimated. The following characteristics were incorporated in the model:[33] (a) gender, via a female dummy; (b) age, expressed through seven dummies denoting as many age brackets (reference category: age 56–65); (c) civil status, articulated in married, single, widowed or divorced (reference category: single); (d) federal region (reference category: Wallonia); (e) level of education, represented by five dummies (reference category: senior secondary school); (f) number of children; (g) working status (reference category: employee). The results are displayed in Tables 10.5 to 10.7.[34]

A foremost feature relates to the coefficients of determination that, at an absolute level, look rather low. The R-squares range, in fact, is between 2 per cent and 40 per cent. Yet in light of the fact that we are dealing with cross-sectional data, this finding is not at all surprising. Quite the contrary, the proportion of the functionings' variance explained by the selected characteristics appears to be relatively large in relation to the usual results for these kinds of analyses.[35]

Confining the analysis to the statistically significant coefficients, one remarks that monetary resources remain in most cases quite relevant, offering some support to the position according to which a multidimensional assessment of the living standard should ideally supplement the income information with other elements, rather than completely

[33] The complete table summarising the main features of the sample can be found in Figure 10.A.1, together with a description of the least obvious variables.

[34] ***, ** and * denote significance at the 1 per cent , 5 per cent and 10 per cent levels respectively. Whenever necessary, heteroskedasticity-consistent standard errors have been computed according to White's covariance matrix with standard errors in parentheses.

[35] As can easily be remarked, a slight difference in the sample size on which the estimations have been performed characterises the results. Such a gap originates from the specificity of the procedures: as the factor analytic technique computes the loadings and, subsequently, estimates the scores for all factors simultaneously, using only complete observations, any individual displaying a missing value on some item is automatically dropped from the analysis. The fuzzy procedure, conversely, computes each functioning separately; this also explains the different sample sizes exhibited by the various fuzzy aggregates.

Table 10.5 *Psychological distress, social interactions and economic conditions with dummies*

Variable	Psychological distress		Social interactions		Economic conditions	
	Factor score	Fuzzy eval.	Factor score	Fuzzy eval.	Factor score	Fuzzy eval. –
Intercept	0.251***	0.217***	0.289***	0.293***	0.517***	0.475***
	(0.014)	(0.014)	(0.011)	(0.013)	(0.013)	(0.019)
Income	0.033***	0.044***	0.032***	0.048***	0.122***	0.185***
	(0.009)	(0.010)	(0.007)	(0.009)	(0.010)	(0.013)
Income sqr	−4.45e-09***	−6.76e-09***	−4.21e-09***	−6.16e-09***	−1.14e-08***	−1.54e-08***
	(1.16e-09)	(1.81e-09)	(1.09e-09)	(1.06e-09)	(2.41e-09)	(2.61e-09)
Effect of children	0.002	0.001	−0.008***	−0.010***	0.007***	0.003
	(0.002)	(0.002)	(0.002)	(0.002)	(0.003)	(0.002)
Female	0.075***	0.088***	−0.059***	−0.071***	0.006	0.004
	(0.005)	(0.005)	(0.004)	(0.004)	(0.004)	(0.006)
Age 16–25	0.068***	0.077***	0.237***	0.248***	−0.058***	−0.071***
	(0.014)	(0.015)	(0.012)	(0.014)	(0.013)	(0.018)
Age 26–35	0.058***	0.065***	0.144***	0.152***	−0.046***	−0.073***
	(0.010)	(0.011)	(0.007)	(0.009)	(0.009)	(0.014)
Age 36–45	0.066***	0.077***	0.084***	0.094***	−0.048***	−0.081***
	(0.010)	(0.010)	(0.007)	(0.008)	(0.009)	(0.013)
Age 46–55	0.046***	0.053***	0.035***	0.035***	−0.027***	−0.045***
	(0.010)	(0.010)	(0.008)	(0.007)	(0.009)	(0.013)
Age 66–70	0.008	0.008	−0.007	−0.006	0.003	0.006
	(0.011)	(0.011)	(0.006)	(0.007)	(0.010)	(0.014)

Table 10.5 (*cont.*)

Variable	Psychological distress		Social interactions		Economic conditions	
	Factor score	Fuzzy eval.	Factor score	Fuzzy eval.	Factor score	Fuzzy eval. −
Age 71–75	−0.012	−0.006	−0.015**	−0.029***	−0.002	−0.013
	(0.011)	(0.012)	(0.006)	(0.007)	(0.011)	(0.016)
Flanders	−0.027***	−0.014***	0.067***	0.067***	0.073***	0.131***
	(0.005)	(0.005)	(0.004)	(0.004)	(0.004)	(0.006)
Brussels	−0.035***	−0.034***	0.009	−0.003	−0.013*	−0.006
	(0.009)	(0.008)	(0.006)	(0.007)	(0.008)	(0.011)
Married	0.002	−0.005	−0.060***	−0.052***	0.054***	0.036***
	(0.007)	(0.008)	(0.007)	(0.008)	(0.007)	(0.010)
Divorced	0.020*	0.020*	−0.024***	−0.013	−0.060***	−0.108***
	(0.011)	(0.011)	(0.009)	(0.010)	(0.009)	(0.013)
Widowed	−0.008	−0.010	−0.059***	−0.055***	0.001	−0.020
	(0.012)	(0.012)	(0.008)	(0.010)	(0.011)	(0.016)
Primary school	−0.006	−0.004	−0.016***	−0.038***	−0.058***	−0.095***
	(0.008)	(0.008)	(0.005)	(0.006)	(0.007)	(0.010)
Junior secondary	0.005	−0.002	−0.001	−0.008	−0.036***	−0.058***
	(0.006)	(0.006)	(0.005)	(0.006)	(0.006)	(0.008)
Third level non uni.	0.002	−0.002	−0.005	−0.004	0.022***	0.041***
	(0.006)	(0.007)	(0.005)	(0.006)	(0.005)	(0.008)
University and over	−0.008	−0.019**	−0.024***	−0.019**	0.038***	0.068***
	(0.008)	(0.009)	(0.007)	(0.008)	(0.007)	(0.010)

Self-employed	−0.012	−0.022**	−0.018**	−0.019**	−0.014*	−0.006
	(0.008)	(0.009)	(0.007)	(0.008)	(0.008)	(0.011)
Student	−0.025	0.014	−0.038	0.053***	−0.056*	−0.019
	(0.033)	(0.012)	(0.029)	(0.013)	(0.032)	(0.015)
Unemployed	0.020**	0.022**	−0.038***	−0.063***	−0.111***	−0.168***
	(0.010)	(0.010)	(0.008)	(0.010)	(0.009)	(0.013)
Retired	−0.014	−0.001	−0.033***	−0.054***	−0.017*	−0.036***
	(0.010)	(0.011)	(0.007)	(0.008)	(0.010)	(0.014)
Home duties	−0.008	−0.006	−0.015**	−0.027***	−0.028***	−0.035***
	(0.010)	(0.010)	(0.006)	(0.008)	(0.009)	(0.013)
Other	0.043***	0.069***	−0.023**	−0.080***	−0.103***	−0.164***
	(0.017)	(0.014)	(0.011)	(0.012)	(0.013)	(0.018)
Adj. R^2	0.1061	0.0919	0.4045	0.3985	0.2645	0.2373
Sample size	5227	6570	5227	6776	5227	6675

Table 10.6 *Cultural activities, working conditions and health with dummies*

Variable	Cultural activities		Working conditions		Health	
	Factor score	Fuzzy eval.	Factor score	Fuzzy eval.	Factor score	Fuzzy eval.
Intercept	0.309***	0.221***	0.664***	0.616***	0.819***	0.669***
	(0.012)	(0.016)	(0.011)	(0.012)	(0.007)	(0.016)
Income	0.062***	0.092***	−0.010	−0.004	−0.005	−0.007
	(0.010)	(0.012)	(0.007)	(0.008)	(0.004)	(0.010)
Income sqr	−7.04e-09***	−1.11e-08***	3.23e-09***	2.11e-09	7.64e-10	2.79e-10
	(2.44e-09)	(2.97e-09)	(1.00e-09)	(1.45e-09)	(5.91e-10)	(1.43e-09)
Effect of children	−0.007***	0.001	0.005***	0.005***	0.005***	0.012***
	(0.002)	(0.002)	(0.002)	(0.002)	(0.001)	(0.002)
Female	0.026***	0.018***	0.019***	0.025***	0.001	−0.047***
	(0.004)	(0.005)	(0.004)	(0.005)	(0.002)	(0.005)
Age 16–25	−0.094***	−0.043***	−0.035***	−0.075***	0.025***	0.070***
	(0.012)	(0.015)	(0.012)	(0.013)	(0.007)	(0.016)
Age 26–35	−0.073***	−0.046***	−0.030***	−0.066***	0.023***	0.067***
	(0.009)	(0.011)	(0.008)	(0.009)	(0.005)	(0.012)
Age 36–45	−0.037***	−0.019*	−0.037***	−0.057***	0.013*	0.042***
	(0.009)	(0.011)	(0.007)	(0.008)	(0.005)	(0.012)
Age 46–55	−0.011	0.003	−0.015**	−0.023***	0.013**	0.033***
	(0.009)	(0.011)	(0.007)	(0.007)	(0.005)	(0.012)
Age 66–70	0.009	0.026**	0.001	−0.001	−0.005	−0.005
	(0.009)	(0.013)	(0.002)	(0.003)	(0.006)	(0.013)

Age 71–75	−0.013	−0.010	−0.001	−0.001	−0.028***	−0.041***
	(0.010)	(0.012)	(0.003)	(0.002)	(0.008)	(0.015)
Flanders	0.032***	0.084***	0.027***	0.016***	0.003	0.022***
	(0.004)	(0.005)	(0.004)	(0.004)	(0.002)	(0.005)
Brussels	0.043***	0.045***	0.005	0.004	0.005	0.019**
	(0.008)	(0.009)	(0.006)	(0.007)	(0.004)	(0.008)
Married	−0.032***	−0.045***	−0.004	0.007	0.002	−0.008
	(0.007)	(0.009)	(0.007)	(0.008)	(0.004)	(0.008)
Divorced	−0.007	−0.012	0.006	0.005	0.001	−0.012
	(0.009)	(0.012)	(0.008)	(0.010)	(0.005)	(0.012)
Widowed	−0.049***	−0.070***	−0.001	0.007	−0.020***	−0.050***
	(0.010)	(0.013)	(0.007)	(0.008)	(0.007)	(0.014)
Primary school	−0.097***	−0.138***	0.002	0.004	−0.023***	−0.051***
	(0.006)	(0.008)	(0.004)	(0.005)	(0.004)	(0.009)
Junior secondary	−0.039***	−0.058***	0.003	0.007	−0.006**	−0.015***
	(0.005)	(0.007)	(0.005)	(0.005)	(0.003)	(0.007)
Third level non uni.	0.070***	0.096***	0.003	0.003	0.006**	0.023***
	(0.006)	(0.008)	(0.005)	(0.006)	(0.003)	(0.007)
University and over	0.122***	0.126***	−0.003	−0.008	0.007*	0.034***
	(0.008)	(0.010)	(0.007)	(0.009)	(0.004)	(0.008)
Self-employed	0.022***	0.011	0.023**	0.042***	0.018***	0.050***
	(0.008)	(0.009)	(0.009)	(0.010)	(0.003)	(0.008)
Student	0.073**	0.140***	0.006	0.027	0.006	−0.003
	(0.030)	(0.014)	(0.036)	(0.047)	(0.013)	(0.012)

Table 10.6 (*cont.*)

Variable	Cultural activities		Working conditions		Health	
	Factor score	Fuzzy eval.	Factor score	Fuzzy eval.	Factor score	Fuzzy eval.
Unemployed	−0.022***	−0.050***	0.005	−0.057***	−0.008*	−0.042***
	(0.008)	(0.010)	(0.004)	(0.005)	(0.005)	(0.012)
Retired	−0.008	−0.023*	−0.019***	−0.097***	−0.027***	−0.083***
	(0.009)	(0.012)	(0.006)	(0.007)	(0.006)	(0.013)
Home duties	0.003	0.002	−0.011**	−0.093***	−0.014***	−0.027**
	(0.008)	(0.011)	(0.005)	(0.006)	(0.005)	(0.011)
Other	−0.023*	−0.065***	0.005	−0.066***	−0.095***	−0.218***
	(0.013)	(0.015)	(0.005)	(0.005)	(0.012)	(0.021)
Adj. R^2	0.2208	0.2277	0.0204	0.0550	0.1786	0.2064
Sample size	5227	6768	5227	6164	5227	6806

Table 10.7 *Shelter*

Variable	Factor score		Fuzzy eval.	
	Coeff.	Std. err.	Coeff.	Std. err.
Intercept	0.757***	(0.011)	0.783***	(0.014)
Income	0.015**	(0.007)	0.051***	(0.008)
Income sqr	5.01e-10	(8.04e-10)	−2.06e-09**	(1.01e-09)
Effect of children	−0.003	(0.002)	−0.023***	(0.002)
Female	0.010***	(0.003)	0.008*	(0.005)
Age 16–25	−0.055***	(0.011)	−0.098***	(0.015)
Age 26–35	−0.066***	(0.008)	−0.099***	(0.010)
Age 36–45	−0.052***	(0.008)	−0.066***	(0.010)
Age 46–55	−0.033***	(0.007)	−0.043***	(0.010)
Age 66–70	0.001	(0.007)	0.001	(0.010)
Age 71–75	−0.002	(0.007)	−0.004	(0.011)
Flanders	−0.010***	(0.003)	−0.017***	(0.005)
Brussels	−0.041***	(0.007)	−0.049***	(0.009)
Married	0.026***	(0.006)	0.032***	(0.008)
Divorced	−0.022***	(0.009)	−0.036***	(0.011)
Widowed	0.027***	(0.008)	0.052***	(0.011)
Primary school	−0.019***	(0.006)	−0.049***	(0.007)
Junior secondary	−0.010**	(0.005)	−0.024***	(0.006)
Third level non uni.	−0.002	(0.004)	0.017***	(0.006)
University and over	−0.006	(0.006)	0.024***	(0.008)
Self-employed	0.017***	(0.006)	0.023***	(0.008)
Student	−0.051*	(0.030)	0.039***	(0.012)
Unemployed	−0.019**	(0.008)	−0.034***	(0.011)
Retired	−0.001	(0.007)	−0.019*	(0.010)
Home duties	−0.010	(0.008)	−0.021**	(0.010)
Other	−0.025*	(0.013)	−0.043***	(0.015)
Adj. R^2	0.0817		0.1192	
Sample size	5229		6694	

neglecting it. Three unusual outcomes, however, stand out: the absence of any income effect on one's health, which is probably to be attributed to the presence of schooling and age variables; its impact on one's psychological conditions, suggesting that extra household resources – at least up to some point – tend to worsen one's mental distress; finally, the irrelevance of additional earnings for one's job satisfaction, stressing how a greater work contentment may well derive from aspects such as a stimulating environment or challenging tasks rather than from the salary one receives.

Some slight gender bias in favour of men can be noted as far as social interactions are concerned, while women seem to be far more subject to psychological distress though more involved in culturally oriented activities and enjoying slightly better working and housing conditions. The latter findings look rather curious. Nevertheless, the peculiar character of the first result has to be reappraised in light of the fact that the 'working conditions' functioning should probably better be seen as a job satisfaction indicator.

Along these lines and besides the possible selection bias in the female work force, it is not difficult to interpret women's higher satisfaction with their job as related to their lower expectations, which – as Clark (1997) suggests – originate in turn from the worse position historically held within the labour market by women in comparison with men. A possible explanation for the connection between housing circumstances and the feminine gender may instead come from the high proportion of women living alone (over 60 per cent) whose sheltering situation exhibits clear improvements with respect to both their male counterpart and to their 'colleagues' living in larger households.

The social group of the Belgian elderly, contrary to the quite common contention according to which they would be psychologically vulnerable, turns out to perform pretty well at the emotional level: both the factor score and the fuzzy evaluation suggest that only people up to fifty-five years old seem to experience depression, insomnia, loss of concentration and analogous symptoms far more frequently than their older 'colleagues', reaching a maximum for the age brackets 16–25 and 36–45. Furthermore, and probably as a consequence of their higher economic attainments, the over-fifty-fives also enjoy the best shelter and working conditions compared with any other age group, while devoting themselves more often to cultural activities. More importantly, the regressions could be interpreted as suggesting that senility (in particular, after the seventieth year of age) makes one more socially isolated. However, due to the structure of the 'social relations' functioning (mainly comprising items related to leisure activities), this result comes as no surprise and, accordingly, it should not be taken as too rigorous an indication of social isolation.

From a geographical point of view, a number of considerable discrepancies in functionings' achievements sharply characterise the country. Flanders appears, in fact, to outperform the remaining regions in what concerns participation in the social life, working and economic conditions.[36] Its inhabitants also score rather well on culture, but the lack of any statistical significance of regional differences for the estimates based on the factor score induces one to rely exclusively on the indications provided by the fuzzy aggregate, according to which Flemish people would experience a more intense cultural involvement. Wallonia can be said to be unquestionably associated with the best housing conditions, whereas the capital holds the opposite position in the rank.

Not astonishingly, the marital condition significantly affects (in a negative way) the achievement of a satisfactory relational life, both in its social and cultural dimensions. The latter deprivation amplifies even more, however, when turning to widowed individuals, in spite of controlling for the presumably probable age effect. Yet widowhood is robustly associated with the highest achievements in shelter, an unusual outcome that is probably to be ascribed to the adaptive preferences of the elderly constituting this social group. Even worse, however, appears the situation of divorced or separated individuals, who are found to experience several forms of deprivation: from large income losses or fairly modest housing conditions to restricted social contacts (at least according to the factorised measure). Besides, the mentally distressing impact of divorce is also robustly captured, even if its significance level is quite large.

Education plays the expected role, improving health, shelter, economic means and, needless to say, increasing the participation in cultural activities. Not too surprisingly in the light of the items defining one's social interactions, the highest level of schooling seems to exert a negative influence on leisure activities involving contacts with other people. The lack of contacts with friends or other people in general,

---

[36] The significance of the differences between the coefficients for Brussels and Flanders has been tested, revealing a lack of statistical significance for regional differences on the functionings 'health' (for the fuzzy aggregate), 'cultural activities' (only the factor score) and 'psychological distress' (both for the factor score and the fuzzy aggregate).

nonetheless, plays a considerable role also with respect to one's working conditions. The results suggest, indeed, that the unemployed, the retired and people entirely devoted to home duties would be particularly concerned by such a risk.[37] They would all also be confronted with low fulfilments in both the economic and, of course, the working dimensions of life, while not enjoying a good health status. In addition, the jobless and irregular workers would face poor shelter circumstances and reveal sporadic involvement in cultural occupations. What's more, corroborating the findings by Sweeney (1998), a clear harmful effect of unemployment on mental health is suggested. The self-employed, on the contrary, exhibit better achievements, no matter the adopted methodology: higher work satisfaction, superior housing conditions, enhanced overall health than traditional employees. Finally, as for students, an undefined influence on shelter conditions would require more careful investigation. However, it is important to stress that this represents the only circumstance where a clear conflict emerges between the two considered methodologies. Otherwise stated, the main finding of the direct observation of the contributions of several personal attributes to individual living standards lies in the extensive resemblance of the resulting snapshots.

From a general point of view, I interpret this as a valuable and reassuring result. However, it is likely to be even more plainly revealed if tackling the issue from a slightly different perspective, i.e. by focusing on the specific portrayal of the most deprived fraction of the entire

---

[37] In light of the already mentioned feature of the factor procedure according to which only complete observations are used, a problem is likely to arise for those respondents having had no type of paid activity during 1998, such as housewives, the unemployed or the retired. Otherwise stated, normally these individuals won't have any score on the 'working conditions' factor. In order to avoid such an event, a statistical solution was adopted in this chapter. Specifically, for the variables making up the 'working conditions' functioning, prior to performing factor analysis the individuals belonging to the above-mentioned categories were attributed a value equal to the mean of each variable (i.e. zero, since the items are standardised). This transformation basically does not affect the overall distribution while allowing one to compute scores also for the respondents without any paid job. Nevertheless, much caution is required in the use of the obtained factor scores for the considered social groups, as for them the resulting 'working conditions' functioning amounts to nothing else than a statistical construct and, therefore, the indications stemming from it do not have much empirical value. Moreover, the adopted solution implies some obvious *a priori* normative assumptions that can be highly debatable.

population according to each functioning. In view of such an exploratory exercise, the bottom 10 per cent of individuals were arbitrarily selected, bearing in mind that this is a purely illustrative choice, implying in no way a judgement concerning the degree of actual deprivation displayed by the data. Tables 10.8 and 10.9 show the results for the subsamples.

As already claimed, women are significantly more distressed than men. Most frequently, these women are either divorced, unemployed or housewives (the latter according only to the fuzzy aggregate), and have a fairly low level of education. Confirming the previous findings, psychological distress seems to be an event that is most likely to occur earlier than one's seventies, with a worrisome presence among youngsters. In the same line, financial limitations mostly tend to involve women between the ages of thirty-six and fifty-five, especially if they are Walloons, living alone as a consequence of being divorced or widowed. Next to them, a sensible presence of the unemployed, individuals having occasional jobs and people devoted to home duties can be noted. Keeping to material dimensions, shelter deprivation is robustly associated with youth as well as with Brussels, while once again the widowed and the self-employed stand out among the best-performing categories. Unhealthiness and social isolation primarily hit elderly women,[38] thus the bottom share of the corresponding functionings logically displays a connection with retirement as well as with widowhood and restricted family size. More significantly, however, a sensible presence of divorced individuals has to be remarked, as well as an obvious (due to the inclusion of some disabled) considerable number of sporadic workers among the unhealthiest. Similarly, the unemployed look rather concerned by the lack of social activities.

Deprived workers mostly belong to the masculine gender, are quite young, live in large families and have a fairly high level of education. The latter finding probably has to be interpreted in light of the well-known higher job expectations commonly cherished by graduates, which are likely to impinge on their judgements. Finally, as for the absence of cultural involvement, some disagreement between the methodologies appears. The picture offered by factor scores mainly points at either young unemployed Flemish men or retired people in their seventies. The fuzzy aggregate, instead, reveals that a low value for cultural

---

[38] Also in this case, some caution is needed in evaluating the relationship of social interactions with senility.

Table 10.8 *Distribution of the 10% most deprived individuals (factor scores)*

Characteristics	Sample	Psych. distr.	Social interac.	Econ. cond.	Cultur. activ.	Work cond.	Health	Shelter
Male	47.0	43.6	30.8	42.5	53.5	60.8	42.5	45.3
Female	53.0	56.4	69.2	57.5	46.5	39.2	57.5	54.7
Age 16–25	13.9	26.7	0.6	9.0	10.7	9.6	2.3	10.9
Age 26–35	18.5	12.4	4.8	16.9	21.8	29.9	9.2	25.5
Age 36–45	22.9	24.3	11.9	25.8	23.5	30.3	16.9	28.6
Age 46–55	16.5	13.6	18.2	19.8	13.0	20.6	15.3	13.5
Age 56–65	11.4	8.8	19.8	11.3	12.6	3.3	18.7	8.1
Age 66–70	5.9	4.1	15.5	6.0	6.9	–	16.0	4.2
Age 71–75	4.6	3.8	22.9	4.9	5.2	–	15.3	2.9
Flanders	56.0	55.8	29.7	32.4	63.1	47.0	51.6	56.4
Brussels	9.0	8.9	15.7	12.1	5.9	9.7	8.8	14.1
Wallonia	35.0	35.3	54.6	55.5	31.0	43.3	39.6	29.5
Married	60.0	59.4	60.0	41.6	70.5	65.6	57.5	53.9
Single	24.3	24.0	7.8	22.6	17.2	24.7	11.3	24.7
Widowed	7.3	5.9	22.2	9.4	7.5	0.9	20.5	4.8
Divorced/Sep.	8.4	10.7	10.0	26.4	4.8	8.8	10.7	16.6
Primary school	14.3	12.4	30.3	29.1	31.3	11.8	30.9	18.9
Junior secondary	25.4	26.4	23.9	36.5	32.3	18.9	28.8	28.8
Senior secondary	32.3	32.6	22.5	23.6	27.3	31.9	25.6	26.1
Third level	19.4	19.7	13.7	8.1	8.0	25.4	11.5	18.0
University	8.6	8.9	9.6	2.7	1.1	12.0	3.2	8.2

Employee	45.0	35.0	18.9	26.8	43.4	–[1]	23.7	47.8
Self-employed	7.0	7.0	3.8	4.4	3.6	–	0.8	5.3
Unemployed	6.0	25.8	6.9	25.1	13.4	–	5.7	14.7
Studies	9.0	7.1	0.2	1.3	0.4	–	0.4	1.3
Retirement	21.0	14.9	50.0	21.3	23.9	–	46.6	14.1
Home duties	9.0	7.2	16.9	11.1	12.8	–	11.5	10.7
Other	3.0	3.0	3.3	10.0	2.5	–	11.3	6.1
Household size								
1	13.0	10.1	24.3	22.9	7.3	10.3	25.0	12.7
2	29.0	25.9	41.0	31.0	29.4	21.2	43.6	25.6
3	20.0	19.9	13.9	21.3	22.4	25.0	12.6	27.5
4 or more	38.0	55.9	20.8	24.8	40.9	43.5	18.8	34.2

[1] Due to the statistical expedient that has been used in the computation of both the factor score and the fuzzy aggregate concerning 'working conditions', it is not possible to depict the most deprived according to their occupation. Such figures would lack, in fact, any empirical meaning as a result of the artificial nature of the construct for jobless individuals.

Table 10.9 *Distribution of the 10% most deprived individuals (fuzzy aggregates)*

Characteristics	Sample	Psych. distr.	Social interac.	Econ. cond.	Cultur. activ.	Work cond.	Health	Shelter
Male	47.0	34.3	29.7	44.1	44.0	61.5	42.2	48.2
Female	53.0	65.7	70.3	55.9	56.0	38.5	57.8	51.8
Age 16–25	13.9	15.3	1.8	13.1	12.6	12.7	3.5	16.8
Age 26–35	18.5	15.6	5.2	16.0	18.0	29.2	7.3	23.9
Age 36–45	22.9	24.7	12.9	28.1	23.1	36.2	14.6	26.5
Age 46–55	16.5	16.7	21.1	18.2	15.9	17.1	16.3	13.2
Age 56–65	11.4	12.2	17.9	9.2	10.7	2.1	19.7	6.5
Age 66–70	5.9	5.3	18.9	4.4	6.3	–	16.6	3.8
Age 71–75	4.6	3.9	15.9	4.7	7.1	–	15.7	3.0
Flanders	56.0	57.3	42.5	28.3	46.3	55.2	54.4	50.1
Brussels	9.0	7.8	11.4	12.7	9.4	9.6	7.1	13.1
Wallonia	35.0	34.9	46.1	59.0	44.3	35.2	38.5	36.8
Married	60.0	53.3	58.4	44.1	62.6	61.8	55.1	52.2
Single	24.3	24.2	9.5	24.0	10.1	27.9	12.4	31.8
Widowed	7.3	6.1	22.9	8.8	17.3	0.7	20.1	2.4
Divorced/Sep.	8.4	16.4	9.2	23.0	10.0	9.6	12.4	13.6
Primary school	14.3	15.9	40.3	24.2	39.4	10.7	33.1	18.8
Junior secondary	25.4	25.5	26.2	36.4	32.9	18.2	30.2	33.4
Senior secondary	32.3	29.8	18.6	27.1	19.8	32.6	22.6	26.6
Third level	19.4	20.5	10.4	9.4	5.9	27.3	10.0	15.7
University	8.6	8.3	4.5	2.9	1.1	11.2	4.1	5.5

Employee	45.0	43.0	14.7	27.4	24.3	–	20.8	45.5
Self-employed	7.0	5.4	2.8	4.4	4.2	–	1.6	5.1
Unemployed	6.0	7.7	8.1	21.9	10.2	–	5.9	10.9
Studies	9.0	9.4	0.7	8.0	0.8	–	2.7	11.9
Retirement	21.0	18.9	50.4	18.9	40.6	–	47.4	11.8
Home duties	9.0	10.2	18.2	10.3	14.4	–	10.5	9.7
Other	3.0	5.4	5.1	9.1	5.5	–	11.2	5.1
Household size								
1	13.0	12.4	24.2	19.3	20.2	11.0	26.8	8.7
2	29.0	31.8	38.6	29.3	36.4	22.1	42.6	20.0
3	20.0	20.1	14.1	21.1	19.4	23.9	13.0	26.3
4 or more	38.0	35.7	23.1	30.3	24.0	43.0	17.6	45.0

Table 10.10 *Pearson correlations among functionings (fuzzy evaluations)*[1]

	Psychol. distress	Social interac.	Econ cond.	Cultur. activ.	Work cond.	Health	Shelter
Psychol. distress	1.00						
Social interactions	0.05	1.00					
Economic conditions	−0.16	0.13	1.00				
Cultural activities	0.07	0.39	0.22	1.00			
Working conditions	−0.13	0.02	0.14	0.03	1.00		
Health	−0.29	0.26	0.17	0.16	0.09	1.00	
Shelter	−0.17	−0.06	0.22	0.06	0.07	–	1.00

[1] One coefficient was omitted because it was not significant. Any other, on the contrary, is significant at 1 per cent

activities is mostly shared by Walloon women, belonging to the same working categories indicated by the factor score, but mostly exhibiting a different marital status (i.e. either divorced or widowed instead of married).

Some resemblance between these sketched-out images and the one proposed by Chiappero-Martinetti (2000) for housewives can be clearly identified, as well as some similitudes in between the categories of the socially and the culturally deprived. The latter phenomenon may lead one to presume that some interaction between these two dimensions is actually going on, especially for fuzzy sets. Factor scores, in fact, by construction are orthogonal to each other, thus uncorrelated. In order to dispel such a doubt, the Pearson correlation coefficients between the various fuzzy evaluations have been computed and reported in Table 10.10. They do not seem only to confirm the suspicions (with a 0.39 coefficient for the two alleged parties) but in addition point to a not surprisingly significant relationship between health and mental distress, as well as to a positive influence of leisure activities on one's physical condition.

What is more notable although not innovative is the claim which seems to be conveyed by the remaining sizeable values, namely the inappropriateness of totally disregarding any financial information, due to its being so intrinsically related to most of the considered aspects of well-being. Still, as both methodologies have clearly been ascertaining, income accounts for only a very limited part of the story and this should definitively be seen as a reason to follow multidimensional approaches like Sen's.

In the light of the analysis that has been undertaken, it is clear that the individual functionings' measures constructed via both factor analysis and fuzzy sets theory exhibit a remarkable similarity and, through the performed exploration, have proven to offer substantially equivalent pictures of the Belgians' living standards, emphasising in particular the deprivation of some social subgroups (unemployed, housewives, retired, divorced) on most dimensions as well as the existence of notable regional disparities.

But where do such similarities stem from? At the end of this exploration, no clear-cut answer this question can be offered; rather, an intuition, suggesting systematic exploration of the formal relationship between the various fuzzy aggregative operators and the factor scores' least squares estimation procedure, as a consequence of the standardisation practice in factor analysis substantially producing analogous effects on the items as the attribution of membership values. My exclusive focus, in this chapter, has been on the empirical consequences of the adoption of a particular procedure on the overall results. I believe, however, that further contributions in this area should, on the one hand, perform sensitivity analyses with the purpose of testing the dependency of the conclusions on the particular dataset which is adopted, and, on the other, try to structure the different approaches more explicitly along the lines of their normative implications.

Concluding remarks

In this chapter a couple of operational interpretations of Sen's functioning approach have been explored in view of assessing the role played by methodological choices in the determination of individual well-being profiles. Some scepticism towards the fuzzy methodology initially triggered this study. Nevertheless, such mistrust had to be reappraised in the light of the encouraging preliminary results that were reported. Clearly, much remains to be done to refine the procedures – particularly the fuzzy one – outlined here. However, an impressive resemblance seems to be borne by the general patterns of functionings' achievements arising from the application of the confronted techniques. The presence of a few discrepancies in the actual shapes of the derived functionings does not seem to significantly affect the indications stemming from the multi-variate analysis. Hence, this overall outcome can be seen as a promising preliminary step in deepening our understanding of the reliability and practicability of the capability approach.

Moreover, the results do not look especially sensitive to the various subjective prior judgements that had to be made. Having examined the robustness of the fuzzy aggregates to changes in the various assumptions that were necessary for their construction, they were found to be rather insensitive to the selection of the specific form taken by the membership function. I feel, however, that further analyses should possibly incorporate a more comprehensive array of tests concerning the choice of the specific parameters on which the sigmoid and trapezoidal specifications are based or, alternatively, consider other membership functions.

The picture of the standard of living resulting from the empirical application does not differ too much from the ones illustrated by some previous studies, namely a relatively high degree of accomplishment in the material dimensions (shelter, working and economic conditions) as well as in health and psychological status, contrasted with relatively poor realisations in social interactions and cultural activities. The degree of reliability of the indications stemming from the latter two dimensions, however, remains quite doubtful owing to their particular definition. A closer look at the apparent contributions of a number of personal characteristics to raising or lowering individual achievements reveals a slight gender bias together with the precarious physical, mental, economic and housing situation experienced by divorced or separated individuals, not to mention the sharp regional disparities in the Belgians' living standards. Poor social life for the retired, for women taking care of the housework as well as for the unemployed, bearing not only a financial but also a remarkable psychological burden consequent upon their condition, is further evident.

I believe an unquestionable merit of both the investigated approaches lies in having stressed that the reality we are often confronted with cannot be fully grasped by the traditional methodological instruments and that, sometimes, the use of essentially equivalent methods borrowed from other areas may allow welfare economists to move further in their investigations. Hopefully, this very preliminary and unambitious exercise was able to convey such messages, while in the meantime stressing that applied work on Sen's approach nowadays probably constitutes the field embodying the main challenges for future research.

Appendix

a) Linear function

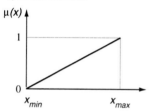

b) Trapezoidal function

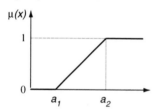

c) Sigmoid function

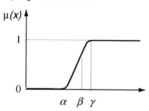

d) Cheli and Lemmi's function

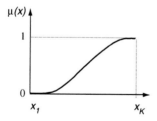

Figure 10.A.1 Graphic representations of membership functions

Table 10.A.1 *Basic indicators*

Functioning's components	Type of indicator	Description of the indicator
Social interactions		
Friends	Categorical (5 mod.)	Frequency of contact with friends
Sports match	Categorical (5 mod.)	Frequency of attending matches
Café	Categorical (5 mod.)	Frequency of going to cafés
Restaurant	Categorical (5 mod.)	Frequency of going to restaurants
Disco	Categorical (5 mod.)	Frequency of going to discos
Games	Categorical (5 mod.)	Frequency of playing games with friends (bowling, etc.)
Going out	Categorical (5 mod.)	Frequency of going out
Sports practice	Dichotomous	Participation at least once a week in a sporting activity
Economic status		
Meet ends	Categorical (6 mod.)	Possibility of making ends meet
Savings	Dichotomous	Regularity in saving
Perceived situation	Categorical (3 mod.)	Perception of the household present economic situation
Economic satisfaction	Categorical (6 mod.)	Degree of satisfaction about one's economic situation
Financial difficulties	Summated scale	Various economic difficulties [1]
Non-affordability	Summated scale	Lack of a number of commodities due to unaffordability [2]
Health		
Health status	Categorical (5 mod.)	Self-assessed health status
Chronic illness	Dichotomous	Presence of chronic illness, handicap or disability
Recent illness	Dichotomous	Interruption of one's activities due to recent illness/accident
Hospital	Dichotomous	Hospitalised during last year
Generalist	Continuous	Number of visits to a generalist in last year

Table 10.A.1 (*cont.*)

Functioning's components	Type of indicator	Description of the indicator
Specialist	Continuous	Number of visits to a specialist in last year
Alternative medicine	Continuous	Number of visits to an homeopath, osteologist, etc. in last year
Cultural activities		
Theatre	Categorical (5 mod.)	Frequency of going to the theatre
Cinema	Categorical (5 mod.)	Frequency of going to the cinema
Concert	Categorical (5 mod.)	Frequency of attending concerts
Museum	Categorical (5 mod.)	Frequency of visiting museums
Conference	Categorical (5 mod.)	Frequency of attending conferences
Creative activity	Dichotomous	Participation in a creative activity (dance, painting, singing, theatre, etc.)
Association	Dichotomous	Membership of a socio-cultural association
Shelter		
Crowding index	Continuous	No. of rooms/equivalence scale
Heating	Dichotomous	Heating availability
Housing satisfaction	Categorical (6 mod.)	Degree of satisfaction about one's housing
Dwelling's problems	Summated scale	Presence of structural problems in the house[3]
Area's problems	Summated scale	Presence of problems due to the location[4]
Psychological distress		
Depressed	Categorical (5 mod.)	Frequency of feeling depressed
No appetite	Categorical (5 mod.)	Frequency of losing appetite
Insomnia	Categorical (5 mod.)	Frequency of difficulty sleeping
Unrested	Categorical (5 mod.)	Frequency of feeling without energy

Table 10.A.1 (*cont.*)

Functioning's components	Type of indicator	Description of the indicator
Nervous	Categorical (5 mod.)	Frequency of being unable to sit quietly
Feel guilty	Categorical (5 mod.)	Frequency of feeling guilty, self-doubting
No concentration	Categorical (5 mod.)	Frequency of being unable to concentrate
Weeping	Categorical (5 mod.)	Frequency of weeping easily
Pessimistic	Categorical (5 mod.)	Frequency of being pessimistic
Irritable	Categorical (5 mod.)	Frequency of being irritable
Need reassurance	Categorical (5 mod.)	Frequency of needing reassurance
Out of sorts	Categorical (5 mod.)	Frequency of feeling out of sorts
Psychological problems	Dichotomous	Interruption of one's activities due to psychological problems
Working conditions		
Work certitude	Categorical (6 mod.)	Degree of satisfaction about the certitude of one's work
Work type	Categorical (6 mod.)	Degree of satisfaction about one's type of activity
Number of hours	Categorical (6 mod.)	Degree of satisfaction about the number of hours spent at work
Work schedule	Categorical (6 mod.)	Degree of satisfaction about one's schedule
Working environment	Categorical (6 mod.)	Degree of satisfaction about one's working conditions and environment
Work distance	Categorical (6 mod.)	Degree of satisfaction about the distance of one's workplace from home
Job search	Dichotomous	Currently looking for an alternative job
Overqualified	Dichotomous	Feeling overqualified for the position currently held

[1] The indicators whose summated rating has been considered are: difficulties in paying the rent; difficulties in paying invoices (water, electricity, etc.); difficulties in paying back loans; difficulties in paying instalments for consumer goods.

[2] The indicators whose summated rating has been considered relate to the impossibility of affording the following items: a car; a TV; a video recorder; a microwave oven; a telephone; a dishwashing machine; a computer; a country house; an alarm system.

[3] The indicators whose summated rating has been considered are: insufficient space; lack of brightness; heating problems; mould or humidity; damaged roof; cracks in the walls; damaged coatings.

[4] The indicators whose summated rating has been considered are: noise from neighbours; noise from outside (street, factories, etc.); environmental pollution; criminality in the area; bad acoustic insulation; slum district; lack of privacy with respect to neighbours.

Table 10.A.2 *Membership functions for the different models*

Functioning	Model 1	Model 2	Model 3
Social interactions			
Friends	Cheli-Lemmi	Sigmoid	Trapezoidal
Sports match	Cheli-Lemmi	Sigmoid	Trapezoidal
Café	Cheli-Lemmi	Sigmoid	Trapezoidal
Restaurant	Cheli-Lemmi	Sigmoid	Trapezoidal
Disco	Cheli-Lemmi	Sigmoid	Trapezoidal
Games	Cheli-Lemmi	Sigmoid	Trapezoidal
Going out	Cheli-Lemmi	Sigmoid	Trapezoidal
Economic status			
Meet ends	Cheli-Lemmi	Sigmoid	Trapezoidal
Perceived situation	Cheli-Lemmi	Linear[1]	Linear
Economic satisfaction	Linear	Linear	Trapezoidal
Financial difficulties	Cheli-Lemmi	Logistic	Trapezoidal
Non-affordability	Cheli-Lemmi	Logistic	Trapezoidal
Health			
Health status	Linear	Linear	Trapezoidal
Doctor[2]	Cheli-Lemmi	Logistic	Trapezoidal
Psychological distress			
Depressed	Cheli-Lemmi	Sigmoid	Trapezoidal
No appetite	Cheli-Lemmi	Sigmoid	Trapezoidal
Insomnia	Cheli-Lemmi	Sigmoid	Trapezoidal
Unrested	Cheli-Lemmi	Sigmoid	Trapezoidal

Table 10.A.2 (*cont.*)

Functioning	Model 1	Model 2	Model 3
Nervous	Cheli-Lemmi	Sigmoid	Trapezoidal
Feel guilty	Cheli-Lemmi	Sigmoid	Trapezoidal
No concentration	Cheli-Lemmi	Sigmoid	Trapezoidal
Weeping	Cheli-Lemmi	Sigmoid	Trapezoidal
Pessimistic	Cheli-Lemmi	Sigmoid	Trapezoidal
Irritable	Cheli-Lemmi	Sigmoid	Trapezoidal
Need reassurance	Cheli-Lemmi	Sigmoid	Trapezoidal
Out of sorts	Cheli-Lemmi	Sigmoid	Trapezoidal
Cultural activities			
Theatre	Cheli-Lemmi	Sigmoid	Trapezoidal
Cinema	Cheli-Lemmi	Sigmoid	Trapezoidal
Concert	Cheli-Lemmi	Sigmoid	Trapezoidal
Museum	Cheli-Lemmi	Sigmoid	Trapezoidal
Conference	Cheli-Lemmi	Sigmoid	Trapezoidal
Shelter			
Crowding index	Cheli-Lemmi	Sigmoid	Trapezoidal
Housing satisfaction	Linear	Linear	Trapezoidal
Dwelling's problems	Cheli-Lemmi	Logistic	Trapezoidal
Area's problems	Cheli-Lemmi	Logistic	Trapezoidal
Working conditions			
Work certitude	Cheli-Lemmi	Sigmoid	Trapezoidal
Work type	Cheli-Lemmi	Sigmoid	Trapezoidal
Number of hours	Cheli-Lemmi	Sigmoid	Trapezoidal
Work schedule	Cheli-Lemmi	Sigmoid	Trapezoidal
Working environment	Cheli-Lemmi	Sigmoid	Trapezoidal
Work distance	Cheli-Lemmi	Sigmoid	Trapezoidal

[1] As a result of this indicator being characterised by three categories only, neither the sigmoid nor the trapezoidal functions could be specified.

[2] Three indicators were merged so as to facilitate their treatment: generalist, specialist and alternative medicine were aggregated into an overall measure (named Doctor) by means of the standard union operator, so as to reflect the position of the least favoured individuals (from the point of view of the necessity of contacts with a physician) in the determination of the corresponding functioning.

Table 10.A.3 *Sample means and variable definitions*

Summary characteristics of the sample	
Characteristics	Sample means (n = 7021)
Male	0.470
Female	0.530
Age 16–25	0.139
Age 26–35	0.185
Age 36–45	0.229
Age 46–55	0.165
Age 56–65	0.114
Age 66–70	0.059
Age 71–75	0.046
Flanders	0.560
Brussels	0.090
Wallonia	0.350
Married	0.600
Single	0.243
Widowed	0.073
Divorced/ Separated	0.084
Primary school	0.143
Junior secondary	0.254
Senior secondary	0.323
Third level non univ.	0.194
University and over	0.086
Employee	0.450
Self-employed	0.070
Unemployed	0.060
Studies	0.090
Retirement	0.210
Home duties	0.090
Other	0.030
Household size	3

Table 10.A.3 (*cont.*)

Summary characteristics of the sample	
Characteristics	Sample means (n = 7021)
Mean household income	28148 Euros
1st decile (% mean)	0.320
9th decile (% mean)	1.750

Income: aggregate household disposable income per year corrected on the basis of the OECD equivalence scale. The resulting amount was further divided by 1 million.
Income sqr: aggregate household disposable income per year corrected by the OECD scale, divided by 1 million and squared.

Cited references

Atkinson, A. B. 1999. 'The contributions of Amartya Sen to welfare economics', *Scandinavian Journal of Economics* 2: 173–190.

Basu, K. 1987. 'Achievements, capabilities and the concept of well-being', *Social Choice and Welfare* 4: 69–76.

Brandolini, A. and D'Alessio, G. 1998. 'Measuring well-being in the functioning space', *mimeo*, Banca d'Italia, Roma.

Cerioli, A. and Zani, S. 1990. 'A fuzzy approach to the measurement of poverty', in Dagum, C. and Zenga, M. (eds.), *Income and wealth distribution, inequality and poverty*, Springer Verlag, Berlin: 272–284.

Cheli, B. and Lemmi, A. 1995. 'A "totally" fuzzy and relative approach to the multidimensional analysis of poverty', *Economic Notes* 24: 115–134.

Chiappero-Martinetti, E. 2000. 'A multidimensional assessment of well-being based on Sen's functioning approach', *Rivista Internazionale di Scienze Sociali* 2: 207–239.

Clark, A. E. 1997. 'Job satisfaction and gender: why are women so happy at work?', *Labour Economics* 4: 341–372.

Filippone, A., Cheli, B. and D'Agostino, A. 2001. 'Adressing the interpretation and the aggregation problems in totally fuzzy and relative poverty measures', *ISER Working Paper*, no. 2001–22, Institute for Social and Economic Research, University of Essex, Colchester.

Harman, H. H. 1976. *Modern factor analysis*, University of Chicago Press, Chicago.

Norwich, A. M. and Turksen, I. B. 1984. 'A model for the measurement of membership and the consequences of its empirical implementation', *Fuzzy Sets and Systems* 12: 1–25.

Sanchez, E. 1986. 'Medical applications with fuzzy sets', in Jones, A., Kaufmann, A. and Zimmermann, H. J. (eds.), *Fuzzy sets theory and applications*, D. Reidel Publishing Company, Dordrecht: 331–347.

Sen, A. K. 1985. *Commodities and capabilities*, North Holland, Amsterdam.

Sen, A. K. 1987. *The standard of living*, Cambridge University Press, Cambridge.

Sen, A. K. 1990. 'Welfare, freedom and social choice: a reply', *Recherches Economiques de Louvain* 56: 451–485.

Sen, A. K. 1992. *Inequality reexamined*, Harvard University Press, Cambridge, MA.

Sen, A. K. 1994. 'Well-being, capability and public policy', *Giornale degli Economisti ed Annali di Economia*, 53: 333–348.

Sen, A. K. 1996. 'Freedom, capabilities and public action: a response', *Notizie di Politeia*, 12: 107–125.

Sweeney, J. 1998. *Why hold a job? The labour market choice of the low-skilled*, Ph.D. Dissertation, Katholieke Universiteit Leuven, Leuven.

Thomson, G. H. 1951. *The factorial analysis of human ability*, London University Press, London.

11 Operationalizing capabilities in a segmented society: the role of institutions

KANCHAN CHOPRA[1] AND ANANTHA KUMAR
DURAIAPPAH[2,3]

Introduction

The world is characterized by the co-existence of excessive opulence and considerable destitution. Some groups have had success in accessing and taking advantage of the opportunities offered by modern economic growth; others have been left behind. It is a well-known fact that societies throughout time have always had this 'two-tier' structure of 'haves' and 'have-nots.' So, the question that arises is this: Is it possible to achieve equality among all groups and among all individuals?

The answer depends in large part on the definition of 'equality' and the subsequent question, 'equality of what?' (Sen 1980). The one simple truism we accept and value is the heterogeneity of human beings. We all come into this world with different natural attributes as well as social and economic endowments – what we might call intrinsic initial conditions. It is the very differences among individuals that provide the incentives to change, adapt and innovate. However, we also need to ask ourselves whether we are willing to accept a world where individuals starve, die from the lack of drinking water, succumb to diseases which could have been treated with little cost, not have homes to live in or the ability for children to go to school and learn. Can we accept these as just manifestations of our intrinsic conditions or can some form of

[1] International Institute for Sustainable Development (IISD), 161 Portage Avenue, Winnipeg, Manitoba, Canada R3B 0Y4; Tel: (204) 958–7720; E-mail: akduraiappah@iisd.org
[2] Institute of Economic Growth, University Enclave, Delhi 110007, India; Tel: (91) (11) 7667288, 7667101; E-mail: kanchan@iegindia.org
[3] Comments and suggestions from Arun Abraham and Flavio Comim as well as two anonymous referees are gratefully acknowledged.

equality be established which at the same time does not destroy our unique values and attributes that make us all so different?

In *Development as Freedom,* Sen formulates a framework that characterizes freedom as the central feature of development (Sen 1999). We shall not dwell on the various definitions of freedom but accept the concept of freedom as Sen uses it in his book: the ability of an individual to achieve valuable doings and beings she has reason to value. Sen argues that by providing freedom – he lists five instrumental freedoms – people, especially the poor, are given the means to become agents of change and are granted the autonomy to achieve the life they would like to lead. According to Sen, what they achieve is almost inconsequential. The important thing is that people have the freedom to decide the life they value doing and being and not have it imposed as most current poverty-reduction policies do.

But the question that begs itself is whether we can have undifferentiated freedoms?[4] A closer analysis of poverty, destitution and deprivation reveals a complex nexus of inter-dependency among individuals and groups – a nexus that creates barriers and constraints for individuals or groups with low or bad initial conditions. Jordan argues in his book, *Poverty and Social Exclusion,* that individuals with similar characteristics form groups to exclude others in order to capture higher rents (Jordan 1996). However, in order for some groups to exclude others, some level of freedom has to be taken away from the individuals or groups excluded. In that perspective, the equality of freedom Sen recommends has been violated. This in turn creates poverty within a society.

To summarize, our key aim is to achieve a world wherein people have equal freedom, not necessarily equal wealth. People require equal instrumental freedoms to exercise the freedom to achieve. However, some individuals and/or groups who capture higher rents by excluding others through their influence over the prevailing institutions compromise the potential for this reality. In this chapter, we focus our attention on the underlying dynamics of institutions and the way they are used by individuals or groups in the game to capture rent by excluding others.

This chapter is presented in the following format. In the second section, an overview of Sen's five instruments of freedom is provided. The main objective of this section is to make the link between his

---

[4] Undifferentiated freedom is when no segment of a society suffers unfreedoms.

framework and institutions. In the third section, we shall investigate the critical factors at play in determining the provision of freedoms. In section four, we present two case studies from India to test our framework provided in section three. We end the chapter in section five with a synopsis of the poverty-institutions-capability nexus by drawing on the results from the two case studies. We shall also provide some plausible policy interventions when a differentiated system of freedom exists.

The Sen paradigm of freedom functionings and capabilities

In *Development as Freedom*, Sen discusses in detail five instrumental freedoms – political freedom, economic facilities, social opportunities, transparency guarantees, and protective security (Sen 1999). He reveals, through a combination of anecdotal and empirical evidence, how these five instrumental freedoms have, and can, play a critical role in granting individuals self-determination. He also stresses the role institutions play in the development of freedoms.

Individuals live and operate in a world of institutions. Our opportunities and prospects depend crucially on what institutions exist and how they function. Not only do institutions contribute to our freedoms, their roles can be sensibly evaluated in the light of their contributions to our freedom. (Sen 1999, p. 142)

We need to digress slightly here. The term institution has many interpretations and definitions. It is often used interchangeably with organizations. In order to prevent any ambiguity, we begin by defining the term institution. In this chapter, we define institutions as the formal and/or informal rules that guide how people within societies live, work and interact with each other (North 1990). In other words, institutions are the rules that govern the game of life.

Within the broad definition of institutions, we identify two types of institutions: formal and informal. The former constitute written and codified rules. Examples of formal institutions would be the constitution, the judicial laws, the organized market and property rights. Informal rules, meanwhile, are rules governed by social and behavioral norms of a society, family and/or community (Ensminger 1997, North 1990). In many instances, informal institutions, over time, evolve into formal institutions. Institutions are highly path dependent and as North asserts, for institutional change to be a stable process, it should be an evolving and continuous process (North 1990).

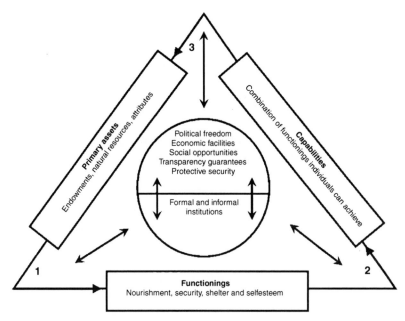

Figure 11.1 A schematic illustration of the process by which resources, endowments and attributes are transformed to functionings and capabilities.

Organizations are defined as players in the game. These are the agents that play by the rules to win the game (ibid). Organizations can include political bodies (governmental departments, political parties), economic bodies (firms, family farms), social bodies (clubs, churches), educational bodies (schools, universities) and more recently non-governmental organizations (WWF, IUCN).

We now return to Sen's paradigm of functionings, capabilities and freedom. In order to see the process through which individuals transform their primary assets (endowments, resources and personal attributes) to achieved lifestyles, we need to draw from his earlier work on functionings and capabilities (Sen 1993). Figure 11.1 presents our attempt to put together the various parts of the puzzle Sen has developed over the years within a single framework.

We do not attempt to validate or challenge the functioning-capability-freedom model of Sen in this chapter. We take that part of his model as given. Our aim here is to analyze how institutions enter his model and to investigate the constraints faced in delivering these institutions in a segmented society. We shall therefore provide only a brief description of the transition path from primary assets (endowments/natural resources/attributes) to functionings, to capabilities and finally, to choices in this chapter.[5]

The endowments/natural resources/attributes box captures the primary asset characteristics of individuals. An endowment describes the economic wealth of the individual at any one point in time. Natural resources describe the collective natural wealth available in the economy. 'Attributes' refers to the personal characteristics of individuals that include intelligence, physical disabilities, age, gender etc.

Functionings are defined as the various things a person may value doing or being (Sen 1999). These can vary from elementary functionings such as nourishment and shelter to complex ones like self-esteem and community participation.

Individuals' 'capability space' refers to the alternative combinations of functionings that individuals can achieve (ibid). The achieved functionings in our figure represent the final functioning vector *chosen or achieved* by individuals. The final link between achieved functionings and primary assets represents the growth in the stock of primary assets and the cycle repeats itself. The cyclical nature of the system highlights the dynamic properties of the process versus viewing the procedure as a static set of changes.

In the model presented above, we have grouped institutions and freedoms together and formulated them as the vortex of a complex nexus of primary assets, functionings, capabilities and choice. The transition from primary assets to functionings, functionings to capabilities, and capabilities back to primary assets, is governed and influenced by the institution-freedom (IF) nexus. The consequences of modeling IF in this manner are discussed in the subsequent paragraphs.

We postulate two points through the first step from primary assets to functionings. First, the initial conditions influence the functioning space of individuals. In other words, a person with a low endowment base will identify functionings that are within the feasibility of that endowment base. But the second point poses a slightly more interesting twist. We say that by linking the transitory path between primary assets and functionings with that of the IF nexus, that even the specification of functionings is itself dependent on the degree of access to the instruments of freedoms. This inadvertently implies that the degree of access

---

[5] A more detailed description can be found in *Inequality reexamined* (Sen 1993).

reduces or enlarges the functioning space of an individual. An example of this is the difficulty women face, in many countries, if they want to pursue a career in the sciences due to societal or cultural stigma (informal institution). This lack of social opportunities is further reinforced by the dearth of support from the formal institutions of higher education. The inadequacies of these two institutions are responsible, among a host of other inadequate or weak institutions, for women being deprived of social opportunities, political freedom and economic facilities.

The next step from functionings to capability is the thrust of the Sen paradigm. The capability set represents the various combinations of possible functionings that the individual can achieve. In the model presented in Figure 11.1, we propose that the IF nexus influences the size of the capability set. For example, if work rules in a country do not allow individuals, especially poor people, to take time off to visit a public health care centre or if the cost of health care is prohibitively high, then the poor are not capable of achieving basic health functioning – a capability. The poor in this case did not have the economic facilities or transparency guarantees to access private or public health care respectively. The institutions that failed in this context would be the labor laws and to a certain extent imperfections in the health sector market.

A distinction needs to be made between different kinds of freedom in this context. Some kinds of freedom are a constituent component and enabler for the enlargement of individual functionings. This freedom is what Sen terms constitutive freedom and we use this term interchangeably with capabilities in this chapter. The presence of some kinds of freedom is a prerequisite for institutions to be put in place. Political freedom is a case in point. Transparency guarantees, meanwhile, serve as both necessary conditions and elements of the process of the evolution of institutions.

Sen discusses a third step that describes the actual vector of functionings achieved. It is the phase whereby the actual achievements of individuals are evaluated against the functionings they wanted to achieve. We leave this third phase out of the model we present here. We shall assume that what is important is the freedom or capability to achieve a desired functioning and if that is available, then whether an individual actually achieves the functioning is not critical. It is more the availability of valuable choices that is important.

We shall argue that the evolution of freedom or capability is the vehicle for the enlargement of functionings, and in turn, the rate at which freedoms or capabilities evolve depends on and determines the rate of evolution and efficiency of institutions. Although Sen does not elaborate on the evolution of freedom, we suggest that the degree of freedom available to individuals at any moment is dependent on the efficiency and effectiveness of institutions.

In the next section, we shall discuss the dynamics of institutions and ways by which they can influence the capabilities of individuals.

Institutions, freedom and exclusion

Sen recognizes that institutions are necessary for the provision of the five instruments of freedom (Sen 1999). The formation of new institutions should ideally create or augment the five instruments of freedom. However, it must also be understood that evolving institutions can be interpreted as attempts to distribute freedom at different tiers in a segmented society.

We must remember that institutions are created by individuals who can act either as independents or as members of an organization or group. Therefore, institutions can be created or modified to further the interests of certain individuals or groups. This unfortunately puts us in the following predicament. First, we live in a resource-constrained society and economic theory tells us that individuals or organizations will always try to capture maximum rent from limited resources (Jordan 1996, Olson 1965).[6] Second, we need institutions to provide all individuals with undifferentiated rights to the five instruments of freedom – in order to allow individuals the autonomy to achieve the lifestyle they want. Third – and this is the Achilles heel of the system – institutions required to provide the different forms of freedom are created by the very same individuals who would, by reason of resource scarcity, try to influence the institutions in order to capture rent (Duraiappah 1998).

Given the fact that there is a differentiated system of freedom or capabilities, we begin by looking at the relationship between the degree of freedom or capability and institutional effectiveness and efficiency.

---

[6] We do recognize that individuals do have motives that go beyond self interest but shall ignore this for the moment in this chapter.

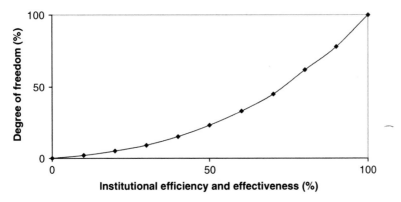

Figure 11.2 Relationship between degree of freedom and institutional efficiency and effectiveness.

The efficiency of institutions is determined by the transaction cost incurred by an individual when using a particular institution. The time and cost of filing land tenure at the land office is a case in point. In some countries, this process is relatively easy and quick, while in others it can be cumbersome, complicated and time consuming. The level of complication of the rules measures the effectiveness of an institution. For example, in the case of the land tenure, the effectiveness is determined by the degree of transparency of the agreement and the time taken to resolve disputes accruing from the land agreement.

In Figure 11.2, we postulate that as institutional efficiency and effectiveness increase, or in other words the transaction cost decreases, the degree of freedom or capability an individual enjoys increases.

The transaction cost of using institutions in turn can be influenced by the degree of influence, control or leverage individuals or groups have over these institutions. Theoretically, institutions are formulated by societies and are meant to be outside the realm of influence by any one or any group of individuals. However, complexities arise when some individuals or groups are able to influence institutions (in a manner that gives them an advantage in the transitory process from primary goods to capabilities) by excluding others from the process. This exclusionary practice in essence, allows the creation of, what we term, a differentiated system of freedom. This forces some individuals or groups to be disadvantaged vis à vis others who are able to capture rents by influencing the institutions underlying the provision of freedoms.

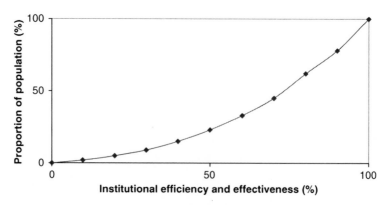

Figure 11.3 Relationship between institutional efficiency and effectiveness with the proportion of people able to access and use institutions.

This brings us to our next postulation – as institutional efficiency and effectiveness increase, the proportion of the population having access to the institutions increases. In other words, as transaction cost decreases, more people are able to make use of the institutions. This is illustrated in Figure 11.3.

The final step we need now is to link Figures 11.2 and 11.3 to get a relationship between the degree of freedom or capability with the proportion of the population having the freedom or capability. We have broken the graph in Figure 11.4 into three sections. Given the fact that there is a differentiated system of freedom, we can characterize freedom or capability into three categories – freedom as a 'private' good, a 'club' good, and finally as a 'public' good. The actual classification is dependent on the proportion of the population having access to the five instruments of freedom through the respective institutions. The ideal situation is when the vast majority of the population have access to the freedoms; then in essence, freedom is a public good – this is region 1 in Figure 11.4.

If, however, only a small segment of the population have access to the freedoms, as shown in region 3, then freedom is a private good bought by individuals within this small elite group. In region 2, freedom is a club good. Only individuals belonging to social organizations enjoy the freedoms offered by the institutions. The principal difference between regions 2 and 3 is that being part of a group versus just being an individual facilitates access to freedoms.

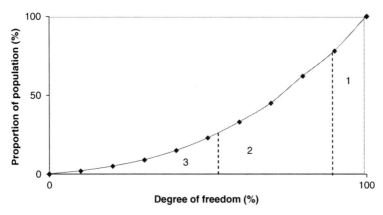

Figure 11.4 Freedom: A public good (1), a club good (2) or a private good (3)?

The costs and benefits of an individual being located in each region determine the level of rent-capture activities and the efficiency of institutions in the country. Although a smaller number of individuals have access to freedom in region 3 and therefore theoretically capture a larger portion of the rent, empirical evidence suggests that the benefits from having a more efficient market outweigh the benefits of rent capture (Olson 2000). It must be noted that the higher the level of rent capture, the lower the efficiency of institutions – and this includes the market. Therefore the question arises: Why does institutional inefficiency occur?

In *The logic of collective action: public goods and the theory of groups*, Olson offers one of the first influential contributions towards the economic analysis of rent capture and group behavior (Olson 1965). He provides a framework to analyze how and why groups behave as they do and the strategic reasons for excluding others in the pursuit of well-being. Olson recommends efforts be made on increasing market competition to reduce the power of specialized groups and therefore diminish the power of excluding the poor – in other words, using the market to move the poor from region 3 to 1. His main contention is that the poor are too disorganized to form groups to capture rent or compete with the richer and more organized groups (Jordan 1996) – moving them from region 3 to 2 will fail.

But we find ourselves in a quandary. How do we improve an institution, the market in this case, when exclusive[7] groups will always try to

---

[7] Exclusive groups refers to groups taking collective action for rent (Jordan 1996).

influence the institutions governing market competitiveness? Although Olson demonstrates that social benefits of perfect institutions outweigh the social costs of imperfect institutions, the individual or group benefits from imperfect institutions provide a strong incentive for these groups to embark on rent capturing activities. In many ways Olson's recommendation poses an enigma – the solution he suggests is the problem.

In the following section we present results from two case studies carried out in India. The case studies illustrate how various poor groups have addressed the dilemma we highlight above. These studies will demonstrate the potency of using informal institutions by the poor to move themselves from region 3 to region 2. The studies will also show the opposite side of the coin whereby some groups have been able to use the formal institutions to their advantage and in the process push others, especially the poor, into region 3. The two case studies will illustrate how individuals and groups move into or out of poverty by decreasing or increasing their capability or freedom respectively through the use of formal and informal institutions.

Case studies on institution development and freedom in segmented societies

The first study presented in this chapter was carried out in the Palamau district in the state of Bihar.[8] The district is besieged with high levels of poverty and land degradation. The community is characterized by a large number of relatively small farms and landless laborers. The second study is from the Udaipur region in the state of Rajastan. High levels of distress migration characterize the district. The main reason for migration has been excessive land and water degradation. The lack of rules governing the use of common land and water systems had created conditions of unequal access and use among the various groups in the community.

Protective security in eastern India

The Palamau district in Bihar, now Jharkhand, is marked by the coetaneous presence of destitution and environmental degradation.

---

[8] The reference here is to the erstwhile state of Bihar, divided since 1999 into Bihar and Jharkhand. Palamau is now part of Jharkhand.

The main problem in the Palamau district is the lack of access to economic facilities and protective security of livelihood for the poor.

Two main reasons can be cited for the deterioration in economic facilities and protective security. The first reason is linked to the excessive and unsustainable 5–7 percent deforestation rates each year (Chopra and Kadekodi 1999). The depletion of forests in turn caused soil erosion, destruction of water catchments and water scarcity across the state. The declining productivity of these natural resources inadvertently caused a reduction in land productivity which inadvertently led to the deterioration in the economic facilities. Moreover, the loss of forest led to the loss of a critical supply of non-timber forest products that the poor relied on, especially during times of crisis – in many instances the only form of protective security they had access to.

The second reason could be traced to badly designed land tenure reforms. The majority of the smallholdings had undergone a series of sub-diversions that subsequently forced many of them to not have the necessary minimum scale requirements for successful water and soil management strategies. This in turn caused many individuals or families owning these farms to adopt unsustainable farming activities that inadvertently caused a further drop in their land productivity. The drop in land productivity in turn forced many of the poor farmers to lose access to the economic facilities they needed to improve their land quality and adopt sustainable management practices.

As we see it, two problems had to be addressed. The first problem revolved around the scale issue to improve the economic facilities of the poor. The second revolved around protective security – in this case environmental security. Recourse to the formal institutions was found to be cumbersome and problematic. The poor who did not have the political clout found the process of approaching the organizations responsible for implementing the appropriate institutions to be a time-consuming, frustrating and humiliating experience (Sharma and Gupta 1987).

Therefore, in order to overcome the formal barriers and the high transaction costs associated with using the formal institutions, an informal institution called Chakriya Vikas Pranali (CVP) was formed by the various stakeholders in the district with the help of an NGO. In Palamau the groups of agents who got together and negotiated the set of rules were:

the owners of scattered bits of degraded land – small or marginal land-owners

the residents of villages in whose jurisdiction these lands were situated

the agents who could provide labor – landless laborers

the providers of technology, capital and organization.

The strength of the CVP lies in the collective approach it advocates towards the provisioning of the five instruments of freedom Sen discusses.

The CVP requires all agents involved to negotiate a set of rules to govern use of resources – in this case land and water. The ownership of land remains with the owners. It is only the way that the land is used and the outputs distributed which are determined collectively. Moreover, participation is voluntary and there is free entry and exit, albeit under certain conditions to prevent free-riding behavior. Chopra and Kadekodi show in their study that the decision to participate was based on the economic opportunity cost of land and labor (Chopra and Kadekodi 1999). The CVP allowed the poor to expand their capability set by offering them an effective and efficient informal institution that gave them access to the various instruments of freedom. The CVP allowed the poor to move from region 3 in Figure 11.4 to region 2. The instruments of freedom were provided to members of an informal club – in this case the CVP.

The success of CVPs can be attributed to the following two properties.

Transparency in decision making

All activities such as land development, water harvesting, plantation, protection, harvesting and marketing of the produce, etc. are guided by community decisions. These decisions are based on a participatory approach, with equal weight given to all members.

Risk minimization

A three-tier plantation programme based on temporal benefits provides a time-differentiated stream of income, allowing the participants greater insurance against risks. The unique strength of the system is that risk is shared uniformly across the whole group and therefore the risk borne by each person is minimized. The three-tier plantation programme offered the environmental security that the poor had lost with the deforestation of the forests.

Transparency in sharing benefits

Another unique characteristic of the CVP is the manner by which benefits are distributed among the participants. The income from the produce is shared between those who have participated. Some income is to be retained for future village development and some is to be reserved as a social net for the needy. The workers or students as they are called are paid regular 'stipends' for their participation in the village eco-development; they save part of it as a worker/student fund for their own future use. The households which have pooled their lands get a share as returns to land. The cycle restarts with another share of the income being kept as a village development fund for further investments and village developments. The cyclic nature of transforming resources to capabilities supported by the CVP is a clear illustration of the cyclic process of the Sen paradigm shown in Figure 11.1.

Ownership of institution

As the CVP was an initiative of the various stakeholders and full participation was allowed, the sense of ownership of the institution is high. Moreover, the degree of participation was found to be high due to the low transaction cost incurred by the various stakeholders.

This now brings us to the second study.

Migration and environmental degradation: expanding capabilities in a rural community in western India

The second study takes us to the Udaipur district of Rajastan in Western India. The district is characterized by higher than normal rates of migration. A study by Chopra and Gulati found prolonged cumulative degradation of the commons as the principal driving factor causing the distress out-migration from this semi-arid region to urban areas (Chopra and Gulati 2001). The vast majority of the migrants were individuals or families who relied on the commons as a buffer against droughts or other extreme events. With increasing degradation, many of these people had no other option but to move to urban centers in search of alternative employment. The economic facilities and social opportunities that the richer and more politically powerful individuals were able to access in times of need were denied to the poor, thus leaving them with no other option but to migrate to the cities in search of employment.

However, in some villages, the migratory trend was beginning to reverse, even in years of drought. The case study analysis presented below highlights some of the key variables responsible for this reversal in the migratory trends. An econometric analysis was carried out where migration was the dependent variable and a host of other explanatory variables were the independent variables.

We shall not provide a detailed analysis of the econometric results in this chapter. The reader can find these in Chopra and Gulati (ibid). Two main results emerge from the analysis.

> The first is that the main independent variable explaining the decline in migration is the creation of informal institutions to manage the commons.
>
> The second is that some groups with power positions accruing from stronger access to formal institutions can form a barrier towards the creation of informal institutions.

The emergence of informal institutions created by the community aimed at improving the condition of common land and water can be viewed as an attempt at expanding the functionings and capabilities of individuals – in this case the poor and the destitute. The institutions revived the freedom of choice available to the poor. The process involved a distribution and redistribution of capabilities across sections of society. In order to accomplish this task, existing sets of social norms and practices were questioned in the context of their appropriateness for the efficient and sustainable management of common resources. The study highlighted the following critical factors that played important roles in the development of the informal institution to manage the commons:

(a) *Ownership*: Consensus building with respect to the need for a new dispensation; this is often the most difficult task. The need for such a dispensation is often traced back to the existence of 'economies of scope' or 'economies of scale' which enable the introduction of a new technology.

(b) *Transparency in rules*: The laying down of detailed rules for working together on specific asset- or income-creation activities. In particular, the rules need to spell out inputs provided by groups or individuals and the returns they can expect from this provision.

At this stage, technologies being used and modes of organizational responsibility for individual tasks need to be formulated carefully. This is the enterprise part of the micro-level initiative, and the economics and technology aspects come in here.

(c) *Accountability*: The putting in place of a system of responsibility for repair and maintenance of assets created.

(d) *Transparency in distribution*: The sharing of output, its time and the manner in which it accrues need to be spelt out as well.

The critical point here is that the institution must be marked by transparency and there should be a sense of ownership by the various stakeholders. This is required for two reasons. The first is to ensure that freedoms of individuals are not compromised, otherwise the whole purpose and intention of the institution becomes meaningless. The second reason is more pragmatic – transparency is needed in order to attract the minimum amount of cooperation from individuals to meet economies of scale requirements.

Other characteristics of the local institution to be noted are:

The more successful interventions were those that related to improving natural capital in the form of augmentation of land and water resources, both private and common.

Building on traditional institutions of mutual help was an important component of success.

Local leadership could be garnered if a complementarity existed between their resource base and the activities undertaken by the new initiatives.

Initial financial (and technological) resources almost always came from the outside: either from a donor agency, a government department, or through the NGO community.

We have till now discussed the creation of an informal institution at the village level to address issues relating to the sustainable use of the commons in order to reduce distress migration in times of drought or other natural calamities. However, the village does not work in a closed economy and at some point in time will need to integrate within the wider framework of the district, state and country. We now turn our attention to this scaling-up dimension and investigate whether and under what circumstances the capability space provided by local informal institutions is widened or narrowed.

The village-led institutional intervention discussed above draws its strength from its ability to improvise rules and conventions of behavior. The institution also draws on existing traditional institutions to set up innovative models of management. However, expansion of its boundaries may bring it into conflict with other institutions that pervade the economy at the macro level. Examples of this are legal- and/or market-generated constraints. Increased productivity of common lands often creates surpluses that can be marketed. To go beyond the basic needs level and to further expand the functioning and capability space of individuals, access to other institutions may be necessary.

The absence of a macro perspective may become a constraint at this stage in its evolution. It was found – example illustrated below – that for local institutions to play an instrumental role in poverty alleviation in a sustainable fashion, a second phase of creating links with the larger and more formalized institutions of society was necessary. An experiment documented from the same region gives some indications.

The village of Gogunda Tehsil in Udaipur district was under the jurisdiction of the NGO UVM from 1987 onwards. This village had created an informal institution to manage and protect its pastureland (Saint 2000). The institution worked with productive results for 8–10 years. However, at a certain point in time, local leaders had decided to exclude a few settler families from being part of the institution. The excluded group then resorted to the formal legal institutions governing the country and was able to get an injunction against the local community leaders' decision on barring the group from accessing the commons. The entry of a new group that now did not have its actions governed by the informal institution meant, in effect, a breakdown in the sustainable use of the common resources. This in turn led to the degradation of the commons.

What does the Gogunda Tehsil experience imply for the development of informal institutions as an expansion of capabilities? We conclude the following:

Increasing the capabilities of the poor may be constrained by formal institutions.

Informal institutions must be flexible to adapt to changing external conditions and this includes new stakeholders with different objectives and status.

Informal institutions need to work together with the formal institutions in order to increase the capability space of the disenfranchised.

Synopsis and recommendations

We began the chapter by asserting that there exists a differentiated system of freedoms and the degree of differentiation is influenced by the effectiveness and efficiency of institutions. We postulated that the more effective and efficient the institutions, the larger the proportion of population that will have access to them. This allowed us to then define freedom as a private, public or club good based on the proportion of the population having access to effective and efficient institutions. In other words, the efficiency and effectiveness of institutions influence the capability space of individuals. The question we posed ourselves at the beginning of this chapter was: What interventions can reduce the degree of differentiation of freedoms among various stakeholders.

The two case studies presented here highlighted the following two critical interventions that can go a long way in addressing the differentiated system of freedoms that exists in many societies:

i. The creation of informal institutions provides an outlet through which the poor can exercise their rights and freedoms to expand their capabilities.
ii. Informal institutions cannot be created in a vacuum. These institutions must be developed in synergy with the formal institutions.

Case study one made it apparent that providing clear land ownership status cannot by itself be a solution to alleviate poverty. Individuals own land but the plots were too small to warrant any economically viable land and water management strategy. The institutions underlying the provision of economic facilities were not accessible by the poor farmers. The next best solution, as the case study supports, is the creation of informal institutions by the indigent groups to balance the inefficiency of the formal institutions. A plausible policy recommendation from the first case study would be to support the organization of the poor and strengthen the informal institutions they use to solve their problems. In other words, let them become their own agents of change.

Case study two provides an important qualification to the recommendations made by the first case study. In the case of the Udaipur district, land is not privately owned. It is the commons, a buffer in times of distress, which was being degraded by mis-management. The creation of an informal institution to correct for the mis-management worked relatively well. However, we observed that the system broke down when existing members denied entry to potential new members from using the informal institution. The refusal of entry in essence violated the formal institutions governing at the macro level and the end result was the breakdown of the informal institution.

In case study one, land was privately owned and entry could be denied or allowed by the informal institutions – there was no conflict with the formal institutions of land ownership and use. Both institutions worked effectively and efficiently, thereby allowing a large number of people access to the institutions and thereby allowing them to expand their capability space. However, in study two, the formal and informal institutions were working against each other and some individuals were able to exploit the dichotomy. This in turn led to the collapse of an institution – an institution that had reduced the transaction costs to a group of stakeholders in the past. The loss of this institution in effect left them with a system that imposed high transaction costs in terms of either: (1) accessing the appropriate formal institutions to provide the necessary buffers the commons provided; or (2) the formal institutions providing some form of sustainable management of the commons. The increased transaction cost implies that the system of freedom is in region 3 or freedom as a private good that is accessible only to a few who could afford the transaction costs.

An interesting two-tier system evolves from the case studies presented in this chapter – a system of formal and informal institutions that needs to be synchronized in order for them to be in synergy and increase overall institutional effectiveness and efficiency. The two-tier system that evolves from this study would suggest that freedom be provided as a public good. Allowing informal institutions to emerge prevents the rent-capture activities of the more powerful groups to influence the formal institutions, thereby increasing transaction costs. The larger the number of informal institutions, the lower the probability of institutional captures. In many ways this result supports the growing number of civil societies in both developed and developing countries that are beginning to play a role in determining policy directions and overall institutional change. The benefits of providing a multitude of these institutions far outweigh the additional transaction costs they may produce (Piore and Sabel 1984; Coleman 1990; Putnam 1993). This result is further supported by recent theoretical work on democracy and community, and the external benefits group interaction has on the economy (Habermas 1984; Dryzek 1990; Hirst 1994). Moreover, this result would be in agreement with the de Tocquevillian system of democracy that argues for the benefits of group interactions (Jordan 1996).

Cited references

Chopra, K and G. K. Kadekodi. 1999 *Operationalizing sustainable develop-ment.* New Delhi, Thousand Oaks California, London: Sage Publications.

Chopra, K and S. C. Gulati. 2001 *Migration, common property resources and environmental degradation: interlinkages in India's arid and semi-arid regions.* New Delhi, Thousand Oaks California, London: Sage Publications.

Coleman, J. S. 1990 *Foundations of social theory.* Cambridge, M.A.: Harvard University Press.

Dryzek, J. 1990 *Discursive democracy: politics, policy and political science.* Cambridge, M.A.: Cambridge University Press.

Duraiappah, A. K. 1998 Poverty and environmental degradation: a review and analysis of the nexus, *World Development* Vol 26, No 12, pp. 2169–2179.

Ensminger, J. 1997 'Changing property rights: reconciling formal and infor-mal rights to land in Africa.' In *The frontiers of the new institutional economics,* (ed.) by J. N. Drobak and J. V. C. Nye. San Diego, U.S.A: Academic Press.

Habermas, J. 1984 *The theory of communicative action.* Boston: Beacon.

Hirst, P. 1994 *Associative democracy: new forms of economic and social governance.* Cambridge, U.K.: Polity Press.

Jordan, B. 1996 *A theory of poverty and social exclusion.* Cambridge, U.K.: Polity Press.

North, D. 1990 *Institutions, institutional change and economic perfor-mance.* Cambridge, U.K.: Cambridge University Press.

Olson, M. 1965 *The logic of collective action: public goods and the theory of groups.* Cambridge, M.A.: Harvard University Press.

Olson, M. 1982 *The rise and decline of nations: economic growth, stagfla-tion and social rigidities.* New Haven: Yale University Press.

Olson, M. 2000 *Power and prosperity*. New York: Basic Books.

Pandey, M. P. 1992 *Land and religious institutions: the scenario in Bihar*. Patna: ANS Institute for Social Studies.

Piore, M and C. Sabel. 1984 *The second industrial divide*. New York: Basic Books.

Putnam, R. D. 1993 *Making democracy work: civic traditions in modern Italy*. Princeton: Princeton University Press.

Saint, K. 2000 'Silviculture management case studies by Ubeshwar Vikas Mandal: Jogiyon-ka-Guda, Keli and Seedh', Natural Resources Institute Report No. 2535, Udaipur, India.

Sen, A. K. 1980 *Equality of what*, The Tanner Lectures in Human Values, Vol 1, University of Utah Press and Cambridge University Press.

Sen, A. K. 1993 *Inequality reexamined*. Cambridge, M.A.: Harvard University Press.

Sen, A. K. 1999 *Development as freedom*. New York: Anchor Books.

Sharma, A. N and S. Gupta (eds.). 1987 *Bihar: Stagnation or growth, spectrum*. Patna: Publishing House.

Sharma, M. 2000 'Dalit rights: whose ponds? who commands? the Hindu survey of the environment 1997 and State of India's Environment: The Citizens Fifth Report, 2000.' Edited by Anil Agarwal, Suinta Narain and Srabani Sen.

PART III

Applications

12 Democracy, decentralisation and access to basic services: an elaboration on Sen's capability approach

SANTOSH MEHROTRA [1]

Introduction

Sen (2000) suggests that there are three arguments in favour of democratic political freedoms and civil rights: their direct importance for basic capabilities, including that of political and social participation; their instrumental role in enhancing the hearing the people get, including their claim to economic needs; and their constructive role in the conceptualisation of the needs. We suggest that the constructive role can be easily subverted by the conspiracy of silence about issues which are central to transforming the lives of the poor. The instrumental role of enhancing the hearing of people can also be effectively blunted if the hearing merely leads to populist rhetoric, and government spending plans to deliver services relevant to the poor, without actual delivery of quality services. The conceptualisation of their needs is more often carried out by well-intentioned, well-educated bureaucrats, neither fully sharing nor understanding the life experiences of the poor, functioning through vertically operated sectoral line ministries.

Thus, while national democracy offers much potential or scope for articulating the needs of the poor for basic social services, in such an environment the potential for the poor to enhance their capabilites is rarely realised except in a highly distorted manner. However, deep democratic decentralisation creates the basis for participation, the collective voicing of needs and collective action to force the government to deliver services effectively.

Sen recognises that there is a danger of overselling the effectiveness of democracy. He notes that India's success in eradicating famines is not

[1] Regional Economic Adviser, Poverty and Governance, The Regional Centre for Asia, Bangkok; santosh.mehrotra@undp.org

matched by that in eliminating regular under-nutrition, or curing persistent illiteracy, or inequalities in gender relations. 'While the plight of famine victims is easy to politicise, these other deprivations call for deeper analysis and more effective use of communication and political participation – in short fuller practice of democracy' (p. 154). It is to this concern – the abiding problems of the ineffective delivery of basic social services (primary health care, reproductive health services, elementary schooling, safe drinking water and sanitary means of excreta disposal) and what governments need to do to trigger this more effective political participation of the poor, their collective voice and local action – to which we turn our attention in this chapter. It is this participation which, from the evidence, ensures effectiveness of service delivery – provided there is a capable state and sufficient authority devolved to the local level to involve the community.

The first section makes three extensions to the capability approach and explains why this extension is necessary in the context of ensuring better accountability of state-delivered basic social services. The second section looks at the problem of why accountability is as weak as it is, and discusses it in the context of the nature of the colonial and post-colonial state. Section three moves on to examine the empirical evidence on the effectiveness of accountability through mechanisms of deep democratic decentralisation. In order to keep the discussion focused, we do this in the context of one basic service – that of ensuring schooling for all the children. However, the argument applies as much to the delivery of other basic services, and evidence is provided from the health sector. A critical ingredient giving teeth to deep democratic decentralisation is the right to information, which is also discussed in this section. Section four examines the spread of decentralisation in the developed and developing world in the last decade – though it finds its precise nature wanting in the features of deep democratic decentralisation. The fifth section finds historical evidence from the now industrialised countries on the role of democracy and decentralisation in ensuring schooling for all in the nineteenth century.

Three extensions of the capability approach

For Sen, a person's 'capability' refers to the alternative combinations of functionings that are feasible for her to achieve. 'Capability is thus a freedom' (p. 75). Functionings are things which a person may value doing or being – *simple* ones like being able to read and write, being well nourished and being free from avoidable disease, or *complex* ones like being able to take part in the life of the community and having self-respect.

Our suggestion is that a group of simple functionings – being adequately nourished, being able to read and write, being free of avoidable disease – is synergistically linked to the more complex functionings in real life. For instance, the functionings (being educated up to elementary level) are very difficult to achieve without being able to participate in society. In the abstract, they are possible to realise separately, but in practice, it is often impossible for the poor to realise even simple functionings without the complex one of participation.[2]

Unless democracy permeates to the lowest level of the powerless poor, and is made effective by their collective action, even elementary functionings will be impossible to realise.[3] Democracy at the macro level is what has always concerned Sen; the India versus China contrast is always referred to. Without democracy at the national level, micro-level democracy is inconceivable.[4] However, without the demand for effective services at the community level coming from 'collective voice and collective action', the supply of services will remain of poor quality and thus ineffective.

We suggested above that simple functionings such as literacy and numeracy might be impossible to achieve without the complex one of being able to take part in the life of the community. The capability set

---

[2] The relationship holds in the opposite direction as well, i.e. with the functionings of literacy and good health, individuals tend to become more effective 'participants' in society. That, however, is not the subject of this chapter.

[3] After the Russian revolution (1917) and the Chinese revolution (1949), simple functionings improved for the vast majority of the peasant and working classes even in the absence of formal democracy in the Western sense. However, two points are fundamental here. First, even though formal democracy did not exist in either the Soviet Union or China, the voice of the poor was being articulated by the Bolsheviks (in whatever distorted form after the first decade) and by the Chinese Communist Party. Second, in the twenty-first century, with the collapse of central planning and 'democratic centralism' of the Soviet variety, the way forward to articulate the voices of the poor has to be different from the Russian/Chinese authoritarian method. It has to be through deep democracy, which goes beyond multi-party elections in a Western democratic sense.

[4] For instance, it is unlikely that under a military regime (e.g. Pakistan 1999–2002) democratic decentralisation is going to make much headway, even though efforts at devolution (in Pakistan the efforts have been similar to those in India in the 1990s) are made.

must include the freedom, and in fact, the *realised* functioning of participation. However, participation by whom? The capability approach – as currently formulated – is so focused on the *individual's* capabilities and functionings that it tends to ignore the powerlessness of the poor individual to realise those functionings, even if a distant government was willing and able to finance/provide services which are the basis of key functionings. In fact, an individual's functioning of participation rarely amounts to more than voting in elections once every five years. A poor individual's ability to participate more than once in five years is limited by her powerlessness.

Meanwhile, intermediaries exploit the distance between the central government and the village where the school (or health centre) is located to foil the objectives of the centre, no matter how well intentioned the centre. In fact, without the state 'enabling' collective action, which emerges as a counterweight to the intermediaries, the delivery of services, and hence the functionings, cannot be realised. Sen rarely mentions the need for such collective action. Yet only hierarchical control of functionaries is rarely effective under such circumstances. Since the poor have little choice of 'exit' (in the Hirschman (1970) sense), 'voice' alone works.

So far, however, Sen's discourse around the complex functioning of participation has largely been concerned with democracy at the national level (or state level in large federal states), multiparty politics and the role of the opposition in such democracy. Democracy at the macro level rarely translates into power for the poor. If it did, we would have more evidence of pro-poor economic growth and dramatic improvements in human development indicators in those Latin American, African and East European countries which became democratic over the 1980s and 1990s. After all, over 100 countries now have democratically elected governments, almost twice as many as at the end of the 1980s (World Bank, 1999). The capability approach is essentially an evaluative one, and thus can be and has been used for normative purposes. If specific functionings (or their elements and concomitant indicators) are defined, then it is possible to measure the distribution of those functionings (or elements) in the population.[5] However, the purpose there is largely evaluative. An essential element

---

[5] For instance, Brandolini and D'Alessio (1998) use such components as education and skills (with their typical indicator years of education, level of education reached), health and access to health care (indicator: contacts with doctors and nurses), and so no. These are used in the Swedish Level of Living Surveys.

in making the approach operational – in the sense of being helpful to the policy-maker – is to define the conditions that would lead to the realisation of the functionings. We suggest that the complex functioning of participation has to be contextualised *at the level of the community* to have operational use. Unless thus extended, none of the simple functionings is likely to be realised, even in democratic states.

The state delivers development services in most developing countries in a top-down, bureaucratic manner through sectoral line ministries down to the local level. But this manner of service delivery defeats one of the greatest sources of technical efficiency in the utilisation of resources – the synergy of interventions in the various social sectors. Without the state making a conscious effort to ensure synergy between interventions in the spheres of health, education, water and sanitation, reproductive health and nutrition within a geographic location, these latent synergies will not be realised.[6] But the state is incapable of delivering these services effectively as long as it operates vertically. Inter-sectoral action is best triggered through 'voice' at the local level, with village-level planning. This synergy between interventions across sectors is likely to be an added benefit to the effective delivery of individual public services – if collective voice at the local level puts pressure on local-level functionaries to respond to local needs and demands, instead of delivering services merely based on resource allocation determined at a higher, bureaucratic level of decision-making.

To sum up this section, in our elaboration on the capability approach there is a case for three extensions in order to make the approach operational. First, Sen's distinction between simple and complex functionings is too watertight; in real life, there is mutual interdependence between simple and complex functionings that Sen does not recognise. Second, Sen's formulation of the capability approach focuses exclusively on the individual, ignoring the collective capability. Third, Sen's articulation of democracy as a desirable condition for enhancing human capabilities is mistakenly conceived only at the national level, when what matters most for genuine participation is local participation, realised only through deep democratic decentralisation. To bring all three points together, the complex functioning of participation that

---

[6] For a detailed discussion of these synergies within basic services, and the synergies between basic services, income-poverty reduction and economic growth, see Mehrotra and Delamonica (2006).

the approach postulates needs to be contextualised not at an individual level but at that of *the community – collective voice and collective action* – to have operational use. Unless thus extended, none of the simple functionings (e.g. the ability to read and write) is likely to be realised, even in democratic states.

Capability-enhancing accountability and the nature of the state

Accountability is a top-down notion. It assumes – rightly – that the government structure is a hierarchical one. In a hierarchical bureaucracy, accountability usually implies answerability to higher echelons of government. Presumably, at the highest level of government are politicians, elected every five years or so, and hence accountable to the citizens (who pay their salaries) only at quinquennial intervals. Underlying the notion of accountability is an assumption that government functionaries deliver a service – inefficiently and corruptly – and if made 'accountable' they will be more effective and less leakage of government funds would occur, and a higher fraction of government assistance would reach the people – rather than be 'absorbed' by the administration. However, the notion of accountability is flawed because it posits the government as a 'structure-in-itself' and for-itself – distinct from the body of citizens which pays for its creation and, in democracies, has voted it to power. Without the citizenry's quiescent sufferance there would be no structure-in-itself.

Accountability of government functionaries which enhances the capabilities of its citizenry, we suggest, is possible only when there is deep democratic decentralisation of the state. The current post-colonial state structure, however, is highly centralised, inherited from colonial administrations. The purpose of colonial administration was its own preservation, and the preservation of its status of distinctness and aloofness from the people they ruled. The function of the colonial administration was to maintain law and order, and ensure a minimum level of infrastructure services in urban areas (where their functionaries usually lived) – e.g. water, electricity, railways to connect the urban centres. These functions were to be maintained so that the objective of surplus extraction for the metropole would continue smoothly and unhindered. Meanwhile, the surplus extraction made it possible for the functionaries of the colonial state to enjoy a standard of living in the colony that was roughly commensurate with that in their homeland – and much higher than that of the vast majority of the natives they ruled.

The post-colonial state inherited the same functions but added on developmental ones to the hitherto minimal one associated with surplus extraction. The developmental functions grew systematically over at least three decades from 1950 to 1980. The state provision of physical infrastructure grew to include the provision of a social infrastructure (health, education). Not satisfied, it further involved the creation and acquisition of productive facilities and services (banking, insurance and trade). The monopolies and public-sector enterprises created by this expansion of developmental activities also created a fertile ground for rent-seeking by politicians, bureaucrats and lower-level functionaries. The scope for rent-seeking grew so much as to make it plausible to argue that the state, by the late 1970s, had turned predatory, while still being developmental.[7] Surplus extraction by the post-colonial state was now no more for an external government – be it based in Paris, London, Lisbon, Madrid, Amsterdam, Tokyo or Rome – but rapid economic growth, compared with economic stagnation in colonial times, enabled rent-seeking to thrive.

This is hardly surprising given that the structure-in-itself of the post-colonial state was merely superimposed on the existing colonial state structure. The existence of democracy might have replaced the hitherto authoritarian state – a certain plus. But the structure's separation from its citizenry survived.

What changed dramatically was the nature of the personnel in bureaucratic/political leadership. The colonial bureaucrat had relatively little reason to be a rent-seeker at a personal level; his primary objective was to facilitate surplus extraction for the metropole. But very soon after independence, comparisons were being made among the post-colonial citizenry between the moral uprightness of the colonial administrators and their post-colonial successors. The colonial administrators could afford to be morally upright at an individual level, even in the absence of democracy, let alone deep democratic decentralisation and accountability to the people. The political role

---

[7] This story largely applies to much of South Asia as well as to Sub-Saharan Africa, naturally with certain variations on this broad theme (on South Asia, see Bardhan, 1984; Wade, 1985, 1989). The story is more complicated in much of East Asia (on the latter, see Khan, 2001) and Latin America (see Ames, 2001).

of the colonial state was surplus extraction, not development (which in post-colonial times has become a route to personal enrichment). When the senior-most administrators were known to be upright, there was little scope for middle and lower-level state functionaries to be engaged in personal aggrandisement on a grand scale. But the post-colonial state's rapidly expanding developmental role and the growth in the state's fiscal base created the scope for government leaders – both in the legislative as well as the executive branches – to engage in grand larceny.

Democratic elections provided the environment for a vicious cycle to be set in motion. Electioneering required finances, and since candidates were not funded by the state, the mobilisation of funds for fighting and winning elections created a fertile ground for industrial groups (domestic and international) and/or landed interests to finance political parties. Electioneering became an increasingly expensive business. Once funds were raised and spent, debts were incurred – both moral and financial. If military juntas overthrew democratically elected government, they inherited the rent-seeking from their civilian predecessors. Those political debts had to be re-paid – by raising more money. Mechanisms emerged to mobilise resources through legal (e.g. taxes or royalties/fees on contracts for natural resource extraction) or illegal means and distribute those resources legally (e.g. through subsidies) or illegally (through patronage).[8] Bureaucratic rent-seeking followed a similar course. The making of appointments in the police, the education system, and the publicly owned utility companies became a 'business'. Appointments, transfers, and promotions could all be bought and sold for a price. Once a bureaucratic post had been 'bought' in a financial transaction, the out-of-pocket costs by the candidate appointed had to be fully recouped and thereafter profits made – the citizenry was the final source of funds. Most payments were made from unaccounted-for sources – creating a fertile ground for the spreading of the black economy.

An aspect of the authoritarian 'corruption-free' colonial state was its monopoly of information. The Official Secrets Act was the means for

---

[8] Anecdotal evidence speaks of three kinds of black money flowing to political parties and their functionaries: first, there was undeclared money flowing to political parties, as institutions, for political purposes; second, there was undeclared money flowing to individuals in the political parties for political purposes; and third, there was undeclared money flowing to individuals in political parties for non-political purposes.

withholding sensitive information which, in the eyes of the colonial state, could be used by the nationalist leaders – struggling for political freedom and independence from the colonisers – against the state. The same Official Secrets Act has, however, continued to exist in the post-colonial period, despite the introduction of five-yearly democratic elections to nascent legislatures and parliaments after independence. Unless Official Secrets Acts are replaced by legislation giving citizens the right to information, voice cannot be articulated. 'Voice' is based on information, and as long as information (and state documents containing information) is the monopoly of state functionaries, the latter can continue to act with impunity in the secure knowledge that the higher echelons – themselves corrupt – will protect them. In fact, if the higher-ups in the hierarchy do not protect the ones lower down – the ones who have the most dealings with the public – the game could be over.

It is not as though the state is not currently 'accountable'. To a whole series of networks (the capitalist both domestic and international, the landed, the labour aristocracy) the two key sets of personnel – bureaucrats and politicians – are to some extent already accountable. So the structure-in-itself is indeed embedded in networks in society. But the kind of accountability we are talking about is that at the community level of the lowest-level functionaries of the state – both elected functionaries (i.e. politicians) and civil servants (e.g. nurse/midwife, school teacher, water engineer). Without that accountability, services cannot be delivered effectively. Without that accountability, nor can the synergy of interventions in health, education, nutrition and water and sanitation be realised.

The international financial institutions (IFIs) launched their neo-liberal 'roll-back the state' campaign after the fiscal deficits of overly stretched developmental states grew to unmanageable levels. The IFIs have attempted to cut the state's functions right down to a similar (though not same) level as that of the colonial state. Underlying this neo-liberal notion of the minimalist state is a notion of market failure – the state should intervene only where there is likely to be market failure (e.g. basic health, basic education and infrastructure). This notion of the state is keenly informed by the literature on government failure. Government failure, in this view, had characterised the pre-1980 state in most developing societies in both its taking on functions in the productive/service sectors of the economy and in not undertaking the required regulatory functions in an even-handed manner (which could have enabled capital accumulation to occur in the private sector). However, state structures which were inherited from the colonial state – created for entirely different objectives – were bound to suffer from 'government failure'. The mere imposition of Westminster-style parliaments in new states was not going to transform structures meant for surplus extraction and law-and-order maintenance into democratic forms of functioning – least of all in largely illiterate societies.

The question is, how to make such states more accountable to their citizenry. How does one ensure that the state at least effectively delivers the services which are recognised to be quasi-public goods and have large externalities – basic education, basic health, safe water? More than 1 billion people lack safe water. Over 2 billion lack safe sanitation. Eleven million children die each year from largely preventable causes. Some 800 million currently suffer from hunger. Nearly 1 billion are illiterate. How does one make sure that the state delivers at least the minimal basic services, so that the simple functionings – the ability to read and write, to avoid hunger and disease – are universally available?

We examine some examples of basic service delivery which have worked on a large enough scale for one to draw some broader conclusions about how accountability could be improved with respect to delivery of basic services.

Making deep democratic decentralisation work

Moves towards democratic decentralisation in India

At least in India, there has been some recognition that central planning, of the kind implemented by the national Planning Commission and top-down delivery of programmes, has not worked. This recognition has led to the constitutional amendment to create district-and-below elected bodies that can engage in micro-planning. The Planning Commission recognises a district (in India usually a district has a population of 2 million) as the lowest unit of planning in all sectoral plans including education. The 1993 constitutional amendments (73rd and 74th) gave a statutory basis to district planning by providing for the constitution of a District Planning Committee to consolidate the plans prepared by village panchayats (elected councils of at least five persons from the village) and town municipalities, and to prepare a draft development plan for the district as a whole. This is clearly a welcome development, but the process runs the risk of replicating the 'top-downness' of planning of an earlier era. To deepen the process, what is needed is collective voice, to enable collective action by the community at the lowest level – thus creating a synergy with the district-level planning process. This is what we mean by deep democratic decentralisation. What is required is a way for micro-level planning at the community level to articulate with and directly influence the outcomes of macro-planning at the district level.

The 1993 Constitutional Amendment (72nd and 73rd) mandated the creation of elected councils in every state at and below the district level – known as the *panchayati raj* institutions (PRI).[9] However, institutions will not grow immediately into their full potential and start performing unless they are nurtured and supported, with adequate funds and powers to perform their functions. Only a positive partnership between the local authority and state governments, supplemented with the collective voice of the community, will ensure that the tasks of school effectiveness, and other local development challenges, will be confronted.[10] This is the evidence from a wide variety of experiences with respect to social service delivery from around the developing world – from Brazil in Latin America, from Africa (as we discuss later) and from India.

The involvement of PRIs in education since 1994, when they were constituted, has been uneven across states. The high-achiever state Kerala – which already had high education and health indicators before PRIs became widespread – has moved vigorously in making PRIs central to development planning, including education.[11] Similarly, Madhya Pradesh – which we discuss in detail later – has attempted to give them a central place, while other states have shown varying responses. In West Bengal – with a Communist Party government in power for over 25 years and where PRIs functioned, unlike the rest of

---

[9] Each state is divided into administrative units called districts, which are further divided into blocks, which in turn are comprised of a number of villages. The elected councils – which had existed in the 1950s and had become moribund – have been made mandatory at each of the three administrative levels.

[10] For an analysis of the unevenness of the powers vested with PRIs in different states, see a World Bank document: 'Overview of Rural Decentralisation in India, New Delhi', September, 2000.

[11] For a discussion of Kerala, see Drèze and Sen (1989), and Krishnan (1997).

India, even before the 1993 Amendments – education has been organised under the *nominated* district primary education councils for
many years. Instead of constituting a body from elected representatives, the state government continues with the nominated councils
(Raina, 2000). In other words, while the constitutional measure – an
enabling action – to mandate the creation of PRIs was taken by the
central parliament, it is the follow-up by the state governments to
empower the PRIs that will result in effective 'voice' becoming possible.
What we will show is that where that 'voice' has been made effective,
the results are impressive.

We demonstrate this with the example of two states in India which
have been known to be under-achievers in primary schooling and
literacy. These two states – Madhya Pradesh and Rajastan – have
made remarkable progress in the decade between Census 1991 and
Census 2001. How voice has played a role in this development is
discussed below. But in order to place the achievement of these two
states in perspective, a few remarks on the state of schooling in much of
the educationally backward states – which is reminiscent of much
of South Asia or Sub-Saharan Africa – is discussed.

Elementary schools: *cake for the rich, fodder for the poor*

India has the largest populations of illiterates in the world; the illiterate
population in 2000 was larger than its total population at the
time of independence from British rule, over half a century ago
(1947). Public schooling, provided mostly by state governments, has
not succeeded in the 50 years since independence in providing universal
access to schooling, so that net enrolment at primary level in the
country is only 82 percent. In addition, public schools are of such low
quality that a third of children enrolled are known to drop out.

Significant proportions of primary schools (grades 1–5) – often with a
minimum of 150 children – have only one or two teachers; hence, multi-
grade teaching is a matter of necessity. Teachers are well paid, but with
little peer pressure, teacher absenteeism is a widespread problem.[12]
Knowledge of subject content of most teachers is questionable. All the

---

[12] Teacher absenteeism is a widespread problem in other South Asian countries and
over much of Sub-Saharan Africa. Schools cannot function if teachers have
second jobs (which is often the case).

evidence from learning achievement tests indicates that minimum levels of learning in language and maths are not achieved by a majority of children.

However, not all states of India are equally afflicted. It is well known that Kerala and Tamil Nadu in the south have done very well with respect to education (and health) indicators. We have, however, drawn on evidence about the effectiveness of deep democratic decentralisation in terms of schooling from the more backward states in the north of the country.

Democratic decentralisation to realise schooling for all – the case of Madhya Pradesh

It is not sufficient for the State to merely take enabling action to *create* democratic institutions at the local level, as it has done for all states in the country. For collective voice to be enabled, and be translated into collective action by the community, state governments have to empower PRIs, as the state government of Madhya Pradesh (henceforth MP) has done. MP is one of the six states in India (Bihar, Uttar Pradesh, MP, Rajasthan, Andhra Pradesh and West Bengal) which account for two-thirds of the children out of school.[13] In other words, it is one of the states where the literacy rate has been well below the national average, along with the other states mentioned. However, in the 2001 Census of India (a decennial event), MP showed an increase of 20 percentage points in its literacy rate, the highest increase of any state (along with Rajastan) during the period 1991–2001. Clearly, the MP government was doing several things right. What were they?

MP was the first state to put the PRI system into effect (after the constitutional amendment was passed by the Indian parliament in 1993). In contrast, Bihar (which has had the worst educational and social indicators in the country, comparable to those in much of Sub-Saharan Africa) was the only state which had not had its PRI elections until 2001. A working PRI system was in place in MP in 1994. It provided a facilitating structure for direct community action. The

---

[13] These are the also the states chosen by Unicef to study the problem of financing of basic education, along with Assam and a relative high-achiever, Tamil Nadu. See Mehrotra *et al.* (2005).

government converted selected programmes, of which primary education was one, into a mission-mode. One of the most remarkable developments in MP was that, in order to find out which children were in school and which were not, the MP state government commissioned a survey in 1996. Instead of academic institutions conducting a sample survey, the democratic decentralisation opened an opportunity to undertake a door-to-door survey of elected people's representatives to discover the names of children in and out of school.

Ironically, this survey was carried out as part of the District Primary Education Programme (DPEP)[14] – which drives home the point about the difference between taking *enabling action* by the state and *empowering the community*. While most states in India took the enabling action of creating the PRI system, none took as much empowering action as Kerala[15] and MP. What makes a difference is not merely voice through Village Education Committees – which exist, at least nominally in all states, but which functioned unevenly – but actual involvement of parents and mobilising the interest and enthusiasm of the local community.

The panchayat leadership was seen by the MP state government as a key player. There were three features. First, instead of using the school teacher for data collection, the responsibility was widened to a local group including the local panchayat representatives and literacy activists. Second, the idea was not just to collect information of which children were in school (from school statistics), but which children (5–14 year olds) from the village were not in school. Third, the objective in surveying children was not one of statistics collection but to lead

---

[14] The District Primary Education Programme has been run on a decentralised and participatory basis, but with many of the top-down elements being retained (see Bashir and Ayyar, 2001). MP also had the largest number of districts covered by DPEP of all Indian states, and hence received a considerable proportion of total DPEP funds disbursed by the central government.

[15] Kerala – already in the mid-1990s a high achiever in health and education indicators – has implemented a real programme for people's participation in the wake of the action to decentralise governance through the PRI. Under the People's Development Planning process in Kerala, each village council (or panchayat) has made its own Ninth Five-Year Plan (1997–2002). In fact, it also took the unprecedented decision to make available 40 per cent of the Ninth Plan funds directly to panchayats for the implementation of these plans, which include education.

the motivational campaign to persuade parents to send their children to school.[16] It was, in other words, intended to consolidate community management of the primary education system in the state.[17]

A remarkable conclusion – with significant policy implications – emerged from the participatory survey. It is well known that government school-based statistics of enrolment are grossly exaggerated, showing inflated enrolment. In fact, the implication of the high government school-reported enrolment statistics is that those children not in school are in fact drop-outs; no wonder the drop-out rate seems so appallingly high in most states (at least based on government data). However, most 'out of school' children contacted through the survey described themselves as 'unenrolled' and not 'dropped out'. The policy implication is that, in addition to the problem of dropout (which, though not non-existent, may be much smaller than believed hitherto), the major problem is that children have *never* gone to school.

In other words, access to schools itself is a problem – despite the government claiming that the norm of provision of one school within a one kilometre distance has been met for 95 percent of India's children. It also knocks the bottom out of the massive central governmental effort, with significant budgetary allocations, to provide non-formal education (NFE centres) to the millions of dropouts around the country since 1979. If children never went to school, how could they drop out? And if they never dropped out, then why provide NFE centres for them? What is needed are formal primary schools for them![18]

---

[16] For an analysis of the MP process, see Srivastava (1999), Gopalakrishnan and Sharma (1999), Vyasulu (1999).

[17] One outcome of the survey was the development of a village education register as a basic record of educational statistics of each village to be maintained in two copies at the village panchayat and the school. The survey was also used as a basis of cohort monitoring for completion of primary schooling.

[18] Concerned about the so-called high drop-out rate in the country despite growing enrolment through the first three decades after independence, the central government in 1978 started a country-wide programme for creating NFE centres, in both villages without a government primary school and those with one. They were supposed to mop up the children who had dropped out, enabling them through 2–3 hours' teaching a day to reenter the formal primary school. However, the NFE centres had little or no impact in increasing enrolment in MP (and elsewhere). Data (collected during the campaign-based survey in MP) suggest that enrolments and drop-out rates in villages with NFE centres remained the same or higher than those without them. In fact the share of

The policy response of the state was to introduce a scheme to guarantee primary schools to all hamlets, not just all villages (given that a village consists of a number of discrete hamlets). Under the scheme (called the Education Guarantee Scheme), if 40 parents in a locality (only 25 in a tribal area) seek a school for their children, routed through the village panchayat, the state government is committed to provide, within 90 days, a lower-paid teacher's salary for the purpose.[19] The village panchayat can appoint the teacher from within the community, and it also has to make arrangements for space where the teacher can organise the children into classes.

The results have been remarkable. While 80,000 schools had opened in the 50 years since independence in MP as part of the regular government primary school system, 30,000 new schools were created within three years of the announcement of the scheme (after January 1997). What is particularly important is that it led to a huge increase in enrolment of tribal children – the very children with some of the lowest enrolment rates among vulnerable groups. It also led to a larger than proportionate increase in girls' enrolment.

Several features of the scheme have to be noted, and offer profound lessons for other similar situations around the world. First, the scheme offers a guarantee from the state to provide a school on demand from the community, but a guarantee that is not legal. This is of interest to those who have argued vociferously for making primary education compulsory by law.[20]

children out-of-school in villages where there was only a NFE centre was higher than those with only a primary school. In other words, despite their much lauded operational flexibility, the NFE centres were not more successful in enrolling children than the formal primary schools with their more rigid timetable and structure. Worse, more girls were out of school in villages with NFE centres than in villages with a primary school, so that even in respect of special targeting of girls (under the central government's NFE scheme, 90 per cent central assistance went to girls-only NFE centres) the NFE scheme is a disaster (Gopalakrishnan and Sharma, 1999). Not surprisingly, the government of India finally cancelled the NFE programme – nationwide – after these discoveries.

[19] One of the main reasons for the success of the EGS is its cost-effectiveness. In regular (non-EGS) schools, teacher salaries account for over 90 per cent of costs at the primary level. School teachers in regular schools are strongly unionised and an important political force, and receive salaries which are high relative to per-capita income (Kingdon, 1994). However, EGS school teachers are paid only a third or less of what regular school-teachers are paid.

[20] Wiener (1991) argued that in order to reduce child labour in India it is essential to make primary education compulsory in India, just as it was in many European

Second, the expansion of schools and enrolment is the outcome of a mutually dependent action by the government and the community. The community's demand for a school ('collective voice') is the initial premise of government action.[21] Even the provision of a school is a reciprocal action, with the community recommending the teacher from among its local people and the government remunerating and training her, the community providing space for the centre, and the government providing educational and other contingency materials. EGS vests the budget with the village panchayat and then extends the responsibility laterally towards the community.

Third, the fact that the teacher comes from the community ensures two things: accountability of the teacher to the community, and of the community as parents to the teacher. Above all, it addresses the endemic problem, underlying the ineffectiveness of schools in many low income countries, of teacher absenteeism. One of the perennial banes of the rural school in India generally, and in the northern states in particular, is teacher absenteeism, together with the problem of arriving late to school and leaving early. The teacher can get away with such behaviour when he does not belong to the community and is accountable only to a distant inspector of schools belonging to the government's department of education. If he is accountable to the panchayat, monitoring becomes so much easier.

Sen has always spoken of the agency role of women in the development process – justifiably so. The constitutional amendment to revive

countries in the nineteenth century. However, in India state governments are permitted to legislate that elementary education is compulsory, and many have done so. There is no evidence to suggest that the states that have compulsory elementary education have any better educational indicators than those which have not. In fact, the international evidence points to exactly the same evidence. See Mehrotra (1998).

21 The community's agency in EGS is critical to its success. This is best illustrated in contrast to another national scheme, the NFE (mentioned above). The proposal for a new NFE centre came from the state government's education department, and after the government's approval, the district panchayat issued the order. The demand did not come from the village panchayat. The assessment of materials needed in the NFE centre was by the education department and it passed on this information to the district panchayat. The role of the panchayats was confined to ratifying official proposals, looking upwards for further sanctions. The dysfunctionality of the NFE is symptomatic of the ineffectiveness of the entire system of basic education. The fact that it took 21 years for the government to finally abandon the scheme is a telling example of the pitfalls of the bureaucratic path to development.

the PRIs requires that at least one-third of the members of the village council should be women. So far, women have tended to play a minor role, even in the village council, being seen as proxies for their husbands. The fact that many of these women may be illiterate does not strengthen their position. Over time, however, it is possible that they will mature into more active agents, especially as active members of parent–teacher organisations and village education committees.

Sen, however, rarely speaks of the community and its agency role. The real difference in the case of the campaign mode of data collection by the panchayat leadership is precisely the agency role being played by the community. Collection of education data as done at present is indicative of the centralised nature of governance and its management of primary education. When accountability structures function in a centralised system of governance, they work vertically upwards towards the higher echelons of the bureaucracy, and never horizontally towards the community.

Schooling: the synergy of collective voice and state action in Rajastan

Like MP, another state that made remarkable strides during the 1990s is the north-western state of Rajastan. Literacy rates between Census 1991 and Census 2001 rose by as much as 21 percentage points (from 41 to 62 percent), slightly higher than MP. This is again remarkable because, like MP, Rajastan is known to be a backward state with respect to every human development indicator. The only two states that continue to live up to their BIMARU (or sick) status with respect to schooling are Uttar Pradesh (with a population the size of Russia or Brazil) and Bihar.

The processes that led to this achievement in Rajasthan are rather similar to those in MP. What started as projects – Shiksha Karmi in 1987 and Lok Jumbish in 1992 – became state-wide processes. Unlike in MP, where the process began well after the creation of PRIs (constitutional amendment of 1993), in Rajastan the process began earlier but has been deepened by the PRIs. First, as in MP, school mapping carried out with full community participation is a defining feature (Ramachandran, 1998; Ramachandran and Sethi, 2001). It was adopted as a means of offsetting the weaknesses of centralised educational planning, which for more than four decades failed to ensure universal access to schooling. The state has a difficult topography, with large parts of it being a desert. School mapping substitutes macro-planning by a central body located in the state capital for micro-planning by the affected community. It not only identifies the children out of school – as opposed to counting those in school as is done in the administrative recording system with highly inaccurate and usually inflated enrolment rates – but it also ensures community mobilisation. In other words, it goes beyond the traditional approach to school mapping, where it is simply an exercise in locating schools based on quantitative criteria (Singh, 2000). Instead, it is a means of generating demand for schooling in communities where the vast majority of parents are illiterate, and hence it is not taken for granted in such households that the child will necessarily go to school when attaining school-going age. In such a situation, only participatory diagnosis of the problem, analysis and then mobilisation can lead to schooling becoming a people's movement for schooling.

The government encourages the creation of a core team responsible for school mapping. At least 50 percent of each core team's members are women. A lynchpin of the core team is the shiksha karmi or locally recruited school teacher (unlike the majority of schools in India where teachers are appointed by the state administration to a civil service of transferable teaching posts within the state). A family-to-family survey about child participation in schooling is followed by the preparation of a village education register. The latter provides the basis to plan enrolment of children in schools. The register pertains to each family in the village, so that their participation in schooling can be monitored. Regular attendance is encouraged through persuasion by the core team or the village education committee.

The village education register, retention register and village education plan are seen as people's documents which are not kept in government custody. This allows the community to have complete access to such records, unlike land records. This is an important issue, and we return later to discuss the people's right to information.

The programme essentially ensures creation of a school in school-less communities or makes an existent but dysfunctional school function again. This requires the hiring of two locally available teachers to substitute for the regular primary school teacher who is frequently absent. It also requires opening of new schools in school-less habitations.

The Village Education Committees are critical to the programme. Members of the VEC are selected in the village council. Village-level bodies have been known in the past to be dominated by the power-elite (usually landed, upper-caste, men); hence they are required by the government to give representation to all hamlets part of the village, most castes, women and even parents of children not of school-going age. The VEC performs a whole series of functions:

Participation in household survey and school mapping.

Enrolment of all children in 6–14 years age group from their locality or habitation.

Taking decisions regarding location and schools timings.

Monitoring participation of children in day schools to ensure that children do not remain absent and if they do, using their influence to get them back to school.

Ensuring availability of textbooks and teaching–learning materials with all children, especially those belonging to poorer sections of society.

Making regular visits to schools to ensure their regular functioning.

Obtaining contributions in cash and kind from the community to improve the physical infrastructure and environment of the local school.

Advising and motivating teachers, and also bringing lack of performance to the notice of higher authorities.

(Singh, 2000).

It is important to emphasise that this programme is not run by an NGO. It is implemented by a board, an autonomous agency under the control of the state education minister. After the setting up of the elected panchayat structure, it has developed links with elected representatives at different levels.

What the experience of Rajastan and Madhya Pradesh demonstrates is that in two of the most low-income Indian states, with the worst social indicators in the country, it is possible to bring about a transformation in schooling for the poor – provided the local government functionaries are mobilised in a participatory manner, and government structures are made to respond to collective pressure from the people. In other words, it involves at least three elements: a functioning state, powers devolved to the local authority and voice of the community.

In both Rajasthan and MP, these programmes had an important role to play in making considerable advances in schooling and literacy noticeable in these two states. However, large improvements in literacy also occurred over the 1990s (1991–2001) in other states as well, as a result of which the national literacy rate rose by 13 percentage points (from 52 to 65 percent). An important reason for these advances lies in the national investment through the donor-driven DPEP, mentioned earlier, which accounted for the increase in public spending on elementary education – a key feature of a functioning state. Another important reason for the increase in primary enrolment was the initiation of the mid-day meal scheme (1996), which in most states offered a 3 kg ration of foodgrain for each child attending school.[22] Other states had these interventions as well. The question remains: why did two of the poorest states, with some of the worst education indicators in India until the early 1990s, exceed the scope and pace of educational advance of other states combined? While it is not argued here that the interventions analysed in this chapter were the only part of the explanation, at the same time it is unlikely that DPEP is the only part of the explanation of the remarkable success in these two states, given that DPEP was implemented in all states, not just in these two.

Health: accountability to the community in Sub-Saharan Africa

Mobilising voice in the health sector has also helped to rejuvenate health services (Mehrotra and Jarrett, 2002). For instance, serious disruption to public health systems occurred during the 1980s in most Sub-Saharan countries, when a severe international economic recession and financial indebtedness led to structural adjustment measures in many countries and a marked reduction in the state's role in the provision of services (Chabot *et al.*, 1995). One approach to this crisis lay in the greater mobilisation of community resources in the development of local health services, recognising that patients seeking care were already beginning to pay considerable sums of money for treatment of various kinds. This was the situation in which the Bamako Initiative arose in 1987, leading in many countries to a reasonably successful example of voice in ensuring access to affordable essential

[22] For an analysis of these programmes, see Govinda, 2002; Mehrotra *et al.*, 2005; and Mehrotra, 2005.

health services for an increasing proportion of people (Jarrett and Ofusu Amaah, 1992).

The Bamako Initiative (BI), implemented to varying degrees in half the countries in Sub-Saharan Africa and fewer countries in Latin America and Asia since the late 1980s, has shown that organised communities can help sustain local public health services, not only by contributing financial resources but by having 'voice' in the management of services. The strategy of the BI is to revitalise public health systems by decentralising decision-making from the national to the district level, instituting community financing and co-management of a minimum package of essential services at the level of the basic health units. The aim is to improve services by generating sufficient income to cover some local operating costs such as the essential drug supply (often imported with donor provided foreign exchange), salaries of some support staff, and incentives for health workers. Funds generated by community financing do not revert to the central treasury but remain in the community and are controlled by it through a locally elected health committee. Thus, a revolving pool of funds helps to sustain the health service. From mere recipients of health care, consumers become active partners whose voices count.

After ten years of implementation of the initiative, community action in most rural health centres in Benin and Guinea has not only enabled nearly half the population to be regular users of the services but has also raised and sustained immunisation levels close to Year 2000 Health for All target levels (Levy-Bruhl *et al.*, 1997). Charging a modest fee to users is seen in some cases to be the most affordable option for the poorest segments of the population who otherwise only have access to more expensive alternatives, although it is less clear whether mechanisms exist to protect indigent members of the community. Much of the success has been in ensuring the supply of affordable essential drugs that are readily available in the health centres, under the scrutiny of the committees. Another factor has been the improved attitude of health workers, traditionally one reason for people, especially women, not to use the service.

Recent assessments have shown that community participation in the Bamako Initiative has actually not been as well defined as originally thought, and that significant community empowerment has not taken place. 'Induced' participation, pushed in many cases by donor demand and often based on political decisions or bureaucratic simplicities, tends to accentuate elite groups in communities, marginalising women and the spontaneous organisations that are already formed to cope collectively with local problems.

However, even with a relatively weak voice exercised by households and communities, significant outcomes have been achieved. It would appear that voice needs to be associated with the retention and use of locally generated resources, and that these go to improving the health service and achieving sustained outcomes. Greater emphasis, however, needs to be put on working with existing local organisations and motivating their participation in the running of services.

The right to information – the steel-frame of deep democratic decentralisation

If deep democratic decentralisation is to succeed, it can only do so armed with the right to information – and the abolition of the Official Secrets Act. At least in all South Asian countries, the Official Secrets Act was operative in almost every country under British colonial rule. Laws to promote secrecy instituted by the British to suit their own agenda of preserving an authoritarian regime, intended for surplus extraction, have been adopted by post-colonial states without regard to democratic principles.

The right to information is recognised in the UN Declaration of Human Rights 1948. Article 19 of the declaration says: 'Everyone has the right to freedom of opinion and expression; this right includes freedom to hold opinions without interference and to seek, receive and impart information and ideas through any media and regardless of frontiers.' Sweden was one of the first countries with laws providing freedom of information. Similarly, the right to information is also recognised in laws passed in Finland, Norway, Denmark, Canada, Australia and the US.[23]

In this context, the first problem is that in most low-income countries the right to information has not been recognised in law (with the exception of India, where it finally was legislated into law in 2005). In Pakistan and Sri Lanka, civil society actors have succeeded in the

---

[23] Thus in Sweden in each department all incoming and outgoing mail is placed in a special press room for an hour every morning for reporters to examine. If any reporter wants further information on a case, she needs only to walk down the hall to examine the department's files (Sachar, 1999).

past few years to provide government with a blueprint for right to information legislation. In Pakistan, the draft ordinance was passed in a highly watered down form by the caretaker Leghari government in the mid-1990s and then allowed to lapse by the new government. The ordinance suggested by civil society groups failed on account of bureaucratic resistance since it gave broad access to bureaucratic decisions, including questions of loans and exposed loan defaulters. Nepal has the right to information guaranteed as a fundamental right in the Constitution, but it has not been used much on account of the ignorance of people about their rights. In India two states (Tamil Nadu and Goa) have passed laws on the right to information while others have tried to enforce it in some form through executive instructions and guidelines.

The further problem in a largely illiterate village in a low-income country is how the poor will muster up the courage to seek out information – assuming that a right to information was recognised in law.[24] The biggest fear of the village level functionary is the possibility that one day the ordinary person in the village will be given the right to ask questions and demand information on how the money for government programmes has been spent (Roy, 1999). Deep democratic decentralisation coupled with the actual use of the right to information would be a good mechanism for ensuring accountability of government functionaries. In other words, it is not just that government programmes for basic services (health, education, water and sanitation) and poverty alleviation have to be delivered through directly and democratically elected village and local councils. To ensure the accountability of local functionaries, the community needs to have access to all relevant documents pertaining to those projects and programmes.[25]

---

[24] Thus in Kerala, not only has the state decided to allocate 40 per cent of plan funds for the village councils, but the right to information has been added to the panchayat raj legislation. However, as Goetz and Jenkins (1999) rightly note, if there is limited uptake of the provision in literate and politically conscious Keralans, this is unlikely to work anywhere else.

[25] The following government instruction shows the kind of transparency that is expected of local councils in India after the creation of PRI system:

> 'Each state should consider passing orders highlighting three different aspects of transparency. First, the panchayati raj institution (PRI), especially the gram panchayat, should display all vital information pertaining to development projects, especially receipt of funds and how they are being spent, in the panchayat offices or on a prominent board outside the school, for the information of the

Further examples of successful service delivery through democratic decentralisation

There is a strong correlation between per capita income and the share of local government in total government expenditure and revenue (Somanathan, 2001). This suggests that richer countries have been generally more successful in devolving power to local governments. It could be that this happens because the demand for government services rises more than proportionately with income.

The good news is that democratic decentralisation is growing in many parts of the developing world. In Latin America, with the exception of a few small countries, virtually all legislative and executive authorities are now elected in 13,000 units of local government. Through much of Latin America popular and indigenous organisations, often based on traditional forms of association, give voice to the poor and deal with immediate needs in health, education and public infrastructure. In the Philippines, Bolivia and Brazil decentralisation laws require local governments to incorporate grassroots organisations in their deliberations and to give such organisations a role in administering services and projects (Manor, 1999). New government forums can increase the voice of marginalised groups especially if ethnic minorities are geographically located in one area. For instance, as a result of the Popular Participation law in Bolivia, municipal councils were created where Quechua and Aymara representatives can contribute to decisions on allocating resources (Garau, 2001). Community participation is occurring in planning (e.g. rebuilding and development programmes in Cape Town), water production (e.g. Haiti and Yaounde), and environmental issues (e.g. implementation of

public. Second, all relevant records should be open to inspection, and third, members should also be able to obtain photocopies of documents pertaining to the development projects as also matters of general public interest by paying a nominal charge. Particularly, all bills, muster rolls, vouchers, estimates and measurement books, also the criterion and procedure for selection of beneficiaries, and list of beneficiaries should not only be available for inspection, but photocopies of these documents should be given on demand.' (N. C. Saxena, Secretary Rural Development, Government of India, in a letter to all Chief Secretaries in state governments, 4th July 1997).

Local Action Agenda 21 programmes in Uganda and Bolivia). Reasons of space preclude a detailed examination of these examples.[26]

Participatory budget-making in Porto Alegre, Brazil demonstrates that having local communities make decisions on the use of municipal resources can be very effective in local development. The most important outcome of deepening of democratic decentralisation – in the form of participatory budgeting – is the output indicators of services delivery. The share of the city population with access to water and sanitation increased from 49 percent in 1989 – when the experiment began – to 98 percent for water and 85 percent for sanitation in 1996. The number of students enrolled in elementary or secondary schools also doubled during this period (De Sousa Santos, 1998; Baiocchi, 1999; Avritzer, 2000).

Another example of the success of deep democratic decentralisation comes from the state of Ceara, in poor north-east Brazil (Tendler, 1997). The rural preventive health programme started in the late 1980s resulted in a few years to vaccination coverage for measles and polio tripling from 25 percent to 90 percent of the child population, and infant mortality falling from 102 to 65 per 1,000 live births.

In the last decade there has been a massive shift in development thinking in favour of decentralisation of government. The World Bank, as part of its public sector reforms, as also of its neo-liberal bias against the state, particularly tried to encourage decentralisation of service delivery through much of the late 1980s and 1990s. However, as one could have known from the beginning, decentralisation would work if it helped to neutralise the power of the local elite in the decision-making process. If it merely substitutes the power of the national elite by the power of a local elite, decentralisation cannot give voice to the people. However, that such ideas have had their influence is clearly suggested by the World Development Report 2000/1 ('Attacking Poverty'), presaged as it was by participatory poverty assessments in dozens of countries: 'To benefit poor people, it [decentralisation] must have adequate support and safeguards from the centre and effective mechanisms of participation' (p. 106).

---

[26] See Manor (2003) for further examples.

An argument often made is that the poor are not prepared for democracy, and that building democratic institutions takes time. For instance, the World Development Report 2001 p. 113 states:

Civil and political liberties, along with competitive elections, are powerful instruments for holding governments accountable for their actions. To translate this potential into reality, many institutions need to be in place to ensure that democratic processes function as they should – among them, independent media to monitor electoral and administrative processes, an independent judiciary to uphold the constitution and rule of law, and strong parliamentary institutions with the capacity to monitor the executive through such mechanisms as public accounts committees. *Building these institutions takes time* ... (emphasis added)

Indeed, it does take time for institutions to take root and acquire a life of their own, independent of their creators. However, institutions can exist for a long time and yet not act in the interests of the poor – as, for instance, the judiciary in many Latin American countries has often acted in the interest of authoritarian regimes that appoint the judges. Or for that matter, in state-level legislatures in the larger, federal South Asian countries, where land is a provincial subject, state governments have habitually prevented land reforms from being enacted – except in West Bengal or Kerala (where the Communist Party of India was in power). Clearly, where the political commitment exists, the priorities of the poor are tackled first. Where the democratic framework already exists at the national (or state) level, democratic decentralisation at the lowest level should take priority. The evidence in the preceding section shows that in *all* the cases discussed deep democratic decentralisation has shown results in less than a decade.

What role might non-governmental organisations have in such democratic decentralisation? NGOs can indeed help to mobilise and empower communities – where they exist. More often than not, the coverage of NGOs is rarely broad enough to make a difference. The evidence from over 60 participatory poverty assessments is that NGOs are few and far between (Narayan *et al.*, 2000). Many of them are engaged in innovative activities, but on a small scale. Scaling up those innovative, pro-poor activities to a national or state level can only be the job of governments. For example, there are some NGOs engaged in extremely useful, innovative activities in elementary education in several parts of India. Unfortunately, it requires the financial muscle and institutional infrastructure of the state to take those activities to scale.

History favours democracy and decentralisation

History is in favour of democracy and decentralisation. Thus Lindert (2000) argues that before the twentieth century there was little social spending of any kind (i.e. tax-based public spending on health care, low-income housing subsidies, education, pensions, welfare and unemployment compensation), mainly because political voice was so restricted. Voting rights were restricted by law limiting the franchise to those who owned some land, earned some minimum income, or paid some minimum value of direct taxes. It has been argued that the social spending share of the economy was restricted in 1780–1880 in OECD countries, rose much between the 1880s and 1980, especially after World War II, and its share has remained roughly constant in the industrialised countries since 1980. As voting rights became less restricted, a shift occurred towards progressive taxation, enabling social spending to grow.

In fact, the interests of those with voice explains why Prussia and laissez-faire North America pioneered the public schools financed from taxes and why Britain fell behind (despite the latter being regarded as the workshop of the world). Lindert (2000) suggests two reasons – which derive from the political economy of these regions. First, there was a systematic influence of the spread of voting rights upon primary schools enrolments (as on social transfer spending as a share of GDP). Countries where a majority of adults (North America, Australia, France) voted had many more children in school than either non-democracies or countries where only a wealthy minority could vote (e.g. Britain, US South). Nearly universal white male voting rights in the US and Canada set the stage for local tax-based funding of a largely public school system, and similarly so in Australia and New Zealand. Britain was an educational laggard mainly because electoral reform was slower in Britain and because Parliament kept central control of school finance. After the Third Reform Act (1884/85) the vote was extended from 31 percent (Second Reform Act, 1867/68) to about 63 percent of males in the UK. Until then the reliance on central government and private sources for school funding delayed the expansion of schooling. France was a laggard until the mid-nineteenth century. The 1848 Revolution gave voting rights for all men, but the Emperor was ambivalent on the education front for two decades thereafter.

A second cause of the spread of schooling was decentralisation. Prussia/Germany and Northern America (Canada, Northern USA) left the decision of how much tax to pay for schools up to the localities. Even though the German national government was undemocratic, local governments raised the taxes and locally elected and appointed officials ran the schools. This was unlike the case in Britain, and other industrialising countries, where education lagged behind. The British Parliament had created barriers to local government initiative by requiring a locality to get a Parliament loaded in favour of church and landed interests to approve new local taxes for schools. Scotland, which was permitted to depend more on local taxation, did much better than England in school enrolments (Lindert, 2001). In France, commitment to education suddenly increased after the defeat at Prussian hands in 1870. What also helped was the law of 1867, which forced communes to raise more local taxes if they wished, and mandated more local schools for girls. The communes responded by raising their local revenues.

There are some implications for prospects for social spending and access to basic services in developing countries from this historical experience. The transfer of power from metropolitan countries to post-colonial governments in Asia and much of Sub-Saharan Africa was accompanied by universal suffrage. Nationalist parties, which had led the anti-colonial movement, naturally were the first to come to power. However, democracy was quickly subverted in many of them, superseded by one-party dominant states. Only in the late 1980s and 1990s was some semblance of democracy restored in several of the African states. Unfortunately, the emergence of democracy had been preceded by an effective collapse of the state, hand in hand with a collapse of output, incomes and public spending through the 1980s. Similarly, there have been few Latin American countries with democracies in the last half-century, though military/authoritarian governments have given way in the 1980s and 1990s to democratically elected regimes. Yet the sharp decline in output and incomes in the 1980s and the growing income inequality and poverty incidence in much of Latin America even in the 1990s have further stratified these societies.[27] Politically, while national governments might be democratically elected, policies are populist and methods of implementation are authoritarian; deep democratic decentralisation is now the way forward.

---

[27] For evidence on worsening distribution of income in Latin America, see ECLAC (2000) and Cornia (2000).

Summing up

1. We would argue for three extensions to the capability approach in order to make the approach operational. First, Sen's distinction between simple and complex functionings is too watertight; in real life, there is mutual interdependence between simple and complex functionings that Sen does not recognise. Second, Sen's formulation of the capability approach focuses exclusively on the individual, ignoring the collective capability. Third, Sen's articulation of democracy as a desirable condition for enhancing human capabilities is mistakenly conceived only at the national level, when what matters most for genuine participation is local participation, realised only through deep democratic decentralisation. To bring all three points together, we suggest that the complex functioning of participation the approach postulates needs to be contextualised *at the level of the community – collective voice and collective action –* to have operational use. Unless thus extended, none of the simple functionings (e.g. the ability to read and write) is likely to be realised, even in democratic states.

2. To have expected accountability from the post-colonial state was to expect the impossible. The post-colonial state was merely superimposed on the structure of the colonial state. The latter was organised along lines intended for surplus extraction; accountability or transparency was not their objective. In fact, it was authoritarian, surplus-extractive, but low on corruption, especially in the top echelons of government. The top bureaucracy lack of corruption had a largely salutary effect on the middle and lower levels. This structure was replaced by a (usually) democratic one, but reliant upon rent-seeking for personal enrichment. The only hope there is for making such a structure accountable is deep democratic decentralisation (DDD).

3. DDD implies three concepts: one, democracy at the national level; two, decentralisation of key functions related to service delivery to local governments; and three, institutions and mechanisms to enable the collective voice of the community in the jurisdiction of the local government. Increasingly in developing countries most states now have democracies, especially since the mid-1980s. In the 1990s the number of states that adopted some form of decentralisation of powers and responsibilities (though much less of

taxing authority) also increased. In the vast majority, the last prerequisite is almost entirely missing. Without all three, states will not finally lose the characteristics they inherited from the colonial state of being a structure-in-itself and for-itself.

4. Communist states may have exhibited forms of participation, so in principle participation and the articulation of collective voice is not entirely inconsistent with undemocratic states. However, increasingly since about 1990, central planning and the associated socialist forms of economic and political organisation have been on the decline; they are not seen as the way forward in most societies in either transitional or developing economies. If we take this fact as a given, then one can argue legitimately that decentralisation of the kind discussed here is consistent only with democratic forms of government at the national level. In other words, it would be sham decentralisation if undertaken by a military or authoritarian government at the national level.

5. The objective of DDD is to enable the community to participate in a collective manner so that the local-level government functionaries can be made to deliver the services they are mandated to do by the central and state governments. In other words, we are not recommending that non-government bodies start to deliver services, rather that voice improves the effectiveness of the delivery of services by the state.

6. A significant role for the central government here is (a) to create local government bodies which can be so influenced, since the effectiveness of programmes or services delivered by central or state governments in a vertical manner is lower than when the same programmes are delivered by local governments; (b) to mandate that local government functionaries, both elected and appointed, are accountable to the local community through mechanisms which are reasonably transparent.

7. Decentralisation should involve a substantive role for local governments to be responsible and accountable for the delivery of basic social services (e.g. water and sanitation, basic education, basic health, nutrition supplementation of pregnant mothers and under-fives, mid-day meals in schools). The evidence presented from a variety of regions of the developing world suggests that DDD does help to improve the delivery of services. Only hierarchical control of functionaries in vertical line ministries is rarely effective in service

delivery. Since the poor have little choice of 'exit' (in the Hirschman (1970) sense), 'voice' alone works.

8. The articulation of collective voice can take a variety of forms and can use different mechanisms. Whatever forms it takes, where it is successful in achieving the goals it is premised upon a three-way interaction between the central, the local and the community – of a mutually inter-dependent nature. For instance, to identify children out of school, evidence suggests that instead of using school-based administrative records, the central/state government should mandate that village council involve the whole community in school mapping, so that the families not sending their children to school would get identified. The out-of-school children can then be monitored through a village register accessible to all. In other words, the task is not left to the school teachers only, who are usually part of the government bureaucracy. If user charges are essential (given that often the poor are paying for certain services already) then they must be retained within the community, not passed on to the state treasury, and used specifically to improve the service, while ensuring community-based exemptions for the poorest.

9. A critical ingredient of deepening democratic decentralisation is the right to information. Legislation is required to place the right to information in the hands of ordinary citizens. But even more importantly, information about use of funds allocated for various services for each local government needs to be openly placed in the public realm – whether it is for a health centre, a school or a water facility.

10. The experience of industrialised countries in the nineteenth century has shown rather systematically that both the spread of the democratic vote, as well as decentralised raising of finances, was responsible for the spread of schooling in those countries which led in schooling in Europe and North America; in those which lagged, both the vote and decentralisation was slower in coming.

We began with Sen's three arguments in favour of democratic political freedoms and civil rights: their direct importance for basic capabilities, including that of political and social participation; their instrumental role in enhancing the hearing the people get, including their claim to economic needs; and their constructive role in the conceptualisation of the needs. Most democratic developing states offer the *possibility* of the first, but in fact it does not translate into effective voice in decision-making on issues affecting the daily lives of the poor. The once-in-five-years exercised right to vote is not participation. Given that the vast majority of the poor in most low-income countries are illiterate and for all practical purposes voiceless, and their access to the 'free' media is limited, democracy also does not play the instrumental role of ensuring hearing of their needs.[28] The conceptualisation of their needs is more often carried out by bureaucrats functioning through vertically operated sectoral line ministries. Thus, while national democracy offers much potential or scope for articulating the needs of the poor for basic social services, in such an environment the potential for the poor to acquire simple functionings is rarely realised except in a highly distorted manner. Deep democratic decentralisation creates the basis for participation, the collective voicing of needs and collective action to force the government to deliver services effectively.

Cited References

Ames, B. (2001), 'The Politics of Public Spending in Latin America', *American Journal of Political Science*, Volume 21, Issue 1 (February, 1977), pp 149–176.

Avritzer, L. (2000), 'Public Deliberation at the Local Level: Participatory Budgeting in Brazil', Paper delivered at the Experiments For Deliberative Democracy Conference, Wisconsin, January.

Baiocchi, G. (1999), 'Participation, Activism, and Politics: The Porto Alegre Experiment and Deliberative Democratic Theory', Paper, Department of Sociology, University of Wisconsin-Madison, baiocchi@ssc.wisc.edu.

Bardhan, P. (1984), *The Political Economy of Development in India*, Oxford: Basil Blackwell.

Bashir, S. and Ayyar, R. V. (2001), 'District Primary Education Programme' in *Encyclopaedia of Indian Education*, Vol 1, J. S. Rajput (ed.), National Council of Educational Research and Training, New Delhi.

Brandolini, A. and D'Alessio, G. (1998), 'Measuring Well-being in the Functioning Space', Bank of Italy, mimeo.

---

[28] If anything, the media is dominated usually by an urban elite, who rarely write about or raise development issues, and are often more driven by concerns of national security, law and order, sports, and international news. See Drèze (1999) for an excellent analysis of the media and its neglect of development (including education) issues in India.

Chabot, J., Harnmeijer, J. W. and Streetfland, P. H. (eds.) (1995) *Africa Primary Health Care in Times of Economic Turbulences*, Royal Tropical Institute, The Netherlands.

Cornia, G. A. (2000), 'Inequality and Poverty in the Era of Liberalisation and Globalisation', UNU Millenium Conference Paper, January.

De Sousa Santos, B. (1998), Participatory Budgeting in Porto Alegre: Toward a Redistributive Democracy, *Politics and Society*, 26, 4: 461–510.

Drèze, J. (1999), 'Militarian, Development and Democracy', Lecture given at the University of Baroda.

Drèze, J. and Sen, A. (eds.) (1989), *Hunger and Public Action*, Oxford University Press: Oxford.

ECLAC (2000), *Social Panorama of Latin America: 1999–2000*, Santiago: United Nations Publications.

Esman, M. and Uphoff, N. (1984), *Local Organizations: Intermediaries in Rural Development*, Ithaca, N.Y.: Cornell University Press.

Garau, P. (2001), 'The Changing Context and Directions of Urban Governance', mimeo.

Goetz, A. M. and Jenkins, R. (1999), 'Right to Information and Panchayati Raj' in *The Right to Information*, Lokayan Bulletin, Contemporary Articles, Vol II, 16.2, September–October, New Delhi.

Gopalakrishnan, R. and Sharma, A. (1999), *Education Guarantee Scheme*, Government of Madhya Pradesh, Bhopal.

Hirschman, A. O. (1970), *Exit, Voice and Loyalty: Responses to Decline in Firms, Organizationa and States*, Cambridge, M.A.: Harvard University Press.

Jarrett, S. W. and Ofusu-Amaah, S. (1992), 'Strengthening Health Services for MCH in Africa: The First Four Years of the Bamako Initiative', *Health Policy and Planning*; 7(2): 164–176.

Khan, M. H. (2001), 'The New Political Economy of Corruption' in Fine, B., Lapavitsas, C. and Pincus, J. (eds.) in *Development Policy in the Twenty-first Century. Beyond the Post-Washington Consensus*, London and New York: Routledge.

Kingdon, G. G. (1994), *An Economic Evaluation of School Management Types in Urban India – A Case Study of Uttar Pradesh*, D. Phil. Thesis, University of Oxford, Oxford.

Krishnan, T. N. (1997), 'The Route to Social Development in Kerala: Social Intermediation and Public Action', in Mehrotra, Santosh and Jolly, Richard (eds.), *Development with a Human Face*, Oxford: Clarendon Press.

Levy-Bruhl, D. *et al.* (1997), 'The Bamako Initiative in Benin and Guinea: Improving the Effectiveness of Primary Health Care', *International Journal Health Planning Management*, Vol 12, suppl.1, S49–S79.

Lindert, P. H. (2000), 'What Drives Social Spending, 1980–2020', mimeo, University of California: Davis.

Lindert, P. H. (2001), 'Democracy, Decentralization, and Mass Schooling Before 1914', Working Paper Series No. 104, Agricultural History Center, University of California, Davis, California.

Manor, J. (1999), *The Political Economy of Democratic Decentralization*, Washington D.C.: The World Bank.

Manor, James (2003), 'Democratisation with Inclusion: Political Reforms and People's Empowerment at the Grassroots', Background paper for Human Development Report 2003, www.undp.org.

Mehrotra, S. (1998), 'Education for All: Policy Lessons from High Achieving Countries', *International Review of Education*, Vol 44, 5/6, pp 461–484.

Mehrotra, S. (ed.) (2005), *The Economics of Elementary Education in India: The Challenges of Public Finance, Private Provision and Household Costs*, New Delhi: Sage Publications.

Mehrotra, S., Panchamukhi, P. R., Srivastava, R. and Srivastava, R. (2005), *Universalizing Elementary Education in India. Uncaging the 'Tiger' Economy*, New Delhi: Oxford University Press.

Mehrotra, S. and Delamonica, E. (2006), *Making Human Poverty History. Macro-economic and Fiscal Policies to Achieve the Millennium Development Goals*, London: Zed Books.

Mehrotra, S. and Jarrett, S. (2002), 'Improving Health Services in Low-Income Countries: Voice for the Poor', *Social Science and Medicine*, Vol 54, 11: 1685–1690.

Narayan, Deepa, Chambers, Robert, Shah, Meera Kaul and Petesch, Patti (2000), *Voices of the Poor: Crying Out for Change*. New York: The World Bank, Oxford University Press.

Narayan, Deepa with Patel, Raj, Schafft, Kai, Rademacher, Anne and Koch-Schulte, Sarah (2000), *Voices of the Poor: Can Anyone Hear Us?* New York: The World Bank, Oxford University Press.

Raina. V. (2000), *Year 2000 Assessment. Education for All. Decentralisation of Education*, New Delhi: Ministry of Human Resource Development, Government of India and National Institute of Educational Planning and Administration.

Ramachandran, V. (1998), 'The Indian Experience' in *Bridging the Gap Between Intention and Action. Girls' and Women's Education in South Asia*, UNESCO.

Ramachandran, V. and Sethi, H. (2001) Rajasthan Karmi Project: An Overall Appraisal. New Education Division Documents No. 7, Education Division of SIDA. Stockholm: SIDA.

Roy, B. (1999), 'The Politics of Waste and Corruption' in *The Right to Information*, Lokayan Bulletin, Elements from the History of Struggle, Vol.1, 16–1, July–August, New Delhi.

Sachar, R. (1999), 'Right to Information – The Constitutional Aspect' in *The Right to Information*, Lokayan Bulletin, Contemporary Articles, Vol II, 16.2, September–October.

Saxena, N, C. (1997), *Policy and Legal Reforms for the Poor in India*, National Research and Resource Centre, LBS National Academy of Administration, Mussoorie – 248179, Paper no.1.

Singh, A. (2000), 'Participatory Micro-Planning for Universal Primary Education' in Year 2000 Assessment. Education for All, Ministry of Human Resource Development, Government of India, and National Institute or Educational Planning and Administration, New Delhi.

Somanathan, E. (2001), 'Empowering Local Government. Lessons from Europe', *Economic and Political Weekly*, October 13.

Tendler, J. (1997), *Good Governance in the Tropics*, Baltimore: Johns Hopkins University Press.

Vyasulu, V. (1999) 'MP's EGS: What Are the Issues?', *Economic and Political Weekly*, 34(24): 1542–3.

Wade, R. (1985), 'The Market for Public Office: Why the Indian State is not Better at Development', *World Development* 13(4): 467–497.

Wade, R. (1989), 'Politics and Graft: Recruitment, Appointment, and Promotion to Public Office in India', in Ward, P. M. (ed.), *Corruption, Development and Inequality: Soft Touch or Hard Graft?*, London: Routledge.

Wiener, M. (1991), *Child Labour and the State in India*, New Delhi: Oxford University Press.

World Bank (1999), *Education Sector Strategy*, Washington D.C.: World Bank.

World Bank (2000), *Overview of Rural Decentralisation in India*, 3 vols, mimeographed, Washington, D.C., 27 September.

World Bank, *World Development Report 2000/1, Attacking Poverty*, New York: Oxford University Press.

13 Reinforcing households' capabilities as a way to reduce vulnerability and prevent poverty in equitable terms

JEAN-LUC DUBOIS AND SOPHIE ROUSSEAU

Introduction

Reducing poverty through appropriate strategies is one of the world-wide current major objectives. Helping those who are already poor to escape from poverty usually does this. Preventing the non-poor from falling into poverty – or the poor from getting poorer – when they are confronted with extreme difficulties could also be a supplementary solution. This second perspective is not frequently raised despite the increase of uncertainty and insecurity in a strongly changing world. All countries, in the developing and industrialised worlds, are facing regular internal and external shocks, which have an impact on their populations' standards of living.

Therefore individuals, households and social groups may see their level of living decrease and the risk of poverty traps appear, with long-term consequences on future generations. This raises the issue of vulnerability and makes the search for security a new objective for the present as well as for the future.

Let us define 'vulnerability' as the probability of having one's situation worsen when facing a dramatic event. Depending on various factors, this worsening may lead to poverty. Therefore decreasing the level of vulnerability could also be considered as part of poverty-reduction policies. It implies to design preventive *ex-ante* actions, besides the usual *ex-post* curative policies. In political terms, such an attitude may also be quite attractive and rewarding, since it corresponds to a reinforcement of the people's global security, which is now emerging as a new social claim.

Such a focus on vulnerability, complementary to that of poverty, implies identifying the threats and, more generally, the risks that people encounter in their daily lives. Assessing their capacity to overcome the social consequences related to the realisation of such risks, i.e. their capacity of resilience, can help define the appropriate means and supportive policies that would improve the global security.

In this context, the 'capability approach' as developed by A. K. Sen appears a natural reference, for it is based on the improvement of the people's long-term capabilities. However, it focuses predominantly on the decrease of poverty through the design of 'human development strategies' (UNDP 1999), improving the access to health and education, to safe water and adequate nutrition, thus leading to an increase in the level of human capital. It also helps to fight against social exclusion by increasing empowerment and participation in public decisions, reinforcing, in this way, the level of social capital.

In the meantime, the improvement of people's capabilities leads them to become less vulnerable to the various risks encountered, because the amount of human capital – and social capital to a certain extent – that they own can be used besides physical and financial capital to face the difficulties that occur. Therefore, focusing on capability allows tackling, at the same time, both issues of vulnerability and poverty. Within this framework, designing equitable policies means not only reducing poverty through the improvement of people's capability but also ensuring security through the decrease of vulnerability.

Through the next pages, we will present, first, the relevance of the capability approach when dealing with vulnerability. Then, by examining the link between vulnerability, risk and capability, we will introduce the idea of vulnerability-reduction policies as preventive options. Finally, to raise the issue of an equitable distribution of security among the people, we will look at some of the social justice criteria that could be used in this context.

The relevance of the capability approach

What does the concept of 'capability' mean? The French language does not include such a concept, which lies between the two notions of *capacité* (ability) and *potentialité* (potentiality). In the available translations from English into French of Sen's work, a series of words also appears frequently, such as *possibilité* (possibility), *faculté* (faculty) *opportunité* (opportunity). But their combination introduces ambiguity into the definition and adds to confusion.

Going back to the *Webster's New Collegiate Dictionary*, the definitions found for 'capability' are: (i) the quality or state of being capable (which means ability), (ii) a feature or faculty capable of development (which expresses potentiality), and (iii) the facility or potential for an indicated use. This third definition, to which we refer in this chapter, includes, in fact, the two dimensions of 'ability' and 'potentiality' as components of the 'capability'.

The basic definition

The capability of a person is usually defined in relation to her ability to function. It reflects what she can actually do or be within a certain context. Living is, for everybody, a combination of various functionings ('being' and 'doing') such as moving, being clothed and sheltered, being able to meet one's nutritional requirements (or being well nourished), being in good health, being socially respected and having the power to participate in the social life of the community (Sen 1987).

The capability of a person results in the achievement of a combination of various functionings. Her well-being is concerned with this achievement (Sen 1993). To achieve these functionings, she has to use a variety of commodities that she will choose according to their specific characteristics (Lancaster 1971). She also needs primary goods to access services and, through these services, she may be able to accumulate and generate assets.

All this increases the person's ability to do things and improve her potentiality dimension. It enables her to live a pleasant life and to become what she wishes to be. These are the objectives proclaimed by the human development strategies which are being implemented in various developing countries. This approach, which is based on the assessment of capability, has brought new insights in the analysis of the population standards of living and the evaluation of poverty situations.

However, in operational terms – i.e. to measure people's capability and to design the corresponding targeted actions – there is a need to distinguish between the various components which interact within the capability definition. For instance, any increase in capability is related to the access to goods and services: i.e. access to public transport, access to education, access to health services, etc. But even if these services are available, people may not have the physical capacity (due to personal handicap or remoteness), or the financial capacity (insufficient level of

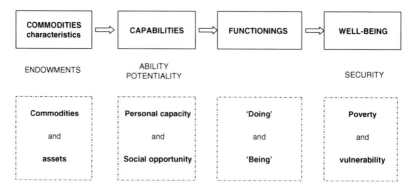

Figure 13.1 Adapting the capability approach

income, big opportunity cost), or the social opportunity (due to rights and constraints) to be able to fully benefit from them. Moreover, the access to these goods may be insufficient to allow the generation of assets through accumulation: human capital through education and health, financial capital through savings, social capital through stable relationships, etc.

Therefore examining the concept of capability itself is a necessary step to understand what are its main components and how they could determine the policy measures that should be designed.

A few of capability's components

We have summarised the main steps of the capability approach in Figure 13.1 which relates commodities (with their characteristics) to the capabilities, the functionings and the level of well-being reached. To introduce vulnerability in this framework, we need to add a few modifications which increase precision while remaining consistent within the overall approach.

First, commodities should be considered in a wider sense to include all type of goods and services. Then the overall endowment of the person will include various type of goods, services and assets, all of them reflecting directly on her capability (see Figure 13.2).

Second, a distinction can be made within the capability concept between the 'ability' and the 'potentiality' dimension and within the functionings between the fact of 'doing' and of 'being'. Capability can be considered as a combination of the 'ability of doing' things with the

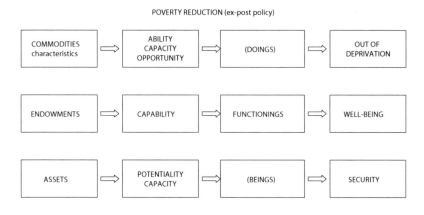

POVERTY REDUCTION (ex-post policy)

VULNERABILITY REDUCTION (ex-ante policy)

Figure 13.2 Two complementary policies: poverty (*ex post*) and vulnerability (*ex ante*)

'potentiality of being' as one wishes. Ability is certainly necessary to escape from poverty by doing the right things at the right time. But potentiality, through the constitution of endowments and mainly assets, prevents the person from falling into poverty. Her various endowments, such as land, durable equipment, savings, human and social capital, etc., can be used as a buffer – by selling part of these assets or by increasing their yield – when facing dramatic events which cause losses in the level or the standard of living. Therefore, she will be less likely to experience a worsening in her situation (Seigel and Alwang 1999).

Third, since the level of potentiality is the result of the ability of doing things regularly during a certain period of time, such an endowment-based view may not be sufficient to ensure that the right reaction occurs to resist downward movements in well-being. On one hand, the person may not have the 'individual capacity' required to use these endowments or assets correctly, because of handicap, illness, despair, lack of information, etc. On the other hand, 'social opportunities' may not exist due to social constraints, i.e. services such as education or health may be available but certain categories of people may not have the right to access them, based on tradition, discrimination or for political reasons. This kind of drawback is relevant both to the ability and the potentiality components of the capability.

According to such an adjusted framework, capability then becomes the result of a combination of 'ability of doing' and 'potentiality of being'. It is based on the constitution of endowments (commodities and assets) as a result of an individual capacity in a context of social opportunities. All these elements – namely endowments, individual capacity and social opportunities – have to be taken into account when assessing people's capability and designing capability-based development policies (see appendix).

However, aggregating these elements through poverty analysis remains an issue since they are located at different levels: capacity at the individual level, endowments at both individual and household levels, and social opportunities at the group level. Discussion on relevant methodology refers then to household economics and social group analysis and is not the objective of this chapter.

Improving capability to reduce vulnerability

Dealing with the issue of vulnerability implies considering capability as a combination of the two components: ability and potentiality. In general terms, vulnerability is the probability of falling to a lower state of well-being. It may be a fall into poverty, which is our main concern, but not necessarily, since many people may be vulnerable but not poor. However, poor people are generally more vulnerable and therefore the willingness to reduce poverty can be related to the one of decreasing vulnerability.

Our objective is to look for ways of making people less vulnerable in order to decrease or annihilate their probability of falling, when confronted with dramatic events. This requires introducing the notion of risk of such events or shocks.

Risk and vulnerability

Vulnerable people are, by definition, people at risk. This means that if a risk occurs and is transformed into a dramatic event, the people may see their situation worsen in terms of level of living (i.e. income and consumption) or standards of living (access to education, health, more generally quality of life).

Analysing vulnerability necessitates taking into account the risk encountered. There is a variety of risk. Some can be considered as social risk, since they are related to changes in the environment – either the macroeconomic environment (i.e. the price increases related to a devaluation), or the social and political environment (job losses, riots, etc.), or the natural environment (i.e. linked to climate changes, natural disasters, floods, etc.). These are external risks for the person or the household. Others are idiosyncratic risks related to the characteristics of a person or a household (i.e. an accident, the death of the household's head, a divorce, etc.). All these risks have one thing in common which is that, when they occur, the related shock on the well-being causes a downward trend in the household's standard of living, even if this does not automatically lead to poverty.

Let's take, for instance, the case of a household facing a sudden cut in the real income (due to job losses through company restructuring or to inflation linked to currency devaluation). This situation affected many families in Africa during the structural adjustment period of the 1980s. It drove some of them to 'monetary poverty'. To improve the situation, expenditures (or opportunity costs) were reduced and some children were taken out of school or put into lower-quality schools. But this induced a kind of 'standard of living poverty', through the non-enrolment of children. It resulted in the reduction of human capital because of the impossibility to accumulate through education: a kind of 'potentiality poverty' is therefore generated.

Consequently, access to the labour market for these children will be more difficult and the level of expected income lower. This transforms their 'potentiality poverty' into a 'monetary poverty'. In this way, poverty has been transmitted from one generation to the other and this poverty interactions mechanism generates a vicious intergenerational cycle, a cycle in which potentiality plays a key role. This means that protecting the household from the risk of falling into poverty would have avoided such a vicious cycle.

Vulnerability and capability

What do people or households do when they are confronted with that shock in order to alleviate the economic and social consequences? They use the means they have in hand to overcome the situation.

For instance, confronted with a loss of income, they may use savings to compensate, sell some land or cattle, take the children out of school, or ask for help from a social group they are related to. In each case, they refer to their own assets, whether these are financial, physical, human or social. It is this capacity to use these assets correctly that enables them to overcome the situation; in other words, it is the potentiality dimension of their capability which is used.

We are, therefore, back to the capability approach which considers the use of commodities for functioning. But in this case, the potentiality component through the assets owned plays a more important role than the ability one. The right combination of various assets, and the capacity of using them correctly, will avoid falling into poverty when faced with a shock.

In general terms, the person's vulnerability increases when facing greater risk but decreases when the level of her capability (through its potentiality dimension) gets higher. This relationship between vulnerability, risk and capability can be expressed by a simple formula:

Vulnerability = Risk / Capability

Since everyone in their daily life faces a pattern of various risks (social and idiosyncratic), it is the set of assets owned which prevents them from falling into poverty. According to their capacity of combining various assets, they will be more or less protected from the consequences of any corresponding shocks.

In this context, 'resilience' is the *ex-post* measure of a person's capability to resist a downward movement of well-being by mobilising her potentiality.

Reducing vulnerability is a preventive attitude

This result shows that any increase in the person's capability, through the development of her potentiality, reduces vulnerability and would, therefore, protect them from falling into poverty. This leads to a complementary way of fighting poverty by preventing its emergence *ex-ante* instead of fighting it only *ex-post* (i.e. once it has occurred) through the usual package of poverty reduction policies.

Of course this does not concern the long-term structural poverty which requires the design of appropriate measures to help people escape from poverty. However, all the current studies on poverty dynamics show that, especially for monetary poverty, a percentage of people are regularly emerging from poverty but some of them may fall into poverty again depending on the various events they encounter (World Bank 2000). We are mainly concerned with this latter category of people.

In this context, two policy orientations can be considered: one focuses on poverty reduction as an *ex-post* policy. This applies a set of measures already used to fight structural poverty. The second focuses on vulnerability reduction as an *ex-ante* policy to prevent the fall into poverty. Figure 13.2 presents these alternatives. In both cases, the capability approach is referred to by introducing the distinction between commodities and assets, ability and potentiality, doings and beings, deprivation and security.

More generally, as vulnerability depends on both the risk and capability levels, an appropriate strategy would be to combine measures that reduce the risks encountered and increase the people's capability (through its potentiality component).

For example, the case of women is a particular and quite interesting one. First, all surveys show that women live in a great state of vulnerability. Their opportunity of accessing work, a regular income, or any kind of asset is never certain, so the risk of downward well-being is permanent. One could even say that they are more vulnerable than poor, compared with men, and this appears through household survey data in a lot of urban as well as rural areas (Lachaud 1999). However, vulnerability has a strong impact on the way they allocate expenditures, savings and time (Ardeni and Andriacchio 2001).

Second, this vulnerability originates in a 'gender inequality chain' with which women are confronted through their whole life cycle and which has consequences on a daily basis (Dubois 2000). This chain begins with the probability of birth which may be influenced by specific policy measures (e.g. the one-child policy in China), then the probability of living after one year (e.g. high female infant mortality rate in India due to the dowry tradition) or even after five years (high child mortality rate in some African countries). All these result in a shortage of women (Sen 1992).

The chain perpetuates through the asymmetric distribution of education: either enrolment rates or the length of studies or the quality of education are lower for women. It later switches to the difficulty of integrating the labour market as some activities do not allow women to receive an adequate salary, i.e. they are paid less and have a higher probability of being made redundant first in case of institutional restructuring. So they have greater difficulty in constituting assets. This chain finally closes with inequalities in the decision-making process either in companies, the public sector (the 'glass ceiling' barrier) or political stances (for this reason a legal obligation of parity was introduced in France).

The gender inequalities chain makes women vulnerable to a lot of external shocks by limiting their capacity of innovation and preventing them from taking the opportunities which would have helped them to avoid poverty. This situation is even more true when the household's head is a woman, for there is no man to compensate for the inequalities or to do the things that women are socially not allowed to do. Such constraints are the result of various discrimination rules established according to legalised traditions on what a woman can or cannot do, which generally does not match their expectations.

Women are, therefore, more exposed than men to the risk of falling into monetary poverty since they obtain lower incomes on a more irregular basis and have greater chances of losing their jobs. When this happens, they have more difficulty, having fallen into poverty, in escaping from it, due to their lower level of education (human capital), the lack of valuable means (assets) and the constraints linked to domestic activities and children. All this increases the probability of falling into a poverty trap, with heavy consequences on the children.

Thus, gender inequality increases vulnerability on a permanent basis and generates long-term poverty which, through the children, can be transmitted to the next generation. We are confronted with the same vicious poverty cycle as previously, which links vulnerability to intergenerational poverty, but in the case of women, gender inequality is the source of the mechanism. Breaking this cycle requires either fighting gender inequality, at the various stages of the chain, or reinforcing the women's capabilities (and more precisely the potentiality component). This is often done, for instance, by a series of actions facilitating the access to literacy and professional education, the use of credit and micro-finance, the constitution of livestock, a reduction in the time devoted to domestic activities such as the search for wood and water, etc. (Droy *et al.* 2001).

Introducing security as a way to relate to social justice

Reducing people's vulnerability leads to an improvement in their security. For instance, if the probability of famine decreases to zero because of the implementation of food stocks, the people will feel less insecure in terms of access to food, i.e. food security has been achieved. A similar policy could be promoted in a lot of areas: access to income, work, health, education, peace, etc. Considering these various dimensions of security, the UNDP has already spoken of 'human security' (UNDP 1994).

Therefore, generally speaking, security is ensured through the reduction of vulnerability and the improvement of potentiality (as a part of the capability approach). A key question remains in terms of social justice: by acting on the level of vulnerability, can we ensure the same level of security for everybody? With such a question we are brought back to the issue of equality.

Back to the issue of equality

The famous debate on 'equality of what?' brought the equality of capability as the best objective for action since the gap of inequality between capability is narrower than the one of utility (measured through income), or of consumption of primary goods, etc. (Sen 1982, Sen 1997). In a way, it can be compared to the equality of opportunity which has become the policy reference for a lot of government and development agencies.

Considering security, it should be noted that security increases when vulnerability is reduced, since they are interrelated. In this case, facing either the distribution of vulnerability or the distribution of security gives a similar answer to the question of equality. Vulnerability increases with risk and decreases with the person's potentiality. Therefore, one can consider that acting on risk (to reduce it) and on capability (to improve it) should be the two main components of a public policy which aims at ensuring security in equitable terms to everyone.

If the poor and the rich were confronted with the same risk, either social or idiosyncratic, the solution would be quite simple: focusing on the equality of capability would be the appropriate solution, i.e. in our case it would be the improvement of potentiality. Unfortunately, the risk is partly related to the level of poverty. Poor people live in places where there is a higher risk of being confronted with natural hazards and environmental damage, illness due to poor hygiene and lack of sanitation, accident either in the work place or outside, or aggression, etc. Therefore one has to take into account the inequality of risk and its distribution among the people, differentiating between social and individual risk.

Criteria for action

Faced with such a complex situation, what are the criteria for action, in terms of social justice, that would ensure an equality of security for all? We suggest reference to the usual alternative 'weak' and 'strong' criteria, both of them requiring, however, more in-depth thought to build relevant solutions.

A 'weak criteria' would focus on decreasing the social risk while improving people's capability through a universal principle of action. The French social protection system is an example of this. In this case, appropriate policies would reduce the potentiality poverty and decrease the part of the risk directly linked to poverty. Both of them contribute to a decrease in vulnerability and an improvement in security. For instance, people may wish to move from a dangerous place to a better one as their level of education increases. Unfortunately, due to the current social rigidities, some of the poor may be unable to do this. This makes the criteria insufficiently sustainable and requires a stronger criterion.

The second criterion, the 'strong criterion', is based on Rawls' difference principle (Rawls 1971) and takes into account the whole range of risk inequalities that the poor face. For each kind of risk that is encountered (and the corresponding level of shock that results), the poor would be encouraged to constitute a certain level of assets in order to face the same level of risk as the equivalent rich. Such a targeted solution is more difficult to implement and requires a lot of information about the levels of risk, vulnerability and the composition of capability.

This means that an important amount of research work remains to be done in conceptual and empirical terms. A set of indicators needed to be produced in order to measure the distribution of the various dimensions of vulnerability, risk and capability through appropriate household investigations and monitoring systems (regular surveys, sentinel site, observatory, etc.).

Conclusion

This chapter shows that the capability approach can be successfully used in the definition of vulnerability. Through this framework, any reduction in vulnerability, and the corresponding improvement in human security, appear as supplementary ways of fighting poverty *ex-ante*, i.e. through a preventive attitude by considering those who may suffer from dramatic events.

The problem is, therefore, to improve the resilience capacity, i.e. the capacity to cope with the economic and social consequences of shocks. The capability approach leads to feasible solutions for it allows the design of human development strategies policies aimed at reinforcing people's capability. However, one should distinguish between the ability component of capability, which is used to act against deprivation, and the potentiality one, which increases the protection towards risk. Vulnerability is directly linked to the level of potentiality achieved when facing risk and through this distinction Sen's capability approach remains appropriate.

Human security, meanwhile, is directly linked to vulnerability. Making people less vulnerable is a necessary step for improving their security (i.e. decreasing their insecurity in its diverse dimensions). This could be done by decreasing the various risks they are facing. However, it is a complex issue because risks are multiform and divided between idiosyncratic and social risks. A second option would be to improve people's capability as already suggested through the design of human development strategies.

In that case, the focus should be put on the constitution of endowments through the accumulation of various assets. This can be understood, in fact, as a reduction of the 'potentiality poverty' which expresses the lack of endowments and which complements the usual 'monetary poverty' and 'standards of living poverty'. It requires, however, the person's ability to function for a long enough period of time so as to constitute such endowments before any shock occurs. The lack of potentiality could be considered as the deepest dimension of poverty. Therefore, public policies aiming at poverty reduction would have to integrate these three dimensions of poverty: monetary (or income), standards of living and potentiality poverty. Moreover, bringing potentiality into the analysis of poverty, through the use of various forms of endowments, contributes to the definition of sustainable human development (Dubois *et al.* 2001), a development that ensures the transmission of potentiality in equitable terms from one generation to the other.

The issue of social justice comes into the debate when confronted with vulnerability and security. It goes back to the famous discussion about 'equality of what?' – the equality of capability suggested by Sen does not automatically imply an equality of security because the vulnerability towards risk may differ from one person to another. Risk has an idiosyncratic component which is also linked to the level of poverty: it decreases when poverty is reduced.

In conclusion, vulnerability relates consistently to the notion of capability and those of security and social justice by referring to the 'potentiality poverty'. It adds new conceptual elements to the design of human development strategies which were originally based on the capability approach for poverty reduction. In this way, it expresses a new responsibility towards human beings for it is better to prevent vulnerable people from falling into poverty, knowing the social consequences on the capabilities of future generations (Sen 2000).

Appendix: elements for a conceptual formalisation

Let us refer to the person i living at date t. She is supposed to have a level of capability C(i,t) which includes two components: her 'ability' to function A(i,t) (for instance 'doing' things to escape from poverty) and her 'potentiality' P(i,t) ('being' what she expects to be using a set of endowments to avoid vulnerability). Her capability is the result of the combination of these two components, a combination which varies according to her life cycle. The capability C(i,t) is therefore as a function F(.) of two arguments [A(i,t), P(i,t)]

First, the 'ability' argument A(i,t) is related to the capacity of using various commodities (goods and services) through their own characteristics c(x(i,t)), in a social context that defines the rules of the game and generates the social opportunities O(i,t) to access to these commodities. This is, for instance, what a woman is able to do when trying to earn a living, to allocate her time between domestic and work activities, as head of a household in a society which does not favour women's work. This can be written (Sen 1987):

x(i,t) as a vector of commodities belonging to person i
c(x(i,t)) a function converting commodities into characteristics
O(i,t) the set of constraints, or social opportunities, the person faces, expressed by a vector of discrete functions

Then considering f(.) as the person's capacity to react in such a context, the ability argument is expressed by A(i,t) = f[c(x(i,t)), O(i,t)].

Second, the 'potentiality' argument P(i,t) is also related to the person's capacity f(.) to use a combination of the various assets (physical, financial, human, social, etc.) that she has in hand. If we call $K(i,t)$ this vector of assets resulting from accumulation over time, then $P(i,t) = f[K(i,t)]$.

The capability being a function $F(.)$ of the person's capacity to combine both ability and potentiality dimensions:

$$C(i,t) = F[A(i,t), P(i,t)] = F.f\ [c(x(i,t)), O(i,t), K(i,t)]$$

If we consider that the person's endowments include both commodities (goods and services) and assets, then $E(i,t) = [c(x(i,t), K(i,t)]$ and the person's capability is expressed by $C(i,t) = F.f\ [E(i,t),\ O(i,t)]$. Capability is a function of the person's capacity $F(.)$ to combine ability and potentiality, to convert her endowments $E(i,t)$ while being constrained by the social opportunities $O(i,t)$.

If we introduce the person's vulnerability $V(i,t)$, where by definition vulnerability is a function $h(.)$ which increases with risk $R(i,t)$ and decreases with the person's potentiality $P(i,t)$ (through the person's capacity to use appropriate assets $f[K(i,t)]$when facing a shock), therefore:

$$V(i,t) = h[R(i,t)\ /\ C(i,t)] = h[R(i,t)\ /\ F[A(i,t), P(i,t)]$$

Moreover, the level of security $S(i,t)$ increases when the level of vulnerability decreases, therefore :

$$S(i,t) = k\{1/V(i,t)\} = k.h\ \{F[A(i,t), P(i,t)]\ /\ R(i,t)\}$$

Cited references

Ardeni P-G. and Andriacchio A. 2001, 'Women and Poverty in Mozambique: is there a Gender Bias in Capabilities, Employment Conditions and Living Standards?' in *Justice and Poverty: Examining Sen's Capability Approach*, Conference 5–7 June 2001, Cambridge.

Droy I., Dubois J-L., Rasolofo P. and Andrianjaka H. 2001, 'Femmes et pauvreté en milieu rural: analyse des inégalités sexuées à partir des observatoires ruraux de Madagascar', *Séminaire sur la pauvreté*, 5–7 février 2001, Antananarivo.

Dubois J-L., Mahieu F-R. and Poussard A. 2001, 'Social Sustainability as a Component of Human Development', Seminar on *Human Development*, 21 June 2001, University of Paris XII Val de Marne.

Dubois J-L. 2000, 'Comment les politiques de lutte contre la pauvreté prennent-elles en compte les inégalités sexuées ?', *Genre, population et développement, les pays du Sud*, Th. Locoh (ed.), Dossiers et recherches de l'INED n°85, Paris.

Lachaud J-P. 1999, *Pauvreté, ménages et genre en Afrique subsaharienne. Nouvelles dimensions analytiques.* Série de recherche n°3. Centre d'Économie du Développement, Université Montesquieu Bordeaux IV.

Lancaster K. J. 1971, 'A New Approach to Consumer Theory', *Journal of Political Economy* 74, pp. 132–157.

Rawls J. 1971, *A Theory of Justice*, Harvard University Press, Cambridge.

Seigel P. and Alwang J. 1999, *An Asset-based Approach to Social Risk Management: A Conceptual Framework*, Social Policy Discussion Paper N°9926, The World Bank, Washington.

Sen A. 2000, *Development as Freedom*, Oxford University Press, Oxford.

Sen A. 1997, *On Economic Inequality*, Expanded edition with a substantial annex by Foster J. E. and Sen A., Clarendon Press, Oxford.

Sen A. 1993, 'Capability and Well-Being', in *The Quality of Life*, Nussbaum M. and Sen A. (eds.), Clarendon Press, Oxford, pp. 30–53.

Sen A. 1992, *Inequality Reexamined*, Oxford University Press, Oxford.

Sen A. 1987, *Commodities and Capabilities*, Oxford India Paperbacks, Oxford University Press, Oxford.

Sen A. 1982, 'Equality of What ?' in *Choice, Welfare and Measurement*, Blackwell, Oxford, reedited Harvard University Press, pp. 353–369.

UNDP United Nations Development Program1994, *New Dimensions of Human Security*, Human Development Report, Oxford University Press, Oxford.

UNDP United Nations Development Program 1999, *The Human Development Report*, CD-Rom, Statistical Data Base, New-York.

World Bank 2000, *Attacking Poverty*, World Development Report 2000, Washington.

14 | *Capabilities over the lifecourse: at what age does poverty damage most?*

SHAHIN YAQUB[1]

Introduction

Consider the capabilities of two people, one an adult and the other a baby. In terms of capabilities, understood as 'alternative things a person can do or be', it is obvious that almost always the adult will have greater capabilities than the baby. This is for the simple reason that most adults have had opportunities to develop their capabilities through social, economic and biological processes commonly called 'growing up'. These processes of development mean that generally the functionings of the adult in different spaces – cognition, physical ability, emotional intelligence, etc. – are more sophisticated than those of the baby. Thus we could say the average adult has greater capabilities than the average baby, and there are variances around each of the two averages (since adults differ amongst themselves in their capabilities and so do babies to some extent). Growing up *is* human development.

The experience of growing-up varies across individuals and, amongst other things, depends on childhood poverty. Increasing evidence shows that childhood partly explains the differing outcomes in adult capabilities. Some babies become poor adults and others not, and the reasons for this are structured partly through unequal opportunities to develop in childhood (Sen 1999b). Data tracking individuals over decades links childhood deprivation to low adult attainments in health, education, income and psychosocial well-being (reviewed below).

[1] I thank Michael Lipton and Robert Eastwood for very helpful comments. This chapter draws on my doctorate, which they supervised. Thanks also to Arnab Acharya, Xavier Cirera, Flavio Comin, Peter Houtzager, and Mohammed Razzaque for their ideas. Funding from the UK's Economic and Social Research Council is gratefully acknowledged. Contact details: shyaqub@unicef.org

437

Babies who end up as poor adults tend to have less nourishment – physically, emotionally and intellectually. One might term this as the lifecourse approach to capabilities (Yaqub 2004).

The lifecourse approach is distinctive from the more widespread perspective that understands variations in adult capabilities mainly in terms of factors prevailing in adulthood (labour markets, health services, etc.). The latter perspective provides many important explanations of inequality in adult capabilities, but it is an ahistorical approach to capabilities that treats all adults as having had the same childhood. The ahistorical approach makes interpersonal comparisons across characteristics like gender, location, class, caste, etc., and we might think of these characteristics as being markers of inequality in long-run development opportunities over the lifecourse.

This chapter draws out an important implication of shifting from an ahistorical approach to a lifecourse approach to capabilities. Many interventions to expand adult capabilities might be made when they are least likely to succeed – or even impossible to succeed (for example, a stunted adult cannot be 'unstunted'). Put another way, in many instances preventing poverty through childhood interventions may be more successful than curing it in adulthood. It raises several important policy issues, including the relative cost-effectiveness of preventing poverty versus curing it, and whether resources are currently optimally allocated across the lifecourse (in terms of the range of interventions available to expand human capabilities from conception to death). These are empirical questions not yet addressed well in the literature.

The objective of the chapter is exploratory, given the paucity of relevant empirical literature. It suggests that when considering interventions to expand capabilities, in addition to knowing the target group and the targeted functionings, another important variable is the timing in the lifecourse. For example, increasing female literacy also involves a choice of intervening with women only or intervening with girls only, or, more likely, some combination of both. The impact of an intervention could depend on its timing in the lifecourse, as well as the characteristics of the intervention itself and its delivery. For instance, it is commonly accepted that children learn more easily than adults – and there is biological evidence for it (Yaqub 2002). Of course, learning propensity would not be the only criterion because a range of economic, social and ethical concerns should enter into the choice of timing. The chapter has a simpler objective of emphasising the importance of thinking about 'timetabling' interventions within the lifecourse and the potential trade-offs involved.

First the chapter explains timetabling in the context of capabilities. Discussions of capabilities commonly ignore the temporal dimension, although clearly individuals evolve over their entire lifecourse. The concept of capability is an attractive organising tool because it readily links to research on functionings by biologists, child development specialists and social psychologists.

Section two presents evidence on economic mobility to show that having a 'good start' in early adulthood influences subsequent lifetime success. It shows that the chances of rising up the income ladder decline with time, and related to this, also the chances of escaping poverty decline with time. Section three winds back the development clock from early adulthood, by including childhood. It looks at the stability of functionings over the lifecourse, e.g. do stronger babies become stronger adults, etc. A basic assumption in antipoverty interventions is that failures in functionings caused by poverty can always be reversed. In other words, the effectiveness of interventions depends on reversibility. Longitudinal evidence on functionings shows that reversibility may be more varied, depending on factors such as when in the lifecourse poverty occurs (early or late age?), its duration (transitory or chronic poverty) and the particular functionings in question (cognitive or emotional or physical?). The final section concludes by arguing that timetabling of antipoverty interventions within the lifecourse offers a way to understand when different interventions may be most beneficial.

Functionings, capabilities and time

Time is implicit in concepts of functionings and capabilities. 'Functionings represent parts of the state of a person – in particular the various things that he or she manages to do or be in leading a life. The capability of a person reflects the alternative combinations of functionings the person can achieve, and from which he or she can choose one collection' (Sen 1993, p. 31). A person with greater capability has more alternatives, and therefore is free to choose the life he or she values (Sen 1999). Capability depends not just on command over commodities but also their use (because people use commodities differently). Each person chooses, *from their own set*, one of several feasible 'personal utilisation functions' which generates a vector of functionings out of a vector of characteristics of commodities (Sen 1987). Income determines command over commodities, but what determines the set of personal utilisation functions? Sen (1987, p. 26) says only that the feasible set of utilisation functions available to an individual is determined by 'personal and social factors'.

Time affects this account in at least three ways. First, command over commodities evolves over time. This is well recognised in economics, for rich and poor countries (Atkinson *et al.* 1992; Yaqub 2003). Income dynamics can be decomposed into age effects (determined biologically and socially), cohort effects (shared shocks unrelated to age, such as technology), serially dependent effects (including effects from past antipoverty interventions) and random events (specific to the individual). Second, the set of personal utilisation functions is likely to be time-dependent also. Like income, the set may be subject to effects related to age, cohort, serially dependent and random components. For example, biology affects use of commodities, or for example sets of personal utilisation functions could be correlated through time due to the effect of experience. Third, capability involves choosing from alternative combinations of functionings that the person can achieve, and some choices have temporal implications (such as investments in physical, human, or social capital). It is recognised that vulnerability to future harm forces the poor to invest in activities with low risk (and low returns), thus trapping them into further poverty. Peer, family and neighbourhood characteristics also influence choice.

The timetabling problem is easy to see from this discussion. Generally antipoverty interventions are designed in two dimensions, with reference to a target human functioning and a target population classified as achieving insufficient levels of that functioning (van de Walle 1998). Timetabling suggests that the lifecourse should be a third dimension for the design of antipoverty, because time influences functionings and capabilities. Each individual's capability sets are linked from babyhood through adulthood (or more precisely, from conception to death). Brim and Phillips (1988) make a similar point using a cube analogy to illustrate the three-dimensional decision-making involved (with functionings, population group and time as the axes). But the cube characterisation itself may be inaccurate because timetabling argues for something stronger. It argues that failing to achieve certain kinds of functionings can narrow a person's options later in time (for example, secondary schooling builds on primary schooling). In this case, a pyramid rather than a cube would better characterise the timetabling problem by indicating how poverty can reduce the space for intervention over time.

This 'shortage of space' to intervene may explain some of the difficulties in expanding capabilities – are resources overly focused on the thin end of the wedge? Calculations of age-specific expenditure on human development are rare. Haveman and Wolfe (1995) estimated that in the USA, 15 percent of GDP in 1992 was spent on 0–18 year olds, who comprised 27 percent of the total population.[2] Moreover residential segregation means that poor children 'face greater than average developmental obstacles, yet tend to have fewer than average resources invested in them' (Danziger and Waldfogel 2000, p. 2). The same applies across countries (arguably another form of residential segregation), since poor children in poor countries face greater development risks but are locked into countries, communities and households with fewer resources. Inequality is partly inequality between generations, and current intergenerational resource allocations to tackle poverty may merely intensify this inequality.

Economic mobility over the lifecourse

Evidence on economic mobility supports the view that the effectiveness of interventions against poverty depends partly on the lifecourse – specifically, how much and what part of the lifecourse a person spends in poverty. Escape from income poverty requires upward economic mobility. The evidence shows economic mobility declines with age. It indicates a relatively small window of opportunity in early adulthood for economic success.

One reason for this could be that the failures in functionings associated with poverty become increasingly difficult to reverse with time. This relies on the idea that income and earnings are material rewards for achievements in certain functionings. Those who develop more

---

[2] This estimate included expenditure by parents, government and non-governmental organisations. The breakdown was as follows (in billions of 1992 dollars): parental direct costs $454.5, parental time costs $112.6, government spending on education $235.6, government social services $8.1, government legal system costs $0.4, federal food programmes $18.3, government spending on housing $7.1, government health care $18.2, government transfers and tax credit $45.8, nongovernmental spending $3. This totalled $898.8 billion dollars in1992, or $13,515 per under-18 year old.

sophisticated functionings over time experience growth in earnings and income, and are upwardly mobile. A good start in early adulthood has lasting implications because capabilities continue to evolve due to adult experiences. Capabilities evolve during adulthood through a range of activities, including employment, social roles, and household formation, as well as through biological processes in ageing – all of which differ between rich and poor.

The economic mobility literature uses longitudinal data that tracks over time changes in incomes and earnings of individuals, sometimes over decades. Geweke and Keane (2000) found that in the USA, already by age 30 years, low earnings strongly predicted low earnings persistence *throughout life*. This result held even after conditioning on race and education. Björklund (1993) found that single-year income inequality in Sweden converged on lifetime income inequality only after age thirty. Table 14.1 shows that in Denmark, Finland, France, Germany, Italy, Sweden, the UK and the USA, earnings mobility was lower at older ages. The table reports two measures of mobility: 1) the correlation between earnings and 'earnings five years later', and 2) the

Table 14.1 *Measures of earnings mobility by age group*

	Shorrocks for Theil0 after 6 yrs				Pearson correlation after 5 yrs			
	< 25 yrs	25–34	35–49	50–64	< 25 yrs	25–34	35–49	50–64
Denmark	0.75	0.85	0.91	0.94	0.23	0.56	0.72	0.78
Finland		Not reported			0.12	0.33	0.46	0.48
France	0.71	0.85	0.91	0.92	0.29	0.64	0.80	0.83
Germany	0.52	0.88	0.93	0.93	0.39	0.73	0.87	0.89
Italy	0.70	0.84	0.91	0.90	0.39	0.70	0.83	0.84
Sweden		Not reported			0.65	0.48	0.70	0.82
UK	0.81	0.85	0.91	0.91	0.48	0.65	0.75	0.76
USA	0.73	0.85	0.91	0.91	0.52	0.63	0.73	0.70

Source: OECD (1996), OECD (1997)

Note: The lower the Shorrocks or Pearson, the greater the mobility. The Shorrocks (1978) measure is the following ratio: inequality of earnings averaged over all years, divided by a weighted sum of inequality in each year (the weights are set equal to the share of yearly earnings in aggregate earnings). The Shorrocks was calculated using the Theil0 inequality index over a six-year accounting period. The Pearson used a five-year accounting period.

Shorrocks (1978) measure of mobility over six years. In both measures, a value of one indicates no mobility. The Shorrocks is based on the fact that inequality of earnings aggregated over several years is less than inequality in a given single year, because of mobility. Data problems restrict the evidence to OECD countries but a similar result is likely in developing countries where labour markets are relatively less efficient.

Those below the poverty line who do not experience upward mobility become chronically poor. In this respect, the effectiveness of anti-poverty interventions at a particular time is influenced by the capability set of the target group at that time. Generally people with greater capabilities can better exploit new resources and opportunities. Expanding the capabilities of those with accumulated problems should prove more difficult than reversing the transitory poverty of those with relatively more options. Evidence on poverty state dependency supports this view. A sorting may exist amongst the poor whereby the chance of exiting poverty falls with increasing time in poverty. Table 14.2 shows this for eight countries, in which generally the chance

Table 14.2 *Chronic poverty: percentage of poor remaining poor after T years of poverty*

T years poor	Absolute poverty				0.5 of median income				Poorest income quintile
	USA	Poland	Neth'lds	Germany	USA	UK	Canada	Spain	Hungary
1	47	60	32	45	62	53	63	24	25
2	64	72	63	69	74	66	73	48	57
3	73	78	75	65	80	78	83		
4	77		80	60	92	68			
5	81		92	58	85				
6	84		91	100	90				
7	85		100	71					
8	87		100	100					
9	88								

Source: Gottschalk and Danziger (1997), Okrasa (1999), Maitre & Nolan (1999), Cantó-Sánchez (1996), Galasi (1998)

Note: Some results presented as reported by authors, and others are derived. Spanish estimate for T = 2 is actually for T = 1.5 years

of escaping poverty is halved by the fourth year in poverty, as compared with the first year in poverty. Spending time in poverty affects the possibility of escaping poverty, possibly because of the long-run harm that poverty causes on functionings.

Functionings over the lifecourse

Evidence that tracks more direct measures of functionings over time shows the long-run harm caused by poverty during different phases of the lifecourse. Direct measures are based on anthropometrics, psychological tests, biological measures, etc. (rather than income and earnings). Like the evidence on economic mobility, it suggests that the possibility of expanding functionings depends partly on timing in the lifecourse. Particularly interesting is that the direct measures of functionings can be tracked from birth. Some of the evidence shows how favourable development in childhood leads into a good start in early adulthood. People have 'sensitive periods' when the development of a particular characteristic is most receptive to influence by environmental factors (Bornstein 1989). Sensitive periods are likely to signal when poverty damages most and antipoverty interventions help most. This is commonly recognised in nutrition, for example in terms of growth curves for stature (Osmani 1992; Payne *et al.* 1994). The same idea can be applied to other physical, mental and emotional characteristics (Yaqub 2002).

The longitudinal evidence shows functionings stabilise with age and become increasingly sufficient to predict later functionings (Bloom 1964). Other functionings are heterotypically stable in that two superficially different functionings are correlated across time, i.e. an (earlier) functioning X_t is a predictor of a (later and different) functioning Z_{t+}, with the stability in this case in some underlying characteristic (Kagan 1971).[3] Studies have looked at stability covering long periods of the lifecourse, even linking prenatal events to adult outcomes. Unfortunately the lack of longitudinal data means there is relatively less coverage

---

[3] These statements follow the discussion in Wohlwill (1980) on different concepts of stability in human development. Additionally ipsative stability refers to the stability through time of the relative performance of different functionings, and homotypic stability refers to continuity of a trait even if there is a change in the underlying process causing that trait.

of developing countries, and even then, shorter periods of the lifecourse are tracked.

Intrauterine predictors

Studies in several countries suggest that physiological development before birth can heighten susceptibility to morbidity throughout life. This is referred to as the 'foetal origins of disease' or 'biological programming' (Barker 1994). A well-studied case is that of foetuses in the Dutch famine of 1944–45. Tracking the health statuses of the 'famine foetuses' over the lifecourse showed they were more vulnerable as adults to diabetes, high blood pressure and coronary heart disease (Stein *et al.* 1975; Lumey *et al.* 1993). The explanation is unclear but research has focused on the idea that famine caused adaptations to the biological structure and metabolism of the foetus (UN ACC/SCN 2000).

Similarly in rural Gambia, people born in the hungry season were ten times more likely to die after the age of 25 than those born in the surplus season (Moore *et al.* 1999). Importantly, in this case, most deaths were from infectious diseases. Anthropometric and haematological status at age 18 months was no different between groups, suggesting an impairment of immune function at some earlier age (Prentice 1998). Perez-Escamilla and Pollitt (1992) reported that in Guatemala infants having suffered intrauterine growth retardation had lower weight-for-age, weight-for-length, and length-for-age right through the first three years of life; had worse psychomotor development at one and six months (even after controlling for confounding factors); and worse verbal and memory abilities at three and four years (after controlling for confounding factors). But by adolescence, this group showed no difference in a range of personality and intelligence tests.

More generally, in several countries low weight at birth (sometimes low weight at 12 months) has been associated with increased risk in adulthood of hypertension, coronary heart disease, diabetes, and autoimmune thyroid disease (Scrimshaw 1997). Low birthweight appears to signal an increased propensity for morbidity conditional on contemporaneous health-determining factors (Scrimshaw 1997). In the UK, low birthweight was associated with a wide range of social and economic indicators in adulthood (Bartley *et al.* 1994). The time scale in these studies makes them highly suggestive of long-run consequences of early poverty.

Childhood predictors

Intelligence scores, such as IQ, can be measured at different points in childhood. IQ scores are interesting because they try to measure aptitude in socially and economically rewarded intellectual tasks and behaviour (even if they do not necessarily capture natural ability or intelligence). In one study five patterns of longitudinal change in IQ were identified between ages 30 months and 17 years, plus a set of cases with idiosyncratic profiles (Wohlwill 1980). After age six years IQ scores become more stable and predictive of later scores (Berk 1996; Siegler and Richards 1982). For example, IQ scores between 5–7 years show a correlation to IQ scores between 17–18 years of 0.86 (Wohlwill 1980). Other studies show that environmental factors, such as absences from school, can cause declines in IQ (Ceci 1999; Gorman and Pollitt 1996). In the UK, Feinstein (2000) reported considerable stability for IQ scores at 22 months, 42 months, 5 years and 10 years, and also showed that the 22 month IQ score could predict educational attainments at age 26 years.

Correlations using broader measures are consistent with results using IQ in showing how capabilities develop over the lifecourse. Walker *et al.* (1994) found in the USA that outcomes at ages 7–36 months in socioeconomic status, IQ (Stanford Binet tests) and early language production were all correlated to outcomes between ages 5–10 years in language, verbal ability and academic achievement (reading and spelling). The authors concluded that students who began schooling at a disadvantage continued along a delayed academic trajectory. In the Philippines, early nutritional status was associated with schooling outcomes 12 years later – malnourished children enrolled late, repeated grades, and learned less per year of schooling (Glewwe *et al.* 1999). In under five year olds who survived severe pneumonia in the Gambia, the main predictor for raised mortality over the next four years was weight-for-age prior to illness (West *et al.* 1999).

Results in several countries show how the timing and duration of income poverty matters. In the USA, the educational attainment of adults was found to depend on parental income (Duncan *et al.* 1994; Duncan *et al.* 1998). Importantly, the effect existed only for parental income in early and middle childhood, and not in adolescence, suggesting the relative importance of early development.[4] Moreover, although transitory income poverty in childhood had an effect, chronic poverty in childhood had a much stronger (negative) effect on IQ and behaviour (Duncan *et al.* 1994). Consistent with this, studies in Canada, the UK, and USA found that the effect of current income on child development is small – and that indicators that capture long-run status have larger impacts, such as background characteristics other than parental income (Haveman and Wolfe 1994; Duncan *et al.* 1998; Blau 1999; Curtis *et al.* 1999; Levy and Duncan 2000; McCulloch and Joshi 2000). Overall the literature suggests that 1) the income effect varies by type of functioning with greater effect on ability measures, and lower impacts on behaviour; 2) the impact of permanent income is much larger; and 3) effects of parental income are bigger at lower income levels.

Other studies show how a person's childhood development can locate that person on the income and employment ladder in early adulthood. For example, in the USA, the duration of childhood income poverty predicted early employment outcomes (Corcoran *et al.* 1992). In New Zealand, the duration of unemployment from age 15 to 21 years was related to characteristics at ages 3–5 years, ages 7–9 years and at age 15 years (Caspi *et al.* 1998). Moreover the risk of adult unemployment was strongly correlated from one age to the next. When characteristics for all ages were included in a single model, only those at 15 years were significant. This suggested that 'the significance of the childhood predictors of unemployment appears to reside in their initiation of a process of cumulative disadvantage and risk, such that by mid-adolescence deficiencies in human, social, and personal capital increase the risk of unemployment' (Caspi *et al.* 1998, p. 442). Similarly in the UK, Feinstein (2000b) found characteristics at age ten years – attentiveness in school, conduct disorder and self-esteem – were correlated to hourly wages and unemployment probabilities at age 26 years.

---

[4] Duncan *et al.* (1994) attempted to fine-tune such effects on IQ and behaviour at age five years, by comparing attainments of those having experienced poverty before age two with those experiencing poverty after age two – no timing effects were detected.

Early adult predictors

Early adulthood can influence lifetime development (a point already made based on economic mobility). Burgess and Propper (1998) found that, amongst males in the USA, consumption of hard drugs and violent behaviour in adolescence (age 16–22 years) predicted lower employment, earnings levels and earnings growth ten years later. Adolescent consumption of alcohol and soft drugs had no such effects. Hauser *et al.* (2000) found that in the USA, the correlation between years of schooling and occupational status *at first job* was 0.77 for men and 0.50 for women, and *at 54 years* 0.54 for men and 0.37 for women. The correlation between adolescent IQ and occupational status was lower but more stable through the lifecycle: at first job it was 0.44 for men and 0.33 for women, and at age 54 years, 0.39 for men and 0.37 for women. In the UK, Hobcraft (1998) found a wide range of adolescent outcomes was correlated to income and employment at age 33. Hobcraft and Kiernan (1999) found that the birth of a first child before age 23 was predictive of adverse outcomes at age 33. Burgess *et al.* (1999) found the effect of early unemployment on employment a decade later depended on class – amongst low-skilled individuals the effect persisted, but not amongst mid- and high-skilled individuals. Moreover career interruptions, with periods unemployed, flatten the lifetime earnings profiles because of lower job experience, and the effect is larger for males than females (Albrecht *et al.* 1999).

Research on adult cognition has found that different cognitive functions can have different time profiles as people age (Horn and Donaldson 1980). The strongest declines occur in fluid intelligence, which is believed to depend more strongly on physiological structures. Fluid intelligence is less socially imparted, is characterised by idiosyncratic strategies of knowledge acquisition and use, and is achievement and output oriented. In contrast, crystallised intelligence refers to more learned abilities, such as verbal comprehension, experiential evaluation, formal reasoning and technical proficiency, and is more analytic and process oriented.

Fluid and crystallised thinking require information via sight, hearing, short-term memory and long-term memory. Importantly, aspects of both fluid and crystallised intelligence require use in order to be sustained. Reasoning aspects of fluid intelligence decline most steeply with age, accompanied by declines in short-term memory. But people showing such declines can simultaneously show *a lack of decline* – or even improvement – in crystallised intelligence and many aspects of long-term memory. One interpretation of this is that adult experiences matter a lot for intellectual time-profiles, because learned aspects are resilient even though the neurological base of intelligence follows a natural deterioration with age.[5]

This is especially important because people have vastly different intellectual experiences in the labour market – Featherman *et al.* (1988) reported the interesting result that adult personality can change as the content of employment changes over the lifecycle. Horn and Donaldson (1980, p. 475) argue 'it may be that a relatively large proportion of the content of intelligence that persists at later ages is acquired in young adulthood' because data indicates that people can recall more information that was current when they were 20–25 years old than information that was current at other periods of their lives. Early experience in the labour market could be important for maintaining later cognition.

Conclusion

Evidence presented in this chapter suggests that, as the lifecourse progresses, achievements in functionings become increasingly determined by past achievements – economic mobility declines with age, the chances of escaping poverty declines with its duration, and functionings at earlier ages are correlated with functionings at later ages. Taken together, one path identifiable from this evidence is that advantages in childhood map into advantages in early adulthood, which then continue to influence capability throughout life. If that is the case, what is the scope for interventions to expand capabilities? The chapter argues that more explicit consideration of the lifecourse would improve the impact of interventions to expand capabilities.

This is not meant to say that adult poverty should be ignored in preference to child poverty. A lot of adult poverty is transitory (Sinha *et al.* 2002). Life is not completely determined at any age, which means events continue to unfold that warrant antipoverty interventions,

---

[5] For example, age leads to loss of brain weight, number of functional neurons, cerebral blood flow, neuronal conduction rate – and gains in brain water content, fissures, inert waste products, and neurofibrillary tangles (Horn and Donaldson 1980, p. 479).

even if the person never experienced poverty before (Danziger and Waldfogel 2000). Moreover capabilities in adulthood are limited by many contemporaneous factors, such as lack of access to finance and markets, absent services in health and education and powerlessness in social and political decision-making (Lipton *et al.* 1998). These factors are regularly identified in the ahistorical approach to diagnosing poverty. Of course, fixing these will expand capabilities regardless of lifecourse issues – but the chapter makes the additional point that the size of impact will depend partly on the timing in the lifecourse when the improvements are made. Growing up poor and starting early adulthood poor, limit how a person can use subsequent opportunities in life, including those offered by antipoverty interventions.

A point of departure between the lifecourse approach and the ahistorical approach is that in the latter poverty is tackled after it occurs – a 'fix it' approach – because the factors believed to cause poverty are mostly contemporaneous to poverty itself. The lifecourse approach points to longitudinal evidence revealing the complex and multidimensional aetiology underlying capabilities. This suggests that curing the harm caused by poverty may not be entirely possible – and quick – for everybody. For many people, the fix-it approach may be too little and too late. The harm from poverty may be irreversible in some aspects of capabilities, and for others, reversal may be slight and slow. On the one hand, this suggests that the task of reversing existing poverty, especially chronic poverty, might yet have been grossly underestimated. On the other hand, this indicates that people need the basic social and economic opportunities to get their lives right in the first place. Timetabling would prioritise antipoverty to when the worst damage from poverty can be avoided, when the most gains in functionings can be obtained, and when the fastest returns accrue.

Cited references

Albrecht, James W., Pers-Anders Edin, Marianne Sundström and Susan B. Vroman 1999. 'Career Interruptions and Subsequent Earnings: A Reexamination Using Swedish Data.' *Journal of Human Resources* V34 N2, pp. 294–311

Atkinson, A. B., F. Bourguignon and C. Morrisson 1992. *Empirical Studies of Earnings Mobility*. Fundamentals of Pure and Applied Economics 52, Harwood Academic Publishers, Chur, Switzerland

Barker, David J. P. 1994. *Mothers, Babies and Disease in Later Life*. British Medical Journal Publishing Group, London

Bartley, M., C. Power, D. Blane, G. Davey Smith and M. Shipley 1994. 'Birth Weight and Later Socioeconomic Disadvantage: Evidence from the 1958 British Cohort Study.' *British Medical Journal* V309 Dec, pp. 1475–1479

Berk, Laura E. 1996. *Infants, Children and Adolescents*. Second Edition, Allyn and Bacon, Boston

Björklund, Anders 1993. 'A Comparison Between Actual Distributions of Annual and Lifetime Income: Sweden 1951–89.' *Review of Income and Wealth* V39, N4, pp. 377–386

Björklund, Anders and Marten Palme 1997. *Income Redistribution Within the Life Cycle Versus Between Individuals: Empirical Evidence Using Swedish Panel Data*. Working Paper 197, Series in Economics and Finance, School of Economics, Stockholm

Blau, David M. 1999. 'The Effect of Income on Child Development.' *Review of Economics and Statistics* V81 N2 May, pp. 261–276

Bloom, B. S. 1964. *Stability and Change in Human Characteristics*. Wiley, New York

Bornstein, M. H. 1989. 'Sensitive Periods in Development: Structural Characteristics and Causal Interpretations.' *Psychological Bulletin* 105, pp. 179–197

Brim, Orville G. and Deborah A. Phillips 1988. 'The Life-Span Intervention Cube.' In: E. Mavis Hetherington, Richard M. Lerner and Marion Perlmutter, *Child Development in Life-Span Perspective*. Lawrence Erlbaum Associate Publishers, London

Burgess, Simon M. and Carol Propper 1998. *Early Health Related Behaviours and Their Impact on Later Life Chances: Evidence from the US*. CASE Paper 6, Centre for Analysis of Social Exclusion, London School of Economics, London

Burgess, Simon, Carol Propper, Hedley Rees and Arran Shearer 1999. *The Class of '81: The Effects of Early Career Unemployment on Subsequent Unemployment Experiences*. CASE Paper 32, London School of Economics

Campbell, Frances A. and Craig T. Ramey 1994. 'Effects of Early Intervention on Intellectual and Academic Achievement: A Follow-up Study of Children from Low-Income Families.' *Child Development* V65 N2 April, pp. 684–698

Cantó-Sánchez, Olga 1996. *Poverty Dynamics in Spain: A Study of Transitions in the 1990s*. Discussion Paper 15, Distributional Analysis Research Programme, STICERD London School of Economics, London

Caspi, Avshalom, Bradley R. Entner Wright, Terrie E. Moffitt and Phil A. Silva 1998. 'Early Failure in the Labor Market: Childhood and

Adolescent Predictors of Unemployment in the Transition to Adulthood.' *American Sociological Review* V63 N3 June, pp. 424–451

Ceci, Stephen J. 1999. 'Schooling and Intelligence.' In: S. J. Ceci and W. M. Williams, *The Nature-Nurture Debate*. Blackwell, Oxford

Corcoran, Mary, Roger Gordon, Deborah Laren and Gary Solon 1992. 'The Association Between Men's Economic Status and their Family and Community Origins'. *Journal of Human Resources* V27 N4, pp. 575–601

Curtis, Lori, Martin D. Dooley, Ellen L. Lipman and David H. Feeny 1998. *The Role of Permanent Income and Family Structure in the Determination of Child Health in the Ontario Child Health Study*. Working Paper 16, Canadian International Labour Network

Danziger, Sheldon and Jane Waldfogel 2000. *Investing in Children: What Do We Know? What Should We Do?* CASE Paper 34, Centre for Analysis of Social Exclusion, London School of Economics, London

Del Rosso, Joy Miller and Tonia Marek 1996. *Class Action. Improving School Performance in the Developing World Through Better Health and Nutrition*. World Bank, Washington DC

Duncan, Greg J., Jeanne Brooks-Gunn and Pamela Kato Klebanov 1994. 'Economic Deprivation and Early Childhood Development.' *Child Development* V65 N2 April, pp. 296–318

Duncan, Greg J., W. Jean Yeung, Jeanne Brooks-Gunn and Judith R. Smith 1998. 'How Much Does Childhood Poverty Affect the Life Chances of Children?' *American Sociological Review* V63 N3 June, pp. 406–423

Featherman, David L. and Kenneth I. Spenner, with Naouki Tsunematsu 1988. 'Class and the Socialization of Children: Constancy, Change or Irrelevance?' In: E. Mavis Hetherington, Richard M. Lerner and Marion Perlmutter, *Child Development in Life-Span Perspective*. Lawrence Erlbaum Associate Publishers, London

Feinstein, Leon 2000a. *Pre-school Educational Inequality? British Children in the 1970 Cohort*. Discussion Paper in Economics 56, University of Sussex

Feinstein, Leon 2000b. *The Relative Economic Importance of Academic, Psychological and Behavioural Attributes Developed in Childhood*. Discussion Paper in Economics 62, University of Sussex

Galasi, Péter 1998. *Income Inequality and Mobility in Hungary 1992–1996*. Innocenti Occasional Paper 64, UNICEF Florence

Garmezy, N. 1983. 'Stressors of Childhood.' In: N. Garmezy and M. Rutter (eds.), *Stress, Coping and Development in Children*. McGraw-Hill, New York

Geweke, John and Michael Keane 2000. 'An Empirical Analysis of Earnings Dynamics Among Men in the PSID: 1968–1989.' *Journal of Econometrics* V96, pp. 293–356

Gittleman, Maury and Mary Joyce 1998. *Have Family Income Mobility Patterns Changed?* Paper presented at the 25th General Conference of the International Association for Research on Income and Wealth, August 1998, Cambridge, England

Glewwe, Paul, Hanan Jacoby and Elizabeth King 1999. *Early Childhood Nutrition and Academic Achievement: A Longitudinal Analysis.* FCND Working Paper 68, IFPRI, Washington DC

Gorman, Kathleen S. and Ernesto Pollitt 1996. 'Does Schooling Buffer the Effects of Early Risk?' *Child Development* V67, pp. 314–326

Gottschalk, Peter and Sheldon Danzinger 1997. *Family Income Mobility – How Much is There and Has it Changed?* Boston College, Massachusetts

Grantham-McGregor, Sally and Christine Powell, Susan Walker, Susan Chang and Patricia Fletcher 1994. 'The Long-term Follow-up of Severely Malnourished Children Who Participated in an Intervention Program.' *Child Development* V65 N2 April, pp. 428–439

Hauser, Robert M., John Robert Warren, Min-Hsiung Huang and Wendy Y. Carter 2000. 'Occupational Status, Education, and Social Mobility in the Meritocracy.' In: Kenneth Arrow, Samuel Bowles and Steven Durlauf, *Meritocracy and Economic Inequality.* Princeton University Press, New Jersey

Haveman, Robert and Barbara Wolfe 1994. *Succeeding Generations: On the Effects of Investments in Children.* Russell Sage, New York

Haveman, Robert and Barbara Wolfe 1995. 'The Determinants of Children's Attainments: A Review of Methods and Findings.' *Journal of Economic Literature* V33, pp. 1829–1878

Hobcraft, John 1998. *Intergenerational and Life-Course Transmission of Social Exclusion: Influences of Childhood Poverty, Family Disruption, and Contact with the Police.* CASE Paper 15, Centre for Analysis of Social Exclusion, London School of Economics, London

Hobcraft, John and Kathleen Kiernan 1999. *Childhood Poverty, Early Motherhood and Adult Social Exclusion.* CASE Paper 28, Centre for Analysis of Social Exclusion, London School of Economics, London

Horn, John L. and Gary Donaldson 1980. 'Cognitive Development in Adulthood.' In: Orville G. Brim and Jerome Kagan (eds.), *Constancy and Change in Human Development.* Harvard University Press

Kagan, Jerome 1971. *Change and Continuity in Infancy.* Wiley, New York

Levy, Dan and Greg J. Duncan 2000. *Using Sibling Samples to Assess the Effect of Childhood Family Income on Completed Schooling.* Discussion Paper 168, Joint Center for Poverty Research, Northwestern University

Light, A. and K. McGarry 1994. *Job Change Patterns and the Wages of Young Men.* Mimeo, Ohio State University

Lillard, Lee A. and Robert T. Reville 1997. *Intergenerational Mobility in Earnings and Occupational Status.* RAND, California

Lipton, Michael with Shahin Yaqub and Eliane Darbellay 1998. *Successes in Anti-poverty.* ILO, Geneva

Lumey, L. H., A. C. J. Ravelli, L. G. Wiessing, J. G. Koppe, P. E. Treffers and Z. A. Stein 1993. 'The Dutch Famine Birth Cohort Study: Design, Validation of Exposure, and Selected Characteristics of Subjects after 43 Years of Follow-up. *Paediatrics and Perinatrics and Epidemiology* V7, p. 354

Mahoney, James 2000. 'Path Dependence in Historical Sociology.' *Theory and Society* V29, pp. 507–548

Maitre, Bertrand and Brian Nolan 1999. 'Income Mobility in the European Community Household Panel Survey.' Working Paper 4, European Panel Analysis Group, University of Essex

Martorell, Reynaldo 1992. 'Long-term Effects of Improved Childhood Nutrition.' *SCN News*, Number 8, Administrative Committee on Coordination/ Subcommitte on Nutrition ACC/SCN, United Nations, Geneva

Mayer, Susan E. 1997. *What Money Can't Buy. Family Income and Children's Life Chances.* Harvard University Press

McCulloch, Andrew and Heather E. Joshi 2000. *Child Development and Family Resources: An Exploration of Evidence from the Second Generation of the 1958 British Birth Cohort.* Working Paper, Essex University

McCulloch, Neil and Bob Baulch 1999. *Distinguishing the Chronically from the Transitorily Poor: Evidence from Pakistan.* Working Paper 97, Institute of Development Studies, Brighton

McDonald, Mary Alice, Marian Sigman, Michael P. Espinosa and Charlotte G. Neumann 1994. 'Impact of Temporary Food Shortage on Children and Their Mothers.' *Child Development* V65 N2 April, pp. 404–415

Meng, Xin and R. G. Gregory 2000. *Impact of Interrupted Education on Earnings – The Educational Cost of the Chinese Cultural Revolution.* Working Paper 40, Canadian International Labour Network

Michael Rutter and the English and Romanian Adoptees (ERA) study team 1999. 'Developmental Catch-up, and Deficit, Following Adoption After Severe Global Early Privation.' In: S. J. Ceci and W. M. Williams, *The Nature-Nurture Debate.* Blackwell, Oxford

Moore, S. E., T. J. Cole, A. C. Collinson, E. M. Poskitt, I. A. McGregor and A. M. Prentice 1999. 'Prenatal or Early Postnatal Events Predict Infectious Deaths in Young Adulthood in Rural Africa.' *International Journal of Epidemiology* V28 N6 Dec, pp. 1088–1095

Myers, Robert 1995. *The Twelve Who Survive: Strengthening Programmes of Early Childhood Development in the Third World.* High Scope Press, Michigan*

Norton, Rebecca 1994. 'Maternal Nutrition During Pregnancy as it Affects Infant Growth, Development and Health.' *SCN News*, Number 11, Administrative Committee on Coordination/ Subcommitte on Nutrition ACC/SCN, United Nations, Geneva

OECD 1996. 'Earnings Inequality, Low-paid Employment and Earnings Mobility.' In: *Employment Outlook 1996*, Organisation for Economic Cooperation and Development, Paris

OECD 1997. 'Earnings Mobility: Taking a Longer Run View.' In: *Employment Outlook 1997*, Organisation for Economic Cooperation and Development, Paris

Okrasa, Wlodzimierz 1999. *The Dynamics of Poverty and the Effectiveness of Poland's Safety Net, 1993–96.* Policy Research Working Paper 2221, World Bank, Washington DC

Osmani, S. R. 1992. 'On Some Controversies in the Measurement of Undernutrition.' In: Osmani, S. R. 1992 (ed.). *Nutrition and Poverty.* WIDER Studies in Development Economics, Oxford University Press

Payne, Philip and Michael Lipton, with Richard Longhurst, James North, and Steven Treagust 1994. *How Third World Rural Households Adapt to Dietary Energy Stress. The Evidence and the Issues.* Food Policy Review 2, IFPRI, Washington DC

Perez-Escamilla, Rafael and Ernesto Pollitt 1992. 'Causes and Consequences of Intrauterine Growth Retardation in Latin America.' *Bulletin of Pan American Health Organisation* V26 N2, pp. 128–147

Prentice, A. M. 1998. 'Early Nutritional Programming of Human Immunity.' In: *Annual Report 1998*, Nestle Foundation for the Study of Problems of Nutrition in the World, Lausanne

Reville, Robert T. 1995. *Intertemporal and Life Cycle Variation in Measured Intergenerational Earnings Mobility.* RAND, California

Rischall, Isaac C. 1998. *The Effect of High School Effort on Future Earnings.* Working Paper 30, Canadian International Labour Network

Robins, L. N. 1984. 'Longitudinal Methods in the Study of Development.' In: Sarnoff A. Mednick, Michele Harway and Karen M. Finello, *Handbook of Longitudinal Research. Volume One: Birth and Childhood Cohorts.* Praeger, New York

Scrimshaw, Nevin S. 1997. 'The Relation between Fetal Malnutrition and Chronic Disease in Later Life.' *British Medical Journal* V315 N7112, 825–826

Seckler, D. 1984. 'The 'Small But Healthy Hypothesis': A Reply to Critics.' *Economic and Political Weekly*, V19 N44, pp. 1886–1888

Seitz, Victoria and Nancy H. Apfel 1994. 'Parent-focused Intervention: Diffusion Effects on Siblings.' *Child Development* V65 N2 April, pp. 677–683

Sen, Amartya 1987. *Commodities and Capabilities*. Oxford India Paperbacks, New Delhi

Sen, Amartya 1993. 'Capability and Well-being.' In: Martha C. Nussbaum and Amartya Sen, *The Quality of Life*. WIDER Studies in Development Economics, Clarendon Press, Oxford

Sen, Amartya 1999a. *Development as Freedom*. Alfred A. Knopf, New York

Sen, Amartya 1999b. *Investing in Early Childhood: Its Role in Development*. Presentation at the Annual Meeting of the Inter-American Development Bank on 'Breaking the Poverty Cycle: Investing in Early Childhood', 14 March 1999, Paris

Shorrocks, A. F. 1978. 'Income Inequality and Income Mobility.' *Journal of Economic Theory* N2, pp. 376–393

Siegler, R. S. and D. D. Richards 1982. 'The Development of Intelligence.' In: R. J. Sternberg (ed.), *Handbook of Human Intelligence*, University Press, Cambridge

Sinha, S., Lipton, M. and Yaqub, S. 2002. 'Poverty and Damaging Fluctuations: How do They Relate?' *Journal of Asian and African Studies*, V372, pp. 387–421

Stein, Z., M. Susser, G. Saenger and F. Marolla 1975. *Famine and Human Development: The Dutch Hunger Winter of 1944–1945*. Oxford: University Press

UN ACC/SCN 2000. *Nutrition Throughout the Life Cycle. Fourth Report on the World Nutrition Situation*. Administrative Committee on Coordination/ Subcommitte on Nutrition ACC/SCN, United Nations, Geneva in collaboration with IFPRI, Washington DC

UNICEF 2000. *Poverty Reduction Begins with Children*. UNICEF, New York

van de Walle, Dominique 1998. 'Targeting Revisited.' *World Bank Research Observer* V13 N2, pp. 231–248

van der Gaag, Jacques and Jee-Peng Tan 1998. *The Benefits of Early Child Development Programs. An Economic Analysis*. Human Development Network, World Bank, Washington DC

Wadsworth, Michael Edwin John 1991. *The Imprint of Time: Childhood, History, and Adult Life*. Clarendon Press, Oxford

Wadsworth, Michael Edwin John 1997. 'Health Inequalities in the Life Course Perspective.' *Social Science and Medicine* V44 N6, pp. 859–869

Walker, Dale, Charles Greenwood, Betty Hart and Judith Carta 1994. 'Prediction of School Outcomes Based on Early Language Production and Socioeconomic Factors.' *Child Development* V65 N2 April, pp. 606–621

Walsh, Vivian 2000. 'Smith After Sen.' *Review of Political Economy* V12 N1, pp. 5–25

West, T. E., T. Goetghebuer, P. Milligan, E. K. Mulholland and M. W. Weber 1999. 'Long-term Morbidity and Mortality Following Hypoxaemic Lower Respiratory Tract Infection in Gambian Children.' *Bulletin of the World Health Organization* V77 N2, pp. 144–148

WHO 1995. *Physical Status: the Use and Interpretation of Anthropometry.* Technical Report Series 854, World Health Organization, Geneva

Wohlwill, Joachim F. 1980. 'Cognitive Development in Childhood.' In: Orville G. Brim and Jerome Kagan (eds.), *Constancy and Change in Human Development.* Harvard University Press

World Bank 1998. *Early Child Development. A Manual for Website Users.* Human Development Network, World Bank, Washington DC

Yaqub, Shahin 2002. 'Poor Children Grow into Poor Adults: Harmful Mechanisms or Over-deterministic Theory?' *Journal of International Development* V14, pp. 1081–1093

Yaqub, Shahin 2003. *Chronic Poverty: Scrutinising Estimates, Patterns, Correlates, and Explanations.* Working Paper 21, Chronic Poverty Research Centre, Manchester University

Yaqub, Shahin 2004. *Born Poor, Stay Poor? Linking Evidence on Intergenerational Poverty, Child Poverty and Adult Poverty to Examine Whether Offspring of Poor Parents Develop into Chronically Poor Adults.* DPhil thesis. Brighton: Sussex University

Young, Mary Eming 1996. *Early Child Development: Investing in the Future.* World Bank, Washington DC

Zimmerman, David J. 1992. 'Regression Toward Mediocrity in Economic Stature' *American Economic Review* V82 N3, pp. 409–429

15 | Social policy and the ability to appear in public without shame: Some lessons from a food relief programme in Kinshasa

TOM DE HERDT[1]

Introduction

The success or failure of poverty programmes crucially depends on the behavioural response they generate from both the 'poor' and the 'non-poor'. Amartya K. Sen discusses this issue in some recent publications on social policy (Sen 1995; 1999), arguing among other things that 'capability-oriented reasonings in dealing with targeting problems have some distinct merits with regard to incentive compatibility' (1995: 19). More specifically, Sen believes that targeting problems could be significantly reduced by structuring social policy initiatives in response to specific capability deprivations, such as illiteracy, sickness, malnourishment, etc. This is the essence of his 'instrumental argument' in favour of the capability approach, besides the better-known 'fundamental argument' (Sen 1999: 131). In the present contribution, I challenge the instrumental argument by proposing a more complex use of capability-oriented reasoning. To this end, I emphasise the *plurality of concerns*, which is in fact also part and parcel of Sen's approach. Indeed, Sen's suggestion that capabilities better reflect the decisional concerns of the potential 'targets' becomes much more convincing if we broaden the inventory of relevant functionings. More specifically, I consider whether the ability to appear in public without shame might be one of the more relevant determinants of human agency and hence of the behavioural response to social policy initiatives. In Sen's work,

---

[1] I wish to thank the participants to the research seminar in Leuven and to the Conference on Capabilities and Justice in Cambridge where this chapter was presented. Many thanks also to the editors of this book and to three anonymous reviewers for their very valuable comments and remarks. Remaining errors are mine.

the term 'agent' refers to 'someone who acts and brings about change, and whose achievements can be judged in terms of her own values and objectives' (Sen 1999: 19). Thus, it is to be sharply distinguished from game-theoretical uses of the concept, as, for example, within a principal-agent framework.

In order to demonstrate our hypothesis, I analyse the case of a food relief programme in Kinshasa (Democratic Republic of Congo). The programme was implemented by an externally sponsored network of healthcare centres in response to the looting that occurred in the capital in 1991. The network was financed and headed by *Médecins Sans Frontières* (MSF) between June 1992 and August 1995. Although the crisis that had ravaged the country's economy and society was far from over, MSF decided to abandon the project, as the programme managers had become aware that it was failing on two counts. First and foremost, those who received assistance under the programme seemed to be trapped in it rather than helped by it. The programme managers attributed this problem to the fact that some mothers effectively used their underfed children as 'meal tickets'. Second, the programme failed to reach the intended target population, not because of inadequate *supply* but because of insufficient *demand*. In other words, the behavioural response by the (potential) target population proved to be a crucial determinant of the programme's (in)effectiveness.

I develop the argument in three steps. In the first section, I fully spell out Sen's 'instrumental argument' for capability-oriented reasoning. A brief presentation of the performance indicators of the food programme in Kinshasa subsequently allows us to identify some weaknesses in his version of the argument. In section two, I focus on the observed behaviour of the (potential) target group. I also include explanations which consider the 'ability to appear in public without shame' as one of the main determinants of human agency. Even though the concept is notoriously vague and ambiguous, I consider it of key importance in explaining the behavioural response of the potential target group to the food emergency programme. In order to be able to take some meaningful steps towards a more operational and unequivocal definition of 'public shame', I specify a set of propositions. An important notion in this respect is that public shame can limit agency both in a direct way and by distorting people's cognitive make-up. After discussing the methodological problems triggered by this peculiar characteristic, I set out to explore the relevance of public shame in the context of the abovementioned food relief programme.

In a third and concluding step, I summarise my own 'instrumental argument' for capability-oriented reasoning. Besides its emphasis on the multifaceted nature of well-being, the capability approach also highlights the importance of seeing 'people as active agents of change, rather than as passive recipients of dispensed benefits' (Sen 1999: xiii). Having established that the 'ability to appear in public without shame' is a basic determinant of human agency, I explore some further connections between 'public shame' and social policy initiatives.

Targeting problems in food emergency programmes

Let us begin by spelling out in some greater detail Sen's 'instrumental argument' for the capability approach. Comparing it to a policy that tries to target the income-poor, Sen sees three advantages in a social policy articulated around basic capabilities (1999: 132–4). First, many functional deprivations, including agedness or physical disability, are hard to simulate for purely tactical reasons because they are beyond the control of the persons afflicted. Second, many functioning-related public services, such as education and healthcare, are nonshiftable and nonsaleable, which guarantees some 'built-in matching' between demand for and supply of social policy. Third, even if none of the former elements applies (or if they apply only partially), the aid may still be assumed to match the requirements of 'those who really need it', as capabilities supposedly better reflect people's personal decisional concerns than a narrow focus on income. As a result, the policymaker can attribute greater weight to (and have more trust in the mechanism of) self-selection, and he or she can be less concerned about the possibility that individuals might try to distort information or adapt their behaviour for purely tactical reasons.

Sociologically speaking, the latter argument is the most challenging of the three, as it makes some important assumptions about human behaviour and decision-making capacity. It is also an argument that can be tested by studying people's responses to a policy of nutritional support involving take-home food rations. Unlike age or gender, the level of malnourishment of a child is, technically speaking, relatively easy for its parents to manipulate. And unlike education, for example, food rations can easily be sold or given away to a better-nourished person by whoever is taking care of the child. In other words, *if* nutritional support for the malnourished is indeed a better policy than monetary support for the income-poor, the argument must inevitably be based on the third of the abovementioned merits, namely that this type of aid better matches the requirements of 'the genuinely needy'. After all, those who *really* need the food aid will no doubt utilise it in the intended way, while those who do not (or no longer) need food aid will surely show no interest. Admittedly, Sen mentions 'occasional reports' of families that deliberately kept one child famished so that they could use it as a 'meal ticket'. However, he goes on to argue that 'in general such incentive effects in keeping people undernourished, or untreated, or illiterate are relatively rare, for reasons that are not altogether astonishing' (1999: 133). In fact, Sen considers these reasons to be so unsurprising that he does not analyse them further.

In the empirical case discussed below, the programme is targeted towards families with children under the age of five and suffering from acute malnutrition. The latter means that either their weight is below 75 per cent of the median for the corresponding height category or they exhibit clinical signs of malnourishment (edema etc.). If the child's weight increases to above 85 per cent of the median for at least three consecutive weeks, it is considered 'cured' and may leave the programme. The programme offers food aid in two ways: not only does it provide food concentrates for malnourished children, but, rather importantly, it also provides a sack of maize, beans and flour for these children's family (the so-called dry ration). It is assumed that the child's malnutrition is caused by scarcity of food (and/or financial resources) at household level, and hence that the symptoms of malnutrition cannot be cured without tackling the root cause of household poverty. The total cost of this *dry ration* per household amounts to $200 a year,[2] which represents about 10 per cent of total food outlays of an average (10-member) household in Kinshasa.[3]

---

[2] Own calculations, based on W. Vanderhaegen, 'Growing importance of emergency aid: healthy or not ?' Unedited document, Antwerp: University of Antwerp (1998). The outlays include the cost of inputs + transportation and storage. Personnel and equipment costs are *not* included.

[3] This is merely a guesstimate, based on the fact that average food outlays in Kisenso, one of the poorest districts, amount to $171.70 (Luzolele and De Herdt 1999).

Free food distribution is considered to be helpful only to the extent that acute child malnutrition is caused by temporary factors beyond its family's control. In other words, *theoretically* (though not in practice), the target group does not include those who are seen to be 'structurally' poor. It is assumed that approximately 5 per cent of the malnourished are 'social cases'. They are a group of vulnerable people who are inclined to 'conceive the supplementary feeding as long-term aid' and who 'existed before and will always exist, since it is difficult to change the causes of their poverty and malnutrition'.[4] Conversely, the aid from MSF was intended for the 'temporarily' poor, i.e. it was targeted towards those families which were unable to guarantee food security to their members because of temporary problems stemming from the prevailing economic and political chaos. Note that this option is central to MSF's policy: a (natural or manmade) disaster calls for exceptional ethical rules that are, by definition, temporary exceptions to 'normal' practice (Boltanski 1993). I will return to this ethical argument for intervention below.

In Tables 15.1 and 15.2 I have brought together the main indicators of programme performance. First, I discuss programme performance by looking at its impact on those receiving aid. While during the first year of operation the percentage of children who left the programme 'cured' reached the target of at least 70 per cent, targets for other indicators were not realised: 17 per cent left the centre before having been cured, and 7 per cent died while receiving assistance under the programme.[5] These indicators actually deteriorated as the programme went on.

Also interesting from our perspective is the category of children who were 'transferred or sent away before having been cured'. This category should comprise the children who were transferred to other centres or to a clinic, but it also includes those who were sent away by local healthcare staff on the basis of evidence (or suspicions) of shirking: a caretaker might, for example, present herself in two healthcare centres in the course of the same week, or, more commonly, she might be suspected of keeping her child malnourished in order to be considered for a dry ration. Here we once again stumble upon 'occasional'

---

[4] MSF-Belgium, 'Thrimonthly report of the project of nutritional assistance to malnourished children in Kinshasa-Zaire; May–June–July 1995', Unedited document, Kinshasa: MSF-archives (1995), p. 4.

[5] This might be an underestimation, as some children who were listed as having 'abandoned' the programme had actually died.

Table 15.1 *The food emergency programme in Kinshasa, 1992–1995, indicators of programme performance*

	Programme performance			Programme
	Year 1	Year 2	Year 3	Targets
Average number of children under treatment	3425	3967	3045	cf. table 2
Of those leaving the programme:				
% were cured	73.6%	57.4%	58.2%	>70%
% abandoning before being cured	16.8%	24.3%	15.5%	<10%
% died	7.3%	7.9%	10.0%	<5%
% transfers + sent away	2.3%	10.5%	16.3%	
average stay (cured children)			100 days	<91 days
% severe / new cases			61.7%	

Source: own compilation, based on MSF-archives (Brussels).

Table 15.2 *Treated and potential population of food emergency programme, Kinshasa 1992–1995*

Year–Month	Number of cases under treatment by MSF-sponsored Centres	% of children of total population acutely malnourished in Kinshasa	Number of children acutely malnourished in Kinshasa	% treated/ malnourished
92–9	2873	5.1%	37 679	8%
93–3	3712	8.9%	69 145	5%
93–9	3538	4.6%	35 738	10%
94–3	4080	10.7%	86 667	5%
94–9	4034	7.5%	60 748	7%
95–4	2689	5.9%	49 985	5%

Source: own calculations, based on various reports of MSF, and on demographic data by Ngondo *et al.* (1993).

evidence of people using a child they are supposed to care for as a 'meal ticket'. Moreover, it appears that the evidence is less occasional than we would perhaps like to believe. From 1994 (year 3), in an attempt to document the problem of shirking, MSF began recording the 'average period of stay' of a cured child, and found that it fluctuated around 100 days. However, the forms that were used in the centres to follow up on the children were designed for a maximum stay of only 13 weeks (91 days), which, from a medical point of view, is more than sufficient to recover from malnutrition. The grassroots healthcare workers were therefore constantly reminded that something appeared to be wrong in some families: why were their children not recovering, despite such long periods of assistance? Why were these families so 'negligent', as one expert put it?[6]

The last variable in Table 15.1 is very significant: apparently, almost two-thirds of all children who were assisted under the programme were so seriously malnourished that they should have been admitted to hospital for 24-hour medical care. This is a first indicator of the programme's performance in terms of who it was able to reach – or to be more precise, who it failed to reach on time. Further evidence is assembled in Table 15.2, where the number of children assisted and the target population are compared.

Admittedly, the figures presented in Table 15.2 are merely indicative and they should be interpreted with circumspection. To begin with, there are some disputable differences in the definition of 'malnutrition' between the two series of data.[7] Further, they *over*estimate the number of children assisted, as some were registered at different centres at the

---

[6] C. Vanrie, 'Programme nutritionnel MSF/Kinshasa; rapport mensuel mois de juillet 1994', Unedited document, Kinshasa: MSF-archives (1994), p. 4.

[7] The representative survey on the basis of which the percentage of acutely malnourished children was estimated considers as malnourished any child weighing less than − 2z-scores for the average child of the same height and sex. However, although the use of the criterion of 75 per cent of the median child of the same height and sex is considered less accurate, this criterion continues to be used almost universally in healthcare centres across the world for pragmatic reasons. Further, given that one standard deviation may be considered to be approx. 10–11 per cent (Mosley and Chen 1984), the criterion of 'weighing less than − 2z-scores' is somewhat more tolerant than the criterion of 75 per cent. But given that the children participating in MSF's food programme weigh up to 85 per cent of the median child (the exit-criterion applied by the food centres), the estimation of the number of malnourished children as published in the table may be regarded as very conservative.

same time. This was a recognised problem. An attempt was made to resolve it by the introduction of a rule under which children could be admitted only to the centre located in their district (from October 1994 onwards).[8] However, by March 1995, it emerged that the measure had apparently never been properly implemented.[9]

Be that as it may, the principal lesson to be drawn from the figures is quite clear to see: the emergency food programme seems to benefit only a small minority of the target group. It should be noted at this point that this is a demand-side rather than a supply-side problem: the network of MSF-sponsored healthcare centres covered almost the entire city, with the exception of the most affluent districts. MSF found it 'problematic' that it was unable to reach all malnourished children. In fact, its programme covered only 5 per cent of the potential population.[10] The organisation responded in a variety of ways. First and foremost, it revisited the families that had abandoned the programme without further notice. Second, it tried to restrain local healthcare workers' inclination to exclude so-called 'opportunistic' mothers, i.e. those who were suspected of deliberately keeping a child malnourished in order to receive the family food package. Deguerry, an external expert,[11] defended the latter measure on the basis of two arguments: first, he pointed out that it is conceivable that a case of serious long-term malnutrition has a deeper cause (HIV-AIDS, TB, for instance), and second, he argued that mothers will not allow their children to go undernourished simply in order to receive a food donation. He felt that their strategy could probably be explained in terms of a catastrophic economic situation and, on this basis, recommended that they be assisted regardless.

However, as can be observed from Table 15.1, these actions probably compromised the programme's effectiveness. The percentage of children who died before they could be cured continued to increase, as did the proportion of children who were transferred. The percentage of children who quit the programme before being cured decreased, but this indicator too failed to even come close to the initial target of less than 10 per cent.

[8] Vanrie, *Programme Nutritionnel*, p. 2.
[9] F. Vautier, F. 'Rapport de mission 3–4/95' Unedited document, Kinshasa: MSF-archives (1995), p. 8.
[10] MSF-Belgium, *Thrimonthly report*, p. 8.
[11] M. Deguerry, 'Rapport de mission (mars)', unedited document, Kinshasa: MSF-archives (1994), pp. 6–7.

In sum, by the end of the third year, the programme seemed to be facing a dilemma between programme effectiveness on the one hand and targeting effectiveness on the other. Being unable to resolve this dilemma, the leading agency opted to terminate its support for the food relief programme.[12]

The question arises: why did the programme fail? For one thing, it seems that it did not encounter merely *occasional* cases of families treating their children as meal tickets: the data on average period of stay would suggest that most families receiving food aid actually belonged to this category. Yet the fact that the programme was unable to reach a large group of families is in apparent contradiction not only with the 'meal-ticket' explanation but also with Sen's argument regarding the merits of capability-oriented reasoning in relation to incentive compatibility. Indeed, why should only a minority be tempted by the highly valuable food package? Is capability-oriented reasoning helpful in trying to understand the behavioural response of potential and would-be beneficiaries of the programme?

Malnourishment and the inability to appear in public without shame

It should be noted that, while there was certainly debate within the organisation about the fact that the target population was inadequately reached, the issue of the apparent failure to effectively eradicate malnutrition among children who *were* assisted had a much deeper impact on programme assessment. This was to be expected: it is a well-known fact that local field organisations tend to measure a programme's efficiency in terms of its effect on those who are reached rather than its general impact on the issue at hand (Elster 1992). Accordingly, they tend to collect information relating to the improvement of 'local' rather than 'overall' efficiency, while their discourse focuses more on 'local' than on 'overall' fairness. The essence of the notion of 'local fairness' as conceived by the fieldworkers is expressed quite aptly in the following citation:

[12] In reality, only MSF opted out. The network remains intact up until today and, in the context of new possibilities for donating food, continues to organise the food emergency programme. However, this implies more irregular provisioning and, above all, a much less valuable dry ration. At present, around 8000 children are enlisted in the programme.

The supplementary feeding programmes may be considered to be based on a tacit contract between the beneficiary's family and the centres. This contract stipulates that the centres should commit themselves to following up each child and to providing food at regular intervals, in return for the family's regular participation and commitment to the child's health (to feed a malnourished child requires time and patience). It is quite understandable, then, that in the case of marginalised families, this contract is not honoured.[13]

It is interesting to note the implicit assumption made in this quote regarding the articulation of norms (i.e. the 'not altogether astonishing reasons' that people have for taking care of their children) and material interests. It is considered to be 'quite understandable' that marginal families fail to honour the contract and are prepared to compromise the health of at least one of their children. In other words, what we, the non-poor, understand to be normal, caring behaviour is seen as a luxury that the poor cannot afford. The poor, therefore, are condemned to living in an amoral world.

It is not my intention to argue the contrary case, i.e. that there is no relationship or tension between norms and interests. However, I do submit that norms are not merely preferences that can be traded off against one another in the light of budget restrictions and the structure of relative prices.

The starting point of my argument is what Sen frequently refers to as 'the ability to appear in public without shame'. He regards this ability to be one of the essential determinants of human agency. The public-shame argument goes back at least to Adam Smith. In his discussion of the ability of the 'industrious poor' to reproduce themselves and their families, he introduces the concept of 'necessary goods', or

the commodities which are indispensably necessary for the support of life, but whatever the custom of the country renders it indecent for creditable people, even of the lowest order, to be without ... Custom ... has rendered leather shoes a necessary of life in England. The poorest person of either sex would be ashamed to appear in public without them (1979: 469–71).

Though not strictly a physical necessity, leather shoes were considered to be such a socially imposed necessity that the effects of a tax increase on potatoes or on leather without a proportional increase in (subsistence) wages would have had a similar impact: in either case, the

---

[13] Author's translation, Vautier, *Rapport de mission*, p. 10.

industrious poor would have been inhibited in reproducing themselves as a social class.[14]

Thus, in the minds of Smith as well as Sen, there is clearly a well-circumscribed set of behaviours and rules of conduct that are so essential that people would rather compromise their own physical existence (or that of their peers) than imperil what Rawls refers to as the 'social bases for self-respect'. In other words, they feel that decent behaviour is anything but a luxury, and that its cost will determine people's degree of commitment to it. Somehow, the 'meal-ticket explanation' seems to miss this important point, suggesting, as it does, that material poverty induces amoral reasoning.

It must be acknowledged that 'public shame' is probably one of the most elusive of the often-cited capabilities. In order to operationalise the concept further – for analytical as well as policy purposes – I would like to refine the definition of 'public shame' by submitting five propositions.

Proposition #1: Public shame does not involve only goods.

First, it should be noted that people do not feel shame only for the way they dress or for their possessions. This would be indicative of the kind of commodity fetishism that Sen is so concerned about when he distinguishes between his perspective and the 'opulence approach'. The reasons for public shame can vary from wearing inappropriate shoes to using inappropriate language, gestures, manners, behaviour, etc. More specifically, not being able to feed your children adequately may be a reason for public shame. I would argue that we come very close to the precise meaning of public shame if we define it in the same terms as Avishai Margalit defined humiliation, i.e. as 'any sort of behaviour or condition that constitutes a sound reason for a person to consider his or her self-respect injured' (Margalit 1998: 9). Accordingly, the 'ability to appear in public without shame' can be interpreted as an ability to appear in public without having good reasons for feeling humiliated. This might be the case, for example, if the person in question is seen, treated or related to as nonhuman (Margalit 1998: 108). In this sense, it is perhaps somewhat unfortunate that public shame is often discussed in the context of relative

---

[14] For a recent use of the concept of 'necessary goods', see Goodin (1988).

poverty: our argument would rather connect it to what Sen calls relational poverty (Sen 2000).

Proposition #2: Public shame differs between social groups within society.

Norms of decency differ not only between societies but also between social groups within the same society (Sen 1999: 88). As Smith asserts, 'in Scotland, custom has rendered [leather shoes] a necessary of life to the lowest order of men; but not to the same order of women, who may, without any discredit, walk about barefooted' (1979: 471).

Sen is not always clear on this point. In his discussion of public shame, for instance, he quotes Adam Smith's example of shoes in England, but he stops short of quoting Smith on the status of shoes in Scotland. Yet, adopting a clear position on this proposition is important, if only because it might exclude many definitions of 'relative' poverty that continue to establish unique poverty lines for all the inhabitants of a particular country or region. While this may be a pragmatic solution, it is worth remembering that it is no more than that.

It should be clear that the humiliation a football player experiences after losing a game is far less severe (in fact it is not severe at all) than the shame of being considered a bad parent. This is probably due to the fact that a bad footballer has no reason whatsoever to consider himself to be nonhuman or subhuman, whereas matters are rather more complicated for bad parents. According to Margalit, 'parents', and to be more precise 'mothers' and 'fathers', are considered to be 'encompassing groups', while he defines 'humiliation' as 'the rejection of an encompassing group or the rejection from such group of a person with a legitimate right to belong to it' (1998: 141). Consequently, rejecting mothers of malnourished children from the group of mothers more generally can rightly be called a humiliation.

Proposition #3: There are different types of public space.

On the one hand, the type of shoes we might wear for, say, going shopping will not necessarily be considered 'decent' enough for attending Sunday morning mass or, for that matter, a conference at Cambridge University. On the other, to be able to appear in public without shame depends, among other things, on what (you think) bystanders know about you, and this is determined at least as much by what you are wearing as by the circumstances in which they happen to see you. Being seen queuing for a food package can therefore be humiliating.

Proposition #4: Public shame is negotiable.

Even though it is reasonable to assume that some people will feel deep shame at their inability to adhere to the rules of 'custom', it is equally likely that others will deviate from the norm simply for the sake of challenging it. More significantly, it may at times, or perhaps even most of the time, be important to know exactly by whom a particular custom is imposed and whose behaviour is consequently judged to be indecent. In concentrating on public shame and on how to avoid humiliation, we should not lose sight of the fact that, quite often, there is someone who imposes the rules, sets the standards and possibly humiliates those who refuse to accept his or her authority. Negotiating over the definition of decent behaviour appears to be an essential ingredient of what is now often referred to as the *politics of identity* (Meyer and Geschiere 1999). Applied to the present case, it might be worthwhile noting that – in Kinshasa at least – the shame of being the parent of a malnourished child is in fact borne by the mother, not the father. This outcome is culture-specific and, no doubt, can be rather convenient for the fathers.

Proposition #5: It is necessary and sufficient to have a sound reason for feeling shame.

Finally, like Margalit, I would like to make a clear conceptual distinction between feeling ashamed and *having a sound reason* to feel ashamed. The latter notion tries to capture an essential aspect of the condition of public shame, which is relatively independent from the empirically verifiable feelings of humiliation or shame those involved may be experiencing.[15] Consequently, Margalit takes into account that people can adopt different tactics to evade, ignore, laugh at or contest an attack on their self-respect. These tactics can vary from an overly sensitive reaction, whereby the humiliator is depicted as a beast, to an 'Uncle Tom' attitude, whereby the supposedly humiliated party shows no sign whatsoever of humiliation or interprets the available evidence in such a distorted manner that no humiliation need be faced.

It is quite clear to see what the implications of proposition #5 are from a normative point of view: the policymaker's concern with public shame should not simply evaporate if those involved do not feel ashamed, much

---

[15] See also the similar reasoning by Sen, who makes a distinction between what people *value* and what people *have reason to* value (e.g. Sen 1999: 63).

as the policymaker should continue to feel concern when the 'mental wreck, ravished by famine and buffeted by disease' has come to accept his or her predicament merely as a way to survive such harsh conditions (Sen 1985: 188; 1999: 62–63). In what follows, I shall focus on the implications of the fifth of the above propositions, approaching it from the perspective of an empirical analysis of the determinants of agency. This will allow us to develop an alternative interpretation of the data gathered on the food relief programme in Kinshasa.

Margalit's strategy of distinguishing between 'feeling humiliated' and 'having reasons to feel humiliated' implies that we should consider the possibility that 'reasons for feeling humiliated' can affect individual agency in two different ways: shame may be a factor that is taken into account at the moment of decision-making, e.g. when deciding whether or not to appear in a particular public space, say a healthcare centre. Alternatively, however, the humiliating conditions might also cause the individual to change his or her cognitions – or beliefs invoked to interpret the situation – so as not to have to feel ashamed. In other words, humiliation can result either in a feeling of shame, which will encourage the humiliated person not to appear in public, or in a distorted view of reality, which would arguably reduce the humiliated person's agency in another way. The latter causal chain connects to the theory of cognitive dissonance reduction, whose primary hypothesis has been summarised aptly by Akerlof and Dickens: people like to think of 'themselves as "smart, nice people". Information that conflicts with this image tends to be ignored, rejected or accommodated by changes in other beliefs' (1982: 308).[16]

However, even if the latter causal chain between public shame and agency can be related to a well-established theoretical psychological concept, we should be aware that there is a difference between the

---

[16] See also Quattrone and Tversky: 'an individual who holds two or more cognitions (i.e. attitudes and beliefs) that are psychologically inconsistent will experience an uncomfortable state of tension, called dissonance. The individual will then be "driven" to reduce dissonance by changing one or more of the cognitions so that they are no longer inconsistent' (Quattrone and Tversky 1986: 39). A similar idea had been expressed *avant la lettre* by Adam Smith: 'Rather than see our own behaviour under so disagreeable an aspect, we too often, foolishly and weakly, endeavour to exasperate anew those unjust passions which had formerly misled us ... and thus persevere in injustice, merely because we once were unjust, and because we are ashamed and afraid to see that we were so' (Smith 1976: 158).

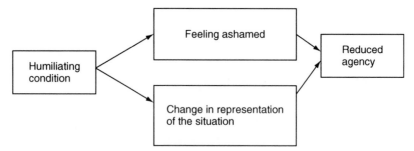

Figure 15.1 Humiliation affecting agency
Source: own survey, Matete (1996)

ordinary assumption that people are reasonable beings and the assumption invoked here that people *like to think* of themselves as reasonable beings. Whereas the ordinary rational choice model prohibits a causal link from motives to cognitions (Elster 1994), this link becomes the essence of the cognitive dissonance reduction model.

Accordingly, I feel we should adopt the methodological principle of being frugal in our use of the cognitive dissonance reduction model as a determinant of human behaviour (Boudon 1996, 1997). It might become more convincing as an argument if the successive steps in the causal chain can be demonstrated. I shall discuss each of these steps in turn and use data from the food relief programme to illustrate each one.

Step #1. The rational-choice hypothesis can be shown to have only limited explanatory value for the case at hand.

As I argued in the first section, the rational-choice hypothesis, which arguably supports the thesis of malnourished children as meal tickets, cannot explain why so few people are interested in the programme in the first place. To reiterate, this lack of interest finds expression in (1) the small proportion of the target population reached, and (2) the high proportion of 'severe' cases among the new clients. In other words, people come too few and too late. Why did MSF fail so badly in reaching the potential population of malnourished children? Certainly the nutritional centres covered by MSF were offering a 'generous' family food package. Furthermore, the package contained a portion of beans, a relatively expensive commodity in Kinshasa that is supplied by air from the Kivu region. The question arises why so many so-called 'social cases' chose not to incorporate MSF's family food package into their survival strategies? Why were they so 'irrational'?

To be more specific, it would be consistent with rational choice behaviour to include 'caring for your children' as one of the preferences in the utility function (Becker 1996). Thus, it could be reasoned that, under a certain income level, poverty obliges people to set priorities and trade off their child's well-being against other needs. Table 15.3 summarises the results of a survey we organised in one of Kinshasa's districts, and which enables us to compare households with children that receive the dry ration with households of a representative sample. The latter group was subdivided into households with well-nourished children aged between 6 and 59 months and households with at least one malnourished child of the same age.

We specified three different and commonly used indicators of income-poverty (see annex): one based on total household outlays, another based on food outlays and a third based on housing quality. For each of these indicators, we found no significant difference between households that received the dry ration and households that did not. We did, however, find a significant difference for all three indicators between the two groups of households with at least one malnourished child and the group of households with well-nourished children only.[17] In other words, the absence or presence of family altruism seems to be related to factors other than (income) poverty. Clearly, then, we need to look for a different explanation.

In a slight variation of the rational-choice hypothesis, family altruism might be considered part of the preference function of only *some* people, while others may be assumed to have preferences that are characteristic of 'amoral egoists'. In this case, we could distinguish between the (moral) 'altruists' (who do not come to the centre) and the (a-moral) 'egoists' (who use one of their children as a meal ticket). While such a model could easily explain the results presented in Table 15.3, there is no rational reason for the egoists to arrive too late at the healthcare centre. Of course, the failure of the rational-choice hypothesis is merely an argument to deem *any* alternative explanation more probable.

---

[17] For technical details on sample composition and the calculation method for income indicators, see T. De Herdt, 'Surviving the Transition: institutional aspects of economic regress in Congo-Zaire', unpublished PhD thesis, University of Antwerp (2000).

Table 15.3 *Wealth characteristics of different types of households in Matete (Kinshasa)*

	Representative sample			F-value	ANOVA- Analysis		
	Well-nourished	Mal-nourished	Children receiving dry ration		Post-hoc analysis°: mean difference between		
					(1) and		(2) and (3)
	(1)	(2)	(3)		(2)	(3)	
Number of cases	64	10	21				
Per adult equivalent FOOD expenditures ($ per year)	282	146	191	2.85*	136*	91*	–45
Per adult equivalent TOTAL expenditures	700	414	428	4.79**	286**	272**	–14
% food expenditures/all real expenditures	62 %	65%	71%	2.66*	–.03	–.09*	–.06

°Least Significant Difference Test if homogeneity of variance can be assumed, and Tamhane's T2 test if homogeneity of variance is rejected by Levene's test.

* p < .1

** p < .05

Source: own survey, Matete 1996.

Step #2. There is ambiguity in the perception of reality, which makes the possibility of cognitive change more plausible.

The shame-induces-cognitive-change argument becomes more probable if we can prove that the set of cognitions is not fully specified, i.e. that there is some room for manoeuvre and interpretation. There are indications that such room exists in this particular case.

To begin with, it may be difficult to recognise that a child's symptoms are indicative of deficient nutrition. Usually the immediate cause of acute malnutrition is *illness*, not malnutrition *as such*. The problem is compounded by the fact that other children who are given the same food ration will not necessarily have the same symptoms. Further, the quantity consumed is less important than the degree of variation in consumption and, more generally, the quality of the food. For all these reasons, 'ordinary' knowledge is not very useful for validating the relationship between deficient food intake and symptoms of acute malnutrition[18] and, concomitantly, an entirely different reading of the symptoms becomes possible.

Further, there are many traditional interpretations of the symptoms of malnutrition to contend with. Sometimes, it is thought that undernourished children have become the target of sorcery or of an 'evil eye' within their (extended) families. If a person falls ill for no apparent reason or without an obvious root cause, sorcery is almost always seen as a possible explanation: perhaps a(n extended) family member sucked the lifeblood out of the child in order to reclaim whatever was previously taken from them.[19] However, while sorcery is sometimes considered as a possible cause, one tends to stop short of making a precise 'diagnosis'. Often, the symptoms of malnutrition are simply used as an argument to accuse a family member of witchcraft. The child's malnutrition is thus attributed to a family conflict, a transgression of certain 'traditional' norms, etc. There are of course different routes to 'resolve' such a conflict, depending on its type and depth, the

---

[18] In our case, the relation between deficient food intake and malnutrition could be categorised as what Boudon calls a 'type II belief', i.e. a belief that can be validated but is not (1996: 125).

[19] By way of illustration, we refer to one of our interviewees, who mentions a boy who used to live with his father after his parents' divorce. However, the stepmother claimed he had been bewitched by his biological mother in an attempt to kill his father. The child eventually decided to run away (Luzolele and De Herdt 1999: 27–8).

type of evildoer, and the type of communication channels between the conflicting parties. One possibility is to call on the services of a traditional healer, who can then give the child an 'antidote' that will protect it from evil forces. Note that readings whereby the symptoms of malnutrition are attributed to sorcery are hard to invalidate, as sorcery is traditionally believed to be practised 'at night' and 'behind one's back'. Furthermore, 'evidence' of sorcery is found precisely in the fact that it is generally accepted as an explanation. While one might assume that ignorance regarding the relationship between deficient food intake and symptoms of malnutrition can be easily resolved by organising training sessions on basic medical care for young mothers, it is a much harder proposition to invalidate witchcraft in a society where the power of nocturnal forces is considered so matter-of-course. Indeed, questioning these forces would be seen to invalidate the questioner rather than the nocturnal forces themselves.[20]

Wrong diagnoses do not necessarily and certainly not unambiguously result in wrong cures. Reading malnutrition in terms of sorcery does not necessarily imply that the child will not be cured. Many 'antidotes' administered by healers actually have a high nutritional value, e.g. the food concentrate from the red fruit of a tropical tree, which is supposed to compensate for any blood that has been sucked out of the child's body by a witch. Although in the case of what is known as *nsanga*, the child's symptoms are associated with unfaithfulness on the part of its mother, this perceived cause is not necessarily disconnected from medical and social reality: not only does sexual intercourse bring about hormonal changes that may affect the production of colostrum, but extramarital intercourse may also be an indicator of diminishing (or indeed total lack of) care for a child, which may in turn affect its nutritional status (Engle and Nieves 1993). To the extent that the latter aspect is significant, 'healing' of the family (e.g. through a 'payment' to the child's lineage as a means of rectifying the transgression of the rule) may indeed have a positive impact on the child that is measurable in terms of its nutritional status.[21]

---

[20] In Boudon's terms, sorcery may be categorised as a 'type III belief': it cannot be validated by an operation of confrontation with the real world (1996: 125).

[21] Future research should inquire into this: given that a growing number of children are brought up in the absence of their natural father, or even their mother, the diagnosis of *nsanga* seems to be rather likely, though it will be much more difficult to 'cure' it in the 'proper' way under these 'modern' circumstances.

Thus, given that reality is sufficiently ambiguous to assume that people will not necessarily make what *outsiders* would consider to be the most rational choice, we can restate the problem. Indeed, the issue is not so much that alternative readings of the symptoms of malnutrition are *ex ante* less probable. It is rather that these alternatives are *systematically favoured* over the explanation that the symptoms of malnutrition are caused by insufficient food intake, which, given the general circumstances, is at least as probable. Compare our argument to the troubleshooting algorithms used by computer experts. The problem is not that the list of alternative explanations for the symptoms of malnutrition is too long, but rather that the algorithm used to test the relevance of each of these symptoms seems to put the 'insufficient food intake' hypothesis last, while time is running out for the child to be cured.

Indeed, parents will tend first to visit a traditional healer or, more generally, to address what they regard to be the root cause of the child's symptoms before turning for help to the nutritional centre. This may also explain why parents do not consider the food that is offered at the nutritional centre to be normal: mothers often assume that 'they put some drug in the food'. As one mother put it, 'why should my child be cured by eating your flour, while it became ill eating my own?'[22] In this sense, the nutritional centres have become a new type of healer, a kind of healer-of-last-resort, that is capable of protecting people against the consequences of the evil eye, or of neutralising the malicious effects of adultery, though without the prospect of healing the root causes of the symptoms or restoring the social fabric surrounding the child.

Step #3. Some plausible cognitions enable people to avoid feeling ashamed.

A further step in our argument is that the insufficient-food-intake explanation is ignored for as long as possible, as such a diagnosis brings with it a sense of failure and humiliation. Some evidence of this line of reasoning is found in the interviews of households from the representative sample that we identified as 'poor' according to the income criterion (Luzolele and De Herdt 1999: 52–63).

---

[22] Quoted in M.-P. Monganza, 'Analyse des représentations sociales de la malnutrition dans la population de Kingabwa comme préalable essentiel pour une intervention nutritionnelle efficace'. Unedited Mphil dissertation, Université de Louvain (1997), p. 127.

In this context, we would, first and foremost, call attention to such frequently heard colloquialisms as 'we eat by the horoscope' and 'we eat by miracle'. To our modern minds, these sayings would appear to be unmistakable signals of crisis, but in fact they also emphasise the religious underpinnings of good health: an individual is healthy and able to feed himself and his family simply because he is blessed by the gods or by fate. Moreover, note that the notion of 'eating by miracle' does not imply that the *Kinois* consider themselves to be powerless or even void of responsibility *vis-à-vis* the supernatural forces that determine their existence. These forces are far from arbitrary, even if they are free to act as they wish. It follows that one can interpret the above expression as a reminder that the ambition of self-control and self-sufficiency is illusory. Thus, it is an admonition that one should show more rather than less respect for social norms; it provides an incentive to take more social responsibility, rather than to be fatalistic about the vagaries of life.

But if survival is seen in religious terms, failure to survive will, in the first place, be interpreted as a conflict with the gods, and, by inference, as a punishment for something that must have upset them. Indeed, the viewpoint that sorcery is a cause of malnutrition basically considers the symptoms of malnutrition as a punishment for transgressing social norms. Whatever may have been at the origin of these norms and explain their dynamics, to the extent that malnutrition is associated with the transgression of social norms by the (foster) parents of the malnourished child, the range of 'cures' is of course of a totally different order in such cases as compared to those where the symptoms of malnourishment are seen simply as an indication of *malnutrition*.

Shame is also connected in a different way with malnutrition. Several interviewees expressed their reluctance to go out and beg for food:

We don't like to beg, as tomorrow they will say 'he came here to beg'. The next visit, you might have gone there for a different reason, but they're going to think that you have returned to ask for money again. This is why we don't do it. To expose everyday problems or basic needs outside the home is almost taboo; to ask for something basic brings shame and it disrupts social ties. (Cited in Luzolele and De Herdt 1999: 58, my translation)

The point that the interviewee is making is not so much that a good relationship must be reciprocal, whereby a gift is returned in due time and with an overall balance between gifts and counter-gifts.[23] Rather, her point is that asking for food would 'spoil' the social relationship in the sense that the beggar can no longer perceive it to be truthful. Once the relationship has become compromised in this way, doubt creeps in, and this will undermine any subsequent attempt to make it intrinsically valuable again. In the same vein, the Kinois describe the poor (*babola*) as the lonely: '*Mobola* is a person without parents; he who lacks food is poor, because, if he doesn't eat, it's because he has no-one to give him food' (cited in Luzolele and De Herdt 1999: 63, my translation).

It is worth noting that the taboo on begging seems to be restricted mainly to the domain of daily needs, and especially food. One can ask for help to pay for tuition fees or healthcare costs, but not food. Although we did not inquire deeply into this issue, we feel the phenomenon may be seen as a remnant of a predominantly agricultural society, where land was abundant and where the amount of food available depended largely on the amount of effort that was put into working the land. In this context, shortage of food is associated with laziness.

Thus, if it is indeed the case that, as the interviewee above stated, 'if someone lacks food, this must be because (s)he has no-one to give him food', participating in a food aid programme is equivalent to admitting that one has failed, not only as a care provider but also, and more importantly, as a social being. Or, as a staff member at the healthcare centre in Kisenso put it:

We see many such cases: persons who, if they don't have money themselves, and even if the sister [i.e. the head of the healthcare centre, TDH] can help them by selling some maize, they don't have the courage to come and ask for assistance. Some children die because of their parents' shame. (Cited in Luzolele and De Herdt 1999: 63, my translation).

Participating in a food aid programme is inevitably seen as an obvious sign of poverty. Why else would a person admit publicly or even privately that (s)he is unable to feed his (or her) children?

Step #4. There are no relevant 'secondary' norms whereby the people involved can define exceptions to the norm that invokes shame in them.

Norms are never absolute: there are inevitably circumstances in which exceptions become permissible. These exceptions are justified through

---

[23] In the vocabulary of the gift economy, asking for food implies that the gift can no longer be given *voluntarily*, and that it is therefore not a gift that unites.

secondary or adjunct norms. Typically, every social norm is accompanied by a set of clearly demarcated loopholes that define exceptions and/or excuses for deviating from the primary norm (Elster 1989; Ainslie 1992). Such loopholes may also be expected to exist in relation to the norm that associates the acceptance of food aid with laziness, social failure and irresponsible behaviour.

One such loophole allows us to reinterpret the behaviour of people who seek assistance from the food aid programme despite the existence of a strong norm against it. The reason for shame disappears if one can blame a child's malnutrition on the irresponsible behaviour of others, or even on the child itself. If, for example, one can say credibly to oneself that the malnourished child has been bewitched and is hence already socially dead, there is no need to feel ashamed. In fact, taking such a child to the healthcare centre may be interpreted by the general public as an act of humanity. At the same time, however, children who are considered socially dead are, for this very reason, likely to face different treatment at home too. They are more likely to be stigmatised, and, if the phenomenon of meal-ticket children were quantifiable, we would probably find a high proportion of such children among them.

Although we were unable to prove this hypothesis directly, we have some evidence concerning a similar group of children. A frequently heard expression is *mwana na mwana na tata naye* ('every child has its own father'). It may be used as an excuse by a child's extended family members (on the mother's side) to deny any responsibility for its health after the father has disappeared, even though the child is growing up in its mother's family.

Table 15.4 summarises some other results of the survey conducted in Matete. It allows us to show the relevance of this excuse in terms of child malnutrition.

Indeed, it appears[24] that there are significant differences between the composition of households with well-nourished children (first column) and those of the two groups of households with malnourished children. Whereas 60 per cent of children in the former group belong to the nuclear bi-parental family that constitutes the backbone of the household, this

---

[24] To be sure, a more complete analysis should control for other, relevant intervening variables, such as income. As has been demonstrated elsewhere, income (or wealth) can indeed influence both the percentage of unmarried mothers and nutritional status, though the net effect of an absent father does not disappear if we control for this (De Herdt 2004).

Table 15.4 Characteristics of children and households in Matete (Kinshasa)

| | Representative sample | | Children receiving Dry ration | F-value | ANOVA- Analysis | | |
| | Well-nourished | Mal-nourished | | | Post-hoc analysis: mean difference between | | |
	(1)	(2)	(3)		(1) and (2)	(1) and (3)	(2) and (3)
Number of household members	10.4	14.8	14.1	6.15***	−4.4**	−3.8***	.61
% not of the nuclear family	34%	35%	33%	.02	−.005	.01	.02
% of same or older generation than household head	18%	3%	2%	6.54***	.15***	.16***	.007
% children 0–6 years	22%	20%	28%	2.79*	.02	−.06**	−.08*
Of which % children of head	60%	23%	27%	6.26***	.37*	.34***	−.04
% (great) grandchildren	32%	77%	73%	9.84***	−.45***	−.41***	.04
% other extended family	8%	0%	0%	1.52	.08**	.08**	–
% of children with father absent	34%	50%	59%	2.86*	−.16	−.26**	−.09

°Least Significant Difference Test if homogeneity of variance can be assumed, and Tamhane's T2 test if homogeneity of variance is rejected by Levene's test of homogeneity of variance.

*p < .1

**p < .05

***p < .001 Percentages are mean percentages.

Source: own survey, Matete 1996.

is only about 25 per cent in the latter group. Moreover, 50 per cent of malnourished children who are not assisted by the food emergency programme are being raised by a lone mother, compared with only 34 per cent of well-nourished children. Among malnourished but assisted children, finally, the proportion is 59 per cent.

However, could one not argue that, even if there are strong moral norms opposing it, the 'exceptional' circumstances of the socio-economic crisis that has ravaged Kinshasa constitute yet another loophole? This certainly seems to have been the reasoning of MSF, whose intervention was triggered by a looting spree in Kinshasa in September 1991. It would appear, then, that this is a valid argument. Still, we cannot possibly judge the exceptional nature of the situation from the outside. While the looting may have been exceptional enough for donors, it is important to note that it was merely another phase in a long process of economic and social decline, and, for that matter, by no means the most exceptional phase. The looting was preceded by major political, macro-economic and monetary shocks in the 1960s, 1970s and 1980s. Three months earlier, Kinshasa had been swept by so-called pyramid games that eventually caused a collapse of the banking sector. Moreover, the looting of 1991 was followed by similar incidents in January 1993, the monetary chaos of October 1993, hyperinflation in 1994, etc. (De Herdt 2002).

Finally, the question arises as to whether the general climate of lawlessness and disintegration of the social landscape in Kinshasa might have provided people with the ultimate excuse for ignoring a social norm. In this context, I would argue against the view that every notion of justice, of rights and duties, has disappeared with the collapse of the modern state. Indeed, the opposite may well be true: as legality became a source of injustice, local notions of justice might have become more salient reference points for identifying the rights and duties of the *Kinois*. As a consequence, in order to be able to appeal to the norms that guarantee one's rights, one must first gain social respect, and this implies that one should assume one's responsibilities. As it turns out, the domain of food is typically an area where mothers bear the brunt of responsibility and where, if they fail, they risk losing their social existence.

I conclude that our considerations of public shame suggest that the implicit contract between the healthcare workers and parents caring for malnourished children is paradoxical. Those who would be interested *ex post* in respecting the terms of the contract actually prefer not to sign it *ex ante*, while those who are inclined to agree *ex ante* do so for the same reasons that prevent them from complying *ex post*. It is precisely because the supplementary feeding programme targets the malnourished that it will not reach the malnourished with caring parents. After all, the latter will want to avoid exhibiting signs of poverty. This will cause them either to avoid being seen in public spaces that are associated with the food relief programme, or to favour those interpretations of reality that enable them to maintain their self-respect. It is, most likely, this inability to appear in public without shame that heavily constrains the agency of the caretakers, and, by implication, undermines the programme's effectiveness.

Capability-oriented reasoning, plural concerns and public shame

The material discussed above allows us, I think, to make some more general observations about capability oriented reasoning in formulating and executing social policy.

As mentioned in the introduction, the effectiveness of targeting sometimes depends, wholly or partly, on decisions by the potential and would-be clients of targeted programmes. I agree with Sen that capabilities may be assumed to better reflect people's personal decisional concerns than the narrow focus on income, and that capability-oriented reasoning may therefore be instrumental to social policy-makers. However, the case study of food relief in Kinshasa also strongly suggests that Sen's instrumental argument for the capability approach is not convincing if one does not take adequate account of the plurality of concerns inherent in capability-oriented reasoning. In this particular case, I have documented the hypothesis that the ability to appear in public without shame is one of the more relevant determinants of human agency and thus of the programme's effectiveness. I also believe that this finding may be generalised to other areas of social policy, including those for which Sen assumes that 'built-in matching' will *prima facie* resolve the incentive problem. Even if literate people have no incentive to attend school and healthy people see no need to visit a medical centre, this only resolves one part of the targeting problem: you still need to secure effective access to all the illiterate and the unhealthy. Taking into account the above analysis, I argue that capability-oriented reasoning that emphasises plural concerns is very useful in identifying the diversity of factors that might effectively exclude people from making use of a particular service. More specifically, one needs to be aware that effective exclusion from social services – which inevitably reduces the effectiveness of these services – is not only a matter of material deprivation.

But there are further connections between the ability to appear in public without shame as one of the fundamental determinants of human agency and public policy initiatives. Consider the following example: 'One way to discourage people [to depend on charity] is to make it very clear that they lower their esteem when they ask for charity. The same psychology can be used to encourage recipients to leave the relief rolls as fast as they can' (Rainwater 1982: 28). The question therefore arises whether public shame can be utilised to improve targeting.

There are, I think, two major arguments against this view. To begin with, the manner in which we operationalised the concept of public shame enables us to disagree with such a strategy. As I noted above (proposition #5), shame is not necessarily a merely additional cost, but it can also influence cognitions. In this particular instance, the really needy might *postpone asking for food relief for too long*, while the would-be needy might exploit a loophole to avoid shame when asking for food. Thus, the tactic of lowering the beneficiaries' self-esteem will not necessarily have the intended result. Further, public shame is not merely instrumentally important as a determinant of human agency, it is also an intrinsic constituent of well-being. Sen himself subscribes to John Rawls's argument that self-respect is 'perhaps the most important primary good' (Sen 1995: 13; 1999: 136). It would thus not be very sensible to have people 'pay' for resolving one kind of deprivation with another.

However, doubt immediately sets in if we try to think the latter argument through. Although self-respect is perhaps the most important primary good, attaining a shameless society should never be a political ideal. I would agree with Margalit's distinction between a *shameless* society and a *decent* society. It might at least be helpful if members of decent societies were ashamed of acts of humiliation and abuse that exist there. Moreover, decent societies should allow each individual as much freedom as possible to express his or her identity with the features that he or she finds most suitable. This inevitably implies that the political game of identity construction, reconstruction and imposition must go on, and, by inference, that the 'losers' of this game will suffer 'public shame'. The elimination of every possible source of shame can probably only be achieved at the cost of the right to self-expression, which is arguably also a constituent of well-being and a determinant of self-respect.

However, we feel that societies striving towards decency should distinguish themselves from other societies mainly in that they try to *regulate* these politics of identity in two ways. As I have previously argued, not every identity is equally important. Bad football players and bad parents are fundamentally different. Societies striving towards decency should thus give priority to eliminating the more important sources of shame. Additionally, the observation that shame varies between public spaces indicates that we can, once again, set priorities in this respect and try to free *the most important* public spaces from the politics of identity. Those institutions that are most powerful and that represent society as a whole are potentially the more harmful humiliators, and they should therefore be given priority in a social policy aimed at combating public shame.

At this point, I return to Rainwater's argument that public shame can be used as a mechanism to improve targeting effectiveness. Food aid is arguably thoroughly humiliating, as it implicitly questions the recipient's membership of some of the most important identities (parenthood, motherhood) and as it is the state itself (through its public healthcare centres) that does the questioning. However, the problem with such aid is perhaps that it is insufficiently targeted towards the 'truly' indigent according to local notions of justice. Food aid must remain a clearly demarcated exception to the local practices surrounding food production, distribution and consumption. I concur with Mackintosh and Tibandebage (2002) that close collaboration between communities and facilities seems the best way to define such exemption schemes if indeed they are deemed necessary.

Annex: Specification of indicators of household wealth

We identified three separate measures of household wealth. Consider the following formula:

$$W(\alpha, \theta)_h = \frac{X_h}{(Adults_h + \alpha Children_h)^{\theta}}$$

with

$w(\alpha, \theta)_H$ = indicator of household h's wealth, function of parameters α
        and θ,

x_H = measure of household-level wealth,

α = equivalence factor to convert children's consumption into
        adult equivalents, $0 < \alpha < 1$, and

θ = factor expressing scale economies, $0 < \theta < 1$.

On the basis of the above formula, we first calculate a child-neutral and scale-neutral measure of total household income as

$$T(.7, .85)_h = \frac{Y_h}{(Adults_h + .7^*Children_h)^{.85}}$$

with Y_h = total real outlays + imputed rent for house-owners.[25]

Further, an indicator supposedly much closer to the indicator of malnutrition is

$$F(.7, 1)_h = \frac{F_h}{(Adults_h + .7^*Children_h)}$$

with F_h = food outlays at the household-level. The scale parameter $\theta = 1$, reflecting the common assumption that there are virtually no scale economies in food consumption.

Finally, there is a variable that measures household quality. This variable is a summary measure of different qualitative aspects of housing infrastructure, like the presence or absence of a toilet, a kitchen, quality of the roof and road paving. It is expressed in terms of monthly rent by means of a simple linear regression between the housing quality variable and the rent paid by occupants. Housing quality is supposed to be dependent neither on the number of household members, nor on the composition of the household:

Cited references

Ainslie, G. 1992. *Picoeconomics; the strategic interaction of successive motivational states within the person.* Cambridge: Cambridge University Press

Akerlof, G. A. and Dickens, W. T. 1982. 'The economic consequences of cognitive dissonance', *American Economic Review* 72, 3: 307–319

---

[25] For a discussion on the choice of the parameter values, see T. De Herdt, 'Surviving the Transition ...' pp. II.9 – II.15.

Becker, G. S. 1996. *Accounting for tastes*. Cambridge MA/England: Harvard University Press

Boltanski, L. 1993. *La souffrance à distance; morale politique, médias et politique*. Paris: Métailié

Boudon, R. 1996. 'The "cognitivist model": a generalised "rational-choice model"', *Rationality and Society* 8, 2: 123–150

Boudon, R. 1997. 'The moral sense', *Rationality and Society* 12, 1: 5–24

De Herdt, T. 2000. 'Surviving the transition: institutional aspects of economic regress in Congo-Zaire.' Unpublished PhD thesis, University of Antwerp

De Herdt, T. 2002. 'Democracy and the money machine in Zaire', *Review of African Political Economy* 93/94: 445–462

De Herdt, T. 2004. 'Hidden families, lone mothers and "cibalabala": Economic regress and changing household composition in Kinshasa' in T. Trefon (ed.) *Re-inventing order in Kinshasa*. London: Zed Books, pp. 138–152

Deguerry, M. 1994. 'Rapport de mission (mars).' Unedited document, Kinshasa: MSF Brussles

Elster, J. 1989. *The cement of society; a study of social order*. Cambridge: Cambridge University Press

Elster, J. 1992. *Local Justice; how institutions allocate scarce goods and necessary burdens*. New York: Cambridge University Press

Elster, J. 1994. 'Rationality, emotions and social norms', *Synthese* 98: 21–49

Engle, P. L. and Nieves, I. 1993 'Intra-household food distribution among Guatemalan families in a supplementary feeding programme: mothers' perceptions', *Food and Nutrition Bulletin* 14, 4: 314–322

Goodin, R. E. 1988. *Reasons for welfare; the political theory of the welfare state*. Princeton New Jersey: Princeton University Press

Luzolele, L. and De Herdt, T. 1999. *La pauvreté urbaine en Afrique Subsaharienne; Le cas de Kinshasa*. Kinshasa: CEPAS

Mackintosh, M. and Tibandebage, P. 2002. 'Inclusion by design? Rethinking healthcare market regulation in the Tanzanian context', *Journal of Development Studies* 39, 1: 1–20

Margalit, A. 1998. *The decent society*. Cambridge MA: Harvard University Press

Meyer, B. and Geschiere, P. 1999. 'Globalization and identity; dialectics of flow and closure' in B. Meyer and P. Geschiere (eds.) *Globalization and identity; dialectics of flow and closure*. Oxford: Blackwell Publishers, pp. 1–16

Monganza, M.-P. 1997. 'Analyse des représentations sociales de la malnutrition dans la population de Kingabwa comme préalable essentiel pour une intervention nutritionnelle efficace.' Unedited Mphil dissertation, Université de Louvain

Mosley, W. H. and Chen, L. C. 1984. 'An analytical framework for the study of child survival in developing countries' in W. H. Mosley and L. C. Chen (eds.) *Child survival; strategies for research Supplement to Population and Development Review* 10: 25–45

MSF-Belgium 1995. 'Thrimonthly report of the project of nutritional assistance to malnourished children in Kinshasa-Zaire; May–June–July 1995.' Unedited document, Kinshasa: MSF-archives

Ngondo, S. De St.-Moulin, L. and Tambashe, B. 1993. *Perspectives démographiques du Zaïre 1984–1999 et population d'âge électoral en 1993 et 1994*. Kinshasa: CEPAS

Quattrone, G. A. and Tversky, A. 1986. 'Self-deception and the voter's illusion' in J. Elster (ed.) *The multiple self*. Oxford: Oxford University Press, pp. 35–58

Rainwater, L. 1982. 'Stigma in income-tested programmes' in I. Garfinkel (ed.) *Income-tested transfer programmes; the case for and against*. New York: Academic Press, pp. 19–66

Sen, A. K. 1985. 'Well-being, agency and freedom; the Dewey lectures 1984' in *The Journal of Philosophy* 87, 4 (April): 169–221

Sen, A. K. 1995. 'The political economy of targeting' in D. Van de Walle and K. Nead (eds.) *Public spending and the poor: theory and evidence*. Washington: IBRD, pp. 11–25

Sen, A. K. 1999. *Freedom as development*. Oxford: Oxford University Press

Sen, A. K. 2000. *Social exclusion: concept, application, and scrutiny*. Asian Development Bank Social Development papers n° 1

Smith, A. 1976 [1790] *The theory of moral sentiments* (ed.) D. D. Raphael, A. L. Macfie, Oxford: Clarendon Press

Smith, A. 1979 [1791] *An inquiry into the nature and causes of the wealth of nations* R. H. Campbell and A. S. Skinner (eds.) Oxford: Clarendon Press (2 vols)

Vanderhaegen, W. 1998. 'Growing importance of emergency aid: healthy or not?' Unedited document, Antwerp: University of Antwerp.

Vautier, F. 1995. 'Rapport de mission 3–4/95.' Unedited document, Kinshasa: MSF Brussels

16

The capability approach and gendered education: some issues of operationalisation in the context of the HIV/AIDs epidemic in South Africa

ELAINE UNTERHALTER[1]

Education appears untheorised in Amartya Sen's writings about the capability approach. In a brief section in the closing chapter of *Development as Freedom* the contrast is drawn between human capital theory, long the dominant trend in analyses of education in the third world, with human capability:

the substantive freedom of people to lead the lives they have reason to value and enhance the real choices they have. (Sen 1999: 293)

Sen describes the way human capital theory and the capability approach emphasise different elements of what is valued. Within a framework of human capital there is a narrow conception of the contribution of education to a limited range of indirect benefits for individuals, for example improving production or family income over generations.

The notion of capability, however, implies a larger scope of benefits from education which includes enhancing well-being and freedom of individuals and peoples, improving economic production and influencing social change (Sen 1999: 293–6). The problematic, but unstated, assumption in this passage and repeated in Sen's writing on education in India with Jean Drèze (Drèze and Sen 1989; Drèze and Sen 1995;

[1] Thanks to Michael Young and Bob Cowen for comments on earlier drafts and to Harry Brighouse, Ingrid Robeyns and Melanie Walker for ongoing conversations and detailed critiques of work in progress on capabilities. An earlier version of this chapter was published as 'The capabilities approach and gendered education: An examination of South African complexities' in *Theory and Research in Education*, Vol. 1, No. 1, 7–22. Thanks to Jenny Parkes for checking the amended manuscript.

Drèze and Sen 2002) is that the form of education linked with substantive freedom can unproblematically be equated with schooling. As stated, it is implied that evaluating only a very limited range of functionings that relates to the domain of schooling, such as enrolment and retention or a narrow notion of literacy, capabilities relating to education can be metonymically assessed.

Sen's writing on capability and justice is concerned with inequality and difference, and he is particularly sensitive to the ways certain social formations may entail women's complicity with gender injustice through adaptive preference (Sen 1995). Given these concerns, his consideration of education, which fails to take sufficient account of contestations and complicities predicated on unequal social relations within schools, is surprising. The analysis he makes in much of his writing where education is mentioned often takes no account of differences in form or outcome of education. It is not concerned, for example, with the questions raised by curriculum in different education systems, particularly issues of the hierarchy of subjects. These are frequently associated with assumptions about learning linked to gender identities, for example that girls cannot or should not learn mathematics or other high status subjects, or boys should not learn about childcare. Nor is his writing concerned with the different modalities of education – processes of learning, teaching, assessment and management – and their differing and sometimes contradictory consequences for different groups. There is a remarkable homogeneity in the way Sen discusses education, a homogeneity that raises problems and leads to difficulties particularly when the passages are read as examples of the capabilities approach operationalised.

In this chapter I want to draw out some of the difficulties with these assumptions on the uniformity of education. This is not because I am hostile to the aspirations entailed in Sen's writing on capability, which I share, but because of the considerable empirical evidence that education, or at least formal schooling in particular contexts, may as much be a case of capability deprivation, as of human capability in development. In thinking about operationalising the capability approach I am concerned with the specific consideration given to complementary social theories that enable us to understand relations entailed by education and schooling. These theories need to be viewed not just as background context to an evaluative space but as having profound implications for how that space is understood.

I want to examine these issues at two levels. In the first part of the chapter I detail the ways in which Sen positions education in his exposition of capabilities. In the second part I look at a policy approach to HIV/AIDS initiated in 2000 by the Department of Education in South Africa and try to consider how the capability approach might be operationalised in evaluating this and what additional information might be needed. In the concluding section I return to a consideration of the capability approach in an attempt to explore how thinking about education raises not only the importance of capability for political and social analysis, which is the way in which Sen has framed the argument (Sen 1993: 45). A more refined theorisation of education raises questions that remain unresolved in the capability approach, questions that entail a consideration of how the approach locates and defines its relationship to political and social analysis.

Education and capabilities

Sen's deployment of the concept of capability, 'the alternative combinations of things a person is able to do or be' (Sen 1993), emerged out of his critiques of utilitarianism and Rawls' theory of justice (Sen 1980). While utilitarianism fails to engage with problems of equality, Rawls' notion of justice as fairness focuses on this as a central concern. Sen's critique aims at a key assumption in Rawls' second principle of difference, which he finds problematic. This principle demands efficiency and equality with regard to the needs of the worst off. These needs are defined in terms of access to primary social goods. Sen points out that if issues of distribution and justice rest on a passive ascription of need regarding primary social goods, key dimensions of inequity that relate to agency and the differences between people with regard to need are occluded (Sen 1980). In developing the concept of capability Sen is able to deploy arguments about freedom and functionings or active constructions of 'doing and being'. Justice is not 'done to', as implied by Rawls' work, but is 'done with' the active participation of individuals. Sen distinguishes between narrow measurements of wellbeing like standard of living, and contrasts these with wellbeing and agency achievement, both signalled by the more expansive and active concept of capability (Sen 1993).

Sen's conceptualisation of capability is, like utilitarianism and Rawls' theory of justice, a normative ethical theory. Harry Brighouse has observed that one cannot simply read off policy implications regarding education from theories that are posed at this level of generality. However, paying attention to the implications of utilising a theory of egalitarian justice in deciding between good and bad education policies yields important insights regarding hitherto unquestioned assumptions (Brighouse 2001). Interestingly, Sen has not scrutinised education policies through the lens of the capability approach in the way in which he has examined general policies regarding poverty and famine (Drèze and Sen 1989; Sen 1999). Although he does utilise education statistics extensively in his work with Jean Drèze, the foundational insights of the work on famine relating to democracy, distribution and differential needs are not discussed in relation to education, although many similar points could be made. I will attempt to undertake aspects of the examination of education policy in relation to the capability approach in the second section of the chapter, but before turning to this I want to point out the ways in which Sen discusses education. In this examination I will concentrate on his writing on capabilities, aimed at a wide readership, in *Development as Freedom* (Sen 1999) and his presentations for an audience specifically concerned with education (Sen 2002; Sen 2003).

Education appears in *Development as Freedom* in three guises. First, it appears as a feature of capability space, a very loosely defined set of facilities or arrangements that *enable* freedom. *Facilities* for education, Sen outlines, are a feature of 'the social and economic *arrangements*' on which freedom depends (Sen 1999: 3; my italics). Here education is an uncontoured space, unmarked by contested power, history, or social division. Education merges into schooling. But this is a problematic assumption. There are some forms of schooling on which freedom does not depend, or where the relationship to freedom is complex. For example, schooling linked to indoctrination into a racial hierarchy, such as what occurred under apartheid in South Africa, could not simply be understood as the social arrangements on which freedom depended. Although undoubtedly that form of schooling, for all its inadequacies, did contribute to the conditions out of which a democratic society emerged, but for many decades it also contributed to the reproduction of repression (Kallaway 1984).

Elsewhere, Sen makes clear that both opportunities (facilities) and processes, for example regarding education, are necessary to give substance to his view of freedom (Sen 1999: 17). But again this formulation does not distinguish between education and schooling. It does not take account of education facilities or processes that might not enhance freedom, such as those evident in village schools within some states in India where girls might learn subordination. This may be because they are forced to sit at the back of classrooms in the dark or because the ways in which they are portrayed in textbooks are always demeaning and derogatory (Kumar 1989). In a number of autobiographical texts written by South African women it is evident that they learn aspects of subordination through schooling. They depict themselves as gaining a wider education about social inequalities through participation in political opposition movements and reflections on the ways their bodies were racialised and gendered (Unterhalter 1999).

A second way in which education appears in Sen's writing on capability is in a causal or influential relationship with individual freedom or functionings. Because freedom is a social *product*, education (a social arrangement) is implied to have a decisive link to freedom.

The central role of individual freedoms in the process of development makes it particularly important to examine their determinants. Substantial attention has to be paid to the social influences, including state actions, which help to determine the nature and reach of individual freedoms. *Social arrangements may be decisively important in securing and expanding the freedom of the individual.* On one side, the social safeguarding of liberties, tolerance, and the possibilities of exchange and transactions influence individual freedoms. On the other side, they are also influenced, by substantive public support in the provision of those facilities (such as basic health care or *essential education) that are crucial for the formation and use of human capabilities* (Sen 1999: 41–2; italics are mine).

It can be seen that Sen uses a loose formulation of the social aspect to point out what may be 'decisively important' in securing and expanding the freedom of the individual. Education and schooling are suggested in this formulation. But later in the paragraph Sen writes that 'essential education', is 'crucial', virtually causal in forming capabilities. If 'essential education' is read as basic schooling, an elision Sen frequently makes, for example in his paper on basic education and human security (Sen 2002), this is too narrow a formulation. Schooling might not always contribute to forming capabilities. Schooling is probably necessary, but not sufficient for this. The point that needs emphasis is that it is quality schooling that encourages learning and reflection, as well as achievement as recognised by the official assessment system that is crucial for the formation of capabilities. The capability approach might indeed help shed light on what quality schooling is and how decisions concerning curriculum or pedagogy are made. I have attempted some of this in my work with Harry Brighouse which considers overlapping dimensions of education that address its intrinsic, positional and instrumental value (Unterhalter and Brighouse 2003). But this more expansive utilisation of the approach is not possible if a narrow reading is made and suggests that any schooling (essential education) is crucial to the formation and use of human capabilities.

Another version of this position sees human capability as co-terminous with education (Sen 1999: 293) in much the same ways as human capital theory viewed human capital formation (skill) as the core of education. Here education not only causes freedom, capabilities and development, it is also constitutive of both. From this vantage point the processes and facilities for education, sketched as conditions or opportunity arrangements, disappear in the first delineation. Education is twinned with freedom or capabilities and the assumption that education will always be beneficial, an enhancement of freedom, and as such a component of capability. This might well be the case given the fullest meaning of education, but it is not necessarily always the case with schooling. An early passage from *Hunger and Public Action* illustrates these elisions at work:

A person's capability to avoid undernourishment may depend not merely on his or her intake of food, but also on the person's access to health care, medical facilities, elementary education, drinking water and sanitary facilities. (Drèze and Sen 1989: 13)

While the general point regarding the expansive and active nature of capabilities is persuasive, questions about the quality of the health care, medical facilities and elementary education the person has access to and chooses to make use of are excluded. To what extent does the capability approach to evaluation of freedom allow us to consider these questions and how might deficiencies in the quality of schooling or health have a bearing on capabilities?

A theory which makes a causal link between education and capability is problematic because sometimes education, particularly that in schools, is not an enlargement of freedom. This is evident for example in the vexed question of the appropriate language of instruction, which in multilingual societies generally entails a curtailment of freedom if a single language is privileged. Another example is the way that subordinated groups, like girls or children of particular racialised or ethnicised groups 'learn their place' of unfreedom when they enter school (for some examples see Aikman 1999; Gillborn 1995; Vally and Dalamba 1999; Unterhalter 1999).

Third, education as described in Sen's work appears as a result of capability in the guise of particular knowledge and basic educational skills that enhance participatory freedom. Here education does not disappear into the general definition of human capability, or find itself neutrally sketched as 'facilities' or 'opportunities'. Rather, education is a particular set of 'hard' outcomes, most notably literacy or other particular skills valued on the labour market, or linked in the case of women's literacy with enhanced child survival, or resulting more generally in enhanced social participation (Sen 1999: 191–2). Because literacy and numeracy are considered measurable outcomes, it is this understanding of education and human capability that has been most widely and powerfully used in comparative studies across countries and regions. It has been a feature of work by Sen and others who draw on his approach (see e.g. Drèze and Sen 1995; UNDP 1990; UNDP 1995). The commentaries in the UNDP reports indicate that gross and net enrolment ratios, school retention rates, and the compilation of an education index are all proxies for indicating the way education is linked to an expansion of freedom (UNDP 2000: 8). But these indicators are generally not understood as proxies by governments and their officials seeking to translate education policy into practice. The indicator of enrolment or achievement in a test is seen as 'education' and this is what teachers and district education officials are instructed to achieve. Thus 'education' becomes a narrow set of performative measures (Unterhalter and Brighouse 2003). This narrow understanding of outcome is in its own way as inadequate as using income levels to measure economic opportunities. Measurements of literacy, even acknowledging them as proxies, can tell us something about education and participatory freedom, but they cannot tell us if certain groups can put their literacy to work to enhance their participation in society. Indeed much of the work in critical literacy studies highlights how difficult it is for dominated groups to utilise their literacy when gender, racial or ethnic discrimination and injustice persists (Street 1995; Prinsloo and Breier 1996; Robinson-Pant 2000). We therefore need to operationalise the capability approach by drawing on a richer informational base.

Sen's exposition of capability thus elides different meanings and connotations of education and schooling – namely aims, processes and outcomes. Why these elisions are not immediately apparent or confusing in his work is because of his common assumption in all discussion that education is linked either through correlation or causation with freedom and that everything that happens in schools is education valorised in this way. Ideally this would be so, but a great virtue of Sen's work is that it is not a mere exercise in 'ideal theory.' It seeks to give guidance for action in the actual, unjust world we inhabit. In this world some forms of education do not enhance freedom, or may do so only partially and in contradictory ways. Sen acknowledged this very briefly in his address to the Commonwealth Ministers of Education, but it has not been a major feature of his work and these comments were not related to the theoretical implications of the capability approach (Sen 2003). It is these diverse effects of education that will be examined in Section two when the capability approach to evaluation is applied in examining a policy response from the South African Department of Education to the HIV/AIDS pandemic.

The capability approach and policy on gender, HIV/AIDs and education in South Africa

South Africa provides an interesting example of complexities and ambiguities in education and thus provides a wide scope for illustrating some of the difficulties in the positioning of education in Sen's writing on capabilities. In this section I want to look at what happens when one attempts to apply the capabilities approach to evaluating policies of the South African government for dealing with some of the gender dimensions of the HIV/AIDS epidemic.

The apartheid regime had used education as a major component of strategies for segregation and inequality (Kallaway 1984; Unterhalter *et al.* 1991). With its end the 1996 Constitution gave all those living in South Africa the right to basic education, including adult basic education, and committed the state 'through reasonable measures' to make education, beyond four years of basic education, 'available and accessible to all' (South Africa 1996: 14). The 1996 Schools Act abolished the different departments of education of the apartheid era that had perpetuated inequity in provision. A range of funding mechanisms, a national qualifications framework, a common curriculum approach and extensive in service training of teachers (in contrast to the previous era) have been used to try to redress some of the inequities in provision from the past. But their impact has been relatively slow to take effect.

The racialised injustices of apartheid education were pre-eminent for those formulating education policy for the new democratic society, but gender injustices in education were not ignored. However, with the exception of some policy in higher education, the national Department of Education has been much less attentive to issues of gender justice than other aspects of equality. It has been particularly slow in implementing the recommendations of its Gender Equity Task Team which reported in 1997 (Wolpe, Quinlan and Martinez 1997; Daniels 2001; De La Rey 2001; Ramagoshi, 2005).

Into this climate of slow but nonetheless significant reform, the scale of the HIV/AIDS epidemic came as a major shock. In the 1980s South Africans saw HIV/AIDS as primarily a disease of gay white men. At the time of the first democratic election the rate of HIV infection was still relatively low in South Africa, compared with central and eastern Africa. However, by the end of the decade infection rates had escalated dramatically. In 2000 it was estimated that 4.2 million people were HIV positive. This meant that at that time South Africa had the largest numbers of people with HIV in the world (UNAIDS 2002). The numbers infected represented nearly one quarter of the population (24.8 per cent) (UNAIDS 2003). However, the numbers affected as partners, children, family members, friends, community members, professionals, political representatives, workmates or employers were much larger. Women were estimated to comprise approximately 56 per cent of those infected, with the single largest group of women comprising those aged 15–34 (Whiteside and Sunter 2000).

Treatment for those who were HIV positive in South Africa had been very limited until the government announced it would make anti-retroviral drugs available in 2003. While access to cheaper treatment will make a difference in the future, to date the time span between infection and death associated with AIDs has been very short. Researchers for the South African Medical Research Council have described the epidemic as a series of waves. The number of people infected with AIDS peaked in 1998 with approximately 930,000 infections a year; the highest number of people living with AIDS was expected to peak around 2006 with 7–8 million infected. The wave of deaths from AIDS-related illnesses is expected to reach a high point in 2010 with an estimated 800,000 deaths a year, although improved access to treatment might have a dramatic effect on this. The numbers of HIV/AIDS orphans is estimated to peak in 2015 with nearly 2 million orphaned children (Bradshaw, Johnson *et al.* 2002).

The level of HIV infection in schools is unknown as of yet. The HIV/AIDS database of the US Bureau of Census using population-based HIV survey evidence for 2002 estimated that in the 15–19 age range in South Africa 7.3 per cent of young women and 4 per cent of young men were HIV positive (US Bureau of Census 2003). A study in 2000 in Kwazulu Natal province estimated that amongst 15–19 years olds, the vast majority of whom are in school, 15.64 per cent of African girls were likely to be HIV positive compared with 2.58 per cent of African boys (Morrell, Unterhalter, Moletsane and Epstein 2001). The equivalent figures for other racialised groups were infection rates of 1.25 per cent for teenage white and Coloured school girls, 0.26 per cent for white and Coloured school boys of the same age and 1.29 per cent for Indian teenage schoolgirls and 0.26 per cent of Indian teenage school boys. The dramatic differences are the result partly of teenage African girls having or being coerced into sex with older men, also a group with high infection rates.

This information on the gendered dimension of HIV infection must be read in conjunction with related material on the high levels of sexual violence in South Africa. In 1998, according to Rape Crisis, there were 49,280 rapes reported. This was the highest rate of reported rape in the world, representing 115.6 rapes for every 100,000 of the population. These reports use a narrow definition of sexual violence when classifying rape. In addition, it is estimated that only 29 per cent of rapes are reported to the police. Extrapolating from these figures and using a wider definition of rape to include oral sex and rape with objects, the Rape Crisis Centre has arrived at a figure of 1,086,200 rapes per year, or an estimated one rape every 23 seconds somewhere in the country (Rape Crisis 2001).

Sexual violence is a significant feature of South African schools. In a Human Rights Watch study published in April 2001, the considerable anecdotal evidence of high levels of rape and other forms of sexual violence in schools collected over many years (see Marks 1987; Wolpe, Quinlan and Martinez 1997; Unterhalter 2002a) was confirmed and augmented (Human Rights Watch 2001). This large-scale study based on extensive interviews with learners, teachers, parents and school administrators in three provinces of South Africa documented how widespread sexual violence is and how it takes place in schools and on the way to school. Male teachers and young male pupils were frequently major perpetrators. The report acknowledges efforts by the government and women's rights organisations to try to deal with this long-existing pattern, but says that in practice the education departments and school governance bodies rarely do anything. The procedures and practices that exist for dealing with sexual violence in schools are grossly inadequate (Human Rights Watch 2001). This work is corroborated by other surveys. A study in Johannesburg in 1998 found that one schoolgirl in three had been raped (Rape Crisis 2001). A survey on the frequency of rape amongst South African women conducted in 1998 with a large nationally representative sample of 11,735 women aged 15–49 by the Medical Research Council found that 159 women (1.6 per cent) had had forced sex before they were 15. Of these, 33 per cent reported the perpetrator as a teacher (Jewkes, Levin *et al.* 2002).

Qualitative ethnographic work confirms these findings. A study of two secondary schools in Durban in Kwazulu Natal, to which I have contributed, found that of fifteen girls participating, three reported a personal experience of rape involving teachers or fellow pupils. All fifteen reported firsthand knowledge of a friend or relative who had been raped (Morrell, Unterhalter, Moletsane and Epstein 2001). In role-play activities dealing with gender undertaken with sixty learners, every single group, when asked to portray a gendered interaction, acted a scene involving a form of violence (Thorpe 2001). In both schools, despite reasonably well functioning management structures, there was failure to respond at a whole-school level to cases of sexual violence involving teachers and learners. These were seen as individual aberrant examples (Moletsane, Morrell, Unterhalter and Epstein 2002; Kent 2004).

A number of studies worldwide are pointing to the links between sexual violence and HIV infection (Gordon and Crehan 1999; Heise, Ellsberg, Gottemoeller 1999; Chingaze, Decosas, Chikore 2000; Garcia-Moreno and Watts 2000; Dunne *et al.* 2003). Research in South Africa confirms what has been noted elsewhere: unequal gender relations and extensive sexual violence often make it impossible for women to insist on condom use, and exposes them to increased risks of infection because of coerced sex (Jewkes *et al.* 1999; Abrahams and Jewkes 2000). In South Africa discourses of masculinity which invoke violence or the ability to enjoy unprotected sex to demonstrate being a 'real man' are commonplace (Morrell 2001; Makhaya 2001; Parkes 2002). However, some alternative discourses of masculinity linked to care and compassion have also been noted (Morrell, Unterhalter, Moletsane and Epstein 2001; Unterhalter 2001).

Thus side by side with South Africa's record on gender equity with regard to adult literacy and access to schooling, we must place the recognition of dangerous social divisions in schools, 'facilities for education', as a key part of the capability space and the conditions that facilitate freedom in Sen's analysis. Going to school for young black South African women may well not provide openings for what they are able to do or be, but may be placing them at grave risk of severe trauma, infection and early death. Education for these young girls may represent a key freedom, the capability to lead a fuller life, to realise themselves as ends not means. But it may, at the same time, signal a different and more sinister meaning of end. The process of education, in an unregulated social facility, literally ends the girl's life, destroying her capability. The high national figures on rape and sexual violence indicate profound gender inequities, and that girls are at risk even when they are not at school. But the failure of management in schools with regard to providing a safe environment for education places the assumption of education simply and unproblematically on enhancing capabilities in question.

The South African government now has ample evidence on the high levels of sexual violence in schools and the extent of HIV infection. The strategies it is putting in place attempt to address some of the links between gender, violence and HIV. Can the capability approach be used to evaluate this response?

Sen's writing on using the capability approach for evaluative purposes stresses that the space for evaluation is neither that of aggregated utilities, that is, the sum benefits for a whole society, nor that of primary goods, the resources needed to realise Rawls' difference principle. Evaluations are to be made in the capability space and what is to be evaluated is substantive freedom of an individual, his or her active empowered capability to choose a valued life. In practice what might be evaluated is realised functionings, that is what a person is and does, but evaluating functionings cannot serve as a substitute for evaluating the capability set of alternatives that a person is substantively free to do (Sen 1999: 74–5). Generally in much of the work that builds from Sen, and in Sen's own writing, functionings are taken as proxies for capabilities. But in the case of South Africa, given the history of a racialised and gendered education system, evaluating functionings is very limited. While evaluating capabilities has wider scope, this task needs to draw on history and social theory to provide an appropriate understanding and thus an adequate form of operationalisation.

A clear statement of the importance given to addressing gender issues in response to the HIV/AIDs epidemic occurs in the Tirisano plan adopted in 2000 by the new Minister of Education. The Tirisano initiative of the Department of Education was directed at consolidating the gains made in the early period of democratic reform in South Africa, where the focus had largely been on changing the legislative framework and creating a de-racialised education system. Tirisano has been directed at deepening the quality of reform, paying attention to curriculum change, teacher development and measures to address poverty. Tirisano used an approach to planning that entailed setting clear objectives and implementation paths to translate generalised policy goals into outcomes. Addressing the HIV pandemic through work in schools was a major goal of the Tirisano plan. Its first strategic objective was to incorporate learning about HIV/AIDS in the school curriculum, generally through the subject called Life Skills and to plan for the effects of the pandemic on the educational system. One of the strategic objectives of Tirisano is:

To promote values, which inculcate respect for girls and women and recognise the right of girls and women to free choice in sexual relations. (Department of Education 2000: 12)

This is accompanied by an intended outcome formulated in terms of:

Change of attitude and behaviour towards *sexuality* including an increased respect for girls and women (ibid, my italics).

Now we can try to evaluate implementation of this policy in terms of its success in securing achieved functionings – that is, firstly, whether certain values promoted throughout the school that enhance respect for women and girls have been put in place, and secondly, whether girls and women consider they are able to reject sexual harassment. We could assess success in achieving these by an outside measurement of success. For example, an examination in the subject Life Skills could be conducted, or an assessment could be made by an inspector on the competence of the teachers and the school management in delivering the Life Skills syllabus and building a school community that supports this. Or we could assess the ways in which Life Skills is working to enhance the status of women and girls in the school through participatory methodologies developed by those inside the school and by working with an outside facilitator. However, an attempt to undertake a combination of these two forms of evaluation in a study of an HIV/AIDs intervention in Durban schools I have participated in demonstrated how limited evaluation of functionings was. Pupils and teachers had a schooled response to the messages about HIV/AIDS, they knew the 'right' answers to provide (Thorpe 2002). Similar shallow understandings of the information taught in Life Skills classes has been documented elsewhere in Kwazulu Natal (Harrison 2002). Participatory methodologies led researchers to being convinced by learners and teachers that if conditions in the school and its surrounding locale supported messages of gender equality, interventions could succeed to put government policy into action (Moletsane *et al.* 2002). However, more detailed ethnographic work in a school where strategies concerning gender equality and HIV/AIDS had been considered successful yielded a more pessimistic conclusion (Kent 2004). In this school certain functionings had been noted and taken as indicative of policy success. Learners and teachers provided examples of girls leading assemblies and teachers making condoms readily accessible to pupils (Moletsane *et al.* 2002). But the ethnographic work showed how little this had changed the texture of the gender regime of the school, where sexual harassment was normalised and girls and women teachers openly derided. The different studies evaluating functionings in one school show how important the historical and social analysis of the school is and how misplaced simple conclusions on the basis of functionings might be. It is difficult to make judgements about achieved functionings without a social theory to interpret the reasons for the patterns one observes.

If we use the capabilities approach for evaluation and consider not simply achieved functionings, but also the vectors of functionings, capabilities – the sets of alternatives girls and boys, men and women associated with the school are free to choose in response to the new curricular initiative – we will be looking for very different elements. At issue here are the feasible alternatives to the given policy. There are many feasible and different ways the policy could be framed and these need to be explored in relation to capabilities. Some public process of evaluation and selection of relevant capabilities would have to take place (Robeyns 2003; Alkire 2002). In this process we would need to ask questions about whether the life skills curriculum enhances freedom and valued choices concerning life and protection from HIV infection or whether it just encourages a superficial under-standing of the nature of the epidemic. We would need to consider whether gender differences in agency with regard to sexuality are enhanced or diminished by the new curriculum relative to some ear-lier baseline ideas about agency, gender and sexuality. We would also need to look at capabilities and approaches to health care and con-sider whether for many girls their capabilities are enhanced relative to a baseline of no formal schooling, which might be less risky. But it is unlikely that selecting these most relevant capabilities one would pay attention to the crucial area of the structures of gender inequality in the society that so profoundly conditions attitudes to sexuality, use of health services and responses to curriculum development initiatives. Just as with evaluating achieved functioning, it is difficult to make sense of the information without a social theory, so too for analysing capabilities. The capability approach to evaluation is likely to be extremely limited in fostering social change without some notion of gender injustice and the ways in which rape and other forms of sexual violence have been normalised in South Africa. Without understand-ing how they have been made an aspect of what is considered the 'provocative behaviour' of girls, and ignored by school managers, a capability based evaluation would be working within too narrow a framework.

The government, in the Tirisano document, locates the problem of the HIV/AIDS epidemic in relation to attitudes to sexuality, not the wider conditions of gender injustice (very different to lack of 'respect') of which non-consensual sex is but one manifestation. This rather preliminary application of the capability approach does not itself reveal this inadequacy of the government response to the HIV/AIDS epidemic through curriculum intervention. The omissions and assumptions become evident only when the capability approach is used with a complementary social theory.

The failure to locate features of the gender regime in schools in plans for dealing urgently with the AIDS epidemic indicates that the government believes that combating the epidemic is a question of changing attitudes through information and curricular change. The social relations that bring the attitudes linked to rape and sexual violence into being are not identified as problematic and the capability approach does not of itself suggest that they should be. Indeed it is hard to know whether in conditions with high levels of complicity in sexual violence by men and women 'free choice in sexual relations' is entirely possible.

Refining the understanding of education in the capabilities approach

The very loose way that Sen identifies social space and education as a social facility or an enlargement of capability, which I outlined in section one, could encourage a lack of critical edge entailed in evaluation utilising the capability approach as I have just sketched. In this final section I want to look at the relation between capabilities and political and social analysis, drawing particularly on what we know of the sociology and politics of schooling.

Sen argues persuasively on the importance of the theorisation of capabilities for political and social analysis. However, he is relatively silent about the relationship of political and social analysis to capabilities, leaving most of his comments gestural and associated with particular cases. See for example his discussion on the need to evaluate markets and their contribution to freedoms *together with* an assessment of democracy and the delivery of equity and efficiency (Sen 1999: 142). The way in which this assessment is to be made is left unspecified.

How are we to understand 'social arrangements' without an adequate social theory? As I outlined above, it might be possible to claim one was utilising the capability approach and view schooling as a space free of contestation, unmarked by race or gender inequalities, whose outcomes were always an expansion of human capabilities. In this reading the South African government policy would be an entirely adequate response predicated on aspects of the notion of capabilities. But schools are not outside society. It seems to me that political and social analysis are crucial to make the capability approach 'real' and that without an explicit acknowledgement of the salience of social theories of inequality, the capability approach lays itself open to becoming a hollow mantra.

Education is difficult to theorise because the word connotes ideas and aspirations, social relations, institutions and specific forms of understanding and skill. It is a process that is socially constructed, reproducing social inequalities and constantly contested, seeking to transform these. Different social theories looking at schooling will emphasise different aspects of these tensions. The importance of education for developing an understanding of the freedom to do and to be and for establishing our humanity is beyond question. But without appropriate social theories that allow us to understand what happens in the socially constructed spaces, in which the capability approach is applied, the reach of the approach can be limited.

Social theories themselves are not beyond critique, but those concerned with questions of egalitarianism have a commitment to social change in common. Social change is powerfully linked with human agency, which is itself central to the capability approach. In taking thinking about the capability approach and education further it seems crucial to consider the ways in which capabilities interface with the social and the political at a theoretical as well as an empirical level.

Cited references

Abrahams, N. and Jewkes, R. 2000. 'Sexual coercion in intimate relations: a risk for HIV/AIDS'. Paper presented at 13th International Conference on HIV/AIDS, Durban, July

Aikman, S. 1999. *Intercultural education and literacy*. Amsterdam: John Benjamin

Asmal, K. 1999. Call to action: mobilising citizens to build a South African education and training system for the 21st Century. *Statement made by the Minister of Education 29 July 1999, on line at www.anc.org.za (accessed April 2001)*

Alkire, S. 2002. *Valuing freedoms. Sen's capability approach and poverty reduction*. Oxford: Oxford University Press

Bradshaw, D., Johnson, L., Schneider, H., Bourne, D. and Dorrington, R. 2002. *Orphans of the HIV/AIDs epidemic*. Pretoria: Medical Research Council, on line at http://www.mrc.ac.za/policybriefs/2policy2002.pdf (accessed January 2004)

Brighouse, H. 2001. 'Egalitarian liberalism and justice in education'. *Inaugural Professorial Lecture*, London: Institute of Education

Chingaze, F., Decosas, J. and Chikore, J. 2000. 'Linking the issues: HIV, gender, human rights and child protection'. Paper presented to Southern African AIDS Training Programme, Harare

Daniels, G. 2001. 'Gender activists slam government'. *Weekly Mail and Guardian* 10 August, on line at http://www.mg.co.za (accessed October 2001)

De La Rey, C. 2001. 'Women and management in higher education in South Africa'. Paper presented to Seminar on Managing Gendered Change in Selected Commonwealth Universities, Association of Commonwealth Universities/ Institute of Education, Johannesburg, February

Department of Education 2000. *Implementation Plan for Tirisano.* Pretoria: Department of Education

Drèze, J. and Sen, A. 1989. *Hunger and public action.* Oxford: Clarendon Press

Drèze, J. and Sen, A. 1995. *India: economic development and social opportunity.* Delhi: Oxford University Press

Drèze, J. and Sen, A. 2002. *India: development and participation.* Delhi: Oxford University Press

Dunne, M., Humphreys, S. and Leach, F. 2003. 'Gender violence in schools'. Background paper commissioned for the UNESCO EFA Monitoring Report, 2003, on line at Http://portal.unesco.org/education/en/file_download.php/ee2258a3769cd087cc22453acdbe3910Gender+and+violence+in+schools.doc (accessed January 2004)

Garcia-Moreno, C. and Watts, C. 2000. 'Violence against women: its importance for HIV/AIDs prevention'. Unpublished paper prepared for World Health Organisation, Geneva

Gillborn, D. 1995. *Racism and antiracism in real schools.* Buckingham: Open University Press

Gordon, P. and Crehan, K. 1999. *Dying of sadness: gender, sexual violence and the HIV epidemic.* New York: UNDP HIV and Development Programme

Harrison, A. 2002. 'The social dynamics of adolescent risk for HIV: using research findings to design a school based intervention'. *Agenda,* No. 53

Heise, L., Ellsberg, M. and Gottemoeller, M. 1999. 'Population reports: ending violence against women'. *Population Reports* Series L, No. 11 Johns Hopkins School of Health, Baltimore, on line at www.jhuccp.org

Human Rights Watch 2001. *Scared at school. Sexual violence against girls in South African schools.* New York: Human Rights Watch, on line at www.hrw.org/reports/2001/safrica (accessed March, 2001)

Jewkes, R., Penn-Kekana, L., Levin, J., Ratsaka, M. and Schreiber, M. 1999. 'He must give me money, he mustn't beat me'. Violence against women in three South African provinces. *Report prepared for CERSA, Medical Research Council, Pretoria*

Jewkes, R., Levin, J., Mbananga, N. and Bradshaw, D. 2002. 'Rape of girls in South Africa'. *The Lancet*, 359, 319–320

Kallaway, P. (ed.) 1984. *Apartheid and education*. Johannesburg: Ravan

Kent, A. 2004. 'Living life on the edge: Examining space and sexualities within a township high school in greater Durban, in the context of the HIV epidemic'. *Transformation* 54, 59–75

Kumar, K. 1989. *The social character of learning*. Delhi: Sage

Makhaya, G. 2001. 'Young men in soccer take action after personalizing the risk of HIV/AIDS'. Paper presented at conference on The Politics of Gender and Education, Institute of Education, University of London

Marks, S. 1987. *Not either an experimental doll: the separate worlds of three South African women*. London: The Women's Press

Moletsane, L., Morrell, R., Unterhalter E. and Epstein, D. 2002. 'Instituting gender equality in schools: Working in an HIV environment'. *Perspectives in Education* 20, 2, 37–53

Morrell, R. (ed.) 2001. *Changing masculinities in a changing society: Men and gender in Southern Africa*. Pietermaritzburg: University of Natal Press

Morrell, R., Unterhalter, E., Moletsane, L. and Epstein, D. 2001. 'Missing the message: HIV/AIDS interventions and learners in South African schools'. *Canadian Woman Studies* 21, 2, 90–95

Parkes, J. 2002. ' "Children also have rights, but then who wants to listen to our rights?" Children's perspectives on living with community violence in South Africa'. *Educate* 2, 2, 59–71

Prinsloo, M. and Breier, M. (eds.) 1996. *The social uses of literacy: theory and practice in contemporary South Africa*. Johannesburg: SACHED Books and Amsterdam: John Benjamins

Ramagoshi, M. 2005. 'National Department of Education Initiatives' in Chisholm, L. and September, J. *Gender equity in South African education 1994–2004*. Cape Town: HSRC Press, 138–142

Rape Crisis 2001. 'Rape Crisis Statistics', on line at www.rape.co.za (accessed April 2001)

Robeyns, I. 2003. 'Sen's capability approach and gender inequality: selecting relevant capabilities', *Feminist Economics*, 9(2–3), 61–92

Robinson-Pant, A. 2000. *Why eat green cucumbers at the time of dying? Women's literacy and development in Nepal*. Hamburg: UNESCO Institute for Education

Sen, A. 1992. *Inequality reexamined* Oxford: Oxford University Press

Sen, A. 1993. 'Capability and wellbeing', in Nussbaum, M. and Sen, A. (eds.) *The quality of life*. Oxford: Clarendon Press

Sen, A. 1995. 'Gender inequality and theories of justice', in Nussbaum, M. and Glover, J. (eds.) *Women, culture and development*. Oxford: Clarendon Press, 259–274

Sen, A. 1999. *Development as freedom*. Oxford: Oxford University Press

Sen, A. 2002. 'Basic education and human security'. Background paper for workshop for the Commission for Human Security, Kolkata, January, on line at http://www.humansecurity-chs.org/activities/outreach/Kolkata.pdf (accessed January 2004)

Sen, A. 2003. 'The importance of basic education'. Speech to the Commonwealth Education Ministers Conference, Edinburgh, on line at http://www.globalpolicy.org/socecon/develop/2003/1028seneducation.htm (accessed January 2004)

Sen, A. K. 1980 'Equality of what?' in S. McMurrin (ed.) *Tanner Lectures on Human Values*, Cambridge: Cambridge University Press and reprinted in Sen, A. K. 1982. *Choice Welfare and Measurement*, 353–369, Cambridge, Massachusetts and London: Harvard University Press

South Africa 1996. *Constitution of the Republic of South Africa*. Pretoria: Government Printer

Street, B. 1995. *Social literacies: critical approaches to literacy in development, ethnography and education*. London: Longman

Thorpe, M. 2001. 'An evaluation of the intervention of Dramaide's programme, "Mobilising young men to care" in two township schools in Durban'. Report to the research project on Gender, Violence and HIV, School of Education, University of Natal, Durban and Institute of Education, University of London

Thorpe, M. 2002. 'Masculinity in an HIV intervention'. *Agenda*, 53

UNAIDS 2002. *Report on the global HIV/AIDS epidemic*. Geneva: UNAIDS, on line at www.unaids.org (accessed January 2004)

UNAIDS 2003. 'National response brief: South Africa'. Report of the United Nations Programme on HIV/AIDS, Geneva: UNAIDS, on line at http://www.unaids.org/nationalresponse/result.asp?action=overall&country=329 (accessed January 2004)

UNDP (United Nations Development Programme) 1990. *Human development report*. New York: Oxford University Press

UNDP (United Nations Development Programme), 1995. *Human development report*. New York: Oxford University Press

UNDP (United Nations Development Programme) 2000. *Human development report*. New York: Oxford University Press

Unterhalter, E., Wolpe, H., Botha, T., Badat, S., Dlamini, T. and Khotseng, B. (eds.) 1991. *Apartheid education and popular struggles*. London: Zed

Unterhalter, E. 1999. 'The schooling of South African girls', in Heward, C. and Bunwaree, S. (eds.) *Gender education and development: beyond access to empowerment*. London: Zed

Unterhalter, E. 2001. 'The work of the nation: heroic masculinity in South African autobiographical writings of the anti-apartheid struggle'. *European Journal of Development Research* 12, 2, 157–178

Unterhalter, E. 2002a. 'Gender, race and different lives: South African women teachers' autobiographies and the analysis of education change', in Kallaway, P. (ed.) *Education and liberation in South Africa: the history of education under apartheid.* New York: Peter Lang

Unterhalter, E. and Brighouse, H. 2003. 'Distribution of what? How will we know if we have achieved Education for All by 2015?' Paper for 3rd Conference on the Capabilities Approach: From Sustainable Development to Sustainable Freedom, University of Pavia, September

US Bureau of Census 2003. *HIV/AIDS surveillance database.* Washington: US Census Bureau, on line at http://www.census.gov/ipc/www/hivtable.html (accessed January 2004)

Vally, S. and Dalamba, Y. 1999. *Racism, racial integration and desegregation in South African public secondary schools.* Johannesburg: South African Human Rights Commission

Whiteside, A. and Sunter, C. 2000. *AIDS: The challenge for South Africa.* Cape Town: Human and Rousseau Tafelberg

Wolpe, A., Quinlan, O. and Martinez, A. 1997. *Gender equity in education. Report of the gender equity task team.* Pretoria: Department of Education

17 Women and poverty in Mozambique: is there a gender bias in capabilities, employment conditions and living standards?

PIER GIORGIO ARDENI AND ANTONIO ANDRACCHIO

Introduction

This chapter presents an analysis of the employment conditions and living standards in Mozambique with particular emphasis on women's conditions. A large strand of the literature has emphasised the existence of a *gender bias* in employment conditions and living standards, particularly in developing countries. Some have also argued about a supposed process of *feminisation of poverty*. In this chapter we try to address that issue by looking at the relationship between employment conditions, consumption expenditure, living conditions or 'capabilities', asset ownership and poverty of women in Mozambique. It is widely believed that women are poorer than men simply *because* they are women: they are discriminated against in the labour market (and so they earn less than men), they are discriminated against at home (and so they do not get the same education attainments as men), they are discriminated against in the family (they often have to work during the day and take care of their family at night). Although this opinion is relatively widespread and held true, it is not clear why it should be so, especially in a society that claims there are no gender barriers. Moreover, it is obviously important to understand what are the determinants of a *greater* poverty for women as opposed to men. In this chapter we will address the issue of whether women are actually discriminated against in the labour market, and, if so, if this leads to a larger percentage of poor among women as opposed to men.

The analysis is based on the data from the national Household Living Standard Survey (HLSS) that was conducted by the Instituto

510

Nacional de Estatìstica (INE) in 1996/97 with support from the World Bank and the International Food Policy Research Institute (IFPRI).[1] Poverty is a pervasive phenomenon in Mozambique, particularly in rural areas, where almost three quarters of the population fall below the poverty line.[2] The starting point of this chapter is a broader research effort supported by ILO and UNDP Mozambique to address the issue of the so-called *feminisation of poverty* (Ardeni 2001). Our claim is that women are not necessarily poorer than men but they are certainly socially and economically more vulnerable which leads them to be more *exposed* to poverty. The labour market is *segmented*, in the sense that there seems to be a *gender bias* in the labour market: women tend to get jobs that are less qualified and they generally earn less than men, even when employment status or work type is same. All other conditions being equal, women generally have jobs that are either informal, less guaranteed, less paid or less qualified. And yet, *they do not appear to be poorer than men*, at least when poverty is measured by consumption expenditure. Women are more present in the informal and low-salary job categories than men and yet they do not spend less. Their working conditions make them more vulnerable as they are socially less protected. The economic consequences are that women's consumption patterns are different from men's, even when their income is the same: women's consumption smoothing has a different and more pronounced profile than men's. This is why women tend to have roughly the same monthly income levels as men but higher consumption expenditures, everything else being equal. When measured by capabilities (education

---

[1] The survey was the first nationally representative survey conducted in Mozambique since the end of the war over a sample of more than 8,000 households and more than 40,000 people. It was vast in scope and objectives and covered several issues concerning living standards, as well as health, housing and economic conditions of the population.

[2] Poverty profiles have already been presented, based on the same source and set of data, in the *Mozambique Poverty Assessment Report* (MPAR) provided by IFPRI together with the Ministry of Finance and Planning and Universidade Eduardo Mondlane, and also in an IFPRI *Discussion Paper* by Datt, Simler, Mukherjee, and Dava (1992). The MPAR covered a wide range of topics including poverty, food security, nutrition, health, education, safety nets, while the IFPRI discussion paper focused on the determinants of living standards and poverty in Mozambique. In this chapter, using the same data source, we focus on the key question of the relationship between poverty and gender.

and health conditions) and wealth (asset ownership), *women do appear to be poorer than men.* In summary, poverty is widespread in Mozambique and affects both women and men. Women do not necessarily spend less but they *are* poorer as they are more vulnerable, have generally lower social status, informal or low-salary jobs and worse working and living conditions.

The chapter is organised as follows. We begin by analysing, in Section 2, the recent trends in female employment in Mozambique, which show that women's participation in the last decades has been rising. Data from various countries show that a considerable share of employment is in the informal sector and that a majority of female employment is in the informal sector. The comparison between formal and informal employment figures shows that there is a considerable gender bias in the labour market also in Mozambique. Income-earning working women are fewer, as a percentage, then men, while on the other hand, unpaid working women are more, as a percentage, than men. Among workers, wage-workers are by far more often men then women, and particularly so in urban areas. Workers are more often paid workers when they live in the city and less so when they live in the country. Putting together all unpaid workers, undeclared income-earning workers and own account workers – a conjoint we term *informal* – it emerges that among women three quarters of total workers are informal in urban areas (as opposed to 50 per cent of men) and 95 per cent are informal in rural areas (as opposed to 88 per cent for men). Income distribution, which we analyse in Section 3, confirms that wage-workers are more often in upper quintiles, while unpaid workers are more frequently in the lower quintiles. Interestingly, this is more so for men than women, as there are comparatively more unpaid working women in the upper quintiles of the distribution.

In most developing countries poverty is typically thought to affect large households with fewer earners relative to the non-poor households, and it is believed that women who earn low incomes and work in the informal sector head a substantial proportion of poor households. Households headed by women in Mozambique amount to less than a quarter of total households and they are relatively more in the cities than in rural areas. Interestingly, also, female-headed households are smaller in size than male-headed households. Women are also more present in female-headed households relative to men than in male-headed households. And yet, their distribution across employment positions and worker statuses does not change significantly between female-headed and male-headed households.

Section 3 analyses the relationship between income, consumption expenditure and gender across households in Mozambique. Although there seems to be a close association between informality and gender bias and the evidence suggests a strong correlation between informality and poverty for women, particularly all over Africa, this is apparently not confirmed for Mozambique. Per-capita consumption expenditure is slightly higher for people belonging to woman-headed households than for those belonging to man-headed households, particularly so in rural areas. Per-capita income, on the other hand, is slightly higher for those who are in man-headed households in urban areas, and is higher for those who belong to female-headed households in rural areas. The correlation between per-capita consumption and household size is apparently negative, which also shows the absence of those 'economies of size' that some think are important in reducing the negative effects of poverty.

In Section 4 three different approaches to the measurement of poverty are studied. In the first one, consumption-based poverty indicators are analysed. Poverty indexes are presented for urban and rural areas and for male- and female-headed households. Interestingly, female-headed households are apparently less likely to be poor, particularly in rural areas, then man-headed households. We then look at capabilities, at least those measured by education and health conditions, from which it appears that women are much worse off then men. Last, we look at asset-based indicators of poverty, which confirm that overall women are worse off then men in Mozambique: they are poor, less secure, less protected. We conjecture that *women spend more because of their worse overall social and employment conditions*.

In conclusion, there is apparently a weak correlation between consumption and employment status across sexes, a slightly more evident correlation between poverty status and work type across sexes, and a high correlation between poverty status (as measured by capabilities and assets) and consumption across sexes. Therefore, we can certainly state that there is a gender bias in living standards and employment conditions, which is reflected in a significant 'feminisation of poverty'.

Formal and informal employment and gender bias in Mozambique

Formal vs. informal male and female employment

In the last decades, female labour force participation in Mozambique has not changed much.[3] Of total female labour force, 96 per cent is estimated to be in agriculture. Thus, differently from most developing countries – where there is evidence of an increasing number of women turning to the non-agricultural sector for jobs, mostly located in urban areas – in Mozambique, in the last three decades, the percentage of women in industry has barely changed. Non-agricultural employment is usually associated with wage labour. According to the HLSS, in Mozambique around 10 per cent of total labour force can be defined as *wage labour force*. As in many other developing countries, a majority of women does not have wage employment: women are mostly self-employed, own-account workers or unpaid workers. According to the available statistics, wage-employed workers accounted for 16.5 per cent of labour force in 1980, whereas female wage labour force was estimated to equal 3.6 per cent of total labour force.[4] Thus, taking into account population growth, the biggest decline in wage labour force – and in female wage labour – seems to have taken place between 1991 and 1997. This is apparently in contradiction with the economic growth and rise in agricultural production observed during that period, and it is probably an indication of informal labour participation rise and increased female informal employment.

The trends we observe in Mozambique have actually been paralleled by similar trends in all developing economies, particularly in sub-saharan Africa. Female employment grew at an impressive rate during the late 1970s and 1980s and, as a consequence, female unemployment

---

[3] According to the World Development Indicators (WB 1999) the percentage of female labour force over total labour force has slowly decreased from 49.2 per cent in 1970 to 49 per cent in 1980 to 48.4 per cent in 1997. In the Mozambique 1997 Population Census data the labour force participation rate is estimated to be 73.5 per cent for men and 66.5 per cent for women (with an employment rate of 93.6 per cent for women).

[4] The 1991 census estimated a 16 per cent share of wage labour force, with a female wage labour share of 5.2 per cent. According to the HLSS, the female wage labour rate can be estimated to be around 4 per cent.

declined. However, growth of female employment in the *formal* economy has also slowed down, apparently, thus implying that informal employment among women has risen.[5] An increase in female employment generally indicates an improvement in female employment quality (especially if it is wage labour). And yet, as we know, the rising share of female wage employment is not necessarily an indicator of improvement in job quality. Much of women's wage employment is in the *informal* category, that is, in the *underground economy* (large firms failing to comply to labour regulations) or in the *informal economy* (micro-enterprises operating outside the recognised institutional framework), with obviously no overall improvement in job quality. It is therefore important to know whether access to formal employment has increased or not.[6]

In most developing countries women's labour force participation has been rising in the last decades. An increasing share of female employment is in the non-agricultural sector, notably in urban areas, and women have been shown to move from non-wage to wage employment, although in Mozambique this happened only until the beginning of the 1990s and it is now slowing down. The majority of women today appear to be in non-wage employment in the informal economy, either as own-account or unpaid workers. A notable characteristic of developing economies is that a considerable part of the production and exchange of goods and services takes place outside the *formal* system, i.e. *outside the legally recognised institutional framework, which regulates economic activity*. Employment in *informal* activities, being outside the institutional framework, is thus termed *informal*, as the units that create such employment have no incentive or means to go formal. Typically, such is the non-wage employment of own-account or unpaid workers, whose magnitude is generally not known, as much of informal employment is also *unrecorded*, i.e. statistically non-observed.

Informal employment consists of *all employment* outside the prevailing and recognised institutional framework. As such it is obviously not homogeneous because it may consist of several different typologies

---

[5] Several studies support this view. See, for instance, the UNDP 1993 World Development Report on 'jobless growth'.

[6] While in some countries and in some periods formal female employment has increased faster than that of men, generally a good share of female employment in trade, and to a certain extent in manufacturing and services, is in the non-wage employment category, i.e. self-employed or unpaid, and often *informal*.

of workers. We can divide informal employment in *wage employment* and *non-wage employment*, i.e. self-employment and unpaid employment. While we may assume that all non-wage employment is informal – almost all own-account and unpaid workers in developing countries operate outside the recognised institutional framework – wage employment can be either formal or informal. Informal wage labour is typically: paid labour of small enterprises, or *micro-enterprises*, which do not comply with the formal standards of the institutional framework and are thus to be considered as part of the informal economy; paid labour of formal enterprises who do not comply with the standards of labour laws and regulations. Employers or heads of micro-enterprises – i.e. *micro-entrepreneurs* – are also counted as part of the informal economy and so are their paid workers. Informal wage employment also includes *independent wage-workers* not attached to any particular enterprise or employer (casual or irregular workers, family workers, domestic servants).[7]

Data on informal employment are mostly taken from surveys, and are usually not very homogeneous across surveys. Employment in the informal sector as a share of urban labour force varies significantly across developing countries, although it is often much higher in Sub-Saharan Africa (Ardeni 2001). Obviously, if the share of labour force in informal employment is high, generally not so high is the share of the informal 'sector' of the economy over total GDP, mostly because of low labour productivity. The available evidence indicates that a majority of female employment in Africa and Asia is in the informal sector, while in Latin America the proportion of women in the informal sector, is

---

[7] There is a vast literature on the subject, and it is beyond the scope of this chapter to review it. See for instance Ardeni (1997). While all definitions of informal economy point to the main feature of being outside the recognised institutional framework, it should be noted that informal employment is not necessarily of lower quality: being informal is usually associated with lower quality but informality in itself is not a *cause* of inferior quality. In fact, informal enterprises generally operate in a different business environment from formal enterprises', as they usually lack the same access to factor and product markets, public resources, funds and loans, information and opportunities as formal enterprises do. Enterprises usually stay informal in order to avoid compliance with most regulations, since this would add to the cost of running their business. Productivity and revenues are generally low and work conditions are poor, as they operate under conditions of 'informality'. Obviously, the extent of informality varies across enterprises and sectors of activity, but in any case it is clear the *extent of informality* is not unambiguously measurable.

probably less because a substantial number of them is in informal (undeclared) wage employment in the service sector. Thus, most of the available evidence demonstrates the existence of a *gender bias* as more women are in poor quality employment and as there are relatively few paid women employees in the informal sector. Women are also over-represented in specific branches and activities within the informal sector, which suggests that women are generally over-represented in low-income activities.

The composition of employment in terms of worker status also provides some indication of the quality of employment in the informal sector. Since wage-workers generally earn less than the self-employed and entrepreneurs, a higher proportion of the former would indicate that overall employment quality is inferior than otherwise. A higher share of unpaid workers would also suggest lower employment quality, as these generally receive almost no income. Income is also an indicator of employment quality. The income of informal workers is lower than that of workers in the formal sector almost by definition. However, income varies considerably even in the informal sector. There is overwhelming evidence suggesting that incomes of women in the informal sector are substantially lower than in the formal sector.[8] Moreover, gender disparity in incomes seems greater in the informal sector. Income differentials between men and women persist not only in the two sectors but also among employment categories. Gender disparity seems to be larger for self-employed and (micro) entrepreneurs than for wage-workers in the informal sector.[9]

This evidence undoubtedly suggests that women are discriminated against even when they are not wage-workers. Some of this differential in earning capacity can be explained by differences in endowments in capital (human and physical), legal status, age of enterprise, location of enterprise. But also, it appears that women enterprises differ from men's in terms of the scale, items sold by traders, extent of diversification, nature of linkages, contacts, and networks, and, most importantly, the type of business premises used by women – typically nearby their residence – which limits access to more productive informal activities.

---

[8] A caveat is important here. While the informal sector includes both wage and non-wage-workers, in the formal sector all workers are wage employees. Therefore one should compare the incomes of self-employed (whether paid or unpaid) and entrepreneurs in the informal sector and formal wage employees, on one hand, and the incomes of wage-workers in both sectors, on the other hand.

[9] In Africa, the evidence is quite significant (see Ardeni 2001).

Overall, the evidence shows that male–female earning differentials in the informal sector are larger than in the formal sector. Within the informal sector, both male and female entrepreneurs have higher income than self-employed workers, who in turn have generally higher incomes than wage-workers, often above minimum wage levels. Clearly, income varies with the type of work and sector of employment, but this is a fairly general pattern. In general, for instance, home-workers, i.e. those working at home on a subcontracting or piece rate basis, earn less compared to women operating on own account without any subcontracting relationship.[10] Is there a gender bias? Are there more women in poor quality employment than men in the informal sector? The evidence, particularly for Africa, shows clearly that a greater proportion of women in the informal sector have poor quality employment than men. As compared with the formal sector, the over-whelming majority of women in Africa are in poor quality employ-ment. Overall, the evidence from all developing countries points to the existence of gender disparity in incomes, as a whole and by branches and employment status.[11] If physical capital is important, the differ-ence in investment in human capital also contributes to explaining gender differences. The evidence suggests, in fact, that improved access to education by women can play an effective role in reducing gender disparities in income in the informal sector.

Formal and informal employment status and type of work

Although in Mozambique there have not been systematic surveys on the informal economy on a national basis (Ardeni 1997), several studies have been conducted in recent years on selected areas of the

---

[10] The absolute level of income is also important, as it tends to reveal the existence of poor quality employment when it is below a certain threshold, e.g. legal minimum wage. Among both formal and informal workers a certain percentage receives low incomes, although one would expect it to be higher for informal workers who, by definition, work outside the recognised institutional framework. Data for various countries indicate that probably a third or more of employment in the informal sector is of poor quality. Also, in most cases the relative share of female employment of poor quality – as indicated by a low level of income – is at least twice as large as the men's share.

[11] The sectorial composition of employment is also illuminating, as there is overwhelming evidence to suggest that women are more concentrated in a few low-income sectors as compared to men.

country and on specific issues. The Household Living Standard Survey offers considerable amounts of information about labour market and gender conditions in Mozambique. Even though employment in the informal sector, either as a share of urban labour force or over total employment, cannot be directly quantified using the HLSS, there are estimates of significant categories of workers. As we said above, in fact, we can assume that all non-wage employment is informal, since almost all own-account and unpaid workers in developing countries, and in Mozambique, operate outside the recognised institutional framework.[12] Wage employment can be either formal or informal: informal wage labour is typically paid labour of (informal) micro-enterprises or paid labour of formal enterprises who do not comply with the standards of labour laws and regulations. Micro-entrepreneurs are also to be counted as part of the informal economy and so are their paid workers. Finally, informal wage employment includes independent wage-workers not attached to any particular enterprise or employer (casual or irregular workers, family workers, domestic servants).

Employment figures in Mozambique – as resulting from the HLSS – show that among all the adult population, 40.8 per cent declare their *employment status* as *working* (these can be either self-employed or wage-workers, and we term these as *income-earning workers*), 2.1 per cent declare to be *employed but not working* or *seeking employment* or plainly *unemployed* (these can be considered *active unemployed*), 14.8 per cent declare to *help a family without payment* while 9.6 per cent declare to be working as *unpaid domestic servant* (implying that, overall, 24.4 per cent of total adult population has a declared unpaid job), 23 per cent are *students*, while the remaining 9.6 per cent has no declared activity.[13] Gender differences are evident at the national level: while 46.7 per cent of men declare an income-earning employment status, only 35.5 per cent of women do, and while only 13.4 per cent of men have an unpaid job, 40 per cent of women do.[14]

---

[12] See the definition by the ILO. Strictly speaking, the ILO definition does not include wage-workers. Instead it mostly includes own-account workers in microenterprises.

[13] We will not report here all the figures. For a detailed analysis, see the Statistical Annex in Ardeni (2001).

[14] In urban areas the picture is even more skewed. While income-earning workers in urban areas are, overall, less (34.2 per cent) than total income-earning workers, and so are urban unpaid workers (21.6 per cent), urban students have a

Table 17.1 *Employment status by area and gender (%)*

	Urban areas			Rural areas		
	Men	Women	All	Men	Women	All
Income-earning workers	30.4	24.9	27.9	69.6	75.1	72.1
Active unemployed	57.6	34.1	49.9	42.4	65.9	50.1
Unpaid workers	23.9	31.3	29.4	76.1	68.7	70.6
Students	45.0	51.6	47.9	55.0	48.4	52.1
Others	29.6	25.2	27.4	70.4	74.8	72.6
Total working-age population	34.2	32.5	33.3	65.8	67.5	66.7

Overall, *paid employment* in Mozambique (both self-employment and wage employment) appears to be predominantly male (54.6 per cent): in particular, women are 40.5 per cent and 47.3 per cent of total income-earning workers in urban and rural areas, respectively. Conversely, women represent, on aggregate, 73.8 per cent of total *unpaid employment* at national level (78.7 per cent in urban and 71.7 per cent in rural areas). The urban–rural distribution of population by employment status shows that while total adult population lives for one third in urban areas and for the remaining two thirds in rural areas, income-earning workers are more concentrated in rural areas (72.1 per cent). Unemployment is mainly an urban phenomenon, as more unemployed live in the city in proportion to urban population (50 per cent), while unpaid work is more concentrated[15] in rural areas (70.6 per cent). Gender differences do exist in the case of the urban–rural distribution, although they seem to be less pronounced in Table 17.1. Only one fourth of income-earning female workers live in cities, as opposed to 30 per cent of income-earning male

larger share of total adult population (33.2 per cent). Gender differences are even more striking. While 41.5 per cent of men are income-earning workers, only 27.3 per cent of women are. Conversely, while only 9.4 per cent of men have a declared unpaid job, 33.3 per cent of women do. Male students are also in larger numbers (35.6 per cent) than female students (30.8 per cent). In rural areas, 49.4 per cent of men declare to be working, as opposed to 39.5 per cent of women. Conversely, while 15.5 per cent of men have an unpaid job, 34 per cent of women do. In rural areas there is also a high percentage of people (almost 10 per cent) that declares some 'other' employment status not included in the ones described above.

[15] In the sense that the proportion of unpaid employed workers in rural areas is greater than the proportion of total adult population.

workers. Conversely, while 31.3 per cent of unpaid women workers live in urban areas, only 23.9 per cent of unpaid men workers live in cities. Also, more than 54 per cent of unemployed men are in cities, while 34 per cent of unemployed women live in urban areas.

The *type of work* – as declared in the HLSS[16] – shows that 45.6 per cent of the people interviewed declared to be *working on own-account*, 0.3 per cent declared to be *entrepreneurs*, and 14.4 per cent declared to be working either for the public administration, some state or private enterprise, or some co-operative. While own-account workers and entre-preneurs can be considered as *self-employed*, those working for some company can be considered as *declared*, i.e. *formal, wage-workers*. Self-employed and wage-workers together sum up to *declared paid workers* (60.3 per cent of total), while *declared unpaid workers* are the remaining 39.7 per cent (Ardeni 2001). Gender differences are pronounced in this case: while, in fact, 78.2 per cent of men are declared paid workers, only 44.4 per cent of women are declared paid workers. Differences between rural and urban areas are also striking: while men are paid workers in 92.2 per cent of the cases when they live in the city and in 73.1 per cent of the cases when they live in the country, women are paid workers in three cases out of four when they live in cities and only 37.5 per cent of the cases when they live in the country.

At the national level, women account for only 38.8 per cent of total paid workers and 74 per cent of total unpaid workers. Interestingly, women account for 52.7 per cent of overall declared paid and unpaid work. The distribution by gender is not very different, in this case, between the city and the country. Conversely, 26.6 per cent of men in the city have a declared job, while only 18.3 per cent of women do: in particular, while in the city 9.6 per cent of men have an unpaid job, only 8.2 per cent of women do, and most of those women having unpaid jobs work in the country (91.8 per cent).[17]

As we said above, informal employment consists of two basically different typologies of workers: *wage employment* and *non-wage*

---

[16] The HLSS is based on dubious definitions of analytical categories, such as 'domestic (unpaid) workers', 'self-employed', 'unpaid family labour', that should reflect people's current activity. For some criticism, see Cramer and Pontara (1998).

[17] HLSS data confirm that also in terms of sector of employment women are concentrated in a few sectors and generally in low-income activities (Ardeni 2001).

employment, including self-employment and unpaid employment. While we assume all non-wage employment is informal, wage employment can be either formal or informal.[18] *Employment status* and *type of work* together allow us to infer the amount of non-wage employment, but not that of informal wage employment (see Table 17.2). Notice that those who declare as their employment status that of *income-earning workers* are more than the sum of those who declare to be *wage-workers*, *own-account workers* and *entrepreneurs*. The difference between the two can be attributed to those who are *undeclared income-earning workers* (i.e. informal workers). Also, notice that those who declare to be *non-earning workers* as their employment status are not in the same number as those who declare to be *unpaid workers* as their category or type of work. As the former outnumber the latter, the difference can be attributed to those *irregular unpaid workers* (i.e. informal workers, too). This is not surprising, as many people (when asked about their employment status) perceive their farming activities (from the *machambas*[19] to *irregular* and *seasonal agricultural activities*) as simply *work* albeit *implicitly paid*, but when they are asked in what employment status they fit they declare to be *domestic workers* (and these are, as well, informal workers). Table 17.2 shows the amount of these types of informal employment, given by the sum of own-account workers, undeclared income-earning workers and unpaid or non-earning workers, thus excluding informal entrepreneurship and informal wage employment (i.e. paid labour of informal micro-enterprises and unregistered wage labour of formal enterprises).

Results are striking, as 84.6 per cent of total workers in Mozambique appear to be *informal* – 92.6 per cent of all workers in rural areas and 65 per cent of all workers in urban areas are in fact informal, according to the criterion indicated above (which excludes informal wage-workers and micro-entrepreneurs). Among women, 95.9 per cent of those working in rural areas and 77.9 per cent of those working in urban

---

[18] Informal wage labour is typically paid labour of informal micro-enterprises, or paid labour of formal enterprises who do not comply with the standards of labour laws and regulations (non-registered labour). Employers or heads of micro-enterprises should also be counted as part of the informal economy and so should their paid workers. Finally, informal wage employment also includes *independent wage-workers* not attached to any particular enterprise or employer (casual or irregular workers, family workers, domestic servants).

[19] In the Portuguese language, small portions of cultivated land.

Table 17.2 *Formal and informal employment* (%)

	Urban Areas			Rural Areas			National		
	Men	Women	Total	Men	Women	All	Men	Women	All
1 Income-earning workers (5 + 6)	74.2	44.0	58.1	72.9	52.0	61.3	73.3	49.8	60.3
2 Wage-workers	39.9	19.4	29.0	8.4	2.3	5.0	17.9	7.1	12.0
3 Own-account workers	25.4	22.2	23.7	61.5	28.0	42.9	50.7	26.4	37.3
4 Entrepreneurs	0.6	0.4	0.5	0.3	0.1	0.2	0.4	0.2	0.3
5 Total declared paid workers (2 + 3 + 4)	65.9	42.1	53.2	70.3	30.3	48.1	69.0	33.7	49.6
6 Undeclared income-earning workers	8.2	1.9	4.9	2.6	21.7	13.2	4.3	16.1	10.8
7 Non-earning workers	16.7	53.7	36.5	24.2	46.2	36.5	22.0	48.3	36.5
8 (of which: declared unpaid workers)	9.3	11.7	10.6	34.8	48.6	42.5	27.1	38.2	33.2
9 Active Unemployed	9.1	2.3	5.5	2.9	1.7	2.2	4.7	1.9	3.2
10 Total work-force (1 + 7 + 9)	100.0	100.0	100.0	100.0	100.0	100.0	100.0	100.0	100.0
11 Informal workers (3 + 6 + 7)	50.3	77.9	65.0	88.4	95.9	92.6	76.9	90.8	84.6

areas are informal workers. Among men, 88.4 per cent of those working in rural areas are informal and 50.3 per cent of those working
in urban areas are informal. Overall (Ardeni 2001), women account
for 59.1 per cent of total informal workers at the national level
(75.8 per cent in rural areas and 24.2 per cent in urban areas). As
77.7 per cent of total informal employment is in rural areas, it appears
that while informal men workers are particularly concentrated in rural
areas (four fifths of total informal male employment), almost one
fourth of informal women workers have a work activity in the city.

Even if we exclude own-account workers, who might not always be
informal (some might be registered and comply with regulations and
fiscal obligations), the share of informal workers over the total reduces
to 47.3 per cent, and in the case of women to 64.2 per cent. Therefore,
even excluding own-account workers, it is clear that in Mozambique
women depend more heavily on their informal sector employment than
men. In sum, *a majority of female employment is informal, particularly
as irregular and unpaid work*. Also, that the share of women own-
account workers is higher than that of men in urban areas seems only to
confirm that most of those own-account activities are in fact informal.
All this confirms the existence of a *gender bias* as more women are in
poor quality employment.

Employment status could also provide some indication of the quality
of employment in the informal sector. Wage-workers generally earn
less than the self-employed and entrepreneurs, so that a higher proportion of the former would indicate that overall employment quality is
inferior than otherwise. A higher share of unpaid workers would also
suggest lower employment quality, as these generally receive almost no
income. In Mozambique, more women than men are in the unpaid
categories of employment, which implies that a higher proportion of
women than men earn low incomes. And even as compared with the
rest of sub-saharan Africa, the proportion of unpaid workers among
women appears to be very high.

The empirical evidence from many developing countries indicates
that the majority of female wage employment appears to be informal.
HLSS data do not allow a direct measure of the amount of informal
wage employment in Mozambique. Only 4.3 per cent of women at the
national level declare to be wage-workers (71.9 per cent of which are
in urban areas, where they represent 21.7 per cent of total declared
wage-workers but are only a fraction of women working in the city,

11.8 per cent). In the face of these figures, we can probably assume that all women wage-workers are *formal* workers, although there is certainly a fraction that is paid below the minimum wage and should therefore be considered as informal.[20] The other three common forms of informal wage employment, i.e. domestic work, irregular wage labour, and wage labour in micro-enterprises have probably been accounted for in the table discussed above.[21] As one can see in Table 17.2, non-income-earning employment – the sum of unpaid domestic work for others and in one's own family – accounts for 45 per cent of total female employment, while undeclared income-earning employment accounts for another 13.4 per cent of the total. Once again, *the incidence of informality appears to be far greater among women than it is among men*: only 21 per cent of men workers are non-income-earning workers and only 4.9 per cent are undeclared income-earning workers. While it is true that some male wage-workers (who are 20.9 per cent of the total) might be informal, it is clear that there are far less informal wage-workers among men than among women.

Income, consumption expenditure, and gender

Income distribution and gender in Mozambique

What we can consume depends on what goods we are able to acquire. In each given social environment, and depending on the legal, institutional, cultural and economic conditions, a person can establish command over some alternative commodity bundles: the set of alternative bundles of goods over which a person can establish such commands is what has been defined as this person's *entitlements*, and it is the basis of Amartya Sen's 'entitlement approach' (Sen 1981). As a person's entitlements depend on her initial endowment and what she acquires through exchange, a lot of the command over goods that she will eventually establish thus depend on the terms of that exchange, i.e. relative prices and her purchasing power. The labour market conditions analysed above have shown that there is a considerable gender bias in Mozambique's labour market which obviously affects women's

[20] It is well known that many formal private firms, even in Mozambique, fail to respect labour laws and regulations.

[21] If we exclude wage-labour in micro-enterprises, on which we have no direct information.

entitlements, ceteris paribus, as we will see below. As women appear to be more likely to get unpaid jobs, informal jobs or simply the worst paid job as compared to men, this will affect their income levels, their purchasing power, and hence their consumption patterns. This in turn will determine women's relative poverty status, and their worse standards of living and capabilities as compared to men's.

In Mozambique, income distribution by employment status appears to be rather uneven, although not so dramatically. The male/female ratio by employment status across quintiles is almost uniform, and the distribution by employment status across income quintiles is fairly even for both sexes. Income-earning workers account for no more than 45 per cent of the total number of individuals across all quintiles (a little less for women and a little more for men). Overall, while 73 per cent of people in the upper quintile are paid workers, only 52.1 per cent in the lower quintile are paid workers. But, while among men 86.6 per cent of those in the upper quintile and 71.2 per cent in the lower quintile are paid workers, among women 59.9 per cent of those in the upper quintile and only 35.3 per cent of those in the lower quintile are paid workers, implying that *almost two thirds of women in the lower income quintile are unpaid workers*! Overall, less than 10 per cent of wage-workers are in the lower income quintile, and more than one fourth of unpaid workers are in the lower quintile. Unpaid workers are well represented among women across all quintiles, both in urban and in rural areas. Finally, while the rich tend to live in urban areas (55.2 per cent among women and 57.5 per cent among men are in the two upper quintiles), the poor tend to live in the country (47.5 per cent among women and 48.1 per cent among men are in the two lower quintiles).

The most relevant differences in employment status between men and women across income quintiles are to be found, once again, in the *payment status* (paid or unpaid). While 40 per cent of women in the upper quintile are unpaid workers, only 13 per cent of men are unpaid workers. Of all unpaid workers, 75 per cent are women, in all income quintiles. Wage-workers' income distribution tends to confirm the conjectures that *declared wage labour appears to be formal, and hence, better paid*. Among women, for instance, wage labour seems to be a condition of relative economic well being, as of all female wage-workers almost 50 per cent are in the two upper quintiles. On the other hand the two lower quintiles of income distribution account for half of women unpaid working population. Women entrepreneurs are also rather penalised in terms of income distribution, as opposed to their male counterparts (almost 45 per cent are in the two lower quintiles). This confirms that wage labour is a rather prominent economic condition, being declared and hence formal, that unpaid labour is on the other hand a rather penalising condition and that particularly women are in the lower income brackets and in the lower quality jobs. Income distribution also shows that woman-headed households are economically worse off than man-headed households. Employment status by income quintiles is apparently not too different across quintiles, but it differs, as we have seen above, according to the household head gender. Those living in urban areas are mostly in the upper quintiles (63.5 per cent for those from MHH and 54.9 per cent for those from FHH): unemployed and students are well represented in this fraction of urban population. Those living in rural areas are mostly represented in the lower quintiles, particularly among FHH. Wage-workers belonging to MHH in the lower income quintile are 19.1 per cent of those workers living in the city and only 3.5 per cent of those workers living in the country. Wage-workers belonging to FHH in the lower quintile are even less, as they are only 4.2 per cent of those living in the city and 1.7 per cent of those living in the country. Conversely wage-workers belonging to MHH in the upper quintile are 65.3 per cent of all workers living in the city but only 8.8 per cent of those living in the country. Wage-workers belonging to FHH in the upper quintile are only one third of those living in the city and just 8.4 per cent of those living in the country. Hence, *being a wage-worker in Mozambique pays if you are from a man-headed household and you live in the city.*

Own account workers are obviously over-represented in the lower quintile when they belong to a MHH, both when they live in the city (40 per cent of all workers in that income bracket) and when they live in the country (almost half of the total). Own-account workers, in any case, are much worse off when they belong to a FHH and they live in urban areas, as they account for three quarters of all workers in the lower quintile, as well as in rural areas, as they account for 63.5 per cent of all workers in the lower quintile. Finally, unpaid workers seem to be worse off when they belong to a MHH, both in urban and in rural areas: they are, respectively, 40 per cent and 50 per cent of all workers in the lower quintile. For those in a FHH, they account for 19.3 per cent and 36.5 per cent of all workers in the lower quintile in urban and rural areas, respectively.

Consumption expenditure, income, and gender

In spite of the recognised importance of Amartya Sen's contributions to the understanding of poverty, most of the indicators used in applied studies on comparative valuations of poverty conditions result from non-linear transformations of some monetary variable like consumption expenditure or income.[22] According to Buvinic (1993), one author who most forcefully argued about the *feminisation of poverty* in developing countries, consumption expenditure is the correct monetary indicator that we should use to look at poverty across households, as there are indivisible costs – i.e. fixed costs – that characterise that type of expenditure. These fixed costs are independent of the number of individuals in a household, so that *it is total household expenditure the right indicator of consumption potential.* This is an argument, however, which makes sense in a developed economy, and does not plausibly apply to a developing economy where food consumption is about three quarters of total consumption, hardly a value that allows for a great amount of fixed costs. Sticking to Angus Deaton's motto 'welfare belongs to individuals', we shall look at *per-capita consumption expenditure* – the total household average monthly expenditure[23] divided by the average number of individuals per household[24] – as it is shown in Table 17.3.

As we said, food, beverages, and tobacco represent three quarters of average per-capita consumption expenditure at the national level, a percentage that is slightly superior in rural areas than in urban areas. Overall, per-capita consumption expenditure is twice as big in urban areas than in rural areas: hence, not only do individuals belonging to rural households represent the majority, but they spend 50 per cent less then individuals belonging to urban households. Table 17.4 shows per-capita income as the sum of wage labour and self-employment income, property income, gross transfers and estimated self-consumption. Interestingly, and differently from consumption, per-capita income in urban areas is only one and a half times as big as income in rural areas. Despite the very low share of wage employment, the contribution of

[22] Sen (1976, 1981) and Atkinson (1987) described these indicators.

[23] In the case of Mozambique's HLS survey, household consumption expenditure has been calculated over a 12-month period, from which an average monthly expenditure per household has been estimated.

[24] Average per-capita consumption could also be calculated as the average of average household consumption expenditure (Deaton 1997).

Table 17.3 *Real per-capita consumption expenditure (Meticais, monthly basis)*

Expenditure Items	Urban Areas			Rural Areas			National		
	MHH	FHH	All	MHH	FHH	All	MHH	FHH	All
Food	131.545	128.440	130.852	106.301	119.948*	109.211	110.950	121.588*	113.238
Beverages and Tobacco	5.477	2.280	4.763	753	400	678	1.623	763	1.438
Clothing	11.179	7.281	10.309	7.408	5.754	7.056	8.103	6.049	7.661
Housing and Fuel	50.780	65.617	54.091	26.790	37.794*	29.136	31.208	43.166	33.780
Health Care	1.891	2.471	2.020	1.158	917	1.107	1.293	1.217	1.277
Transport and Communication	5.287	4.328	5.073	2.778	2.506	2.720	3.240	2.858	3.158
Education and Entertainment	3.087	3.374	3.151	967	499	867	1.357	1.054	1.292
Others	6.291	6.244	6.280	1.167	864	1.102	2.110	1.903	2.066
Total	215.536	220.035	216.540	147.322	168.682	151.876	159.884	178.598	163.909

*Significant at 5% (student's *t*)

Table 17.4 *Real per-capita income (Meticais, monthly basis)*

Income source	Urban Areas			Rural Areas			National		
	MHH	FHH	All	MHH	FHH	All	MHH	FHH	All
Wage Labour	55.817	40.218	52.874	10.328	3.650*	9.231	19.343	11.946	18.088
Self-employment	47.653	45.342	47.310	71.220	77.092	72.348	65.460	67.088	65.926
Self-consumption	9.107	11.007	9.503	6.197	8.224*	6.549	6.695	8.578*	7.046
Property Income	4.144	4.779	4.279	23.678	34.484	25.534	19.406	26.439	20.703
Transfers (gross)	7.059	15.617*	8.763	4.728	10.159*	5.647	5.130	11.062*	6.192
Other Receipts	498	1.064	574	2.159	2.248	2.178	1.784	1.897	1.809
Total	124.278	118.027	123.303	118.310	135.858*	121.487	117.819	127.011	119.765

*Significant at 5% (Student's *t*)

wage labour income to per-capita income looks significant in the cities and very low in rural areas. Conversely, self-employment income (in per-capita terms) appears to be rather constant across areas.

The comparison between FHH and MHH shows that, overall, individuals belonging to woman-headed households spend more both in urban and in rural areas (Table 17.5). However, only for those living in rural areas and belonging to FHH per-capita consumption expenditure appears to be significantly higher than that of those belonging to MHH.[25] Individuals belonging to MHH have, on average, a higher per-capita income if they live in the city and a lower per-capita income if they live in the country than that of those belonging to FHH (Table 17.4), albeit statistically non significant. Per-capita income is significantly higher for individuals in FHH living in the country. On the whole, per-capita income seems to be slightly higher whenever a woman heads the household (but not significantly higher). This contrasts with the argument that FHH are worse off than MHH. Even if we only consider food consumption, the evidence seems to favour woman-headed households.

Total household consumption expenditure, however, is greater for MHH than for FHH, both in rural and in urban areas (Ardeni 2001). This obviously leads us to question the importance of household size, as age does not seem to be a significantly different factor across households. As we said above, FHH are significantly smaller than MHH.[26]

The correlation between per-capita consumption and household size is negative and significant. Therefore, in the case of Mozambique, the household size effect is important, although it favours FHH, which have a smaller average size than MHH. As this is an economy where food consumption is so important (68.9 per cent in Table 17.3 above),

---

[25] Statistically, the student's *t* test is significant for food and housing expenditures.

[26] The kernel estimate of the number of household components shows that the density of FHH is concentrated around a value that is systematically lower than that of MHH. As we have seen above, the distinguishing feature of household composition in Mozambique is the larger size of MHH as compared to FHH (5.08 vs. 3.96). We know there are several reasons to explain the demographics of Mozambique: years of prolonged war, with the consequent displacement and men toll, migration to neighbouring South Africa and Zimbabwe, particularly of young men. In our sample, of all women heads of households, 40 per cent are widows and 25 per cent are divorced or separated. Less than 20 per cent of women heads are actually married (as opposed to 80 per cent of men). Deaton (1997) states that in his opinion this is a sort of 'stylised fact': 'In all household survey data of which I am aware, total household expenditure rises with household size, but not so rapidly, so that per-capita expenditure decreases with household size.'

Table 17.5 *Per-capita consumption by area and gender of household head by employment status (Meticais, monthly basis)*

	Urban Areas			Rural Areas			National		
	MHH	FHH	All	MHH	FHH	All	MHH	FHH	All
Income-earning workers	199455	212386	201775	135370	157503	139021	146347	167721	149926
Active unemployed	201844	267292	216281	180255	144473	173970	187681	194895	189063
Unpaid workers	180255	143135	173388	119142	126730	120404	130159	130013	130134
Students	200356	232058	206674	117205	140032	121668	144373	170587	149530
Others	139497	149185	141680	106541	126896	110192	112053	131596	115716

it should not come as a surprise that per-capita expenditure and household size are inversely correlated. One could argue that most MHH, thanks to their larger size, could better exploit some sort of scale economies. However, as we will see below, this argument does not sound too robust (it is difficult to think of any economy of scale with regard to food consumption, as two persons generally eat twice as much as one person).

The comparison between per-capita consumption of male-headed and female-headed households by the household head's marital status is also interesting. As Drèze and Sen (1981) pointed out for rural India, the household head's marital status can be an important element for a deeper analysis of poverty conditions. FHH in which the household head is a widow or divorced are more disadvantaged in relative terms not only vis-à-vis the correspondent man-headed households, but also vis-à-vis the entire FHH group (Ardeni 2001). Conversely, FHH with an unmarried head have access to a per-capita consumption level greater than that of married or cohabiting heads of households. In any case they both have a per-capita consumption level greater than the correspondent MHH.

All the estimates discussed above ignore the composition of households: households with more or less children are, in fact, different. In the medical literature, as well as in some economic literature, it is acknowledged that the necessary caloric requirement of individuals is not uniform across age (and maybe sex) and may be different across households, living conditions, climate, and so on. Atkinson (1998), in referring to the per-capita consumption level to be used as the threshold beyond which one gets the sad qualification of 'physically poor', states: 'The term *absolute* can, however scarcely, be used in the same sense of physical sciences and there is a scope for a great deal of disagreement about where the line should be drawn.' It is beyond the purpose of this chapter to discuss the complex question of how to ponder individual consumption expenditures in order to account for the different energy requirements. Yet following the WHO indications (WHO 1985), we may treat household composition by weighing all household components according to their age and sex, thus obtaining a 'WHO-adult-equivalent' number of components for every household.[27] Adult-equivalent estimates of consumption expenditure and income confirm the above evidence: FHH spend more than MHH, both in urban and in rural areas. This is not surprising, as the *average household*

---

[27] Adult-equivalent estimates of per-capita consumption are not shown here.

composition is not as different between FHH and MHH as much as the *average household size*. Conversely, per-capita income is higher for MHH living in urban areas but slightly lower for those MHH living in the country (Ardeni 2001).

It was recalled above that the entitlements of a person are the set of alternative commodity bundles that that person can acquire. Ceteris paribus, women's exchange entitlements have been shown to be often worse than men's. Consequently, we expect different employment conditions by gender and household type affect consumption patterns differently, and in favour of men. Table 17.3 shows that this is actually not the case. In urban areas, individuals belonging to FHH have higher per-capita consumption expenditures than individuals belonging to MHH if they are income-earning workers, unemployed, or out of the labour force, while they have lower consumption levels when they are unpaid workers. In rural areas, individuals belonging to FHH have higher consumption levels all the time except when they are unemployed (but per-capita consumption is much lower anyway). Table 17.5 partly explains this result. Formal workers (wage-workers) living in urban areas are better off when they belong to FHH, while those living in rural areas are better off when they belong to MHH (but their per-capita consumption is much lower). Informal workers (own-account and unpaid workers) are in the opposite condition: when living in the city they are better off if they belong to MHH, when living in the country they are relatively better off if they belong to FHH. Once again, it is confirmed that women are able to work out less penalising living conditions only when they have access to the more protected and less vulnerable job market positions.

In conclusion individuals belonging to woman-headed households show higher per-capita consumption levels both in urban and in rural areas. The correlation between per-capita consumption and household size is negative and significant. Also, per-capita income seems to be slightly higher whenever a woman heads the household. And yet, individuals in woman-headed households have higher per-capita consumption expenditures when they have an income-earning (mostly formal) job or are either unemployed or out of the labour market. Conversely, they have lower per-capita spending levels when they have an unpaid (mostly informal) job. Considering that individuals belonging to female-headed households living in urban areas are only 7 per cent of total population, and that 95 per cent of women living in

Table 17.6 *Per-capita consumption by area and gender of household head by type of work (Meticais, monthly basis)*

	Urban Areas			Rural Areas			National		
	MHH	FHH	All	MHH	FHH	All	MHH	FHH	All
Wage-workers	248699	316246	257578	157053	148860	156191	208810	253536	214188
Own-account workers	169937	165583	168918	139886	161387	144238	143401	161965	147229
Entrepreneurs	260254	114500	230665	204864	138746	196168	231793	123856	213681
Declared unpaid workers	134605	126970	133117	121658	129143	122671	122329	128974	123249

rural areas have an informal job, we can conclude that *women are generally worse off than men*, i.e. *poorer* (entitlement failure coupled with capability deprivation).

Poverty and gender in Mozambique

Formal and informal employment, gender and consumption-based indicators of poverty

The recent literature has brought about a large amount of evidence purporting that the labour market in most developing countries is characterised not only by a gender gap but also that the gender gap is larger in the informal sector. In other words, there should be a close association between informality and gender bias. Several explanations have been suggested, and yet the differences in 'human capital' endowments (as measured, for instance, by education and schooling) can explain only a small portion of the gender disparity in wages and very little of the gender gap in employment status and type of work. The gender gap seems to be more attributable to the labour market structure, i.e. to several labour market 'imperfections' and plain discrimination. Not only are women more likely to find informal (as opposed to formal) employment, but they typically receive lower incomes than men and have lower quality jobs. What the results above suggest, in fact, is that individuals who have informal jobs also have lower per-capita expenditures when they belong to a woman-headed household, and therefore *women who have informal jobs (and possibly get lower incomes) have lower per-capita expenditures, too.*

In developing countries, a substantial proportion of women have informal employment, a proportion that is generally higher for women than for men. This is confirmed in Mozambique too. Women who have an informal employment usually earn low incomes, and that is often associated with low levels of human capital and various labour market imperfections and segmentations. Women's income also tends to be lower than men's. However, as we have seen above, in Mozambique, declared per-capita income seems to be higher in woman-headed households, particularly in those living in rural areas (Table 17.4).

Since in most cases women with an informal employment are the main 'bread winners' in the family, it turns out that those families which depend on women's contribution to the household income are more likely to live in poverty. In particular, in most developing countries, woman-headed households are more likely to live in poverty than man-headed households. Yet, women in FHH are not always the chief earners, and the importance of women's contribution to household income varies. In any case, there is apparently a clear tendency showing that the poorer the women and their working conditions the higher the likelihood of being chief earners in their family. In particular, it appears that the proportion of women who work in the informal sector and are the sole earners in the family is considerably high in most developing countries.

Poverty seems to be a distinguishing feature of woman-headed households around the developing world. Empirical evidence shows, in fact, that the share of FHH over the total number of household is usually not too big, while it is generally higher among low-income households. Thus, households headed by women are more likely to be below the poverty line compared to households headed by men: woman-headed households are over-represented among poor households.[28] Now, as we said above, the proportion of individuals who earn low incomes is larger in the informal sector than in the formal sector. This implies that households that depend on the informal sector are more likely to be poor. All across Sub-Saharan Africa there appears to be a strong association between poverty and type of employment.[29] The incidence of poverty is found to be higher among women household heads who are self-employed in the informal sector,[30] although not always so.

The proportion of poor people working in the informal sector is also high, although not all poor are in the informal sector (a significant

---

[28] The evidence from Sub-Saharan Africa seems to support the hypothesis of a gender bias: FHH are three times more likely to be poor in Burkina Faso, twice as likely in Cameroon and Mali and just as likely in Madagascar (Lachaud 1994). The share of FHH was 14.9 per cent and 4.4 per cent among the poor and the non-poor, respectively, in Burkina Faso, 25.9 per cent and 12.1 per cent in Cameroon, 14 per cent and 11 per cent in Madagascar, and 10.6 per cent and 5.5 per cent in Mali (Lachaud 1994).

[29] In several African cities large numbers of informal workers belong to poor households (Lachaud 1996).

[30] For instance: 100 per cent in Ouagadougou, as opposed to 86 per cent of men household heads; 88 per cent in Yaounde as opposed to 50 per cent of men household heads.

number of low-income workers is in fact to be found in the formal sector).[31] Moreover, for a large majority of women their main job is in the informal sector, mostly in the low-income activities. In recent years the pressure on women to enter the labour market, and hence the informal sector, has dramatically increased because of the decline in real income, particularly in Africa.[32] Women's income has contributed to a reduction in the level of poverty of many households: although the importance of women's contribution to household income varies, it appears that the size of contribution is particularly significant for poor households. Women's employment in the informal sector thus contributes to a reduction in household poverty, particularly among the poorest households. Inevitably, then, women in poor households are more actively involved in some work activity than women in non-poor households. And yet, they are more likely to work in the informal sector, thus earning low incomes.

In sum, the evidence suggests a strong correlation between women, informality, and poverty, in all developing countries, particularly in Africa. Women from the poorest households are able to reduce their poverty thanks to their informal employment, despite low earnings, and thus the number of poorest household actually tends to decline as women's participation in the informal sector rises.

In the case of Mozambique and with the available data, how can we assess whether women are poorer than men? Obviously, there are many ways one can define 'poverty' and they are all fundamentally relative to some 'consumption norms' or some 'poverty line'.[33] How can we measure 'poverty'? From the 'biological approach' to the 'inequality approach' to the 'relative deprivation approach'; all have been criticised on several grounds. In what follows we will first present a set of measures based on *consumption expenditures* (in this section)

---

[31] According to Lachaud (1988), in Abidjan (Cote d'Ivoire) in 1986, 83.3 per cent of the absolute poor were self-employed own-account workers, as opposed to the 25.9 per cent of those belonging to the high-income group.

[32] Between 1980 and 1986 real income in 27 African countries has declined by about a third (Lachaud 1994), and by 1990 it was about a third lower than ten years before. In the decade, female heads of households have increased their labour force participation rate by about 20 per cent.

[33] See Sen (1981) for an interesting and thorough discussion on the concepts and measures of poverty.

and then compare them with a different set of measures based on *capabilities* (in the next section).

All the above comparisons in terms of consumption patterns between man-headed and woman-headed households can be summarised by means of indexes of *relative poverty intensity*, through different versions of the so-called 'Foster-Greer-Thorbecke' index. More precisely, the Head-Count Index (HCI) represents the share of people below the poverty line ('incidence'), the Poverty Gap Index (PGI), the normalised sum of the deviations from the poverty line ('depth'), and the Squared Poverty Gap Index (SPGI), the squared normalised sum of the deviations from the poverty line ('severity'). The poverty line is taken here as being equal to 163,000 Mt per months, i.e. 5,264 Mt per day (about half a US dollar) and is almost equal to the one used by IFPRI. The poverty line is taken as approximately equal to the 50th-quintile (not the median) household expenditure. This means that we are measuring *relative poverty* through the *distribution* of consumption expenditure across household. In our opinion this is preferable in as much as it is closer to the concept of inequality, being the case of a comparison among monetary aggregates. All of these measures allow us to qualify what we already stated above when we discussed the distribution of consumption expenditure among households, as poverty indexes are just a non-linear transformation of expenditure measures.

According to these measures, it appears that in Mozambique *poor* households are the great majority (67 per cent), less in urban areas (62 per cent), and more in rural areas (69 per cent). Poor FHH are proportionally less frequent than non-poor MHH nation-wide, as well as in rural areas. In urban areas FHH are more likely to be poor than MHH. For woman-headed households poverty intensity is significantly higher in urban areas, while it is significantly lower in rural areas. Table 17.7 shows all of these poverty indexes.

Ultra-poverty indexes show a similar picture (ultra-poverty is defined as half the value of the poverty line). While in urban areas FHH are significantly ultra-poorer than MHH, in rural areas almost 50 per cent of individuals belonging to a man-headed household are ultra-poor. The results are slightly ambiguous, as in urban areas MHH tend to be slightly less poor than FHH, although in rural areas there live more than 70 per cent of all households included in the sample.

Table 17.7 *Poverty and ultra-poverty indexes*

	Urban area			Rural area			National		
	MHH	FHH	All	MHH	FHH	All	MHH	FHH	All
Incidence (HCI)	0.61	0.65	0.62	0.70	0.64*	0.69	0.67	0.64	0.67
Depth (PGI)	0.26	0.29	0.27	0.30	0.26*	0.27	0.29	0.27	0.28
Severity (SPGI)	0.14	0.17*	0.15	0.16	0.13*	0.15	0.15	0.14	0.15

Ultra-Poverty

	Urban area			Rural area			National		
	MHH	FHH	All	MHH	FHH	All	MHH	FHH	All
Incidence (HCI)	0.34	0.41*	0.36	0.39	0.33*	0.38	0.37	0.35	0.37
Depth (PGI)	0.11	0.14*	0.12	0.12	0.10	0.11	0.11	0.11	0.11
Severity (SPGI)	0.05	0.07	0.06	0.05	0.04	0.05	0.05	0.05	0.05

In this raw comparison of poverty indexes between FHH and MHH sensitive to household size (which we have seen is substantially lower for FHH than for MHH), we find that in general per-capita consumption expenditure seems to be sensitive to household size, although it tends to decrease with the number of household components. In urban areas there appear to be no size economy effect. In rural areas, there is a noticeable size economy effect only for very large numbers of household components. If we separate MHH and FHH we get a slightly different picture. In urban areas, per-capita consumption in FHH does show a rank reversal as size increases, although the general tendency is not clear. In rural areas, there is a more definite size economy effect, apparently, both for MHH and FHH. Per-capita consumption decreases with size up to seven components and then it increases as the size rises. Yet, it seems that this effect cannot be attributed uniformly to any gender bias in household composition, as the size effect is very similar across households of different heads. In sum, the relationship between poverty indexes and household size appears to be negative, although very weak, and in any case not sufficient to justify some 'rank reversal' of the poverty profile discussed above.

Table 17.8 *Poor people by area and gender of household head by employment status and work type (percentage belonging to poor households)*

		Urban areas			Rural areas		
		MHH	FHH	All	MHH	FHH	All
1	Income-earning workers	64.1	67.2	64.7	77.6	67.6	75.8
2	Wage-workers	61.4	61.8	61.5	66.7	73.6	67.5
3	Own account	65.8	70.4	67.1	94.2	67.1	87.3
4	Entrepreneurs	42.3	85.7	51.5	45.8	80.0	51.7
5	Total declared paid workers	63.1	67.2	63.9	90.1	67.5	84.7
6	Undeclared income-earning workers	76.7	66.7	75.2	53.6	69.0	54.4
7	Non-earning workers	71.1	82.1	73.4	80.0	79.8	79.9
8	Declared unpaid	72.1	75.4	72.7	78.9	78.8	78.9
9	Active unemployed	72.4	68.9	71.7	78.6	66.7	76.6
10	Total work-force $(1 + 7 + 9)$	67.1	72.9	68.3	78.5	71.7	77.4
11	Total informal workers $(3 + 6 + 7)$	69.6	76.4	71.1	79.3	71.8	78.0
12	Formal workers $(2 + 4)$	61.1	62.4	61.3	66.0	74.0	66.9
13	Students	16.6	65.4	36.0	80.8	77.3	80.1
14	Others	78.2	78.2	78.2	84.8	81.7	84.2
15	Total working-age population	59.7	70.9	62.5	79.6	74.0	78.6

Poverty status shows also a weak correlation with employment status and a stronger correlation with work type across sexes (Ardeni 2001). Active population in urban areas is generally better off than in rural areas. In urban areas, women wage-workers tend to be in higher proportion than men wage-workers among the non-poor. In rural areas, women are less represented than men among wage-workers. Being a paid worker helps men more than women, both in urban and in rural areas. Employment status and work type together give the amount of formal and informal work, and it is interesting to look at its correlation with poverty status (Table 17.8). While informal workers belong to a poor family in 71.1 per cent of the cases when they live in the city and in 78 per cent of the cases when they live in the country, formal workers are from a poor family in 61.3 per cent of the cases in urban areas and in 66.9 per cent of the cases in rural areas. Hence, *informal workers are more likely to be from a poor household*. Informal workers are poorer when they are from a woman-headed household and live in urban areas while they are generally poorer when they are from a man-headed household and live in rural areas. On the other hand, formal workers are poorer when they are from an FHH, no matter where they live (although in rural areas they are worse off and more frequent). Hence, being informal does not help woman-headed households much more than man-headed households in terms of poverty status.

Capabilities as indicators of well-being and poverty

As Sen has several times pointed out the concept of well-being must be complemented by individual autonomy and responsibility. By considering explicitly the problem of the *'capacity to choose'*, standard poverty measures like the Headcount Index, the Poverty Gap Index and the Squared Poverty Gap Index have been widely criticised, and yet remain some of the most widely used rough indicators of poverty. Sen (1981, 1992) has strongly insisted on the so-called 'capability approach' to the measurement and assessment of poverty. 'Formally, a person's *capability* is a set of functioning bundles, representing the various alternative "beings and doings" that a person can achieve with his or her economic, social, and personal characteristics'. While the *'entitlement* is a set of commodity bundles, the *capability* of a person is a set of alternative functioning bundles' (Drèze and Sen 1989, p. 13).

For the scope of an evaluation exercise, like the one we are actually performing, a consumption-based measurement of well-being is informationally limited to the extent that the available observations do not include some important functionings such as 'being in good health, avoid escapable morbidity/premature mortality', and 'having a good education'. Of course, a necessary condition for this kind of comparison is the viability of detailed and complex micro-data on education and health outcomes, which has been, in the case of Mozambique, a very limiting condition. The conversion of consumption (or income) into capability and function, is complex, and may vary across individuals – in Sen's words there is a parametric variation in income-capability relationship (Sen 1992, p. 124). But, on the other hand, consumption patterns may reflect differences in functionings and corresponding disparities in elementary capabilities. For example, why has a FHH got a high share of education expenditure? Is it actually not so poor or has it got a lack of capabilities?

It is in this spirit, therefore, that in this and in the following sections, we will account directly for some basic functionings, regarding the education, health, and asset ownerships. When we depart from a pure resources-based measurement of well-being then we can show that differential female deprivation is in fact of extraordinary proportions, especially in terms of 'being able to read and write', and, generally, in all educational outcomes. In an important sense, the direct accounting of functioning, can be relevant for an analysis of the dynamic aspects of capability deprivation, to the extent there may be a cyclical situation of disparities; this is the case, for example, for the difference we find in the school attendance of the children.

Moreover, patterns of unequal distribution of capabilities between males and females may be persistent by means of inherited wealth, as we will see in the next section. From a theoretical point of view, the unequal distribution of capabilities and functionings may be set in causal relationship with the patterns we shall observe in terms of asset ownership, and, certainly, they complete the scenario of vulnerability of which females suffer in Mozambique. If we merge these pieces of evidence on functionings with the inability of the FHH to have 'a good and socially protected job', that we have dealt with in the first section, we might understand why Sen is right when he says that it is possible that gender differences, in developing countries, are often inadequately captured by expenditure levels.

Consider first literacy rates by area and gender by age group (Table 17.9). As expected, these are reasonably high in urban areas and dramatically low in rural areas, particularly for women. Gender inequalities tend to be large in all age groups and tend to increase with age. In rural areas, for instance, only one woman out of ten older than thirty is literate and the FMR for that age group is 0.21. Children under 14 (especially girls) appear to be particularly penalised when they live in rural areas. Hence, being a child in Mozambique is a rather difficult condition, particularly if one lives in the country. The most fortunate are those living in the city, as they can get some education (literacy) in 75 per cent of the cases. Being a little girl in Mozambique is an even more difficult condition, as in less than one case out of ten one would get some elementary education, and only in one case out of four when

Table 17.9 *Literacy rates by area and gender and female–male ratios by age groups (percentages)*

Age groups	Urban areas				Rural areas				National			
	Men	Women	Total	Female Male Ratio	Men	Women	Total	Female Male Ratio	Men	Women	Total	Female Male Ratio
7–10	53.72	51.93	52.83	96.7	11.93	9.21	10.54	77.2	25.26	22.40	23.82	88.7
10–14	77.70	73.45	75.48	94.5	35.04	25.59	30.36	73.0	48.90	42.25	45.55	86.4
15–19	88.51	84.06	86.33	95.0	54.93	40.36	48.06	73.5	67.28	57.11	62.42	84.9
19–24	92.59	83.36	87.81	90.0	59.22	31.63	42.68	53.4	73.19	49.27	59.58	67.3
24–30	93.07	75.81	84.02	81.4	59.35	26.07	39.51	43.9	72.35	41.91	54.96	57.9
30–59	87.68	56.27	71.70	64.2	53.27	11.18	30.19	21.0	64.77	24.69	43.29	38.1
>59	63.57	28.47	45.42	44.8	28.18	3.87	17.17	13.7	36.51	10.88	24.48	29.8

Table 17.10 *Distribution of individuals by area and gender by years of schooling (percentage over total)*

	Urban area		Rural area		National	
Years of schooling	Men	Women	Men	Women	Men	Women
No schooling	21.9	43.2	57.5	75.3	44.2	59.3
Some primary	37.9	30.8	30.6	20.1	33.4	25.5
Complete primary	21.2	15.4	10.1	3.7	14.3	9.6
Some Secondary	8.9	4.2	1.2	0.6	4.1	2.4
Complete Secondary	4.3	3.6	0.2	0.0	1.8	1.8
Technical school	4.5	2.4	0.2	0.0	1.8	1.2
Higher education	1.3	0.3	0.2	0.3	0.5	0.2
Total	100	100	100	100	100	100

older (between 10 and 14). Gender inequalities are striking, especially in rural areas, where not even three girls for every four boys get literacy.

The distribution of individuals by area and gender by years of schooling (Table 17.10) confirms these results. One again, gender inequalities are striking. In urban areas, 43.2 per cent of all women have no schooling (as opposed to 21.9 per cent of men). In rural areas, 75.3 per cent of all women have no schooling (as opposed to 57.5 per cent of men) and 20.1 per cent did not finish primary school. The lack of education is thus astounding, as is the gender bias: less than 16 per cent of all women in urban areas has completed primary school or some higher level of schooling. In sum, not only is there a dramatic lack of education but education is certainly gender biased in Mozambique.

The gender bias is confirmed in the way children are raised (Table 17.11). In man-headed households, among those attending school the share of boys is systematically higher than that of girls, both in urban and in rural areas. At the same time, among those who do not attend school, girls predominate. In woman-headed households, the pattern is not too different, particularly in rural areas, while in urban areas there is a slighter preference for girls. Girls are therefore penalised in primary education. The gender bias is all too homogeneous across the country: girls receive less education than boys.

Health conditions show no better picture of deprivation and poverty in Mozambique. Women are more frequently sick, and yet they see a

Table 17.11 *Children by school attendance and gender of household head by area and sex (percentages)*

	Children (7–14 years old)	MHH			FHH			All		
Area		Attend school	Do not attend school	Total	Attend school	Do not attend school	Total	Attend school	Do not attend school	Total
Urban	Boys	52.2	45.7	50.9	44.9	45.2	45.0	50.8	45.6	49.5
	Girls	47.8	54.3	49.1	55.1	54.8	55.0	49.2	54.4	50.5
Rural	Boys	57.0	44.9	50.6	53.8	45.9	49.9	56.4	45.1	50.5
	Girls	43.0	55.1	49.4	46.2	54.1	50.1	43.6	54.9	49.5
Total	Boys	54.9	45.0	50.7	49.9	45.7	48.1	53.9	45.2	50.2
	Girls	45.1	55.0	49.3	50.1	54.3	51.9	46.1	54.8	49.8

Table 17.12 *Health conditions of children and adults by area and gender of household head*

	Urban areas		Rural areas		National	
	MHH	FHH	MHH	FHH	MHH	FHH
Mean days lost to illness in the last 30 years						
Boys	1.46	2.04	1.12	1.63	1.35	1.66
Girls	1.48	1.75	1.11	2.12	1.37	1.61
Men	2.12	1.28	1.43	1.91	1.20	1.89
Women	1.75	3.01	2.66	3.79	2.38	3.50
Anthropometric indicators (under 5 years of age only): Stunting(%)						
Boys	28.71	34.42	50.57	46.08	43.84	42.04
Girls	28.36	30.08	48.19	49.08	42.54	43.30
Wasting(%)						
Boys	18.33	23.26	33.70	30.22	28.97	27.48
Girls	15.10	14.68	23.45	25.56	21.01	21.95
Percent of sick household members who saw professional medical workers						
Children	76.2	67.5	50.1	46.0	57.9	54.2
Adults	73.0	63.8	40.8	36.1	49.3	45.8
Children under 10 getting vaccine by sex						
Boys	51.4	53.1	48.9	48.3	49.9	50.4
Girls	48.6	46.9	51.1	51.7	50.1	49.6

doctor or medical professional less frequently than men, particularly in rural areas. Anthropometric indicators are more favourable to boys, although girls in rural areas are more likely to be vaccinated.[34]

In conclusion, education and health indicators show that in terms of capability deprivation, Mozambique is still quite behind and much in line with other developing countries. Gender inequalities are as evident as one can possibly see from the simple data at hand. This confirms that women are not given the same opportunities as men, and hence the same capabilities, which reinforces the claim that they are deprived not just of the basic material needs but also of the capabilities to achieve

[34] HLSS data do not allow for any consideration about mortality rates or morbidity rates, which could possibly be taken from census data.

better living conditions in the future. Women in Mozambique face the prospect of a poor life, poor in terms of current consumption possibilities (income and employment conditions) and future consumption possibilities (education and health).

Asset-based indicators of poverty

All consumption-based indicators of poverty measure *actual* expenditure, implicitly assuming that rational individuals do act primarily to satisfy their needs and interests[35] so that their expenditure patterns reveal their *state* and levels of deprivation. Income-based indicators measure *actual* purchasing *capacity*: under the same rationality assumption this reveals individuals' *possible* expenditure pattern and their possible ending *state* and eventual levels of deprivation. All of these measures have been widely criticised, and yet remain the most used indicators of poverty. Sen's capability approach to the measurement and assessment of poverty gives alternative measures not so much of expenditure patterns as about capability (choice) *potentials*.

The poverty measures based on actual or potential expenditure patterns do not consider one important and fundamental variable that generally has a profound influence on consumption profiles: the *ownership of assets*.[36] There is growing empirical evidence, at the microeconomic level, on the relationship between ownership and distribution of assets and poverty.[37] In most developing countries, credit markets are 'rationed' and the initial distribution of wealth can be a strong impediment to change and improvement in households' economic conditions. Social, economic and cultural conditions (i.e. traditions) are strongly intertwined and can play a big role. In the case of land, for instance, it is very important to understand how legislation on property rights evolves and, in particular, how norms, customs, and rules condition inheritance practices, sometimes penalise women or

---

[35] See the interesting discussion on what motivates individual 'consumption', whether interest, well-being or advantage, in Sen (1999) and the consequences thereof.

[36] Another important missing variable in consumption-based measures of poverty is consumption of public goods.

[37] A widely studied relationship, beginning with the seminal article by Deininger and Squire (1998), has been that between assets and long-run economic growth (through series of not always convincing cross-section estimates).

children.[38] The problem of asset ownership is, thus, clearly related to the capability approach, to the extent that it may influence women's initiative and agency, and balance economic and social power between women and men. In other words, asset ownership is linked to the question of social capability and empowerment of women.

Mozambique's economy is still based on agriculture, with an agrarian structure where land – especially the *machamba*, the vegetable garden for household use – is one of the most widely owned assets. Almost every single household has its own *machamba*, and most use it just for own consumption. It is therefore important to consider that the vegetable garden can be an important source of consumption goods that does not necessarily fall into the statistically observed commodity bundle accounted for by the HLSS. It is true that own-consumption goods have supposedly been accounted for in the survey, but the ownership of such an asset has a consumption *stabilisation* function that cannot be accounted for in the consumption bundle. Livestock is also an important asset playing the same function: security in the provision of food for the lean times, security for the value as collateral it can offer.

We have explored the possibility of creating an *index of assets owned by the household* to verify the conjecture that assets do affect consumption patterns and hence poverty levels.[39] An index of assets owned must capture *heterogeneity in the access to ownership* among household groups and between MHH and FHH. We have included land (number of households owning *machambas*, average size in hectares), livestock, house, and durable goods. Durables include TV, radio, transportation vehicles and all other goods characterising 'living conditions' and 'housing characteristics', like water sources (wells, taps), type of fuel used for cooking and heating, are all considered as important indicators of

---

[38] In Mozambique, for instance, the 'land law' promulgated in December 1998 ignited a fierce debate on what should have been the relationship between property rights – still exclusively pertaining to the state – and the several tenure options allowed, including individual, communal, municipal and traditional ones.

[39] With annual data, it is actually difficult to explore such a conjecture. From the stock of animals and land owned it is difficult to quantify the flow (net sale transactions) having just one annual figure. Households can in fact, use livestock transactions in the medium and long run to overcome situations of temporary economic stress.

household *permanent income*, and hence an important element in discriminating between temporary and prolonged deprivation.

Filmer *et al.* (1998) and Filmer and Pritchett (1999) have recently studied the relationship between asset ownership and children's school attendance in a few developing countries (after controlling for the presence of schools in the vicinity and roads). Sahn and Stifel (2000) have shown how an aggregate asset ownership indicator can be an important discriminating factor for poverty comparisons over time and across space.

In the construction of an *index of assets owned by households* we could 'condense' in one index the relative distribution of land, livestock, durable goods and housing characteristics across households. The problem of constructing such an index is thus the problem of constructing a measure:

$$A_J = \beta_1 \, a_{i1} + \beta_2 \, a_{i2} + \beta_3 \, a_{j3} + \ldots + \beta_k \, a_{ik} \qquad (1)$$

where $j = 1, \ldots, N$ are households and $i = 1, \ldots, K$ are assets owned. Besides the problems that can arise because of qualitative differences among assets (which in principle could require specific corrective mechanisms), the construction of an asset index, once the quantities owned by every household are known, is no different from the estimation of the β weights. If asset market prices were known exactly, one could use prices as β weights. In the case of Mozambique, the only prices available are those included in the document attached to the HLSS survey questionnaire.[40] Also, it is not always clear how to evaluate asset values, whether at current values (what obsolescence rate?) or at purchasing values (what current market prices?).

An alternative method to construct *index of assets owned by households*, which we will attempt here, is that of using a 'principal components' statistical estimate.[41] As we know, principal components analysis seeks linear combinations of a number of variables able to capture the largest possible variability and to replace them with a more

---

[40] At the 'Poverty Alleviation Unit' of the Finance Ministry in Mozambique, in order to determine the 'use value' of the durable goods owned by households, market prices have been used. Yet, those prices do not look too reliable: most of them were (informally) observed in some street markets, in the capital city of Maputo alone.

[41] See Sahn, D. and D. Stifel (2000).

synthetic and sufficiently 'close' (in terms of distance) index. From an economic point of view, this is like assuming that for every household in the sample there exists one single 'factor' (say 'wealth') that determines the variability in asset ownership (a strong and arguable assumption). From a statistical point of view, considering the data sample variance–covariance matrix, it is possible to project orthogonally[42] the standardised data matrix thus obtaining linear combinations of the data known as *principal components*. It is easy to show that the first such combination is the first principal component, that is, the one that captures the largest possible variability in the data. In practice, in the construction of an aggregate index, one usually extracts only the first principal component, and the coefficients of that linear combination are chosen as the β weights for constructing the index itself.

At the same time, the different categories (values for discrete variables) of a variable can be attributed a 'score', representing increasing degrees of asset ownership, going from a minimum to a maximum of 'satisfaction' for the possession.[43] Atkinson (1999) has recently proposed the technique of attributing scores to categories, as an alternative to the simple opposition between ownership and no ownership used in several studies.[44] Once the β weights have been calculated, scores can be multiplied by their respective weights and the index constructed.

The index of assets owned has thus been constructed with the following β weights: 0.35 (durables), 0.38 (water), 0.37 (fuel), 0.35 (sanitation), 0.32 (housing characteristics). Obviously, such an index has to be interpreted cautiously, as it is very sensitive to types of goods included (some might also have been considered as completely non-influent by families, thus inducing a strong bias in the index). Moreover, as Deaton has pointed out, asset distribution can be a degenerative one.[45] Given these warnings, we can then rank all households in our sample according to such an asset index. By fixing at the 50th percentile (as we did for the poverty line) the cutoff value for a 'theoretical' *asset poverty line,*

---

[42] Such a projection is made through the matrix, whereby the columns represent eigenvectors corresponding to the eigenvalues ranked in decreasing order of the data sample variance–covariance matrix.

[43] For instance, for durables, a score of 1 could represent the category 'no durable goods owned', a score of 2 'one or two goods', and so on, up to a maximum of 4.

[44] See also Klasen (2000).

[45] In our case, one further problem was the existence of so many missing values for several variables.

Table 17.13 *Asset ownership by area and gender of household head and asset poverty*

	Urban areas		Rural areas		National	
	MHH	FHH	MHH	FHH	MHH	FHH
Assets Ownership (Land and Livestock)						
Household with cultivable land, machambas (%)	45.84	47.79	97.75	96.28	82.61	81.10
Cultivable land per household (hectares)	2.53	2.23	1.95	1.57	2.44	2.11
Household owing livestock(%)	14.69	9.52	40.26	27.52	32.81	21.88
Asset Poor*	0.12	0.23	0.71	0.80	0.54	0.63
Asset Poor and Household Size						
0–3	0.20	0.35	0.78	0.86	0.65	0.75
4–6	0.14	0.21	0.73	0.77	0.57	0.58
7–10	0.07	0.08	0.63	0.63	0.42	0.40
11+	0.04	0.01	0.40	0.57	0.13	0.19
Quintiles of per-capita expenditure						
1st quintile	0.35	0.49	0.84	0.88	0.75	0.76
2nd quintile	0.22	0.30	0.73	0.85	0.62	0.73
3rd quintile	0.11	0.17	0.69	0.83	0.53	0.62
4th quintile	0.05	0.16	0.41	0.74	0.47	0.57
5th quintile	0.05	0.10	0.57	0.72	0.32	0.49

*Percentage of households below the 50th percentile of the *index of household asset ownership* distribution

we can then say that every household whose index value is below that line is 'asset poor'. Obviously, the meaning of poverty, in this context, is different from the one used above.[46]

Results are shown in Table 17.13. In the first part, some aggregate data are shown. While it seems there are not many differences between man-headed and woman-headed households in terms of land owner-ship (they both own some cultivable land in about the same percentages in urban and rural areas), it appears that MHH have larger pieces of

---

[46] Filmer and Pritchett (1999) claim that the rankings deriving from the two approaches are consistent.

land, on average (this can be probably explained with the larger house-hold size of MHH), and many more MHH than FHH own livestock. On average, then, we can say that MHH are wealthier (less asset poor) than FHH.

The incidence of 'asset poverty' is shown in the next line (Table 17.13). It is the percentage of households whose asset index falls below the 50th percentile of the asset index distribution. Interestingly, this confirms the poverty analysis discussed above. In urban areas, there are more asset poor households among FHH than among MHH, although their share is far lower than that of the poverty HCI. In rural areas, the 'asset poverty' index and the HCI are consistent, and FHH are asset poorer than MHH. Overall, 63 per cent of woman-headed households are asset poor, as opposed to 54 per cent of man-headed households.

The other results are also interesting. There appears to be an interesting *inverse* relationship between household size and asset poverty. Among small families (0–3 members), 65 per cent are asset poor when man-headed and 75 per cent are asset poor when woman-headed. As the size of the household increases, the share of asset poor household decreases: overall, among families with 11 or more members only 13 per cent are asset poor when man-headed and 19 per cent are asset poor when woman-headed. Therefore, smaller families are the poorest, and larger families are the wealthiest.

Per-capita expenditure patterns also confirm the above results. Individuals in households belonging to the 1st quintile are by and large asset poor, particularly in rural areas. As per-capita consumption increases, families are less and less likely to be asset poor, particularly in urban areas. Yet, FHH still appear to be largely worse off than MHH: in rural areas, 72 per cent of woman-headed households belonging to the 5th expenditure quintile are asset poor. Therefore, while for man-headed household consumption patterns and asset ownership go together (the richer the higher spending), for woman-headed household consumption patterns cannot rely on any asset stabilisation effect.

Asset distribution in Mozambique shows how uneven asset property is, particularly in rural areas where the majority of the population lives. The share of 'asset poor' households is dramatically high, particularly for woman-headed households, which actually shows that their con-sumption behaviour, and their poverty profile, are justified by a con-dition of greater insecurity, greater instability and greater vulnerability.

Conclusions and further work

This chapter has shown that in Mozambique women are worse off than men and actually are poorer than men in several ways. Women are worse off than men in the labour market, they are less likely to be income-earning workers or just wage-workers, and they are more likely than men to be own-account workers or simply non-earning workers. Female-headed households are more likely to get an average income that is lower than man-headed households' when they live in the city, and they are better off than man-headed households when they live in the country. Per-capita consumption levels seem to be higher for woman-headed households, particularly in rural areas (where the large majority of the population lives). Although it appears that declared income receipts are low (as is normal in this kind of survey) and lower than consumption expenditures (as is not so normal but happens), it is clear that there is apparently no correlation between per-capita expenditure and income levels. Most importantly, there is no evident correlation between employment condition and per-capita expenditure, and hence, poverty status. Women receive less education, they are more likely to be illiterate, and enjoy worse health conditions than men. Finally, female-headed households are also more likely to be poor in terms of assets.

How do we justify that people living in female-headed households, who are apparently those who are worse off both in terms of income distribution, employment condition, and asset distribution, show a consumption-based poverty profile that is not different – actually is better – from that of those who live in man-headed households? We conjecture three possible answers to that question.

From a monetary point of view, the first conjecture is that there is an *aggregation effect* that masks the true underlying relationships. While in fact employment conditions refer to individuals as such, per-capita expenditure – and hence poverty status – are calculated as averages within households. As an example, consider a household where the head is a man with a regular job as wage-worker, who has a wife and two young children. Typically, for most men with regular jobs in the formal sectors, wives undertake informal activities as a way to increase the household income. Unskilled women have more access to informal jobs, as formal employment is usually not viable or difficult to obtain. Now compare overall consumption expenditure of this household with that of a female-headed household with two children, where the head is a widow and one of the children works as an informal own-account artisan with the help of the mother. Now, this family might well be better off than the other in terms of per-capita expenditure, and yet the former is certainly more protected and less vulnerable in social terms. The aggregation effect – pooling together all the household members – wipes off the differences in terms of individual consumption between the two different households, so that in the end it will look as if the wage-worker man enjoys the same living standards as the own-account worker woman (while he actually earns *more*). This is a problem that, given the data source at hand, is impossible to overcome: expenditure and income data are (household) *averages* while employment data are individual data. Therefore, strictly speaking, the two pieces of information are not comparable. We are not speaking of what women actually spend *individually* (we do not have that information), we are speaking of the per-capita spending of the household women belong to.

The second conjecture is that aggregate data blur actual differences at a less aggregated level. In the first place, the data we have analysed are national: regional and local differences are certainly important, and it might be that in a more regionally detailed analysis significant differentiated patterns emerge. Aggregate data also do not highlight the possible different effects of the major determinants of poverty which might affect people differently: human capital endowments (education), location, land and asset property, access to health care and other services and utilities. We conjecture that economies of size, for instance, might be effective depending on asset property (and its absolute value) and land use.

The third conjecture is that consumption smoothing is different according to employment condition or asset ownership, *because women's permanent income is different from men's*. Thus, even though *at first glance* it looks as if individuals with different employment statuses have the same consumption behaviour, their overall life-cycle consumption patterns are different. As an example, consider two individuals, a man and a woman. Suppose the man has a regular job in the formal sector as a wage-worker (e.g. a State employee). Suppose the woman is an informal wage-worker in a small artisanal factory, with no contract, as a seasonal worker. In other words, suppose the woman has been hired as a temporary worker with no future guarantee. Typically, these two individuals have completely different expected lifetime income paths and expenditure patterns. While the man will be able to save and maybe accumulate savings – what is called *consumption smoothing* – the woman will not have any chance to save and accumulate – her consumption smoothing will be totally different. Yet, empirically, it might well be that in any given moment in time consumption expenditure is the same for the two individuals, actually probably higher for the woman than for the man.[47] If this is true, then, looking at consumption expenditure will *not* be the right indicator of the level of poverty of the two individuals. And this is probably the reason why any measure of poverty based on some monetary value of expenditure in any given moment in time will not be the right indicator of overall living standards. Consumption smoothing is related with asset property, like house or land, vicinity to infrastructures and services, human and physical capitals, which do affect life consumption expenditures and living standards. Poverty measures simply based on a punctual estimate of consumption expenditure are just deemed to be uninformative and biased.

One indirect way to test for the permanent-income hypothesis is to look at variability of consumption expenditures: if it is true that men spend less because their expected future income pattern is more stable (and secure), or because of the asset they own, then their consumption variability will be *lower* – consumption will be *smoother* – than women's. Estimated standard errors of average per-capita consumption expenditure by gender of household head and area confirm our conjecture: *women's consumption patterns are less smooth than men's*. Per-capita consumption of FHH has a systematically higher variability than that of MHH. It would be interesting to explore this conjecture further, but data from a simple HLSS do not allow for any intertemporal comparison.

Without any doubt, our main conclusion is that the well-being comparisons based on consumption per capita are misleading. This is an important point in the case of comparison between FHH and MHH.

---

[47] An extreme example of this might be the following. Compare two individuals: one has a regularly paid job and earns $1,000 a month, the other has no job and has just got $1,000 in a given month. Clearly, the consumption patterns of the two individuals will be different, and the second will probably spend *more* on that given month although, on average, along her lifetime she will spend *less*.

Table 17.14 *Per-capita consumption by area and gender of household head average value and standard errors (Meticais)*

Average	Urban Areas			Rural Areas			National		
	MHH	FHH	All	MHH	FHH	All	MHH	FHH	All
	215,536	220,035	216,540	147,322	168,682	151,876	159,884	178,598	163,909
S. E.	13920	19683	13647	3870	5169	3491	4078	5541	3794
% S. E.	6.45%	8.94%	6.30%	2.62%	3.06%	2.22%	2.55%	3.10%	2.31%

In a series of different works Amartya Sen has stressed that, when we adopt a pure consumption based measure of poverty, the differences in relative poverty between women and men, in the case of the third world countries, are often hidden.

To the extent that we left a monetary representation of well being, and we introduced some basic measures of capabilities and functionings in our data, we showed that the results of a simple exercise of multivariate statistical analysis can confirm Sen's arguments.

The consumption based measures of poverty, used in most empirical works, are not able to point out some important differences in individual inequality, such as that deriving from assets ownership.

Moreover, as Sen has explained, the relationship between the 'functionings' and per capita consumption is often unstable, and the same variability as we found in the relationship between informality and the relative poverty of the women in Mozambique. This chapter has tried to dig through the data of a household living standard survey to look for a sensible support to the hypothesis that poverty in Mozambique affects women more than men. We have come to the conclusion that women are more vulnerable in the job market, they have worse employment conditions, they receive worse education and live in worse health conditions, the households they head are not as wealthy as those headed by men but, on average, the households they belong to do not show any consistent sign that they are poorer than men's, at least in terms of consumption-based poverty indicators. It may be that those indicators do not offer the proper picture. If we look to all the evidence we have considered, we answer a qualified yes as a response.

Cited references

Ardeni, P. G. 1997, 'The Informal Economy in Mozambique: A Preliminary Study', Proceeding of Conference on Informal Sector and Economic Policy in Sub-Saharan Africa, Bamako, March, AFRISTAT, Paris.

Ardeni, P. G. 2001, 'Women and Poverty in Mozambique: Is There a Gender Bias in Living Standards and Employment Conditions?', ILO-UNDP Report, Maputo.

Atkinson, A. B. 1987, 'On the Measurement of Poverty', *Econometrica* 4: 749–764.

Atkinson, A. B. 1989, 'Poverty', in J. Eatwell, M. Milgate and P. Newman (eds.) *Social Economics: The New Pelgrave*, Norton, New York.

Atkinson, A. B. 1999, *The Economic Consequences of Rolling Back the Welfare State*. Cambridge, MA: MIT Press.

Atkinson, A. and Hills, J. (eds.) 1998, 'Exclusion, Employment and Opportunity', CASE Paper 4, Centre of Analysis of Social Exclusion London School of Economics, London.

Buvinic, M. 1993, 'The feminisation of poverty? Research and policy needs', in J. Figueireido, Z. Shaheed, (eds.) *New Approaches to Poverty Analysis and Policy*, Volume II, ILO, Geneva.

Buvinic, M. 1997, 'Women in Poverty: A New Global Underclass'. *Foreign Policy* 108: 38–53.

Bruck, T. 2001 'Determinant of Rural poverty in Post-War Mozambique: Evidence from a Household Survey and Implications for Government and Donor Policy', *QEH Working Papers Series*, Oxford, University of Oxford.

Cramer, C. and Pontara, N. 1998, 'Rural Poverty and Poverty Alleviation in Mozambique: What's Missing from the Debate', *The Journal of Modern African Studies* 36: 101–138.

Dasgupta, I. 2000, 'Women's Employment, Intra-household Bargaining, and Distribution: A Two-sector Analysis', *Oxford Economic Papers* 52: 723–744.

Dasgupta, P. 1990, 'Well-being and The Extent of Its Realization in Poor Countries', *The Economic Journal* 100: 1–32.

Dasgupta P. 1993, *An Inquiry into Well-being and Destitution*. Oxford: Clarendon Press.

Datt G., Simler K., Mukherjee S. and Dava G. 1992, 'Determinants of Poverty in Mozambique: 1996–97'. International Food Policy Research Institute (IFPRI) Discussion Paper n. 78, Washington, D.C.

Deaton, A. 1997, *The Analysis of Household Surveys*. Baltimore: The Johns Hopkins University Press.

Deininger K. and Squire L. 1998, 'New Ways of Looking at Old Issues: Inequality and Growth', *Journal of Development Economics* 57 (2): 257–285.

Drèze, J. and Sen, A. 1989, *Hunger and Public action*. Oxford: Clarendon Press.

Drèze, J. and Sen, A. 1990, *The Political Economy of Hunger*, Volume 1, Oxford: Clarendon Press.

FAO/WHO/UNU 1985, *Energy and protein requirements*. Technical Report Series 724. Geneva: World Health Organization.

Filmer D., King E. M. and Pritchett L. 1998, 'Gender Disparity in South Asia: Comparisons Between and Within Countries', World Bank Development Research Group, Working Paper.

Filmer D. and Pritchett, L. 1999, 'The effect of household wealth on educational attainment: evidence from 35 countries', *Population and Development Review* 25 (1): 85–120.

Foster J., Greer J. and Thorbrecke. E. 1984. 'A Class of Decomposable Poverty Measures', *Econometrica* 52: 761–765.

ILO-JASPA 1991, *Africa Employment Report*, Addis Ababa, Ethiopia, International Labour Office.

Klasen S. 2000, 'Measuring Poverty and Deprivation in South Africa', *Review of Income and Wealth*, 46 (1): 33–58.

Lachaud, J-P. 1988, *Le marché du travail urbain en Cote d'Ivoire: structure et segmentation*, ILO International Institute for Labour Studies, Labour Market Programme Discussion paper DP/12/1988, Geneva.

Lachaud, J.-P. 1994, *The Labour Market in Africa*, ILO International Institute for Labour Studies, Research Series 102, Geneva.

Lachaud, J-P. 1996, *Les femmes et le marché du travail urbain en Afrique Subsaharienne*, Centre d'Economie du developpement, Université Montesquieu – Bordeaux IV, Bordeaux, Série de Recherche, 1.

Lanjouw P. and Ravallion M. 1995, 'Poverty and Household Size', *The Economic Journal* 105: 1415–1434.

MPAR 1998, 'Understanding Poverty and Well-being in Mozambique: The First National Assessment (1996–97)', Ministry of Planning and Finance, Eduardo Mondlane University and International Food Policy Research Institute (IFPRI), Washington, D.C.

Sahn, D. and Stifel, D. 2000, 'Poverty Comparison Over Time and Across Countries in Africa', *World Development*, 28: 2123–2155.

Sen, A. 1976, 'Poverty: An Ordinal Approach to Measurement', *Econometrica* 46: 437–446.

Sen, A. 1981, *Poverty and Famines*. Geneva: ILO.

Sen A. 1992, *Inequality Reexamined*. Oxford: Oxford University Press.

Sen, A. and Drèze J. 1995, *India: Economic Development and Social Opportunity*. Oxford: Oxford Unversity Press.

Sen, A. 1999, *Commodities and Capabilities*. Oxford: Oxford India Paperbacks.

Sethuraman, S. V. 1987, 'Employment and Incomes in Rural and Urban Botswana', ILO – Southern African Team for Employment Promotion, Geneva, Unpublished draft report.

UNDP 1993, *Human Development Report*. New York, Oxford: Oxford University Press.

World Bank 1999, *World Development Indicators*. Washington D.C.: World Bank.

18 From the quantity to the quality of employment: an application of the capability approach to the Chilean labour market

KIRSTEN SEHNBRUCH[1,2]

Introduction

Analysing a labour market based on the development of its unemployment rate is as simplistic as assessing a country's level of development based solely on its GDP per capita figures. Yet this is precisely what most labour market analysts do.

This chapter will show how an application of Amartya Sen's capability approach to the Chilean labour market breaks up such a perspective by obliging us to take into account a series of other variables related to the quality of employment that are at least as important to individual wellbeing as having a job in the first place.

Employment is a subject very much neglected by the development literature, even though it is the central factor in an individual's wellbeing once his or her most basic needs have been covered. The capability approach therefore has much to contribute to any debate on the labour markets of developing countries. This chapter uses the results of a survey specifically designed and implemented by the author to create an indicator of the quality of employment, and will demonstrate the uses of such an indicator in order to show how the capability approach can be used as a policy making tool to capture the capabilities and functionings associated with employment far better than other measures such as an unemployment rate.

[1] Senior Scholar and Lecturer, Center for Latin American Studies, University of California Berkeley; ksehnbruch@yahoo.com
[2] I would like to thank Flavio Comim, Dante Contreras, Javier Nuñez and Claudio Santibañez for their helpful comments. The usual disclaimers apply.

This chapter also applies the capability approach to a country with a higher level of development than most of the examples that have been used so far to illustrate the approach.[3] This is because for a country like Chile, which has reached a relatively advanced stage of development, indicators such as longevity, morbidity and literacy have reached levels almost comparable to those of the most industrialised or developed countries. However, this does not mean that the standard of living in Chile is comparable to these countries, at least not for the vast majority of the population. Other variables therefore need to be considered in order to monitor the progress of countries in such an 'intermediate' phase of development. Often quantitative indicators are no longer appropriate for this purpose, and one has to turn to variables that consider quality at least as much as quantity, such as the quality of education, the quality of healthcare, or the quality of employment.[4]

The overall objective of this chapter is to broaden and stimulate the debate on labour policy in developing countries, and direct attention away from the single variable of the unemployment rate and thus oblige policy makers to take into account a broader range of issues that capture the capabilities of individuals.

The labour market in the context of development thought

Labour market developments as a fall out of other development policies

Within the area of development and welfare economics, the labour market is a particularly neglected topic, especially if we compare it with the attention that other policies have received. A significant amount of

---

[3] Although I am aware of the fact that the capability approach has been applied to some countries with higher levels of development (in particular Belgium and Italy), the approach is still mainly applied to less developed countries. The papers presented at this conference bear out this point: of those papers dedicated to a practical application of the approach, almost three quarters use cases from the developing world.

[4] An example that aroused much attention in Chile is the result of a study undertaken by Bravo and Contreras, which shows that although the literacy rates that the country records are very high, the ability of those who are officially considered literate to understand the most basic written instructions, is extremely limited. The study concludes that the focus of education policy should now turn to the quality of education provided rather than just aiming at ensuring an appropriate quantity (extent) of education (Bravo and Contreras, 2001).

research exists on growth strategies, structural adjustment programmes, privatisations, the liberalisation of markets, targeting social
policies, or on the effects of successive financial crises that have hit
developing countries. In all of these cases, employment remains a
secondary issue, and employment policies become a fall out of other
economic policies. Analysts rarely go beyond looking at how unemployment rates and wage levels are affected by these policies. This has
led to a complete neglect in the literature of the link between employment and individual well-being.[5]

Even in the Chilean literature, which has produced extensive analysis
on the country's labour market, the focus on employment rates and
income levels clearly predominates.[6] In the Chilean case, analysts
typically discuss employment in relation with the economic crises of
1975 and 1982, showing how a more flexible, deregulated labour
market and a liberalised economy in 1982 allowed the unemployment
rate to decline faster than after the 1975 crisis. The quality of the jobs
created in order to bring about this rapid decrease in the unemployment
rate is, however, rarely mentioned.

Although both Sen and other analysts have written about the labour
market in relation to the capability approach, their work mainly refers
to issues of employment versus unemployment.[7] So unemployment
rates remain the main point of focus in the literature, even though it
has been evident for a long time now that unemployment is not really
the main problem in labour markets of developing countries. Already
in 1981 Paul Streeten wrote that the concepts of

---

[5] Bosworth, Dawkins and Stromback, for example, have written an entire book
about labour economics, which discusses the supply and demand features of the
labour market in great detail, as well as other issues such as human capital
functions and the relationship between economic growth and labour. But it
completely neglects to mention that there is a connection between the
characteristics of the labour market and the well-being of the individual
(Bosworth, Dawkins and Stromback, 1994).

[6] A paper by Paredes (1996) typifies this approach: he states that the objective of his
paper is to highlight the most salient characteristics of the Chilean labour market
between 1970 and 1996, and then goes on to discuss data that relates purely to
participation rates, unemployment rates and wage levels, without mentioning any
other variables that may be equally important.

[7] See for example Sen 1997, 1999a (pp. 94–96) and Ootegem and Schekkaert
(1990).

employment and unemployment make sense only in an industrialised society where there are employment exchanges, organised and informed labour markets, and social security benefits for the unemployed ... 'Employment' as interpreted in industrial countries is not the appropriate concept. ... to afford to be unemployed, a worker has to be fairly well off. To survive, an unemployed person must have an income from another source. The root problem is poverty, or low-productivity employment, not unemployment. Indeed, the very poor are not unemployed but work very hard and long hours in unremunerative, unproductive forms of activity. (Streeten, 1981: 12–13)[8]

In other words, the *quality* of employment matters as much as the *quantity* of employment. Policy focusing exclusively on unemployment rates is overlooking the 'working poor' and the lack of functionings and capabilities that result from low quality jobs.

The labour market as a vehicle of individual development and expanded capabilities

In a developing country, employment is the principal vehicle which generates individual capabilities. It not only provides the income with which a person can fulfil her basic needs (and those of her dependants), but it also determines the coverage and extent of social security benefits that the individual is entitled to.

Generally speaking, developing countries have a limited ability to afford fully fledged welfare states, which can support individuals through any personal or economic crisis. Although state subsidies do exist in many developing countries, they are rarely enough to sustain the individual and their dependants if they have no additional source of income (e.g. support from other family members or informal jobs). And furthermore, even these limited benefits often depend on the type of job a worker holds.[9] So even if universal entitlements to welfare benefit

---

[8] The view that unemployment is a luxury few can afford is echoed by numerous case studies, see Agacino and Echeverria (1995), Echeverria *et al.* (1998) and Garcia Huidobro (1999).

[9] Child benefit in Chile, for example, amounts to just over US$4 per child per month for those with the lowest income levels and are paid out through the worker's payroll. This means that they are limited to wage-earners with written contracts and not received by the self-employed.

Traditional unemployment benefits were so low that the take-up rate of the benefits amounted to only approximately 15% of the unemployed. These benefits have now been replaced with a new unemployment insurance scheme based on

payments do exist, these have only a marginal impact on individual wellbeing as they are aimed at fulfilling only the most basic needs.

What matters much more, especially in middle income countries like Chile, is what kind of benefits your job entitles you to. An open-ended employment contract means workers contribute to a health insurance as well as to a pension plan. It means they have accident and disability insurance and that their dependants receive death benefits in the extreme case. Such contracts also mean that workers have a regular income, which enables them to plan their expenditure and manage credit should they so desire. They also generate the right to legal protection against unfair dismissals or the contravention of other regulatory conditions, representation through unions, maternity benefits and childcare facilities, and regulated working hours and schedules. Above all, the type of job held will determine the level of financial compensation the individual is entitled to if made redundant for economic reasons.[10]

Given the structure of labour legislation in Latin America, workers without written contracts are not entitled to any of the benefits listed above, and thus have to fall back on minimal state social security services should they need them. The self-employed are also excluded from all of the benefits enumerated here unless they contract them voluntarily, which, in Chile at least, few choose to do. And workers with atypical contracts (part-time, fixed-term or project based) are only partly covered by them.

To developing countries a labour policy strategy is even more relevant because they have to adjust to conditions of global competition without ever having reached the standard of living attained by more developed countries. In terms of employment conditions, this means that they have never reached certain minimum standards for the labour force as a whole. A segment generally referred to as the 'informal sector' has always remained marginalised, both in terms of holding lower quality jobs as well as being excluded from most provisions of labour market legislation. Without a specific effort to integrate this segment more fully into the labour force, tougher competitive

individual savings. For further explanations on this subject, see Sehnbruch 2006a and 2006b.

[10] Chilean workers who have a written open-ended contract and are made redundant for reasons not attributable to themselves are entitled to a severance payment of one month's salary per year of service from their employers.

conditions will penalise it further, thus increasing its marginalisation. In Latin America, the proportion of the informal sector has[11] generally not diminished despite fluctuating (and in the case of Chile decreasing) unemployment rates.

These mechanisms illustrate the important role of employment and labour market policy both as a filter for economic wealth and social security benefits as well as a determinant of other factors that contribute to the individual's capabilities. If we thus consider the labour market from this perspective, we must consider job characteristics as much as whether a person has a job. This is why it is so simplistic to think about the labour market in terms of unemployment rates and wage levels, as has indeed been recognised by some experts.[12] This leads us to the concept of *quality of employment*, which implies a comprehensive and all-inclusive approach to the labour market that considers all aspects of work. The following section discusses how the capability approach transforms the way employment should be viewed, and defines the quality of employment based on this view.

Applying the capability approach to employment: defining the quality of employment

Sen has discussed employment in terms of capabilities himself in his work. In his early writings, he recognised work as one of the key components of the entitlement exchange ('own labour'). Work and the income we receive in return for 'selling our labour power' generate functionings, capabilities and ultimately utility for the employed person (Sen, 1981: 2 and 46). Selling their labour power in one way or another is the only input into the entitlement exchange that the vast majority of people have at their disposal. This is particularly true of more developed economies, like Chile, where subsistence farming and sharecropping have been virtually abandoned. From the very beginning, employment has thus formed an integral part of the capability approach. Aside from what public policy can provide by constructing an appropriate infrastructure (e.g. health or education facilities), work, and the human capital that is its prerequisite, are the individual's

---

[11] As defined by the ILO.
[12] See ILO, Labour Overviews, various years.

principal input factors into his or her own function of wellbeing, as well as into that of any dependants.

The importance of employment has also figured in Sen's writings on unemployment and its associated deprivations, particularly in the context of inequality (Sen, 1997 and 1999). While recognising the benefits associated with work other than income (e.g. as an opportunity of having a fulfilling occupation), he mainly contrasts not having a job with having a job, and thus considers unemployment as one of the 'spaces' in which inequality manifests itself.

If we are to consider the 'quality of employment' according to the capability approach, the concept should therefore be defined as *the capabilities and functionings generated by a job*, capabilities and functionings, which the individual has reason to value. This definition is the direct consequence of applying the capability approach to employment, or, to put it differently, it is the definition that integrates employment into the framework of the capability approach. It is an all-inclusive definition, one that defines employment in a manner which properly reflects its implications beyond income generation in the broadest possible terms and applies a different perspective to the labour market than those habitually considered in the literature.[13]

In his work, Sen typically mentions some general capabilities that the individual has reason to value, as well as some basic capabilities that are necessary to the individual's mere survival. Among the former he categorises the ability to participate in the life of the community, the ability to appear in public without shame, and among the latter are the capabilities of being adequately fed, housed and in good health. Work provides us with a set of capabilities very comparable to these examples. Any psychological study of the effects of unemployment on the individual illustrates that work provides us with a series of factors other than the basic income which provides the means to our survival.[14] Issues such as self-respect and self-worth, personal growth, social integration and participation are some of the key functionings generated by work. In addition, we must consider the more basic functionings of being fed, housed, healthly, and assured future income (e.g.

---

[13] In this chapter, the term 'quality of employment' is used as opposed to the ILO's term 'decent work' in order to emphasise the difference that applying the capability approach to the labour market makes.

[14] See for instance Burchell *et al.* (2000). Sen mentions these issues himself in Sen (1997c).

through job security, pension, disability and unemployment insurance). These factors are not solely dependent on the income earned from employment.

The quality of employment is thus a function of all these characteristics (and many more) which leads to a given set of functionings, capabilities and ultimately utility. This leaves us with a clear and simple – although not easily applicable – definition of what constitutes *quality of employment*.

Applying the capability approach to employment: from the quantity of employment to the quality of employment

Any overview of the literature on labour markets shows that a comprehensive approach to the labour market like this one is rarely applied in practice, least of all in the case of developing countries. The ILO's own publications, but also those of other international organisations, show how limited the available data is so that the concepts which examine or require a broad range of employment variables cannot be applied to existing data.[15]

This leaves any labour market analyst with the question of what do we look at if we are not experts and want to get a quick impression of the situation of a labour market?

This point brings us back to the example of Chile and of how this problem surfaced there during its recent economic downturn, during which the unemployment rate virtually doubled in the space of one year (1998–1999). Typically, it is the press which looks for a single figure and then stimulates public debate and opinion, which in turn orients public policy. Accordingly, the only figure that the Chilean press ever commented on during the downturn was the unemployment rate. And consequently, the only figure that public policy seemed to focus all its attention on, especially as this was during an election year, was the unemployment rate. This means that only this one facet of the

---

[15] See the ILO's World Employment reports, the World Bank's Development Reports, the UNDP's Development Reports, etc. At most, these publications refer to employment and wage levels when including the labour markets in their analysis. But the available statistics never go beyond the most basic data, even in the case of the regional employment reports of the ILO (e.g. Labour Overviews for Latin America) where the only additional variable considered is the distinction between the informal and formal sector.

employment crisis was commented on. Other factors, such as under-employment, the sudden informalisation of jobs, or large shifts towards contingent employment, were ignored by the commentators who live in a country where an employment crisis will fill the capital's public transport vehicles with ice cream vendors almost overnight.

This type of problem raises the question whether it would not be better to create a more inclusive indicator of labour market developments, even if we have to recognise that such an indicator cannot ever be a faithful reflection of all the characteristics of employment and the preferences and circumstances of the individuals employed.

A similar debate emerged regarding the measurement of human development and welfare and has been extensively discussed in the literature, especially with regard to the construction of the Human Development Indicator (HDI) first proposed by the UNDP in 1990. In his preface to ul Haq's *Reflections on Human Development*, Streeten writes: 'Such indexes are useful in focusing attention and simplifying problems. They are eye-catching. They have considerable political appeal. They have a stronger impact on the mind and draw public attention more powerfully than a long list of indicators combined with a qualitative discussion. The strongest argument in their favour is that they show up the inadequacies of other indexes, such as gross national product (GNP)' (ul Haq, 1995: xi). The same could be said about a quality of employment indicator.

It has thus become an accepted wisdom that it is not enough to talk about income per capita when thinking about economic development, but indispensable to include other variables in the debate, specifically variables that enhance the capabilities of individuals (e.g. education), as well as variables that humans have reason to value for their own sake (e.g. longevity).

As employment has an important impact on the quality of life and on individual well-being, Sen's arguments are all relevant to the debate about how to look at the labour market as well. In the same way that GNP/capita is a very narrow measure of well-being, the unemployment rate is too narrow a measure to capture the development of the labour market as it fails to consider any other aspect of work other than its availability. Moreover, looking at the labour market only from the perspective of unemployment rates is as simplistic and arbitrary as analysing human well-being only from the perspective of income levels.

The capability approach forces us to ask different questions about employment that are far wider ranging than those ordinarily asked. We cannot simply observe the participation rate and its development, but must ask whether all people who want to work are capable of doing so. This includes the inactive in our universe. Similarly, it is not enough to consider the unemployment rate; we must ask whether the unemployed have the capability to successfully reintegrate themselves into the labour market, without getting stuck in a segment of precarious employment. And rather than simply looking at the employment rate, we must also consider the quality of jobs, i.e. the functionings and capabilities that they generate. Most importantly, this considers what individuals can achieve with a given set of job characteristics, which means that their needs and personal circumstances are taken into account. This makes the capability approach the only theoretical approach to focus on human development as an end, not as a means. By defining capabilities as the space of comparison, it asks what the means are that we need to foster in order to achieve certain ends.

One obvious problem with applying the capability approach to the labour market is that employment indicators are not as clear cut as the indicators of well-being that Sen looks at. For example, we can agree that the longer we live, the better, i.e. a longer life and lower morbidity rates are desirable. The same goes for education: it is difficult to disagree with the intrinsic value of education, if only for its own sake. Similarly, it is difficult to disagree with the idea that a higher level of income generally offers the opportunity for realising more functionings and enhances capabilities.

However, the desirability of different job characteristics depends largely on the personal needs and circumstances of the worker. A few simple examples will illustrate the point: a part-time job requiring late afternoon shifts may be perfect for a student wanting to earn extra cash. Yet the same job would probably be a highly unsatisfactory one to the same student once he has graduated and is aiming to build a career. Similarly, a job offering a short term contract for the duration of a project may be perfect for a young person not yet sure of what she wants to do and without significant financial commitments. Yet the same job with a high degree of insecurity may be a cause of stress to an individual who heads a household and has to provide a steady flow of income to finance a mortgage or the education of children. As for social security, how many people would prefer to not pay their contributions, and rather run the risk of falling ill or growing old without protection, simply because they consider cash in hand now to be preferable to future income. In the case of Chile, 75 per cent of the self-employed take this view.[16]

So even for the objective criteria (e.g. type of contract or social security coverage) there is no straightforward and objective order of preference in the answers. In addition, we have to consider the criteria that would perfectly legitimately form part of the concept of quality of employment, while being totally subjective. These include job satisfaction, career development, personal fulfilment, job stability, or levels of responsibility. Again, one can take the view that these can be measured objectively, if one were to assume average criteria, but by and large, these criteria are subjective by nature.

The economic crisis in Chile led to a sharp increase in the unemployment rate between 1998 and 1999, but the survey results that this chapter is based on also showed other significant developments in the Chilean labour market. For example, there were sharp declines in the proportion of new jobs created during 1998/9 with open-ended contracts (down from 42 per cent to 21 per cent). Similarly the proportion of jobs created which contribute to a pension plan fell dramatically compared to the previous year (61 per cent to 47 per cent). Conversely, the percentage of atypical jobs and jobs without contracts or social security coverage increased proportionately. These developments also produce a deterioration of the job characteristics of the labour force in general.

Given these results and the fact that they were not considered (and still are ignored) both by public debate as well as public policy makers, the idea of forming an indicator of the quality of employment, which would include all aspects of these developments, seemed even more pressing. Unfortunately, this chapter cannot present the results of this survey in detail.[17] However, it is the careful analysis of these results that lead to the selection of the component variables of the indicator presented below.

An indicator of the quality of employment

The objective of simplicity guided the conceptualisation of this index with the aim of making it easily understandable and replicable. The

---

[16] According to the results from the employment survey described below.
[17] All the statistics referred to and more can be found in Sehnbruch, 2006.

index will first be presented here in descriptive form before explaining how the variables were measured and the reasoning for constructing it in this way. (Appendix III presents a more formal tabulation of its composition.)

The following employment characteristics were chosen to be included in the index:

1. Income
2. Social security coverage
3. Contractual status
4. Employment stability
5. Professional training received.

All five variables were standardised into three subcategories, each of which were awarded zero, one or two points. The points scored for each variable by the members of the sample were then added up (leading to a range of 0–10 points) and divided by five thus allocating every person in the sample an individual score. The higher the individual's score, the better the quality of employment. This method also means that all variables included in the index are all equally weighted, an issue which will be discussed in section V.6.

The five component variables of this index and the rankings of their various subcategories were chosen for the impact they are likely to have on the functionings and capabilities of the individual, either due to the nature of the variable itself or due to the regulatory issues attached to it. We will look at each variable in turn to explain how it was measured and why it was included in the index.

Income

The data on income was obtained by asking for the last monthly wage received by the respondent.[18] Wages were then divided into three categories defined as multiples of the minimum wage: less than two minimum wages, 2–4 minimum wages and more than four minimum wages. They were calculated on an hourly basis net of taxes and other deductions.

In the case of income, the choice of the variable and its scores are relatively obvious: income covers basic needs and creates functionings

---

[18] Although it would be preferable to consider a more long-term indicator of income such as average wage over the last year, this survey could not gather this data due to budget constraints.

and capabilities, and more income is generally better than less. The individual subcategories of the variable expressed in multiples of the minimum wage were chosen as arbitrary cut off points and because measures of poverty levels could not be taken into account as the survey did not gather household income. The classification assumes that anything less than double the minimum wage is not enough to constitute a decent level of income based on the author's calculation of the income needed to satisfy the basic needs of a four-person household. The average wage at the time of the survey in Chile consisted of about 2.5 minimum wages. Although this constitutes the average wage of the labour force, it still cannot be considered a 'good' level of income, a category which this indicator defines as more than four minimum wages.[19] It is important to note that all workers earning above a certain cut off point (in this case ten times the minimum wage is considered appropriate) are automatically considered as part of the high quality employment category, as this amount of income allows them to take care of all necessary expenses, such as pension and health insurance. Furthermore, jobs in such an income category record almost without exception the best employment conditions in all the other variables.

Ideally the stability of income should be included in this indicator as well, but this variable is more complicated to measure than the level of income. It is therefore assumed that the stability of income will be picked up by the other component variables such as, for example, the variables tenure and type of contract. One of the reasons why self-employment scores fewer points than the salaried sector is because its income flow is less stable and predictable. Also, whether the individual is contributing to social security or not is an indicator of income stability as workers with irregular incomes generally do not contribute.

Social security
Social security coverage refers to whether the individual was contributing or not contributing to a health insurance scheme, which could be either private or public. Contributions also had to be up to date.

---

[19] These levels of income are based on the average number of persons per household in Santiago and the average number of workers per household. They represent the minimum level of income that should be earned by an individual with family dependants in order to achieve a reasonable or a good standard of living.

Health insurance coverage is included in this index as it is obviously one of the most important inputs into the functionings and capabilities of the individual. Sen himself has focused on the variable health in all his work related to welfare.[20] As the public emergency services for the extremely poor only provide minimum coverage, contributing to an insurance scheme must be considered a priority, even if many workers do not agree, or optimistically believe that they will never fall ill and therefore decide they do not need an insurance plan.

The score allocated within the variable is dictated by the quality of services to be expected by the type of insurance coverage. A private insurance generally delivers better services than the public system, which in turn provides a better service than the emergency scheme which covers those not insured.

As the correlation between those who contribute to a health insurance scheme and a pension scheme is almost 100 per cent since employers deduct contributions either to both or to neither from the worker's wage, only one of the variables is used in the index. Including pension insurance separately would effectively mean according social security a double weighting. The variable health was chosen above pension contributions, mainly because with a health insurance plan it is easier to distinguish between public or private insurance.

A number of other variables that would perhaps normally be considered to be part of social insurance are excluded from this index. They include insurance for accidents and illness at work, unemployment insurance, and other forms of benefits or income support. In Chile, any insurance related to accidents and health risks at work is covered by a separate insurance system that the employers pay for. It can generally be assumed that all wage-earners with a written contract will be covered by such insurance, so that the issue is covered by the variable contractual status. As regards unemployment insurance, the best variable for capturing its coverage is the combination of the variable type of contract, tenure, and the level of income. And income support (e.g. family allowances) again depends on whether the individual has a written contract.

---

[20] See for example his analysis of infant mortality, life expectancy, or stunting in Drèze and Sen 1995a and 1995b.

Contractual status

The variable 'contractual status' considered whether the respondent had an open-ended contract, an atypical contract (either short term, project based or fee paid), or no written contract at all in the case of wage-earners. In the case of the self-employed, the variable considered whether they were employers or self-employed. The self-employed were divided into professional or non-professional self-employed according to whether they had attained a higher educational qualification or not. Given the structure of Chilean labour legislation and its social security systems, almost all working conditions depend on the contractual or occupational status.

The contractual status of a worker must be considered as one of the most important aspects of the employment relationship because the individual's legal protection is largely determined by the type of contract, and indeed by its very existence in written form.[21] A salaried job without a contract is considered the worst situation, even though the job may be relatively stable, or relatively well paid, simply because the worker would not be automatically covered by the labour statutes. In addition, a written contract or documented income is a prerequisite for subscribing to any health or pension insurance plan, so that not having a contract automatically implies a lack of protection in that sense, too. Apart from that, for employers the point of not giving their workers written contracts is to avoid the payment of social security contributions, while for the employee the motivation for accepting such work is often to take home more pay in cash by not paying the contributions.

An open-ended contract scores more points than an atypical one, not because it is considered preferable *per se*, but because it is the only form of contract that assures some form of compensation and legal protection in case of loss of employment, which in practice acts as unemployment insurance.[22] For the majority of workers with atypical contracts, it can be

---

[21] Theoretically, in case of a dispute with an employer, a verbal contract should also be considered as a valid basis for an employment relationship. However, as it is extremely difficult to prove the existence of a verbal contract, this effectively leaves the worker in a very weak position.

[22] This continues to be the case despite the implementation of an unemployment insurance system in Chile in 2002. The benefits that can be obtained from this insurance depend in large part on the existence of a written open-ended contract, and on the tenure of a worker's previous employment. For details about this new insurance system, see Sehnbruch 2006a and 2006b.

assumed that they are obliged to look for a new job every year as, in theory at least, it is forbidden to renew short term contracts more than once. This leaves them facing unemployment at regular intervals without any form of income support, as they are not entitled to any compensation for the loss of their jobs when their contracts terminate. In an efficient labour market, this aspect should be compensated for by means of a higher wage, but in practice, this survey showed their wages to be lower.

In the case of the independent sector, employers and the professional self-employed score the highest points, mainly because their status implies a high level of protection due to the income levels they are likely to earn, as well as essentially being part of the formal sector by means of their legal status (declared and legal activity, payment of taxes, etc.). The survey's results showed that the majority of the employers or professional self-employed were in the highest income category. They also have a sufficient level of knowledge to make informed choices regarding their social security situation. The non-professional self-employed are, however, considered as a lower quality of employment classification. A number of factors contribute to this ranking. They include instability of income, a low rate of social insurance contributions as they are not obliged by law to contribute either to pension or health insurance, and little consideration by employment legislation. The combination of these factors leave them highly vulnerable to any kind of emergency situation where they are rarely able to cover its financial demands out of their own pockets alone. The main advantage of being self-employed is the degree of independence on the job and the much lower risk of unemployment. However, the latter is to an extent undermined by the instability of incomes in economic downturns.

In general, the variable contractual status is also important because many other aspects of employment are highly correlated with it. For example, open-ended contracts are likely to be held in larger companies with independent work establishments, systems for accident prevention, maternity benefits, and mechanisms for worker representation. Jobs without contracts or the self-employed, on the other hand, are often found in smaller companies, in small workshops or in the open air under inadequate health and safety conditions or without appropriate sanitary facilities.

Stability of employment: tenure
Employment stability for the purposes of this index was measured by the tenure of the current job held. The different lengths of tenure

were then divided into three separate categories: less than three years, 3–5 years, and more than five years.

The variable tenure was included in the index because, as we saw in the previous chapter, it determines the level of compensation payments and benefits from the unemployment insurance scheme that salaried workers are entitled to. Within this variable, only more than five years of tenure is considered to be the quality category, as this period would cover an unemployed person for the average duration of unemployment during non-crisis times in Chile (five months) by their own means.

In the case of the self-employed, the length of time they have been exercising their occupation is also an indicator of stability as the survey results showed that the longer the self-employed work in the same occupation, the less their business is likely to go bankrupt resulting in loss of employment. For the self-employed, the survival of their business is crucial as they would not be entitled to any form of unemployment benefit or income support should they have to give up their employment.

Again the scores allocated to the different options of this variable reflect a judgement on the risks that the individual faces in each occupational position, rather than a value judgement *per se*. A relatively short tenure may well be a positive sign for some segments of the labour force as individuals change jobs in order to improve their prospects, income or further their career in general. However, this survey showed that the majority of employment changes occurred out of necessity rather than desire. In addition, given the provisions of the Chilean labour market legislation for severance payments in case of redundancies, a short employment tenure means an increased risk for the worker whatever the reasons for the short tenure, and it is this risk that this indicator captures.

The variable 'tenure' also implicitly considers a worker's periods of unemployment as workers with short job tenures are likely to pass through unemployment every time they switch jobs. These workers therefore score a lower score than those with longer job tenures.

Training
The fifth variable that the index considers is whether the worker has received any formal training during the last year, whether he has received on the job training, or none at all.

The variable training is included in this indicator as it is the best measure of personal, skill and career development of the individual. Within this variable, a formalised training course is considered to be preferable to on the job training as it generally constitutes a more planned form of training oriented specifically towards the needs and skill development of the individual and may be useful in other jobs too, whereas on the job training is often company specific and not as easily transferable to other jobs.

In comparison with the possibility of earning more money or the risk of losing one's job without being entitled to any form of unemployment insurance, the issue of training could be considered as secondary. Yet at this point it is important to remember that we are considering the labour market from the capability perspective. What is training if not one of the most important means of enhancing the capabilities of the individual? In the case of training it is the *associated benefits* rather than the *prospective risks* that this index intends to capture.

First, in an environment in which technological changes are happening ever faster, training is the one factor that can ensure a worker's skills do not become obsolete, which would entail the risk of being dismissed or of career stagnation by making it more difficult to move to another job. Second, training, whether on the job or external to the work establishment, supplies the individual with one of the best means of improving her position within the establishment, both in terms of career progression as well as income, even if this is not immediately apparent. And third, a higher qualification is one of the best means of insurance against the misfortune of prolonged unemployment spells as it increases the worker's chances of finding a new job should he lose his current one, and furthermore, provides a degree of insurance against having to accept a job with worse characteristics (e.g. a less advantageous contract, salary, pension and health insurance plans).

With all of these criteria that form part of this index, it is clear that one could argue that they are not as straightforward as they seem. Not having a contract does not necessarily imply job instability. Or having a short term contract could also be a positive if that is what the individual wants. Or short term duration may be due to positive career progression. And so on. In each of these cases, the index should pick up either the risks or benefits associated with these scenarios through the other variables included in the index.

Weighting

The component variables of this index are all equally weighted. Methods of equal weighting such as have been used for creating the HDI or the ILO's decent work indicator have the advantage that they reduce any interference from the method of calculating the weights to a minimum. They are also a convenient solution when there is no consensus view on how the variables should be weighted as is the case in all of these methods mentioned above.

In the case of this index, maintaining simplicity has also been a concern. It is vital that policy makers understand the index, and that it is easily replicable. What is most important is that every year (and in every country where it is applied) the index is calculated in the same way so that time series and cross country comparisons can be made.

Potential uses of the index

The indicator proposed in this chapter allows for several different types of analysis. First, since it allocates each individual a score, we can analyse the quality of employment of particular groups of the labour force, and observe how they develop over time. For example, it would be possible to determine how the quality of employment develops in specific economic sectors, regions, or types of companies. The advantage of such an analysis is that it enables policy makers to identify precisely which regions, types of companies, or segments of the economy are generating better jobs than others. This, in turn, can give useful hints regarding which of these should perhaps receive additional policy support to enable them to expand, while also showing which sectors of the economy need closer monitoring, different legislation, or other types of support in order to help them improve the types of jobs they are generating.

Second, the index allows us to group individuals into categories of high, medium, low or very low quality employment. These categories can then be analysed and related to other variables included in the survey (e.g. age, sex, education, economic sector, size of company), so that we can analyse which groups of the labour force are particularly affected by low quality employment. Like the analysis described above, this would enable policy makers to focus attention on those groups of the population which are most disadvantaged by the labour market and need additional support.

Both of the methods of analysis described above would also provide us with extremely important information on the types of jobs which are likely to generate unemployment or the groups of the population most likely to suffer from it, since the analysis of the survey data showed that people with low quality jobs are far more likely to become unemployed than others.

The index also enables us to calculate an overall score for the quality of employment of the entire labour force. If calculated on an annual basis, an impression can be obtained of how the labour market has developed over time. Similarly, the distribution of the quality of employment can be calculated for the entire labour force, which would enable us to track how different quality jobs are distributed among the population.

Finally, if such an indicator were to be produced in several countries (e.g. in the whole of the Latin American region), we would be able to rank countries according to their labour market performance and track their relative and absolute performance over time. This would provide governments with an additional incentive to improve their labour conditions, which are increasingly being monitored by the international community as an input factor into unfair trading conditions, as well as being a sticking factor in the negotiation of free trade agreements. The ranking and comparison of different countries is the main purpose of the HDI, and while debates are still going on about whether such rankings have actually had an impact on the policy making decisions of governments, it is obvious that such indicators at least are of interest to international organisations who have to allocate funding and identify the weakest aspects of a country's development that need the most support. The ILO's decision to produce a similar indicator to measure decent work is proof of the importance of such information.

The component variables have all been chosen with the possibility of reproducing the index in other countries in mind. The variables required for the index are likely to be part of standard household or labour market surveys, and if they are not, they should be included as they are absolutely fundamental to any labour market analysis. If the variables should not be available in existing surveys, they can easily be produced by adding a few simple questions to existing surveys. Also, given that the legislative frameworks of Latin American labour markets are relatively similar, as are the problems that they face, the variables can be applied without much adaptation to the scenarios of other countries in the region.

Of course, apart from allowing us to undertake international comparisons, one of the main functions of the index has to be to enhance the analysis that can be done of a particular labour market, such as the Chilean one.

Segments of the labour force with low quality employment

The most important result that we obtain from this indicator is that just under half of the Chilean labour force has jobs of either very low or low quality (13 per cent and 34 per cent respectively). This means that their jobs show at least two serious defects, e.g. no social security and no contract. Table 18.1 shows that while 33 per cent of the labour force has jobs of medium high quality, only 19 per cent have high quality jobs.

This type of analysis shows that we should be concerned about the quality of employment of a far greater proportion of the work force than if we look simply at figures related to workers with very low income, or at workers without written contracts. The proportion of low quality jobs produced by this indicator is higher than even the proportion of the informal sector that official ILO statistics define.

Table 18.2 shows that twice as many women have very low quality jobs than men, although the proportions even out at the next level of employment quality, where more men than women have low quality jobs. Roughly the same proportions of men and women have medium and high quality jobs.

Table 18.1 *Quality of employment of the labour force*

Quality of employment	Total	Cumulative
Very low quality	13.1	13.1
Low quality	34.2	47.3
Medium quality	33.4	80.7
High quality	19.2	100.0

Note: calculations based on a representative survey of the Greater Santiago labour market undertaken in 1999 by the author. An extensive analysis of this survey data beyond this indicator of the quality of employment can be found in Sehnbruch 2003.

Table 18.2 *Quality of employment by sex*

	Men	Women	Total
Very low quality	10.6	21.0	14.8
Low quality	40.3	33.1	37.4
Medium quality	32.7	29.2	31.3
High quality	16.4	16.7	16.5
Total	100.0	100.0	100.0

Table 18.3 *Quality of employment by age group*

	14–19	20–25	26–35	36–45	46–55	56–65	>65	Total
Very low quality	61.9	16.8	15.2	10.4	10.1	8.3	14.3	14.8
Low quality	35.7	45.5	34.1	35.7	31.5	47.6	57.1	37.4
Medium quality	2.4	25.9	32.7	32.2	39.9	32.1	21.4	31.3
High quality	0.0	11.9	17.9	21.7	18.5	11.9	7.1	16.5
Total	100.0	100.0	100.0	100.0	100.0	100.0	100.0	100.0

Numerous studies have shown that women earn less than men and that the overall quality of their employment is inferior to men's[23] and an index such as this one would help bring gender issues into the mainstream of public policy debate and help policy makers monitor the matter with consistent data over time.

Almost all 14–19 year olds have very low or low quality jobs, a situation that improves significantly with the over 20 year olds (Table 18.3). The best jobs are clearly held between the ages of 35–55, after which the situation again reverses. Although a lower proportion of older people work in the lowest quality job category, their number increases in the low quality category and also declines in the high quality category. Again this data would enable policy makers to monitor the quality of employment in different age groups over time and direct specific policies at those groups that most need supporting.

[23] See for example ILO, 1998a, ILO, 1999, Oxman and Galilea, 1999.

Table 18.4 shows the contrast between the quality of employment of workers who achieved a higher level of education with those who did not and is an important result as it suggests that higher education is the only key to a better quality job. There is little gradual increase in the quality of jobs as the level of education improves, there is simply a sharp contrast between those with and without higher education. Again this is an important fact for labour policy to consider and bear in mind when devising new legislation.

There are no particularly sharp differences in the quality of jobs that the various economic sectors generate as the proportions in each category do not vary dramatically from the totals (Table 18.5). Variations are relatively minor, although it is interesting to note that the construction sector, which is often maligned for offering the worst jobs, actually has proportionately fewer workers in the lowest quality sector. It is also noteworthy that the highest proportion of good jobs is found in the services sector, although the 'other' sectors also seem to provide high quality jobs. In a survey such as this one, which was limited to the Greater Santiago area, this is likely to be explained because the 'other' component includes the financial services and communication sectors, which offer some of the best jobs available. A closer examination of the types of jobs that different economic sectors generate should be one of the most important principles guiding long-term public policy, and an index such as this one would help integrate this aspect into the policy debate.

Table 18.6 relates the quality of employment to the size of the employer and clearly shows that the larger the size of the company, the better the jobs they provide. A real shift, however, occurs in companies with more than 50 employees. In companies below this size, the employment offered is clearly of a lesser quality, with the worst jobs found in the category with five employees or fewer, or among those who work completely independently. While this conclusion reinforces the idea that the better jobs can be found in what the ILO classifies as the 'formal sector', it is important to note that this conclusion is not without significant exceptions, something that cannot be found in the table above which relates the level of education to the quality of employment. People with no more than primary education stood very little chance of obtaining a high quality job, whereas the chances for somebody working in smaller companies to achieve better quality employment are much better. This result clearly reflects the

Table 18.4 *Quality of employment by level of education*

	Primary school			Technical secondary school		Secondary school			
	None	Complete	Incomplete	Complete	Incomplete	Complete	Incomplete	Higher education	Total
Very low quality	15.4	20.9	23.4	7.6	19.2	13.0	20.2	6.3	14.8
Low quality	84.6	46.5	46.9	38.2	48.1	36.2	47.4	15.8	37.4
Medium quality	0.0	29.1	25.5	34.4	25.0	36.7	30.7	33.2	31.3
High quality	0.0	3.5	4.1	19.8	7.7	14.1	1.8	44.7	16.5
Total	100.0	100.0	100.0	100.0	100.0	100.0	100.0	100.0	100.0

Table 18.5 *Quality of employment by economic sector*

	Industry	Construction	Commerce	Services	Other	Total
Very low quality	14.5	10.0	15.7	14.0	8.7	13.1
Low quality	31.1	46.2	40.7	29.7	32.0	34.2
Medium quality	36.3	31.0	30.5	34.3	33.7	33.4
High quality	18.1	12.8	13.0	22.0	25.7	19.2
Total	100.0	100.0	100.0	100.0	100.0	100.0

Table 18.6 *Quality of employment by size of employer*

	1	2–5	6–10	11–50	51–100	101–200	>200	Total
Very low quality	22.4	16.2	16.0	11.2	8.3	5.1	2.4	13.1
Low quality	48.2	38.4	29.3	32.1	25.3	25.7	21.5	34.2
Medium quality	26.4	33.7	38.2	37.5	34.1	33.7	32.1	33.4
High quality	3.0	11.8	16.6	19.1	32.4	35.4	44.0	19.2
Total	100.0	100.0	100.0	100.0	100.0	100.0	100.0	100.0

number of professionals working independently or for very small companies that provide specialised services, and shows that small companies cannot always be classified as 'informal', as is presumed by the ILO definition of informal sector.

We should again note that the relationship between the quality of employment and different sized companies is an important consideration for labour policy. This highlights the role that an indicator such as this one could play in the policy making process.

None of the results described above is particularly surprising. In fact, they mirror those that were obtained when analysing the survey data according to categories of type of contract and occupational position. Similarly, an analysis of the same data by income category would also reflect this picture, as would an analysis by size of company or type of social insurance. What is different about this index is that it summarises these results in a single variable. And this variable draws attention to a group of highly vulnerable workers who are not explicitly considered by a labour policy which focuses mainly on the unemployed.

The tables presented so far allow us to consider a number of important questions that any comprehensive labour market policy should address. They show which economic sectors are producing higher quality jobs, that men hold better jobs than women (although perhaps not as consistently as some analysts would have us believe), and that larger companies generate better jobs than smaller companies. They also show that older people are vulnerable to having poor quality jobs, as well as younger workers who are in the crucial stage of family building. The results can thus help to identify particular areas that should be the focus of policy making.

This index has not been designed to replace the variable unemployment. Instead, it is intended to be used in addition to the unemployment rate, following the logic that the unemployed face different problems than the employed, and should therefore be subject to different policy measures. However, it is very important to note that an analysis of the jobs held by the unemployed who participated in this survey shows that they score very poorly on the variables considered by this index. Most of the unemployed are young, unqualified, held jobs with atypical contracts or none at all, therefore did not contribute to pension and health insurance, were not trained professionally on their jobs, and had very short job tenures. This is a long-term policy consideration that is completely ignored by policy makers in Chile who mainly focus on managing the unemployment rate in the short-term.

As we can see, the capability approach as it is applied to the labour market here would oblige policy makers to take into consideration a broader range of variables in order to foster quality employment. And their success in doing so could be monitored by the development of this index over time.

Individuals in the index

Table 18.7 shows how workers with different combinations of variables would be classified according to this index. These five cases are classified as having either low or very low quality jobs. As a result they would have a very low level of capabilities. Yet there is no government labour policy that focuses on cases like these simply because they are all employed. And as this chapter discussed above, official labour policy focuses mainly on the unemployment rate. The people described in the

Table 18.7 *Classification of workers according to this index*

	Contract	Income	Health insurance	Tenure	Training received	Quality of employment category
Julio, construction worker	Atypical	Min. wage	Public	9 months	None	Very low
Verónica, 3 jobs as a maid	None	1.5 × min. wage	None	7 years	None	Very low
Andrés, sells fruit in the streets	Self-employed	<1 min. wage	None	5 months	None	Very low
Rosario, massage therapist	Self-employed	2.5 × min. wage	None	6 years	None	Low

table above were all picked out of the survey's sample. They all voiced frustration about their working conditions and described their inability to improve their situation without temporary support from an alternative source.

Julio, a construction worker, for example, mainly complains about his contract. He has to look for a new job at least once a year and never knows exactly how long each contract will last. Although his health and pension contributions are covered, it is unlikely that he will accumulate enough funds in his account to qualify for a minimum pension, and he thus considers that his pension contributions are wasted. He also complains that he simply does not earn enough to put aside money for the periods when he is without work. He lives with his family in his mother's house and during periods of unemployment relies on his mother's support. In between jobs he always spends a couple of months travelling all over Santiago asking at the various different building sites whether they need help. He says his friends are the most useful source of information about prospective employment. Although municipal jobs centres do exist in Chile, Julio claims they are useless as employers hardly ever advertise their jobs there. He has given up going to them.

Verónica, who works as a part-time maid in several households, voiced concern about her lack of pension and health insurance. Every time she or one of her children is ill, she has to go through a process of obtaining a certificate that allows her to receive free emergency medical care, which she says is of very low quality. Yet she cannot contribute to either a pension scheme or health insurance, first because she would not be able to afford it, and second because she cannot prove that she has regular income, as none of her employers has offered her a contract, and she dare not ask them for fear of losing her employment.

Andrés lost his job as a construction worker two months prior to being interviewed by this survey, and was unable to find a job on another site. He now sells fruit from a basket in the streets of central Santiago because he cannot afford to be without any income. His wife's earnings as a part-time maid are not enough to cover the family's expenses. In reality, he is unemployed, but since he is receiving an income from selling the fruit, any employment survey in Chile would register him as employed, even though he says he is looking for other work with the help of his friends. This case is common in the Chilean labour force, but there is no specific public policy directed at such cases since they are not officially registered as unemployed.

Rosario, a massage therapist, on the other hand, explained that she can barely make ends meet as she has to support a large family. If she could obtain more qualifications, she could charge a higher price for her services and thus earn more, but the loss of income that she would experience during her period of training makes this an impossible option. A loan with low interest rates from the government would enable her to overcome this difficulty, but there is no such programme in Chile for the self-employed.

One of the most important reasons for creating this index is to focus attention on cases like the ones described above. Micro credit, professional training, low motivation to contribute to private health and pension systems, or unstable employment are all issues that public policy should address in order to enhance the functionings and capabilities of the individual.

In a country like Chile, which despite having attained a certain degree of development still offers the unemployed no benefits or security to speak of,[24] the question of having a job or not having one predominates in the labour market debate, almost to the exclusion of all other topics. While government and public concern about this is certainly justified, it is also short-sighted. The quality of employment is what will ultimately ensure the development of the economy, foster growth, social cohesion and welfare. A low unemployment rate is merely a component of this. Creating an index of the characteristics that constitute quality of employment should hopefully reduce the issue of unemployment to the status of a 'component variable' and have the same effect of broadening public debate that the creation of the HDI did. Ultimately, if human functionings and capabilities are to be enhanced, this requires a long-term view, and also a broad, inclusive view.

Aside from stimulating debate, the proposed index will also provide useful information to public policy makers. Its main purpose could be to help identify those sectors of the economy, or regions of a country, which are generating better jobs than others, or those segments of the work force which are particularly marginalised.

---

[24] The new, privatised unemployment insurance scheme that was introduced in Chile in 2002 will not significantly change this, as it protects least those most vulnerable to becoming unemployed. See Sehnbruch 2006a and 2006b for details on this system.

Just as unemployment rates can vary from sector to sector or according to geographic location, it is perfectly possible that some sectors within an economy may have better ratings than others or improve their rating while others decline. By the same logic, some regions may improve their quality of employment while others deteriorate. This sends important signals to policy makers as to which areas should receive particular attention.

In addition we should consider that unemployment rankings may differ substantially from quality of employment rankings, in the same way that the human development indicator varies from plain GNP rankings. The strength of the quality of employment indicator is that it will pick up on issues that the unemployment rate simply does not consider. A particular region could perhaps register a very low unemployment rate, but this may be entirely due to atypical contracts or short term contracts such as those that are used in areas with activities predominantly in the agricultural or mining sectors, which could mean that the region is particularly vulnerable to job losses in situations of economic downturn.[25]

Or a region may have a very high unemployment rate although its quality of employment indicator is very good. This may indicate to public policy makers that the unemployed in this region do not have the qualifications needed in order to integrate themselves into the labour market, so that special training programmes or relocation programmes could be designed to better match the skills of the labour force with the requirements of their environment.

Similarly, trends over time may vary. For instance in the Chilean case where unemployment rates dropped steadily over a long period of time, this positive development almost completely distracted attention from the fact that increasingly jobs were being created with inferior qualitative characteristics. Ultimately, this has even led to a failure on behalf of the government to legislate appropriately. Atypical contracts, part-time work or subcontracting, for example, are all issues that are still not comprehensively defined in the Chilean Labour Code.

It should be considered that all indices, whether poverty lines, unemployment rates or GNP/capita are ultimately arbitrary. Their main

---

[25] In the case of Chile, most regions in the country depend predominantly on one particular type of industry or sector, e.g. mining in the north, fruit and agriculture in the middle, and forestry in the south.

value must be seen in the comparative perspective that they open up for us, which allows us to monitor developments over time and across different regions or countries. Bearing this purpose in mind, the methodology presented here was specifically designed to be applicable to other countries apart from Chile, especially countries where similar sources of data are available, and which have similar labour market structures. All the Southern Cone countries of Latin America, for example, would fall into this category.

Ultimately this index aims to produce a change in the way we think about the labour market. It intends to produce what could be described as a cultural change, a shift in emphasis away from unemployment to a broader, more inclusive concept. This does not mean that having a job is not supremely important to those who want to work, but it does mean that other issues should also be considered.

Conclusion

This chapter has demonstrated how the capability approach changes our perspective of the labour market by focusing our attention on the freedom and well-being of the individual rather than on the labour market's macro- and microeconomic functions. By considering the labour market's role as a filter of social and economic policies that impact the individual's wellbeing, labour policy is placed in a position of critical importance in the context of a country's development, on a par with fiscal, economic and social policy. This means that the development literature should accord labour policy the importance it deserves rather than continuing to ignore the role that employment plays in both individual welfare and macroeconomic development.

Applying the capability approach to the Chilean labour market has led to the suggestion of an alternative measure of labour market performance: the quality of employment indicator, which constitutes a useful analytical tool for the process of policy making. The results of the quality of employment indicator suggest that the main problems of the Chilean labour market are low incomes, too much informality within the formal sector, too many atypical contracts and too much self-employment, little professional training, low coverage of health and pension insurance, and low stability of employment. This leads to the conclusion that slightly less than half of the Chilean labour force has low or very low quality jobs. This is a considerably more complex result than a conclusion that merely considers whether the country's unemployment rate is too high.

Inspired by the work of the late Mahbub ul Haq, the originator of the Human Development Index (HDI), this author took the view that 'a measure of the same level of vulgarity as the unemployment rate was needed, which would not be as blind to the other aspects of employment as the unemployment rate'.[26] Although at first sceptical of ul Haq's view, Sen, in his own words, later came to appreciate it, as he accepted that no combination of tables would be able to replace the convenience of a single number, so that in order to broaden the debate, this single number would have to simply incorporate several components.[27]

The index and method proposed in this chapter are arbitrary and their elaboration is but a preliminary suggestion. However, it respects the overall objectives of an approach which consistently emphasises that the functionings and capabilities of an individual depend on more than just income (or GNP/capita). While therefore not pretending to be a perfect summary measure of the labour market, it does broaden the basic criteria which the employment debate normally focuses on to include capability enhancing aspects.

The chapter has suggested that labour market policy should form an integral part of any development strategy. Once the population of a developing country is fed, healthy and literate, employment should form the central and most important focus of its development strategy as the conditions associated with employment determine the capabilities and wellbeing of individuals more than any other variable.

---

[26] The original phrase is 'We need a measure of the same level of vulgarity as GNP – only a number – but a measure which is not as blind to the social aspects of human life as is GNP' (UNDP, 1999: p. 23).

[27] See the article written by Sen in the Human Development Report, 1999: p. 23.

Appendix

Table 18.A.1 *Quality of employment index*

Variable	Score
Professional position	
Indefinite contract	2
Atypical contract	1
No contract	0
Employer	2
Professional self-employed	2
Non-professional self-employed	1
Income	
Less than 2 minimum wages	0
2–4 minimum wages	1
More than 4 minimum wages	2
Health insurance	
None	0
Public	1
Private	2
Employment stability	
Less than 3 years	0
3–5 years	1
More than 5 years	2
Training received	
None	0
On the job	1
Training courses	2
Total points scored / 5	
High quality job	1.6–2.0 points
Medium quality job	0.8–1.4 points
Low quality job	0–0.6 points

Cited references

Agacino, R. and M. Echeverría (eds.) 1995. *Flexibilidad y Condiciones de Trabajo precarias.* Santiago: PET

Bastelaer, A. van and R. 2000. Hussmanns *Measurement of the Quality of Employment.* Geneva paper presented at a joint Eurostat and ILO Seminar

Beatson, M. 2000. *Job 'Quality' and Job 'Security'.* London: Labour Market Trends

Bosworth, B., R. Dornbush and R. Labán (eds.) 1994. *The Chilean Economy: Policy Lessons and Challenges.* Washington D.C.: Brookings Institution

Bravo, D. and D. Contreras. 2001. *Competencias Básicas de la Población Adulta.* Santiago: Universidad de Chile, Ministerio de Economía and CORFO

CERC. 1999. *Barómetro CERC,* Santiago: Centro de Estudios de la Realidad Contemporánea

Chakraborty, A. 1996. 'On the Possibility of a Weighting System for Functionings'. *Indian Economic Review,* 31 (2): 241–250

Clark, D. A. 2000. *Capability and Development, An Essay in Honour of Amartya Sen.* University of Lincolnshire and Humberside: Working Paper 39

Cypher, J. M. and J. L. Dietz. 1997. *The Process of Economic Development.* London and New York: Routledge

Drèze, J. and A. Sen. 1989. *Hunger and Public Action.* Oxford: Clarendon Press

Drèze, J. and Sen, A. 1995a. *The Political Economy of Hunger.* Oxford: Clarendon Press

Drèze, J. and A. Sen. 1995b. *India: Economic Development and Social Opportunity.* Oxford: Clarendon Press

Drèze, J. and A. Sen. 1996. *Indian Development: Selected Regional Perspectives.* Oxford and Delhi: Oxford University Press

Echeverría, M., V. Solis and V. Uribe-Echevarría. 1998. *El Otro Trabajo.* Cuaderno de Investigación N° 7, Departamento de Estudios, Santiago: Dirección de Trabajo

Edwards, S. and N. Lustig (eds.) 1997. *Labour Markets in Latin America: Combining Social Protection with Market Flexibility.* Washington D.C.: Brookings Institution Press

Eßner, K. 2000. *Nationalstaat und Marktwirtschaft in Lateinamerika – Chile als Vorbild?* Working Paper, Bonn: Friedrich Ebert Stiftung

García Huidobro, G. 1999. *Problemas de medición de empleo.* Estadística y Economía Vol 18, Santiago: Instituto Nacional de Estadísticas

ul Haq, M. 1995. *Reflections on Human Development.* New York and Oxford: Oxford University Press

ILO *World Employment Report,* various years, Geneva: ILO

ILO *Labour Overviews for Latin America (Panorama Laboral)*, various years, Lima: ILO

ILO 1998a. *Chile: Crecimiento, empleo y el desafío de la justicia social*, Santiago: ILO

ILO 1999. *Decent Work*, Geneva: ILO

Infante, R. (ed.) 1999. *La calidad del Empleo: La experiencia de los países latinoamericanos y de los Estados Unidos*, Lima: ILO

Jenks, C., L. Perman and L. Rainwater. 1988. 'What is a Good Job? A Measure of Labour Market Success.' *American Journal of Sociology*, Vol 93, No. 6: 1322–1357

Maloney, W. 1998. *The Structure of Labour Markets in Developing Countries*. Policy Research Working Paper 1940, Washington D.C.: World Bank

Meier, G. and J. Rauch. 2000. *Leading Issues in Economic Development*. Oxford: Oxford University Press

MIDEPLAN 1998. *Encuesta CASEN 1998*. Santiago: MIDEPLAN

Nolan, J.P., I.C. Wichert and B.J. Burchell 2000. 'Job Insecurity, Psychological Well-being and Family Life', in *The Insecure Workforce*, edited by E. Heery and J. Salmon. London: Routledge

Ootegem, L. van and E. Schokkaert. 1990. 'Sen's Concept of the Living Standard Applied to the Belgian Unemployed.' *Recherches Economiques de Louvain*, 56 (3–4), 429–450

Oxman, V. and S. Galilea (eds.) 1999. *Políticas de Igualdad de Oportunidades entre Mujeres y Hombres en el Trabajo*, SERNAM, Santiago

Paredes, R. 1996. *Mercado Laboral e Instituciones: Lecciones a Partir del Caso de Chile*, unpublished paper, Santiago: Universidad de Chile

Rodgers, G. 1997. *The Quality of Employment: Issues for Measurement, Research and Policy*, unpublished paper, ILO

Ruiz-Tagle V.J. 1999. *Chile: 40 años de desigualdad de ingresos*, Working paper No.165, Santiago: Universidad de Chile

Scott, C. 1996. 'The Distributive Impact of the New Economic Model in Latin America in Chile,' in Bulmer-Thomas, Victor (ed.) *The New Economic Model in Latin America and its Impact on Income Distribution and Poverty*. London: Macmillan

Sehnbruch, K. 2003. 'From the Quantity of Employment to the Quality of Employment: An Application of Amartya Sen's Capability Approach to the Chilean Labour Market.' Unpublished PhD Thesis, Cambridge University

Sehnbruch, K. 2006a. 'Individual Savings Accounts or Unemployment Insurance?', *International Social Security Review*, vol. 1

Sehnbruch, K. 2006b. *The Chilean Labor Market: A Key to Understanding Latin American Labor Markets*. New York: Palgrave Macmillan

Sen, A. 1981. *Poverty and Famines: An Essay on Entitlement and Deprivation.* Oxford: Clarendon Press

Sen, A. 1992. *Inequality Reexamined.* Oxford: Oxford University Press

Sen, A. 1997a. *Development Thinking at the Beginning of the 21st Century.* LSE working paper, London: Suntory Centre

Sen, A. 1997b. *What's the Point of a Development Strategy?* LSE working paper, Suntory Centre

Sen, A. 1997c. *Inequality, Unemployment and Contemporary Europe.* LSE working paper, London: Suntory Centre

Sen, A. 1999. *Development as Freedom.* Oxford: Oxford University Press

Sen, A. 1999. Address by Prof. Amartya Sen to the International Labour Conference, Geneva, 1–17th June 1999, www.ilo.org/public/english/10ilc/ilc87//a-sen.htm

Stewart, F. 2000. *Income Distribution and Development.* QEH Working Paper Series N°37, Oxford: Oxford University

Streeten, P. 1981. *First Things First: Meeting Basic Human Needs in the Developing Countries.* World Bank, Washington D.C., Oxford: Oxford University Press

Todaro, Michael P. 1994. *Economic Development.* London and New York: Longman

UNDP 1998. *Overcoming Human Poverty.* New York: UNDP

UNDP 1999. *Human Development Report.* New York: Mundi Prensa

UNDP 2000. *Human Development Report.* New York: Mundi Prensa

World Bank. 1997. *Poverty and Income Distribution in a High Growth Economy: 1987–1995,* Washington

World Bank. 1999. *World Development Report.* Washington D.C., Oxford: Oxford University Press

Index

Lightning Source UK Ltd.
Milton Keynes UK

172212UK00002B/16/P